DECISIVE
THE WEST

A

From th

DECISIVE BATTLES OF THE WESTERN WORLD

and their influence upon history

VOLUME II

From the defeat of the Spanish Armada to Waterloo

MAJOR GENERAL
J. F. C. FULLER
CB CBE DSO

CASSELL&CO

Cassell & Co
Wellington House, 125 Strand
London WC2R 0BB

First published in 1955
This edition 2001

British Library Cataloguing-in-Publication Data
A catalogue record for this book is available from the British Library

ISBN 0-304-35868-1

Printed and bound in Great Britain by
Creative Print & Design (Wales), Ebbw Vale

To

FRANCIS NEILSON

Contents

Maps and Diagrams

The rivalry between England and Spain

The commercial centre of gravity of Europe moved westward with the discovery of the New World and of the Cape route to the East Indies. Henceforth it was steadily to be drawn from the Mediterranean lands toward those bordering the Atlantic. Because of this, Spain, Portugal, and England, and later the United Provinces and France, were to become the rivals for world trade and the possession of the newly discovered countries. Henceforth, until recent times, the urge of imperialism moved toward oversea colonization and empires increasingly tended to become maritime in form.

The first phase of the struggle, between England and Spain, opened peacefully enough. When, on November 17, 1558, Elizabeth I (1558–1603) succeeded her half-sister Queen Mary, wife of Philip II, England and Spain were in alliance against France. The next year so firm appeared their friendship that during the negotiations preceding the signing of the Treaty of Cateau Cambrésis, Philip tried on Elizabeth's behalf to recover Calais, which on January 6, 1558, had been wrested from Mary by the Duke of Guise. Next, he offered to marry Elizabeth, but was refused.

Philip's eagerness to support England was wholly self-interested, and his policy pivoted on Mary Queen of Scots (1542–1587), great grand-daughter of Henry VII of England and daughter of James V of Scotland and Mary of Guise. In Catholic eyes she was the legitimate heir to the English throne, and on April 24, 1558, she had been married to Francis II (1559–1560) of France. At the time, her uncle, the Duke of Guise, was all powerful in France, and by means of Mary he aimed to unite France, England, Scotland, and Ireland into a great Guise empire. As this would be fatal for Spain, for 12 years from 1558 Philip tried at all costs to maintain Elizabeth on the throne as a counterpoise to Mary. To Spain the importance of a friendly England was vital, because England flanked the Spanish sea communications with the Netherlands, and since the loss of Calais, England's command of her home waters was insecure as long as the Netherlands were Spanish.

These two strategical questions dominated Spanish and English policy throughout the reigns of Philip and Elizabeth.

In spite of Philip's support, Elizabeth's position was precarious. She did not want a foreign war, for England, divided between Catholics and Protestants, was politically unstable. But the aim of the Calvinists in England was to support Calvinism anywhere on the Continent, and added to this, because England had become a naval power and was a rising commercial one, the anti-Spanish party in England saw in the fleet a means of challenging the Spanish monopoly of the New World. "Military and seafaring men all over England," writes Camden, "fretted and desired war with Spain. But the Queen shut her ears against them." Nevertheless Elizabeth was not strong enough to hold them completely in check.

Soon after her accession a sudden change took place when on December 5, 1560, Francis II died, and was succeeded by his brother, Charles IX (1560–1574), under the regency of his mother, Catherine de' Medici. In August, 1561, Mary returned to Scotland. There, after the murder of her second husband, Lord Darnley, in 1567, she was forced to abdicate, and in 1568 sought refuge in England, where she was imprisoned by Elizabeth for the rest of her life. These events and the growing ascendency of the anti-Spanish party in England caused a change in Philip's policy toward Mary. As she was no longer the direct tool of the Guises, instead of protecting Elizabeth against her, he began to use Mary as the fulcrum of conspiracy and intrigue against Elizabeth, and in this he was supported by Pope Pius V who, in 1570, excommunicated the English queen.

Besides these political changes, an economic cause of friction was antagonizing Spain: it was the pirating of the African slave trade, a Spanish royal monopoly, by John Hawkins of Plymouth. So lucrative was this illicit business that in 1567 the Queen went into partnership with Hawkins and lent him one of her own ships, the *Jesus*. He set sail in her from Plymouth on October 2, and accompanied by the *Minion* and *Judith*–the latter commanded by Francis Drake–Hawkins first made for the Guinea coast. There he either captured or bought some 500 negroes and sailed for the West Indies where surreptitiously he sold them to the Spanish colonists. On his way he put into San Juan de Ulua for water and shelter, fortified the harbour at its entrance, and denied entry to the Spanish. The Plate fleet arrived with the incoming Viceroy of New Spain, Don Martin Enriques, who feared shipwreck because of a storm, and he made a compact with Hawkins that if he were allowed in he would not molest the English in any way but let them water, reprovision, and depart. A few days later Enriques suddenly opened fire on Hawkins's ships. A battle followed in which the *Jesus* had to be abandoned, but the *Minion* and *Judith* cleared the roadstead and after a perilous voyage returned to Plymouth in January, 1569.

When Hawkins was homeward bound, another incident occurred and a more serious one. For years past Huguenot privateers had plundered Spanish ships on their way from Spain to Flanders, and many of them belonged to John Hawkins's brother William, mayor of Plymouth, whose vessels, in order not to implicate the Queen, sailed under letters of marque from Condé or William of Orange. In 1568, 50 were working under Condé's flag and no fewer than 30 of them were alleged to be English. In December, a group of these privateers chased a Spanish squadron into Fowey, Plymouth, and Southampton, and when the bullion it carried was found to belong to Genoese bankers, payable at Antwerp to the Duke of Alva – Philip's general in the Netherlands – Elizabeth impounded it and with Genoese consent borrowed it for her own use. In retaliation Alva seized English ships and goods in the Netherlands and Elizabeth then did the same with Spanish ships and goods in England. On top of this came the news of the loss of the *Jesus* to add fuel to the glowing antagonisms. Thus England and Spain drifted apart, Philip supported the English Catholics and Elizabeth opened England as a refuge to the Dutch Protestant rebels.

Meanwhile William of Orange (1559–1584) built a fleet, and, in 1569, 18 of his ships took to the seas – the beginning of that sea power which during the following century was to cover the oceans with Dutch fleets and to plant colonies in many lands. Their influence on the situation was immediate; for, in 1570, his sailors, known as *gueux de mer* (sea beggars), captured 300 vessels, and to make good their lack of ports of refuge, Elizabeth winked at their use of English harbours until, in 1572, they surprised Brill and turned it into an impregnable base of their own. Henceforth, and in spite of her inborn aversion to rebels, Elizabeth's policy was increasingly directed toward keeping the insurrection alive, not only in order to exhaust Spain, but also to prevent the Dutch in despair offering the sovereignty of their country to the king of

France. So acute grew the crisis that, although Alva was against an open declaration of war, Philip was so incensed that he gave encouragement to the Ridolfi conspiracy of 1571, the aim of which was to foment a Catholic rebellion in England supported by 6,000 of Alva's men; to assassinate Elizabeth; and to place Mary on the throne and restore the Catholic faith in England. The plot was discovered and quashed, and its sole result was to heighten antagonisms.

In order to strengthen her position, in April, 1572, Elizabeth concluded with Catherine de' Medici a defensive alliance against Spain. But it failed in its object, for immediately afterward the French Huguenots won Charles IX to their side, and Elizabeth, who feared that France would occupy the Low Countries, turned toward Spain; Catherine, who feared that the Huguenots would draw France into war with Spain, on August 24 engineered the massacre of St. Bartholomew. It has been estimated that during it 50,000 people perished in France. As it brought the House of Guise back into power Elizabeth opened negotiations with Philip and trade relations, which had ceased in 1568, were in the spring of 1573 restored between the two countries.

A year later Charles IX died and was succeeded by his brother Henry III (1574–1589), and in March, 1576, Don John of Austria, the victor of Lepanto, was appointed Governor of the Netherlands. On his arrival he found that the Spanish army was in mutiny and that its excesses had reawakened the revolt. When he learnt that Elizabeth was financing the rebels he urged upon Philip the invasion of England. But Philip's finances were in chaos and instead he sent Bernadino de Mendoza to placate Elizabeth and to reopen the Spanish embassy in London, which had remained closed since 1572.

Soon after Mendoza's arrival in England, Don John died and the suppression of the rebellion in the Netherlands was entrusted to Alexander Farnese, Duke of Parma, the ablest soldier of his age and a veteran of Lepanto. In a series of brilliant campaigns he regained Bruges, Ghent, Antwerp, and most of the southern Netherlands, and in desperation the rebels offered the sovereignty of their country to Henry III's brother, the Duke of Alençon.

Although Philip continued to hold back from an open declaration of war on England, Pope Gregory XIII (1572–1585) nearly forced him into action by preparing two expeditions against Ireland. One, in 1578, completely miscarried; the other, in 1580, in which a few Spaniards were involved, landed in Ireland, but its members were soon slaughtered. In 1577, Drake, with five ships, had set out on the voyage which was to lead to his circumnavigation of the world. On his way he raided Valparaiso; looted Tarapaca; captured the great treasure ship *Cacafuego*; and sailed into San Francisco Bay where he took possession of the land in the name of Queen Elizabeth and called it "New Albion." He returned in September, 1580, with an immense booty and was knighted by Elizabeth on the quarter-deck of his flagship, the *Golden Hind*.

When Drake sailed round the world, another event took place which was to have a profound influence on the Anglo-Spanish quarrel. In 1578, in a fit of antiquated chivalry, the young King Sebastian of Portugal invaded North Africa and on August 4, at Alcazar Kebir, he was killed and his army annihilated. He left no children and was succeeded by his great uncle Cardinal Henry, childless and 77 years old, after whom came a host of claimants. Among these Philip had the strongest legal claim, and Don Antonio, an illegitimate son of Louis Duke of Béja (son of King Emanuel of Portugal) was the most popular. It was this question of succession which, in 1579, induced Philip to go gently with England so that he might be free to occupy Portugal on Henry's death. He did not have long to wait. Henry died on January 31, 1580, and soon after Philip sent the Duke of Alva and an army into Portugal. Don Antonio was routed at Alcantara on August 25 and Philip then annexed Portugal and the Portuguese empire. Not only did he gain vast territories in which there was no religious barrier, but also the shipping and seamen of an intensely maritime people.

Don Antonio fled to France after his defeat and later sought refuge in England. As he styled himself King of Portugal, it was open to Elizabeth to recognize him as such and to permit her subjects to act upon his commissions.

This change in the balance of power threw both Elizabeth and Catherine de' Medici, the French queen-mother, into panic. The latter fitted out a fleet under Filippo Strozzi and in 1582 sent it with Don Antonio to seize the Azores, the focal point of the Spanish communications with the New World. There, off the island of Terceira, it was scattered by the Marquis of Santa Cruz, who had commanded the reserve squadron at Lepanto. The following year the French Admiral Aymard de Chaste, accompanied by Don Antonio, was disastrously defeated by the Marquis of Santa Cruz, again off Terceira. The effects of these two victories were great indeed; they confirmed the impression gained at Lepanto that the Spanish fleet was invincible, and they secured the Portuguese Atlantic bases, which were essential to Philip in order to strike at England.

Shortly after the second of these battles, when still at Terceira, the Marquis of Santa Cruz wrote to Philip to urge that only by an invasion of England could the Netherlands be regained. The idea was by no means new, for in 1569 the Duke of Alva had suggested it, and after Lepanto Don John of Austria had considered the task an easy one. Philip demurred; but soon after two events persuaded him to accept it.

First, in January, 1584, because of his complicity in the Throckmorton plot, Elizabeth ordered Bernadino de Mendoza, Spanish Ambassador in England, to leave the country. In reply, Philip laid an embargo on all English shipping in Spanish ports, to which Elizabeth retaliated in kind. She also ordered Drake to ravage the West Indies. On September 14, 1585, he set out with Martin Frobisher, sacked Porto da Praia in the Cape Verde Islands; ravaged San Domingo; plundered Cartagena (in Colombia); threatened Havana and destroyed St. Augustine in Florida.

Meanwhile Parma consolidated his gains, a task in which he was greatly aided by the assassination of William of Orange on July 10, 1584. After his death the situation in the Netherlands grew so critical that Elizabeth, who regarded the rebels as "an ungrateful multitude, a true mob," in August, 1585, reluctantly made a treaty with them and sent the Earl of Leicester and 5,000 soldiers to the Netherlands to hold the breach until William's son, Maurice of Nassau (1584–1625) could establish himself. This was the second event: at length, after 27 years of peace, Elizabeth embarked on war, all but in name.

Philip at last was brought to see that in order to re-establish his authority in the Low Countries there was no alternative to the invasion of England. All along he had avoided so desperate an undertaking, but the intervention of Leicester brought him to recognise that it was imperative. So it came about that on March 12, 1586, Santa Cruz resubmitted his project; but as he now asked for 510 ships and 94,222 men, and estimated the cost of the expedition at 3,800,000 ducats,[1] Philip substituted for it a less ambitious scheme. It was that instead of conveying an army of

[1] A ducat in English money was then worth 9s. 4½d.

invasion from Portugal to England, Santa Cruz's task should be limited to gaining command of the English Channel, after which Parma's army in the Netherlands would be ferried across it.

At this moment, most opportunely for England, Elizabeth was able to secure her kingdom from internal revolt before the storm broke. In the spring of 1586 the English adherents of the captive Mary Stuart, who believed that no invasion could succeed as long as Elizabeth lived, entered into a conspiracy—known as the Babington Plot—to assassinate her. Mendoza, then ambassador at the court of France, and Mary Stuart were involved. The outcome was that Elizabeth's chief ministers, Lord Burghley, Lord High Treasurer, and Sir Francis Walsingham, Principal Secretary of State, much against the Queen's wishes, persuaded her to bring Mary to trial. On February 1, 1587, she was condemned to death and seven days later was beheaded at Fotheringay.

CHAPTER I

The defeat of the Spanish Armada, 1588

Before Calais was lost in 1558 the security of England depended theoretically on defending her shores by fighting battles on the Continent, which was looked upon as the counterscarp of England's defences. After the loss of Calais this dependence had to be replaced by the command of the English Channel; yet, when the crisis of 1586 occurred, although Queen Elizabeth possessed a private fleet of 34 warships, which in time of war could be augmented by many armed merchantmen, no national navy existed, and so things stood until the days of the Commonwealth. Added to this, there was no standing army—the feudal levies had long disappeared—and though, as in the days of the Saxon *fyrd*, her Majesty's Lieutenants were still authorized to call out levies of armed men, except for those in London they were little more than undisciplined bodies of soldiers which, at their best, would have been unable to meet in the field the highly organized soldiers of Spain.

The trouble was that, as Fortescue says of Elizabeth, "she hated straight dealing for its simplicity, she hated conviction for its certainty, and above all she hated war for its expense."[1] These three idiosyncrasies, particularly the last, persuaded her to rely on diplomacy, and because she lacked the force necessary to make it effective she was outwitted consistently by the Duke of Parma who, until the Armada sailed, covered his preparations in the Netherlands by constant proposals of peace, which Elizabeth largely accepted at face value.

Nevertheless, because of the Babington Plot it became apparent that a crisis had been reached, and on December 25, 1586, Elizabeth was persuaded to order the mobilization of her fleet at Portsmouth and to hold a squadron in the Channel during the winter of 1586–1587 to frustrate any possible attempt by the Guises to rescue Mary Queen of Scots. In March, 1587, Mary was dead, and while the main fleet was mobilized at Portsmouth,

---

[1] *A History of the British Army*, the Hon. J. W. Fortescue (1910), vol. I, p. 130. Regarding the expense of war, Queen Elizabeth's yearly income did not permit her to indulge in war without aid from Parliament.

Sir Francis Drake was making ready at Plymouth 23 sail "to impeach the joining together of the King of Spain's fleets out of their several ports, to keep victuals from them, to follow them in case they should be come forward towards England or Ireland and to cut off as many of them as he could and impeach their landing. . . ."[1] As usual, as soon as these orders were issued Elizabeth feared that they might precipitate a war and greatly modified them;[2] but Drake, who knew what to expect, put to sea on April 2, before he could receive her counter-order and arrived at Cadiz on April 19. "We stayed there," he writes, "until the 21st, in which meantime we sank a Biscayan of 1,200 tons, burnt a ship of the Marquess of Santa Cruz of 1,500 tons, and 31 ships more of 1,000, 800, 600, 400 to 200 tons the piece; carried away four with us laden with provisions, and departed thence at our pleasure. . . ."[3] Next, being "furnished with necessary provisions," he made for Lisbon, from where on April 27 he writes: "There was never heard of so great a preparation [as] the King of Spain hath and doth continually prepare for an invasion. . . ."[4]

Lisbon was where the ships of the Armada were being assembled, and though Santa Cruz had established his headquarters there, as yet he had not mustered a man. It was a powerfully defended port. Outside the bar and to the north was an anchorage commanded by Cascaes Castle, and close to it lay the strong fortress of St. Julian. On May 10 Drake cast anchor in Cascaes Bay. The port was thrown into consternation, every vessel cut her cables and sped for the nearest refuge. Thousands of tons of shipping and a vast quantity of stores were then destroyed; the Spanish return puts the loss at 24 ships with cargoes valued at 172,000 ducats.[5] Drake, who had no land forces with him, could not hold the port, so he made for Cape St. Vincent–the strategic point between Lisbon and the Mediterranean. "We hold this Cape," writes Thomas Fenner–Drake's Flag-Captain–"so greatly to our benefit and so much to their disadvantage as a great blessing [is] the

[1] *Camden Society Misc.*, "Sir Francis Drake's Memorable Service, etc.," (1843), vol. v, p. 29.
[2] Elizabeth's counter-order reads: ". . . that her express will and pleasure is you shall forbear to enter forcibly into any of the said King's ports or havens, or to offer violence to any of his towns or shipping within harbouring, or to do any act of hostility upon the land . . ." (*Papers Relating to the Navy during the Spanish War*, 1585–1587, edited by Julian S. Corbett, Navy Record Soc., 1898, p. 101).
[3] *Ibid.*, pp. 107–108.
[4] *Ibid.*, p. 111.
[5] *La Armada Invencible*, Captain Cesaero Fernandez Duro (1884), doc. 15 bis, vol. I, p. 335.

attaining thereof. For the rendezvous is at Lisbon, where we understand of some 25 ships and 7 galleys. The rest, we lie between home and them, so as the body is without the members; and they cannot come together by reason that they are unfurnished of their provisions in every degree, in that they are not united together."[1]

Near St. Vincent immense damage was done to the Portuguese Algarve fisheries and thousands of tons of hoops and pipe-staves for casks were destroyed.[2] Could Drake have remained there he might well have prevented altogether the assembly of the Armada, but this was not possible unless he were reinforced. On May 17 he wrote to Sir Francis Walsingham: "If there were here 6 or more of her Majesty's good ships of the second sort, we should be the better able to keep the forces from joining and haply take or impeach his fleet from all places in the next month and so after, which is the chiefest times of their return home, which I judge, in my poor opinion, will bring this great monarchy to those conditions which are meet."[3]

This was not to be and he set out for the Azores. Sixteen days out from St. Vincent, on June 8, he sighted a large vessel off St. Michael's and took her the next day. She was the *San Felipe*, the King of Spain's own East Indiaman, with a cargo valued at £114,000 and papers which revealed the long-kept secrets of the East India trade.[4] On June 26 Drake was back in Plymouth. He had wrecked all possibility of the Armada sailing that year. This was most fortunate for England, for had the Armada been able to put to sea before the end of September, as Philip intended, Parma might have crossed the Channel. As he writes in a letter to the King: "Had the Marquis come when I was first told to look for him, the landing could have been effected without difficulty. Neither the English nor the Dutch were then in a condition to resist your fleet."[5]

Meanwhile Santa Cruz hastened to make good the damage done and to be ready by the end of February, 1588; but he died suddenly on January 30. Again the expedition was delayed. His

---

[1] *Papers Relating to the Navy during the Spanish War*, 1585–1587, p. 139.
[2] See *ibid.*, pp. 131 and 137. As all salt provisions, wines and water, etc., had to be carried in casks, the importance of this loss may readily be understood.
[3] *Ibid.*, p. 133.
[4] *Ibid.*, p. xlii. These papers so stirred the London merchants that later they formed the East India Company, the foundations of the British Empire of India.
[5] Quoted from *History of England from the Fall of Wolsey to the Defeat of the Spanish Armada*, James Anthony Froude (n.d.), vol. xii, p. 324.

death proved to be as great a calamity to the Spaniards as Drake's raid, for he was the ablest sailor in Spain. In his stead Philip appointed Don Alonzo Perez de Guzman, Duke of Medina Sidonia, who, though a grandee of highest rank, had never seen service either with the fleet or with the army. He wrote to the King asking to be excused,[1] but Philip appointed a competent seaman, Don Diego de Valdez to be his naval adviser and nominated the Duke of Parma commander-in-chief of the entire expedition once Medina Sidonia had sailed up the Channel and joined him.

While Medina Sidonia made ready, the main preparations of the Duke of Parma were the cutting of a ship canal from Antwerp and Ghent to Bruges; the building of 70 landing-craft on Waten River, each to carry 30 horses and equipped with embarking and disembarking gangways; the building of 200 flat-bottomed boats at Nieuport; the assembly of 28 warships at Dunkirk; the recruiting of mariners in Hamburg, Bremen, Emden, and other ports; the construction of 20,000 casks at Gravelines; and near Nieuport and Dixmude the building of camps for 20,600 foot, and at Courtrai and Waten for 4,900 horse.[2]

The operations which were soon to follow are better understood by examination of the naval developments of this period.[3]

The factor which differentiated the warship of the sixteenth century from what she had been in previous centuries was the heavy cannon; for though man-killing ordnance began to be mounted in ships in the fourteenth, it was not until the fifteenth century that a heavy enough gun to smash a ship came into existence. This weapon was of two distinct types, a breech-loader and a muzzle-loader. In its original form the former was what is called a "built-up gun"–that is, a piece fashioned by welding together bars of iron, as already described. Its powder chamber was separate from the barrel, and before discharge was screwed into it by means of an uninterrupted thread. Of this type belong *Dulle Griette* of Ghent and *Mons Meg* of Edinburgh; the latter a cast piece of bell-metal with barrel and chamber in one, and equipped with trunnions.

[1] See Duro, vol. I, doc. 53, pp. 414–415.

[2] Emanuel Van Meteren's Account of the Armada, *Hakluyt Voyages* (Everyman's Library), vol. II, pp. 375–376.

[3] Most of the following is based on Professor Michael Lewis's "Armada Guns: A Comparative Study of English and Spanish Armaments," in *The Mariner's Mirror*, vols. 28 and 29 (1942–1943), and his *The Navy of Britain* (1948).

There were two main types of muzzle-loading pieces – the cannon and the culverin, both mounted on trucks. The former was a true battering-piece that threw a heavy iron shot at medium range, and the latter a longer piece from which was fired a lighter shot over greater distance. The characteristics of these two pieces were as follows:

Type	Bore	Weight of shot	Calibres	Point blank range[1]	Random range
Cannon ..	$7\frac{1}{4}$ in.	50 lb. (about)	18	340 paces	2,000 paces
Culverin ..	$5\frac{1}{4}$ in.	17 lb.	32	400 paces	2,500 paces

Besides these there was a demi-cannon, which fired a shot of 32 lb., and a demi-culverin – a nine- to ten-pdr. There were many smaller members of the culverin class, the more important were the Saker, a five-pdr.; the Minion, a four-pdr., and the Falcon, a two and a half to three-pdr.;[2] but these pieces were wholly man-killers. Another piece, which at this period was falling into obsolesence, was the Perier, a gun of comparatively short range that threw a 24-lb. stone ball.

Up to the opening of the sixteenth century two main types of vessels sailed the seas – namely, the hulk or round ship, and the galley or long ship. The former was used to carry merchandise, and the latter was *par excellence* the warship. But ocean voyaging and improvement in cannon soon began to change ship construction; sails became more important on the ocean than oars, and the sailing ship could better be adapted to broadside fire.

The first transition set in with the introduction of small man-killing naval ordnance in the fifteenth century. They were mounted in two castles,[3] one built over the bow (forecastle), and the other over the stern (rear castle) of the ship, and were pointed to sweep the waist to destroy boarders. Henry VII's Great Ship, the *Regent*, housed 225 of these man-killing guns – mainly swivel-pieces.

The next transition came with Henry VIII, who adopted the

[1] "Point-blank" range was the distance at which the shot began to fall appreciably, and "Random" was the maximum range.
[2] For these and many other pieces of this period see *Papers Relating to the Navy during the Spanish War*, appendix A.
[3] Previously, elevated platforms had been built for archers.

muzzle-loading, ship-smashing cannon. As this weapon was too heavy to be housed in the castles and was unsuitable as an anti-boarding weapon, it had to be mounted on the upper-deck, or better still the main-deck, with port-holes cut in the sides of the ship. The first of these heavy-gunned ships was the *Mary Rose*, built in 1513.

The last transition was that with this type of ship the castles became less necessary, and that as the weight of broadside fire demanded increased deck space, the round ship was developed into what was to become the ship of the line, a vessel the length of which was three beams or more, instead of the average round ship's two beams. In the sixteenth century the most renowned of these ships was Francis Drake's *Revenge*, a ship wholly of English design. This type of ship was "race-built," or what Monson calls "flush-decked"—that is to say, though her poop and forecastle were not flush with the waist, they were from 25 per cent. to 45 per cent. lower than the great Spanish ships and galleasses. This made many of the English ships of war appear smaller than the Spanish; but the largest ships of the two navies were approximately of the same tonnage. The galleon, which was not peculiar to Spain, was "a sailing-ship—usually four-masted—with the ordinary ship-rig of the time, but with the hull built to some extent on galley lines, long for its beam, rather straight and flat, and with a beak low down, like a galley's, instead of the overhanging fore-castle of the ship."[1] The crew of the English warship at this time was approximately two men a ton burden; in the Spanish ships it was three or more.

The influence of the gun on naval tactics was even more radical than on naval construction. In the days of the galley the primary weapon was the beak protruding from the bow and the main tactical operation was ramming. Though the approach might be made in column of galleys, the attack formation was that of line abreast, and, as in land warfare, the battle culminated in an assault or charge. In the gun-ship, the bulk of the primary weapons—the heavy ship-smashing cannon—were not in the bow but along the sides. When the gun-ship neared an enemy, in order to bring a broadside to bear she had to wear or wheel to port or starboard—virtually suicide for the galley. In consequence, with the gun-ship the attack had to be made at right-angles to her line of advance, and in order to carry out this manœuvre methodically

[1] *The Sailing-Ship: Six Thousand Years of History*, Romola and R. C. Anderson (1926), p. 126.

and so to concentrate the maximum hitting power on the enemy, the approach had to be made in line ahead.

This radical change was not yet recognized, fleets went into action in coveys or swarms of ships and the main aim was to board each other's ships. But during the various engagements of the Armada in the Channel line ahead began to take form, and the reason is to be sought in the differences between the armaments of the contending fleets, which Professor Lewis gives as follows:[1]

Fleet	No. of ships	Cannon	Periers	Culverins	Total
English	172	55	43	1,874	1,972
Spanish	124	163	326	635	1,124

The English then, had three times as many long-range pieces as the Spaniards and the Spaniards had three times as many heavy-shotted medium-range pieces as the English. These differences in range and smashing-power dictated the respective tactical policies: the English concentrated on long-range fighting and the Spaniards on medium- and short-range action. Whereas the Spanish tactical aim was to reduce a hostile ship to impotence and then to board her, the English was to sink the enemy or to force her to strike her flag. Although the English culverin had the greater range, it was not powerful enough decisively to batter a ship at long range. Equally important, the inaccuracy of its fire was such that at long range few shots hit their target. Inaccuracy of fire dogged naval warfare, as it also did that on land, until the introduction of the rifled gun and musket. Theoretically therefore, the Spanish, who relied on close-range battering power, were in advance of their enemy as artillerists.

Philip realized clearly the type of tactics the English would adopt and, before Medina Sidonia sailed, he gave him this warning: "You are especially to take notice that the enemy's object will be to engage at a distance, on account of the advantage which they have from their artillery and the offensive fireworks with which they will be provided; and on the other hand, the object of our side should be to close and grapple and engage hand to

[1] *The Mariner's Mirror*, vol. 29, p. 100. Besides the 1,124 heavy ordnance, the Spanish ships carried 1,307 lighter man-killing pieces, mainly in the castles.

hand."[1] But apparently he did not realize so fully that the true advantage of the English lay not in their longer range ordnance, but in their superior seamanship and in the fact that their ships were handier than the Spanish. The Spaniard was a fair weather sailor, the Englishman was not; the Spanish ships were looked upon more as fortresses than vessels and were crowded with soldiers and undermanned with sailors, who were considered little better than galley slaves. In the English ships their crews not only manned but fought them, and though pressed into service received fourpence a day. The greatest difference and advantage of all was that the Spaniard continued to make use of the galley tactics of line abreast in groups, whereas Drake or Howard introduced a rough formation of line ahead in groups and so began to revolutionize naval fighting.

For the English admirals, the greatest difficulty during the months immediately preceding the sailing of the Armada was Elizabeth. Though a woman of pronounced personality and force of character, she was one of the most parsimonious sovereigns who ever sat on the English throne. She was genuinely afraid of Spain, and with reason—it was the greatest military and naval power in the world. Rightly she wanted peace, yet she could not understand that so long as she encouraged privateering and supported the Netherlands peace was not possible.

During the autumn a small English squadron under Sir Henry Palmer, in conjunction with a Dutch squadron, in all some 90 warships of small burden "meete to saile upon their rivers and shallow seas,"[2] blockaded the havens of Flanders; but it was not until November 27[3] that the Queen assembled a council of war to discuss such problems as likely landing places; the employment of land forces; the weapons to be used; and internal security. On December 21 she appointed Lord Howard of Effingham "lieutenant-general, commander-in-chief, and governor of the whole fleet and army at sea."[4] She selected him instead of Drake—her most able admiral—not only to enhance the prestige of her fleet,

[1] Duro, doc. 94, vol. II, p. 9.
[2] *Voyages*, Richard Hakluyt, vol. II, p. 379.
[3] *The Naval Tracts of Sir William Monson*, edit. by M. Oppenheim (1902), vol. II, pp. 267–286.
[4] *State Papers, Relating to the Defeat of the Spanish Armada*, edit. John Knox Laughton (1894), vol. I, p. 19. She denotes him as "knight of our illustrious order of the Garter, High Admiral of England, Ireland, Wales, and of the dominions and islands thereof, of the town of Calais and the marches of the same, of Normandy, Gascony and Aquitaine, and Captain General of the Navy and marines of our said Kingdoms of England and Ireland. . . ."

but because it was essential to have in command a man of so high a rank that he could command obedience. Drake was later appointed vice-admiral to reinforce Howard on the technical side. Of Howard, Thomas Fuller says: "True it is he was no deep seaman; but he had skill enough to know those who had more skill than himself and to follow their instructions, and would not starve the Queen's service by feeding his own sturdy wilfulness, but was ruled by the experienced in sea matters; the Queen having a navy of oak and an Admiral of osier."[1]

Ever since his return from Cadiz and Lisbon, Drake had pressed for a repetition of his audacious raid–an attack on the Spanish fleet in its ports of departure–and had he been allowed to repeat it, the high probability is that the Armada would never have sailed. At length, two days after Howard's appointment, he received a commission to proceed with 30 ships to the Spanish coast. But as soon as this commission had been given the Queen, fearful of antagonizing Spain, cancelled it and ordered that the crews of the fleet be reduced to half their strength.[2] This wavering brought forth a strongly worded letter from John Hawkins to Walsingham on February 15, 1588.

"We have to choose," he wrote, "either a dishonourable and uncertain peace, or to put on virtuous and valiant minds, to make a way through with such a settled war as may bring forth and command a quiet peace. . . . Therefore, in my mind, our profit and best assurance is to seek our peace by a determined and resolute war, which no doubt would be both less charge, more assurance of safety, and would best discern our friends from our foes both abroad and at home, and satisfy the people generally throughout the whole realm."[3]

Hawkins's idea was, like Drake's, that the offensive is the surest defensive. But soon after he had written this letter, the Queen learnt of the death of the Marquis of Santa Cruz. She believed that the Armada could not now sail, and as she also knew that the Duke of Parma was in a difficult situation[4] she fell into the trap the latter had set and sent peace commissioners[5] to the Netherlands.

[1] Quoted in *Drake and the Tudor Navy*, Julian S. Corbett (1898), vol. II, p. 186.
[2] *State Papers*, vol. I, p. 33.   [3] *Ibid.*, vol. I, pp. 59–60.
[4] On March 20, 1588 – that is, about a month later – Parma informed Philip that he had but 17,000 effectives left out of some 30,000 men. Also he writes: "It may be that God desires to punish us for our sins by some heavy disaster." (See Oppenheim's Introduction to the *Monson Tracts*, 1902, vol. I, p. 167.)
[5] They were Henry, Earl of Derby; William, Lord Cobham; Sir James à Crofts, and Doctor Valentine Dale and Doctor John Rogers.

Concerning this, Howard wrote to Walsingham on March 10: "I pray God that her Majesty take good care of herself, for these enemies are become devils, and care not how to kill. . . . I pray to God her Majesty do not repent this slack dealings."[1] Meanwhile, report after report came in that the Armada was soon to sail.[2]

Had Elizabeth been less diplomatically inclined she would have realized that Parma's peace proposals were a blind and that war was inevitable because Philip believed himself to be the instrument of the Almighty. He saw the whole undertaking as a crusade to return England to the fold of the Catholic Church. Day by day, in 50,000 churches, Masses were said; Philip's ships bore the names of saints and apostles; their crews were forbidden to swear, quarrel, gamble, or consort with loose women, and above them floated the imperial banner, on which were embroidered the figures of Christ and the Virgin and the motto: *Exurge Deus et vindica causam tuam.*

Philip wrote to Medina Sidonia: "When you have received my orders, you will put to sea with the whole Armada, and proceed direct for the English Channel, up which you will sail as far as the point of Margate, then open communication with the Duke of Parma, and ensure him a passage across."[3] He warned him to avoid the English fleet, and said that should Drake appear in the Channel, except for rearguard actions he was to ignore him. He also gave Medina Sidonia a sealed letter for Parma in which he informed the duke what to do should the expedition fail.[4]

Philip placed at Medina Sidonia's disposal 130 ships: 20 galleons; 44 armed merchantmen; 23 *urcas*, or hulks; 22 *pataches*, or dispatch-vessels; 13 *zabras*, or pinnaces; four galleasses, and four galleys.[5] These ships aggregated 57,868 tons burden, were armed with 2,431 guns, were manned by 8,050 seamen, and carried 18,973 soldiers. With galley slaves and others the total number of men was 30,493.[6]

The whole fleet was divided into 10 squadrons as follows:

(1) The squadron of Portugal, Medina Sidonia, 10 galleons and two pinnaces.

(2) The squadron of Castile, Diego Flores de Valdez,[7] 10 galleons, four armed merchantmen, and two pinnaces.

---

[1] *State Papers*, vol. I, pp. 106–107.   [2] *Ibid.*, vol. I, pp. 84, 90–92, 107, 122.
[3] Duro, doc. 94, vol. II, pp. 5–13.   [4] Duro, doc. 96, vol. II, p. 17.
[5] The actual number of warships may be taken as between 60 and 70.
[6] For supplies carried, see *The Royal Navy*, Wm. Laird Clowes (1897), vol. I, p. 560, following Duro, doc. 110, vol. II, pp. 82–84.
[7] de Valdez accompanied Medina Sidonia in his flag-ship the *San Martin*.

(3) The squadron of Andalusia, Pedro de Valdez, 10 armed merchantmen and one pinnace.

(4) The squadron of Biscay, Juan Martinez de Recalde, 10 armed merchantmen and four pinnaces.

(5) The squadron of Guipuzcoa, Miguel de Oquendo, 10 armed merchantmen and two pinnaces.

(6) The squadron of Italy, Martin de Bertendora, 10 armed merchantmen and two pinnaces.

(7) The squadron of *Urcas*, Juan Gomez de Medina, 23 ships.

(8) The squadron of *Pataches*, Antonio Hurtado de Mendoza, 22 ships.

(9) The squadron of four galleasses, Hugo de Monçada.

(10) The squadron of four galleys, Diego de Medrado.[1]

While the Spaniards made ready and Elizabeth dallied with Parma, Drake fretted at Plymouth. On March 30, unable to endure further delay, he wrote a strongly worded letter to the Queen's Council in which, Corbett states, he enunciated "the root ideas of the New English school that Nelson brought to perfection."[2]

"If her Majesty and your Lordships," he wrote, "think that the King of Spain meaneth any invasion in England, then doubtless his force is and will be great in Spain: and thereon he will make his groundwork or foundation, whereby the Prince of Parma may have the better entrance, which, in mine own judgment, is most to be feared. But if there may be such a stay or stop made by any means of this fleet in Spain, that they may not come through the seas as conquerors—which, I assure myself, they think to do—then shall the Prince of Parma have such a check thereby as were meet.

"My very good Lords, next under God's mighty protection, the advantage and gain of time and place will be the only and chief means for our good; wherein I most humbly beseech your good Lordships to persevere as you have begun, for that with fifty sail of shipping we shall do more good upon their own coast, than a great many more will do here at home; and the sooner we are gone, the better we shall be able to impeach them."[3]

Again, on April 13, he wrote in similar strains to the Queen, and added: "The advantage of time and place in all martial actions is half a victory; which being lost is irrecoverable."[4] And again on April 28 he wrote:

[1] This squadron did not sail.
[3] *State Papers*, vol. I, pp. 124–125.
[2] *Drake and the Tudor Navy*, vol. II, p. 139.
[4] *Ibid.*, vol. I, p. 148.

"Most renowned Prince, I beseech you to pardon my boldness in the discharge of my conscience, being burdened to signify unto your Highness the imminent dangers that in my simple opinion do hang over us; that if a good peace for your Majesty be not forthwith concluded–which I as much as any man desireth–then these great preparations of the Spaniard may be speedily prevented as much as in your Majesty lieth, by sending your forces to encounter them somewhat far off, and more near their own coasts, which will be the better cheap [the more advantageous] for your Majesty and people, and much the dearer for the enemy."[1]

The outcome was that Howard was ordered to carry the bulk of his fleet to Plymouth, after he had detached a squadron under Lord Henry Seymour to watch the Channel.[2] He set out from the Downs on May 21 and joined Drake two days later. He then took over supreme command and appointed Drake his vice-admiral; as such he became President of the Council of War.[3] After this, Howard wrote to Burghley: "I mean to stay these two days to water our fleet, and afterwards, God willing, to take the opportunity of the first wind serving for the coast of Spain, with the intention to lie on and off betwixt England and that coast, to watch the coming of the Spanish forces. . . ."[4]

Meanwhile rumours and reports arrived from Spain and the high seas. In April it was rumoured that the Armada would make for Scotland,[5] and on May 16 it was reported that 300 sail had assembled at Lisbon, and "that they stand greatly upon their guard hearing but of the name of Drake to approach them."[6] On May 28 it was reported that the Armada was ready to sail.[7] Howard accordingly put to sea on May 30 and Drake's daring project seemed about to be attempted, but on June 6 the fleet was forced back into the Sound by contrary winds. A few days later a dispatch from Walsingham was received which showed that timidity had again crippled the Council; Howard was ordered not to take his fleet to Spain, but instead "to ply up and down in some indifferent place between the coast of Spain and this realm. . . ."[8] Howard, on June 15, answered:

[1] *Ibid.*, vol. 1, p. 166.
[2] At this time Justinian of Nassau (a natural son of Prince William I) and Jan Gerbrandtzoom with two Dutch squadrons were cruising off Dunkirk and the coast of the United Provinces.
[3] Under Drake came Lord Thomas Howard, Lord Sheffield, Sir Roger Williams, John Hawkins, Martin Frobisher, and Thomas Fenner.
[4] *Ibid.*, vol. 1, p. 179.   [5] *Ibid.*, vol. 1, p. 170.   [6] *Ibid.*, vol. 1, p. 173.
[7] *Ibid.*, vol. 1, p. 183.   [8] *Ibid.*, vol. 1, p. 193

"Sir, for the meaning we had to go on the coast of Spain, it was deeply debated by those which I think [the] world doth judge to be men of greatest experience that this realm hath.

"And if her Majesty do think that she is able to detract time with the King of Spain, she is greatly deceived which may breed her great peril. For this abusing [of] the treaty of peace doth plainly show how the King of Spain will have all things perfect, [as] his plot is laid, before he will proceed to execute. . . .

"The seas are broad; but if we had been [on] their coast, they durst not have put off, to have left us [on] their backs. . . ."[1]

Even more disastrous than this faulty strategy of Elizabeth and her Council was their administration. Again and again we find complaints by Howard of lack of victuals, a lack due partly to contrary winds, partly to the inefficiency of the period, but mainly to the parsimony of the Queen and her Councillors. Already, on May 28, Howard had written to Burghley: "My good Lord, there is here the gallantest company of captains, soldiers, and mariners that I think ever was seen in England. It were pity they should lack meat when they are so desirous to spend their lives in her Majesty's service."[2] Again he appealed, this time to Walsingham, on June 15, and from then on much of Howard's and Drake's correspondence falls under two headings: "let us attack," and "in heaven's name send us food." Thus, on June 15, Howard wrote to Walsingham:

"The opinion of Sir Francis Drake, Mr. Hawkyns, Mr. Frobisher, and others that be men of greatest judgment [and] experience, as also my own concurring with them in the same, is that [the] surest way to meet with the Spanish fleet is upon their own [coast], or in any harbour of their own, and there to defeat them. . . .

"Sir, our victuals be not come yet unto us; and if this weather hold, I know not when they will come."[3]

At length, on June 17, the Council gave way on the first point and authorized Howard to do what he "shall think fittest."[4] On June 23 the victuals had arrived and Howard informed the Queen that he was about to sail. He added: "For the love of Jesus Christ, Madam, awake thoroughly, and see the villainous treasons round about you, against your Majesty and your realm, and draw your forces round about you, like a mighty prince, to defend you.

[1] *Ibid.*, vol. I, pp. 202–204.
[3] *Ibid.*, vol. I, pp. 200–201.
[2] *Ibid.*, vol. I, p. 190.
[4] *Ibid.*, vol. I, p. 217.

Truly, Madam, if you do so, there is no cause to fear. If you do not, there will be danger."[1]

Directly the ships were provisioned–probably on June 24–Howard, Drake, and Hawkins put to sea. Howard kept the body of the fleet together in mid-Channel while Drake, with a squadron of 20 ships, stood out toward Ushant, and Hawkins, with an equal number, lay toward Scilly. Soon afterward the wind shifted into the south-west and the fleet had to return to Plymouth, from where, on July 16, Howard informed Walsingham: "We have at this time four pinnaces on the coast of Spain; but, Sir, you may see what [may co]me of the sending me out with so little victuals, and the [evil of the same]";[2] which suggests that it was not the wind alone which forced him back. Lastly, on July 17, we find him writing to the same Minister: "I never saw nobler minds that be here [in our] forces; but I cannot stir out but I have an inf[inite number] hanging on my shoulders for money."[3]

Such was the condition of the English fleet, which in four days was to face the Armada. It consisted of the Royal Navy, 34 ships with *The Ark Royal* (800 tons) as flagship; the London squadron, 30 ships; Drake's squadron, 34 ships; Lord Thomas Howard's squadron (merchant ships and coasters), 38 ships; 15 victuallers and 23 voluntary ships, and Lord Henry Seymour's squadron–off the Downs–which numbered 23 ships.[4]

On May 20, while the English fleet gathered at Plymouth, the Armada dropped down the Tagus and put to sea,[5] but was so buffeted in the Atlantic that, on June 9, Medina Sidonia sought refuge in Coruña, where to his consternation he found that much of the provisions was putrid and much water had leaked out of the newly-made casks. He also found that so many ships needed repair and so many men were sick, that on the advice of a council of war he sent a message to the King recommending a postponement of the expedition until the following year. This Philip refused to consider, so after fresh supplies had been requisitioned, on July 12, in spite of the stormy weather, the Armada sailed again. On July 19 the Lizard was

[1] *Ibid.*, vol. I, p. 217.   [2] *Ibid.*, vol. I, p. 245.
[3] *Ibid.*, vol. I, p. 273.
[4] See *ibid.*, vol. I, p. 167; vol. II, pp. 323–331. Many of these ships did not take part in the fighting. In battle, both sides relied on only a small proportion of their total strength, the English on the Queen's ships and a few others, and the Spaniards on their galleons, great ships (armed merchantmen) and galleasses.
[5] Duro, doc. 115, vol. II, p. 106, and doc. 118, vol. II p. 113. All dates are Old Style, for New Style add 10 days.

sighted, and there Medina Sidonia rested for a few hours until all his ships had come up. The following day he sailed eastward and shortly before midnight learnt from a captured English fishing boat that the Admiral of England and Drake had put to sea that afternoon.[1] This was untrue.

As soon as the Armada sighted the Lizard, Captain Thomas Fleming–who commanded one of the four pinnaces Howard had left in the Channel–reported its approach. The surprise was complete and Howard and Drake found themselves in the very position they had intended for their enemy–namely, "to meet the Spanish fleet upon their own coast, or in any harbour of their own, and there to defeat them." Nevertheless, on this Saturday, July 20, "his Lordship, accompanied with 54 sail of his fleet . . . plied out of the Sound; and being gotten out scarce so far as Eddystone, the Spanish army was discovered, and were apparently seen of the whole fleet to the westwards as far as Fowey."[2] Howard then struck sail and lay under bare poles.

Because no fighting instructions are known to have been issued during the reign of Elizabeth[3] it is impossible to say what order of battle Howard adopted. There was probably no order, other than "follow my leader," since, as yet, his fleet was not even organized into squadrons. And although the formation the Spanish fleet was found in was described as that of a crescent, no records support this. All that is known for certain is that it was divided into the usual main battle, vanguard (right wing) and rear guard (left wing). Corbett suggests that to meet the assumed strategical situation these three groups of ships were probably formed into two divisions or quasi-independent fleets:[4] the main battle, under Medina Sidonia in advance, to hold off Howard, who was supposed to be at Dartmouth, and the van and rear guards, in rear, to hold off Drake, who was known to be at Plymouth. The diagram illustrates his suggested distribution, which if viewed from the rear might well appear to look like a crescent.

As Drake had not been met with in the Channel, Medina Sidonia concluded that he had been caught napping and was still at Plymouth. The opportunity to destroy him was so apparent that Don Alonzo de Leyva, Captain-General of the Armada, and

[1] *Ibid.*, vol. II, pp. 222, 229.
[2] *State Papers* (Howard's Relation of Proceedings), vol. I, p. 7.
[3] *Fighting Instructions 1530–1816*, edit. Julian S. Corbett (1895, Navy Record Soc.), p. 27.
[4] *Drake and the Tudor Navy*, vol. II, pp. 210–219.

others urged Medina Sidonia to attack him before he could get out of the Sound. This was common sense, because in order to carry out their broadside tactics the English required sea-room to manœuvre in and the Spaniards, dependent on boarding, required a fight in narrow waters. Had de Leyva's suggestion immediately been adopted, it is possible that the English fleet might

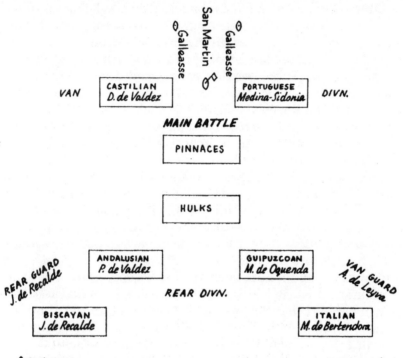

have suffered as disastrous a defeat as the Turkish fleet did at Lepanto. But the King's orders stood in the way, and Medina Sidonia refused to listen to de Leyva.[1]

Strangely enough, so it would appear, during the whole of July 20 the English fleet was unseen by the Spaniards, and it was not until one o'clock the following morning that they discovered from some prisoners that both Drake and Howard were out of Plymouth. Medina Sidonia at once anchored and ordered his squadron leaders to form order of battle.

[1] Duro, doc. 109, vol. I, p. 67.

While they did this, the moon rose and revealed their position to the English. Next, when the attention of the Spaniards was riveted on a small squadron of eight English ships beating out from Plymouth to windward between the shore and the port side of the Armada, which was erroneously assumed to be the van of the English main fleet, Howard and his 50 odd ships "recovered the wind of the Spaniards two leagues to the westward of Eddystone. . . ."[1] and at daybreak Medina Sidonia was dumbfounded to discover a large enemy fleet to windward of him, bearing down to the attack. He realized that he could not avoid battle and ran up the royal standard – the signal for a general engagement.

The English got the weather gauge[2] and drew up in a single long line – *en ala* as the Spaniards called it.[3] Then, writes Corbett, they passed the Spanish vanguard "which formed the starboard and leeward wing of the rear division, firing upon it at long range as they went, and fell on the rearguard, a manœuvre they can only have executed close-hauled in line-ahead. . . . The effect was immediate . . . a number of rearguard captains began crowding in a disgraceful panic upon Sidonia's division."[4] To check the rout, Recalde came up with the *Gran Grin*, and was at once surrounded by Drake, Hawkins, and Frobisher, who poured into his ship a murderous fire "such as never before had been seen at sea." Next, Pedro de Valdez in the *Nuestra Señora del Rosario*, was also engaged, and a little later Medina Sidonia in the *San Martin* came into action. But it was not until Recalde's vessel was completely disabled that Medina Sidonia could collect sufficient ships to relieve him. Howard then broke off the engagement, and soon after this the *San Salvador*, carrying the Paymaster-General of the Armada and his chests, blew up and dropped out of the fleet in flames. Howard signalled to his ships to make sail for the burning wreck, which resulted in a fresh fight, after which he again signalled the retreat.

This engagement, the first between the two fleets, was of outstanding moral importance. It showed that the English ships and gunners were vastly superior to the Spanish. The latter were

[1] *State Papers*, vol. I, p. 7.
[2] The weather gauge is the position of a ship to the windward of another, giving the possessor the initiative and advantage in manœuvring. It facilitates bringing an enemy to action and massing on part of his fleet. Also, the cannon smoke drifting to leeward blinds the enemy.
[3] Duro, vol. II, p. 154, and *Drake and the Tudor Navy*, vol. II, pp. 208 and 221. Whether this line was fortuitous or concerted it is impossible to say.
[4] *Ibid.*, vol. II, pp. 222 and 223.

greatly depressed by their failure to board, and also by the abandonment of the *San Salvador*. As Medina Sidonia says: "the enemy's ships were so fast and handy that there was nothing which could be done with them."[1]

That night, "his Lordship appointed Sir Francis Drake to set the Watch. . . ."[2] and then assembled a council of war in the *Ark Royal*, at which the general opinion held was that the Spaniards would make for the Isle of Wight—obviously the correct thing to do—in order to establish a base on English soil and to gain an anchorage for the fleet. This was the course the Spanish captains persuaded Medina Sidonia to adopt; for the English tactics had led to so excessive an expenditure of Spanish ammunition that they considered it essential for Medina Sidonia to occupy a port or roadstead on the south coast of England—actually the Isle of Wight—whence the Armada could cover the necessary flow of munitions from Spain and stand fast until action had been concerted with Parma.[3] To prevent such a contingency, the English war council decided to give chase to the enemy: Drake lit the great poop lantern of the *Revenge* and set out to lead the fleet through the night.

As the night wore on, suddenly his light disappeared, and immediately many of the ships astern of him hove to, while others held on their course. The result was confusion, and when the sun rose on July 22 the *Revenge* was nowhere to be seen.

What had happened was that when he heard that Don Pedro de Valdez's ship lay helpless, Drake extinguished his lantern and put about, for he had been told that she contained much treasure. In the morning he captured her,[4] sent her into Torbay, and rejoined the Lord Admiral. Apparently his privateering spirit had got the upper hand, which so incensed Frobisher that he exclaimed: "He thinketh to cozen us of our shares of fifteen thousand ducats; but we will have our shares, or I will make him spend the best blood in his belly. . . ."[5]

---

[1] *Ibid.*, doc. 165, vol. II, p. 230.   [2] *State Papers*, vol. I, p. 8.

[3] Duro, doc. 160, vol. II, p. 221.

[4] Drake embraced Don Pedro and gave him very honourable entertainment, feeding him at his own table and lodging him in his cabin.

[5] *State Papers*, vol. II, p. 102. Drake's explanation is, that "in the growing light" of the early morning of July 22 he saw three or four strange craft stealing past him. Thereupon he put out his light and tacked toward them. On discovering that they were German merchantmen, he proceeded to take station and fell in with Don Pedro's ship (*Drake and the Tudor Navy*, vol. II, p. 231). This is not very convincing because if dawn were breaking, there should have been little resultant confusion after the lantern was extinguished.

The respite granted to Medina Sidonia by the confusion in his enemy's fleet enabled him to reorganize his rear division. He now placed it under the command of de Leyva, but continued to maintain the van division as it was, because Seymour's squadron was still unaccounted for; then he set sail again. But the English fleet could not be got together until the evening of July 22, when the wind died away and both fleets were becalmed within cannon shot of each other between Portland and St. Alban's Head.

At dawn the following day the wind rose from the north-east, and as this gave the weather gauge to the Spaniards, Medina Sidonia signalled a general engagement, and fighting was resumed. Soon Frobisher's ship, the *Triumph* (1,100 tons and the largest English ship) and five others got into trouble, and when he saw this ". . . the Duke of Medina Sidonia . . . came out with 16 of his best galleons to impeach his Lordship [Howard] and to stop him from assisting the *Triumph*. At which assault, after wonderful sharp conflict, the Spaniards were forced to give way and to flock together like sheep." Howard's account continues: "This fight was very nobly continued from morning until evening, the Lord Admiral being always in the hottest of the encounter, and it may well be said that for the time there was never seen a more terrible value of great shot, nor more hot fight than this was; for although the musketeers and harquebusiers of crock [a rest or swivel] were then infinite, yet could they not be discerned nor heard for the great ordnance came so thick that a man would have judged it to have been a hot skirmish of small shot, being all the fight long within half musket shot of the enemy."[1]

The next day, Howard informs us, "there was little done," as much ammunition had been spent; therefore he sent "divers barks and pinnaces unto the shore for a new supply of such provisions", and divided his fleet into four squadrons, respectively commanded by himself, Drake, Hawkins, and Frobisher. Here for the first time we find a clear attempt to bring order out of disorder. Hitherto, with the possible exception of their first engagement, the English had fought their ships in swarms, in which the ships of their most noted captains had done the bulk of the fighting. Now these captains were to lead their own squadrons, and although this did not mean that Howard and Drake had decided henceforth to fight in line ahead, because each squadron had its own leader it was a definite step in that direction. Further, to facilitate his

[1] *Ibid.*, vol. 1, p. 12.

attack, Howard arranged that during the night six armed merchantmen from each squadron should keep the Spaniards in
constant alarm.

Unfortunately, the wind fell and these distracting attacks had to
be abandoned. Meanwhile Medina Sidonia told off 40 ships as a rearguard to protect his rear and then continued on his way, but soon
after he was becalmed a few miles to the south of the Isle of Wight.

The following morning–Thursday, July 25–Howard noticed
that Recalde's flagship, the *Santa Ana*, was "short of her company
to the southwards" and ordered Sir John Hawkins to lower some
boats and attack her. Immediately three galleasses rowed toward
the boats, and were "fought a long time and much damaged" by
"the Lord Admiral in the Ark, and the Lord Thomas Howard in
the Golden Lion." The wind then rose, the fleets clinched, and for
several hours the fighting was intense. This is noted by Sir George
Carey, who writes: ". . . with so great expense of powder and
bullet, that during the said time the shot continued so thick
together that it might rather have been judged a skirmish with
small shot on land than a fight with great shot on sea. In which
conflict, thanks be to God, there hath not been two of our men
hurt"[1]–somewhat of an anti-climax to so desperate a struggle.

Medina Sidonia had hoped much of this day–St. Dominic's,
his patron-saint–but when he found his ships again outclassed he
abandoned all idea of seizing the Isle of Wight, sent ahead a
dispatch boat to warn Parma of his arrival, and stood out for
Calais. Howard then made for Dover to link up with Lord Henry
Seymour and Sir William Wynter.

This day's fighting really decided the fate of the whole enterprise. The Spaniards had not yet been beaten, for so far their
losses were insignificant, but the English tactics of refusal to close
–that is, refusal to be pounded by the Spanish heavy cannon–had
exhausted the ammunition of both sides,[2] and whereas Howard
could replenish his from coastal ports near by, Medina Sidonia
could not do so until he had reached Flanders.

---

[1] *Ibid.*, vol. I, p. 324.

[2] The English ran out of both powder and shot, the Spaniards of shot only. Before
starting out, the provision of powder for the Armada was, according to Duro (vol. II,
p. 83) 517,000 lb., and according to Meteren (Hakluyt, vol. II, p. 373) 560,000 lb.,
and of shot 123,790 (Duro, doc. 110, vol. II, p. 83). Though not exactly known, the
English supplies were much less. Of this day's fighting, Meteren says that the two
fleets were at times engaged "within one hundred, or an hundred and twentie yards
one of another" (Hakluyt, vol. II, p. 387), which suggests that both sides were out of
heavy shot, and which, when read in context with Carey's statement, points to the
extreme inaccuracy of the lesser ordnance.

When Friday, July 26 dawned, "The Spaniards," says Howard, "went away before the English army like sheep," not out of fear, but for want of round shot. On Saturday evening, when he was near Calais, Medina Sidonia cast anchor between the town and Cape Gris-Nez and the English fleet anchored "within culverin shot of the enemy."[1] Howard had been joined by Seymour's and Wynter's squadrons and had in all under his command 136 ships, 46 of which were "great ships," whereas the ships of the Armada had been reduced to 124.

The tactical situation was changed completely, for Howard, who had been able, in part at least, to replenish his powder and shot, whereas Sidonia had been unable to do so, could, whenever he wished, close in to small arms range and use his culverins as true ship-battering pieces. The crisis had been reached – the Armada was cornered. But to board the Spanish ships would clearly be both a desperate and a costly operation, for their soldiers were trained and armed to meet this type of attack.

This situation had been foreseen, and some days before the Armada put into Calais Roads Walsingham had sent orders to Dover to collect some fishing craft, pitch, and faggots, to make fire-ships. This suggestion must have come from Howard and Drake, who could not have failed to see that if their enemy could not hold the Channel he would be compelled to put into some roadstead or port.

Early on Sunday, July 28, a council of war was assembled in the main cabin of the *Ark Royal*,[2] at which it was decided that so urgent was it to attack there would not be sufficient time to bring the fire-craft from Dover. Instead eight ships of 200 tons or under were selected from the fleet and prepared so hastily that not even their guns were removed.

Immediately he reached Calais, Medina Sidonia sent his secretary to Parma to urge haste; but no sooner had he gone than another messenger, who had been sent by boat sometime before, returned to say that Parma was at Bruges and that so far no men had been embarked. Then the secretary returned to say that it was impossible for Parma to get his army on board under a fortnight.

The truth would appear to be not that Parma's embarkation was delayed, but that, because of the Dutch fleet under Justinian

[1] *Ibid.*, vol. I, p. 15. See also Duro, doc. 165, vol. II, p. 238.
[2] *Ibid.*, vol. I, p. 15, and vol. II, p. 1.

of Nassau, Parma could not get out of port. It was useless to embark his men before Justinian's ships were driven away. Had it not been for the Dutch blockading fleet, which played a vitally important part in the campaign, in spite of Lord Henry Seymour's squadron, Parma might have chanced a crossing to Margate when the Armada was off the Isle of Wight. Emanuel van Meteren is definite on the effectiveness of the Dutch blockading fleet. "The shippes of Holland and Zeeland," he says, "stood continually in their sight [in the sight of Parma's ships] threatening shot and powder, and many inconveniences unto them: for feare of which shippes, the Mariners and Sea-men secretly withdrew themselves both day and night, least that the duke of Parma his souldiers should compell them by maine force to goe on board, and to breake through the Hollanders Fleete, which all of them judged to bee impossible by reason of the straightnesse of the Haven."[1]

On board the Armada there was discouragement because the Governor of Calais had warned Medina Sidonia that the roadstead was highly dangerous, and because of the bad news received from Parma. "We rode there," writes Don Luis de Miranda, "all night at anchor, with the enemy half a league from us likewise anchored, being resolved to wait, since there was nothing else to be done, and with a great presentiment of evil from that devilish people and their arts. So too in a great watching we continued on Sunday all day long."[2] This is not altogether correct, because the opportunity for an attack by fire-ships was so obvious that Medina Sidonia had ordered out a flotilla of patrol boats to intercept them, should they be launched.

Midnight struck and passed, when early on Monday, as all lay still, the Spanish sentries saw several shadowy ships approach them and then burst into flames. The memory of the "hellburners" of Antwerp, which three years before had destroyed a thousand of Parma's men, flashed across the minds of the terrified Spaniards. Medina Sidonia gave the fatal order for cables to be cut. He meant to reoccupy the anchorage once the fire-ships had passed by, but a panic followed and in confusion many of his ships crashed into each other in the dark and were borne out to sea. "Fortune," wrote a Spanish officer, "so favoured them [the English] that there grew from this piece of industry just what they counted on, for they dislodged us with eight vessels, an exploit

[1] *Voyages*, Hakluyt, vol. ii, p. 389.   [2] Duro, doc. 169, vol. ii, p. 269.

which with one hundred and thirty they had not been able to do nor dared to attempt."[1]

As soon as the fire-ships had drifted clear – they did no damage – Medina Sidonia ordered a signal gun to be fired for the fleet to regroup at Calais. The *San Marcos* (a Portuguese galleon) and one or two others obeyed the signal, but most of the ships, with two anchors lost and unable to get at their spare ones, drifted north-eastward along the coast. When at last he realized that because the wind blew from the south-south-west it would be impossible for these ships to close in on the *San Martin*, Medina Sidonia weighed anchor and stood out to sea to follow the rest.

When morning broke, a triumphant sight greeted the eyes of Howard's men: right along the coast toward Dunkirk the Armada lay scattered, with no possibility of regaining Calais Road, where, stranded on the sand, close under the guns of the town, lay the *Capitana* galleasse with Don Hugo de Monçada and 800 men on board. Now was Howard's chance to attack and overwhelm his enemy, and he set out to seize it, but when he saw the great galleasse, she proved too tempting a bait. Instead of following the fleeing enemy, he made for the galleasse and took her after a stiff fight, in which Monçada was killed.

Drake, Hawkins, and Frobisher crowded on all sail and set out after the Armada. As they were short of powder and shot they closed in on their enemy so that every shot should tell. This they could do at little risk because the Spanish cannon shot had been exhausted. In this running fight their aim was to cut off the weathermost of the Spanish ships and to drive the rest to leeward on to the banks of Zeeland. Meteren writes of this action:

"Wherefore the English shippes using their prerogative of nimble stirrage, whereby they could turne and wield themselves with the winde which way they listed, came often times very neere upon the Spaniards, and charged them so sore, that now and then they were but a pike's length asunder: and so continually giving them one broadside after another, they discharged all their shot both great and small upon them. . . ."[2]

The battle was continued along the coast toward Dunkirk, and at about nine o'clock the two fleets were engaged off Gravelines. The fight lasted until six in the evening.[3] On the Spanish side

---

[1] *Ibid.*, doc. 171, vol. II, p. 283. See also Pedro Estrade's account in *Monson* (vol. II, appendix A, p. 306) and Wynter to Walsingham (*State Papers*, vol. II, p. 9).
[2] Hakluyt, vol. II, p. 392.
[3] Wynter's account, *State Papers*, vol. II, pp. 10–11.

Estrade's account is interesting, because it describes the severity of the English fire:

"So we bare out of the north and north-east," he writes, "with great disorder investing one with another and separated; and the English in the wind of us discharging their cannons marvellously well, and discharged not one piece but it was well employed by reason we were on so nigh another and they a good space asunder one from the other. The Vice-Admiral St. Martin went before, shooting her artillery. This day was slain Don Philip de Cordova, with a bullet that struck off his head and struck with his brains the greatest friend that he had there, and 24 men that were with us trimming our foresail. And whereas I and other four where, there came a bullet and from one struck away his shoe without doing any other harm, for they came and plied so very well with shot."[1]

This praise of English gunnery is corroborated by Sir William Wynter who, on August 1, wrote to Walsingham: "I deliver it unto your Honour upon the credit of a poor gentleman, that out of my ship there was shot 500 shot of demi-cannon, culverin, and demi-culverin; and when I was furtherest off in discharging any of my pieces, I was not out of the shot of their harquebus, and most times within speech one of another. And surely every man did well; and, as I have said, no doubt the slaughter and hurt they received was great, as time will discover it; and when every man was weary with labour, and our cartridges spent, and munitions wasted [expended]–I think in some altogether–we ceased firing and followed the enemy, he bearing hence still in the course as I have said before [*i.e.* NNE and N by E]."[2]

As the crisis of the battle approached–it was six o'clock in the evening–it seemed that the Armada was doomed to inevitable destruction, when, to the relief of its sorely tried men, a squall of wind swept down upon the contending fleets. Then Howard and Drake broke off the fight,[3] and the *Maria Juan* of 665 tons–one of Recalde's ships–foundered. With the squall the battle ended, and as Medina Sidonia had been forced out of the Channel and to leeward of Dunkirk the possibility of joining hands with Parma grew more and more remote.

As night closed in the wind freshened to a half-gale and the *San Mateo*, the *San Felipe*, and a third ship were driven on to the Zeeland coast. When Tuesday, July 30, dawned, Medina Sidonia

---

[1] Monson, vol. II, appendix A, pp. 307–308.   [2] *State Papers*, vol. II, p. 11.
[3] They were now out of shot and in any case could no longer continue it.

looked from his flagship to see 109 English sail little more than half a league astern of his scattered fleet. In his *Relation* we read:

"The Duke fired two guns to collect his Armada, and sent a pinnace with a pilot to order his ships to keep a close luff, seeing that they were very near the banks of Zeeland. For the same cause, the enemy remained aloof, understanding that the Armada must be lost, for the pilots on board the flagship, men of experience on that coast, told the Duke at the time that it would not be possible to save a single ship of the Armada, and that with the wind at N.W., as it was, every one must needs go on to the banks of Zeeland, God alone being able to prevent it. The fleet being in this danger, with no kind of way of escape, and in six and a half fathoms of water, God was pleased to change the wind to W.S.W., and with it the fleet stood to the northward, without damage to any vessel, the duke having sent orders to every ship to follow the motions of the flagship at peril of driving on the banks of Zeeland."[1]

Throughout the entire week's fighting, and in spite of "upwards of 100,000 rounds of great shot" expended by the Spaniards, no English ship was seriously damaged and only one captain and a score or two of seamen were killed.[2] On the other hand, in the battle of Gravelines alone the Spaniards lost 600 killed and 800 wounded.

On the evening of July 29 Medina Sidonia summoned a council of war, which decided that if the wind changed the Armada would regain the Channel, in spite of the fact that his ships were short of provisions and out of great shot. But, should it not regain the Channel, the sole course open was to return to Spain by way of the North Sea. As the wind did not change the latter course was adopted.

It was a desperate venture, for not only were many of the ships now unseaworthy, but they were not provisioned for so long a voyage. Nevertheless, though driven northward by an evil wind and pursued by Drake, to whom had been allotted the post of honour in the chase, it was still possible for Medina Sidonia in part to redeem the disaster. This he could have done if he had landed in the Forth and raised Scotland against the Queen. But his one thought was to get back to Spain; he sailed past the mouth

---

[1] Duro, doc. 165, vol. II, pp. 244–246.
[2] *The Navy of Britain*, Michael Lewis (1948), p. 443.

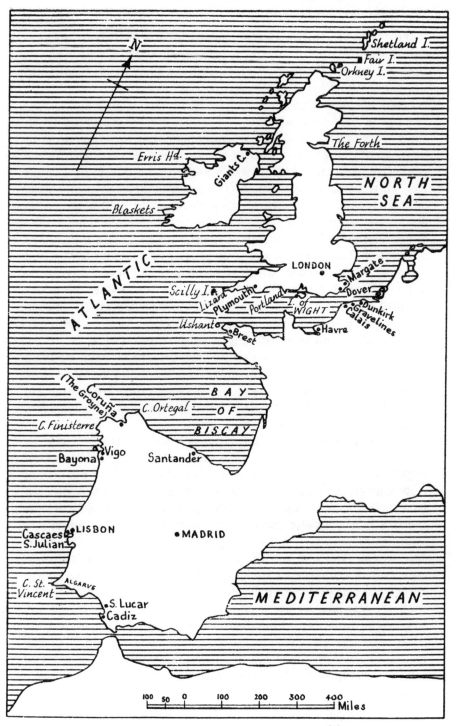

I. THE ARMADA CAMPAIGN, 1588

of the Forth on August 2, and in a single body the Armada stood out for the Orkneys. The next day Howard abandoned the chase, and, on August 7, his ships recovered the Downs, Harwich, and Yarmouth.[1]

From Margate Road, on August 8, he wrote to Walsingham: "I pray to God we may hear of victuals, for we are generally in great want." To guard against an enemy return, he urged Walsingham to look to the country's defences, and then added: "Some made little account of the Spanish force by sea; but I do warrant you, all the world never saw such a force as theirs was; and some Spaniards that we have taken, that were in the fight at Lepanto, do say that the worst of our four fights that we have had with them did exceed far the fight they had there; and they say that at some of our fights we had 20 times as much great shot as they had there . . . Sir, in your next letters to my brother Stafford [Ambassador at Paris] I pray write to him that he will let Mendoza [Spanish Ambassador in Paris] know that her Majesty's rotten ships dare meet with his master's sound ships; and in buffeting with them, though they were three great ships to one of us, yet we have shortened them 16 or 17: whereof there is three of them a-fishing in the bottom of the seas." To this letter he added the postscript—"Sir, if I hear nothing of my victuals and munition this night here, I will gallop to Dover to see what may be got there, or else we shall starve."[2]

The rest of the story, a dramatic one, is soon told, for during the Armada's dreadful voyage home, the galleasse *Girona* went to pieces near Giant's Causeway, and carried to their deaths her crew and Don Alonso de Leyva; the *El Gran Grifon* sank off Fair Island; the *Rata Coronada* was wrecked on the coast of Erris; the *Duquesa Santa Ana* was lost in Glennagiveny Bay; and the *Nuestra Señora de la Rosa* was beaten to pieces on the Blaskets. The *San Marcos, San Juan, Triniada, Valencera,* and *Falcon Blanco Mediano* were lost off the coast of Ireland, and the *San Pedro Mayor,* blown off course, was wrecked in Bigbury Bay, near Plymouth.

Of the 130 sail which stood out from Lisbon in May, 63 are believed to have been lost. Two were abandoned to the enemy; three were lost off the French coast; two were lost off Holland; two were sunk off Gravelines; 19 were wrecked off Scotland or Ireland; and the fate of 35 is unknown. The English did not lose a ship.

[1] *State Papers,* vol. I, p. 18.　　　　[2] *Ibid.,* vol. II, p. 59–61.

Even more horrible than the fate of the castaways on the Irish coast, most of whom were butchered, was that of the crews who were not shipwrecked; thousands of men died of untended wounds, of fever, of hunger, and of thirst—some ships were without water for 14 days. At length, in the middle of September, a messenger arrived post-haste at the Escorial from Santander with the news that Medina Sidonia had returned to that port on September 12. When the messenger gave the King this fatal news, Philip was sitting at his desk. Without change of countenance he observed: "Great thanks do I render Almighty God, by whose generous hand I am gifted with such power, that I could easily, if I chose, place another fleet upon the sea. Nor is it of very great importance that a running stream should be sometimes intercepted, so long as the fountain from which it flows remains inexhaustible."[1]

It was God's will, and so he accepted his defeat. Yet he was not unconscious of the sufferings of the brave men who had risked and undergone so much in this disastrous crusade. He did all in his power to alleviate their ills, and instead of blaming Medina Sidonia, he ordered him to return to Cadiz, there to resume his former governorship.

Very different was the behaviour of Queen Elizabeth, whose first consideration was to cut expense. Unlike Philip, there was nothing either chivalrous or generous in her character, and though Professor Laughton goes out of his way to exonerate her meanness,[2] there is no shadow of doubt that, had she been a woman of heart as well as of head, it would have been impossible for her to have left her gallant seamen to die by scores of want and disease immediately after the victory was won.

The correspondence of Howard proves this conclusively. On August 10—that is, three days after his return from the pursuit— he wrote to Burghley: "Sickness and mortality begins wonderfully to grow amongst us; and it is a most pitiful sight to see, here at Margate, how the men, having no place to receive them into here, die in the streets."[3] Again, on August 29, he wrote to him: "It were too pitiful to have men starve after such a service. . . . Therefore I had rather open the Queen Majesty's purse something

---

[1] Quoted from Motley's *History of the United Netherlands* (1860), vol. II, p. 535. Shortly after the battle of Gravelines a report was received by Philip that the Armada had been triumphant; next, that it had been defeated, but to what extent was uncertain. Not until Medina Sidonia's return did he receive the full news.
[2] See *State Papers*, vol. I, XLIV, XLVI–XLIX.   [3] *Ibid.*, vol. II, p. 96.

to relieve them, than they should be in that extremity for we are to look to have more of their services; and if men should not be cared for better than to let them starve and die miserably, we should very hardly get men to serve."[1]

Although little realized at the time, the influences of this campaign on naval strategy and tactics were profound, and out of them gradually emerged many of the principles which were to govern warfare at sea until the advent of the steamship.

First, the campaign showed the vital importance of bases in relation to command of the sea. Drake's 1587 attack on Cadiz and Lisbon was in idea a more certain method of protecting England against invasion than to meet and beat the Armada in the Channel, and had it been repeated in 1588, as it readily could have been, the high probability is that the Armada would never have sailed. Conversely, the lack of a Spanish naval base near England was the fundamental reason why the Armada was unable to carry out its task. Hence onward, because it is seldom possible to compel an enemy to accept battle at sea, to bottle-up his fleet in its home ports and simultaneously to deny him naval bases near her shores, became the foundations of England's naval policy.

Secondly, the campaign had shown clearly the futility of reliance on armed merchantmen in battle. They took next to no part in the Channel fighting, and the best that can be said of them is that they added grandeur and with it, possibly, terror, to the respective fleets. As raiders, they were of use, but as ships of the line, an impediment rather than a support. Had the English done without them much money could have been saved without in any way jeopardizing the issue.

Thirdly, as artillerists both sides had failed to achieve their respective ends. The English culverins were neither powerful enough nor sufficiently accurate to hit and smash a ship except at close range, and though the Spanish cannon could do so, their ships were not nimble enough nor their seamen sufficiently skilful to bring their superior armament within close range of their enemy. Hence the indecisive nature of the fighting and the tendency for cannon increasingly to become the primary naval weapon in battle.

---

[1] *Ibid.*, vol. II, p. 183. Professor J. E. Neale excuses this parsimony thus: "It is a sad thought that while battle slew a mere hundred during the fight with the Armada, epidemic disease afterwards raged in the fleet and slew its thousands. But once again there was no novelty in the fact: disease also decimated the Spaniards" (*Queen Elizabeth, 1934*, p. 299).

Historically, the importance of the defeat of the Armada was, as Merriman says, that it constituted "the supreme disaster of Philip's reign."[1] Nevertheless the war meandered on until 1604, to end in a peace of exhaustion which was neither creditable nor profitable to England, nor of any great consequence to Spain. It did not add an acre to Spanish territory, nor subtract an acre from English. It did not change the dynasties of England or Spain, nor did it modify the policies of the contending parties or influence their respective religions. Wherein, then, lay the decisiveness of the battle?

To answer that it spared England from invasion is true, but only conditionally so, for the part played by Justinian of Nassau was as important in gaining the victory as that played by Howard and Drake. Even had these two never put to sea, it is improbable that the Armada could have dislodged the Sea Beggars of Brill, because their nimble, light draught ships could sail the shallow coastal waters of Flanders and Zeeland and the cumbersome and larger Spanish ships could not. Yet, even should this hypothesis be set aside, the defeat of the Armada is to be reckoned the most decisive English battle fought since Hastings—it saved England and it mortally wounded Spanish prestige. It showed to the world at large that the colossus had feet of clay; that the edifice of Spanish power was built upon sand, and that the security of her empire was largely a mirage. It was this illusion which for nearly a century had imposed itself upon the credulity of the world to an extent unwarranted either by the resources, the wealth, or the population of Spain.

Since the conquest of Granada in 1492, Spain had accomplished extraordinary things. Suddenly her sons had stretched out their hands and seized the limits of the known world. They conquered Mexico and Peru, planted colonies in southern, central, and northern America, spanned the Indian Ocean, and established the myth of their invincibility. They accomplished these marvellous things because they believed themselves to be the chosen instruments of God. The defeat of their Armada shattered this faith and destroyed the illusion that had fortified their fanaticism. Thirty years later Spain became decadent, not because the war with England had been long and exhausting, but because the loss of faith in her destiny was catastrophic.

There was another reason for this moral collapse: it was that, before the Armada sailed, the Spaniards had failed to grasp the

[1] *The Rise of the Spanish Empire* (1934), vol. IV, p. 552.

true meaning of sea power. Had they done so they would have sought command of the sea before they attempted to gain full command of their scattered lands. Command of the sea was vital to them if they were to prevent the interruption of their trade with the New World and the Indies and to secure their hold over the Netherlands. It was lack of this command which enabled Hawkins, Drake, and others with impunity to sail the Spanish Main; to pillage Spanish treasure ships; to plunder Spanish colonial towns; and to sail into the ports of Cadiz and Lisbon and insult the Spanish flag. It was lack of command of the sea which lost the United Provinces and which led directly to the defeat of the Armada; for power to command the sea was not Spain's, and least of all when the Armada sailed up the Channel to gain it. Though more clearly seen today than in 1588, the Armada was doomed from the start, not only because it was outclassed in navigation and tactics, but because its commanders had little sea sense.[1]

Strange though it may seem at first, the only two peoples who were not spellbound by the Spanish myth were the English and the Dutch, both small nations. But it appears less strange when it is recognized that both were sea powers who could, even if precariously, command their home waters. It was because they could do this that they were able to defeat the fleets of Spain and so set out on their imperial courses which, in less than a century, made them rivals.

What these two peoples learned was that small nations with limited resources and little native power, so long as they command the sea, can win and hold great oversea dominions; whereas great nations, though they may gain vast oversea territories, unless they command the sea, cannot hold them once they are challenged seriously.

The defeat of the Armada whispered the imperial secret into England's ear; that in a commercial age the winning of the sea is more profitable than the winning of the land, and though this may not have been clearly understood in 1588, during the following century the whisper grew louder and louder until it became the voice of every Englishman.

[1] Only after his supreme disaster did Philip set out to build an ocean-going navy and begin to establish Spanish command of the sea. In order to secure the treasure he drew from the Indies, he abandoned carrying it in great fleets—and brought it to Spain in fast, armed vessels of 200 tons, called *gallizabras*, which could sail without escort. Although, as ships of war, they could not help him to win his war against England, by denying to the English raiders their former booty, they did prevent England winning the trade war—actually the real war.

In the "Epistle Dedicatorie" to the first edition of his *Voyages*, published in 1589, and addressed to Sir Francis Walsingham, Richard Hakluyt voices this imperial spirit in the following panegyric:

"So in this most famous and peerlesse government of her most excellent Majesty, her subjects through the speciall assistance, and blessing of God, in searching the most opposite corners and quarters of the world . . . have excelled all the nations and people of the earth. For, which of the kings of this land before her Majesty, had theyr banners ever seene in the Caspian sea? which of them hath ever dealt with the Emporor of Persia, as her Majesty hath done, and obteined for her merchants large and loving privileges? who ever saw before this regiment, an English Ligier in the stately porch of the Grand Signor at Constantinople? who ever found English Consuls and Agents at Tripolis in Syria, at Aleppo, at Babylon, at Balsara, and which is more, who ever heard of Englishman at Goa before now? what English shippes did heeretofore ever anker in the mighty river of Plate? passe and repasse the unpassable (in former opinion) straight at Magellan, range along the coast of Chili, Peru, and all the backside of Nova Hispania, further than any Christian ever passed, travers the mighty bredth of the South sea, land upon the Luzones in despight of the enemy, enter into alliance, amity, and traffike with the princes of the Moluccaes, and the Isle of Java, double the famous Cape of Bona Speranza, arive at the Isle of Santa Helena, and last of al returne home most richly laden with the commodities of China, as the subjects of this now flourishing monarchy have done?"[1]

The historical importance of the defeat of the Armada is this: it laid the cornerstone of the British Empire by endowing England with the prestige Spain lost. And it was this prestige, this faith in her destiny, that urged the English along their imperial way, until their flag floated over the greatest empire the world has so far seen: the empire of the oceans and the seas, which from rise to fall was to endure for over 300 years.

[1] Vol. I, pp. 3–4.

The disruption of Christendom

The passing of feudal Europe into the Renaissance; the decay of scholasticism and the rise of humanism; the over-secularization of the papacy and the steady emasculation of the Empire; the budding forth of rationalism and absolute monarchies; the introduction of the printing press and the development of firearms; the discovery of the New World and the sea route to India, coupled with the growth of city life, of wealth, luxury and poverty, of commerce, trading monopolies and usury, reached flash-point in what is called the Reformation–the religious expression of the general ferment.

The two great detonators were Luther (1483–1546) and Zwingli (1484–1531), to be followed by a still greater, Calvin (1509–1564). In order to reinstate, as they conceived it, the pristine purity of religion, these men turned to the doctrine of predestination: that man is irredeemably evil, and however he may live and whatever he may do, from all eternity God has destined a chosen few for paradise and the vast majority for hell. This doctrine, which shifted the centre of gravity from God to the devil, together with the dogma that the Bible was to be the rule of all doctrine and worship, became the two great abutments of the reformers' cult.

Of these three men, the most portentous was Calvin, a fanatical organizer. He looked upon himself as the Oracle of God, whose orders carried with them divine sanction. At Geneva, where he established himself and his police-state, he assumed the infallibility he denied to the Catholic Church, and created a new type of man, the "Puritan", and a new régime, which aptly has been called "Bibliocracy."

"The Reformation," writes Oswald Spengler, "abolished the whole bright and consoling side of the Gothic myth–the cult of Mary, the veneration of the saints, the relics, the pilgrimages, the Mass. But the myth of devildom and witchcraft remained, for it was the embodiment and cause of the inner torture, and now that torture at last rose to its supreme horror."[1] The law of love was

[1] *The Decline of the West*, English edit. (1928), vol. II, p. 299.

rejected for the law of hate. Soon there grew up an immense Protestant literature on the devil which polluted true religion.

Today, it is difficult to grasp how such a creed offered any attraction. Nevertheless men of conviction were carried away by the thunderous theology of Luther and the cold logic of Calvin. The challenge was so immense and the propaganda so vitriolic that they appealed to all who were discontented. Swarms of monks and degenerate priests saw in the new creed an opportunity to rid themselves of obligations which had become irksome; princes found in it a means to fortify themselves against the Empire and to increase their domains by plundering the Church; the rising money-power discovered in it a sanction which favoured usury and the new economic conditions, and the oppressed masses a doctrine offering liberty and licence to all.

The turmoil which resulted cannot be discussed here, but in order to end it, on September 25, 1555, a compromise was reached at Augsburg, mainly between Ferdinand, who represented his brother, the Emperor Charles V, and Augustus, Lutheran Elector of Saxony. According to its terms, all Lutheran princes were granted freedom from episcopal jurisdiction and were permitted to retain ecclesiastical property secularized before the Treaty of Passau in 1552. Each secular prince had the right to decide, according to the principle of *cujus regio ejus religio*, which religion should be binding on his people, which meant that the faith of the German people was determined for them by their territorial princes instead of by the Church. And though a clause, known as the "ecclesiastical reservation", imposed forfeiture of land and dignities of Catholic bishops who forsook their faith, the Lutherans declared that they did not consider themselves bound by it.

The Calvinists were not included in this compact, nor was any allowance made for the growth of the Protestant religion, which rapidly spread over the Empire. All that the Peace of Augsburg accomplished was to establish a truce, it left Germany divided into two omnipresent factions, and as Lord Bryce says: "Two mutually repugnant systems could not exist side by side without striving to destroy one another." This destruction was made inevitable by the rising power of Calvinism and the newly constituted Society of Jesus, the one aim of which was the extirpation of Protestantism.

The storm centre became Prague, where Calvinism had strongly entrenched itself. In 1526 Bohemia had passed to the House of Habsburg, and in 1575 Maximilian II's eldest son Rudolf was crowned king. He succeeded his father as emperor in 1576, made Prague his imperial capital, and in 1609 was compelled by his Protestant subjects to grant them the so-called "Letter of Majesty", by which their religion was guaranteed and safeguarded by a body of men known as the Defenders. In 1611, Rudolf was deposed by his brother Matthias, who in May was crowned king of Bohemia and a year later elected emperor.

Meanwhile, after the Treaty of Augsburg, two champions had come forward to personify the elements of strife; Maximilian Duke of Bavaria, the Catholic, and Prince Christian of Anhalt, the Calvinist. The former regarded the treaty as a legal settlement to which all question should be referred; the latter believed that Protestantism had to get rid of the House of Austria, or the House of Austria would get rid of Protestantism. Incident followed incident, until, in 1607, Maximilian occupied the free city of Donauwörth. This led to the creation of the Evangelical Union under Christian of Anhalt the following year. Challenged by this show of force, Maximilian formed the Holy Catholic League. A conflict was nearly certain, because Matthias was childless and his successor to both the Empire and Bohemia was likely to be the Archduke Ferdinand of Styria, the grandson of Ferdinand I, a fanatical Catholic. Matthias feared trouble and postponed his election until 1617, when a decision became imperative. When Spain agreed to support Ferdinand's candidature, on the understanding that when he became emperor he would surrender the Habsburg fiefs in Alsace to the Spanish crown, on June 17 the king's councillors, all of whom were fervent Catholics, elected Ferdinand heir to the Bohemian throne. At once the Bohemian Protestants, headed by Count Thurn, refused to recognize Ferdinand, and in December, when the Archbishop of Prague, in violation of the Letter of Majesty, ordered the suppression of Protestant services in the churches which had been built on his domains, the Defenders summoned a Diet to meet at Prague. It assembled there on May 21, 1618, and the following day, after a violent altercation, the king's most trusted councillors, Martinitz and Slawata, and their secretary Fabricius, were hurled out of a window of the Hradcany Palace, an event to become known as the Defenestration of Prague. Immediately after this the Bohemians established a provisional government and proceeded to raise an army under Count Thurn. Hostilities with Austria opened in July and, little thought of at the time, they were destined to develop into the first of the great European wars and to last for 30 years.

On March 20, 1619, the death of Matthias accelerated events. The Confederate States, Bohemia, Lusatia, Silesia, and Moravia, declared the election of Ferdinand invalid, and on August 26 they elected as their king Frederick V Elector Palatine, a fervent Calvinist, whose wife, Elizabeth, was the daughter of James I of England.

Two days later the Electoral College met at Frankfort to decide who should succeed Matthias. It was the controlling organ of the Empire, and without its consent the Emperor could not call a Diet, impose a tax, make an alliance, or declare war. It had been created by the Golden Bull of 1356 and consisted of three spiritual, and four temporal princes. The former were the Catholic Electors of Mainz, Cologne, and Trèves, and the latter, the King of Bohemia, the Elector Palatine and the Elector of Brandenburg, both Calvinists, and the Elector of Saxony, a Lutheran. Therefore, as long as the King of Bohemia was a Catholic, the Catholic princes dominated; but should he be replaced by a non-Catholic, they would be in a minority. In this balance within the Electoral College where lay the root trouble of the Thirty Years War.

At Frankfort, only the three spiritual princes attended in person, the other four members of the College were represented by ambassadors, among whom Frederick's was instructed in the first instance to vote for Maximilian Duke of Bavaria (a Catholic), but should the other Electors vote for Ferdinand, he was to agree. As they did so, Ferdinand was elected Emperor under the title of Ferdinand II (1619–1637). No sooner had the decision been made than the news was received that he had been deposed from the Bohemian throne. As this was a challenge, not only to Ferdinand, but to the whole imperial system, the crisis at once became a European problem.

Because Ferdinand had no army wherewith to eject Frederick, he turned to Maximilian, the only prince in Germany who possessed a standing army, and on October 8, 1619, Maximilian agreed to support Ferdinand on the understanding that he had complete control of operations in Bohemia, and on the defeat of Frederick would be given his electoral titles. Also, at the price of Lusatia, Ferdinand gained the support of John George of Saxony, who detested the Calvinists. Further, Philip III (1598–1621) of Spain, promptly granted Ferdinand a subsidy to raise 10,000

2. THE THIRTY YEARS WAR, 1619–1648

troops and lent him 8,000 more from the Netherlands. On the other hand, the princes of the Union recognized Frederick, as also did the United Provinces, Denmark, and Sweden, while Bethlen Gabor, Prince of Transylvania, entered into alliance with the Bohemians.

In July, 1620, the army of the Catholic League, 25,000 strong, under command of Maximilian, Tilly, and Bucquoy, crossed the Austrian frontier, and at the same time Spinola and 24,000 men set out from Flanders for the Palatinate. On November 8 the former came up with the Bohemians, under Christian of Anhalt, at the White Hill, near Prague, and routed them; Spinola overran the Palatinate.

These disasters broke up the Evangelical Union and might have ended the war had Ferdinand been more tolerant. But his principle, "Better to rule over a desert than a country full of heretics," urged him on; his persecutions exasperated the Calvinists. The result was that the fragments of the Bohemian army, reinforced by numbers of desperate men, rallied round the Calvinist general Count Ernest von Mansfeld, an able mercenary, soon to become known as the "Attila of Christendom", who carried the war into the Upper Palatinate. In the spring of 1622 he was joined by Christian Duke of Brunswick and George Frederick Margrave of Baden Durlach. A series of engagements followed, which in June was ended by a decisive defeat of the Calvinists at Höchst; whereupon Mansfeld and Christian retired into Alsace and later quartered themselves in east Friesland. Lastly, in August, 1623, Christian of Brunswick was crushed at Stadtlohon, and the conquest of the Palatinate was completed.

Ferdinand had, in January, 1621, unconstitutionally placed Frederick under the imperial ban, and in January, 1623, in fulfilment of his promise to Maximilian, he decided to transfer Frederick's electorship to him. As he could not call a Diet on his own authority, he assembled a general Electoral Meeting at Regensburg to sanction the transfer. Apart from Maximilian's brother, the Elector of Cologne, almost every important prince in Germany, as well as the King of Spain, was opposed to it. Nevertheless Frederick was deposed on February 23 and two days later Maximilian was invested with his titles. A storm of protest followed and the Electors of Saxony and Brandenburg refused to recognize their new colleague.

The alarm of the Protestant princes was fully justified. Not only did the unconstitutional deposition of Frederick threaten their individual securities, but, because of the change in the balance of power made by the investiture of Maximilian, they feared that they would be deprived of the ecclesiastical property they had seized since 1555, which included two archbishoprics and 120 abbacies. To prevent this they turned to Christian IV (1588–1648) of Denmark, a Lutheran prince, who, in May, 1624, accepted their cause. The war now entered its second phase; from a European problem it became a European conflict.

Compared with the Danish army, the army of the Catholic League was weak, and Ferdinand consequently was placed in a quandary; he did not wish to barter further territory for allied support. Suddenly the difficulty was overcome by Count Albrecht von Wallenstein (1583–1634), a Czech adventurer of great wealth, who offered to raise for the Emperor an army of 40,000 men free of charge so long as the appointment of its officers remained in his hands. Ferdinand at once accepted the offer and conferred upon Wallenstein the title of Duke of Friedland. Thus, at length, the Empire obtained an army of its own, which cost nothing and which could be maintained indefinitely in the field as long as it was engaged in war, because Wallenstein's maxim was that "war should feed war".

While Ferdinand was thus engaged, James I, at length had espoused the cause of his son-in-law and had quarrelled with Spain. At the same time Cardinal Richelieu (1585–1642), first minister of Louis XIII (1610–1643) of France, whose policy was to break the Habsburg circle which had surrounded France ever since the days of Charles V, concluded an alliance with England, the United Provinces, and Denmark. Thus the French policy of intervention in German affairs was inaugurated, a policy which has agitated central Europe ever since. Because Richelieu was paralysed by a Huguenot rising and James was afraid to summon Parliament, intervention was left to Christian IV, who was eager to extend his influence over the North Sea ports, and in 1626 he took the field.

In April, Wallenstein also set out. He moved against Mansfeld and defeated him at the Bridge of Dessau, then he overran Mecklenburg and Pomerania and increased his army as he went until it numbered some 80,000. On August 27, Christian IV was routed by Tilly at Lutter by the Barenberg and Brunswick was overrun.

As the occupation of the Palatinate had freed the middle Rhine and thereby reopened it as the main line of communication between Italy and the Spanish Netherlands, which was of vital importance to Spain, Wallenstein set out to establish Ferdinand's authority over the Baltic principalities. He flooded the Danish mainland with his troops and in March, 1628, was rewarded when the Emperor conferred upon him the duchies of Mecklenburg. This high-handed act, even more than the raising of Maximilian to an Electorate, showed the Protestant princes that none of them was safe, and that the time was approaching rapidly when the whole of Germany would become an Austrian province. So they concerted on the overthrow of Wallenstein, but how to effect it in face of his 80,000 men was beyond their grasp.

The subjection of the Baltic lands was pushed steadily, and when Hamburg and Lübeck rejected Ferdinand's offer of alliances Wallenstein set out to bring the Hanseatic League to heel by an advance on Stralsund. An army of 25,000 men, under his lieutenant, Arnim, appeared before the town in April, but its councillors were not taken unawares. They had already entered into relations with Christian IV and Gustavus Adolphus of Sweden (1611–1632), and Munro's regiment of 900 Scots–then in the Danish service–400 Danes, and 600 Swedes, were sent by sea to the town. On June 23 a 20-year alliance was signed by Gustavus's agent and the municipality. That same day Wallenstein assumed the conduct of the siege, but after two vain assaults he learnt that Christian and an expeditionary force were off the island of Rügen and on July 24 he raised it.

Christian landed his army to the south-east of Stralsund and occupied Wolgast as the first step toward an invasion of Mecklenburg. There, on August 12, he was intercepted by Wallenstein and routed. Early in 1629 peace negotiations were opened and on June 7 they were concluded by the Treaty of Lübeck. Nearly all the European powers were affected.

Wallenstein now had 125,000 troops under arms, and after Christian's defeat, as there was no enemy left in sight, he indiscriminately billeted them on friend and foe. Certain detachments were quartered in Saxony, and as this was done without the Elector's permission, John George, supported by Maximilian, appealed to the Emperor. Both feared the growing power of Wallenstein, and so also did Ferdinand, who was becoming little more than his puppet. But before the latter tackled this knotty problem, now that his power was supreme, he decided to carry out his long cherished wish–the return of the Church lands wrongfully usurped since 1555. Because he knew that no Diet would sanction this, he decided to effect it by imperial decree, and, on March 6, 1629, he promulgated his Edict of Restitution to a defenceless Germany.

But how to get rid of Wallenstein remained a problem, and although Ferdinand did not set out to solve it, his next act precipitated the solution. At the instigation of Spain he became involved in a war against the French duke of Mantua when he agreed to send troops to Italy, a decision that antagonized the Pope and divided the Catholic Church. This prompted Richelieu to arrange a truce between Sweden and Poland in order to release Gustavus as a Protestant champion against the Empire, and as the Swedish occupation of Stralsund and Pillau[1] would enable Gustavus to wage war on Poland with dangerous effect, Sigismund III of Poland agreed to a six-year truce, which was signed at Altmark on September 26, 1629.

Wallenstein, who was violently opposed to the Edict of Restitution because he saw that a quiescent Germany was essential in order to face Europe's hereditary foe, the Turks, began still further to increase his army, so that he might meet Gustavus should he intervene. But because of Ferdinand's Spanish agreement, in May, 1630, he was instructed to send 30,000 men to Italy. Next, Spain demanded Ferdinand's help to subdue the Dutch, and led by Maximilian the Electors refused to discuss the question as long as Wallenstein remained in power; John George further demanded the withdrawal of the Edict of Restitution.

By abandoning Wallenstein, Ferdinand might pacify the Catholic Electors, and by withdrawing the Edict he might bring Saxony and Brandenburg to heel. He decided on the former course, and on August 17, when at Regensburg, he discussed with his councillors how best he could dismiss his formidable general. Surprisingly enough, when Wallenstein was informed of the Emperor's wish he made no complaint, and on August 24 he tendered his resignation. Rid of Wallenstein, Ferdinand set aside all thoughts of revoking the Edict of Restitution, handed over the imperial army to Maximilian and Tilly, and reverted to the position he had been in at the opening of the war. This was the very moment when Gustavus, who on July 6 had landed his army at Peenemünde on the Island of Usedom, was consolidating his base in Pomerania.

---

[1] Pillau had been ceded by the Elector of Brandenburg to Gustavus in 1627.

The Battles of Breitenfeld and Lützen, 1631 and 1632

The military importance of the two great battles fought by Gustavus Adolphus in Germany lies in that they stemmed from an improvement in tactics and leadership which was profoundly to influence the art of war. Therefore, before inquiring into the events out of which they arose, first it is as well briefly to review the development in land warfare which preceded them; next to take stock of Gustavus's generalship; and then to consider the tactical modifications he introduced.

Although there had been no lack of military inventions since the latter half of the Hundred Years War,[1] and men like Leonardo da Vinci (1452–1519) had even speculated on what were to become submarines, tanks, and aircraft, the main tactical problem before the introduction of cannon was not so much how to defeat an enemy in the field, but how to winkle him out of his fortifications. Not until the castle had been mastered during the second half of the fifteenth century, did the problem of how best to use firearms on the battlefield arise.

Its solution was indicated at the bloody battle of Ravenna, won by Gaston de Foix over the army of the Holy League in 1512, for in it artillery began to play a decisive part. But it was not until the introduction of the improved Spanish matchlock musket, first used at the siege of Parma in 1521, that musketeers set out to prove their worth. This new weapon was six feet long, weighed 15 lb., and was fired from a fork-shaped rest. Its tactical use was developed rapidly by the Marquis of Pescara. In 1522, at the battle of Bicocca, he demonstrated on a large scale the value of musketeers acting independently in the open, and for the first time

---

[1] The following list gives some indication: Hand-grenades, 1382; smoke-balls, 1405; time match, 1405; case shot, 1410; corned gunpowder, 1429; fire balls, 1400–1450; matchlock or arquebus, 1450; bronze explosive shell, 1463; explosive bombs,1470; wheeled gun-carriage, about 1470; pistols, 1483; incendiary shell, 1487; rifling, 1520; wheellock and Spanish musket, 1521; improved hand-grenade, 1536; wheellock pistol, 1543; paper cartridges, 1560; a type of shrapnel shell, 1573; hot shot, 1575; common shell, 1588; fixed cartridges (powder and ball in one), 1590; rifled pistols, about 1592; and percussion fuze, 1596.

pikemen became no more than their auxiliaries. The year following, at Pavia, the steady shooting and manœuvring of Pescara's musketeers won for the Imperialists the most decisive battle of that generation; a battle which founded modern infantry fire tactics. Until the introduction of the bayonet, the musket and pike remained the dominant arms. In all this, it was the Spaniards who led the way, which to a large extent was because they had raised out of the veterans of the conquest of Granada professional bodies of soldiers known as *tercios*. Usually, these Spanish "battles" consisted of 2,000 to 3,000 foot soldiers, one-third musketeers and two-thirds pikemen, and as some of the *tercios* had for their honorary colonels princes of the royal house—the *Infantas*—the new foot soldiers became known as *infantaria*—infantry. In the sixteenth century these heavy "battles" were marshalled in oblongs of men 30 ranks deep with squares of musketeers at their corners, but by the opening of the seventeenth century, because of the progress made in artillery, their depth had frequently been reduced to 10 ranks.

Because of the increasing reliance on the pike, in order to protect the musketeers cavalry charges became more and more restricted, with the result that the Spanish troopers were trained to rely more on the newly introduced wheellock pistol than on sword or lance. They were heavily armoured against musket fire and marshalled in deep squadrons which, rank by rank, rode up to the enemy pikemen and methodically fired their pistols *dans le tas*; each rank after firing wheeled and filed to the rear to reload.

The foot usually were massed in the centre with the field artillery in front covered by skirmishers, and the cavalry drawn up in rear or on the wings. Battles were almost invariably fought in parallel order, open ground was sought with, when possible, the sun and wind behind. Pursuit was seldom attempted and the Spanish baggage trains were usually enormous, accompanied by numerous non-combatants and women. All told, the Spanish tactics were slow, methodical, and cumbersome, yet nearly invincible against a less well-trained enemy.

At this date most other armies still largely relied upon mercenaries. In peacetime their leaders, who were professional soldiers, would keep in hand a small staff of experts in recruiting and training, and when they received a war contract would rapidly fill their ranks with men, regardless of race or religion. Switzerland and northern Italy were always ready to supply large numbers. The men took an oath to their personal leaders, and when captured or on termination of their contract, frequently changed sides. In winter these mercenary forces were usually disbanded, to be recruited again in the following spring for the next summer campaign. Compared with the well-trained and equipped *tercios*, they were often little more than an armed rabble.

Equally important was the influence of firearms on politics. Not only did they proletarianize war by enabling, as Cervantes (1547–1616) says: "a base cowardly hand to take the life of the bravest gentleman," but they centralized power in the hands of the monarchy. The cost of artillery and the expense entailed in equipping large numbers of arquebusiers soon became too great to be borne by any individual, and in consequence had to be met by the State. Further, this concentration of power in secular hands raised the monarchy above the Church; war became a political instrument and ceased to be a moral trial. The seventeenth century saw the rise of standing armies, the development of competitive armaments, and the introduction of the balance of power as a policy. Military service ceased to be the perquisite of a class and began to be a national profession. The development of mass-fighting, if not of mass armies, was a characteristic of the age, and it became manifest in the Thirty Years War.

Because the Spanish military system was universally copied by the European powers, it was the Spanish type of army that Gustavus was called upon to meet.

Gustavus was the eldest son of Charles IX of Sweden (1604–1611) and was born at Stockholm on December 19, 1594. His grandfather was the great Gustavus I, who founded the Vasa dynasty, a commercially-minded man who had favoured the middle class against the nobles and had introduced the Protestant religion into Sweden. Gustavus Adolphus succeeded his father in 1611. That same year he experienced his first taste of war against the Danes. Like Alexander the Great, he set out on his military career when still a boy. In many ways, as more than one writer has noted,[1] he bore a resemblance to the great Macedonian; he

---

[1] Gindely (*History of the Thirty Years' War*, 1884, vol. II, p. 41) says: "When we look around us for a historical person with whom he can be compared, we find but one – Alexander the Great." And Dodge (*Gustavus Adolphus*, 1890, vol. I, pp. 73 and 401) writes: "Few young monarchs have ever been so harassed on taking up the reins of government. Gustavus's situation recalls forcibly that of Alexander" . . . "Except Alexander, no great captain showed the true love of battle as it burned in the breast of Gustavus Adolphus. Such was his own contempt of death that his army could not but fight."

largely created an epoch, blazing the trail for France, as Alexander had done for Rome, and he also resembled him in character. Though reserved in small things, he was passionate in great. A fine horseman and athlete, he possessed a brilliant imagination, a restless temperament and a love for perilous adventures; in battle he was always in the van. Of quick temper, he was nevertheless forgiving: "I bear my subjects' errors with patience," he once said, "but they too must put up with my quick speech."[1] Faithful to his friends, he was merciful to his enemies; a man of high convictions he never sacrificed principle for advantage. Wise in his choice of subordinates, he was also wise in the selection of his heroes, among whom Maurice of Nassau was his special favourite. A student of his opponents, he was also a student of history and his favourite books were the *De Jure Belli ac Pacis* of Hugo Grotius and the *Anabasis* of Xenophon. In his studies he was helped by his remarkable gift of languages; for, besides his mother tongue, he understood Latin, Greek, German, Dutch, Italian, Polish, and Russian. In religion he was firmly Protestant, and in politics passionately Swedish; he never lost sight of his dominant aspiration—the *Dominium Maris Baltici*.

As a general, Gustavus is among the few great Captains, and Napoleon says of him: "*Gustave-Adolphe était animé des principes d'Alexandre, d'Annibal, de César.*"[2] His greatness lay in the novelty of his ideas and the courage with which he applied them. Since the age of 17 he had constant experience of war, and was always learning, inventing, improving, and daring to do. For him it was possible to achieve so many things in war precisely because the generality of men supposed them impracticable. His main contribution to his art was that he was the first general during the modern age who realized that mobility is founded upon discipline, and discipline upon efficient administration and leadership. Most of his officers were young men—he did not like generals of 60 and over—and they were compelled to look after their men. Gindely says: "As he provided food, so did he also clothing for his men. He furnished them with fur-lined coats, he kept tents in readiness to protect them against the inclement weather, and secure them a more humane existence. Low and slanderous speech, drunkenness and gaming were banished by rigid penalties from the camp-life. Nor did he tolerate loose women; he insisted that those girls who

---

[1] Quoted from *Gustavus Adolphus*, Theodore Ayrault Dodge, vol. 1, p. 400.
[2] *Correspondance*, vol. xxxi, p. 354.

followed the army should each be connected with some soldier by marriage."[1] Furthermore, he was one of the first since the classical age to base tactics upon weapon-power instead of on convention. As a general, Chemnitz sums him up as follows:

"No one ever equalled Gustavus Adolphus in leading his army against an enemy, or conducting a retreat so as to prevent loss, nor in encamping his troops, or strengthening his camp with field works. No one knew fortification, attack, and defence so well as he did. No one could divine the intention of his enemy, or take advantage of the chances of war, more ably than he did. He took in at a glance the whole position, and drew up his army so as to profit by every opportunity. The three points that he exceeded all others in were tactics, organisation, and arms."[2]

Another contemporary estimate of him reads:

"He did animate his soldiers rather by fighting, than exhorting; nor did he challenge to himself any advantage above the meanest of them, but honour and command. . . . He well understood that faith and loyalty are not to be expected where we impose thraldom and servitude, and therefore at times he would be familiar, as well with the common soldier, as the commander. His invention and execution of all military stratagems were ever twins; for in all his conquests he owed as much to his celerity, as valour. When his foes were in their tents securely discoursing of him, as afar off, he, like a wolf, broke into their fable, to their irrecoverable astonishment. They could not withstand the force of his fame, much less that of his arms. One feather more I must add, without which his victories had not been fully plumed, nor could have soared so high, and that was this: he never persuaded any man to an enterprise, in which he would not himself make one. He taught them as well by hand, as tongue. I may add, that neither antiquity can, nor posterity ever shall produce a prince so patient, of all military wants, as of meat, drink, warmth, sleep, etc. . . . All his great achievements were ever attended by devotion within, and circumspection without. He first praised God, and then provided for man, at once having an eye on his enemies' next designs, and his soldiers' present necessities. The greatest of his glories, purchased with blood and sweat, could neither change the estate of his mind, or copy of his countenance. The true greatness of his spirit was such, that in all his actions he placed ostentation behind,

---

[1] *History of the Thirty Years' War*, vol. II, p. 435.
[2] Quoted from *A Précis of Modern Tactics*, Colonel Robert Home (1892), p. 226.

and conscience before him, and sought not the reward of a good deed from fame, but from the deed itself. . . ."[1]

Though others equalled him in tactical ability and strategical foresight, probably no single soldier, with the exception of Philip of Macedon, excelled him as a military organizer, and so all-embracing were his reforms that he created the epoch of modern warfare. Not only did he reorganize each arm and combine their tactics, but he founded his whole system on interior economy and an efficient service of supply. He realized that the military methods of his day were out of date, for every army had copied the Spanish system without change, and by the opening of the Thirty Years War it had become extremely cumbersome.

Gustavus reviewed military organization as he found it and saw clearly that the superior weapon was the musket. Accordingly, he decreased the number of pikemen, shortened their pikes from 16 to 11 ft., lightened their armour, and combined them with the musketeers to form companies, exclusive of officers, of 72 musketeers and 54 pikemen, which, with the pikes in the centre, stood in line in files six deep. Four companies formed a battalion, eight a regiment, and two to four regiments a brigade. In each of these formations the right and left wings were composed of musketeers and the centre of pikemen. The musket he lightened in order to dispense with the crutch or rest. By degrees he substituted the wheellock for the matchlock, introduced paper cartridges, and provided his men with bandoliers to carry them.

He employed two types of cavalry, cuirassiers and dragoons; the former were partially armoured and the latter were mounted infantry. The former were formed into squadrons of three instead of 10 ranks deep, and were trained to charge at the gallop instead of the trot, with their pistols used only in the mêlée. They rode in lines of squadrons, one behind the other, or else chequerwise, the last line was the reserve. Though Gustavus marshalled his cavalry on the wings of his infantry, which was the usual procedure, he also placed them behind each infantry line and frequently mixed parties of "commanded musketeers" with them. Generally his cavalry charged under cover of the smoke of the artillery bombardment, and once they had driven back the enemy skirmishers, they retired to allow the infantry to advance. Next, under cover of another bombardment, they charged again, this time on the

---

[1] *The Great and Famous Battle of Lützen* . . . translated from the French, printed in 1633 and published in *The Harleian Miscellany* (1809), vol. IV, pp. 197–209.

enemy's flanks to drive them in on the centre and to create confusion; for the maintenance of an ordered and unbroken front was essential to success.

Yet, in spite of the excellence of his infantry and cavalry, it was on the power of artillery[1] that his battles were founded. As Mahomet II was the first great siege gunner, Gustavus was the first great field gunner. In order to render the gun mobile, he shortened it, lightened its carriage, and reduced the number of calibres. He adopted three main types—siege, field, and regimental. The first two consisted of 24-, 12- and six-pounders, the siege pieces weighed 60-, 30- and 15-cwt., and the field pieces 27-, 18- and 12-cwt. The regimental pieces were light four-pounder guns, two to a regiment, and were provided with fixed ammunition in wooden cases which enabled them to fire eight rounds to every six shots of a musketeer. They replaced his famous leather guns, which he had used in his Polish campaign of 1628–1629.[2] The projectiles usually fired were grape and canister by field and regimental guns, and round shot by siege.

For supply Gustavus depended upon well-found and fortified magazines, to which were attached a regular staff of commissaries. The baggage wagons he reduced in number and allowed 10 to a squadron and eight to a company. Promotion was by seniority; punishments were humane and no flogging was permitted. His Chief of Staff was General Kniphausen, and his General of Artillery, Torstensson, a remarkable soldier, who, in 1630, was only 30 years of age.

Wallenstein's advance along the Baltic brought Gustavus Adolphus into the war, the nature of which he clearly grasped, for at about that time he wrote to his Chancellor, Axel Oxenstierna (1583–1654): "All the wars that are on foot in Europe have been fused together, and have become a single war."

Four years earlier, in 1624, James I and Louis XIII had approached him; but as his terms were no divided command, an advance of payment for his troops, and the occupation of two ports, one on the Baltic and the other on the North Sea, the two kings found them too onerous and turned to Denmark. Charles I, who succeeded to the throne of England on March 27, 1625,

---

[1] His cavalry and artillery were mainly Swedish, and his infantry consisted of a nucleus of Swedes, the rest were Scots, Germans, and other soldiers of fortune.

[2] They were invented by Colonel Wurmbrant, and consisted of a copper tube bound with iron rings and rope and covered with leather. Without its carriage, the gun weighed 90 lb.

agreed to support the war, which was the beginning of his undoing. But when Wallenstein overran Schleswig and Jutland,
gained Mecklenburg and laid siege to Stralsund, Gustavus saw
that the design of the House of Habsburg was to master the Baltic
and the Sound. Therefore, at Altmark, on September 26, 1629, he
had patched up a six-year truce with Poland and had written to
Oxenstierna: "If we await our enemy in Sweden, all might be lost
by a defeat. By a fortunate commencement of a war in Germany
everything is to be gained. We must carry the war abroad. Sweden
must not be doomed to behold a hostile banner upon her soil."[1]
It was for this reason that he sent a Swedish garrison to Stralsund,
so that he might secure a landing on the Pomeranian coast.

France also was perturbed. Soon after La Rochelle surrendered,
in October, 1628, and the Huguenot rising was at an end, Richelieu
sent an ambassador to Sweden to gain Gustavus's help. His plan
was to make Gustavus the tool of French aggrandizement: the war
was not to be carried into the interior of Germany, but instead was
to be waged in the area of the Emperor's hereditary possessions,
that is to say up the Oder into Silesia, Bohemia, Moravia, and
Austria, and Gustavus was to be subsidized by the French, English,
and Dutch. But the Swedish king had no intention of playing the
part of stalking-horse to France. He was free of his Polish war, he
realized that because of the severity of his rule Wallenstein's stock
was falling, and he knew that the Edict of Restitution had terrified
the Protestant Electors. He speedily prepared for war. Thus it
came about that, on July 6, 1630, he landed on the island of
Usedom at the head of 13,000 men, later to be reinforced to
40,000. From Usedom he advanced on Stettin and compelled
Bogislav Duke of Pomerania to surrender the city to him. Thence
he marched into Mecklenburg, reinstated its deposed dukes and,
early in August, sent a detachment of Swedes under Colonel
Falkenberg to help to hold Magdeburg.

Once established in Pomerania, Gustavus was faced by a
stupendous task. His resources were insignificant compared with
his enemy's[2] and no powerful allies welcomed him. John George
of Saxony held aloof and throughout was his secret enemy, for he
stood for the solidarity of Germany and looked upon Gustavus as
a foreign conqueror, and the Elector of Brandenburg offered him

[1] Quoted from *Lives of the Warriors of The Thirty Years' War*, Lieut.-Gen. the Hon.
Sir Edward Cust (1865), part I, pp. 142–143.
[2] In 1630 the population of Sweden and Finland was about 1,500,000; that of the
Empire some 17,000,000.

no support. Had Ferdinand withdrawn the Edict of Restitution at this moment, he would have won over both and have rendered Gustavus's task impossible. Further, Denmark, though neutral, was hostile; France shifty; Holland jealous; England untrustworthy; and Poland as "bitter as gall". This situation should be borne in mind, for out of it was developed the strategy of the next two years. This was governed by three factors.

Firstly, it must be realized that one of the reasons why Germany was divided into so many small princedoms was the original lack of Roman roads east of the Rhine. Secondly, because Gustavus's main base was in Sweden, before he could move inland it was essential for him to gain control of the Baltic coast in order to secure his advanced base in Pomerania as well as his sea communications. Thirdly, the main Catholic power lay west of the Rhine and south of the Danube—that is, in the old Roman territory—the communications of which enabled Spain and Austria to join hands about the middle Rhine. In part to compensate for this advantage, the main reaches of the great rivers, the Oder, Elbe, and Weser—the thoroughfares of the day—ran through Protestant lands and into a sea which was surrounded by Protestant powers.

Gustavus understood this clearly enough, but it was impracticable for him to move south until his base was secure. Winter now intervened, and though the Electors continued to remain obdurate, France came to terms with Sweden and a treaty between the two countries was signed at Bärwalde on January 23, 1631, by which Gustavus was to provide an army of 30,000 foot and 6,000 horse in return for a lump sum of 12,000 thalers and an annual subsidy of 400,000 thalers for the following five years. Gustavus was to guarantee freedom of worship for Catholics and to leave unmolested the lands of Maximilian.

The spring campaign of 1631 was opened by Tilly, who stormed New Brandenburg while his fiery lieutenant, Count Pappenheim, besieged Magdeburg. In order to draw off the former, Gustavus moved on Frankfort-on-the-Oder, which he occupied on April 13; but the crafty Walloon did not follow him but marched on Magdeburg and joined Pappenheim.

Frankfort occupied, Gustavus's one idea was to succour Magdeburg; but he could not set out on an unauthorized march through Brandenburg and Saxony lest either, or both their Electors should fall upon his rear. After much argument he obtained George William's permission to occupy Küstrin and then was forced to spend the next three weeks in haggling before he could gain his permission to enter Spandau. Meanwhile John George of Saxony was not to be moved, and as he commanded an army 40,000 strong Gustavus was compelled to leave Magdeburg to its fate.

Tilly, at the head of 25,000 men, arrived at Magdeburg, and with Pappenheim pressed the siege. On May 20 the city was stormed, sacked and set on fire; 30,000 people died in the flames.[1] At once, as Professor Gardiner writes, "A great fear fell upon the minds of all Protestant men," and Gustavus used terror to counteract terror. He marched on Berlin and at the mouth of his cannon compelled George William of Brandenburg to renounce his neutrality. Joined by William of Hesse-Cassel and Prince Bernhard of Saxe-Weimar, Gustavus entrenched himself at Werben and repulsed an attack of Tilly's, when unexpectedly fortune played into his hands. Cut off on all sides and with his army starving, Tilly invaded Saxony at the head of 40,000 men, threatened to deal with Leipzig as he had with Magdeburg, and compelled its surrender. At once John George abandoned his neutrality and entered into alliance with Gustavus. The two allies met at Düben on the Mulde on September 15. Their combined armies numbered about 47,000 men and the following day they set out for Leipzig to offer battle.

As Düben was only 25 miles to the north of Leipzig, retreat for Tilly was out of the question, and as his troops, now in a land of plenty after months of starvation, were out of hand, his best course would have been to hold fast to Leipzig, to stand a siege, and to await reinforcements. But Pappenheim, who considered him senile, thought differently. On September 16 he set out on a reconnaissance during which, to force Tilly's hand, he sent back a message that he had sighted the enemy moving south from Düben, and that, as it was not possible for him to return without great risk, he must immediately be supported. Thus he engineered the fateful battle of Breitenfeld.

Tilly moved out of Leipzig and took up a position some five miles north of it, on a slight rise with the village of Breitenfeld on his left and that of Stenberg on his right. The field was known as "God's acre," because in former times other battles had been fought there. According to an old topographical work it was a "pleasant and fruitful plain, abounding with all necessaries and pleasures, constantly mowed twice, and sometimes thrice a year,

[1] It was not destroyed deliberately; Tilly needed it badly to supply his troops.

besides having pleasant woods, and many fine orchards, with all sorts of fruit."[1]

Tilly, an old general, born in 1559, was a sound and conventional soldier. Quoting Marshal de Grammont's memoirs, James Grant describes him as: "Short in stature, he was meagre and terrible in aspect; his cheeks were sunken, his nose long and pointed, his eyes fierce and dark. When not sheathed in gilded armour, he usually wore a slashed doublet of green silk, a preposterously broad-brimmed and conical hat, adorned by a red ostrich feather; a long beard, a long dagger and mighty Toledo. . . ."[2] A past master in the Spanish tactics, Tilly set up his battle order in one or possibly two lines of *tercios*; 17 great squares of foot of 1,500 to 2,000 men each with heavy columns of cavalry on their right and left. His army probably numbered 40,000 men, of which a quarter was cavalry. He commanded the infantry and allotted the left wing cavalry to Pappenheim and the right wing to Fürstenberg and Isolani. He had only 26 guns. The heavy guns he placed between his centre and right, and the light in front of his centre. Monro says he had advantage "of Ground, Wind and Sunne."[3]

On September 16, Gustavus, at the head of his army, came upon Tilly from the north and bivouacked one mile from the Imperialist position. He spent the night in his travelling coach discussing the forthcoming battle with Sir John Hepburn, Field-Marshal Horn, Field-Marshal Baner, and General Teuffel, all sheathed in complete mail.

The following morning, "As the Larke begunne to peepe,"[4] the trumpets in the Swedish bivouac sounded to horse and the drums called a march. The entire plain was covered with a haze through which the Swedes could see the line of red fires which marked Tilly's position. Prayers were said, then Gustavus drew out his order of battle in parallel order to his enemy's; but instead of making use of heavy battles, he marshalled his infantry in brigades or half brigades in such a way that the musketeers were covered by the pikemen and could file between the ranks of the latter, deliver their volley and retire. Thus, instead of an immovable square castle, says an old writer, "each brigade was like a little movable

---

[1] Quoted from *Memoirs and Adventures of Sir John Hepburn*, James Grant (1851), p. 95.
[2] *Ibid.*, p. 71.
[3] *Monro His Expedition*, etc., Colonel Robert Monro (1637), part II, p. 64.
[4] *Ibid.*, part II, p. 63.

fortress with its curtains and ravelins, and each part would be able to come to the assistance of the other."[1]

He drew up his army with the Swedes in the centre and on the right, the Saxons held the left. Of the Saxon formation nothing is known; the Swedish was as follows: In the centre were drawn up four brigades of foot in first line, supported by a cavalry regiment and Monro's and Ramsay's infantry brigades; in second line were three infantry brigades, including Hepburn's Scots,[2] supported by one cavalry regiment; the whole under Teuffel and Hall. In reserve behind the centre were two regiments of cavalry. The right wing, under Baner, consisted of six cavalry regiments in first line with bodies of musketeers between them; in support there was one regiment, and in second line four regiments. To the left wing, under Horn, were allotted three regiments of cavalry in first line with musketeers, and two regiments in second line. The regimental pieces were drawn up in front of the regiments and brigades, and the heavy artillery, under Torstensson, was massed in front of the centre. On the left of Field-Marshal Horn stood the Saxons. The whole array, probably 47,000 men, pinned green branches in their hats; the Imperialists wore white ribands. The Swedish battle-cry was *Godt mit us*, and their enemy's, *Sancta Maria*.

Monro states that Gustavus "ordered his Armie, and directed every supreame Officer of the Field, on their particular charge and stations committed unto them, for that day: as also he acquainted them severally, of the forme he was to fight unto, and he appointed Plottons of Musketiers, by fifties, which were commanded by sufficient officers to attend on several Regiments of horse, and he instructed the Officers how to behave themselves in discharging their duties on service. Likewise he directed the Officers belonging to the Artillery, how to carry themselves. . . ."[3]

"With Trumpets sounding, Drummes beating, and Colours advanced and flying," the battle opened, and soon, as Monro says, ". . . the enemy was thundering amongst us, with the noise and roaring whistling of Cannon-Bullets; where you may imagine the hurt was great; the sound of such musick being scarce worth hearing . . . then our Cannon begun to roare, great and small, paying the enemy with the like coyne, which thundering continued alike on both sides for two hours and a half, during which

---

[1] Quoted from *Gustavus Adolphus*, C. R. L. Fletcher (1923), p. 190.
[2] There were many Scots in the Swedish Army, including an "Anthony Haig of Bemerside"—a spirited young cavalier.
[3] *Monro His Expedition*, part II, p. 64.

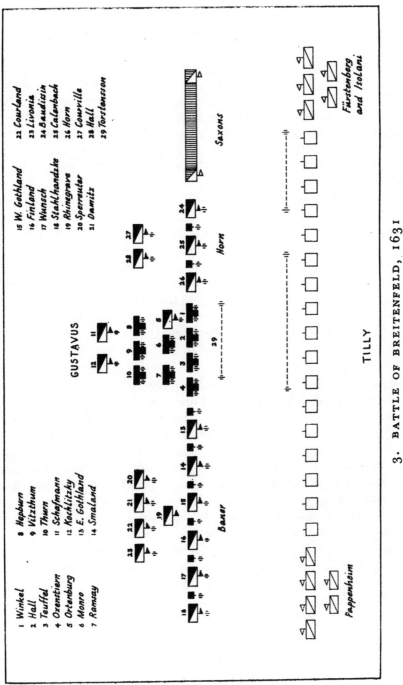

1 Winkel
2 Hall
3 Teuffel
4 Oxenstiern
5 Ortenburg
6 Monro
7 Ramsay

8 Hepburn
9 Vitzthum
10 Thurn
11 Schafmann
12 Kochlitzky
13 E. Gothland
14 Smaland

15 W. Gothland
16 Finland
17 Wunsch
18 Stahlhandske
19 Rhinegrave
20 Sperreuter
21 Damitz

22 Courland
23 Livonia
24 Baudissin
25 Calenbach
26 Horn
27 Courville
28 Hall
29 Torstensson

GUSTAVUS

Baner

Horn

Saxons

Fürstenberg
and Isolani

Pappenhsim

TILLY

3. BATTLE OF BREITENFELD, 1631

time, our Battailes of horse and foot stood firme like a wall, the Cannon now and then making great breaches amongst us, which was diligently looked unto. . . ."[1]

The Swedish guns, more numerous and which fired three rounds to the Imperialists' one, so galled the enemy that Pappenheim, a high-spirited commander, could stand their fire no longer and, without waiting for orders, at the head of 5,000 horse charged the Swedish right wing. It was a foolish act, and Tilly, who knew it, exclaimed in rage: "They have robbed me of my honour and glory." Not only was it a mistake, but it failed, for the pistols of the horsemen were no match for the muskets of the "commanded musketeers"[2] placed between the Swedish cavalry regiments, and these groups poured salvo after salvo into the dense ranks of the Imperialist horsemen. Seven times Pappenheim charged and each time he was repulsed; on the last occasion Baner hurled his reserve upon him and drove him in rout from the field.

Fürstenberg and Isolani, on Tilly's right, apparently mistook Pappenheim's advance as the signal for a general engagement and charged the Saxons who, at the first shock, fled the field. John George spurred his way to Eilenburg. Not only did this compensate for Pappenheim's mistaken initiative, for Gustavus's total strength was now reduced by over a third, but Tilly, who was an able tactician, at once took advantage of it. He saw that the Swedish left was now uncovered and was overlapped by his right, and ordered a move obliquely to the right to be followed by a left wheel, in order to bring his right down on his enemy's left flank. Simultaneously he ordered Fürstenberg to attack the Swedish rear.

The probabilities are that had he been faced by antagonists other than the Swedes the movement would have proved decisive. But as Gustavus's men could manœuvre twice as fast as the Imperialists, the advantage was not Tilly's. At once King Gustavus Adolphus ordered Horn to wheel his wing to the left in order to meet Tilly's change of front, and simultaneously he brought forward the brigades of Vitzthum and Hepburn from the second line of the centre and reinforced Horn's left.

The Scots advanced in dense column. Monro's account of their action is as follows:

---

[1] *Ibid.*, part II, p. 65.
[2] It should be remembered that, in accordance with the Spanish tactics, the charge was carried out at the trot and with the pistol, the sword being used only after the enemy's ranks had been disorganized by pistol fire. The Swedish charge was the opposite; it was delivered at the gallop and with the sword, the pistol being used for the mêlée.

"The enemies Battaile standing firm, looking on us at a neere distance, and seeing the other Briggads and ours wheeling about, making front unto them, they were prepared with a firm resolution to receive us with a salvo of Cannon and Muskets; but our small Ordinance [regimental pieces] being twice discharged amongst them, and before we stirred, we charged them with a salvo of muskets, which was repaied, and incontinent our Briggad advancing unto them with push of pike, putting one of their battailes in disorder, fell on the execution, so that they were put to the route.

"I having commanded the right wing of our musketiers, being my Lord of *Rhees* [Reay's] and *Lumsdells* [Lumsden's], we advanced on the other body of the enemies, which defended their Cannon, and beating them from their Cannon, we were masters of their Cannon, and consequently of the field, but the smoake being great, the dust being raised, we were as in a darke cloud, not seeing the halfe of our actions, much less discerning, either the way of our enemies, or yet the rest of our Briggads: whereupon, having a drummer by me, I caused him to beate the *Scots* march, till it cleared up, which recollected our friends unto us, and dispersed our enemies being overcome; so that the Briggad coming together, such as were alive missed their dead and hurt Camerades."[1]

While this action was fought, Gustavus seized the opportunity to deliver the decisive blow. He rode over to the right and ordered Baner to send the West Gothland Horse down the Swedish front to charge the left flank of Tilly's battles. Then Gustavus placed himself at the head of four regiments and bore up the slope where the enemy's guns still stood. He swept through them, fell upon the left flank of Tilly's line, and pounded the Imperialists with their own cannon. Simultaneously Torstensson wheeled round the reserve artillery and poured its shot into the dense Spanish squares. A desperate fight ensued; but its end was certain. Soon the Imperialists lost all order and stampeded. They lost 7,000 killed, 6,000 wounded and captured, all their artillery, 90 flags, and the whole of their train. Gustavus's losses, including the Saxons's, "did not exceed three thousand men," most "killed by the enemies Cannon."[2]

The bulk of the Swedish army then bivouacked: "Our bone-fiers," writes Monro, "were made of the enemies Ammunition waggons, and Pikes left, for want of good fellowes to use them; and all this night our brave Camerades, the *Saxons*, were making use of

[1] *Ibid.*, part II, p. 66.   [2] *Ibid.*, part II, p. 67.

their heeles in flying, thinking all was lost, they made booty of our waggons and goods [the Swedish supply and baggage column], too good a recompence for Cullions that had left their Duke. . . ." But 1,500 Swedish horsemen did not halt, and Gustavus at their head pursued Tilly's fugitives; captured 3,000 at Merseburg on September 19, and on September 21 abandoned the pursuit at Halle.

Thus the battle ended, epoch-making not only because it was the first great test and trial of the new tactics against the old, and therefore the first great land battle of the modern age, a victory of mobility and fire-power over numbers and push of pike, but because, for good or for evil, it shattered the reviving forces of the League and decided that Germany was not to become a Catholic power under the House of Austria. It was, as Professor Gardiner says: "the grave of the Edict of Restitution" and "the Naseby of Germany."[1] Perhaps also, as Lord Bryce writes, it "saved Europe from an impending reign of the Jesuits."[2]

From September 17, 1631, until his death, Gustavus became the hero of the Protestant world and the "common men" in the north of Germany looked up to him "as a redeemer, and as such deified him."[3] He gave spirit and direction to the war, without which the Protestant cause would have collapsed and the history of the western world would have been different. With insight Professor Gardiner writes:

"Those tactics were, after all, but the military expression of the religious and political system in defence of which they were used. Those solid columns just defeated were the types of what human nature was to become under the Jesuit organisation. The individual was swallowed up in the mass. As Tilly had borne down by sheer weight of his veterans, adventurers like Mansfeld and Christian of Brunswick, so the renewed Catholic discipline had borne down the wrangling theologians who had stepped into the places of Luther and Melanchthon. But now an army had arisen to prove that order and obedience were weak unless they were supported by individual intelligence. The success of the principle upon which its operations were based could not be confined to mere fighting. It would make its way in morals and politics, in literature and science."[4]

Breitenfeld fought and won, the question has often been asked:

[1] *The Thirty Years' War*, pp. 139–140.
[2] *The Holy Roman Empire*, James Viscount Bryce (1928), p. 383.
[3] *The Thirty Years' War* Anton Gindely, vol. II, p. 85.
[4] *The Thirty Years' War*, p. 140.

"Why did not Gustavus march on Vienna and impose his will upon Ferdinand?" Several historians consider that he should have done so, and Folard compares him with Hannibal after Cannae. But the comparison is inapt, for circumstances were entirely different. Firstly, the road which ran to Vienna was bad; it passed through the forests of the Erzgebirge and the devastated lands of Bohemia, and winter was near. Secondly, Vienna was not the capital of a united nation, but the residence of a shadow emperor, therefore it possessed even less political significance than Madrid did during the Peninsula War (1808–1814). Thirdly, Gustavus, hundreds of miles from his base, could not afford to risk a rising behind him; the loyalty of the Electors of Brandenburg and Saxony was suspect and Bavaria would hug his flank. Fourthly, by moving to the Rhine, as eventually he did, though he would upset Richelieu by carrying war into Catholic territories, he would be able to base himself on the Protestant Palatinate and also to supply his army, for "the Priests Lane," as it was called–Würzburg, Bamberg, Fulda, Cologne, Mainz, Worms, and Spires–included the richest districts in Germany, and they had furnished many men and much money to the armies of the League. Lastly, and not least in importance, by occupying the Palatinate he would cut the Spanish connexion between the Netherlands and Italy. Therefore he decided to advance on the Rhine, while the Elector of Saxony carried war into Bohemia.

Gustavus occupied Würzburg on October 18, pushed on to Frankfort-on-Main, and thence to Mainz which, after a two-day siege, surrendered. Within three months of his great victory he had subdued the whole of the Rhineland; had formed alliances and appointed governments; had forced neutrality on all the Catholic princes of the Rhine; had driven the Spanish troops back to the Netherlands; and was firmly established on both banks of the middle Rhine, in Alsatia, the Lower Palatinate, and Cologne, much to the annoyance of Richelieu, who was alarmed by this prodigiously rapid and thorough conquest. "Means must be devised", he said, "to check this impetuous Visigoth, since his successes will be fatal to France as to the Emperor." Nor were his alarms unfounded, for Gustavus turned definitely toward the formation of a *Corpus Evangelicorum*, a federation of Protestant princes under his leadership. This meant the destruction of the Imperial system, which Richelieu did not want destroyed, but made impotent.

Set upon this idea, in the spring of 1632 Gustavus advanced against Tilly, who had recruited another army since Breitenfeld and, joined by the Duke of Lorraine with 12,000 men, headed some 40,000 men in all. Gustavus crossed the Danube at Donau-wörth and caught up with the enemy on the river Lech. There, under cover of a smoke cloud and an artillery bombardment, he bridged the river and defeated Tilly on April 16. Tilly was severely wounded and died a fortnight later.

Ever since he had dismissed Wallenstein, Ferdinand had regretted the act, and no sooner had it taken effect than he contemplated his recall, in spite of the fact that he feared this formidable man who, though typical of his age, could see beyond it. Wallenstein's aim apparently was to consolidate the Empire under a *fainéant* monarch with himself as Mayor of the Palace. To accomplish this end, Wallenstein saw that the religious disputes must cease; that tolerance must be established, and that, in order to govern a tolerant State, money was the instrument which alone could bit and bridle the greeds of men. He based everything on calculation. Astrologer, man of business, utterly without morals and mercenary, he accumulated enormous wealth. Silent, reserved, mysterious, no man dared question him. He was the typical product of the power-age then dawning, and the kind of man who in days to come was to be venerated and honoured as a captain of industry or a banker prince.[1]

In desperation, Ferdinand turned to him again and Wallenstein imposed the most drastic terms:[2] absolute and unconditional control of the army; complete subservience of the Emperor, who was to issue no orders without his consent; control of all confiscated territories; the speedy revocation of the Edict of Restitution; and probably also an Elector's hat. These terms were accepted, and the Czech came back as the "General of the Baltic and Oceanic Seas" to deliver Ferdinand from the hands of the king of the Baltic and the Protestant territories.

Wallenstein's first action was an attempt to win over John

---

[1] When, in January, 1622, Ferdinand II debased the coinage by 75 per cent. of its value, Hans de Witte and others carried out a gigantic fraud by reducing it by a further one-tenth of its value. Wallenstein at once took advantage of this. "He was not fastidious about his means; they consisted in the robbing of an unfortunate female cousin, and in the purchase of a great share of the confiscated lands which he paid for chiefly in debased coin." (See Gindely's *The Thirty Years' War*, vol. I, pp. 289–290 and 380.)

[2] The full terms are not known; see *The Thirty Years' War*, C. V. Wedgwood (1938), p. 315.

George of Saxony, and his second to shake the faith of George William of Brandenburg in the Swedish cause. But he did not succeed and in April, 1632, he marched into Bohemia, then occupied by the Saxons. He seized Prague and forced the Saxons to retire, and, on June 27, united his army with the forces of Maximilian of Bavaria and so raised his total strength to 60,000. He moved on Amberg and came into collision with a Swedish force at Neumark; whereon Gustavus withdrew to Nuremberg. He was followed by Wallenstein who, on July 16, arrived at Fürth, in its immediate vicinity, and there entrenched.

For weeks the two armies faced each other, while "all Germany and all Europe," as Gindely writes, "waited with anxiety and hope for news."[1] On September 4, supplies were short and Gustavus assaulted his opponent's position to be repulsed at a loss of some 3,000 men. Fourteen days later, when sickness had claimed thousands of his troops, Gustavus abandoned the siege and decided to march on Vienna in order to draw Wallenstein away from Saxony. But the latter saw through his enemy's plan, and instead of following him he set out for Saxony, while Maximilian retired with the remnants of his forces to defend Bavaria. Next, Wallenstein sent word to Holk and Pappenheim, then on the Weser, to join him with the intention to effect a general concentration against Saxony and to drive John George out of the war.

Directly this became apparent, John George frantically appealed to Gustavus to come to his aid. The king was already on his way, and on October 22 was back in Nuremberg. On November 2 he was joined by Berhnard of Saxe-Weimar at Arnstadt, and on November 8 he occupied the Kösen defile at Naumburg, from where he urged John George, whose army was at Torgau, to join him with all available forces.

In the meantime Leipzig had been occupied by Holk, and with winter imminent Wallenstein, who assumed that Gustavus would call off the campaign and go into winter quarters, entrenched his army around Lützen. To prevent overcrowding, he sent Pappenheim and his cavalry to occupy Halle.

Though, thus far, Wallenstein's defensive strategy had got the better of his adversary, in face of so astute a general as Gustavus this division of his army was a risky decision. When, on November 14, Gustavus learnt of it, he decided to bring his enemy to battle and in spite of his own numerical inferiority.

[1] *The Thirty Years' War*, vol. II, p. 135.

At one o'clock on the morning of November 15 he set out for Pegau to unite with the Saxons. There he halted for four hours, but as nothing was heard of them he marched for Lützen in the hope that he would surprise his enemy while still divided, but the road was so bad that he was much delayed. At Rippach he fell in with a body of Croats and scattered them after a tough fight. That night he lodged "in the playne feildes, about an English mile from Litzen, where the enimies randavow was,"[1] and there held a council of war. Though Kniphausen was for manœuvre and Bernhard of Saxe-Weimar for attack, Gustavus had already made up his mind. He said that "the die was now cast; that he could not bear to have Wallenstein under his beard and not make a swoop upon him," because, as he explained: "I long to unearth him, and see how he can acquit himself in a campaign country."[2]

In his enemy's camp Wallenstein, afflicted with an attack of gout which necessitated his being carried in a sedan chair, "spent that whole night in digging and intrenching, in embattling his army, and planting his artillery. . . ." for he "was infinitely desirous to avoid the combat."[3] When he learnt of Gustavus's proximity, at 2 a.m., on November 16, he sent an urgent message to Pappenheim. "The enemy is advancing," he wrote. "Sir, let everything else be, and hurry with all your forces and artillery back to me. You must be here by tomorrow morning–he is already over the pass [of Rippach]."[4]

The plain of Lützen, upon which the two armies now lay bivouacked, is low and flat, and across it from south-west to north-east runs the Leipzig Road, built on a raised causeway, and flanked on each side with a ditch; and about two miles east of Lützen runs the Flossgraben, a small, sluggish stream, fordable in most places. Wallenstein, who intended to fight a purely defensive battle as he had done at Nuremberg, marshalled his order of battle in one line, a little north of the Leipzig Road; his right flank rested on a slight rise of ground immediately north of Lützen, upon which were some windmills, and his left rested upon the Flossgraben. The ditches along the Leipzig Road he dug into trenches and lined with musketeers. His exact strength is not

---

[1] "George Fleetwood's Letter to His Father," *The Camden Miscellany* (1847), vol. I, p. 6.
[2] Quoted by Cust in *Lives of the Warriors of the Thirty Years' War*, part I, p. 211.
[3] "The Great and Famous Battle of Lützen. . . ." *The Harleian Miscellany*, vol. IV, p. 201.
[4] Quoted from *Gustavus Adolphus*, C. R. L. Fletcher, p. 277. This letter, drenched in Pappenheim's blood, is to be seen in Vienna.

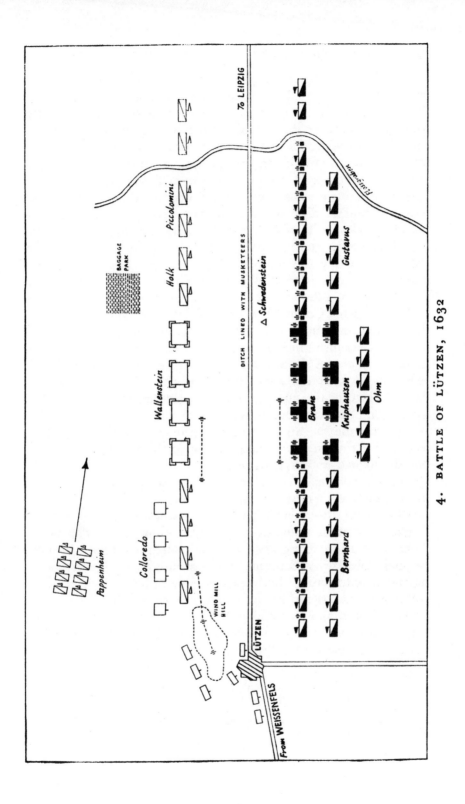

4. BATTLE OF LÜTZEN, 1632

known, it probably was 25,000 men without counting Pappenheim's 8,000. He divided his army into a centre, right, and left;
the first consisted of four great *tercios* of infantry under his own
command, and the second and third of Colloredo's and Piccolomini's cavalry. He held Lützen, which he set on fire, and
posted his 60 to 66 guns in two groups, one in front of the right
wing and the other in front of the right centre.

Gustavus moved forward "by the peep of day"–about eight
o'clock; "but so thick and dark a mist arose" that he was compelled to halt. He then addressed his men.[1] His object was to cut
off Wallenstein from Leipzig, not only to deprive him of his
base, but to free the road for John George, whom he hourly
expected. His army probably numbered 18,000, and he drew it up
in two lines as follows: four and a half brigades in the centre of
each line under Count Brahe and Kniphausen, and on each of
their flanks his cavalry ordered as at Breitenfeld. The right wing
he held under his immediate command, the left he gave to Bernhard. Further, he drew up a reserve of cavalry in rear of the
centre under Colonel Ohm. In front of the infantry he posted a
battery of 26 heavy guns, and his 40 regimental pieces stood in
front of the "commanded musketeers."

When the mist began to drift away "the cannons played a while,
but we were presently under ffavour of their canons. And the
battaile ioyned aboute tenn of the clock," writes Fleetwood. He
continues: "it being then a faire day; but just as the battaile ioyned
there fell so great a miste that wee could not see one another. . . ."[2]
It was during this short interval of clearness that Gustavus led
forward the right wing cavalry, and, according to Fleetwood,
"The King at the first charging of the graft [the ditches along the
Leipzig Road] was shott throug the arme and his horses neck,"
but refusing to retire, "he leaped over the graft and charged the
enimie."[3] He scattered Wallenstein's musketeers, routed a body of
Croatish horse, and then charged Piccolomini's heavy cavalry and
drove them back. Meanwhile Bernhard led forward the left wing,
and pushed back Colloredo's cavalry, and the centre moved

---

[1] See *The Harleian Miscellany*, vol. IV, p. 200.
[2] *The Camden Miscellany*, "Fleetwood's Letter," vol. I, p. 7.
[3] *Ibid.*, p. 7. There is no doubt that time and again Gustavus needlessly risked his
life; yet many leaders did the same. Hand-to-hand encounters between generals-in-
chief were frequent during this war, such as the battle duel between Archduke
Leopold and Piccolomini at the second battle of Breitenfeld, November 2, 1642.
Marshal de Rantzau, who died in 1650, lost in the course of his service, an eye, a leg,
an arm, and an ear.

forward and captured Wallenstein's central battery, but soon lost it.

Because of the mist, no two accounts of this phase of the battle tally. Apparently Gustavus, when he heard that his centre was in retreat, headed a regiment of horse and rode toward it. Separated from his men in the fog, he and three companions rode into a party of enemy cavalry, and he was shot through the head and body and killed; two of his companions were cut down, but the third escaped.

His death, instead of disheartening his men, filled them with a fanatical fury, and as Saxe-Weimar, who took over command, led them forward, Pappenheim came on the field. He fell on the Swedish right wing and drove it back to its original position. At this juncture he was killed and the battle became a frantic mêlée. The King's body was recovered, Wallenstein's guns were retaken, then lost and captured again, but after this the Swedes carried all before them and the imperial army broke up and scattered as night crept over the field. "Thus", writes Fleetwood, "concluded our famous battaile, farr exceeding that of Lypsick [Breitenfeld], for had not our foote stoode like a wall, there had not a man of us come of alyve, they being certen twyce our number."[1] There was no pursuit, and the losses are uncertain. Fleetwood says the Imperialists lost between three and four thousand killed and the Swedes about fifteen hundred. Also he writes: "And I am confident, had it pleased God that he [Gustavus] survived this day, he had putt a period to all the warrs in Germany. . . ."[2]

This is probable, for as Gindely writes: "It lies not beyond the range of possibility that he would have gained his purpose . . . of founding a dominion in Germany, and thus hastening by more than a hundred years the political and mercantile evolution of the country's resources."[3] And Bryce writes: "In four campaigns he destroyed the armies and the prestige of the Emperor; devastated his lands, emptied his treasury, and left him at last so enfeebled that no subsequent successes could make him again formidable."[4] Like Alexander, Gustavus died before his work was accomplished, and like him, he left behind a task too grand in idea for those who followed him.

---

[1] *Ibid.*, p. 9.   [2] *Ibid.*, p. 9.
[3] *History of the Thirty Years' War*, vol. III, p. 147.
[4] *The Holy Roman Empire*, pp. 383–384.

The war would have ended had it not been for Richelieu. The Empire was in collapse, Wallenstein discredited, turned traitor and was assassinated in 1634. But as French control of the left bank of the Rhine had not been gained the war went on and Richelieu treated "the old German frontierland as having no rights against the King of France."[1] "His will", writes Mr. Stanley Leathers, "fanned the flames of war from the Oder to the Ebro. Dangling before his deluded allies the prospects of a general peace, in which all interests should be secured, ceaselessly impressing on all concerned that a separate arrangement could be neither profitable nor trustworthy, he gradually wore down the strength of the Habsburgs and recovered the ground lost in twenty years of irresolution or of impotence."[2]

Nevertheless Richelieu was not a success as a strategist; though a statesman of the first order, he never understood war as an art.

The next turning point came with the battle of Nördlingen on September 6, 1634, in which Bernhard of Saxe-Weimar was beaten decisively by the Emperor's son Ferdinand of Hungary, Matthias de Gallas, and the Cardinal Infante. By the spring of the following year the whole of southern Germany was again in the Emperor's hands. The treaty of Prague (May 30, 1635) followed, and by it peace was signed between the Emperor and John George of Saxony, and the League was dissolved.

Because Sweden, backed by France, refused to accept this peace, the war entered its final stage of invasion and conquest; in which France and Sweden were ranged against Austria and Spain. The aim of the former, as always, was to break the Habsburg circle. Ferocity now took control. All ideals vanished; that of Ferdinand; that of Gustavus; and that of Wallenstein. The war became a conflict of Bourbon against Habsburg—a gladiatorial encounter for power. The peasants revolted, soldiers alone could live, and soon hordes of starving women and children, like packs of jackals, followed the armies.[3] Werth raided almost up to the gates of Paris and threw its inhabitants into panic. Battles were won and lost and entire regions depopulated, until, slowly out of the agony, the desire for peace gathered Protestants and Catholics about the Emperor and a semblance of national unity began to appear.

Ferdinand II died on February 15, 1637. By his will he directed

---

[1] *The Thirty Years' War*, Samuel Rawson Gardiner, p. 167.
[2] *The Cambridge Modern History*, vol. IV, p. 141.
[3] Gindely (vol. II, p. 334) quotes a case of an army of 38,000 fighting men being followed by 127,000 women, children and followers.

that all his hereditary kingdoms and principalities should remain for ever undivided, and so founded the Austrian monarchy. Richelieu died on December 5, 1642, the creator of monarchial France. Louis XIII died on May 4, 1643, to be succeeded by his son Louis XIV, born in 1638. Fourteen days later the battle of Rocroi was fought, in which the Great Condé put an end to the Spanish military system. Torstensson, one of the most remarkable of the many remarkable generals of the war, won the decisive battle of Jankau on March 6, 1645, which led to peace between Saxony and Sweden, and the war ended in the autumn of 1648 where it began, with the Swedish siege of Prague.

Thus the conflict collapsed, for Ferdinand III (1637–1657) could no longer resist the pressure of France, and as his empire was now a wilderness he was unable to feed his armies. Peace had for long been discussed, and on October 24, 1648, it was signed by the Empire and France at Münster, and by the Empire and Sweden at Osnabrück. The treaty, known as the Peace of Westphalia, for a century and a half remained the norm in the relations between the States of the new Europe created by it, which with slight variations retained its form until 1789.

By the Treaty of Westphalia Calvinism was placed on an equal footing with Lutheranism, and New Year's Day, 1624, was fixed upon as the date on which all religious disputes were to be tested. Thus an epoch was wound up and the Reformation established by law.[1] The sovereignty of Rome was abrogated and the disruption of Christendom sealed. So despiritualized had western Europe become that, when, on November 26, Innocent X denounced the treaty in his bull *Zelo domus Dei*, Europe laughed.

The map of Europe was redrawn according to the treaty. The Upper Palatinate went to Bavaria; the Lower to Charles Louis, son of Frederick, the unfortunate "Winter King". Brandenburg received the bishoprics of Halberstadt, Minden, Cammin, and part of that of Magdeburg; Sweden, Upper Pomerania, Bremen, Verden, Mecklenburg, Stettin, and the island of Rügen; and Saxony retained Lusatia and part of the bishopric of Magdeburg. The Swiss republic was declared a sovereign state, as were the United Provinces, and France, now the enemy of the repose of Europe, received Upper and Lower Alsace, Metz, Toul, Verdun,

---

[1] But it was a very different Reformation from the one contended for by Luther and Calvin, for the Protestant piety was dealt a blow from which it never recovered. It all but ceased to be a religion, and became instead a political programme.

Breisach, and Pignerol, with the right to garrison Philippsburg. Germany was split into some 300 petty, autocratic states in which serfdom was reintroduced and superstition became rampant.[1] With the schools destroyed, there was a lack of education and literature and art suffered accordingly. Long before 1648 the whole country had been barbarized and brutalized, the orderly and prosperous life of the German burgher had perished, as had that of the housewife, dragged about as she had been at the tail of mercenary armies, "half a prostitute and half a gipsy".

In 1880, Prince Hatzfeldt, German Ambassador in London, told Lord Granville that "Germany had not yet recovered from the effects of the Thirty and the Seven Years Wars; and that a determination to prevent the recurrence of similar disasters ought still to be the keynote of German policy"[2]—and no wonder. The entire country had been ruined more completely than on any previous occasion in history, not excepting the Hun and Mongol invasions. Eight million people are said to have perished, besides 350,000 killed in battle. In a district in Thuringia where, in 1618, 1,717 houses had stood in 19 villages, only 627 remained in 1649, and of the 1,773 families which inhabited them, only 316 could be found to occupy the 627 houses. In the same district 244 oxen remained out of 1,402, and of 4,616 sheep—not one. In Bohemia, of 35,000 villages only 6,000 are said to have survived, the population sank from about 2,000,000 to 700,000, and in the County of Henneburg 75 per cent. of the people and 80 per cent. of the livestock perished, and 66 per cent. of the houses were destroyed.[3] And the worst was that the richest areas suffered most.

The peace of Westphalia was one of the great landmarks in history. The Habsburgs turned toward the east, and when a generation later the Ottoman empire began to crumble, they sought on the Danube compensation for their losses on the Rhine. Sweden, until the battle of Poltava, in 1709, became a great power; the leadership of Germany passed into the hands of the Hohenzollerns; and France, her security strengthened by the disruption of Germany, continued her war with Spain. Meanwhile two new powers rose in the north, the United Pro-

---

[1] In 1625 and 1628, the bishop of Würzburg is said to have burnt 9,000 persons for witchcraft, and in 1640–1641 1,000 were burnt in the Silesian principality of Neisse.
[2] Quoted from *The Cambridge Modern History*, vol. IV, p. vi.
[3] None of these figures is very reliable. On this question see *The Thirty Years' War*, C. V. Wedgwood, pp. 510–516.

vinces, a growing commercial empire, and England under
Cromwell. As the future *roi soleil* played in his nursery and the
signatures of the Treaty of Westphalia were barely dry, the head of
Charles I of England rolled into the executioner's basket at
Westminster, the challenge of emerging plutocracy to the divine
right of kings.

The constitutional struggle in England

When the Thirty Years War boiled over in Bohemia, a collateral struggle simmered in England, a struggle which was to lead to the disruption of the kingdom and eventually to the establishment of a constitutional monarchy. Its root cause went back to the Hundred Years War, when military service was commuted for payment, and paid armies were substituted for feudal levies. Until then the sword had been the symbol of authority, henceforth, more and more, the purse was to challenge the sword, and those who held its strings were not the feudal barons, but the moneyed and trading classes from whom the early parliaments were largely recruited.

With the advent of standing armies in the late fifteenth and early sixteenth centuries another change set in. Because no continental nation could feel secure without a permanent army, in all countries which could afford them they became an essential instrument of the king's government. Further, because they endowed the king with power to enforce his will both in peace and in war, continental sovereigns soon began to dispense with their parliaments. Thus, in Spain, they practically disappeared and in France the Estates General ceased to be summoned between 1614 and 1789.

It was because of her insular position that England remained unaffected by this change, and when, on the accession of James I in 1603, her sole land frontier disappeared, the only possible reason for raising a standing army vanished with it. It was because of this that the parliamentary system took firmer root in England, for without an army the king could neither crush popular opposition nor control the power of the purse. Another radical difference between England and continental countries was that when the latter dispensed with their parliaments the dissolution of the monasteries by Henry VIII added vast wealth to those classes from which so many parliamentary members were recruited. The result was that the Lords and Commons became a plutocracy which, sooner or later, was bound to challenge the authority of the king in what so far had been his recognized domains of government.

Nevertheless it must not be overlooked that until the passing of the Bill of Rights in 1688 it was not parliament, but the king and his self-appointed ministers who governed; parliament was little more than the instrument which voted his supplies. To conceive of government without a king was tantamount to conceiving the Catholic Church without the pope. Further, there was nothing in law or the constitution that compelled an English sovereign to summon parliament before he needed its assistance, and, so far as the country was concerned, could he carry on his government without parliament, so much the better for the taxpayer. Therefore, as long as the king could rule without parliament—that is, within his legal income—far from tyranny, his personal rule was a sign of good government.

Since good government meant that the king had to live within his means he was encouraged to practise economy, not to antagonize his people, and above all to refrain from foreign wars. The first two policies were difficult enough, because ever since the discovery of the New World the enormous influx of bullion had caused a fall in the value of money, and this not only led to social unrest, but decreased the purchasing power of much of the king's revenue and so rendered it increasingly difficult for him to pay his way. The inadequacy of her finances was one of the reasons why Elizabeth's policy had, at one and the same time, aimed at the prevention of war and the encouragement of privateering. The former enabled her to govern within her income, and the latter to add considerably to it without call on parliament. It was also the main reason for James I's pacific foreign policy which, after his peace with Spain, in 1604, included the projected marriage, first of his son Henry, and on his death, of Charles, with the Infanta Maria, daughter of Philip III. Then, in 1618, came the outbreak of the Thirty Years War, and in order to subsidize his daughter Elizabeth, wife of the Elector Palatine, in 1621 James summoned his third Parliament, which voted as a token of its loyalty the paltry sum of £140,000 and was dissolved soon after. Next, in February, 1623, Charles, accompanied by his bosom companion, James's favourite, George Villiers, Duke of Buckingham, journeyed to Madrid to ask for the Infanta's hand in the hope that her father's marriage gift to him would be the restoration of the Palatinate to his brother-in-law. As the negotiations hung fire, on his return to

England Buckingham put himself at the head of the **popular movement against** Spain, and, in 1624 James reluctantly summoned another Parliament, which recommended the dissolution of the marriage treaty and an attempt to recover the Palatinate–incompatible proposals.

Buckingham–the virtual ruler of England–steered for war with Spain, and in need of an ally, he set out to arrange a marriage between Charles and Henrietta Maria (1609–1666), sister of Louis XIII and daughter of Henry IV. At the same time he sent a rabble of 12,000 ill-armed men under Mansfeld–then in England seeking aid–to Holland where, without money or provisions, most perished miserably of sickness and famine.

Such was the situation when, on March 27, 1625, James died, and to tackle it successfully a very different type of man from his son was needed. Charles lacked his father's common sense, was both pliant and pigheaded, and incapable of appreciating the motives of others; but like his father he was a stickler for prerogative and was possessed by an exalted idea of kingship. He postponed difficulties, dallied with opportunities, and though swayed by his friends, obstinately held to his cherished beliefs. Temperamentally artistic, he was a highly cultured man. He loved reading Shakespeare, which shocked his puritanical subjects, and Rubens calls him: *le prince le plus amateur de la peinture qui soit au monde*. His private life was impeccable, and in Clarendon's opinion he was "the worthiest gentleman, the best master, the best friend, the best husband, the best father and the best Christian that the age in which he lived produced." In a revolutionary epoch he was out of place, and even had times been normal, he was more fitted to adorn the drawing room than the throne.

Most unfortunately for him, he set out on his reign under two baneful influences. First, his marriage with Henrietta Maria–a Catholic–which took place by proxy on May 1, antagonized his puritanical Parliament and Protestant subjects. Secondly, his subservience to Buckingham–a flamboyant political gambler, vain, passionate, forceful and reckless, a man who deluded himself with grandiose schemes and impracticable crusades–blinded him to the fact that, in order to govern at all, the essential was to follow his father's wise, pacific policy.

But Buckingham was bent on war, and as it could not be waged without money one of Charles's first acts was to issue writs for the election of a new parliament. On June 18 it assembled. It was intolerantly Protestant, and although Charles had already entered upon engagements totalling nearly £1,000,000, it voted him subsidies of no more than £140,000. Further, in order from the outset to place him in its pocket, instead of granting him the customary revenue of tonnage and poundage for life–for long the established usage–it conceded them to him for one year only. Thus, within three months of Charles's accession, a deadlock was reached which could be resolved only by capitulation or by the sword. On August 12 Parliament was dissolved.

Buckingham impressed some 8,000 vagabonds and ruffians and on October 8–with a touch of Drake in the air–they were sent to seize Cadiz. But the expedition, unlike Drake's, ended in a disorderly fiasco and gave rise to so critical a situation that Charles was compelled to summon his second Parliament. On February 6, 1626, it met, and at once launched a violent attack on Buckingham. On May 8 it impeached him at the bar of the House of Lords, and though Charles had not received a penny, in order to save his favourite he dissolved Parliament on June 15.

In desperate financial straits, Charles resorted to forced loans and Buckingham, not content with one war on his hands, plunged the country into another, this time with France. An expedition to La Rochelle followed, which ended in an even greater fiasco than that at Cadiz, and to raise a second expedition he persuaded Charles to summon his third Parliament. It assembled on March 17, 1628, and was violently hostile. On May 28 it drew up the Petition of Right, in which the effective paragraph was that no man was to be compelled "to yield any gift, loan, benevolence, tax, or suchlike charge without the consent of both houses of Parliament". At first Charles jibbed; but Buckingham, still determined on his subsidies, persuaded him to accept the Petition. Then came an attack on Buckingham and an argument whether tonnage and poundage were a tax–they were not–and Charles lost patience. On June 26 he prorogued Parliament.

The first great turning point in his reign arrived when Buckingham was assassinated on August 23 by John Fenton while he was at Portsmouth preparing his expedition. The expedition sailed without him, and the story of its predecessors was repeated.

When Parliament reassembled in January, 1629, the extremists, under John Pym, launched a furious attack on the Crown and a religious offensive against the Church, Charles's last stronghold, for only through the Church could he grip the hearts of his people. On March 2 he dissolved his third Parliament, not because he wanted to govern–as government was then understood–without Parliament, but because it was impossible for him to do so with Parliament. On April 24 he made peace with France, and on November 5, 1630, with Spain. Thus Buckingham's disastrous policy was abandoned.

Although Charles was now free to rule without a parliament, the crucial problem remained unresolved. Parliament did not want to overthrow the constitution–far from it–but it did want to pocket the king and to use him as its "rubber stamp". Without the king it would be unable to find a constitutional basis of government. The king must, therefore, continue to reign–that was the first essential; in order that Parliament might govern in his name –that was the second. Therefore, now that he was free from foreign entanglements, Charles's one aim should have been to ward off internal troubles. This he failed to do.

His two chief advisers were Sir Thomas Wentworth (later first Earl of Strafford) and William Laud, Archbishop of Canterbury. The former was one of the ablest statesmen of his age and early in 1629 Charles made him president of the Council of the North. As such he was idolized by the common people, but by righting their grievances he antagonized the powerful capitalist cloth-makers of Yorkshire. In 1632 he was transferred to Ireland as Lord Deputy. There he put down the speculators of the rich London merchants; laid the foundation of a small and efficient army paid for by the Irish Parliament; and founded the Ulster linen industry. Had circumstances permitted him to continue his creative work there can be little doubt that, though it would still further have antagonized the plutocrats, it would have placed Charles in so popular a position that as long as he was careful not to antagonize the people there would have been no need for him to summon another parliament.

That Wentworth's good work was brought to nought was due almost entirely to Laud, who was a tactless, fussy, pedagogic and zealous religious reformer. Bent on tidying up the Church, which was certainly lax, his two chief instruments were the courts of Star Chamber and High Commission which, though they had been accepted as organs of law under the Tudors, were now looked upon as arbitrary. In the face of violent opposition Laud cleaned up the Church in England and then turned his attention to Scotland.[1] It was an act of supreme folly, because the Scots were mostly fanatical Calvinists, and were Scotland to rebel it would be necessary for Charles to raise an army, which he could not pay for without calling Parliament.

Undaunted, Laud set out to purge the Scottish Church. Scottish bishoprics were filled with Anglican zealots, new canons were forced upon the Kirk, and an attempt was made to impose upon it the Anglican prayer book. The result was that, when, on July 23, 1637, the Dean of Edinburgh began to read from it in St. Giles Cathedral, a violent tumult followed.

A lengthy manifesto, known as the Covenant, was at once published by the general assembly of the Kirk. It was a frenzied document, the aim of which was to sweep away the King's Church government and to set up a Presbyterian theocracy. The Scots began to arm, and so did Charles; but they could call upon many veterans of the Thirty Years War, under Alexander Leslie Earl of Leven, who had served with Gustavus Adolphus, and all he had at his disposal were the local trained bands, a worthless and ill-armed rabble. But money had to be found to pay them, and when he failed to raise a loan in the City, in June, 1639, Charles negotiated a truce with the Scots at Berwick. In September he summoned Wentworth to London, who, as Earl of Strafford—for thus he became in January, 1640—advised him to issue writs for a new Parliament. This Charles did, but though he needed at least £100,000 a month to maintain his army, when, on April 13, Parliament met, instead of voting him a grant in aid, under Pym and Hampden it entered into a treasonable intrigue with the Scottish Commissioners then assembled in London. Three weeks later it was dissolved, to become known as the Short Parliament.

Strafford suggested that the army in Ireland be brought over to England, but before anything could come of this the Scots took the initiative. They crossed the border, routed a body of Charles's men at Newburn, and occupied Newcastle. For Charles there was nothing left to do but to issue writs for yet another Parliament.

The Long Parliament, as it came to be known, assembled at Westminster on November 3, 1640. It was an undisguisedly revo-

---

[1] Laud's zeal had an important influence on the growth of the British Empire. Until he set to work, the supreme problem in the newly formed American colonies was how to increase their populations. This his persecutions most successfully accomplished, some 20,000 people—mostly Puritans—left for Maine, New Hampshire, Massachusetts, etc., between 1628 and 1640. Later, Cromwell's intolerance sent many thousands—mainly Royalists—to the New World.

lutionary body. It impeached Laud of high treason; on a trumped up charge it brought before the Lords a Bill of Attainder against Strafford, and simultaneously introduced in the Commons a Bill prohibiting the dissolution of Parliament without its own consent. Both Bills were read a third time on May 8, 1641, and to bring pressure to bear on Charles, Pym, an adept in psychological warfare, loosed the London rabble in thousands against the Palace of Whitehall, where the King and his family were in residence. Charles had promised Strafford "on the word of a King, you shall not suffer in life, honour or fortune", but afraid that the Queen and her children would be lynched by the mob, after agonizing hesitation, instead of vetoing both Bills—as he legally could—on May 10 he gave them his assent. Two days later Strafford was beheaded on Tower Hill. Thus Charles in the supreme crisis of his reign, which on his part demanded a flash of audacity, morally degraded himself and weakly sent to his death the sole man in the kingdom who might have mastered his enemies. Derisively the Act Suspending the Constitution lived on to become his own death warrant.

A host of reforms followed: a Triennial Bill, which provided for the calling of Parliament every three years with a session of at least 50 days, was made law; the judges were removed from the King's authority; the courts of High Commission and Star Chamber were abolished; the collection of ship-money was declared illegal, and tonnage and poundage in future were to be granted for only a few weeks at the time. With the King thus politically and financially hamstrung, Pym and his followers launched an attack on the Church. Their aim was to exclude the bishops from Parliament, and to seize Church property in order to pay ransom to the Scots and to relieve the burden of the English taxpayer. Further, a treaty with the Scots was negotiated, after which, on August 10, Charles set out for Scotland, apparently on an attempt to bring together the distracted halves of his kingdom. It was an unfortunate move, for it presented Pym with the opportunity to raise a scare about army plots and thereby to work on the nerves of the people. Equally unfortunate for Charles, the fear of a military *coup* in the north was stimulated by the outbreak of rebellion in Ireland, where, since the execution of Strafford, the old corruption and exploitation had returned.

Pym, bent on bringing the growing crisis to a head, decided to launch a national appeal against the Crown in the form of a lengthy document known as the Grand Remonstrance. He intended that Parliament should endorse this before Charles returned from Scotland. Every act of Charles's reign was reviewed in this document and all grievances were attributed either to the papists, the bishops, or to the King's counsellors. It also set forth the good deeds of the existing Parliament, and in conclusion the King was begged to deprive the bishops of all temporal powers.

Charles returned on November 25 and six days later a deputation, headed by Pym, presented the Remonstrance to him. When it had been read, Charles dismissed the deputies with an evasive answer, and Pym, who saw that the constitutional line of approach was now barred to him, decided to force the King's hands by accusing the Queen in Parliament "of compromising against the public liberty and of secret intelligence of the rebellion in Ireland" –that is, of high treason.

It would have been better if Charles had ignored the threat, for if it had been carried out most of the nation would almost certainly have rallied to the Queen. Instead, as he had when in Scotland obtained evidence of Pym's treasonable intrigues with the Scots, on January 3, 1642, he instructed the Attorney-General to present to the Lords articles of impeachment for treason against Pym, Hampden, and three other members, as well as one of the peers. In order to gain time, the Lords appointed a committee to consider whether the impeachment was in order. Charles did not act immediately and have the five members arrested in their beds, but hesitated, and not until the following day, and then only after the Queen had flung at him the stinging words, *"Allez poltron!"* did he go to the House with some 400 armed men to make the arrests. But Pym and his colleagues had learnt of his approach and had scrambled into a boat and sought refuge in the City. When he entered the Commons, to quote his own words, Charles found that "the birds had flown." It was an unforgivable blunder, not that it was attempted, but that it failed.

Charles felt no longer safe in London and with his family moved to Hampton Court. The Queen set out for Dover from there with the crown jewels and on February 23 she crossed to Holland. Before her departure Charles had arranged with her that as the people north of the Humber were overwhelmingly loyal, he intended to make York his headquarters. On March 19 he set out for that city, and, again through hesitation, instead of seizing Hull –which he could have done–where a large munitions depôt had been established, he secured Newcastle as his base port, and the Queen shipped there his first consignment of cannon, muskets, pistols, and powder.

At length, as the rebels were mobilized their forces, on August 22, a day of wind and storm, the King ordered the royal standard to be unfurled on Castle Hill, Nottingham; an appeal to his people and a challenge to Pym's Perpetual Parliament.

The Battle of Naseby, 1645

The Wars of the Roses were a conflict between two royal houses, the Great Rebellion was a clash between two social classes, one representing the dying feudal world, the other the emerging capitalist. Neither side was prepared for war, hence its chaotic character. Armies rose, struggled and faded away, and each county may be said to have had its own war, in which sieges abounded. This, in no small part, was because of the peacefulness of preceding years. Joshua Sprigge wrote in 1647: "Through the great goodness and long-suffering of God, England hath been a quiet habitation these eighty years,"[1] and "Peace", remarks Dalton, "hath so besotted us, that as we are altogether ignorant, so are we much the more not Sensible of that defect. . . ."[2] As so often happens, a long and prosperous peace had bred self-seeking and irresponsibility. Hobbes diagnoses this as his seventh and last cause of the Rebellion:

"Lastly, the people in general", he writes, "were so ignorant of their duty, as that not one perhaps of ten thousand knew what right any man had to command him, or what necessity there was of King or Commonwealth, for which he was to part with his money against his will; but thought himself to be so much master of whatsoever he possessed, that it could not be taken from him upon any pretence of common safety without his own consent. King, they thought, was but a title of the highest honour, which gentleman, knight, baron, earl, duke, were but steps to ascend to, with the help of riches; they had no rule of equity, but precedents and custom, and he was thought wisest and fittest to be chosen for a Parliament that was most averse to the granting of subsidies or other public payments."[3]

Another reason for the chaos of the war was the lack of a standing army. The so-called trained bands were only quarter-trained county and city militias, and when an army had to be raised—for instance, when James I reluctantly agreed to assist Mansfeld—it

---

[1] *Anglia Rediviva: History of the Army under Sir T. Fairfax* (1854 edit.), p. 8. Sprigge was Fairfax's chaplain.
[2] *Life of Sir Edward Cecil, Viscount Wimbledon* (1885 edit.), vol. II, p. 399.
[3] *Behemoth or The Long Parliament*, Thomas Hobbes (1889 edit.), p. 4.

was even worse than the trained bands. Of Mansfeld's, Dalton says: "Such a rabble of raw and poor rascals have not lightly been seen . . . they go so unwillingly that they must rather be driven than led."[1] This was because of impressment. "In England," wrote Barnaby Rich in 1587, "when service happeneth we disburthen the prisons of thieves, we rob the taverns and alehouses of tosspots and ruffians, we scour both town and country of rogues and vagabonds."[2] And on the outbreak of the Great Rebellion recruiting was on identical lines.

When Charles raised his standard at Nottingham, the north and west of England largely supported him; the south and east mostly favoured Parliament.[3] The people were split into three groups; those who favoured either Charles or Parliament, and those who politically were neutral and wanted to be left alone. The last group vastly outnumbered the other two.

The manufacturing centres, seaports, and large towns—above all London—were mostly Puritan; therefore material and financial advantages overwhelmingly favoured Parliament. It may be said that money was the decisive factor in the war, for whosoever had it could always raise troops from the common people, who would only serve for pay or plunder. Further, as the navy[4] was against Charles, Parliament was able to gain command of the coasts and also to secure the customs' duties of the ports, which amounted to more than £250,000 a year.

Leadership at first was definitely on Charles's side, and though numbers were against him, in the first days of the war lack of men was of no great account because both sides were so little organized. But lack of ships and money impeded Charles from free communication with France and Holland and from purchasing supplies from abroad. In consequence, sea power played a decisive part in his defeat. Nevertheless, during the initial phase of the war, these advantages were largely wasted by Parliament's

---

[1] *Life of Sir Edward Cecil*, vol. II, pp. 74, 79.

[2] *A Pathway to Military Practice*, quoted by C. H. Firth in his *Cromwell's Army*. In another pamphlet—*Dialogue between Mercury and an English Soldier*, written in 1574, Rich says: "The pety constable, when he perceyveth that wars are in hand, foreseeing the toyles, the infinite perills, and troublesome travayles that is incident to souldyers, is loth that any honest man, through his procurement should hazard himselfe amongst so many daungers; wherefore if within his office there hap to remayne any idle fellow, some dronkerd, or setitiouse quariler, a privy picker, or such a one as hath some skill in stealing a goose, these shall be presented to the service of the Prince."

[3] The population of England was then about 5,000,000, including some 350,000 in London.

[4] Thanks to Charles's resort to ship-money, it was in good condition and consisted of 16 warships in the Downs and two in Irish waters.

committee system of command, which led to endless debates, half-measures, and waste of time.

When Charles, at Nottingham, gathered in his followers under the Earl of Lindsey, a tired old soldier of 69, the Roundhead[1] forces assembled at Northampton under the Earl of Essex. Both sides were short of money and irregularity of pay led to indiscipline and constant desertions. Weapons and ammunition were scarce and confidence in inefficiency unbounded. First, subscriptions of men and horses were appealed for; next, officers were commissioned to raise new regiments while existing ones were allowed to die from lack of recruits. Lastly, impressment was resorted to and arbitrary levying of supplies enforced. Neither army can be said to have represented an organized fighting force, and in these circumstances the arrival from Holland of Prince Rupert (1619–1682) with his younger brother Maurice, was a heaven-sent acquisition for Charles.

Rupert, the third son of the unfortunate Elector Palatine, and, therefore, Charles's nephew, although only 23 years old, was already a veteran soldier, for since his fourteenth year he had served in the Danish and German wars. On his arrival, Charles gave him the command of his horse and wisely made him independent of Lindsey. He was a man of reckless courage, headstrong, flamboyant and versatile.[2] Dressed in a scarlet coat richly laced with silver, and mounted on a black Barbary horse, he rode about accompanied by a pet monkey, whom the Puritan pamphleteers dubbed "the little whore of Babylon", and a white poodle named "Boy", who had been taught by him the trick:

> Who name but Charles he comes aloft for him,
> But holds up his Malignant leg at Pym."[3]

Rupert was exactly the type of man needed to give *esprit de panache* to the Royalists, and, like Murat in after years, he was a superb cavalry leader who had adopted the shock tactics of Gustavus of charging home at the gallop sword in hand. Although he has been compared unfavourably with Cromwell, it must be remembered that at the opening of the Civil War circumstances were very different from what they were when the latter made his

---

[1] The Puritan members of the Parliamentary Army were thus called because they usually wore their hair short; the Cavaliers wore theirs in ringlets.

[2] He was one of the earliest mezzotint engravers, and was interested in science and gunnery. He was as able a sailor as a soldier.

[3] Quoted in *Charles and Cromwell*, Hugh Ross Williamson (1946), p. 108.

name. Unlike Cromwell, Rupert had no time to train his men, who mostly were young and headstrong Cavaliers. To manœuvre them was difficult enough, and to hold them in hand at the gallop nearly impossible, as happened again as late as Waterloo. Therefore he fitted his tactics to their lack of training and excess of enthusiasm, led them in whirlwind offensives against his as yet unsteady enemy, and earned for the Royalists such renown that his name was as great a terror to the Roundheads as Drake's had been to the Spaniards. "He put that spirit into the King's army that all men seemed resolved," says Sir Philip Warwick, "and had he been as cautious as he was a forward fighter, and a knowing person in all parts of a soldier, he had most probably been a very fortunate one. He showed a great and exemplary temperance, which fitted him to undergo the fatigues of war, so as he deserved the character of a soldier."[1]

Although the strategy of the war was complicated the opposing strategical aims were simple. For the Parliamentarians they were, firstly to hold fast to London, their political and administrative base, and secondly, in order to legitimize their rebellion, to capture the King, for without his authority they could not justify their cause in the eyes of the people. Thus Essex's commission read: "to rescue his Majesty's person, and the persons of the Prince [of Wales] and the Duke of York, out of the hands of the desperate persons who were then about him."[2] The aim of the Royalists was to occupy London, the heart and mainstay of the rebellion. This could not be done through blockade, because Charles had no fleet; nor could it be done by siege, for London was still walled and Charles had no siege train. The only course open to him was to inveigle the Roundhead forces away from London, to crush them in the field, and then, under cover of the demoralization caused by their defeat, to rush the city before it could be more strongly fortified.

To carry out this strategy required more men than Charles had at Nottingham—namely, 10,000, against Essex's 20,000 at Northampton. He decided to move westward to Shrewsbury and the Welsh border, where his cause was favoured, and there to recruit a force capable of meeting Essex. Then, after a pause in order to train and organize, he would advance rapidly on London, defeat Essex wherever met, and hope that his defeat would stimulate a

---

[1] Quoted in *The Cambridge Modern History*, vol. IV, p. 307.
[2] *Ibid.*, vol. IV, p. 306.

Royalist rising in the City while his victorious army closed in on it. It was a gamble, but in no sense a reckless one.

On September 13 Charles broke camp at Nottingham and set out for Shrewsbury, where he arrived on September 20. Once there he seized Chester, which commanded the approach to Wales–his most fruitful recruiting ground–and from which he could contact Ireland. Mystified by this move, Essex did nothing until September 19, when he marched to Worcester in order to place himself between Shrewsbury and London and so to cover the latter. Fighting had broken out all over the country and Portsmouth was lost to the King.

Charles set out from Shrewsbury on October 12 and moved by way of Bridgnorth, Birmingham, and Kenilworth. His intention was to turn Essex's northern flank, and next, by coming down on his rear, cut him off from London. The King's advance alarmed Parliament and repeated orders were sent to Essex to bring him to battle; at the same time the London trained bands were marshalled under the Earl of Warwick to defend the City. Essex turned eastward, strained every nerve to get in touch with Charles, and on October 22 reached Kineton. The King was then at Edgcott, about seven miles to the east.

On October 23 the battle of Edgehill was fought. Though fiercely contested, it was indecisive, but when Essex fell back on Warwick and Coventry the following day, Charles had nothing between him and London. But his army was disorganized, out of powder and shot, and it was impracticable for him to press on before he had established a base. Therefore he decided to make for Oxford, where he arrived on October 29. There he hesitated whether to go into winter quarters or to move on. At length, urged by Rupert to take the latter course, he set out, but so much time had been lost that Essex was able, by way of St. Albans, to reach London before him. On November 12 Rupert drove the Roundhead outposts out of Brentford, and on the next day came up with Essex's army at Turnham Green. Outnumbered by two to one, the odds against Charles were too great to risk an attack against an entrenched enemy; therefore, after a brief cannonade, he returned to Oxford, which was to become his headquarters for the rest of the war.

The importance of London was so great that Charles decided on another attempt to secure it. His plan was to assemble two sub- sidiary armies to cooperate with his own at Oxford; one under the

Earl of Newcastle at York, and the other under Sir Ralph Hopton in Cornwall. Next, when all three were ready, while the Oxford army advanced on London by way of the Thames Valley, Newcastle and Hopton were to move on London, the one from the north and the other from the south, to join hands below the city and to blockade it by stopping the passage of all ships up the Thames, while the King's army cut off its landward supplies.

On paper, it was a brilliant scheme, but with the amateur troops at Charles's disposal, a far too elaborate one. Local levies never liked leaving their home districts for fear that in their absence they would be overrun. Further, as the Roundheads were strongly entrenched at Hull and Plymouth, and because neither Newcastle nor Hopton had sufficient troops to mask them and simultaneously to move on London, unless they were first captured this contingency might easily arise.

The Queen returned from Holland while this plan was discussed and throughout the first half of 1643 local actions were fought all over the country, in one of which, at Chalgrove, on June 18, John Hampden was mortally wounded. On July 26 Rupert stormed Bristol, the second city in the kingdom, and with its capture Charles's fortunes reached their zenith.

The time seemed propitious to launch the threefold attack on London. But no sooner was it set in motion than Newcastle's men refused to go south while Hull remained a Parliamentary port, and Hopton's men insisted upon the reduction of Plymouth before they marched eastward. The Welsh were uneasy over Gloucester, held by a Parliamentary garrison, because it menaced the loyalists in south Wales, and as Charles could not move on London until Hull and Plymouth fell, he decided to take Gloucester. On August 10, he laid it under siege. Essex was sent to its relief; a Home Counties Army was formed under Sir William Waller, and the Eastern Association was ordered to raise 10,000 foot under command of the Earl of Manchester.

On September 5, as Essex approached Gloucester, Charles raised the siege and took up a position in the Cotswolds, from which, outmanœuvred by Essex, he fell back on Newbury. There, on September 20, an obstinate battle was fought, and had Charles pressed it on the following day the probabilities are that Essex would have been beaten and cut off from London. Instead, during the night, Charles set out for Oxford, and never again was London to be threatened.

With Charles thus occupied, Pym took a momentous decision. Ever since 1640 there had been a tacit alliance between the Opposition leaders and the Scots; now both Houses agreed to revive it in an active form, and in July they decided to send a deputation to Scotland to seek military assistance. On August 7 the Parliamentary Commissioners arrived at Leith.

When he learnt what was on foot, James Graham Marquis of Montrose, a leading Royalist in Scotland, made his way to the King's camp before Gloucester. He urged Charles to allow him to gather in the loyal forces in Scotland and deliver the first blow. But Charles, always a stickler over legal niceties, refused to listen to Montrose; not even to forestall an attack on himself would he agree to draw the sword against his subjects.

Pym had no such scruples. When the Commissioners proposed at Leith a civil league and the Scots rejected it and substituted a religious Covenant, similar to that of 1638, the Commissioners accepted it. This meant the abolition of the episcopacy and the supplanting of the Church of England by a Presbyterian Church on the lines of the Church of Scotland. Further, it meant that Catholicism was to be extirpated in Ireland.

Early in September the agreement took final form, and on September 25 it was sworn by the Assembly of Divines and the House of Commons. Thus, in conflict with the wishes of most of the people of England and Ireland, Presbyterianism was to be established on a uniform footing throughout the three kingdoms, and in return for this monstrous surrender the Scots agreed to send an army to the assistance of the English Parliament, which nevertheless was to pay for its maintenance.

In two ways the Solemn League and Covenant, as this contract was called – the last work of Pym, who died on November 8 – was a most fateful agreement. Firstly, it enabled Parliament to win the First Civil War, and secondly, it led to the rise of the Independents (Congregationalists),[1] those people who maintained the right of every congregation to govern itself, and because of them, as we shall see, it led to the eventual break between Parliament and the Army. In its turn, this led to the Second Civil War, to the execution of the King, and to the establishment of the Protectorate under Cromwell.

---

[1] Whereas episcopacy represented the principle of religious rule in a monarchial form, Presbyterianism stood for the rule of an official aristocracy in religion exercising collective control, and Independency for the principle of democracy in religion.

On January 19, 1644, a Scottish army of 18,000 foot and 3,000 horse, under Leven, crossed the Tweed, and in order to block its path, Newcastle hurried north and reinforced the Royalists at Newcastle. He had no more than 5,000 foot and 3,000 horse at his disposal, and when, on April 11, Lord Fairfax, who commanded the Parliamentary forces in Yorkshire, and his son, Sir Thomas Fairfax, stormed Selby, afraid that he would be crushed between them and the Scots, Newcastle fell back and, on April 18 shut himself up in York. Leven followed close on his heels and on April 20 effected a junction with the two Fairfaxes at Tadcaster; soon afterward they laid siege to York. On June 2 they were joined by Manchester with the troops of the Eastern Association.

At Oxford, it was apparent to Charles that if York fell the north would be lost and his cause jeopardized. Therefore, York had to be relieved, and this could only be done by drawing upon forces in the south, reinforcing Rupert, then at Shrewsbury, and sending him to the relief of York. To do so meant risking the loss of Oxford, for Essex was at Aylesbury and Waller at Farnham. This risk had to be accepted, and on May 16 Rupert set out from Shrewsbury. Meanwhile Montrose, who, on February 13, had been appointed the King's Lieutenant-General in Scotland, had led a minute army across the border to create a diversion.

Rupert, who marched by way of Lancashire and increased his forces as he went, first relieved Lathom House, and next, on June 11, occupied Liverpool. From there he advanced through the Aire-Ribble gap in the Pennines, debouched on the Yorkshire Moors and reached Knaresborough on June 30. Early the next day, when he learnt that the enemy forces at York had raised the siege and were encamped near Long Marston, barring his road from Knaresborough to York, he wheeled his army northward, crossed the Swale at Thornton Bridge, and was joined by Newcastle.

Though Newcastle considered a battle inadvisable, Rupert was full of fire, and on July 2 he marched to Marston Moor and drew out his army facing the Parliamentarians and Scots, who were in position between the villages of Tockwith and Long Marston. Each side had about 7,000 horse but the Royalist infantry, 11,000 strong, was outnumbered by nearly two to one.

The battle opened at 5 p.m. and ended in an overwhelming Royalist defeat, largely because of the skilful handling of the Roundhead left wing cavalry under Cromwell. It was the greatest battle of the war, and for Charles a disaster of the first magnitude. Newcastle abandoned all hope, fled to Scarborough and thence to the Continent, and Rupert collected together some 6,000 cavalry and withdrew to Richmond, from where he made his way back to Lancashire. On July 16 York surrendered, two days after the Queen had sailed from Falmouth for France, never to see the King again.

The fate of the war now lay in the hands of Parliament, for all that remained to be done was for the Fairfaxes and Leven to march south to link up with Essex and Waller, who had been engaged upon a fumbling campaign around Oxford, and to round up Charles. But instead, the three armies in the north separated: Leven marched off to besiege Newcastle; Manchester returned to Lincolnshire; and the Fairfaxes set out to reduce Pontefract, Scarborough, and other Royalist strongholds in Yorkshire. In the south, Waller's army, composed largely of trained bands, began to melt away, and Essex marched into Cornwall, where, in August, he was shut up in Fowey, and on September 2 his infantry were forced to capitulate. Nevertheless, for the Parliamentary cause Marston Moor was the great turning point in the war, for it brought to eminence and trust the man who, above all others, had won it. That man was Oliver Cromwell.

A gentleman farmer of Huntingdon and descended from a nephew of Thomas Cromwell, Earl of Essex and minister of Henry VIII, Oliver was born on April 25, 1599; was elected member for Cambridge on April 13, 1640, and at the outbreak of the war was commissioned captain of the 67th Troop of Horse. After Marston Moor, Rupert nicknamed him "Ironsides", a name which well fitted him; but it was not until the war ended that it was generally applied to his troops. Born and bred a civilian, Cromwell was in no way trained for war; nevertheless he possessed those rare qualities of command and resolution which no training can impart. Further, at the outset of his career as a soldier, he was favoured by the many relatives who cooperated with him and enabled him to gather around himself a veritable Cromwellian military clan. His son Oliver was a cornet in the 8th Troop; Henry Ireton, his future son-in-law, captain of the 58th Troop; John Hampden, his cousin, colonel of the 20th Regiment of Foot; Valentine Walton, his brother-in-law, captain of the 73rd Troop; Edward Whalley, his cousin, cornet of the 60th Troop; and Lord Mandeville, later Earl of Manchester, his neighbour, colonel of the 10th Foot. Out of this clan, under Cromwell's inspiration, came the idea of association, and it cannot be doubted that, because of this, on October 22, 1642 – the day before the battle of Edgehill – Parliament approved the formation of county defence unions, from which emerged the Eastern Association of Norfolk, Suffolk, Essex, Hertfordshire, Huntingdon and Lincoln, grouped around Cambridge, whose member of Parliament was Cromwell. This Association became the backbone of the Parliamentary cause.

Whether on the next day Cromwell, the spiritual if not physical originator of the Association, took part in the battle of Edgehill is uncertain; yet it was about this time that the memorable conversation between him and Hampden took place, which 15 years later he referred to in a speech to his second Parliament. He said:

"At my first going out into this engagement, I saw our men were beaten at every hand. . . . 'Your troopers', said I, 'are most of them old decayed serving-men, and tapsters, and such kind of fellows; and', said I, 'their troopers are gentlemen's sons, younger sons and persons of quality: do you think that the spirits of such base mean fellows will ever be able to encounter gentlemen, that have honour and courage and resolution in them? . . . You must get men of spirit: and take it not ill what I say – I know you will not – of a spirit that is likely to go on as far as gentlemen will go: – or else I am sure you will be beaten still'."[1]

This was his grand idea, that leadership is useless without disciplined followership, and that discipline demands not only that officers and men know what they are fighting for, but "love what they know", for without affection discipline is sterile. He, therefore, sought out men who had the fear of God before them, "and made some conscience of what they did."[2]

Cromwell returned to Cambridge in January, 1643, and set to work to infuse this spiritual urge into his troop. During March he converted it into a regiment of five troops and was promoted colonel. By the end of the year, he added nine more troops, and Baxter informs us: "He had a special care to get religious men into his troop: these men were of greater understanding than common soldiers . . . and making not money, but that which they took for the public felicity, to be their end. . . ."[3] Again, in May, 1643, a

---

[1] Speech XI, Carlyle's *The Letters and Speeches of Oliver Cromwell* (edit. S. C. Lomas, 1904), vol. III, pp. 64–65.
[2] *Ibid.*, vol. III, p. 66.
[3] Quoted from *Oliver Cromwell*, Frederic Harrison (1898), p. 61.

newsletter writer states: "As for Colonel Cromwell, he hath 2,000 brave men, well-disciplined; no man swears but he pays his twelve-pence; if he be drunk, he is set in the stocks, or worse; if one calls the other roundhead he is cashiered: insomuch that the countries where they come leap for joy of them, and come in and join with them. How happy were it if all the forces were thus disciplined!"[1]

In September 1643, Cromwell wrote two remarkable letters in which he gives a clear idea of what he had in mind. To Sir William Springe he wrote: "I beseech you be careful what captains of Horse you choose, what men be mounted: a few honest men are better than numbers. Some time they must have for exercise. If you choose godly honest men to be captains of Horse, honest men will follow them; and they will be careful to mount such. . . . I had rather have a plain russet-coated captain that knows what he fights for, and loves what he knows, than that which you call a gentleman and is nothing else. I honour a gentleman that is so indeed."[2] And to Friend Oliver St. John Esquire on September 11, 1643, he wrote: "I have a lovely company; you would respect them, did you know them. They are no Anabaptists, they are honest, sober Christians: they expect to be used as men!"[3] In these last seven words lies the secret of the whole system of Cromwell's discipline.

After Marston Moor and the abortive peace negotiations[4] that followed it (November, 1644, to February, 1645), which were in no way assisted by the execution of Laud[5] on January 10, Cromwell saw that nothing except drastic action could set the army right. Manchester, leader of the Presbyterians, was for peace;[6] he also was for peace, but peace through victory. As the crisis

---

[1] *Ibid.*, p. 62.

[2] Letter XVI, Carlyle's *The Letters and Speeches of Oliver Cromwell*; vol. I, p. 154.

[3] Letter XVII, *ibid.*, vol. I, p. 156.

[4] "The concessions which Charles was prepared to make adumbrated the final settlement which was to bring the whole matter to its conclusion in 1689. . . . 'There are three things', he said to the Parliamentary Commissioners, 'I will not part with – the Church, my crown and my friends.'. . . And it was precisely on those three things, from this moment to the end of his life, that every negotiation foundered" (*Charles and Cromwell*, Ross Williamson, p. 130).

[5] His trial was even more disgraceful than Strafford's, the Commons arrogated to themselves the right to declare any crime they pleased treasonable (see *History of the Great Civil War*, Samuel R. Gardiner, 1889, vol. II, p. 48).

[6] "If we beat the King ninety-nine times," said Manchester, "yet he is King still, and so will his posterity be after him; but if the King beat us we shall all be hanged and our posterity will be slaves." Manchester, at least, saw where he was going; Cromwell did not. The latter had no plan, no defined goal, and each turning point in his path was solved by prayer. Gardiner says of him: "Cromwell needed the impact of hard fact to clear his mind, but when once it had been cleared he saw his way with pitiless decision and purpose." (vol. II, pp. 18–19).

deepened, instinctively men turned toward where leadership lay
–to Cromwell and the Eastern Association. Already Sir William
Waller had informed Parliament that an army of local levies
would never win the war.

Cromwell resolved to take up the question of leadership in
Parliament and to insist on a clean sweep of political generals,
like Manchester and Essex. This took the form of the Self-denying
Ordinance, according to which members of both Houses were
excluded from offices and commands, both military and civil. On
December 19 it passed the Commons, and was reluctantly accepted by the Lords on April 3, 1645. Meanwhile, on November
23, the Committee of Both Kingdoms had been directed by the
Commons to "consider a frame or model of the whole militia."
It recommended that there should be established an army of
22,000 men–14,400 foot and 7,600 horse and dragoons–and that
it should be regularly paid from taxes "assessed on those parts of
the country which were suffering least from the war." On January
11 the New Model Ordinance passed the Commons, and on
February 15 was accepted by the Lords. Shortly after this a national
army came into being, a standing and professional army to be
disciplined in accordance with Cromwell's grand idea. This idea
carried with it more than a military revolution; for, as Frederic
Harrison writes: "To organise the New Model on the frame of the
Ironsides was to put the sword of the State into the hands of
Independency and of radical reform;" for the New Model was
much more than an army, it was a body of Bible warriors. "It
was itself a Parliament–a Parliament larger, more resolute, and
far more closely knit together in spirit and will than the Parliament
which continued to sit officially at Westminster. From this hour
the motive power of the Revolution passed from the House of
Commons to the army."[1]

Once agreed to, on the motion of Cromwell, Parliament voted
that Sir Thomas Fairfax, a straightforward soldier, free from
sectional interests, then aged 33, should be given the chief command. Under him and next in rank came a Lieutenant-General
as Commander of the Horse; a Sergeant-Major-General as Chief
of Staff and General of Foot; a Lieutenant-General of Ordnance
and a Scout Master General. There were also Quartermaster and
Adjutant Generals, both of Horse and Foot.[2] All these and the

[1] *Oliver Cromwell*, pp. 85, 86.
[2] For the complete establishment of the senior officers, see Fortescue's *A History of
the British Army* (1899), vol. I, pp. 220–222.

subordinate officers were carefully chosen, though, as Sprigge says, some were "better Christians than soldiers." They could live on their pay, which was generous.

The recruiting of the infantry was less satisfactory. Though no more than 14,400 were required, Waller's army could supply but 600, Essex's some 3,000 and Manchester's 3,500. Therefore, to make up the deficit, press gangs were again set to work. Yet, in spite of this, in May, 1645, the infantry were still between 3,000 and 4,000 short of establishment. They were organized in 12 regiments, each of 10 companies averaging 120 strong, divided into 78 musketeers and 42 pikemen ordered in files of six men each. Recruiting for the cavalry appears to have been less difficult; 6,600 were required as well as 1,000 dragoons. The former were organized in 11 regiments of six troops of 100 men each, armed with sword, two pistols, a "pot" or helmet, and a light cuirass, known as "back and breast". The dragoons were formed into a regiment of 10 companies, armed with the musket, and were mounted infantry. Their normal formation was in 10 ranks, and when in action one rank supplied the horse-holders for the other nine.

The artillery, which had hitherto been neglected, was reorganized. The army was provided with a powerful train eventually brought up to 56 guns, some of 6 in. and 7 in. calibre, without counting a number of 12 in. bomb throwing mortars for siege work. Each gun crew consisted of three men, a gunner and two mates; the powder was carried either in cartridges or barrels; two regiments of "firelocks" were raised as escort, but the drivers remained, as before, a heterogeneous collection of carters and hackney coachmen. The train included a body of engineers; but, then as now, the English soldier detested spade-work, and when sieges were undertaken, such as that of Edinburgh Castle, in 1650, English and Scottish colliers were impressed for the work.

Other items of interest are that, though the red coat was not unknown as a uniform,[1] and Cromwell had already adopted it for the infantry of the Eastern Association,[2] it was not until the New Model was formed that it became general, to remain so until 1914.

---

[1] Edward Davies in *The Art of War*, 1620, writes that the dress of the soldier should be in colour "red, murry, tawney, and scarlet, which maketh a gallant show in the field."

[2] At the relief of Newark in March, 1644, "Norfolk Redcoats" are mentioned, and later "Redcoat" and "soldier" are used as synonymous terms: see *The Red-Coat's Catechism*, 1659.

The men carried knapsacks, but no water bottles, also tents in sections, and their staple rations were bread and cheese. Although no field hospitals were provided to repair their bodies, a Judge Advocate General and a Provost Marshal General with a small force of mounted police attended to their moral welfare. Flogging was permitted, but never more than 60 lashes, and though the army contained a multiplicity of saints, it did possess one frail sinner, whose career as a warrior was, in July, 1655, interrupted "by the birth of a young soldier."[1]

This remarkable army, destined to subdue both King and Parliament, was assembled at Royal Windsor where, under Sergeant-Major-General Skippon, it received its scarlet uniform and carried out its training.

While the New Model ("New Nodel"[2] as the Royalists called it) was shaped, Charles, at Oxford, furtively looked in two directions: westward toward Cornwall, Devon, Somerset, and Dorset, in order to establish himself on the coast and to form a Royalist Western Association which would counterbalance the Roundhead Eastern Association, and northward toward Scotland where Montrose's successes had furthered his cause. In order to effect the former plan, he sent Lord Goring to lay siege to Taunton, where he arrived on March 11, 1645. Walker informs us that the latter idea was Rupert's, because he wished "to be revenged on the Scots for the Defeat he had received the Year before".[3]

In preparation for the northern campaign, Rupert went to Gloucester and Hereford to impress soldiers, while Charles made ready at Oxford to join him, but suddenly everything was changed. On April 20 Cromwell[4] was ordered to move west of Oxford to impede the junction between Charles and Rupert. This he did during the following seven days by taking several strong Royalist posts and sweeping the countryside clear of horses. No sooner was

---

[1] Firth's *Cromwell's Army*, p. 301.
[2] *Anglia Rediviva*, Joshua Sprigge, p. 13.
[3] *Historical Discourses upon several occasions relating to Charles I*, Sir Edward Walker (1705 *edit.*), p. 125. Walker was the King's Secretary of War. Clarendon says that, throughout the winter, Rupert had "disposed the king to resolve 'to march northwards and to fall upon the Scottish army in Yorkshire, before Fairfax should be able to perfect the new model to that degree, as to take the field' ". (*The History of the Rebellion and Civil Wars in England*, Edward Earl of Clarendon (1807 edit.), vol. II, part II, book ix, p. 973.)
[4] Under the terms of the Self-Denying Ordinance, 40 days were allowed between its passing and the expiration of the appointments of those officers it affected. This period had not yet elapsed.

this done than Parliament, alarmed over Taunton, ordered Fairfax and his half-formed army, 11,000 strong, to move from Newbury to its relief. Fairfax set out on April 30 and arrived at Blandford on May 7.

Because Cromwell's raid had immobilized Charles–whose lack of draught horses prevented him moving his artillery–Rupert was called in to Oxford, and when it was found that his cavalry was insufficient to protect the King's march, Goring also was instructed to return. He handed the siege of Taunton over to Sir Richard Grenville, and on the day Fairfax marched out of Newbury, Goring set out on his return to Oxford. There, on May 7, Charles held a council of war, at which he was urged to postpone his march north and instead to fall upon Fairfax, then at Blandford. Rupert objected, apparently because his Northern Horse, under Sir Marmaduke Langdale, wished to return home, and because "he was jealous of having a Rival in Command, and so feared Goring who had the Master Wit. . . ."[1] Thereupon Charles, always over pliant, decided on a half measure which, though it might please both parties, was the root cause of his ultimate ruin. He divided his factious little army of 11,000 men and allowed Rupert to move north while Goring moved west.

This decision caused another change, for directly it was known that the King was moving, Fairfax received an order to countermarch and lay siege to Oxford. "This", says Walker, "staggered our Designs." Clarendon points out that, as "Oxford was known to be in so good a condition . . . the loss of it could not in any degree be apprehended," and that therefore nothing could have been more advantageous for Charles "than that Fairfax should be thoroughly engaged before it."[2] Nevertheless the king and his council were undecided; should the army proceed north and link up with Montrose who, on May 9, had won a brilliant victory at Auldearn, or should it turn south and meet Fairfax? Again a half measure was agreed upon, which, as it was thought, would draw Fairfax from Oxford and simultaneously avert a southward march. It was concluded, says Clarendon, "that the best way to draw him from

---

[1] *Historical Discourses*, Sir Edward Walker, p. 126. Clarendon says: "The Prince found that Goring, as a man of a ready wit, and an excellent speaker, was like to have most credit with the King in all debates; and was jealous that, by his friendship with the Lord Digby, he would quickly get such an interest with his Majesty, that his own credit would be much eclipsed." (*The History of the Rebellion*, etc., vol. II, part II, book IX, p. 975.) In 1644 Rupert had quarrelled with Digby and with his own subordinates Goring and Wilmot. Charles, as usual, supported each in turn.

[2] *The History of the Rebellion*, etc., vol. II, part II, book IX, p. 978.

thence [Oxford] would be to fall upon some place possessed by Parliament."[1]

The nearest town of importance which fitted this proposition was Leicester, then commanded by Sir Robert Pye and a good garrison. Therefore it was decided to take it, and on May 31, at considerable loss, it was stormed and occupied. A few days later Charles wrote to the Queen saying: "I may, without being too much sanguine, affirm, that since the rebellion my affairs were never in so hopeful a way."[2]

Actually, Charles had placed himself in a perilous position between Leven in the north and Fairfax in the south, and instead of remaining at Leicester and gathering in his detachments, he plunged into his last and most disastrous muddle. He had summoned Goring from the west and Gerard with his 3,000 foot and horse, then on his way to south Wales, to unite with him, but he counter-ordered the movement of the former and instructed Goring to occupy Newbury and from there either to compel Fairfax to raise the siege of Oxford, or, failing this, to embarrass his operations, while he himself marched directly from Leicester on Oxford. When he had decided on this movement he set out for Daventry, where he halted for five days in order to collect droves of sheep for the revictualling of Oxford, and on June 13 learnt to his consternation that Fairfax had abandoned the siege and had advanced with a strong army, much superior to his own, nearly to Northampton—15 miles to his east.

, What had happened was that when Parliament learnt of the fall of Leicester, it instructed Cromwell to secure the Isle of Ely, in order to protect the eastern counties, and Fairfax "to rise from before Oxford, and to march to defend the association."[3] This the latter did, and, on June 5, he set out in a north-easterly direction. On June 7, at Sherington, he was joined by Colonel Vermuyden and 2,500 horse. Here a council of war was held at which a request was made to Parliament that Cromwell should fill the still vacant appointment of Lieutenant-General and take over command of the horse. On June 9, the army counter-marched to Stony Stratford, and, on June 12, was at Kislingbury on the Northampton Road—some eight miles from Daventry.

This advance took Charles by surprise. Sprigge says: "the King was a-hunting, the soldiers in no order, and their horses all at

Ibid., vol. II, part II, book IX, p. 978.
[2] Anglia Rediviva, Joshua Sprigge, p. 27.   [3] Ibid., p. 30.

grass, having no knowledge of our advance;" but, as Fairfax's infantry had not yet come up, "it was not thought wisdom to make any further attempt."[1] Therefore Fairfax's army bivouacked, and at about six o'clock the following morning, as a council of war was held, in rode Cromwell with 600 horse and dragoons, "who

5. THE CAMPAIGN OF NASEBY, 1645

was with the greatest joy received by the general and the whole army."[2] Charles did not lose a moment, but gathered in his scattered men and withdrew to Harborough (Market Harborough) meaning to return to Leicester and there to gather in troops from Newark, when in the evening it was learnt that Ireton had driven a party of Rupert's men out of Naseby. A council of war was assembled, which cancelled the project to retire on

[1] *Ibid.*, Sprigge, p. 34.   [2] *Ibid.*, p. 35.

Leicester, "and a new one as quickly taken 'to fight'; to which there was always an immoderate appetite, when the enemy was within any distance."[1] Accordingly, early on June 14, Charles drew out his army on the long swelling ridge a mile south of Harborough.

Some seven miles south of Harborough lies the village of Naseby, on a hill-top. The ground surrounding it was then moorland, unenclosed and free from woods, split up by broad, blunt clayey ridges known as "hills", and it was on one of these, the one lying between the villages of East Farndon and Oxenden Magna, that Sir Jacob Astley, who commanded the Royalist infantry, drew up his foot. As the Roundheads did not appear, at about eight o'clock Rupert grew impatient and sent forward his Scout Master to find where they were. On his return, with no news of Fairfax's army, Rupert rode forward, mounted the rise south of the village of Clipston, and saw, as he imagined, his antagonist in full retreat. He at once sent back an order to Astley to move forward to Dust Hill, which he did, and abandoned his good defensive position.

Though at the time Rupert was unaware of it, what actually took place was this. At three o'clock on the morning on June 14, Fairfax paraded his troops at a spot four and a half miles south of Naseby, and in the belief that Charles would retire, ordered a direct advance upon Harborough, by way of Clipston. This done, he and his generals rode forward and soon discovered that instead of retiring the Royalists were advancing to the south of Harborough. As Fairfax watched his distant enemy, Cromwell suggested to him that Mill Hill appeared to be a more suitable position than the one which lay north-east of Naseby and directly south of the East Farndon–Oxenden Magna ridge. So it was toward Mill Hill that the army was counter-marched, and when the leading troops were marshalled by Skippon, he received orders to withdraw them from the northern to the southern slope of the hill. Of this movement Sprigge says: "But considering it might be of advantage to us to draw up our army out of sight of the enemy . . . we retreated about one hundred paces from the edge of the hill, that so the enemy might not perceive in what form our battle was drawn, nor see any confusion therein, and yet we to see the form of their battle." It was this retrogade movement which

---

[1] Clarendon, vol. II, part II, book IX, p. 983. According to Warburton (*Memoirs of Prince Rupert*, 1849, vol. III, p. 102) Rupert counselled retreat.

persuaded Rupert that his enemy was in retreat, and which led to the abandonment of the good defensive position with so much haste that, as Sprigge informs us "they left many of their ordnance behind them."[1]

Charles next marshalled his army. It numbered no more than 4,000 horse and 3,500 foot;[2] these he drew up in three lines. In the first Astley commanded the infantry in the centre with Rupert's cavalry on his right and Langdale's on his left, both in two lines of squadrons. The second line consisted of Howard's infantry with squadrons between regiments, and the third of the King's and Rupert's regiments of foot and the King's Horse Guards, about 500 strong.

In parallel order stood Fairfax's army of 6,500 cavalry and dragoons and 7,000 foot in two lines. In the former Skippon held the centre with his infantry and a forlorn hope in front, with Cromwell's cavalry on his right and Ireton's on his left; the second line consisted of three regiments of infantry. In order to protect the left flank of the order of battle, Okey's regiment of dragoons was drawn out along Lantford hedge, which ran across the field of battle from Fairfax's left to Charles's right.

At 10 o'clock the battle was opened when the Royalists poured down into Broad Moor, and began to climb the opposite ridge. As they did so, the Roundheads moved forward to its crest and, when Ireton was severely wounded by a musket ball, his wing fell into disorder. Rupert took in at a glance what had happened and forthwith charged home, pushed his opponent's first line of squadrons back upon his second line, and then drove both pell-mell from the field. As usual, he could not hold his men, and in a headlong gallop they chased their enemy to Naseby. At Naseby, Rupert ordered Fairfax's train to surrender, but was driven back by its escort of firelocks.

Meanwhile in the centre, Walker tells us: "Presently our Forces advanced up the Hill, the Rebels only discharging five Pieces at them, but overshot them, and so did their Musquetiers. The Foot on either side hardly saw each other until they were within Carbine Shot, and so only made one Volley; ours falling in with Sword and butt end of the Musquet did notable Execution; so

---

[1] *Anglia Rediviva*, pp. 38, 39. See also Walker's *Historical Discourses*, p. 130. Charles had 12 small field pieces, none of which appears to have been brought on to the field.
[2] The numerical strengths of the two armies have been exhaustively examined by Lieut.-Col. W. G. Ross in *The English Historical Review* (1888), vol. III, pp. 669–679.

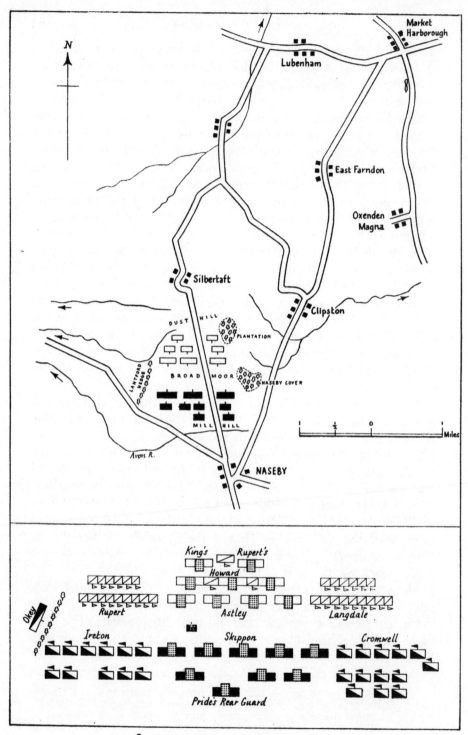

6. BATTLE OF NASEBY, 1645

much as I saw their Colours fall, and their Foot in great Disorder. And had our left Wing but at this time done half so well as either the Foot or right Wing, we had got in few Minutes a glorious victory."[1] In the contest Skippon was severely wounded, and his front line was driven back in confusion. Rightly, says Professor Gardiner: "Whichever leader could bring a preponderant force of horse to bear upon the confused struggle of men in the centre would have England at his feet."[2]

That leader was Cromwell who, at the head of 3,600 horse, moved down the slope to meet Langdale's regiments then advancing up it. When near them Cromwell ordered the charge,[3] and the whole Roundhead right flank trotted forward. Whalley's divisions on the left routed "two divisions of Langdale's, driving them back to prince Rupert's regiment . . . whither indeed they fled for shelter and rallied. . . . In the meantime, the rest of the divisions of the right wing, being straitened by furzes on the right hand, advanced with great difficulty, as also by reason of the unevenness of the ground, and a cony-warren. . . . Notwithstanding which . . . they came up to the engaging the residue of the enemy's horse on the left wing, whom they routed, and put into great confusion."[4]

It was now that Cromwell showed his skill as a cavalry general. Instead of following up his success with a headlong pursuit, like Rupert, he ordered three regiments forward against the beaten enemy horse, and then wheeled the rest of his command left and fell upon Astley's exposed left flank. As he did so Charles moved forward with his reserve cavalry to meet the onrush of the three pursuing regiments, when an extraordinary misunderstanding occurred. Clarendon describes it as follows: "The King . . . was even upon the point of charging the enemy, in the head of his guards, when the Earl of Carnewarth, who rode next to him (a man never suspected for infidelity, nor yet one from whom the King would have received counsel in such a case), on a sudden, laid his hand on the bridle of the King's horse, and swearing two or three full mouthed Scottish oaths (for of that nation he was),

---

[1] *Historical Discourses*, pp. 130–131 (wrongly numbered p. 115), Clarendon gives an almost identical account.

[2] *History of the Great Civil War*, vol. II, p. 213.

[3] Cromwell's horses were trained to charge at the trot. At Grantham, in 1643, Cromwell says: ". . . we came on with our troops a pretty round trot . . . and our men charging fiercely upon them" (Letter X, Carlyle's *The Letters and Speeches of Oliver Cromwell*, vol. I, p. 135).

[4] *Anglia Rediviva*, Joshua Sprigge, p. 40.

said, 'will you go upon your death in an instant?' and, before his Majesty understood what he would have, turned his horse round; upon which a word ran through the troops 'that they should *march* to the right hand'; which led them both from charging the enemy, and assisting their own men. Upon this they all turned their horses and rode upon the spur, as if they were every man to shift for himself.''[1]

The Royalists' centre was left isolated, and while Cromwell held it in front and attacked it in flank, Okey moved forward from the hedge along which his dragoons had been posted, and attacked it in rear. The confusion was complete, and as the Roundheads closed in on their enemy, regiment after regiment of Royalists threw down their arms. At this juncture Rupert returned. He realized that it was hopeless to attempt to rescue the infantry and he galloped past the fugitives and rejoined the King. His horses were blown, and as he was about to meet an onrush from Cromwell, his men refused to face it, wheeled about, and galloped from the field with the Roundheads at their heels. The remnants of Charles's horse swept through Harborough and did not draw rein until they reached Leicester.

The victory was complete, and as Clarendon says, "the King and the kingdom were lost in it."[2] Five thousand prisoners, 12 guns, and the entire train and baggage of the Royalist army fell into Fairfax's hands, as well as 8,000 stands of arms, 40 barrels of powder, and 112 colours. The number of Royalist killed and wounded is not known exactly, but it is supposed to have been some 700 in the battle and 300 in the pursuit; among whom must be reckoned almost 100 Irish prostitutes who were brutally knocked on the head, whereas the faces of the English harlots were gashed "in order to render them for ever hideous."[3]

The King's most important loss was the capture of his private cabinet, which mostly contained drafts or copies of his letters to the Queen.[4] From these it was discovered that he had sought the help of Irish and foreign troops, and had contemplated the abolition of the laws against the English Catholics. At once Parliament printed so much of this correspondence that was thought would blacken him, and concealed all parts which would

---

[1] *The History of the Rebellion, etc.*, vol. II, part II, book IX, pp. 986–987. Walker gives a rather confused though similar explanation.

[2] *Ibid.*, p. 988.

[3] Clarendon includes "wives of officers of quality" (*ibid.*, p. 988).

[4] See *Harleian Miscellany*, vol. v, p. 514.

have vindicated him.[1] Of this particularly shady though astute transaction, which did the King infinite harm,[2] Warburton remarks: "If the dark and crafty Cromwell's, or the deep and plotting Pym's most private correspondence had been laid open to the world by their enemies, how would it stand in comparison? The former of these two professed that it was lawful to play the knave with a knave, and the latter acted on the axiom."[3]

The most important result of Naseby was not Charles's defeat, nor his defamation; it was that the battle was won by the New Model Army, an army mainly composed of Independents. As Margaret James points out: "What little vitality the Presbyterian system possessed was further weakened by the victory of the Independents at Naseby. According to Dr. Shaw[4] the triumph of the army struck a death-blow at Presbyterian discipline by withdrawing the civil arm which had lent strength to its censures."[5]

This, above all things, was what the Presbyterians feared, and the immediate reaction to the victory was the censoring by Parliament of Cromwell's brief report on the battle. From Harborough, on the evening of June 14, he sent his report to the Speaker of the Commons. It ended with the words: "Honest men served you faithfully in this action. Sir, they are trusty, I beseech you in the name of God, not to discourage them. I wish this action may beget thankfulness and humility in all that are concerned in it. He that ventures his life for the liberty of his country, I wish he trust God for the liberty of his conscience, and you for the liberty he fights for."[6] This was a direct challenge to Presbyterian autocracy, and the House of Commons saw it as such and omitted this paragraph when the report was printed and published.

The battle of Naseby differs from Marston Moor in that, whereas the latter, had it been followed up with vigour would have led to the triumph of Parliament over the King, the former led to the

[1] Also Mr. Williamson writes: "Whatever they published and whatever they suppressed they at least knew now what the Royal epistolary style was. Earlier in the war, they had invented for purposes of propaganda letters which purported to come from Henrietta in Holland, which began: 'Most royal and illustrious Monarch of Great Britain, my great, my good and worthy liege the most regal object of my loving heart, best affection and utmost endeavours.' They now discovered that her letters invariably began: 'My dear Heart.'" (*Charles and Cromwell*, p. 137.)

[2] Gardiner (vol. II, p. 224) says: "The effect of their publication was enormous."

[3] *Memoirs of Prince Rupert*, vol. III, p. 112; see also *King Charles the Martyr, 1643–1649*, Esme Wingfield-Stratford (1950), pp. 116–120.

[4] *History of the Church of England during the Civil Wars, and under the Commonwealth* (1900), vol. II, p. 136.

[5] *Social Problems and Policy during the Puritan Revolution, 1640–1660* (1930), p. 12.

[6] Letter XXIX, Carlyle's *The Letters and Speeches of Oliver Cromwell*, vol. I, p. 205.

triumph of the Independents over Parliament. It saved England from the paralysing autocracy of the Kirk[1] and imposed upon that country the stimulating autocracy of Cromwell. During the years of the Interregnum are to be sought the influences of the battle of Naseby upon history.

For another year the war dragged on and to the ever-increasing detriment of Charles, until his situation grew so desperate that, fearful of falling into the hands of Parliament, on May 5, 1646, he surrendered to the Scots, who in settlement of the arrears due to them, which amounted to £400,000, in January, 1647, traded him to the English Parliament and left Newcastle.

Thus Parliament regained the King and with him the fount of all constitutional authority, and in order to be free to use it to establish Presbyterianism throughout England, in March, 1647, a scheme to disband the whole of the infantry of the army was accepted by both Houses. But Ireton and Cromwell, who knew that the army was the sole instrument which could restrain the persecuting zeal of the Presbyterians, had in mind a very different plan. They saw that, because the King was the fount of all authority and the army the source of all power, were the two brought together, the position of the Independents would be irresistible. Therefore, on May 31 – the day before the army was due to be disbanded – Cromwell instructed Cornet George Joyce to ride to Holmby, where the King was held prisoner, to seize his person and to bring him to army headquarters at Newmarket. There on June 7, in order to escape impeachment, Cromwell joined Fairfax.

On July 17, Ireton, the most fanatical of the Independents, and in disposition far more decisive than Cromwell – who was always referring his troubles to the Lord – sketched out a policy for the army called the "Heads of the Proposals." According to this, the bishops were to be deprived of their coercive jurisdiction; the Covenant was to be set aside; complete religious freedom was to be provided for all Protestant denominations; the existing Parliament was to dissolve itself; in future Parliaments were to be biennial; and a Council of State, subject to Parliament, was to conduct foreign policy and control the militia and fleet. It was a statesmanlike policy and, after it had been presented to Parliament, the army was ordered to march on London, which it entered on August 6.

[1] See *History of Civilisation in England*, Henry Thomas Buckle (The World Classics, 1920), vol. III, chap. IV.

From then until the end of October, Cromwell did everything in his power to ensure the restoration of the King on the terms of the "Heads of the Proposals." But Charles did not intend to accept any arrangements other than those which he would have insisted upon had he been victor. Instead, he entered into a secret treaty with the Scots, whereby the latter undertook to restore him to the throne on his promise to establish Presbyterianism for three years in England and to suppress all sectarians. This led to the outbreak of the Second Civil War, which, on August 17, 1648, was extinguished by Cromwell at the battle of Preston.

Ireton lost all patience with Charles and in October drew up the "Remonstrance of the Army", in which the sovereignty of the people was insisted upon and the speedy trial of the King demanded. Parliament feared Ireton more than Charles and refused to be dictated to by the Army. Thereupon, in order to remove from the Commons all who might favour the King, on December 6 Ireton sent Colonel Pride and a regiment to the House, and at its door he arrested 40 members and turned back about a hundred. The remainder became known as the "Rump".

Shortly before Christmas, Charles was brought to Windsor, where final overtures were made to him. But when he refused to see Lord Denbigh, the representative of the Lords, the Commons passed an ordinance establishing a court to charge the King with treason. When the Lords—now fewer than 12 in number—rejected it, the Commons ignored their decision and, on January 6, passed a Bill setting up a Court of 135 Commissioners, which had no constitutional or legal authority, to try the King. On January 19 the trial opened and Charles very rightly challenged the authority of the court. His challenge was overruled, and on January 27 he was condemned to be beheaded. On January 30, with dignity and calm, he met his end in front of his palace of Whitehall before a silent and horror-stricken crowd.

Why Cromwell, who until Charles refused to see Lord Denbigh had struggled to save him, finally played the leading part in his trial[1] is impossible to fathom until we appreciate what manner of

---

[1] Wingfield-Stratford suggests, "It was a decision for which—being the man he was—he had certainly sought and obtained the endorsement of the Lord. That would enable him to overcome any scruples he might otherwise have felt on the score of morals. . . . No doubt Cromwell figured the king's refusal to treat as a kind of omen, a manifest token that the Lord had hardened his opponent's heart and devoted him to destruction. To hesitate longer would be sinful, the sin of Saul. The Lord's patience like that of His servant, was in fact exhausted." (*King Charles the Martyr, 1643–1649*, p. 309.)

man Cromwell was. Clarendon, a fair though hostile witness, says
of him:

"He was one of those men whom his very enemies could not
condemn without commending him at the same time: for he could
never have done half that mischief without great parts of courage,
industry, and judgment. He must have had a wonderful understanding in the natures and humours of men, and as great a
dexterity in applying them; who, from a private and obscure birth,
(though of a good family), without interest or estate, alliance or
friendship, could raise himself to such a height, and compound and
knead such opposite and contradictory tempers . . . he attempted
those things which no good man durst have ventured on; and
achieved those in which none but a valiant and great man could
have succeeded . . . yet wickedness as great as his could never have
succeeded nor accomplished those designs, without the assistance
of a great spirit, an admirable circumspection and sagacity, and
a most magnanimous resolution."[1]

Although this seems to be a just estimate, it does not bring out
clearly the extraordinary complexity of Cromwell's character.
There was no single Cromwell—that is, a clear-cut individual who
can be summed up without profound analysis. Instead, there was
a multiplicity of Cromwells, each linked to the other by his
enormous vitality, for everything he did was forceful. Firstly, there
was the very human, simple and compassionate man, a romantic
and a visionary. Secondly, there was a violent, boisterous and
irascible bully. Thirdly, there was the resolute and iron-willed
general, whose common sense principles were seldom if ever
violated. Fourthly, the calculating politician, the man of expedi-
ents, who had no guiding principles. And lastly, there was "the
sword of the Lord and of Gideon" (the subconscious Cromwell),
who, as the interpreter of God's will, was capable of committing
any atrocity.

What he was in his own eyes, we know. He liked to compare
himself to a good constable "set to keep the peace of the parish",[2]
and would have been glad to have lived under his woodside
tending his flock of sheep, rather than undertake the government
of the land.[3] Though we have no right to doubt his veracity, this
worthy, bucolic policeman is largely a figment of his imagination,

---

[1] *The History of the Rebellion*, vol. III, part II, book xv, pp. 983–984.
[2] Speech XI, Carlyle's *Letters and Speeches*, vol. III, p. 63.
[3] Speech XVIII, *ibid.*, vol. III, p. 188.

for he was a man of violence and thunder; a man who with hat on head and sword in hand bursts into Ely Cathedral and shouts to the preacher in the pulpit: "Leave off your fooling, sir, and come down"; a man who dismisses his factious Parliament with such epithets as "whoremasters", "drunkards", and "corrupters", and a man who, when faced by Lilburne's mutinous regiment, suddenly wheels round his horse and with sword drawn charges headlong into its ranks, scatters the mutineers in panic and forces them to shoot their ringleader.

As a politician he was wholly an opportunist. Why he mounted so high—as he once said—was because he did not know the end ordained to him. In fact, he never had a policy other than complete surrender to the Lord. Therefore, he dealt with each situation as the Lord commanded; he saw the necessity, but never the consequence. Preaching toleration, he was intolerant; insisting upon open discussion, he suppressed it, and not until he found himself in Charles's place did he grasp what the King's problem really was. And, then, how did he set out to solve it? By following in Charles's footsteps, but with a tyranny incomparably more ruthless.

As "the sword of the Lord and of Gideon" he lived in a world of predestined happenings, in which the finger of God had already traced out the script. Nothing that he could do was worthwhile; therefore, when faced with a problem, he set out to solve it by praying to God for some visible evidence, and when it was vouched him, he identified the march of events with the workings of Providence. Like all Puritans, he was what may be called an "automatic hypocrite," because a justification for every human act, however atrocious, could always be found in the Bible. Thus, through self-deception, he deceived others.

His doctrine of divine leading is defined in a letter he addressed from Waterford, on November 25, 1649, to the Speaker of the Commons. This is what he wrote:

"Whereupon, seeking God for direction, they resolved to send a good part of horse and dragoons under Colonel Reynolds to Carrick. . . .

"The enemy, being not a little troubled at this unsuspected business (which indeed was the mere guidance of God) marched down with great fury towards Carrick. . . .

"Sir, what can be said of these things? Is it an arm of flesh that doth these things? Is it the wisdom, and counsel, or strength of man? It is the Lord only. God will curse that man and his house that dares to think otherwise. Sir, you see the work is done by divine leading."[1]

This doctrine, which was the source of his strength, was also the cause of his many barbarities. In his Declaration "For the Undeceiving of Deluded and Seduced People" of Ireland, a long ranting epistle issued from Youghal in January, 1649, we read:

"I will give you some wormwood to bite on: by which it will appear God is not with you. . . .

"You are a part of Antichrist, whose kingdom the Scripture so expressly speaks should be laid in blood; yea 'in the blood of the Saints. You have shed great store of it already:—and ere it be long, you must all of you have blood to drink; even the dregs of the cup of the fury and the wrath of God, which will be poured out unto you!' . . .

"But as for those who, notwithstanding all this, persist and continue in arms, they must expect what the Providence of God (in that which is falsely called the chance of war) will cast upon you."[2]

This was indeed an ominous phrase, for when Cromwell assumed the duties of the Lord's constable, and the delinquents happened to be papists, the vision of Samuel hewing Agag in pieces before the Lord in Gilgal invariably possessed him.

At Drogheda, Wexford and other places, the garrisons and, so it would seem, the civil inhabitants also, were indiscriminately slaughtered, and the massacre sometimes continued for days on end. Priests taken alive were at once hanged and officers who surrendered "knocked on the head", while the soldiers were either killed in cold blood or shipped to the Barbados. Of this savagery, on September 17, 1649, Cromwell wrote to the Speaker of the Commons: "I am persuaded that this is a righteous judgment of God upon these barbarous wretches. . . . And therefore it is good that God alone have all the Glory."[3]

That these happenings have been exaggerated on the one hand and minimized on the other, does not alter the fact that in the 12 years of war in Ireland some 500,000 lives were sacrificed and the population fell to below 1,000,000.[4]

At the trial of Charles, when Cromwell was constantly on his

---

[1] Letter CXVI, ibid., vol. I, pp. 508–512.
[2] Ibid., vol. II, pp. 5–23.
[3] Letter CV, Carlyle's Letters and Speeches, vol. I, pp. 469–470, see also Letter CIV.
[4] History of Ireland, Stephen Gwynn (1923), chaps. xxv–xxix.

knees seeking its justification, the Spirit of the Lord again descended upon him. Not only did he sign the death-warrant before
the verdict was pronounced, but when it had been pronounced
and some of the judges were unwilling to sign the warrant, he
dragged one to the table, held his hand with the pen in it and
forced him to sign his name, and from the hand of another he
seized the pen and in a frenzy smeared it across his face and then
burst into hysterical laughter.[1]

Such was the man–masterful, violent, unstable and God-drunk
–who on Charles's execution took over the reins of government,
and set out to rule Great Britain for 10 years.

Had the quarrel between Charles and Parliament been wholly
a question of finance, it might have been amicably settled on his
death. But at bottom it was a religious dispute, and as the religious sentiments of the Independents were as hostile to those of
the Presbyterians as they were to those of the episcopalians, the
outcome of the King's execution was to transfer Charles's share
of the broil to Cromwell. How the latter played his part in it does
not concern us here, except that, in order to distract popular
attention from his despotic behaviour, he adopted an aggressive
foreign policy which to implement it first of all demanded the
creation of a powerful navy. This, and not his suppression of the
monarchy, was the true and permanent dividend of the battle of
Naseby.

Although with some justification it may be said that, because
the ship-money fleets built by Charles excluded the employment
of armed merchantmen, they originated the English professional
navy, they were so experimental that it is usually accepted that
such a force only took permanent form under the Commonwealth,
during the 11 years of which no fewer than 207 new ships were
added to the Royal Navy.

In 1638 Charles had appointed a single Lord High Admiral to
command his fleet, and when, on the outbreak of the rebellion, the
navy declared for Parliament, the Earl of Warwick was given that
office. At the same time Parliament substituted for the old Navy
Board a body of Navy Commissioners, and, in 1649, abolished the
post of Lord High Admiral and replaced it by a Committee of
Admiralty, the members of which, in 1652, became the Commissioners of the Admiralty. It was these two bodies–the Navy
Commissioners and the Committee of Admiralty–which, under

[1] See *King Charles the Martyr, 1643–1649*, pp. 346–347.

the Council of State, set to work to create the New Model Navy. The former introduced generous and regularly paid wages, looked after the well-being of the sailors and standardized victualling. The latter was concerned with jurisdiction, and it issued the first version of those "Articles of War" which became the basis of all subsequent naval law and discipline. Under the Committee were appointed three "Generals at Sea", Edward Popham, Richard Deane, and Robert Blake, who were responsible for the distribution and movement of the ships. Of these three men, Blake had a profound and enduring influence on naval command and tactics.

In 1649, Blake was aged 50. By profession he was a merchant who had considerable knowledge of the sea, and as in his day all merchantmen were armed to fight pirates and privateers, he may have had some experience of sea fighting. In the First Civil War he had commanded a regiment in the New Model Army, and because of this and his sea experience he was selected by Cromwell as one of his generals at sea,[1] who soon were to be known as admirals. Of him Clarendon says:

"He was the first man that declined the old track, and made it manifest that the science might be attained in less time than was imagined; and despised those rules which had been long in practice, to keep his ship and his men out of danger; which had been held in former times a point of great ability and circumspection; as if the principal art requisite in the captain of a ship had been to be sure to come home safe again. He was the first man who brought the ships to contend castles on shore, which had been thought ever very formidable, and were discovered by him to make a noise only, and to fright those who could rarely be hurt by them. He was the first that infused that proportion of courage into the seamen by making them see by experience, what mighty things they could do, if they were resolved; and taught them to fight in fire as well as upon water, and though he hath been very well imitated and followed, he was the first that gave the example of that kind of naval courage, and bold and resolute achievement."[2]

Backed by the growing power of his fleet, Cromwell set out on the lines of Gustavus Adolphus's *Corpus Evangelicorum* to establish a Protestant empire in Europe under the leadership of England.

[1] Popham and Deane were also colonels in the New Model Army. The former had in his younger days been a ship's officer, and the latter, like Blake, probably had sea experience in the merchant navy.
[2] *The History of the Rebellion*, vol. III, part II, book XV, p. 913.

Later, in 1653, he went so far as to make the astonishing proposal to the Dutch that England and the United Provinces should divide the habitable globe outside Europe between them. But the Dutch, who during the Rebellion had filched from England most of her carrying trade, and who no longer were threatened by France, shied off becoming the junior partner in a proposal which must inevitably have led to their commercial subordination. When they refused the offer Cromwell came down to earth, and on October 9, 1651, replied with the Navigation Act, which prohibited the importation of the produce of Asia, Africa, and America, in any but English and Colonial bottoms, and of the goods of European countries save in English ships or those of the countries of their origin. As this struck at Dutch commercial supremacy, instead of a Protestant union the outcome was a Protestant fracas – the First Dutch War – which opened on May 19, 1652, when the Dutch Admiral Tromp refused to comply with the English right of search, and which ended on April 5, 1654, to the advantage of England.

Frustrated in his attempt to form a Protestant empire in Europe, no sooner was the Dutch War at an end than Cromwell decided to support France against Spain, and this time to seek a more practical empire oversea. Again his motives were mixed. On the one hand, to expel the Spaniards from their colonies would be a service to God, and on the other, according to R. Coke, to gain "Mountains of Gold"[1] would be a service to England. When he recommended his projected expedition against the West Indies, Cromwell said to his Council: "We consider this attempt because we think God has not brought us hither where we are, but to consider the work that we may do in the world as well as at home."[2] As Spain was a Catholic country and, therefore, predestinately damned, he did not consider a surprise attack on her in any way dishonourable. In December, 1654, the expedition sailed and seized Jamaica, which uncalled-for act of brigandage caused Spain to declare war on England. Next, Cromwell entered into an offensive alliance with France on the understanding that the French, helped by the English fleet and 6,000 soldiers, were to conquer for him the Spanish towns of Dunkirk, Gravelines, and Mardyke, in order that he might establish a bridgehead on the

---

[1] *Social Problems and Policy during the Puritan Revolution*, Margaret James, p. 71, quoting *A Detection of the Court and State of England* (1697), p. 387.
[2] Quoted from *History of the Commonwealth and Protectorate, 1649–1656*, S. R. Gardiner (1903), vol. IV, p. 120.

Continent from which to support the Protestant cause in northern Europe. Strange to say, the French agreed to this, and in May, 1657, the English contingent landed at Boulogne. Mardyke surrendered on September 25; the battle of the Dunes was fought and won on June 14, 1658, and Dunkirk surrendered and was handed over to Cromwell. The conquest of Gravelines, Oudenarde, Menin, and Ypres followed rapidly.

On September 3, 1658–the anniversary of the battles of Dunbar and Worcester–Cromwell died, and Spain, now exhausted, came to terms with France and England and the Peace of the Pyrenees was signed on November 7, 1659. According to its terms Avesnes, Roussillon, Philippville, and Marienburg were ceded to France, also Alsace and Lorraine–the latter under certain conditions– and Spain agreed to the marriage of the Infanta Maria Theresa, daughter of Philip IV, with Louis XIV, with the proviso that on the payment of her dowry she would renounce her claims to the Spanish succession. But, as it was never paid, later Louis set this proviso aside.

Although the Dutch war had some economic justification for England, the Spanish war was a disaster. It left France supreme on the Continent; it ruined English trade to the benefit of the Dutch; it caused a deep economic depression throughout England and raised the public debt to over £2,500,000.[1] "The political instability of the Interregnum", writes Margaret James, "had been paralleled by its economic instability, and it is not surprising that London, which had been the backbone of resistance to Charles I, should have welcomed his successor with open arms."[2]

Nevertheless, in spite of the failure of his foreign policy and his complete inability to establish parliamentary government at home, Cromwell left his country a supremely great legacy. In 1647 he had said: "A man never mounts so high as when he does not know where he is going," and in an occult way he was right. Nine years later he said: "These issues and events have not been forecast, but were providences in things," and again he was not altogether wrong. As Margaret James comments on the problems of this period:

"At home, the doctrine of an active faith helped to sanctify a growing industrialism. Abroad it helped to sanctify the shadowy

---

[1] For this and much else see *Social Problems and Policy during the Puritan Revolution*, pp. 71–77.
[2] *Ibid.*, p. 77.

beginnings of imperialism. In the same way as chosen individuals were held to glorify God by rising to a higher position than their fellows, so a chosen nation was thought to exalt Him by dominating its neighbours. Nations, said one writer, should always be on the alert to attack and acquire fresh provinces as well as to defend existing possessions, 'for as Christian saith to him that hath (using it well) shall be given. This riches is your strong tower.''[1]

Thus industrialism and imperialism crept out of the religious mists of Puritanism to become the abutments of English civilization. And though it was not the civilization Cromwell and his Major-Generals had dreamed of, it was the civilization woken by their power-politics since Naseby. The sacrifices had been burned, the oracles were propitious, a new age had opened in which England was soon to play the part of ancient Rome, and for 250 years to cast her imperial net over the seven seas.

[1] In *European Civilization its Origins and Development* (1937), vol. v, p. 91.

The ascension of France

Although the Peace of the Pyrenees extinguished the last sparks of the Thirty Years War, it did not settle the problem France had set out to solve; for by leaving Lille, Besançon, the two Sicilies, and the Milanese in the hands of Spain, in case of need Spain could still effect a junction with the Empire, and together they could encircle France. The consequence was that, when Mazarin died in 1661 and Louis XIV, a young man of 25, burning to emulate Charlemagne and make France supreme and glorious, assumed full powers, the problem of how to break the Habsburg ring became his political inheritance.

In its solution he was greatly assisted by his two great ministers –Louvois and Colbert. The former centralized the administration of the army, and by eliminating the power of the nobles made the King's authority paramount. Besides enforcing honesty, he improved equipment, introduced the bayonet, replaced the matchlock by the flintlock (*fusil*), raised the status of infantry and engineers, and brought the artillery into line with the other arms. Further, he established well organized magazines and made provision for disabled soldiers by building the *Hôtel des Invalides*. But his greatest influence upon Louis was that he dangled before him as the objects of his reign, war, glory and dominion, toward which Louis by nature was only too well inclined. Colbert reorganized the navy and raised it from the 20 warships he found in 1661 to 196 effective vessels in 1671 and to 270 in 1677. He renovated the old harbours and arsenals, modernized Toulon, Rochefort, Brest, Le Havre, and Dunkirk (bought from Charles II in 1662), and, helped by Vauban, laboured to make impregnable the fortresses of France.

Louis had not long to wait for an opportunity to initiate his aggressive policy. On September 17, 1665, Philip IV of Spain died and was succeeded by his half-witted son, Charles II, a boy of four years old. But as Charles was Philip's son by his second marriage, and Maria Theresa the only surviving child of his first, on the strength of a local custom in Brabant and Hainault, the so-called *jus devolutionis*, according to which children of a first marriage had precedence over those of a subsequent one, Louis, in the name of his wife, claimed the whole of the Spanish Netherlands.

England was at war with the United Provinces (Second Dutch War), and because by treaty Louis was engaged to aid the Dutch, in January, 1666, he declared war on England. But Charles II, who was in no way prepared to add to his enemies, in March, 1667, came to a secret understanding with him not to oppose his projected invasion of the Netherlands if, in his turn, Louis withheld all assistance from the Dutch. Shortly after this agreement, the French crossed the Netherland's frontier and seized Lille. Next, in order to prevent the Spaniards, who held Franche-Comté, from reinforcing the Netherlands from Italy, on February 4, 1668, Louis invaded Franche-Comté and overran it in a fortnight.

Before he carried out this aggression, in order that he might assure himself of the Emperor Leopold I's neutrality, in January Louis had induced him to agree to a treaty of partition of the Spanish empire should Charles II, as seemed probable, die without issue. The arrangement was that Spain, the Americas, and the Milanese were to go to Leopold, and Louis was to receive the Two Sicilies, the Spanish Netherlands, Franche-Comté, Spanish Navarre, the Philippines, and the Spanish possessions in Africa.

The immediate results of Louis's aggressions were that on July 31, 1667, Charles II came to terms with the Dutch and agreed to the Peace of Breda, and on February 13, 1668, Spain made peace with Portugal and recognized her independence. At the same time–January to April, 1668–a triple alliance between England, the United Provinces, and Sweden was formed to resist Louis, and he, feeling that he had gone far enough for the present, decided on peace, which, on May 2, was signed at Aix-la-Chapelle. According to its terms, he received Charleroi, Binch, Ath, Douai, Tournai, Oudenarde, Lille, Armentières, Courtrai, Bergues, and Furnes, and gave up Franche-Comté, Cambrai, St. Omer, and Aire. These surrenders he could well afford, because by the terms of the secret agreement with Leopold it had been arranged that, on Charles's death, these places should go to France.

Still bent upon gaining the Spanish Netherlands, Louis set out to disrupt the Triple Alliance, and as a first step toward this, in June, 1670, he entered into a secret agreement, known as the Treaty of Dover, with Charles of England, by which the latter agreed to support France in a war against the Dutch. With his left flank thus secured, he set out to secure his right flank by occupying Lorraine and entering into treaty with the Elector of Bavaria, which established a friendship between the two countries that was to last until 1813. Lastly, in April, 1672, the Triple Alliance vanished altogether when Sweden was won over by a large sum of money.

Meanwhile, on March 17, Charles had declared war on the Dutch, and in May Louis followed suit. At first the French advance, under Condé and Turenne, was rapid, but soon after it was checked when the Dutch cut their dykes. Next, William of Orange was proclaimed Stadtholder of Holland and Zeeland, and thoroughly alarmed, both the Emperor and Frederick William of Brandenburg (the Great Elector), as well as Spain, entered the contest against France.

At sea, in what in English history is known as the Third Dutch War, de Ruyter defeated the English and French in two battles, and had rather the better of them in two more. At length, in 1674, the general fear of the rising power of France, as well as hatred of the French navy, whose barefaced defection in action had led to the loss of the above battles, caused the English Parliament to compel Charles to make peace with the Dutch, which, on February 19, was sealed by the Treaty of London. On land the war continued until 1678, and to the advantage of France, but all the belligerents grew weary and it was ended by a series of separate treaties, which together became known as the Peace of Nymegen (August, 1678, to February, 1679).

This peace placed France in a far stronger position than the one she had gained by the Treaty of Westphalia; for by it she acquired a large slice of the Spanish Netherlands, Alsace, Lorraine, Freiburg, Breisach, and Franche-Comté. Nevertheless England was the real gainer, for during the war, quite unwittingly, France had expended her blood and treasure to no other end than that England should become her most formidable colonial and maritime rival. As part of her spoil, England obtained New Amsterdam (New York)[1] and New Jersey, which enabled her to link together her northern and southern American colonies; also she obtained St. Helena[2] as a base for her East Indian merchantmen. But more important, after her peace with the United Provinces in 1674, because of the continuance of the war, the bulk of the Dutch carrying trade passed to the English flag. Thus, when the Peace of Nymegen was signed, England was left the leading naval and

---

[1] In September, 1664, the Duke of York had obtained New Amsterdam from the Dutch, and had renamed it New York. In 1673 the Dutch reoccupied it, and in 1674 it was restored to England.

[2] Occupied by the British East India Company in 1651. Taken by the Dutch in 1673, and soon after reoccupied by the Company.

commercial power in the world. As such, her homeland was secure, and because of this and her command of the sea, the colonies of all other nations were at her mercy.

In these wars, Louis was not only aided by Charles II, but also by the Turks, who throughout this period were engaged in their final struggle with the Empire, which impeded the Emperor's intervention in strength in the west. Happily for Europe, during the Thirty Years War the Ottoman empire was in one of its periodical states of anarchy, but in 1656, under Mahomet IV (1648–1687) order was restored. In 1663, war was declared on the Empire; but the following year, on August 1, the Turks were routed by Montecuccoli, the Imperialist general, at the battle of St. Gothard. The next Turkish move was made against Poland, where, after several campaigns, on November 11, 1673, a great Turkish army under Ahmad Kiuprili was destroyed by John Sobieski at Khoczim. Ten years later, in order to cripple Leopold, Louis persuaded the Sultan again to march against the Empire. Louis's idea was that were Austria overthrown, Germany would be forced to appeal to him, when, as champion of the Cross, he would restore to France the imperial crown of Charlemagne. Mahomet fell in with Louis's suggestion and assembled an army, reputed to be 250,000 strong, under Kara Mustafa, which crossed the Drave and laid siege to Vienna. At once, Sobieski, now John III of Poland, and Charles of Lorraine, at the head of 70,000 Poles, Bavarians, Saxons, and Germans, marched to its relief, and on September 12, 1683, routed the Turks. Nevertheless the war continued; the Turks suffered a crushing defeat at Har-Kány, near the field of Mohács, on August 12, 1687, and another at Zenta on the river Theiss, at the hands of Prince Eugene, on September 11, 1697. Two years later, on January 26, 1699, this crowning victory led to the Peace of Carlowitz, by which all Hungary and Transylvania were ceded to Austria, and Podolia and the Ukraine to Poland. Thus ended the Turkish peril, which had terrorized eastern Europe since the battle of Manzikert: it was the final echo of the Crusades.

The rout of the Turks before Vienna in 1683 and the accession of James II (1685–1688) to the throne of England on February 16, 1685, placed Louis in a difficult position. The former meant the strengthening of Austria and the latter that, should James, a bigoted Catholic, be unable to retain his throne, the only alternative to him was William of Orange, who had married James's daughter Mary in 1677. Therefore, policy demanded that James's position should be stabilized; but Louis played his cards so badly that the very thing he was most anxious to prevent occurred. Shortly after James's accession he withdrew all toleration from the French Huguenots by revoking the Edict of Nantes, and to make matters worse, James set out to emulate him by attempting by unconstitutional means to force the Catholic religion on his subjects. The result was the "Glorious Revolution" of 1688, by which James was compelled to fly the kingdom and to make way for his son-in-law and daughter, who became joint rulers of England in his stead. "Thus for the divine right of kings", writes Lord Acton, "was established the divine right of freeholders:" government by one of two parties of gentry, the Whigs and the Tories, the one representing the great landowners, merchants and tradesmen, and the other the smaller landowners and country clergy. Power was thus finally transferred from the Crown to Parliament, the former became a constitutional monarchy; freedom of the Press was established; and in 1694 the Bank of England was founded, whereby the English banking system was instituted, which in years to come was to make money all-powerful.

The revolution of 1688 initiated the long duel between England and France for colonial domination, which was to last for over a century, and because at this time France possessed the most powerful army in the world and a formidable navy, when, in 1688, Louis invaded the Palatinate, all the princes of Germany began to rally against him. In order to consolidate this resistance, in 1689 William of Orange, now William III of England (1688–1702), formed the Grand Alliance of England, the United Provinces, and the Empire, and war against France was placed on a more equal footing. On June 30, 1690, the same day that James II in Ireland was defeated at the battle of the Boyne, the allied fleets were severely beaten by Admiral Tourville off Beachy Head; and on May 19–24, 1692, Tourville was defeated decisively by the English and Dutch fleets, under Admiral Edward Russell (later Earl of Orford) at the battle of Barfleur-La Hogue. The importance of this victory cannot be overestimated; there were but few troops in England, and had the battle been lost, 30,000 men under Marshal de Bellefonds were waiting to cross the Channel to invade England and to restore James to his throne.

Although this victory enabled William to devote the whole of his attention to the war in the Netherlands; nevertheless he was nearly uniformly unfortunate. In 1692 he lost Namur and was defeated at Steinkirk, and the following year defeated at Neerwinden. In 1697, largely because of English naval successes in the Mediterranean, Louis expressed his willingness to surrender all conquests made during the war. This, on September 20, led to the Peace of Ryswick, by which William III was recognized by Louis as King of Great Britain and Ireland, and the Princess Anne, second daughter of James II, heiress to his throne. The Grand Alliance was then dissolved, and France was left the strongest power in Europe.

It would seem probable that one reason for the Peace of Ryswick was that Louis, expecting the early demise of Charles II of Spain, wished to conserve the strength of France in order to push the claim of his House to the Spanish throne when that event occurred and, as Mignet says, the Spanish succession was "the hinge on which the whole reign of Louis XIV turned."

Unfortunately for Europe, the hinge was a three-fold one, for on Charles II's death there would be three claimants to his throne. Besides Philip Duke of Anjou, the grandson of Louis XIV, there was the Archduke Charles of Austria, son of the Emperor Leopold, and Joseph Ferdinand, the Electoral Prince of Bavaria, son of the Bavarian Elector Maximilian Emanuel, who had married Leopold's daughter Maria Antonia. Both Louis and Leopold were grandsons of Philip III, and both had married their first cousins, the daughters of Philip IV.

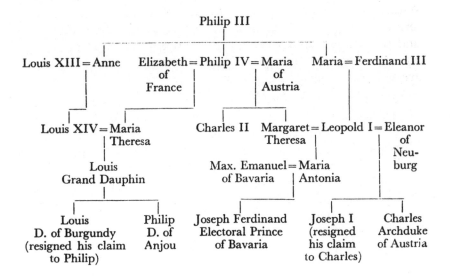

Because Louis would not agree to the whole of the Spanish empire going to the House of Austria, and because Leopold would not agree to its going to France, in order to avert war the sole solution was that on Charles II's death he should be succeeded by Joseph Ferdinand, for under him the Spanish empire would remain independent of both France and Austria. This solution, as Professor Trevelyan points out, would suit England well, because from the reigns of William and Anne to that of George V, it was commercial rivalry and the maintenance of the balance of power on the Continent which constrained England to take part in all continental wars which threatened her in either of these directions. In the present case, the Spaniards, because of their incapacity to conduct their industry and commerce for themselves, during recent years had allowed English and Dutch merchants, disguised under Spanish names, to do it for them and to carry on trade between Spain and her colonies. Therefore, were the Spanish empire to go to France, not only would this very profitable trade be lost, but the Mediterranean would be closed to their ships and both England and the United Provinces would be threatened by the French in the Netherlands.

Neither Louis nor Leopold would, without compensation to themselves, agree that Joseph Ferdinand should succeed Charles, and in October, 1698, in order to overcome these objections, a half-measure, known as the First Partition Treaty, was resolved upon by France, England, and the United Provinces. By this, most of the Spanish empire was to go to Joseph Ferdinand, Milan to the Archduke Charles, and France was to receive Naples and Sicily. Although this was advantageous for Austria, Leopold refused to abandon the whole of the Spanish inheritance for his son, and Spain—which is more understandable—violently opposed partition in any form whatsoever.

Thus things stood until February, 1699, when the whole situation was changed by the unexpected death of Joseph Ferdinand. Louis and William then drew up the Second Partition Treaty. This time the Archduke was to become king of Spain and the Indies and ruler of the Netherlands; France was to receive Naples and Sicily, and the Duke of Lorraine was to surrender Lorraine—already practically a French possession—to France, and in compensation be given Milan.

With incredible folly Leopold again refused to agree. Also the English merchants strongly objected to Naples and Sicily going to

France, because they considered that this would lead to the closing of the Mediterranean to English shipping, and the Spaniards, still opposed to partition, decided to offer the Spanish crown to Philip in preference to Charles, because Louis was better placed than the Emperor to defend the Spanish empire.

At length the crisis boiled over. On November 1, 1700, Charles II died, and by his will he left his undivided empire to Philip, but on the proviso that should Louis not accept it in his name, it was to go to the Archduke Charles. Since this meant that, were Louis to refuse the offer, France would be as fully encircled as she was in the days of Charles V, in spite of his treaty obligations he had no choice but to accept the will and to send Philip to Madrid. Next, in February, 1701, under pretext of protecting them, Louis invaded the Spanish Netherlands and also occupied the Milanese. Then he committed an act which made war inevitable; he seized the Dutch Barrier fortresses,[1] which were guaranteed by treaty. If this were not sufficient aggravation, he excluded English merchants from the American trade, which meant that England had either to fight or abandon her commercial prosperity to France.

The answer to these aggressions was the revival of the Grand Alliance of 1689, and on September 7, 1701, the treaty was signed at The Hague by England, Austria, and the United Provinces. In its original form, the allies accepted the rule of Philip over Spain and the Indies, on condition that the crowns of France and Spain should never be united, and they bound themselves to obtain Milan, Naples, Sicily, and the Netherlands, for Austria. Further, they demanded that the commercial privileges they had enjoyed under Charles II should be guaranteed to them by Philip. Other treaties were made with the King of Prussia, the Elector of Hanover, and other German princes, to raise troops at the expense of England and the United Provinces.

Ten days after the Grand Alliance was formed, James II died at St. Germain-en-Laye, and in defiance of the Treaty of Ryswick Louis acknowledged his son as James III of England. If this were not cause enough to stir England to the core, he added economic injury to dynastic outrage by prohibiting the importation of British goods into France. Retaliation was immediate. In October the House of Commons, which two years before had disbanded most of the army, voted supplies to raise 40,000 English sailors and

---

[1] A line of fortresses in the Netherlands which, according to the Treaty of Ryswick was garrisoned by Dutch troops.

40,000 soldiers, of whom 18,000 were to be British and the remainder foreigners in English pay. Preparations for war were then put in hand. As they proceeded, William III was thrown by his horse and sustained injuries from which, on March 8, 1702, he died. He was succeeded by his sister-in-law, Princess Anne (1702-1714), daughter of James II.

CHAPTER 4

The Battle of Blenheim, 1704

To all outward appearances the death of William III left France supreme and her hoped-for hegemony assured. England was ruled by a woman of no marked ability; the United Provinces were thrown into consternation, and the Empire was in its usual state of decrepitude. Yet again the unexpected happened: fate brought forth the man of destiny, John Churchill, first Duke of Marlborough (1650–1722).[1] Further, fate provided him with an able helpmate, his wife, born Sarah Jennings, who as confidante of the Queen played a dominant part in the direction of affairs.

Son of Sir Winston Churchill, John Churchill was born at Ash, near Axminster, on June 6, 1650, and between 1667, the year he was gazetted an ensign in the King's Regiment of Foot Guards (now the Grenadier Guards), and August 8, 1701, when William III appointed him Ambassador Extraordinary to the United Provinces and Captain-General of the Confederate Armies, he saw much service both on land and sea:[2] at Tangier in 1668; with the Duke of York and Marshal Turenne between the years 1672 and 1674; in the Monmouth Rebellion of 1685; and in Ireland in 1690. These experiences stood him in good stead, for they brought him into touch with the realities of war and, being a man of insight, they enabled him to plumb the French character and to measure up many of his future adversaries.

Soon to prove himself one of the greatest military geniuses his country has known, it was only natural that he was unmercifully traduced by the smaller men of his age. Nevertheless he was far from impeccable in character, and had he been so probably he would never have risen to the position he attained, for in his day, more often than not, intrigue was an ingredient of success. Therefore, in order to judge him as a man, he must be judged by the standards of his age. He was accused of avarice, peculation, and treason, and though it is true that he corresponded with the Jacobites at the Court of St. Germain-en-Laye, for which, in 1692,

---

[1] Created a duke in December, 1702.
[2] At the battle of Solebay, May 28, 1672, in the Second Dutch War.

he was incarcerated in the Tower of London; yet, in 1701, he was the man whom the aggrieved party, William III, appointed as his military successor. The appointment was a wise one, for it demanded above all things tact, an essential of intrigue and diplomacy.

Whatever may have been his failings as a man, as a general and a statesman Marlborough stands high above his contemporaries. Courteous and patient, he possessed what so few men of genius are endowed with—ability to tolerate fools gladly. Though his courage was of the highest, his imagination vivid, and his common sense profound, his master characteristic was his self-control. Nothing unbalanced him, whether it was the stupidity of his allies, the duplicity of the politicians, or the ability of his enemies. As a general he possessed the rare virtue of seeing a war as a whole, and of being able to relate sea power with land power and strategy with politics. Nothing escaped his observation, and no detail, tactical or administrative, was too minute to be overlooked. A master of stratagems, he consistently mystified his enemy; a master of detail, his men were never left in want. In the planning of a campaign he took infinite pains, and in its execution infinite trouble. In an age which believed that the defensive was the stronger form of war, he invariably sought to bring his enemy to battle, and proved conclusively that a vigorous offensive is usually the soundest defence. A contemporary says of him:

"Kirke has fire, Lanier thought, Mackay skill and Colchester bravery, but there is something inexpressible in the Earl of Marlborough. All their virtues seem to be united in his single person. I have lost my wonted skill in physiognomy if any subject of your Majesty can ever attain such a height of military glory as that to which this combination of sublime perfections must raise him."[1]

And Captain Robert Parker, who served under Marlborough in the 18th Royal Irish Regiment, writes:

"As to the Duke of *Marlborough* . . . it was allowed by all men, nay even by *France* itself, that he was more than a match for all the Generals of that Nation. This he made appear beyond contradiction, in the ten Campaigns he made against them; during all which time it cannot be said that he ever slipped an oppor-

[1] The Prince of Vaudemont to William III, quoted by C. T. Atkinson in *Marlborough and the Rise of the British Army* (1921), p. 130.

tunity of fighting, when there was any probability of his coming at his Enemy: And upon all occasions he concerted matters with so much judgment and forecast, that he never fought a Battle which he did not gain, nor laid seige to a Town which he did not take. . . . He was peculiarly happy in an invincible calmness of temper and serenity of mind; and had a surprising readiness of thought, even in the heat of Battle."[1]

Such was "Corporal John", as his men affectionately called him, and it is remarkable that 100 years later even a greater than he was called by his men *Le Petit Corporal*. The one was the forerunner of the other, as well as heir of Gustavus Adolphus; for by breaking down the formalities of late seventeenth-century warfare and returning to the ways of the great Swede, Marlborough opened the road for Frederick and Napoleon. To understand this, it is necessary to appreciate the changes in the art of war which had taken place since 1648.

During this period, communications remained primitive, armies were still of moderate size, and as cavalry remained the decisive arm, strategy was largely circumscribed by forage. Water transport and grass were all-important, also the establishment of magazines, which in its turn led to the predominance of siege warfare over field battles, and the general acceptance that the defensive was more important than attack. This led to the avoidance of battles by means of what may be called the "strategy of evasion," which consisted in manœuvring rather than fighting. The great Turenne (1611–1676) was a past-master in such operations, though never a slave to them;[2] but his most noted opponent, Montecuccoli (1609–1650), laid it down that "The secret of success is to have a solid body so firm and impenetrable that wherever it is or wherever it may go, it shall bring the enemy to a stand like a mobile bastion, and shall be self-defensive."[3]

Marlborough broke away from this type of warfare and returned to the offensive strategy of Gustavus and the attack tactics of Condé and Cromwell. He did so because he was imaginative enough to see into the military changes of his day and appreciate their meaning. Since 1648 there were two supremely important changes – the universal adoption of the flintlock and the replace-

---

[1] *Memoirs of the most remarkable Military Transactions from the Year 1683 to 1718*, Captain Robert Parker (1747), pp. 214–215.
[2] See Jules Roy's *Turenne sa vie et les institutions militaires de son temps* (1884), pp. 449–450.
[3] *Mémoires, ou principes de l'art militaire*, R. de Montecuccoli (1712), p. 223.

ment of the pike by the bayonet.[1] Besides fusiliers, in 1667 grenadiers were introduced, who later were formed into companies, each battalion being provided with one. Therefore, between 1650 and 1700, we find four kinds of infantry—pikemen, musketeers, fusiliers, and grenadiers—which, by 1703, had been reduced to one main type armed with the flintlock and socket bayonet.

This reduction in the number of weapons led to a simplification in formation and tactics, the firing-line of four, and often of three ranks, replaced the column and six rank lines. Battalions, usually 800 strong, were organized into right and left wings, each divided into divisions, platoons, and sections; a platoon in the English service was 50 strong, and in the French 100 strong. Firing, which hitherto had been by successive ranks, was usually delivered by divisions or platoons at close range—30 to 50 paces—and under cover of the smoke of the discharges the assault was driven home with the bayonet.

Marlborough realized that these changes favoured the attack; therefore both his strategy and tactics were offensive. By persistent infantry attacks, he pinned his enemy down and then broke him by the shock action of his cavalry, the squadrons of which were marshalled in three lines and, like Cromwell's, with sword in hand charged at a brisk trot. At Blenheim, Parker tells us that the cavalry were ordered "to advance gently, until they came pretty near [their enemy] and then ride in a full trot up to them."[2] And Kane informs us that Marlborough "would allow the Horse but three Charges of Powder and Ball to each Man for a Campaign, and that only for guarding their Horses when at Grass, and not to be made use of on Action."[3] Further, for the infantry, great emphasis was laid on fire-drill and musketry.

---

[1] The word "bayonet" is supposed to have been derived from the *bayonette*, a short dagger made in Bayonne toward the end of the fifteenth century. The plug-bayonet, which was fixed into the muzzle of the musket, and therefore prevented it from being fired, is mentioned in 1647, was carried by English soldiers at Tangier in 1663, and was issued to French fusilier regiments in 1671 and to the English Royal Fusiliers in 1685. In 1678 a ring-bayonet, which, though it did not block the muzzle easily fell off it, was introduced, also a socket-bayonet, which could be more solidly fixed, is mentioned. In 1687 Vauban proposed to Louvois the use of the latter, and two years later it was adopted by the French army and after 1697 by the English and German. By 1703 the pike was entirely abandoned by the French and nearly so by the English. According to Colonel Home: "The introduction of the bayonet marks the end of the medieval and the beginning of modern war. . . . Tactics were revolutionized by a dagger some 12 ins. long" (*Stray Military Papers*, 1897, p. 23).
[2] Parker, p. 108.
[3] *Campaigns of King William and the Duke of Marlborough*, Genera R. Kane (1747), p. 110.

It must be remembered that the armies Marlborough commanded were composed of national contingents – Dutch, German, and English – which considerably added to his difficulties. When hostilities opened, the English soldier, unlike the English seaman, was not compulsorily recruited. Each colonel enlisted his own men and was given a grant to pay and clothe them. This led to widespread corruption and to the wholesale drafting of criminals into the ranks. Discipline was, therefore, rigorous. Trevelyan mentions a guardsman in 1712 who was ordered 12,600 lashes and who nearly died after he had received the first 1,800.[1] In 1703–1704 this system of raising troops gave way to a series of recruiting Acts which within certain limits rendered compulsory enlistment legal. Usually the summer months were given over to campaigning and the winter to recruiting and teaching the men the elaborate drill of the day.

When, on May 15, 1702, war was declared, the situation that confronted Marlborough was as perplexing as any general has ever been faced with. France and Spain formed a united block, but the Grand Alliance was split into two groups, England and the United Provinces on the one hand, and Austria on the other. To the west of Austria lay Bavaria, still neutral though doubtful, separated from France by Baden, whose ruler, the Margrave Louis, had thrown in his lot with Leopold. To the east of Austria lay Hungary, seething with revolt, and to the south were the Spaniards in Italy. Therefore Austria was threatened from three sides, and because Victor Amadeus II of Savoy was in alliance with France, with his connivance the French had already occupied the valley of the Upper Po and, therefore, could reinforce the Spaniards in the Milanese. While France could operate on interior lines, either against the United Provinces or Austria, Spain could either directly support France or operate against Austria from Italy.

Marlborough's strategical task was first to prevent the United Provinces being overrun by the French, and secondly to prevent Austria being overwhelmed by the French and Spaniards. The former demanded the defeat of France in the north, with the United Provinces as the base of operations, and the latter the defeat of Spain in the south. As regards the latter, Spain's position had been greatly strengthened by the alliance Portugal had made with her and France in June, 1701, and as this had closed the

[1] *England under Queen Anne, Blenheim*, George Macaulay Trevelyan (1930), p. 227.

Portuguese ports to both the English and Dutch, before an attack could be made on Spain, either in the Iberian Peninsula or Italy, to gain a naval base within, or near the Mediterranean, was the first essential.

To fit the strategical situation, Marlborough decided on a two-fold plan. Firstly, while Louis of Baden blocked the defiles of the Black Forest, he would strike at Marshal Boufflers who, at the head of 90,000 men, held all the fortresses on the Maas except Maestricht, and who had occupied the Electorate of Cologne and so had blocked the communications between the United Provinces and Austria. Secondly and simultaneously, Admiral Rooke and an Anglo-Dutch expeditionary force would seize Cadiz and establish there a base for the fleet, from which it could set out to gain command of the Mediterranean, cut the sea communications between Spain and Italy, and threaten France from the south.

The campaign of 1702 opened in Italy, where Prince Eugene of Savoy (1663–1736) in command of the Imperial forces, found himself outnumbered by the French and Spaniards under Marshal Vendôme and was hard put to it to maintain himself in the Modenese. Next, in July, at the head of 40,000 men, Marlborough took the field, and on four separate occasions was prevented from bringing his enemy to book by the timidity and obstruction of the Dutch deputies attached to his headquarters. Nevertheless the French were expelled from the valleys of the Maas and Lower Rhine, and the navigation of the Maas from Liège downward was gained, without which the march to the Danube in 1704 could never have been attempted.

In August, Rooke appeared before Cadiz with 14,000 troops under the Duke of Ormonde, and through faulty planning, lack of initiative, and the disgraceful behaviour of the men, the attempt to seize the port ended in fiasco. On the way home, in October, in order to cover the disgrace, an impromptu attack was made on Vigo. Not only was the Plate fleet, then in harbour, destroyed, but 15 French ships of the line were either taken or burnt and an immense booty captured. Though Vigo was not held as a base, this astonishing *coup de main* accomplished all that the capture of Cadiz could possibly have done, but this success was more than offset by an event which had immediately preceded it. In September Bavaria joined France on the understanding that Maximilian Emanuel's territories would be greatly extended, and that, once the Emperor had been defeated, he would succeed to the Imperial throne, the House of Wittelsbach replacing the House of Habsburg. This alliance permitted Louis XIV to pass from the defensive to the offensive and to advance on Vienna.

Marlborough, in control of the Maas and Lower Rhine, invaded the Electorate of Cologne in 1703, and, on May 18, captured Bonn. Called back to the Netherlands, his well-conceived scheme to occupy Antwerp was ruined by the insubordination of the Dutch general Cohorn.[1] In the meantime Villars, the ablest of the French marshals, who had defeated Louis of Baden at Friedlingen on October 14, 1702, in the spring of 1703 seized Kehl–opposite Strasbourg–crossed the Black Forest and in May linked up with the Elector of Bavaria near Ulm. He at once urged a march on Vienna, but the Elector refused and instead carried his army into the Tyrol, in order to add it to Bavaria, to collect reinforcements, and to establish a link between Bavaria and Italy. Meanwhile Villars was left to cover this operation by watching Louis, who had come up from Stolhofen and had been joined by Field-Marshal Styrum and 19,000 Austrians. At the same time Vendôme, on the Po, was ordered by Louis XIV to join hands with the Elector by way of the Brenner, and to "finish the war by carrying it into the heart of the Empire." But Vendôme wasted so much time that in August the Bavarian garrisons Maximilian Emanuel had established in Tyrol were driven out, and when he found his road to the Brenner blocked by the Tyrolese mountaineers, Vendôme was unable to effect a union.

Had Louis of Baden and Styrum remained together during the Elector's absence Villars might have been overwhelmed; but foolishly they separated their forces. Villars parried the Margrave's attack on Augsburg, fell upon Styrum, and on September 20 decisively defeated him at Höchstädt. At once Louis abandoned Augsburg and retired into winter quarters, and although the season was late for campaigning, Villars again urged the Elector to attempt a dash on Vienna, then seriously menaced by the Hungarian insurgents. But the Elector refused and, after a violent quarrel, Villars was recalled to France and replaced by Marshal Marsin, a far less able soldier. At the same time Marshal Tallard

---

[1] See *The Correspondence, 1701–1711, of John Churchill, First Duke of Marlborough and Anthonie Heinsius Grand Pensionary of Holland,* edit. B. Van 'T Hoff (1951), 136, p. 85. Marlborough's annoyance is sharply expressed in a letter to Heinsius on September 3. He writes: "The difference of opinions I am afraid will incorage the enemy, for it is most certaine thay know all that passes here; so that if I might have millions given mee to serve another yeare and be obliged to doe nothing but by the unanimous consent of the Generals, I would much sooner dye. . . ." (*Ibid.,* 142, p. 90).

captured Old Breisach and in November occupied Landau, thereby greatly improving the communications between France and the 40,000 French troops wintering in Bavaria. By the close of 1703, the situation of Austria was so desperate that Leopold recalled Eugene from Italy and entrusted him with the fate of the empire.

This series of disasters was in part offset by two events advantageous to the allied powers. The first was the defection of Portugal from France, and the second the abandonment of France by Savoy. The former was largely due to the skilful diplomacy of the Methuens—father and son—successive British envoys to the court at Lisbon, coupled with the news of the attack on Vigo, which swung Peter II of Portugal over to the allies, and in May led to the signing of the Methuen Treaty. By its terms Portugal agreed to accept English cloth in exchange for her wine, which was to be imported into England at a rate one-third less than was charged on French wine—thus port ousted claret. In their turn the allies agreed to send an Anglo-Dutch force to Lisbon and to proclaim the Archduke Charles king of Spain.

As regards Savoy, Victor Amadeus had always been distrustful of French sincerity and felt that the stronger they grew the less sincere they would become. When Vendôme demanded that Turin should be handed over to him, he threw in his lot with the allies, and, on October 25, entered into treaty with the Emperor. The importance of this defection was that, for the time being at least, Austria would be secure on her southern flank.

Yet, in spite of these important gains, in the autumn of 1703 the situation was so critical that Marlborough threatened to relinquish his command unless his subordinates obeyed his orders. On October 12 he wrote to Herr Guildermalsen, the Field Deputy: "I consider it my duty, as well as in the interests of the public . . . to inform you that I am more and more convinced both by the experiences of this campaign and the last one, that the little success we have gained is due to the want of discipline in the army, and until this is remedied I see no prospect of improvement."[1] He then returned to England to think out his plan for the following year.

By now it was obvious to Marlborough that, in the forthcoming campaign, the French would attempt to drive the Emperor out of

---

[1] *The Letters and Dispatches of John Churchill, First Duke of Marlborough* (1845), vol. I, p. 198.

the war. This done, they would be in a position to concentrate most of their troops in the Netherlands.

To prevent this, Marlborough's task was to devise a plan which simultaneously would succour the Emperor and be acceptable to the Dutch, or failing this, to be hidden from them. His last two campaigns had convinced him that, because of the formidable French lines and fortresses, a rapid decision in the Netherlands was not to be gained, and he decided that the sole course open to him was to transfer his army to the Upper Danube and to prevent the French and Bavarians forcing their way to Vienna. He clearly saw where the decisive area of operations lay, and as clearly he realized that the Dutch would never agree to his proceeding there. Even were they to do so, the manœuvre was an exceedingly dangerous one. Not only was the distance considerable for a large army to traverse rapidly, but the manœuvre involved a flank march across the French centre, and the sole force Marlborough had to cover it was Louis of Baden's small army, now at Stolhofen, which was quite inadequate for the task. Therefore, it was essential that the ultimate aim of the march should be concealed from the French on the Moselle and in Alsace as well as from the Dutch who, were they to learn of it, would fall into panic. Further, in accordance with the Methuen Treaty, he decided that Admiral Rooke should escort the Archduke Charles and an expeditionary force to Lisbon, and after they had been disembarked, Rooke was next to proceed to the Riviera, and with land forces supplied by Savoy, and helped by the Camisards (Huguenot rebels) of the Cevennes, to carry out a combined attack on Toulon to destroy the fleet in harbour there and to draw the French south.[1]

Who first suggested that the main blow should be struck on the Danube is not known. Coxe says that this decision was arrived at "through the agency of Prince Eugene", with whom Marlborough "had secretly arranged the whole plan of campaign."[2] This is

---

[1] Rooke and the expeditionary force reached Lisbon toward the end of February, 1704, and once the soldiers had been disembarked and the Archduke proclaimed Charles III of Spain—which started an eight-year war in the Peninsula—Rooke carried the fleet to Toulon; but he found that the Duke of Savoy was unable to spare any troops for the joint enterprise and he returned to the Straits, where strong reinforcements brought his fleet to over 50 sail. He then decided to carry out an enterprise which had been for some time contemplated—the capture of Gibraltar. This was effected with little difficulty on August 4; the Rock was weakly held and indifferently fortified. Three weeks later he severely repulsed a French relieving fleet of 50 sail, under Admiral Toulouse, off Velez Malaga; a battle which gained for England control of the Mediterranean, for during the remainder of the war the French made no serious effort to challenge her supremacy in those waters.

[2] *Memoirs of the Duke of Marlborough*, W. C. Coxe (1820), vol. I, p. 316.

unlikely, because at the time Marlborough and Eugene were unacquainted, and no correspondence is known which supports this
contention. What is known is that in August, 1703, Marlborough's plan for 1704 was to invade France by way of the
Moselle, and that during the autumn he received numerous
communications from Count Wratislaw, the Imperial Envoy,
pointing out that, if unaided, Vienna was as good as lost. Nevertheless it would appear that until March 1704, Marlborough held
fast to the Moselle plan.[1] In January he crossed over to The Hague
and discussed it with the Dutch States-General who, fearful that
it would uncover the United Provinces, strongly objected to
it. On his return home in February he received further urgent
appeals from Wratislaw. Finally, in April, Wratislaw presented
"a memorial" to Queen Anne, in which he represented to her
"the extraordinary Calamity, and imminent Danger, the Empire
was exposed to since the Elector of Bavaria had received a
Numerous Army of French," and implored that she "would be
pleas'd to Order the Duke of *Marlborough* (Her Captain-General)
. . . to conduct part of the Troops in Her Majesty's Pay beyond-
Sea, to preserve *Germany* from a total Subversion. . . ."[2] Shortly
after this appeal, Marlborough made mention of the idea. On
May 1 he informed Godolphin, the Lord Treasurer, "When I
come to Philipsburg, if the french shall have joined any more
troops to the elector of Bavaria, I shall make no difficulty of
marching to the Danube."[3] And again, on May 15, he wrote to
him: "If they [the French] send no more [than 15,000 troops] and
there is no misfortune in Germany before I go to the Danube, I
hope we may have success. . . ."[4] Thus, at length, a campaign on
the Danube was substituted for one on the Moselle, and part of
the new plan was that Eugene should replace Styrum and be
ordered by the Emperor to take the field in Germany alongside
Marlborough and Louis of Baden.

Marlborough had decided on his plan in the greatest secrecy,
and returned to the United Provinces on April 21, 1704. He

---

[1] See *Heinsius Correspondence*, 165, p. 101.
[2] *A Compleat History of the Late War in the Netherlands*. Thomas Broderick (1713),
pp. 93–94. See also *Heinsius Correspondence*, 168, p. 103.
[3] *Memoirs of the Duke of Marlborough*, W. C. Coxe, vol. I, p. 320. On May 2, writing
to his wife he said: "But I shall not continue in this country [the Moselle region] long,
for I intend to go higher up into Germany, which I am forced as yet to keep here a
secret, for fear these people [the Dutch] would be apprehensive of letting their troops
go so far." *Marlborough: his Life and Times*, Winston S. Churchill (1934), vol. II, p. 308.
[4] Quoted from *Marlborough: his Life and Times*, vol. II, p. 319.

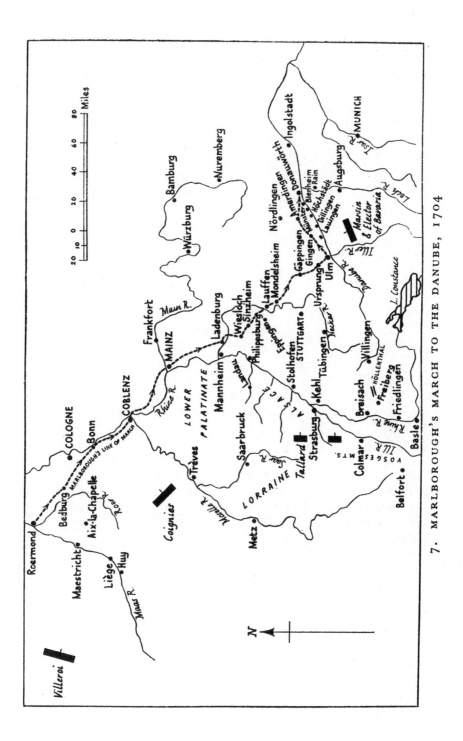

7 · MARLBOROUGH'S MARCH TO THE DANUBE, 1704

arrived at Maestricht on May 10 and there he found the situation as follows: Facing him was Villeroi, who lay within the lines of Mehaigne (Antwerp – Diest – Namur) with Count de Coignies and 10,000 men watching the Moselle. Round Vienna lay the Imperialist army, 30,000 strong, watched from Ulm by the Elector of Bavaria and Marshal Marsin with 45,000 men. In April, 10,000 more had crossed the Black Forest by the gorge of Höllenthal and were on their way to join them. Louis of Baden with 30,000 was at Stolhofen and did nothing to impede the advance of these reinforcements; Eugene, who had only 10,000 under his command, was too weak to hamper their advance. In order to cover these reinforcements and to protect the French line of communications with Bavaria, Tallard with an army of 30,000 lay at Strasburg and Kehl.

Though this distribution of forces was formidable, the main difficulty remained the Dutch. Therefore, in order to disembarrass himself from their control, before he left England Marlborough had arranged that all troops in English pay should come under his direct command. This was a fortunate decision, for when he informed the Dutch deputies that the forthcoming campaign was to be on the Moselle, they at once began to obstruct him. Nevertheless, handing over the defence of the United Provinces to General Auverquerque and 70,000 men, he fixed the first *rendezvous* of his own army at Bedburg, 20 miles west of Cologne, for May 16. In all he had under his command 90 squadrons of horse and 51 battalions of foot, of which 19 and 14 respectively, with 38 guns, constituted the British contingent. From Bedburg he wrote to Mr. Stepney, the English representative at Vienna, requesting him to inform the Emperor of his intention of marching to the Danube, but on no account to let the Dutch hear of it.[1] On May 18, he reviewed his troops, and two days later the army marched for the Rhine. Bonn was entered on May 23. There he learnt that Villeroi had crossed the Meuse and was menacing Huy; that Marsin had been reinforced, and that Auverquerque, on his own initiative, was sending him reinforcements. The advance is described by Parker as follows:

"We frequently marched three, sometimes four days, successively, and halted a day. We generally began our march about three in the morning, proceeded about four leagues, or four and a half each day, and reached our ground about nine. As we marched

[1] *Marlborough Dispatches*, vol. 1, pp. 258–259.

through the Countries of our Allies, Commissaries were appointed to furnish us with all manner of necessaries for man and horse; these were brought to the ground before we arrived, and the soldiers had nothing to do, but to pitch their tents, boil their kettles, and lie down to rest. Surely never was such a march carried on with more order and regularity, and with less fatigue both to man and horse."[1]

On May 25 Marlborough and the cavalry reached Coblenz, and four days later, when the infantry had come up, instead of marching up the Moselle, the army crossed two boat bridges and headed for Mainz. All were dumbfounded, as Parker[2] relates, and not least the French, who now conjectured that their enemy was making for Philippsburg, because bridges had recently been constructed there. On June 3 the cavalry, reinforced by various German contingents, crossed the Neckar at Ladenburg, and on June 7, instead of moving on Philippsburg, from Wiesloch the army turned toward Sinzheim. No longer able to keep his final move secret, Marlborough informed the States-General of his true destination, and Tallard, who was waiting at Landau to confront him once he had crossed the Rhine at Philippsburg, was thrown into consternation by his change of direction, as was the Court directly the news was received in Paris. With his right flank protected by the Black Forest, Marlborough headed for Lauffen.

On June 10 Mondelsheim was reached, and there Prince Eugene and Louis of Baden joined the army. At Gingen, which was entered on June 27, the tasks were distributed. It was decided that Louis of Baden and Marlborough were to work in conjunction, while Eugene was to command on the Rhine and prevent Villeroi and Tallard reinforcing the Bavarians. At length, having marched 250 miles, at the head of 200 squadrons, 96 battalions, and 48 guns, in all about 70,000 men, Marlborough came into contact with Marsin and the Elector entrenched about Dillingen with 60,000 men, 25 miles north-east of Ulm. Eugene, with 30,000 men in the Stolhofen lines, faced Villeroi at Strasburg at the head of 60,000 men.

On June 30 Marlborough moved to Balmershofen, and, on July 1, to Amerdingen, which lies some 15 miles west of the important fortress of Donauwörth, a stronghold it was essential that

---

[1] *Memoirs of the most remarkable Military Transactions from 1638–1718* etc., Captain Robert Parker, pp. 94–95.
[2] *Ibid.*, p. 94.

he should occupy with the least possible delay, for once in his hands he would gain the road to Nördlingen and thus be able to open a new line of communications, as well as to seize the Danube bridge and open the road to Augsburg and Munich. To lay siege to Donauwörth was out of the question because its reduction would have taken several weeks. Further, were Marlborough to attempt it, not only was Tallard well placed to cut his communications, but by advancing he could fall upon Marlborough's rear while Marsin and the Elector attacked his front. Already, on June 30, the Elector hurriedly had sent Marshal Count D'Arco and 14,000 men to Donauwörth, where they had at once begun to entrench the Schellenberg, an oval-shaped hill which dominated the fortress.

As a siege was out of the question, Marlborough decided on a *coup de main*, and in spite of the objections of his generals that after a 15-mile march the troops would be tired, he ordered that on July 2 the Schellenberg was to be stormed. He saw that it was vital not only to deprive D'Arco of 24 working hours, but that during this time Marsin and the Elector would be able to reinforce the Schellenberg by crossing the Danube at Dillingen and moving up its northern bank. Strategically, the whole problem hinged on the fact that Marlborough was 10 miles closer to Donauwörth than Marsin and the Elector. It was this advantage of half a long day's march that decided him not to postpone the attack until July 3, as his generals suggested.

Therefore, early on July 2, the British advanced guard moved out of Amerdingen, and "the way being very bad, long and tedious," it was not until noon that it reached the Wörnitz River immediately west of Donauwörth,[1] where a three-hour halt was made in order to bridge it. Here, apparently, in order to mislead D'Arco into supposing that no attack would be launched until July 3, the allied quartermasters began to pitch camp. Meanwhile Marsin and the Elector moved to the support of Donauwörth, and D'Arco was busily entrenching.

Marlborough's plan of attack was as simple as it was audacious. He decided to assault the Schellenberg on its western and strongest flank; not only because it was the nearest to him, but because, protected as it was by Donauwörth, the attack would be least expected. To do so he assembled two columns, the left one, mainly

[1] *A Compendious Journal of all the Marches, famous Battles and Sieges of the Confederate Allies in the late War.* John Millner (1733), p. 95.

English infantry, was to assault on the north-western extremity of the works, and either to carry them, or if that proved impossible, by furious attacks to draw in D'Arco's reserves and pin them down, and so pave the way for the right column. This column, under the command of the Margrave, was to move be-

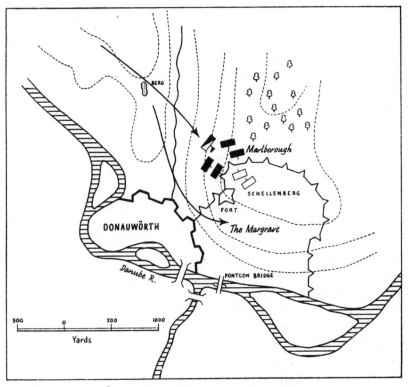

8.   THE SCHELLENBERG, 1704

tween Donauwörth and the south-western extremity of the Schellenberg and assault the position in the rear.

At 5 p.m. Marlborough's artillery opened fire; but it was not until an hour and a quarter later that Lieutenant-General Goor led forward the left column, 6,000 men in three lines, with eight battalions in support, eight in reserve and 35 squadrons of cavalry. What followed, is described by an eye-witness:

"So steep was the slope in front of us that as soon almost as the enemy's column began its advance it was lost to view, and it came into sight again only two hundred paces from our entrenchments. . . . The rapidity of their movements, together with their loud yells, were truly alarming, and as soon as I heard them I ordered the drums to beat the 'charge' so as to drown them with their noise, lest they should have a bad effect upon our people. . . . The English infantry led this attack with the greatest intrepidity, right up to our parapet, but there they were opposed with a courage at least equal to their own. . . . It would be impossible to describe in words strong enough the details of the carnage that took place during this first attack, which lasted a good hour or more. We were all fighting hand to hand, hurling them back as they clutched at the parapet; men were slaying or tearing at the muzzles of guns and the bayonets which pierced their entrails; crushing under their feet their wounded comrades, and even gouging out their opponents' eyes with their nails, when the grip was so close that neither could make use of their weapons. I verily believe that it would have been quite impossible to find a more terrible representation of Hell itself than was shown in the savagery of both sides on this occasion."[1]

The assault was repulsed and the men fell back into the dip north of the hill. A similar fate lay in store for the second assault and also the third; nevertheless, at great cost these attacks accomplished their object; they fixed D'Arco's reserves, and in consequence opened the way for the right column.

According to de la Colonie, the town commandant of Donauwörth, instead of lining the "covered way", which linked the fortress to the Old Fort–built by Gustavus Adolphus–on the south-western flank of the Schellenberg, had withdrawn his men into the main works. This not only facilitated the Margrave's advance; but, because of the formation of the ground, the garrison of the Schellenberg was prevented from noticing the movement. Besides, D'Arco considered the day already his, because strong reinforcements would arrive from Augsburg by nightfall. "It was now nearly seven in the evening", and only one regiment, that of Nectancourt, "was strung out in single rank" along the southern face of the hill. Next, writes de la Colonie:

"They arrived within gunshot of our flank, about 7.30 in the evening, without our being at all aware of the possibility of such a thing," when "I noticed all at once an extraordinary movement on the part of our infantry, who were rising up and ceasing fire

[1] *The Chronicles of an Old Campaigner*, M. de la Colonie, *1692–7171* (1904), pp. 183–185.

withal. I glanced around on all sides to see what had caused this behaviour, and then became aware of several lines of infantry in greyish-white uniforms on our left flank. From lack of movement on their part, their dress and bearing, I verily believed that reinforcements had arrived for us, and anybody else would have believed the same."[1]

At this moment Marlborough drove home his final assault, and caught between two fires the enemy broke. At once the 35 squadrons were launched in pursuit "and a terrible slaughter ensued, no quarter being given for a long time."[2] Thus ended this quite extraordinarily audacious battle; an operation of tremendous risks, yet a sure proof of Napoleon's saying that in war *qui ne risque rien, n'attrape rien.* It had lasted a little over an hour and a half, and as it ended the Elector's reinforcements arrived, but only to witness D'Arco's annihilation, for out of his total force he lost some 10,000 men. Marlborough's casualties were heavy–1,400 killed and 3,800 wounded.

The results of the battle were commensurate with the audacity of its conception and execution. Donauwörth fell, and both the road to Nördlingen and the bridge over the Danube were won. Thus, simultaneously, a line of retreat was opened and a line of advance into Bavaria gained. When he heard of the defeat, the Elector at once broke down the bridge over the Lech and entrenched himself at Augsburg. Marsin appealed for assistance to Tallard who, on July 1, had crossed the Rhine, and, on July 16, when about to lay siege to Villingen, received the first full news of the disaster. On July 22 he raised the siege and marched to Ulm, where he arrived on July 29. This move at once placed Eugene in a difficult position, for obviously he would have to follow Tallard, yet simultaneously he had to watch Villeroi. Ostentatiously he marched northward to Tübingen, where he arrived on July 27, and misled Villeroi into believing that he was not following Tallard. Next he vanished among the Swabian hills and headed his army for Donauwörth.

The vital bridge gained, the second act in this amazing campaign opened. With Tallard approaching–and so perfect was Marlborough's intelligence that two days after the French had crossed the Rhine news of their advance had been received by him –it was of the utmost importance to bring the Elector to book. As he refused battle, and because Marlborough could not risk a siege

<hr/>

[1] *Ibid.*, p. 191.   [2] *Memoirs, etc.*, Robert Parker, p. 97.

as long as Tallard was in the field, on July 8 he crossed the Lech and began devastating Bavaria[1] and the terrified inhabitants appealed to their prince for protection or peace. On July 13, under persuasion of the Electress, daughter of John Sobieski, the Elector was on the point of coming to terms when he heard of Tallard's approach. In consequence he continued the struggle and foolishly dispersed most of his army in order to protect his estates. This was a definite gain for the Allies; but as Tallard was now drawing near, autumn approaching, and Parliament would again assemble in November, a victory became a necessity, and to win one it was essential for Marlborough to disembarrass himself of the Margrave, a slow-witted man whom he did not trust; therefore he fell in with his request to lay siege to Ingolstadt. On July 31 he wrote to Eugene outlining his plan, which was: while a detachment of his troops was to join the Margrave at Ingolstadt, Eugene and the remainder were to unite with Marlborough's army, not only in order to cover the siege, but also to bring the combined forces of Tallard, Marsin, and the Elector to battle.

On Saturday, August 10, Tallard and his allies set out north-ward to cross the Danube at Dillingen, and the next day, from his camp at Münster—two hours' march from Donauwörth—Eugene wrote to Marlborough saying: "The enemy have marched. It is almost certain that the whole army is passing the Danube at Lauingen. . . . The plain of Dillingen is crowded with troops. . . . I am therefore marching the infantry and part of the cavalry this night to a camp I have marked out before Donauwörth. Every-thing, milord, consists in speed [*diligence*] and that you put your-self forward in movement to join me tomorrow, without which I fear it will be too late."[2] At once Marlborough set out to support his colleague.

Meanwhile Tallard moved forward to Höchstädt, some five miles down the Danube from Dillingen, where he learnt that Marlborough was joining Eugene. Presupposing that, as the Margrave was absent, Marlborough would fall back on Nörd-lingen, the Elector (in nominal command) urged an attack. Tallard doubted the wisdom of this and a half-measure was agreed

---

[1] Mr. Churchill exonerates this attack on the civil population and writes: "It was not senseless spite or brutality, but a war measure deemed vital to success and even safety. . . . Its military usefulness cannot be disputed." (*Marlborough: his Life and Times*, vol. II, pp. 409–410.) And Marlborough gives his reasons for it to Heinsius in a letter dated July 31, 1704 (*Heinsius Correspondence*, 200, p. 121).

[2] Quoted from *Marlborough: his Life and Times*, Winston S. Churchill, vol. II, pp. 426–427.

upon–to advance three miles downstream to a position a little west of the village of Blenheim (Blindheim); this they did on August 12. There they flattered themselves they had victory in their hands, imagining that Marlborough would be compelled to retire. As Taylor points out, they were incapable of believing that Eugene and Marlborough could be so neglectful of the rules of war as to deliver a frontal attack upon a numerically superior force occupying a strong position.[1] "That night," Count de Mérode-Westerloo[2] informs us, "spirits were at their highest in the Franco-Bavarian camp, for no one doubted that Marlborough and Eugene would be forced to withdraw."

The Franco-Bavarian camp was pitched on the top of a gentle rise about a mile west of a shallow marshy brook called the Nebel. Its right rested on Blenheim, close to the Danube, where Tallard established his headquarters. Through it ran a boggy brook, the Maulweyer, and about one and a half miles up the Nebel, on its left bank, was situated the village of Unterglau, and a mile and a half farther up Oberglau, where Marsin pitched his headquarters. A mile and a half to the west of Oberglau lay the village of Lutzingen in broken country, here was the Elector's headquarters. The camps were, therefore, protected by these four villages or bastions and the Nebel formed a moat in front of the first and third. Defensively it was, therefore, a strong position, flanked on the right by the Danube and on the left by woodland and hills.

At daybreak on August 12 Marlborough reconnoitred his enemy's position by means of his "prospective-glass", and, as Serjeant Millner informs us, at "About One in the Afternoon we saw their Quarter-Master General set up their Camp Standard, and mark out the Camp from Blenheim to Lutzing."[3] What the strengths of the opposing armies were is not known exactly; Millner[4] computes the Allies at 52,000 and the Franco-Bavarians, at 60,000, and Mr. Churchill[5] writes that the former consisted of 66 battalions, 160 squadrons, and 66 cannon[6]–56,000 men in all; whereas the latter numbered 84 battalions, 147 squadrons, and 90 cannon, or about 60,000 fighting men.

When the Franco-Bavarian camps were wrapped in sleep, all

[1] *The Wars of Marlborough, 1702–1709*, Frank Taylor (1921), vol. I, p. 204.

[2] *Mémoires de Mérode-Westerloo* (1840), p. 298.

[3] *A Compendious Journal*, etc., p. 110.

[4] *Ibid.*, pp. 124–128.

[5] *Marlborough: his Life and Times*, vol. II, p. 442.

[6] Marlborough's own figures, as given to Heinsius on August 16, are 160 squadrons and 65 battalions (*Heinsius Correspondence*, 204, p. 123).

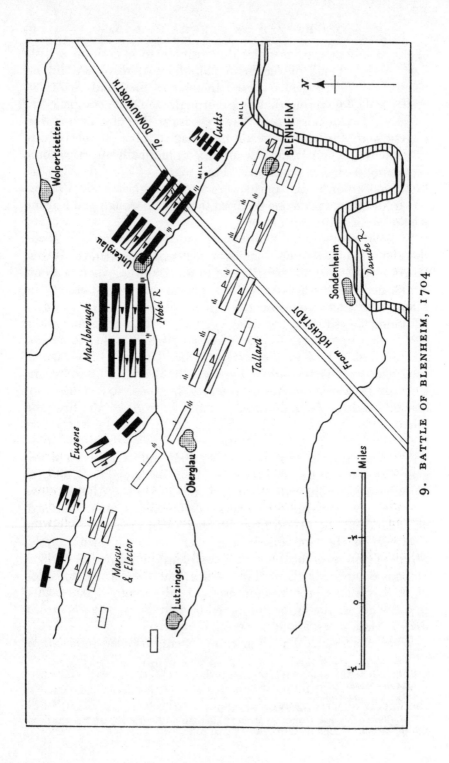

9. BATTLE OF BLENHEIM, 1704

was alive in those of Marlborough and Eugene, and at two o'clock, on the morning of August 13, the joint armies each formed up in four columns and, preceded by 40 squadrons, advanced westward along marked tracks, and an hour later crossed the Kessel Stream by prepared bridges. The morning was dark and misty; Eugene's army marched on the right, Marlborough's on the left, the artillery and pontoons followed the main road to Höchstädt. On the Reichen Stream, a little west of the village of Tapfheim, a halt was made in order to call in the outposts, in all 20 battalions and 15 squadrons, including three brigades of British infantry. These were formed into a ninth column to march on the left, and were placed under the command of Lord Cutts, known as "Salamander". The advance was next continued to Schwenningen, where another halt was made. Marlborough and Eugene with the above 40 squadrons rode forward to the high ground north of Wolpertstetten to reconnoitre the enemy's position. It was now six o'clock, and when an hour later the mist rose, the enemy took alarm and fired two pieces of cannon.

Though the surprise was complete, even now the two French marshals and the Elector were still so obsessed by the idea that their enemy could do nothing other than retire, that at first they judged the advance to be a covering operation to protect the withdrawal of the main body. Even at this moment, about seven o'clock, Tallard wrote to Louis XIV to notify him of his enemy's withdrawal.[1] Next, as the columns came steadily on, Tallard, suddenly realised the truth, ordered the drums to beat and the trumpets to sound, and all was pandemonium in the Franco-Bavarian camps. Although not present at this battle, M. de la Colonie, from the reports of eye-witnesses, gives the following instructive account of this surprise:

"Signal guns", he says, "were fired to bring back the foragers and their escorts; the 'Alarm' and the 'Assembly' were beaten hurriedly, and, without attempting to strike the tents, every effort was devoted to forming line of battle in front of the camp. The hurry and precipitation of all this brought confusion and fear in its train, whilst the foraging parties and their escorts, alarmed by the unexpected signals, returned one by one, rather a prey to misgivings than animated with any desire to fight. The difficulty of having to think of many things at once in the actual presence of the enemy reacted upon the nerves of those in command, and,

[1] *Campagne de monsieur le maréchal de Tallard en Allemagne 1704* (1763), vol. II, p. 140.

above all, upon those who had their carriages packed with the valuables accumulated during their period of winter quarters; such a state of unreadiness is a serious disadvantage in the case of a battle of these dimensions, the preparation for which should have been made much earlier.''[1]

At about half-past eight the allied army came under cannon shot, to which the English batteries replied. Meanwhile Tallard hastily decided on his plan, and as time was too short to do otherwise, he assumed the defensive. Besides, his two flanks were well protected by the Danube and the wooded hills, and his four miles of front by the swampy Nebel. That the two armies, his and Marsin's and the Elector's, took up position as two separate forces instead of one, was a matter of custom, and in any case it was too late to do anything else.

Tallard decided that, while he held the right from the Danube to Oberglau (exclusive), Marsin should hold the centre and the Elector the left. He also decided that the left and centre should take up position close to the right bank of the Nebel and dispute all attempts to cross it, whereas the right would hold back 1,000 yards from that stream, in order that the enemy's left, once it had crossed it, would be caught between the fire of Blenheim and Oberglau, when it could be counter-attacked in front by the French cavalry and driven back into the swamps. Though this plan has been much criticized, when one takes into consideration the shortage of time it was a sound one against any ordinary enemy.

In accordance with this plan, Tallard distributed his forces as follows: (1) To Blenheim he allotted nine battalions as garrison, with seven in support and 11 in reserve in rear of the village; (2) between Blenheim and Oberglau he drew up 44 squadrons (5,500 strong) in two lines supported by nine battalions and four squadrons of dismounted dragoons; (3) on their left he posted 32 squadrons of Marsin's cavalry with 14 battalions in Oberglau; (4) to their left 32 squadrons and 17 battalions—also Marsin's; (5) and on their left, under the Elector, 51 squadrons with 12 battalions in Lutzingen, of which a number was thrown back *en potence*.[2]

From their reconnaissance Marlborough and Eugene saw that the enemy's right was stronger than his left; therefore, as at the

---

[1] *The Chronicles of an Old Campaigner*, pp. 225–226.
[2] The totals of infantry and cavalry are impossible to ascertain, as each account of this battle varies as regards numbers.

Schellenberg, they decided that he would least expect an attack in that direction, and accordingly they arrived at the following general idea; that Eugene should vigorously attack the enemy left, in order to distract the Franco-Bavarian command, and that the decisive blow was to be delivered by Marlborough against the right.

Marlborough saw that Tallard's distribution defensively was an able one, hinged as it was on the villages of Blenheim and Oberglau. If their garrisons were not contained, the risks to his advance would be great; therefore he decided to attack these two villages in such strength that their infantry would be too busy defending themselves to counter-attack in flank his central advance between the villages.[1] If either was carried, so much the better; if not, in any case they would be held and their teeth drawn. Further, as he did not know whether he would be allowed to cross the Nebel unmolested, he drew up his order of battle in an unconventional way. He formed it in four lines; the first consisted of 17 battalions of infantry to gain the right bank; the second and third of 36 and 35 squadrons for the main assault; and the fourth of 11 battalions to hold the ground beyond the Nebel and to cover the withdrawal of the cavalry should the assault fail. On the left of this distribution he drew up Cutts's column; its task was to assault Blenheim. Lastly, he ordered up his engineers to build five bridges across the stream and to repair one which had been broken.

While Eugene's columns toiled over the hilly and wooded ground west of Wolpertstetten, Cutts cleared the left bank of the Nebel immediately east of Blenheim; drove the French out of the water mills, and gained the right bank of the stream. Next, he posted his column in a bottom close to the village, where for several hours his men "with wonderful Resolution . . . stood the Fire of six Pieces of Cannon" planted on the rise beyond it.[2] For four hours the artillery duel was kept up, during which, in order to sustain the *morale* of his troops, Marlborough ordered the chaplains to conduct a service. Also, in full view of the French gunners, he cantered down the line to set an example to his men. A round-shot struck the ground beneath his horse, and to the horror of those watching him, for a moment he was lost to sight in a cloud of dust.

It was now eleven o'clock, and, perturbed because he had heard

[1] See *Memoirs, etc.*, Robert Parker, p. 104.
[2] *A Compendious Journal*, etc., John Millner, p. 115.

nothing from Eugene, Marlborough sent galloper after galloper to the right to ascertain the reason. About this time the situation is vividly described by Taylor: "The sun shone brilliantly on acres of yellow grain, slashed with long, glittering lines of scarlet, blue and steel. The music of both armies rose and fell in challenging paeans. And always the cannon boomed across the marshy stream, and men and horses were cut down, now singly, and now in swathes, and the dismal procession of wounded trailed slowly to the rear. The heat became intense, for it was now high noon. The day was half spent, and already the casualties of the allies amounted to 2,000, when an aide-de-camp of Eugene's came racing from the distant right. The moment had arrived."[1]

It was now half past twelve o'clock, and Marlborough, turning to his generals, said: "Gentlemen, to your posts." Fifteen minutes later Cutts ordered his leading British brigade, commanded by General Rowe, to assault Blenheim, under cover of which the troops on Rowe's right were to move toward the Nebel. Rowe ordered that not a man was to fire until he had struck with his sword the pales of the palisades the French had erected, and then advanced to within 30 paces of the enemy before a withering volley struck him down and a third of his men. The brigade pressed on, and in blinding smoke so uncertain seemed the contest that Lieutenant-General the Marquis de Cléambault, who commanded the troops in Blenheim, called in his seven supporting battalions, and shortly after apparently lost his head, and called the 11 battalions in reserve as well. Thus, 12,000 additional men were jammed into the village, many of whom were not able to move. Parker writes: ". . . we mowed them down with our platoons . . . and it was not possible for them to rush out upon us . . . without running upon the very points of our Bayonets. This great body of Troops therefore was of no further use to *Tallard*, being obliged to keep on the defensive, in expectation that he might come to relieve them."[2]

Nevertheless the assault failed, and a second was delivered and beaten back. Next, the French Gendarmerie, the finest cavalry of France, moved forward on both flanks of Blenheim, and were soon driven back. On the northern flank they were met by Colonel Palmes, who with five squadrons scattered eight by simultaneously charging them in front and on both flanks. A third assault was in preparation, but Marlborough called it off, for he saw that his

[1] *The Wars of Marlborough, 1702–1709*, vol. I, p. 213.
[2] *Memoirs, etc.*, p. 105.

object had been attained, because the French were fixed in the village. Further, his leading infantry were now over the Nebel and the main body of his cavalry was crossing it.

While the battle rolled around Blenheim, a dangerous crisis arose at Oberglau. There 10 battalions, under the Prince of Holstein-Beck, had advanced on that village and had been severely repulsed by the Marquis de Blainville at the head of nine battalions, which included the Irish brigade, known as the "Wild Geese". Driven pell-mell back on the Nebel, the right of Marlborough's centre was left open to attack; whereupon Marsin marshalled a large force of cavalry in rear of Oberglau preparatory to a charge through the gap on the right of his enemy's centre. The situation was critical in the extreme. Marlborough realized it, galloped to the scene, and at once sent an aide-de-camp to Eugene to request him to detach Fugger's cavalry brigade and order it to protect the gap. Though Eugene was fighting a desperate battle in most difficult ground and was also in a critical position, he at once complied, and as Marsin's horsemen charged down toward the Nebel, Fugger struck them on their left flank and drove them back. The charge saved Holstein-Beck, who again advanced and this time drove de Blainville's infantry back into Oberglau, where he "kept those within it besieged", so that, as Campbell says, the allies could now "march before it and attack the cavalry of the enemy with great liberty."[1]

Though Marlborough saw this clearly, for, at three o'clock in the afternoon, the two bastions of Blenheim and Oberglau had been deprived of their offensive power, to the common eye victory was going to the French. The day was advancing; Eugene was at death grips with the Elector, but was making little headway, and if the allies could not advance they would be forced to retire, and to fall back before the French cavalry, as yet little used, meant a rout. But Marlborough knew that victory was his as long as Eugene held on, because so much of the French infantry was locked up in its now purely defensive bastions of Blenheim and Oberglau. There they lay besieged, and between them yawned the gateway to Tallard's doom.

Although Eugene knew that on his front no decision could be gained; Marlborough knew that one was certain on his, as long as Eugene held fast to his enemy. Thus the cooperation between the two generals was complete, and by four o'clock, when the

[1] *The Military History of Eugene and Marlborough*, John Campbell (1736), vol. i, p. 159.

whole of Marlborough's centre had crossed the marshes, he changed his order of attack and formed his cavalry into two lines in front with two lines of infantry behind them. He had at his disposal an overwhelmingly superior force at the decisive point, for against Tallard's 50 to 60 squadrons and nine battalions he marshalled 90 and 23 respectively. He waited until 4.30 p.m., when he heard that Eugene was working round Lutzingen, and then set the whole of his centre in motion. Only then did Tallard realize what was in his enemy's mind; he ordered up his nine reserve battalions and drew them up to the south of Oberglau to impede the advance. At once Marlborough ordered up three Hanoverian battalions and some cannon, and a desperate fight took place: the Hanoverians were driven back and the whole of Marlborough's line of cavalry recoiled. Now was Tallard's last fleeting chance, but his cavalry hung fire.

At about 5.30 p.m., the Duke ordered his cannon to pour grape on to the nine heroic battalions, and under cover of their fire he ordered a general advance. "With trumpets blaring and kettle-drums crashing and standards tossing proudly above the plumage and the steel," writes Taylor, "the two long lines, perfectly timed from end to end, swung into a trot, that quickened ever as they closed upon the French."[1]

Panic struck most of the enemy horse, who did not wait to receive the shock. Wildly firing their carbines and pistols, the French troopers, including the famous Maison du Roi, swung their horses about and galloped from the field. Some made for Höch-städt and others for the Danube, where some 30 squadrons plunged headlong over its steep bank near Sondenheim into the marshes and river below. Meanwhile the nine battalions were cut down to a man. "I rode through them next morning", writes Parker, "as they lay dead, in Rank and File."[2]

The Franco-Bavarian armies were now rent asunder. In vain did Tallard appeal to Marsin; for at this moment Eugene was storming round the village of Lutzingen. His appeal only pressed home the sense of the general danger, and Marsin and the Elector ordered a withdrawal before their right flank could be overlapped. It was now seven o'clock, and the Duke drew rein and hastily scribbled on the back of a tavern bill this pencil note to his wife: "I have not time to say more, but to beg you will give my duty to

---

[1] *The Wars of Marlborough, 1702–1709,* vol. I, p. 215.
[2] *Memoirs, etc.,* p. 110.

the Queen, and let her know Her Army has had a Glorious Victory. Mons. Tallard and two other Generals are in my coach and I am following the rest: the bearer, my Aide-de-Camp Col. Parke will give Her and (*sic*) account of what has pass'd. I shall doe it in a day or two by another more att large.''[1] Within 10 days this message was delivered at Windsor.

After he had scribbled this note and while his cavalry pursued the beaten French and Eugene pressed after Marsin and the Elector, Marlborough turned his attention to Blenheim, where 27 battalions were still held by Cutts, now reinforced by Lord Orkney. Cléambault had galloped for the Danube, had plunged into its stream, and was drowned. At nine o'clock his leaderless men surrendered and the battle ended.

What were its costs? The allies had lost 4,500 killed and 7,500 wounded, including 2,000 British, that is, about 20 per cent. of their original strength. Their enemies, according to Millner, lost 38,609 in killed, drowned, wounded and prisoners, including deserters.[2] That there was no sustained pursuit of Marsin and the Elector is no slur on Marlborough, for he had no fresh reserves at hand, night was falling, and he was encumbered with 15,000 prisoners as well as an immense booty.[3]

Marlborough was elated by his overwhelming victory, and well he might be. Writing to his "dearest soul" on August 14, he called it "as great a victory as has ever been known," and so it was, for Blenheim put an end to the grand design of Louis XIV. It decided the fate of Europe, and as Mr. Churchill writes, "it changed the political axis of the world."[4] Had Marlborough been defeated, the Elector of Bavaria would have replaced the House of Habsburg on the Imperial throne; Munich would have ousted Vienna; and the Empire itself would have become a satrapy of France. Instead, the Elector was chased from his dominions, which were annexed to Austria. Equally important, Blenheim at one stroke cancelled the designs of the House of Stuart; for, had

---

[1] *Memoirs of the Duke of Marlborough*, William Coxe, vol. I, p. 413.

[2] On August 28 Marlborough informed Heinsius that the enemy acknowledged a loss of 40,000 men (*Heinsius Correspondence*, 210, p. 128).

[3] "100 pieces of cannon, great and small, 24 mortars, 129 colours, 171 standards, 17 pair of kettle-drums, 3,600 tents, 34 coaches, 300 laden mules, 2 bridges of boats, 15 pontoons, 24 barrels and 8 casks of silver." (*History of the Reign of Queen Anne digested into Annals*, Abel Boyer, 1703–1713, vol. III, p. 87.) Regarding the prisoners, Marlborough wrote: "We can't march from hence til we can find some way of disposing all the prisoners . . . for we have noe garrisons to send them to" (*Heinsius Correspondence*, 206, p. 125).

[4] *Marlborough: His Life and Times*, vol. II, p. 478.

France gained a hegemony over the entire west and centre of Europe, there can be little doubt that single-handed England would have had to fight her because of the Pretender's claims.

For England, Blenheim was the greatest battle won on foreign soil since Agincourt. It broke the prestige of the French armies and plunged them into disgrace and ridicule. From 1704 onward Louis XIV sought peace with honour, and though the war continued for another eight years, adding the victories of Ramilles (1706), Oudenarde (1708), and Malplaquet (1709), to Marlborough's fame, Louis's one object was to end it. At length, in 1711, England yearned for peace wherein to reinstate her trade.[1] So it came about that negotiations were opened on January 29, 1712, and at Utrecht a series of peace treaties was signed on April 11, 1713. France retained her hold on the left bank of the upper Rhine, and, on the understanding that the crowns of France and Spain should never be united, Philip of Anjou was recognized as Philip V of Spain and the Indies. Thus Louis broke the Habsburg ring, completed the work of Richelieu and Mazarin, and gave France security until 1792. Further, he recognized the Protestant succession in England. Austria was given the Spanish Netherlands, henceforth to be known as the Austrian Netherlands, as well as Naples and Milan, which she retained until 1866. The United Provinces were allotted certain Barrier fortresses, and Savoy, raised to a kingdom, received Nice and Sicily, which island, in 1720, was exchanged for Sardinia. Of all the booty hunters England obtained what eventually was to prove the lion's share: from France, Acadia (Nova Scotia), Newfoundland and the region around the Hudson–thus the expulsion of the French from North America began–and from Spain, Gibraltar and Minorca, which guaranteed her naval power in the western Mediterranean. Further, an advantageous commercial treaty was signed between England and Spain, in which the most profitable clause was the grant to the former of the sole right to import negro slaves into Spanish America for 30 years.[2]

With the signing of the Treaty of Utrecht, England was left

---

[1] "In 1710 the number of vessels cleared from English ports is quoted as 3,550; in 1711 as 3,759; in 1712 as 4,267; in 1713 as 5,807; in 1714 as 6,614. The shipping in London is stated to have increased in these five years from 806 to 1,550" (*The Cambridge Modern History*, vol. v, p. 439).

[2] The *Asiento* or "Contract" for supplying Spanish America with African slaves, which permitted the slave traders to carry on the smuggling of other goods. "This *Asiento* contract was one of the most coveted things that England won for herself in the war and pocketed at the Peace of Utrecht." (*Blenheim*, G. M. Trevelyan, p. 139.)

supreme at sea and in the markets of the world, and as Admiral Mahan says, "not only in fact, but also in her own consciousness." "This great but noiseless revolution in sea-power", writes Professor Trevelyan, "was accomplished by the victories of Marlborough's arms and diplomacy on land . . . it was because Marlborough regarded the naval war as an integral part of the whole allied effort against Louis, that English sea power was fixed between 1702 and 1712 on a basis whence no enemy has since been able to dislodge it."[1]

But the revolution went deeper still; for it was the machinery of the Bank of England and the National Debt which enabled England to fight wars with gold as well as iron. William's war had lasted for nine years and had cost over £30,000,000, and the War of the Spanish Succession dragged on for 12 years and cost about £50,000,000. Only half this vast sum of £80,000,000 was met out of taxation, the remainder was borrowed and added to the National Debt. Thus a system was devised whereby the prosperity of the future was underwritten in order to ease the poverty of the present, and war was henceforth founded on unpayable debt. The banker merchants of London steadily gained in political power over the landed interests, and, therefore, increasingly into their hands went the destinies of the nation and the Empire, whose frontiers had become the oceans and the seas.

[1] *Blenheim*, p. 248.

CHRONICLE 5

The rise of the Muscovite Empire

Two new powers now step on to the stage of western history, Russia and Prussia, and, as related in Vol. I, Chronicle 12, the history of the former opened in the middle of the tenth century with the occupation of the lake Ilmen region by the Norsemen and the establishment at Novgorod of the House of Rurik. The next great event rapidly followed; it was the forceful conversion of the Varangians and their subject peoples to Christianity by Vladimir Prince of Kiev (980–1015). Married to Anna, sister of the Emperor Basil II, the faith Vladimir chose was that of the Orthodox Church. Though this conversion constitutes the first true cultural contact of Russia with the west, the adoption of the Greek faith alienated the Russians from Catholic Europe.

In 1147 another event occurred, which went far to change the whole course of Russian history. It was the founding of a military colony on the Moscova by Yuri Dolgoruki, Prince of Suzdal. Moscow, then no more than a tribal village, grew in power and became the centre of the Great Russians. Not only did it turn the course of eastern Slavonic history away from Europe; but because, strategically, the region of Moscow—an island in a sea of land—possessed no defensible frontiers, the urge to make it secure demanded the establishment of a military state which, in its turn, led to territorial expansion in all directions. Further, this orientation caused a definite split between the western and eastern Slavonic tribes; the one gravitated around Vilna and the other around Moscow. In the thirteenth century, contact between eastern Slavdom and Europe became still more restricted by the decline of the Byzantine empire after the capture of Constantinople by the Crusaders in 1204.

The next great event was the arrival of the Mongols (Tartars) under Batu and Ogotai, grandson and nephew of Genghis Khan. They overwhelmed the Russian chivalry in three great battles, that of Kalka in 1224, and those of the Oka and Sit in 1238, and, with the exception of Novgorod, between these dates every town of importance in Russia was sacked and burnt. Though, soon after, the colossal empire built by Genghis Khan collapsed, the

Golden Horde under Batu firmly established itself in the steppes of the lower Volga, and from his capital of Saray, (near present-day Stalingrad) Batu dominated Russia, which for more than 100 years was entirely estranged from western civilization.

Once subdued by the Tartars, the princes of Russia became their tax-gatherers and police agents, an occupation which proved so profitable that Ivan Kalita ("Money Bags") Grand Duke of Vladimir grew sufficiently powerful to annex Moscow and out-distance all his rivals. The most notable event of his reign was the transference of the Metropolitan see from Vladimir to Moscow, which soon became a capital city of importance. Nevertheless, the supremacy of the Tartars, though on the decline, held firm until the coming of Timur, who, between 1390 and 1394, overran the Golden Horde and so weakened the Tartar hold on Russia that the grand dukes of Muscovy regained contact with the Byzantine empire until its fall in 1453. Although for a century onward contact with the west was all but lost, through the marriage in 1472 of Ivan III, The Great (1462–1505), Grand Duke of Mus-covy, with Zoe (Sophia) Paleologus, niece of Constantine XI, last of the eastern Roman emperors, Moscow became the capital of the Orthodox Church and its dukes heirs of the Byzantine Caesars. Ivan declared his independence from Tartar rule and assumed the title of Tsar (Taesar = Caesar) and devoted his reign to emanci-pation of Russia from the slackening yoke of the Tartars, and the extension of Muscovite rule. He doubled the size of his duchy and invited Italians to his court, one of whom, Pietro Antonio Sulari, of Milan, built for him the palace of the Kremlin.

When, in 1505, Ivan III died, the expansion of Muscovy was continued by his son Vasili III (1505–1533) and also by his grand-son Ivan IV (1533–1564), surnamed "The Terrible", because his vices and atrocities were abnormal even for a Muscovite Tsar. He was a complete autocrat who, like Stalin 400 years later, reduced his subjects to a uniform level of abject proletarian subservience. He warred with the khan of the Crimea who, in 1571, burnt Moscow, and, for reasons to be related, between 1557–1560, conquered Livonia. After he had established his authority over the Cossacks of the Don, he founded the Asiatic power of Russia by pushing his armies over the Urals and carrying war to the terri-tory between the Irtysh and the Ob. An intelligent beast, he was one of the greatest of the Tsars, and a model for all future Slavonic autocrats.

It was during his reign that, to all intents and purposes, Russia was rediscovered by the west. In 1553, during the reign of Edward VI of England, Sir Hugh Willoughby and Richard Chancellor set out in three ships to discover the North East passage to China,[1] and when they reached the coast of Lapland, one of the ships–the *Edward Bonaventure*–with Chancellor on board, was carried into the White Sea. Chancellor landed at the mouth of the Dvina and unexpectedly discovered that he was in Muscovy. He journeyed to Moscow and was so well received by Ivan that on his return Queen Mary sent a special envoy to the Tsar to open trade relations between the two countries. As the White Sea was blocked with ice during many months of the year, in order to establish a more suitable route, in 1557, Ivan invaded Livonia, an aggression which was followed by a seven-year war (1563–1570) with Poland, during which the Swedes and Danes intervened on their own account.

Thus trade brought the West to Russia and war brought Russia to the West, and the isolation in which she had existed since the thirteenth century was broken. The effects were immediate, for before the sixteenth century had run its course the old fear of an Asiatic invasion of Europe reawoke. The policy of the western maritime powers was to open trade with Russia, but that of the eastern European nations was to keep her confined within her barbaric limits by preventing western ideas and manufactures adding to her strength. So alarmed did the king of Poland become over the trade agreements between England and Russia, that he protested to Queen Elizabeth, "in the interests of Christianity" and because Russia was "the enemy of all free nations," against the trading of munitions of war to that country.

In 1580, Ivan, in a fit of ungovernable fury, killed his eldest son, and when he died in 1584 he was succeeded by his second son, Theodore. Thirty years of anarchy followed. On Theodore's death, in 1598, the House of Rurik came to an end, and in 1605 the Poles occupied Moscow. Eight years later they were ejected and Michael Romanoff (1613–1645), son of the Metropolitan Philaret–by marriage connected with the late dynasty–was elected Tsar, and the Romanoff dynasty was established. It was to last until Nicholas II and his family, in circumstances of

[1] See Hakluyt's *Voyages* (Everyman's edit., 1939), vol. I, pp. 266–294. "The newe Navigation and discoveries of the kingdome of Moscovia, by the Northeast, in the yeere 1553; Enterprised by Sir Hugh Willoughbie knight, and performed by Richard Chancelor Pilot major of the voyage: Written in Latine by Clement Adams."

Ivanic horror, were, on July 16, 1918, assassinated at Ekaterinburg by the Jew Yourkovsky.

War with Poland continued throughout most of Michael's reign and during that of his successor Alexis (1645–1676), and had not Charles X of Sweden intervened, the high probability is that the war would have led to the annexation of White Russia. That Charles did intervene was in no way because of the demands of security, but wholly because of military ambition.

Charles, the nephew of Gustavus Adolphus, in 1654 had succeeded to the Swedish throne on the abdication of his cousin, Queen Christina. His outlook was that of a soldier, and no sooner was he king than he attacked Poland and started a conflict which involved Brandenburg, Russia, Denmark, and Holland, and grew into the First Great Northern War. Helped by the unwilling Elector of Brandenburg, after he had subdued most of Poland, Charles entered into alliance with the Cossacks of Little Russia (the Ukraine). Alexis then came to terms with the Poles, made common cause with them against Charles, and wrested from him Livonia, which had been acquired by Sweden in 1621. At length, in 1661, the Swedes and Russians came to terms, and by the Peace of Kardis Livonia was restored to Sweden. But because the Poles refused to execute the treaty, the Russo-Polish war was renewed and dragged on until 1667, when it was concluded by the Treaty of Andrusovo, which restored Smolensk to the Tsar and gave him Little Russia up to the Dnieper. Thus a march toward the west was gained.

The Peace of Kardis left Sweden master of the Baltic, and so the situation remained throughout the reign of Charles XI (1660–1697). After a successful war with Denmark, he made himself autocrat of Sweden and devoted the latter part of his reign to the peaceful rehabilitation of his country. On his death in 1697, he left his son Charles XII (1697–1718), then a boy of 15, an empire including the whole of the Scandinavian peninsula (less Norway), Finland, Carelia, Ingria, Estonia, Livonia, western Pomerania, Wismar, Bremen, and Verden, as well as most of the Baltic islands. Thus the Swedes not only controlled the Baltic; but, except for the Nieman and Vistula, the mouths of all the great rivers flowing into it–the Neva, Duna, Oder, Elbe, and Weser. Imposing though this empire was, it invited destruction. In the east it blocked Russian expansion to the Baltic; in the south it was threatened by the Empire and Brandenburg, and in the west by Denmark and Norway.

Meanwhile Alexis died in 1676, and was succeeded by his son Theodore (1676–1682), who in 1682 was succeeded by his step-brother Peter (1682–1725), to become known as Peter the Great. That he was ever able to regenerate Russia and force her into the orbit of western civilization was due in no small way to the first three Romanoff tsars, who had brought access to western ideas within reach of Russia. Nevertheless, at the time of his accession Russia was still a barbaric country: its tsar owned the land and the people. Of liberty there was none; justice was bought and sold; taxation was on the level of brigandage; corruption, drunkenness and violence abounded; unspeakable forms of vice were universal, as were the grossest superstitions, and the West was held to be the land of the damned. Kotoshikhin, who in the reign of Alexis sought refuge in Sweden, informs us that "The Russians are arrogant and incapable, because they get no education except in pride, shamelessness, and lying. They will not send their children abroad to learn, fearing that if they came to know the mode of life and the religion of other folks and the blessing of freedom, they would forget to return home. It was indeed one of the *arcana imperii* of the Tsars to hinder their subjects from travelling, lest they should behold the spectacle of liberty elsewhere. . . ." It is against this dismal background that the reforms which Peter the Great carried out and the means he employed to enforce them must be judged, and the importance of his victory over Charles XII at Poltava, which enabled him to accomplish them, measured.

CHAPTER 5

The Battle of Poltava, 1709

"Peter is Russia," writes his biographer Waliszewski, "her flesh and blood, her temperament and genius, her virtue and her vices. . . . Never, I should think," he adds, "have the collective qualities of a nation, good and bad, the heights and the depths of its scale of morality, every feature of its physiognomy, been so summed up in a single personality, destined to be its historic type."[1]

Born on May 30, 1672, physically Peter the Great was a man of commanding stature and powerful build; morally a mixture of strength and weakness, of Asiatic cunning and Slavonic shrewdness. He was impulsive, coarse, brutal and lacking in self-control. A cynic and a debauchee, he was sometimes cowardly, sometimes brave. Subject to sudden fits of uncontrollable temper, restless and changeful, he nevertheless persevered in his aim of transforming his country into a pseudo-European power, and the qualities which gave his obstinate determination force were his indifference to fatigue and sentiment. Not only did he inquire into everything that attracted his attention, but forthwith he would set about to master whatever it might be. He learnt the use of the mariner's compass, the sword, the plane, axe and saw, and even of dental forceps, and seldom failed to put his knowledge into immediate practice. He built a frigate with his own hands, drilled his soldiers, at times did his own cooking, made his own bed and extracted the teeth of his subjects. He frequented low company and rarely passed a day without being the worse for drink. In his orgies his greatest joy was to make his female companions drunk, and in the torture chamber he would lash his victims with the knout. Yet, all in all, he was the greatest of the Russian tsars, for through sheer force of will and intolerant brutality he forced his reluctant subjects to westernize themselves. And had he not been what he was, a ferocious organizer, remembering what his subjects were like, he would certainly have failed. Brutes by nature, they demanded a super-brute as master.

Peter inherited two tasks: the first was to secure the frontiers

---

[1] *Peter the Great*, K. Waliszewski (1898). pp. vi and 69.

of Russia, particularly the southern and western, from attack, and the second was the consolidation of the Russian peoples. In part both had been tackled by his immediate predecessors, but it was not until 1667, when the centuries old feud with Poland was brought to an end by the Treaty of Andrusovo that it became possible to do much in either direction. Next, in 1686, by the Treaty of Moscow, the truce was converted into a Russian-Polish alliance, which enabled Peter in 1696 to wrest Azov from the Turks. It was the first Muscovite victory ever won over the Turks, and it added so greatly to Peter's prestige that he resolved to send a Grand Embassy to the principal western powers to solicit their cooperation in an anti-Turkish crusade.

The Grand Embassy set out on March 21, 1697, and Peter attached himself to it as a volunteer sailor, under the name of Peter Mikhailoff, that he might better study shipbuilding and mix more freely with the common people. The journey carried him through Germany, Austria, France, Holland and England, and in England he worked as a shipwright at Deptford. On his return journey, when he was headed toward Venice, he received news of a serious revolt of the *Strelsy* (Musketeer Corps) at home. At once he changed the course of his journey eastward to Cracow, but when he learnt that the rebellion had been suppressed, he halted at Rawa (east of Lodz) to spend a few days with Frederick Augustus Elector of Saxony, who in 1697 had been elected King of Poland.[1] At his court he became party to an alliance which was to precipitate the second Great Northern War and make Russia a pseudo-European power.

The origins of this portentous event were as follows. In the reign of Charles XI of Sweden, a Livonian squire named John Reinhold Patkul, who had been deprived of his estates, entered the service of Frederick Augustus and, in 1698, persuaded him to form a coalition with Denmark and Russia in order to partition the Swedish empire. When this subject was broached to him, Peter, who saw in the Baltic a more profitable opening than in the Black Sea, agreed to participate. The plan was that, while Frederick IV of Denmark drew Charles XII's forces toward Charles's western provinces, the Saxons and the Russians would simultaneously invade his Baltic provinces. The time seemed propitious, for Charles XI had died the year before and the

---

[1] The noted Marshal Maurice de Saxe was his natural son by Aurora von Königsmark; Saxe's great-great-grand-daughter was George Sand.

government of Sweden was now in the hands of a youth of sixteen.

The tour of Europe had convinced Peter of the inherent superiority of the foreigner, and on the night of his return to Moscow, with characteristic impulsiveness, he determined forthwith to inaugurate the new era of enlightenment. He began with externals, and on the following day he assembled his chief boyars round his wooden hut, and to give them the appearance of foreigners, with a large pair of shears he cut off their long beards andm oustaches. Next, to teach the *Strelsy* that revolt did not pay, he spent the following six weeks in torturings and executions in which he and his favourites played the parts of inquisitors and headsmen.

Soon after another reform followed; by *ukase* the wearing of Russian costumes was prohibited, thenceforth Saxon or Magyar jackets and French and German hose were prescribed. A little later he locked up his wife, the Tsaritsa Eudoxia, in a nunnery, and made Alexander Danilovich Menshikoff, a vendor of meat-pies in the streets of Moscow, his favourite. Meanwhile he set about concluding peace with the Porte, and in July, 1700, a 30-year truce was concluded between Turkey and Russia. On August 8, the day after he received news of this, Peter ordered his army to invade Livonia. But unfortunately for Augustus and Peter they had miscalculated the abilities of Charles XII, who though little more than a boy, at once proved himself to be one of the most remarkable soldiers in history.

Born on June 17, 1682, Charles was knight errant and berserker in one. He lived for war, loved its hardships and adventures even more than victory itself, and the more impossible the odds against him, the more eagerly he accepted them. Wrapped in an impenetrable reserve, his faith in himself was boundless, and his power of self-deception unlimited—nothing seemed to him to be beyond his reach. The numerical superiority of his enemy; the strength of his position; the weariness of his own troops; their lack of armament or supplies; foundering roads, mud, rain, frost and scorching sun appeared to him but obstacles set in his path by Providence to test his genius. Nothing perturbed him, every danger and hazard beckoned him on. High-spirited, but always under self-control, faithful to his word and a considerate disciplinarian, from the moment he took the field he became a legend to his men, *un étandard vivant* which endowed them with a faith in his leadership that has never been surpassed. His

10. THE GREAT NORTHERN WAR, 1700–1721

fearlessness was phenomenal, his energy prodigious, and added to these qualities he possessed so quick a tactical eye that one glance was sufficient to reveal to him the weakest point in his enemy's line or position, which at once he attacked like a thunder-bolt. Such was the boy king whose Baltic provinces the self-indulgent Augustus and the boorish Peter over their wine-cups had decided to filch and divide between themselves.

With an eye on opening "a window upon Europe", Peter, accompanied by 40,000 men, under Field-Marshal Golovin, reached Narva on October 4, 1700, and when the siege artillery came up the city was invested. The besiegers, we are told, marched around the fortress "even as a cat might march around a basin of hot soup."[1]

While thus occupied, suddenly the most astonishing news was received in the Russian camp. Charles, who was supposed to be in clinch with the Danes, was rapidly approaching Narva at the head of an "innumerable army". Unknown to Peter, events in the west had not turned out as planned. Frederick IV, trusting in his superior fleet to hold the Sound against a Swedish attempt to cross it, in April had invaded Holstein. But under cover of a friendly Anglo-Dutch naval demonstration, Charles had slipped across the narrow channel and invaded Zeeland. Since this bold move directly threatened Copenhagen, the Danish War collapsed, and on August 18 it was brought to an end by the Peace of Traventhal.

Freed from the Danes, Charles at once struck eastward. On October 6 he reached Pernau, in Estonia, intending to relieve Riga, which was pressed by the Saxons; but when he heard that Narva was besieged, he turned northward, halted for five weeks at Wernburg to collect his army, set out again on November 13, and on November 19 reached Lagena, nine miles from Narva.

It was only then that Peter became aware of the imminence of his enemy, and so sudden was the surprise that he took panic, appointed the Prince de Croy to the chief command, and with Field-Marshal Golovin he fled the field. In no way disconcerted by his enemy's five to one superiority, on the following day, at the head of 8,000 men, Charles set out under cover of a snow storm to attack the Prince. "Now is our time, with the storm at our backs," he shouted. "They will never see how few we are."[2]

---

[1] *A History of Russia*, V. O. Kluchevsky (1926), vol. IV, p. 50.
[2] Quoted from *Charles XII of Sweden*, Eveline Godley (1928), p. 56.

Half an hour later the outer siege works were stormed and the Russian army put to headlong flight.

After the victory, Charles went into winter quarters at Dorpat (Tartu); his intention was to attack Augustus after the spring thaws. Though he has been severely criticized for not pursuing Peter, strategically he was right, for to advance eastward on Moscow with Augustus free to operate against his communications would have been an act of sheer folly.

Charles left 15,000 men to defend the Baltic provinces, and in June, 1701, he set out on his Polish campaign. On July 8 he crossed the Duna under cover of a smoke cloud, routed 30,000 Saxons and Russians at Dünamünde, and overran Courland. In January, 1702, he set out for Warsaw, which he occupied on May 14, and on July 2 routed the Saxons and Poles at Klissow. Three weeks later, with only a cane in his hand, he stood before Cracow, "and captured it by an act of almost fabulous audacity."[1] Again on April 21, 1703, he defeated the Saxons at Pultusk, and on June 6 he proclaimed Augustus dethroned and appointed in his stead Stanislaus Leszcznski Palatine of Posen. In all these battles he was outnumbered by two or three to one.

While Charles warred in Poland, Peter recovered his nerve and invaded Ingria, where on January 7, 1702, he surprised a Swedish force under General Schlippenbach at Errestfer, and again surprised a Swedish force at Hummelsdorf on July 18. After these successes, on December 11 he occupied the small town of Nöteborg and renamed it Schlüsselburg (Key City). Peter had conquered the historic estuary of the Neva, from which in the ninth century the Varangians had passed southward to Novgorod, and on May 16 the following year, he founded St. Petersburg. Thus, at length, he opened the window upon Europe that he had sought.

In the spring of 1704, after ravaging Ingria, Peter laid siege to Dorpat and Narva. The former surrendered on July 24, and a month later the latter was taken by General Ogilvie–a Scot in the Russian service–and its inhabitants massacred. Peter would now have made peace, but as Charles would not contemplate the suggestion, in 1705 the former decided to help Augustus, and in June Ogilvie appeared before Pultusk. The Swedish general, Adam Lewenhaupt, then fell back on Riga, and the Russians, after occupying Courland, went into winter quarters at Grodno.

---

[1] The Cambridge Modern History, vol. v, p. 592.

In January, 1706, Charles suddenly appeared in eastern Poland, but Ogilvie at Grodno refused to come out of his entrenchments. At the same time Augustus advanced from Grodno into Posen in order to crush a small Swedish army under General Rehnskjöld, a preliminary move to falling upon Charles's rear while Ogilvie attacked his front. The plan failed, for on February 3 Rehnskjöld routed the Saxons at Fraustadt (north of Glogau), and Peter ordered Ogilvie to abandon his heavy artillery and baggage, and to withdraw across the frozen Niemen. Charles pursued him as far as Pinsk, then, to the intense relief of Peter, withdrew into Volhynia. He billeted his troops there and hurried back to Saxony to finish with Augustus.

The appearance of Charles and his army in the very heart of the Empire threw the courts of Europe into consternation. The battle of Ramillies had recently been won by England and her allies, and as they suspected that Louis XIV had bought over the Swedes, the Duke of Marlborough was sent to Leipzig to interview Charles. He came to the conclusion that Charles had no intention of helping the French and Marlborough counselled the Government of Vienna to temporize with him.[1] The outcome was that, on September 24, 1706, the Elector's ministers at Dresden concluded with Charles the Peace of Altranstädt, which was ratified by Augustus on October 20. By its terms Augustus renounced his alliance with Peter and recognized Stanislaus as King of Poland. As this isolated Peter, he tried again to come to terms with Charles, but as Charles refused to communicate with him, Peter prepared to carry on the war single-handed. The plan he decided upon was to avoid pitched battles and to draw his enemy into a devastated country in the trust that "General Winter" would accomplish the rest. "The Tsar, as he expressed it," writes Waliszewski, "was to set the Russians against every Swede, and time, and space, and cold, and hunger were to be his backers."[2]

In the spring of 1707 Peter set to work; bands of Tartars and Kalmuks were sent into Poland toward the Silesian frontier to ravage far and wide, and many villages and towns, including Rawicz and Lissa, were burned to the ground. At the same time the defences of Moscow and the fortifications of the Kremlin were repaired and strengthened; precautions which so terrified the Muscovites that, according to Pleyer, the Austrian agent,

[1] *Marlborough's Dispatches* (1845), vol. III, p. 390.
[2] *Peter the Great*, p. 316.

"Nobody spoke of anything except flight or death."[1] There was nothing astonishing in this, for Charles's prestige now stood so high that, with the exception of a few clear-sighted observers, all Europe predicted that he would crush the Tsar and dictate peace from the Kremlin.

Early in September Charles left Silesia at the head of 24,000 cavalry and 20,000 infantry, the best equipped and most powerful army he had ever commanded; and, when he learnt of his advance, Peter concentrated his main army, 35,000 strong, at Grodno, supported by his cavalry at Minsk. Charles encamped for four months at Slupce on the Vistula, and though the reason for so long a halt is unknown, it probably was to wait until the winter frosts had consolidated the roads and rendered the rivers crossable, for all bridges had been broken or burnt by the Russians. Charles left General Krassow and 8,000 men in Poland to support Stanislaus's unstable throne, and on New Year's day, 1708, he crossed the Vistula and set out for Lithuania, but instead of taking the usual road through Pultusk, Ostrolenka, and Lomza, he marched through the forests and swamps of Masuria, as some think, simply in order to pass by a road which hitherto no army had travelled along.

Peter heard of his advance and hastened to Grodno, and when this was reported to Charles on January 26, at the head of 900 cavalry he rode forward, brushed aside an advanced party of 2,000 Russian horse guarding the bridge over the Niemen, and entered the fortress to find that two hours earlier Peter and his army had abandoned it. From Grodno Charles marched north-east to Smorgonie on the Velya, and thence south-east to Radoszko-wicze, north of Minsk, where he encamped his army until June. Two courses now lay open to him, either to recover his Baltic provinces or to follow up Peter. Unfortunately for the Swedes, he decided on the latter, whereas Peter, who thought that he would adopt the former course, began to remove such of the inhabitants who might sympathize with his enemy. At Dorpat, Pskof, and other towns, young, old, sick and dying, in the middle of winter were packed upon sledges and transported into the interior to reinforce the Russian labour corps.

On June 17 Charles broke camp at Radoszkowicze, and on June 29 he forced the Berezina at Borisov. Next, on July 4, he came up with the Russians under Menshikoff and Sheremétief

---

[1] *Peter the Great*, Eugene Schuyler (1884), vol. II, p. 94.

on the river Wabis (Bibitch), near Holowczyn, and defeated
them. Nevertheless the Russians put up a stout fight; they had
learned much since the siege of Narva, but unfortunately for
the Swedes Charles held his enemy in such complete contempt
that he had learnt nothing at all. From Holowczyn Charles next
marched to Mogilev on the Dnieper, which opened its gates to
him on July 8.

When Charles was at Mogilev, an embassy arrived at his
headquarters from Ivan Stephanovich Mazeppa,[1] Hetman of
the Ukraine, with a proposal that, if Charles would take the
Ukraine under his protection, Mazeppa would support him with
a force of 30,000 Cossacks.[2] Though, at the time, the Ukraine
nominally belonged to Poland and Russia, to all intents and
purposes it was independent, and in the past had often been the
determining factor in the wars between Russians, Poles, and
Tartars. Mazeppa had rendered signal service to Peter during
his Turkish War, and had since been befriended by him; but
frightened by his reforms and afraid that they would lead to the
loss of his independence, when Charles appeared on the scene
he decided to throw in his lot with the Swedes. Charles saw in
his offer a solution of his supply problem, for the Ukraine was
rich in grasses, cereals, flocks and herds, therefore exactly the
terrain needed to subsist his army, and fell in with Mazeppa's
proposal. As he had sufficient supplies at Mogilev to feed his
troops for some time, he decided to wait there for the arrival
of Lewenhaupt from Riga with 11,000 men, a supply column, and
an artillery train, as well as for the news of the outbreak of the
insurrection in the Ukraine. He was too impatient to wait long,
and on August 16 he crossed the Dnieper and marched toward
Tcherikov on the river Sozh. Peter and the main body of the
Russian army then moved from Gorki to Mstislavl, and Charles,
turning northward, met the Russians at Dobry on September 9,
and on their withdrawal after a two-hour fight, followed them to
the Russian frontier at Tatarsk, from which spot the Swedes were
appalled to see stretching before them nothing but the flames
and smoke of burning Russian villages.

For the first time in his life, uncertain what to do, Charles

---

[1] He was the natural son of a Polish nobleman, and in his youth, when a page at
the court of John Casimer, King of Poland, for seducing the Queen he was bound
naked on a horse and let loose upon the Ukrainian steppes. Rescued by Cossacks, in
1687 he was elected their Hetman (Hauptmann or Headman).
[2] Kazak is a word of Tartar origin meaning "a free vagabond".

assembled a council of war, at which General Rehnskjöld prudently advised him to await the arrival of Lewenhaupt, whose supply column had now become indispensable, and then to retire into winter quarters in Livonia. But Charles refused to consider a retreat, and most unfortunately for him, while the council sat, he received an urgent message from Mazeppa in which he "begged him not to delay his march, lest some of his Colonels should change their minds and discover all that had passed to the Czar."[1] This appeal decided the question; Charles refused to wait for Lewenhaupt, then nearing Shklov on the Dnieper, 60 miles away, and set out southward to join Mazeppa, in order that his presence might prevent a betrayal of the plan.

What the plan was exactly is unknown; but according to Adlerfeld it was agreed that while the Swedes wintered in Severia –the region between the rivers Desna and Sozh–Mazeppa was to mobilize his Cossacks and bring into alliance the Cossacks of Byelgorod and the Don, as well as the Kalmuks and, if possible, the Tartars of the Crimea. Further, he was to gather in supplies from the fertile provinces of the Ukraine and Byelgorod. These activities, Adlerfeld considered, "would oblige the Tsar to retreat northwards of the town of *Moscow*, and the river *Volga*, where the country is not near so fruitful as that on the south, and in no wise sufficient to subsist an army so large as his: this together with the fears of the *Russians* that they might be obliged to make head against us in the open field, though they were three times our superiors in number, would put the *Swedish* army in a condition to give laws everywhere, whilst the Tsar must be infallibly lost, and his army wanting subsistence, and a great part of it discontented, would be obliged according to all appearances, to disband themselves, or submit to the conqueror."[2]

In conjunction with this over-optimistic operation, King Stanislaus and General Krassow were to enter Russia with two columns, one to march on Kiev and the other on Smolensk, and General Lybecker from Finland was to invade Ingria at the head of 12,000 men and burn Petersburg. "All these projects", writes Adlerfeld, "were so well concerted, and so dexterously conducted, that every reasonable man who had examined them, must have foretold, humanly speaking, a successful issue for *Sweden*."[3]

---

[1] *The Military History of Charles XII, King of Sweden*, written by the express Order of his Majesty by M. Gustavus Adlerfeld, Chamberlain to the King (English trans. 1740), vol. III, p. 207.
[2] *Ibid.*, vol. III, pp. 193–194.   [3] *Ibid.*, vol. III, p. 196.

Nothing could be further from the truth. Not only was Charles a man of impulse who never worked to plan, but, as Napoleon points out, in this campaign he violated all the principles of war: he failed to concentrate his forces; he abandoned his line of operations; cut himself off from his base; and made a flank march in face of his enemy's army.[1] Outside an offensive idea, Charles had no plan, and in spite of the urgency of Mazeppa's situation, not to wait for Lewenhaupt was an act of strategical insanity. From now onward Charles's actions increasingly show that either his faith in himself, or his contempt for his enemy, or both combined, had unbalanced his mind.

Early in May, Lewenhaupt, then at Riga, had been ordered to make ready 11,000 troops, an artillery and ammunition train and a supply column sufficient to subsist his own force for 12 weeks and the entire army for six. Next, at the beginning of June orders were sent to him to march to the Berezina, but they reached him so late that he was unable to set out before July, and when he did he was not informed that Charles had decided to march south and join Mazeppa.[2] At Shklov, which he reached on September 28, to his consternation he learnt that Charles had already set out southward, and the order he received there was to cross the Dnieper and the Sozh and march to Starodub in the Ukraine. He felt that it was his death warrant, for most of the Russian army stood between these rivers; but as he had no option but to obey, he issued false reports, then slipped across the Dnieper, and on October 9 reached Liesna, a few miles from Propoisk on the Sozh. There he was attacked, and a fierce battle ensued under cover of which the supply train moved on to Propoisk. By nightfall his position had grown so critical that he buried his artillery, burnt his ammunition wagons, mounted many of his exhausted men on their horses, and withdrew to Propoisk. He found it impossible to get the supply train over the Sozh, ordered it to be burnt, and advanced down the river until he found a ford and crossed it. On October 21, with 6,000 men out of the 11,000 he had set out with from Riga, he succeeded in joining Charles and his army.

Meanwhile, in the north, Lybecker had also met with disaster. He took the field in September and had succeeded in crossing the Neva, but when he neared St. Petersburg, he found it too

---

[1] *Correspondance de Napoléon ier*, vol. XXXI, pp. 362–364.
[2] Adlerfeld, vol. III, p. 207.

strongly defended to attack and he had been forced to retire on Viborg, which he did at a loss of 3,000 men, 6,000 horses, and all his heavy baggage. Thus the whole plan of campaign, described with so much confidence by Adlerfeld, was wrecked; two of the three subsidiary armies had been cut up in detail, and Charles with the main army was isolated on the borders of the Ukraine.

Charles's hope now rested on Mazeppa being able to rouse the Cossacks of the Ukraine and to supply him with the necessities of war. But the news of the recent Swedish disasters had so depressing an effect on many of Mazeppa's subordinates that the plot was betrayed to the Tsar.

On November 6 Charles reached the small town of Horki, where he was joined by Mazeppa and 1,500 Cossacks, and on the following day his arrival was reported by Colonel Skoropadsky, the Commander of Starodub, to Peter, who forthwith ordered Menshikoff with all speed and before the Swedes could do so, to occupy Baturin, Mazeppa's capital. He did so on November 13, and "this loss", writes Adlerfeld, "was the more considerable, as there was at that place a great magazine of all sorts of ammunition, of powder, cannons, as well as brass and iron; but above all a great quantity of provisions."[1] Five days later, Mazeppa was deposed, and Colonel Skoropadsky appointed Hetman in his stead. The insurrection then fizzled out, and the Swedish army was left like a lake in a desert, cut-off from all its feeding rivers. Even worse was in store, for one of the severest winters ever experienced in Europe was about to engulf the unfortunate Swedes.

Charles reached the Desna on November 15 to find the Russians lining its far bank; yet, nothing daunted, he rafted his men across the river and put his enemy to flight. Next, he moved on to Romni on the Sula, where his starving men found "in abundance all sorts of provisions . . . with forage, both hay and corn for horses and beasts of burthen."[2] Meanwhile, the Russians, who had marched parallel to their enemy, occupied Sumi and Lebedin on the Psiol, and were daily reinforced by thousands of Cossacks, who constantly harried the Swedish foragers.

In December, a little before Christmas, "so rigorous and hard a frost began that," Adlerfeld says, "the memory of man could

[1] *Ibid.*, vol. III, p. 213.   [2] *Ibid.*, vol. III, p. 214.

produce nothing equal to it,"[1] and it gripped the entire continent of Europe. The Baltic was frozen over, as were the Great Belt and the Ore Sound. In France, the Rhône was frozen; in Italy the canals of Venice were covered with ice; also the estuary of the Tagus. In central Europe fruit trees were killed by the frost, and on the plains of the Ukraine the cold was so intense that birds fell dead as they flew through the air, and casks of spirit froze into solid blocks of ice.

Though Charles was comfortably placed at Romni, the proximity of the Russians insulted his vanity, and Peter, who correctly gauged its depth, drew him into a trap by directing most of his army toward the town of Gadiatz, then occupied by four battalions of Swedes, and at the same time he ordered a strong detachment to occupy Romni should Charles move out of it. In spite of the intense cold and against the advice of his generals, Charles, when he heard that Gadiatz was threatened, forthwith marched to its relief. At once the Russians occupied Romni, set fire to Gadiatz and withdrew from that place. When Charles arrived at Gadiatz he found that over one-third of its houses had been burnt and that there were not enough left to shelter his troops.

In the march from Romni to Gadiatz the suffering endured by the Swedish soldiers is indescribable; ill-fed and ill-clothed, some 3,000 were frozen to death and many more were disabled by frostbite. Yet Charles exacted nothing from his men that he did not cheerfully undergo himself, and to him this appalling disaster was but another item for his saga. Early in January, in retaliation for the loss of Romni he took the small town of Veprik, and toward the end of February with only 400 men he scattered 7,000 Russians at Krosnokutsk (west of Kharkov), and at Oposzanaya defeated 5,000 men with 300 men. Both these engagements were won more by the terror of his name than by force of arms.

At the end of February, the frost broke, and the spring thaws put an end to active operations for several months. Peter set out for Voronezh to inspect his Black Sea fleet, while Charles encamped his army at Rudiszcze between the Psiol and the Vorskla. When Lewenhaupt joined him, his army had numbered 41,000 men, now it had shrunk to 20,000, of whom some 2,000 were crippled; his artillery had been reduced to 34 pieces, and most of the remaining powder was spoilt. Nevertheless, Charles was

[1] Adlerfeld, vol. III, pp. 214–215.

well-contented with what he had accomplished, and on April 11 he wrote to Stanislaus: "I and the army are in very good condition"; but Count Piper, his First Minister, had another story to tell. At about the same time, in a letter to his wife, he said: "The army is in an indescribably pitiful state."[1]

By the spring of 1709 the situation had become so critical that the Swedish generals urged Charles to return to Poland. This he refused to do, for he was still confident of final success. Only recently he had sent orders to Stanislaus to join him with Krassow's army by way of Volhynia; also he had come to an agreement with the Zaporogian Cossacks to attack the Russians from the south, and he was still hopeful that he would gain the assistance of the Tartars. With Charles it was always the same: once he had decided upon something, he concluded that either it was accomplished or inevitably would be. "A general," once wrote Napoleon, "should never paint pictures, it is the worst thing he can do," by which he meant that he must base his calculations on facts and not on fancies. Yet never did a general so easily fall victim to his fancies as did Charles. He was always painting pictures with himself in the foreground; they were nothing other than portraits of his imagination in which realistic detail was either totally lacking or of no interest. All he sought was an excuse for self-expression.

Nevertheless, in spite of these imaginings, time had to be gained, for Stanislaus was 900 miles away. More important still, supplies were nearly exhausted, and in order to replenish them as well as to strengthen his position, against the advice of all his generals, Charles decided to lay siege to Poltava, a small fortified town and depôt on the Kiev-Kharkov Road, close to the western bank of the Vorskla, which ran due north and south. That his artillery was inadequate and its powder mostly spoilt; that he had not sufficient force to complete the investment, and that in the vicinity Menshikoff with 80,000 Russians lay ready to march on the sound of his guns, in no way ruffled his calculations. When, on May 2, the siege was opened, Charles was astonished that the town did not yield at the first shot. "What!" he exclaimed, "I really believe the Russians are mad, and will defend themselves in a regular way!"[2] Six weeks later they were still defending themselves.

[1] Quoted from *Peter the Great*, Eugene Schuyler, vol. ii, p. 142.
[2] *Ibid.*, vol. ii, p. 146.

No sooner had the siege begun than Menshikoff advanced his army to the eastern bank of the Vorskla opposite Poltava and entrenched it; a Swedish covering force lined the opposite bank. Meanwhile Peter was engaged in putting down a rising of the Zaporogian Cossacks, which had been instigated by Mazeppa, and it was not until their great water-fortress (*syech*) among the islands of the Dnieper had been stormed that he was free to rejoin his army, which he did early in June. First, he decided to send out raiding parties to restrict his enemy's foraging, and next, under cover of a feint crossing of the Vorskla to the south of the fortress, to carry the bulk of his army over to its western bank to the north of Poltava: this he planned to start on June 17.

While the siege was pressed, the position of the Swedes steadily grew worse, until the situation became so critical that Charles sought the advice of Lewenhaupt, who again counselled him to retire across the Dnieper and regain contact with Poland. Brushing this counsel aside, early on the morning of June 17 – his twenty-seventh birthday – alarmed by the noise of Peter's feint attack, accompanied by Lewenhaupt he rode out toward the Vorskla. They approached the enemy within musket shot, and first Lewenhaupt's horse was shot under him, and then Charles was hit by a ball in the foot. He refused to dismount, but continued his reconnaissance, and only on his return was 'it discovered that the ball had penetrated the whole length of the sole from heel to toes. The wound was so serious that it placed Charles *hors de combat* at the very time when his presence was most needed. For the Swedes it was a crowning misfortune.

When he heard of Charles's mishap, Peter, who thus far had on principle avoided battle, at once resolved to accept it, and in order to draw his enemy into the open field, under cover of night he evacuated the entrenched camp he had built since June 17, north of Poltava, and moved downstream, where he built another one within two miles of the town. Like the first, it was in the form of an entrenched quadrilateral; its eastern face rested on the Vorskla and its southern was covered by a wood intersected by ravines.

While Charles lay prostrate, he received news from Stanislaus and Krassow that they were so fully engaged they could not leave Poland, and that the Sultan would neither directly nor indirectly, through the Tartars, come to his aid. From this it became clear that, as

Charles refused to raise the siege and retire, to avoid defeat through starvation the sole alternative left him was to attack. On June 27 he assembled a council of war at which, after appointing Field-Marshal Rehnskjöld to command in his stead, he ordered him to attack the Russian camp on the following day. Thereupon Lewenhaupt, in order that the maximum numbers of attacking troops might be concentrated, proposed that the siege should first be raised. But Charles would not agree to this; therefore 2,000 men were detailed to observe the fortress, 2,400 more to guard the baggage, and 1,200 to remain on the western bank of the Vorskla to prevent a force of Russians still posted there from taking the Swedish attack in flank. These detachments decided upon, Rehnskjöld was left with barely 12,500 troops, half infantry and half cavalry, and the former were so short of powder and ball that they were ordered to carry out the attack with the bayonet. Also, except for four light cannon, it was decided to leave the whole of the artillery behind.

This may seem to be a policy of despair; yet it is nothing of the kind, for Charles's tactics were not based on numbers or fire power, but on speed and shock; his aim was always to strike so decisive a blow at the opening of a battle that his enemy's equilibrium would be irretrievably unhinged. Like Alexander the Great's cavalry assaults against poorly disciplined and indifferently led troops, Charles's system of attack had succeeded again and again; but this time it was destined to fail, not so much because of Russian numerical superiority, but because Russian discipline and leadership had improved, and above all because, on account of Charles's wound, Swedish unity of command was non-existent.

We are told that Rehnskjöld had no plan,[1] and this is understandable, because Charles had no intention of relinquishing the chief command, and when he appointed the Field-Marshal in his stead he never intended him to be more than his deputy. It is important to bear this in mind, for otherwise the battle of Poltava becomes unintelligible.

Charles had a very definite plan, or better stated, idea of attack, though it was not set down in writing. But before defining it, it is necessary to describe the battlefield.

As mentioned, Peter's entrenched camp was an extensive quadrilateral with its eastern face on the Vorskla, therefore it

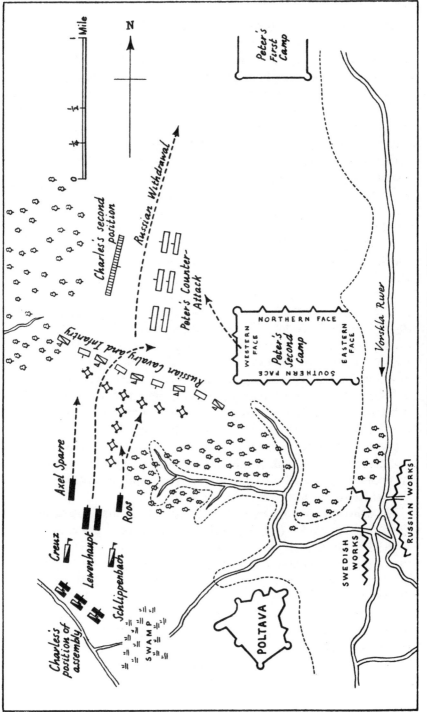

II. BATTLE OF POLTAVA, 1709

could not be attacked on that side. Its southern face, because
of a wood intersected by ravines, was also unattackable, or at
least quite unsuited to a Carolingian attack by *élan*. Westward of
its western face stretched a considerable plain beyond which
lay a wood, and between this wood and the one on the south side
of the camp was a gap of open ground. In order to attack the
camp from the direction of Poltava, it was necessary to pass
through this gap, and Peter had had the prevision to block it
with six redoubts. Further, to restrict the use of the gap as an
entrance, he was, at the time of the battle, building four more
redoubts southward of, and at right angles to, the first six, in
order, tactically, to narrow down the use of the gap by cutting
it into two channels.

To any other general except Charles, the forcing of the gap
would have entailed a methodical operation in which artillery
would have been used to reduce the redoubts, and thereby open
the door to the battlefield—the plain. Charles would have none
of this, he was not a "bombarding" general, he was an "assaulting" general. Therefore his intention was to rush the gap without
attempting first to reduce the redoubts, next, by shock to scatter
any enemy troops in rear of the redoubts, and lastly, by rapidly
wheeling his army to the right, to drive these scattered troops
pell-mell into the entrenched camp and enter it on their heels.

Had he not been wounded, he might have succeeded in his
aim; for, as was his wont, he would have directed the whole
attack by galloping from one point to another as the battle
proceeded. But compelled to take the field in a horse-litter, his
usual activity was greatly restricted. The result of this is noted by
Adlerfeld, who comments on the battle:

"In short, that wonderful activity which had appeared in
our troops when the King himself led them before he was wounded,
and when he used to fly to all quarters to animate them, was not
observable on this day. In a word, his wound was the source of
all our misfortunes. . . ."[1] And again: "All this might have been
yet remedied, if the King had not been wounded; but as he lay
on his litter . . . it being impossible to convey him quick enough
from one place to another to distribute his orders, there was in
reality no true command on that day in the army and confusion
at last beginning to arise, every one would act according to his
caprice."[2]

[1] Adlerfeld, vol. III, p. 232.   [2] *Ibid.*, vol. III, p. 231.

Yet, it may be asked, could not his deputy Rehnskjöld, have acted for him? The answer is "No", because in the type of war practised by Charles, which depended above all things upon personality and tactical eye, Rehnskjöld could no more replace Charles than Parmenio could have replaced Alexander. With this background in mind, the chaotic nature of the battle becomes fully understandable.

After he had assembled his 12,500 troops, in order to surprise his enemy at dawn, at midnight on June 27 Rehnskjöld made a night advance to a position facing the gap; but unfortunately for the Swedes, though all possible care was taken to prevent the Russians ascertaining what was on foot, Peter got wind of the movement and drew up a considerable force of cavalry and foot in rear of the redoubts.[1]

At dawn the Swedish infantry advanced in four columns, two on either side of the four unfinished redoubts, with the cavalry following in six columns. But from what happened during the battle it would appear that the order of attack adopted was one of a central column of infantry under Lewenhaupt, flanked by two wings, the left consisting of General Axel Sparre's infantry division, followed by one-half of the cavalry under General Creuz, and the right of General Roos's infantry division and the rest of the cavalry under General Schlippenbach. The left wing advanced on the western and the right wing on the eastern side of the four unfinished redoubts,[2] the former was accompanied by Charles and Rehnskjöld.

Because of the four redoubts, which acted like a breakwater, the battle at once developed into two separate actions, and without great difficulty the left wing drove the Russians behind their redoubts, "which", says Adlerfeld, "we passed in the midst of a violent discharge, both from their small arms and cannons, which latter played incessantly on the spaces between the redoubts".[3] Nevertheless, the Russian infantry was routed and their cavalry stampeded toward the Vorskla.

In this attack we sense the presence of Charles, for the Swedes paid no attention to the fire of the redoubts and rushed the gaps

---

[1] *The History of the Wars of his late Majesty Charles XII, King of Sweden,* by a Scots Gentleman in the Swedish Service (compiled by Daniel Defoe, second edit., 1720), p. 178.

[2] How the centre advanced is not mentioned; but presumably on the right of. or n rear of, the left wing.

[3] Adlerfeld, vol. III, p. 227.

between them with their usual *élan*. But with the right wing it was different, for Roos attempted "to carry them [the redoubts] sword-in-hand one after another, instead of passing through the intervening spaces, as the King had done with his column."[1] The result was that Roos's losses were heavy, and worse still, his command became separated from the rest of the army. Peter noticed this and sent forward 10,000 troops under General Rensel to cut him off, and at about the same time General Schlippenbach, who as a cavalryman probably understood Charles's tactics better than Roos did, realized Roos's predicament and accompanied by Captain Palmfeld, galloped forward to seek the King and acquaint him with the situation, but unfortunately he rode into one of Rensel's patrols and was captured. Shortly after, Roos saw a large body of troops advancing toward him and sent out Captain Funck to discover who they were. Funck, seeing General Schlippenbach among them and mistaking them for Swedes, also fell into Rensel's hands. Immediately after Roos's men were surrounded.

When this disaster occurred, the Swedish left wing entered the plain and was halted by Charles between "the enemy's grand entrenchment and the redoubts". Charles saw Rensel's corps in the distance, mistook it for Roos's division, and sent General Gyllenkrok back to Mazeppa to bring up the artillery and the troops he had with him "to assist in and support the attack on the entrenchment"; because, writes Adlerfeld, "This had been the King's resolution on the morning before the battle began, for he found that if he had then stayed to bring up the ordnance he should have lost too much time, and delayed the execution of his design of passing hastily through the redoubts."[2] But when he approached Rensel's corps and recognized it to be Russian, Gyllenkrok hastily returned to the King, who shortly after learnt that Roos had been taken prisoner and his men either dispersed or killed.

It would appear that immediately after this there occurred the much disputed incident of the whole battle. While Roos was surrounded and Charles formed up in the plain, Lewenhaupt with the centre, broke through the line of redoubts, entered the plain, and was about to advance against the western side of Peter's entrenched camp and storm it, when he received an order—

[1] Adlerfeld., vol. III, p. 227.
[2] *Ibid.*, vol. III, p. 229.

so he says—from "a loyal servant of the King" to halt.[1] Though amazed and indignant, for he believed that he had victory within grasp, he had no option but to obey it. Who sent the order has never been made clear; Rehnskjöld vigorously denied that he had done so, and so did Charles. The truth would seem to be that throughout the battle Charles and Rehnskjöld gave orders alternatively, and that after the initial success of the Swedish left wing, confusion reigned and orders and counter-orders chased each other over the battlefield.

Once Lewenhaupt had halted, the fleeting opportunity passed, and Peter, who after the first success of Sparre and Creuz had been on the point of flying, encouraged by the capture of Roos's corps, ordered up every gun he had to meet the final Swedish assault which he saw Charles preparing; for Charles had decided not to wait for Mazeppa and the artillery, but to strike, as he believed, "while the iron was hot".

Unfortunately for Charles the iron was now cold, for Peter, who had recovered his nerve, had, while Charles waited for Roos, drawn 40,000 troops out of his entrenched camp, supported them with some 100 cannon, and formed them into line of battle. Nothing daunted, Charles gave the order to advance, and 4,000 Swedish infantry with cavalry on their flanks moved forward, "directly to the enemy, charging them with great Fury and good Success", so writes the anonymous Scots Gentleman of Defoe's history. He adds: "but the Cannon from the entrench'd Camp advancing, the Troops opening in several Places for their playing upon us, it was impossible our Foot could keep their Order, or the Men stand the Fire of 70 Pieces of Cannon, loaden with Cartouches of small Shot. . . ."[2] It would seem that about half the Swedish infantry was mown down and the remainder was swallowed up in the Russian masses as they closed in from all sides. About noon the battle ended.

Peter behaved with conspicuous bravery during the action, and was hit by three musket balls, one through the hat, one in the saddle, and one glanced off a metal cross suspended round his neck. Charles, as usual, was in the midst of the fray. Twenty-one out of his 24 bearers and attendants were killed or wounded and his litter was smashed by a cannon ball. He was lifted on to

---

[1] For this incident see *Charles XII and the Collapse of the Swedish Empire*, R. Nisbet Bain (1902), pp. 186–187.
[2] *The History of the Wars*, etc., p. 180.

a horse and in the rout led from the field. A few hours later the *débris* of the Swedes was collected in the camp they had quitted the day before, when it was found that of the 12,500 who had gone into battle some 3,000 had been killed and wounded and 2,800 made prisoners. Among the latter were Field-Marshal Rehnskjöld, four generals, and five colonels. The Russian casualties were about 1,300 in all.

Peter's joy was so extreme that he did not pursue his retreating enemy but sat down to a banquet to which he invited the most distinguished of his prisoners, and it was not until five o'clock in the afternoon that he sent Prince Michael Galitsin to follow the Swedes.

Charles drew in his detachments and collected the fragments of his army, then set out down the Vorskla for the Dnieper, and on June 29 arrived at the small town of Perevolotchna, at the junction of the two rivers. There it was found that all boats and bridging material had been either destroyed or removed, but sufficient rafts were built to allow Charles, Mazeppa, and some 1,000 horsemen to be ferried across the Dnieper. Charles left Lewenhaupt in command of the army, and with his escort rode as fast as his wound permitted to the river Bug and thence to Bender on the Dniester, where he was well received by the Turks. In the meantime Lewenhaupt attempted to cross the Vorskla and march for the Black Sea; but he found it impossible to accomplish and on June 30 he surrendered with over 12,000 men on terms to Menshikoff.

When Peter received the news of the capitulation, he wrote to Admiral Apraksin, "Now, with God's help, the last stone has been laid to the foundation of St. Petersburg."[1] He then sent part of his army to Riga and another part to war against Stanislaus in Poland and proceeded to Kiev. There, in the Church of St. Sophia, a solemn thanksgiving service was held, at which Theofan Prokopovitch, the rector of the Bratsky monastery, in a panegyric on the victory said: "When our neighbours hear what has happened, they will say, it was not in a foreign country that the Swedish army and the Swedish power ventured, but rather into some mighty sea! They have fallen in and disappeared, even as lead is swallowed up in water."[2] These were prophetic words, as other would-be conquerors of Russia were to discover in times to come.

---

[1] *Peter the Great*, Eugene Schuyler, vol. ii, p. 152.
[2] *Peter the Great*, K. Waliszewski, p. 326.

The campaign which followed Poltava very nearly cancelled out everything Peter had won. He had learnt nothing from the mistakes of his great antagonist and committed the self-same blunder which had brought Charles to ruin—he plunged deep into an enemy country in defiance of communications and supply. Instead of leaving well alone, he instructed his ambassador at the Porte to demand the extradition of Charles and Mazeppa. The Turks considered it to their advantage to prolong the Russo-Swedish war, and urged on by Charles, who now showed as much skill with his pen as he had with his sword, in October, 1710, the Porte threw the Russian ambassador into prison and sent Baltaji Mehemet, the Grand Vizier, and 200,000 men to the Russian frontier.

The situation became so threatening that, in March, 1711, Peter declared war, and, in June, General Sheremétief, in command of his army, soon found the land so wasted by the Turks that it was impossible to provision his men. Next, Peter joined him and, like Charles, foolishly decided to continue the advance. On July 16 he reached Jassy. There the difficulties of supply became insuperable, and when he learnt of Baltaji's approach, he fell back on to the Pruth and entrenched his army, reduced through starvation to 38,000 men. On August 11, the Grand Vizier, at the head of 190,000 troops, assaulted the Russian camp and was repulsed. Had he then but invested it, Peter's position was so desperate that, within a few days, his capitulation would have been certain, Muscovy would, in all probability, have revolted, and the whole course of history have been changed. Instead, the Grand Vizier opened negotiations, with the result that Peter was allowed to withdraw his starving army on the engagement that he ceded Azov, dismantled Taganrog and other fortresses, ceased interfering in Polish affairs, and granted Charles a free passage to Sweden. Charles, who had provided the Grand Vizier with the plan of campaign, was furious when he learnt of these terms, accused him of treason, and procured his dismissal.

A series of intricate negotiations and half-cock declarations of war on the part of the Porte followed, and dragged on until 1713, when the Sultan, who feared the temper of his Janissaries, requested Charles to leave Turkey. This he flatly refused to do, and on February 1, when at Bender, he was besieged by his host. For eight hours, with no more than 40 men, he defended his unfortified house against 12,000 Turks and 12 guns, and not until

13

200 of them had been killed – 10 falling to his own sword – was he overpowered and taken prisoner. Negotiations with Russia were then resumed, and finally the differences between Russia and the Porte were, on July 16, settled by the Peace of Adrianople.

At length, on September 20, 1714, Charles left Turkey, and rode, almost unattended, across Austria and Germany. In November he unexpectedly appeared at Stralsund, which, throughout 1715, he defended with all but superhuman heroism against a coalition of Great Britain (Hanover), Russia, Prussia, Saxony, and Denmark. On December 23, with Stralsund reduced to a heap of rubble, he escaped to Sweden, raised another army and, on December 12, 1718, while besieging the Norwegian fortress of Fredriksten, was shot dead in his trenches. Thus died, surely, the most extraordinary soldier in the history of war.

Sweden was now nearly exhausted, and in September, 1719, in order to continue the war with Russia, she came to terms with Hanover, Prussia and Denmark, and ceded Bremen and Verden to the first and Stettin to the second. For two more years she gallantly held out, after which, physically unable to continue the contest, negotiations were opened with Russia. These negotiations, on August 30, 1721, led to the end of the Second Great Northern War and the signing of the Peace of Nysted. By its terms, Russia gained Livonia, Estonia, Ingria, the Finnish province of Keksholm and the fortress of Viborg, and Sweden ceased to be a great power.

The battle of Poltava was more than the usual tussle between two neighbouring peoples, for it was a trial of strength between two civilizations, that of Europe and of Asia, and because this was so, though little noticed at the time, the Russian victory on the Vorskla was destined to be one of the most portentous events in the modern history of the western world. By wresting the hegemony of the north from Sweden; by putting an end to Ukrainian independence, and by ruining the cause of Stanislaus in Poland, Russia, an essentially Asiatic power, gained a foothold on the counterscarp of eastern Europe.

But at the time, the importance of Poltava lay more in what it established than in what it overthrew. It showed Peter that his principal task was to create a regular army and a Baltic fleet, in order to maintain his position *vis à vis* Europe. Further, it showed him that the upkeep of these forces demanded financial reforms, and that these reforms demanded the substitution of

European for Oriental administration. As Kluchevsky writes: " . . . his capital legislative Acts belong exclusively to the post-Poltavan period, and therefore war must have been the factor that converted his administrative legislation into institutional, and himself, originally only a builder of ships and a military organizer, into an all-round purveyor of reforms." Kluchevsky further points out that " . . . since the driving-power of Peter's activity was always war, and the initial field of operations of that activity was military reform, and its ultimate goal was financial reorganization, Peter began his work by reforming the State's defensive resources, and only when that had been done went on to reform the State's internal system."[1] Therefore, had he been crushed at Poltava, these mighty schemes would never have taken shape. The most ominous for Europe was that by the close of his reign he had created a regular army of 210,000 men supported by 109,000 irregulars, and had built a fleet of 48 ships of the line and 787 galleys and lesser vessels. Like the hordes of Xerxes, this vast host gloomed over the eastern horizon of the west, a portent of yet another Asiatic invasion. In shadowy form Poltava was Marathon in reverse.

Besides these major reforms, Peter's fertile brain poured forth innumerable minor ones: such as the prohibition of compulsory marriage; the freeing of women from the *terem* (a species of purdah); the paving of Moscow; the establishment of hospitals, medical schools and sanitary inspectors; the introduction of a new alphabet; the opening of iron, copper and silver mines; and the reaping of corn by scythes instead of sickles. He stood for western efficiency, cost what it might.

The barbaric conditions of his people and the ruthlessness of his will compelled him to resort to terror and compulsion. "The Russia of Peter the Great", writes Waliszewski, "is a factory and a camp", for he made his "Russians a nation of officials, of labourers and of soldiers."[2] In 1708, he sent a forced labour corps of 40,000 men to build St. Petersburg, and when they perished in the swamps of the Neva another 40,000 were conscripted, and yet another. These arbitrary measures caused so much opposition that, in 1713, "informers were invited to report all cases of defalcation to the Tsar, and promised the rank and property of those whom they denounced."[3] Thus were born the

---

[1] *A History of Russia*, vol. IV, pp. 59–60.   [2] *Peter the Great*, p. 561.
[3] *Cambridge Modern History*, vol. V, p. 534.

ancestors of the Tcheka and the Ogpu. In the course of his reign, Waliszewski informs us: " . . . the diminution of the population was calculated at twenty per cent. This does not allow for the terrible holocaust offered up on the altar of civilization, in the prisons and torture-chambers of Prebrajensköie, on the Red Square at Moscow, and in the dungeons of the fortress of St. Peter and St. Paul."[1]

The brutalities of his reign reached their climax during the trial and execution of his son, the unfortunate Tsarevitch Alexis, when an orgy of terror was let loose in St. Petersburg. "There have been so many accusations in the town," wrote La Vie in January, 1718, "that it seems like a place of disaster; we all live in a sort of public infection, everyone is either an accuser or an accused person."[2] People were broken on the wheel; mutilated by loss of tongue, ears and nose, and pressed on red-hot iron bars. Alexis was put to the torture, forced to make a false confession, and condemned by 127 judges who voiced their sovereign's will. It would appear that he was knouted to death.

Peter married this brutality to European efficiency, and out of their union emerged Russia, not only as an empire, but also as a pseudo-western power, and the official birthday was October 22, 1721. On that day, after a solemn thanksgiving service in the Troitsa Cathedral at St. Petersburg in celebration of the Peace of Nysted, Peter was proclaimed "Father of the Fatherland, Peter the Great, and Emperor of all Russia", which at the time extended from the Baltic to the Sea of Okhotsk and from the Arctic Circle to Astrabad on the Caspian.

Such was the harvest which followed Poltava. "You can believe", wrote Leibniz, "how much the revolution in the north astonished many people. It is commonly said that the Tsar will be formidable for all Europe, and will be like a northern Turk."[3] A new threat to Europe had arisen; again Asia was on the move, but this time her Mongoloid hordes were girt in the panoply of the West.

---

[1] *Peter the Great*, p. 560.   [2] *Ibid.*, p. 536.
[3] Quoted from *Peter the Great*, Eugene Schuyler, p. 160. In 1869 the French economist C. T. Delamarre wrote: " It is Europe as a whole which was defeated with Charles XII at Poltava. On the morrow of this victory the Muscovites for the first time gained a foothold in Europe by taking possession of Little Russia (Eastern Ukraine)." *Le problème de l'indépendance de L'Ukraine et la France*, Emanuel Evain (1931), pp. 80-81.

The rise and expansion of Prussia

Better described as the Brandenburg-Prussian State, Prussia was the second of the new powers which emerged during the seventeenth century; yet her origins, like those of Russia, dated from the tenth century, and also like Russia, her expansion was caused by military necessity, for she was a land-locked country surrounded by hostile powers.

In the year 919 (see Chronicle 12 (Vol. I) the Saxon Duke Henry the Fowler founded the Mark of Brandenburg (Brennibor) as a bulwark against the Slavs, and a great colonizing movement began, which in three centuries added all the lands between the Elbe and the Oder to Germany and Christendom. In 1226 the region of the Spree was acquired and Berlin was founded. During the same year the Polish Duke of Masonia appealed to Hermann von Salza, Grand Master of the Order of the Teutonic Knights, to convert the pagan Prussians, a Slavonic tribe inhabiting the region between the mouths of the Vistula and the Niemen. The result was that, between 1231 and 1310, the land–later to become known as East Prussia–was conquered; the towns of Elbing, Königsberg and Danzig were founded, and the Prussians were largely exterminated and replaced by German settlers. In 1313, the headquarters of the Order was permanently established at Marienburg.

With its missionary task ended, coupled with the decline of the Hanseatic League, the union between the Scandinavian States, and the rise of Poland under the Jagello dynasty, the Order fell into a decline, and, in 1410, on the field of Tannenberg, its knights sustained a crushing defeat at the hands of the Poles, from which they never recovered. Seven years later the margravate of Brandenburg passed to Frederick Hohenzollen, Burgrave of Nuremberg, and, in 1466, in accordance with the Perpetual Peace of Thorn, Prussia was divided into two parts. West Prussia, re-named Royal Prussia, including Danzig, became part of Poland, and East, or Ducal Prussia, was restored to the Order as a Polish fief. Lastly, in 1618, on the outbreak of the Thirty Years War, Ducal Prussia was permanently united with Brandenburg and seventeenth-century Prussia was born.

The Thirty Years War was both the death-bed of German medieval civilization and the cradle of Franco-German rivalry, which was to distract Europe for 300 years. When the war ended in 1648, France was powerful and centralized, Germany disrupted and exhausted, and though Brandenburg lost nearly half its population and all its industry and trade, Prussia was untouched. Balked from expansion northward by the English Channel and southward by the Pyrenees, French aggrandizement flowed eastward into Germany, and between the Peace of Westphalia, in 1648, and 1704, when the French were decisively defeated at Blenheim, western Germany was invaded repeatedly. "Louis XIV," writes the Duc de Broglie[1] in his *Frédéric II et Maria Theresa,* "sent his armies so many times across the Rhine needlessly and without a pretext that at length patriotism awoke from its slumber. There are certain faults which Providence punishes by denying them oblivion. The soldiers of Turenne little knew to what an undying hatred on the part of Germany they devoted the very name of their country, when they inscribed it with letters of blood and fire on all the hills of the Palatinate." Thus was German nationalism fostered, as French nationalism had been during the Hundred Years War, and in Brandenburg it began to take form when in December, 1640, Frederick William succeeded to the margravate of Brandenburg.

First he set out to colonize his devastated territories, and by offering complete religious toleration to all comers, thousands of Dutch, French, and other peoples migrated to Brandenburg to become the "true-born Prussians" of later days. Next, he realized that the power of a State is to be measured by its fighting forces, and he improved upon the small standing army created by his father in 1637, and raised it to 25,000 strong. He used it both as a diplomatic and strategical weapon, prevented Ducal Prussia from falling into the hands of the Poles and Swedes, and in 1675 he routed the latter at Fehrbellin, after which he became known to history as the "Great Elector". On his death, in 1688, he was succeeded by his son Frederick, who at Königsberg, on January 18, 1701, crowned himself Frederick I King of Prussia. In May, 1702, as a member of the Grand Alliance against France, Frederick put 14,000 men into the field, a contingent eventually raised to 40,000 strong, which played a notable part at Blenheim,

---

[1] Jacques Duc de Broglie (1821–1901) was the great-grandson of Frederick the Great's opponent at Rossbach.

Ramillies, Oudenarde, and Malplaquet. Though Prussia gained little from the Peace of Utrecht, the part played by Frederick's army in the War of the Spanish Succession was so considerable that when it ended in 1713 the peoples of Brandenburg-Prussia emerged as the Prussian nation–a standing challenge to France.

Frederick I died two months before the Peace of Utrecht was signed, and was succeeded by his son Frederick William (1713-1740), then aged 24 and a figure of great historical importance. Like his contemporary, Peter the Great, he was a man of enormous industry, violent, brutal, and possessed of the manners of a drill sergeant. He instituted rigid economies in every department of state; put the finances of his kingdom in order, and settled 40,000 south Germans in East Prussia. His parsimony, which was remarkable for an absolute monarch, enabled him to raise the strength of his army from 50,000 to 80,000 officers and men; the latter he either impressed or kidnapped in slave-hunts, and the former he conscripted, all nobles of military age were compelled to serve after training in *Cadettenhaüser* (Military Schools). The strength of his army lay not so much in its size as in its discipline and training, which were so brutal that under his son active service was considered a relief from barrack life. His one hobby was his regiment of giant grenadiers, for which he kidnapped men in every country, including Ireland. No abnormally tall man was safe; even the Abbé Bastiani was sand-bagged and collared while celebrating Mass in an Italian church, and any girl who in inches matched his grenadiers was seized in order to mate with them.

Vigorous in everything he did, his queen presented him with 14 children; the fourth, born on January 24, 1713, was christened Karl Frédéric, and is known to history as Frederick II and the Great. His behaviour toward him was nearly as abominable as was that of Peter the Great toward Alexis. He spat in his food to prevent him eating too much; in 1730 he attempted to strangle him with a curtain cord; later he had him condemned to death, and when his councillors refused to be party to his son's murder, he shot his friend Katte before his son's eyes. On May 31, 1740, Frederick William I died, and when those around him sang the hymn, "Naked I came into the world and naked I shall go," he had just sufficient strength to mutter, "No, not quite naked; I shall have my uniform on."

Frederick II found himself at the head of a highly efficient

State, with a well filled treasury and the best trained army in Europe. But Prussia was strategically weak, for she had no natural land frontiers and was surrounded by aggressive neighbours. These circumstances demanded that, in order to remain strong, she must expand; but to do so demanded a pretext, however flimsy, and this Frederick found ready-made for him in the question of the Austrian Succession.

When the Emperor Joseph died without male issue in 1711, his brother Charles succeeded him as the Emperor Charles VI. As Charles also had no son, a family compact, known as the "Pragmatic Sanction", was agreed upon. According to this, Charles's daughter, Maria Theresa, was given priority of succession to the Habsburg dominions over Joseph's daughter, Maria Amalia, who in 1722, became the wife of Charles Albert of Bavaria. After prolonged negotiations, this compact was recognized by every important court in Europe, except the Bavarian. Thus matters stood, when on October 20, 1740, Charles VI died.

Realizing that the compact was fragile, that the States of Europe were at sixes and sevens, and knowing that Austria was unprepared for war, Frederick mobilized his army and sent Count Gotter to Vienna with a letter in which he recognized Maria Theresa's (1740-1780) succession and offered her military assistance in case of need, in return for which he proposed to occupy Silesia, pending the settlement of his claim to it, which he based on the long annulled *Erbverbrüderung* (Heritage-Brotherhood) of 1537 between the Margrave of Brandenburg and the Duke of Liegnitz. Frederick received an emphatic denial of his claim and on December 16 he ordered his army to cross the Silesian frontier and march on Breslau. Thus was precipitated the War of the Austrian Succession.

At once Maria Theresa appealed to the guarantors of the Pragmatic Sanction for assistance; but their standard of honour was no higher than Frederick's, and it was not until the Austrians were badly defeated by Field-Marshal Schwerin at Mollwitz on April 10, 1741, that the conflict became general. Charles Albert of Bavaria set out to gain the Imperial Crown by an invasion of Bohemia; the French, who wanted predominance in Europe, crossed the Rhine as Bavaria's ally; and the Saxons and Savoyards joined in the attack on Maria Theresa while the English and Dutch hastened to support her indirectly by preparing to attack

France. Frederick again defeated the Austrians at Chotusitz on May 17, and entered into alliance with France, when, on the promptings of England, Maria Theresa came to terms with him and ceded to him Lower Silesia, so that she might concentrate against the French and Bavarians. Then Frederick withdrew from the war and Saxony followed suit.

Freed from Prussia and Saxony, Maria Theresa set out to annex Bavaria in compensation for Silesia. In the depths of winter she forced the French out of Prague, and on the Rhine, on June 27, 1743, to add to this reverse, the French were defeated by the English and Hanoverians at Dettingen. Alarmed by these events, and as he realized that an Austrian triumph might lead to the ruin of Prussia, in September, 1744, Frederick re-entered the war and invaded Austria, but was outmanœuvred by Marshal Traun. Slowly the tide turned in favour of the French, Marshal de Saxe beat the English at Fontenoy on May 11, 1745, and again at Lauffeld on July 2, 1746. Meanwhile Frederick, who had been forced out of Austria, was followed by the Austrians and Saxons, who advanced into Silesia and were, on June 4, 1745, defeated at Hohenfriedberg. Next, on December 15, 1745, at the hands of Leopold of Anhalt-Dessau, the "Old Dessauer", who had fought at Blenheim, came the Austro-Saxon defeat at Kesselsdorf, which was sufficiently decisive to compel Maria Theresa again to come to terms with Prussia. This suited Frederick well, for in order not to be left at the mercy of France, he did not seek too complete a victory over the Austrians.

Peace was signed between Austria and Prussia at Dresden on Christmas Day, 1745. By its terms, Silesia and Glatz were ceded to Frederick, and in return he guaranteed the Pragmatic Sanction. Thus he added 16,000 square miles and 1,000,000 new subjects to his realm, and on his return to Berlin was acclaimed "the Great".

Although the war dragged on for another three years, Frederick took no further part in it. At length all belligerents, except Austria, were weary of the conflict, and a general peace was signed at Aix-la-Chapelle in October-November, 1748. By its terms, Frederick's acquisitions were guaranteed, a few small territorial adjustments were made; and a return to the situation prevailing before the outbreak of the war was agreed to. Though Frederick was well pleased with the results of his aggression, the Peace of Aix-la-Chapelle was to be no more than an armistice.

CHAPTER 6

The Battles of Rossbach and Leuthen, 1757

Though Carlyle calls him "the last of the Kings", Frederick the Great was a new type of monarch, representative rather of the Classical tyrants and the princes of the Italian Renaissance than akin to the declining absolute and rising constitutional kings of his age.

A man of culture as well as a soldier, he mixed philosophy with war, and is both so self-revealing and contradictory in his voluminous writings that it is most difficult, if not impossible, to discover what he really was like, not only to his contemporaries but in himself. For instance, few great soldiers have been so callous in provoking wars; yet, throughout, he seems to have realized the futility of attempts to achieve permanent worth by their means. In his *Military Instructions* he writes: "With troops like these [his soldiers] the *world itself* might be subdued, if conquests were not as fatal to the victors as to the vanquished."[1] Again, in one of his many poems he alludes to war as "this brazen-headed monster, the War Demon athirst for blood and for destruction", and he terms Bellona "that woeful, wild woman, beloved of ancient Chaos".[2] Yet he insists that "we must not satirize war, but get rid of it, as a doctor gets rid of fever"; and he writes to Voltaire, for years his companion:—

"How can a prince, whose troops are dressed in coarse blue cloth and whose hats are trimmed with white braid, after having made them turn to the right and to the left, lead them to glory without deserving the honourable title of a brigand-chief, since he is only followed by a heap of idlers obliged by necessity to become mercenary executioners in order to carry on under him the honest occupation of highwayman? Have you forgotten that war is a scourge which, collecting them all together, adds to them all possible crimes? You see that after having read these wise maxims, a man who cares even a little for his reputation, should avoid the epithets which are only given to the vilest scoundrels."[3]

[1] *Military Instructions from the late King of Prussia, etc.*, fifth English edit. (1818), p. 6.
[2] *L'ode de la guerre.*
[3] *Letters of Voltaire and Frederick the Great*, trans. Richard Aldington (1927), Letter CXCII, October 9, 1773, p. 343.

In spite of this wholehearted condemnation of war, his outlook on peace was profoundly cynical. When discussing with Voltaire the Abbé de Saint-Pierre's *Project de Paix Perpétuelle*, he declared: "The thing is most practicable, for its success all that is lacking is the consent of Europe and a few similar trifles."[1] From these and other sayings one is brought to the conclusion that the sole thing he really believed in was "original sin", and this is borne out in a conversation he once had with his inspector of education, Sulzer. When the latter remarked that in former times it was held that man was naturally inclined to evil, but now that his inborn inclination was toward good, the reply he received from Frederick was: "Ah, my dear Sulzer, you don't know this damned race!"

As a king he was broad-minded and liberal. He said: "I and my people have come to a satisfactory understanding. They say what they like and I do what I like." He tolerated all religious sects, because he considered that everyone must "get to heaven in his own way". He freed the Press, abolished torture, developed scientific study, fed free the poor and opened almshouses for thousands of old women; but with characteristic economy made them spin. Nevertheless he could be exceedingly brutal. In one place he explains that a way of gaining intelligence is to seize a rich man, to dress him poorly and to send him into the enemy's country, with the threat that if he does not return within a certain time "his houses shall be burned, and his wife and children hacked to pieces".[2] Also, "If we are in a Protestant country," he writes, "we wear the mask of protector of the Lutheran religion, and endeavour to make fanatics of the lower order of people, whose simplicity is not proof against our artifice. In a Catholic country, we preach up toleration and moderation, constantly abusing the priests as the cause of all the animosity that exists between the different sectaries, although, in spite of their disputes, they all agree upon material points of faith."[3]

He would seem to have been a mixture of Puck and Machiavelli welded together on the anvil of Vulcan by the hammer of Thor.

Except for Alexander the Great and, possibly, Charles XII, Frederick was the most offensively-minded of all the Great Captains. Colin says of him: "Frederick II breathes nothing but the offensive—the offensive always, in every situation, in the operations as a whole as on the field of battle, even if he is in the

---

[1] *Ibid.*, Letter LXVI, April 12, 1742, p. 161.
[2] *Military Instruction, etc.*, p. 61.   [3] *Ibid.*, p. 66.

presence of a superior army. He is activity itself. . . ."[1] On one occasion Frederick said he would cashier any officer who waited to be attacked, instead of attacking: he always attacked and nearly always struck first. "The whole strength of our troops lies in attack," he said, "and we act foolishly if we renounce it without good cause".[2]

He disliked long wars, not only because of their cost, but because soldiers deteriorate during them, and be it remembered that in the eighteenth century offensives largely depended upon drill (skill in moving). Further, he was aware that, as "battles determine the fate of nations",[3] and as "the first object in the establishment of an army ought to be making provision for the belly, that being the basis and foundation of all operations",[4] the longer a war lasts the more difficult becomes supply. Nevertheless, by always attacking, like Charles XII, he suffered more than one disastrous defeat.

Napoleon's estimate of him is interesting. He says:

"He was above all great in the most critical moments, this is the highest praise which one can make regarding him."[5]

.   .   .   .   .

"What distinguishes Frederick the most, is not his skill in manœuvring, but his audacity. He carried out things I never dared to do. He abandoned his line of operations, and often acted as if he had no knowledge whatever of the art of war."[6]

.   .   .   .   .

"It is not the Prussian army which for seven years defended Prussia against the three most powerful nations in Europe, but Frederick the Great."[7]

When his campaigns are examined, we find that it was not only his audacious spirit but also his ability to grasp the tactical conditions of his day and to learn from his own mistakes that made him so great a general. He realized how artificially slow

---

[1] *The Transformations of War*, Commandant J. Colin (1912), p. 195.
[2] Quoted from *A Review of the History of Infantry*, Colonel E. M. Lloyd (1908), pp. 160–161.
[3] *Military Instruction, etc.*, p. 125.
[4] *Ibid.*, p. 7. Frederick provided hand-mills for each company, p. 11.
[5] *Correspondance de Napoléon 1er*, vol. XXXII, p. 238.
[6] *Sainte-Hélène, Journal inédit (1815–1818)*, Général Gourgaud (edition 1899), vol. II, pp. 33, 34.
[7] *Récits de la captivité de l'Empereur Napoléon a Sainte-Hélène*, Comte de Montholon (1847), vol. II, p. 90.

and heavy were the tactics of his age, and from the outset of his career he determined to base his system of war on what these tactics lacked–mobility and rapidity of fire. He states: "A Prussian battalion is a moving battery . . . the rapidity in loading is such that it can triple the fire of all other troops. This gives to the Prussians a superiority of three to one."[1] Nevertheless, in his earlier campaigns, he relied more on the bayonet than the bullet, but soon discovered his mistake; for in his later battles he did his utmost to develop the power of both his muskets and cannon. He was a great artillerist and the creator of the first true horse artillery ever formed, a weapon so little thought of that, from 1759 onward for 30 years, the Prussian was the only horse artillery in Europe. Also, because the Austrians, who acted usually on the defensive, were prone to hold their reserves behind the ridges occupied by their firing lines, he was a great believer in the howitzer. Yet, strange to say, he never fully grasped the value of a trained light infantry, and this is all the more surprising because at the battle of Kolin the Austrian light troops–Croats and Pandours–were largely responsible for his defeat.[2]

From his minor tactics, Frederick developed his major, or grand tactics. Hitherto extreme slowness of deployment usually led to a frontal engagement, hence the head-on battles of the seventeenth and eighteenth centuries. But what Frederick grasped was that, should the mobility of one side greatly exceed that of the other, once the slower had deployed, it would be possible to march against one of its flanks, deploy, and attack it before it could change front. This was the essence of his grand tactics, which were so simple that, though they could easily be copied, they were unlikely to succeed unless the attacker possessed superior mobility. It was for this reason that Napoleon said: "His (Frederick's) Oblique Order could only prove successful against an army which was unable to manœuvre."[3]

Frederick explains this order as follows: "You refuse one wing to the enemy and strengthen the one which is to attack. With the latter you do your utmost against one wing of the enemy which you take in flank. An army of 100,000 men taken in flank

---

[1] *Histoire de mon temps*, Frédéric le Grand (1879), p. 201.

[2] For more information on this subject and for the rising value of light infantry, see my *British Light Infantry in the Eighteenth Century* (1925), pp. 66–72; also Frederick's *Military Instruction, etc.*, pp. 80–82.

[3] Quoted from *Préceptes et Jugements de Napoléon*, Lieut.-Colonel Ernest Picard (1913), p. 125.

may be beaten by 30,000 in a very short time. . . . The advantages of this arrangement are (1) a small force can engage one much stronger than itself; (2) it attacks an enemy at a decisive point; (3) if you are beaten, it is only part of your army, and you have the other three-fourths which are still fresh to cover your retreat."[1]

In order to attain the maximum of mobility and rapidity of fire, Frederick relied upon drill, about which much nonsense has been written. It is true that it was severe and even brutal; yet it is quite untrue that Frederick looked upon it as anything other than a means to an end. Also, it is true that he had no very high opinion of the soldiers of his age. In his *Military Instruction* he writes: "An army is composed for the most part of idle and inactive men, and unless the general has a constant eye upon them . . . this artificial machine . . . will very soon fall to pieces, and nothing but the *bare idea* of a disciplined army will remain."[2] Also: "If my soldiers began to think, not one would remain in the ranks."[3] Further, "All that can be done with the soldier is to give him *esprit de corps*, i.e. a higher opinion of his own regiment than of all the other troops of the country, and since the officers have sometimes to lead him into the greatest danger (and he cannot be influenced by a sense of honour) he must be more afraid of his officers than of the dangers to which he is exposed."[4]

Although he wrote like this, toward his men he was by no means unkindly, at times he could be friendly and familiar. On one occasion a deserter was brought before him. " 'Why did you leave me?' said the King to him. 'Indeed, your Majesty,' replied the grenadier, ' . . . things are going very badly with us.' 'Come, come,' rejoined Frederick, 'let us fight another battle to-day: if I am beaten, we will desert together to-morrow;' and with these words he sent him back to his colours."[5]

Though, later on, the Prussian drill came to be taken for the art of war, Frederick never so interpreted it. He "laughed in his sleeve," says Napoleon, "at the parades of Potsdam, when he perceived young officers, French, English and Austrian, so infatuated with the manœuvre of the oblique order, which was fit for nothing but to gain a few adjutant-majors a reputation."[6]

[1] Quoted from *A Review of the History of Infantry*, Colonel E. M. Lloyd, p. 162.
[2] *Military Instruction, etc.*, p. 5.
[3] Quoted from *The Biology of War*, Dr. G. F. Nicolai (1919), p. 65.
[4] Quoted from a *Review of the History of Infantry*, Colonel E. M. Lloyd, p. 153.
[5] *Frederick the Great: His Court and Times*, edited by Thomas Campbell (1843), vol. III, p. 138.
[6] *Correspondance de Napoléon 1er*, vol. XXXII, p. 243.

The truth is, that unless Frederick's drill was animated by Frederick's spirit, it was a delusion.

A few extracts from his *Instructions* will show that he was far from being solely a drill-master:

"The army of the enemy should be the chief object of our attention" (p. 49).

"In war the skin of a fox is at times as necessary as that of a lion, for cunning may succeed when force fails" (p. 52).

"It is an invariable axiom of war to secure your own flanks and rear, and endeavour to turn those of your enemy" (p. 101).

"The conquering wing of your cavalry must not allow the enemy's cavalry to rally, but pursue them in good order" (p. 118).

"To shed the blood of soldiers, when there is no occasion for it, is to lead them inhumanly to the slaughter" (p. 120).

"Though our wounded are to be the first objects of our attention, we are not to forget our duty to the enemy" (p. 121).

"You are never to imagine that *every* thing is done as long as *any* thing remains undone" (p. 122).

"My officers . . . are expected to profit by my mistakes, and they may be assured, that I shall apply myself with all diligence to correct them" (p. 126).

"Those battles are the best into which we force the enemy, for it is an established maxim, to oblige him to do that for which he has no sort of inclination, and as your interest and his are diametrically opposite, it cannot be supposed that you are both wishing for the same event" (p. 126).

Though Frederick wanted peace, and after the Peace of Aix-la-Chapelle had exclaimed: "Henceforth I would not attack a cat except to defend myself," it would appear that he failed to appreciate the implications of his successful aggression. It had rendered Austria resentful and France fearful; in fact it had provided both with a common grievance which, were they only willing to sink their traditional enmity, could be developed into a common cause. Unfortunately for Frederick, this was what Prince von Kaunitz, Maria Theresa's Chancellor of State, realized. He saw that Frederick's aggression had rendered the traditional rivalry between France and Austria obsolete and suggested to the Queen that France should be approached with a view to obtain her aid in regaining Silesia, in exchange for which she should be offered the Austrian Netherlands. As she loathed Frederick and had been stung by his gibes, Maria

Theresa favoured the suggestion and Kaunitz approached the French Court. Firstly, he pointed out that Frederick alone could gain from a continuance of the rivalry between France and Austria; secondly that, as the Tsarina Elizabeth, whom Frederick had insulted by calling "the Apostolic Hag", was eager to acquire East Prussia; as Saxony could be bought over by an offer of Magdeburg; and Sweden by a promise of Pomerania; if, in exchange for the Austrian Netherlands, France would agree to support Austria, a coalition of 70,000,000 people could be formed which would wipe Prussia and her 4,500,000 inhabitants off the map.

Although this proposal ran counter to French traditional policy, Madame de Pompadour, then the real power at the French Court, whom Frederick had also insulted by calling her "Mlle. Poisson"–her mother was reputed to be a fishwife–readily gave her support. But before a final agreement could be reached, England took a step which precipitated a crisis.

Concerned over the security of Hanover while occupied in their undeclared colonial wars with France, the English Government bought with a large subsidy the Tsarina's guarantee to protect Hanover by concentrating her army on her western frontier.

Frederick's suspicions were aroused, and when he got wind of Kaunitz's negotiations, in his turn he approached England and offered to guarantee the integrity of Hanover. His offer was accepted, and the agreement with the Tsarina, which had not been ratified, was cancelled by the English Government. Next, in January, 1756, according to the terms of the Convention of Westminster, an alliance was entered upon between England and Prussia, and as it was wholly a defensive one, it did not violate Frederick's obligations with France. Nevertheless, as Frederick was well aware, the invasion of Hanover would of necessity in another war become part of the French plan. Lastly, in the following May, in order to offset this Convention, France concluded a defensive alliance, known as the Treaty of Versailles, with Austria. Thus, by the summer of 1756, Europe was divided into two hostile camps–England and Prussia, and France and Austria, supported by Russia, Sweden, and Saxony.

Though for Austria, Kaunitz's scheme was a triumph, for France it was a disaster in disguise. The War of the Austrian Succession had shown how vulnerable the French colonies were, and as already in Ohio and in India an undeclared colonial

war was in progress between France and England, the high
probability was that a new war in Europe, in which France
could not help but play a prominent rôle, would lead to the
extinction of most of the French oversea empire. And this is what
did happen.

Frederick learnt from his spies that the Tsarina was urging
Maria Theresa to hasten her military preparations and saw that
to wait until she was ready would be fatal for Prussia. He decided
to strike first. "After all," he wrote, "it was of small importance
whether my enemies called me an aggressor or not as all Europe
had already united against me."[1]

Though the geographical position of Prussia enabled Frederick
to operate on interior lines, which in the circumstances was an
enormous advantage, Prussia had no defensible frontiers and in
face of the alliance her army was outnumbered by about three
to one. In the south, when the Austrians had joined up with
the Saxons, they would be 40 miles from Berlin; in the north, the
Swedes, when they had concentrated at Stralsund, would be
within 130 miles; in the east, when the Russians had crossed the
Oder, they would be but 50 miles; and in the west, on entering
Prussian territory near Halle, the French would be 100 miles
from Berlin. Yet there was a saving clause: all these armies were
in various stages of preparation; the Austrian had not yet joined
the Saxon; the Russian had still to cross the roadless wastes of
Poland; the Swedes the Baltic; and the French the Rhine.

In July, Frederick demanded an assurance from Vienna that
the Austrian troop concentrations in Bohemia were not directed
against Prussia, and received an evasive answer. He waited no
longer, but detached 11,000 men to watch the Swedes; 26,000 to
watch the Russians; left 37,000 to defend Silesia, and on August 29,
1756, with 70,000 men, suddenly and without a declaration of
war invaded Saxony. On September 10 he occupied Dresden.
Frederick then blockaded Pirna, and in October came up with
the Austrians at Lobositz and defeated them.

Frederick's invasion of Saxony was the signal for a violent
outburst of moral indignation which stirred the Imperial Diet,
which believed that Frederick would be overwhelmed, to place
him under its ban, an action tantamount to outlawing him. More
to the purpose, the Coalition determined to put 500,000 troops
into the field and crush the aggressor.

[1] Quoted from *Frederick the Great*, F. J. P. Veale (1935), p. 181.

Frederick waited until the passes were free from snow, then advanced on Prague, and when he came up with the Austrians there, on May 6, 1757, he again defeated them. He blockaded the city, and advanced southward, and, on June 18, at Kolin, recklessly attacked an Austrian army, under Marshal Daun, nearly twice the size of his own. He suffered a crushing defeat, in which he lost 13,000 men out of 33,000, and was compelled to raise the siege of Prague and to withdraw into Saxony.

Encouraged by Daun's victory, the allies determined to enclose Frederick in a ring of fire. Their plan was as follows: Prince Joseph of Saxe-Hildburghausen, in command of the Reich Army, 33,000 strong, was to unite with Marshal Soubise and his 30,000 men and reconquer Saxony; Marshal d'Éstrées and the Duke of Richelieu and 100,000 men were to advance against the Duke of Cumberland in Hanover; 17,000 Russians, who had taken Memel, were to invade Prussia; 17,000 Swedes, under Baron Ungern Sternberg, were to land in Pomerania; and 100,000 Austrians, under Prince Charles of Lorraine and Field-Marshal Daun, were to operate against the remnants of Frederick's Kolin army. Thus, nearly 390,000 men were to be concentrated against Frederick who, undaunted, withdrew 25,000 men from before Daun and marched 170 miles to Erfurt, then threatened by Soubise.

On May 1, 1757, Louis XV concluded the Second Treaty of Versailles with Maria Theresa, which granted her a yearly subsidy of 30,000,000 livres to pay for her Russian support. In June d'Éstrées began to move, and, on July 26, by accident he defeated Cumberland at Hastenbeck, near Hamelin. Both generals had ordered a retreat, but the unauthorized intervention of a small detachment gave the French the victory. D'Éstrées was superseded by the Duke of Richelieu, who concluded with Cumberland the ignominious Convention of Klosterzeven, according to the terms of which the Anglo-Hanoverian army was to pack up and go home. Though a few weeks later the convention was repudiated by both the English and French governments, Richelieu, instead of joining up with Soubise, in traditional French fashion began to plunder the country. Still advancing—and plundering—Soubise moved on Magdeburg, an important Prussian arsenal, after which he intended to make for Berlin.

Meanwhile the Russians advanced into Prussia, where they

perpetrated unheard-of barbarities.[1] To halt them Frederick ordered Field-Marshal Lehwaldt with 25,000 men to attack 80,000 of them at Gross-Jägerndorf. On August 30, he did so and was defeated. Thus the road to Berlin was unbarred, but as so often has happened, the Russian army melted away through lack of supplies. Nevertheless, by October Frederick's position was so desperate that it seemed to him the war was irretrievably lost.

Though he realized how slight his chances were, because he could not stand still he decided to move against the French. He left the Duke of Bevern with 41,000 men in Lusatia to oppose Prince Charles of Lorraine's 112,000, and on August 25 he set out for Dresden to assemble his army. From there he marched to Erfurt, where he arrived on September 13; whereupon Soubise retired to Eisenach. Frederick then paid Richelieu a bribe of 100,000 thalers to remain inactive, followed up Soubise, cleared Gotha, and left General Seydlitz there to watch him. On September 19 Soubise and Hildburghausen advanced on Gotha, but were met by Seydlitz and hastily withdrew.[2]

With Frederick thus engaged, Bevern was pushed back on Breslau, and Count Hadik, with 3,500 Austrians, advanced on Berlin. On October 16 Hadik entered the Prussian capital and was paid a ransom of 300,000 thalers to depart. When he heard of Hadik's raid, Frederick left 7,000 men under Marshal Keith to guard the Saale, and set out to save his capital; but, on October 20 he learnt that he was too late and decided to return. During his absence, Soubise, who had been reinforced by 15,000 men under Marshal de Broglie, invaded Saxony, and, on October 27, reached Weissenfels, from where he summoned Keith at Leipzig to surrender the city, but was met by a blank refusal.

---

[1] "They hung innocent inhabitants from trees, ripped open their bodies, tore out their hearts and their intestines, cut off their noses and ears, broke their legs, fired villages and hamlets, formed a circle round the burning houses, and drove back their fleeing inmates into the flames. Their wanton brutality was especially wreaked on the nobles and the clergy: these they tied to the tails of their horses, and dragged them after them, or stripped them naked, and laid them upon blazing fires. . . . Their senseless revenge was exercised even on the dead; they opened the graves, and scattered abroad the mutilated corpses." (*Frederick the Great: His Court and Times,* edited by Thomas Campbell, vol. III, p. 102.)

[2] At this time the French Army was in a shocking state of discipline. This may in part be gauged by the booty they left behind them in this retreat: "Pommades, perfumes, powdering and dressing-gowns, bag-wigs, umbrellas, parrots: while a host of whining lacquays, cooks, friseurs, players and prostitutes, were chased from the town to follow their pampered masters to Eisenach." (*Frederick the Great: His Court and Times,* edited by Thomas Campbell, vol. III, p. 109. See also *Histoire Critique et Militaire des Guerres de Frédéric, II,* Lieutenant-General Jomini (1818), vol. I, p. 198.

On his return, Frederick rejoined Keith, and so brought his army up to about 22,000, and when he learnt this Soubise fell back to the Saale. Frederick left Leipzig on October 30, entered Weissenfels the following day, and instantly attacked the French outposts, but found the bridge broken. Keith also found the bridges at Merseburg and Halle destroyed. Although Frederick's position was now dangerous, Soubise foolishly abandoned the Saale, and fell back to Mücheln. Frederick repaired the three bridges, crossed the river on November 3, and encamped at Braunsdorf, near Mücheln. He at once advanced 1,500 cavalry under Seydlitz, raided his enemy's camp, and decided to attack it in force on the following day. But this surprise raid persuaded Soubise to move during the night to a securer position, and as Frederick found it too strong to attack, on November 4 he moved his camp to Rossbach.

Soubise's timidity had much exasperated his officers, among whom was Pierre de Bourcet, who had gained great fame in the campaigns of 1744-1747 in the Cottian and Maritime Alps. He realized that Frederick's position was precarious and suggested to Soubise that he should swing round Frederick's left flank and cut his line of retreat. Further, as Lloyd points out, because Soubise and Hildburghausen outnumbered Frederick by nearly two to one,[1] they were so elated "that they resolved to attack him the next morning, and so finish the campaign; the fatigues of which their troops seemed no longer able or willing to endure."[2]

Once decided upon, no preparations for Bourcet's manœuvre were put in hand until the morning of November 5, when, with some of the allied troops out foraging, Soubise received the following message from Hildburghausen: "Not a moment is to be lost in attacking the enemy. From his manœuvre of yesterday it is obvious that he will not attack us, but instead is more likely to cut our communications with Freibourg. Therefore I am of opinion we should advance, gain the heights of Schevenroda and attack him from that side."[3] Not till then did Soubise make ready.

The field upon which the battle was about to be fought was

---

[1] Tempelhoff gives Frederick's strength at 24,360: infantry 18,800; cavalry 5,160; and artillery 400. (*The History of the Seven Years' War in Germany by Generals Lloyd and Tempelhoff* (1783), vol. I, p. 265.)

[2] *The History of the Late War in Germany, etc.*, Major-General Lloyd (1781), Part I, p. 95.

[3] Quoted from *La Guerre de Sept Ans*, Richard Waddington (1899), vol. I, p. 618.

a wide open plain destitute of trees and hedges, with the village of Rossbach on a low eminence from which the allied camp could be seen clearly. Between Rossbach and Merseburg ran a small stream, south of which gently rose the Janus and Pölzen Hills, which Carlyle describes as "sensible to waggon-horses in those bad loose tracks of sandy mud, but unimpressive on the Tourist, who has to admit that there seldom was so flat a hill."[1] To the south of the plain flowed the Saale and the small town of Weissenfels lay a few miles distant and south-east of Rossbach.

When he received Hildburghausen's message, Soubise sent out a body of French cavalry, under the Count of St. Germain, to Gröst, three miles west of Rossbach, to observe the enemy's camp and also to protect the left flank of the manœuvre. Soubise ordered his camp to be struck at 11 a.m. and moved off in three columns. The advanced guard was of Austrian and Imperial cavalry, followed by French and Imperial infantry, with the French horse in rear. At Pettstädt the advanced guard halted and was joined by the French horse, and after a conference of generals the advance was continued and a half-left wheel made in the direction of Reichartswerben. The march was exceedingly slow and "*tout ce qu'ils avaient de musiciens et de trompettes faisaient des fanfares; leurs tambours et leurs fifres faisaient des rejouissances, comme s'ils avaient gagné une victoire*".[2]

These various movements were watched closely by Frederick. He posted on the roof of the Herrenhaus at Rossbach an officer, Captain Gaudi, and sent out patrols, several of which penetrated the abandoned French camp and learned from the peasants that Soubise had taken the Weissenfels Road. Yet he was not certain whether his enemy was making for Freiburg, because he was short of supplies; or for Weissenfels, which was not likely, because the bridge there was still broken; or for Merseburg, in order to cut him off from the Saale.

When the king was at dinner, at two o'clock Gaudi rushed into the room and reported that the enemy had reached Pettstädt and was wheeling toward the Prussian left. Frederick mounted to the roof, from where a moment's gaze revealed to him his enemy's intention to attack him in flank and rear and drive him away from his communications. At 2.30 p.m. he issued his orders, which were so rapidly carried out that a French officer declared

---

[1] *History of Frederick II of Prussia*, Thomas Carlyle (1888 edit.), vol. VII, p. 333.
[2] *Oeuvres de Frédéric le Grand* (1847), vol. IV, p. 151.

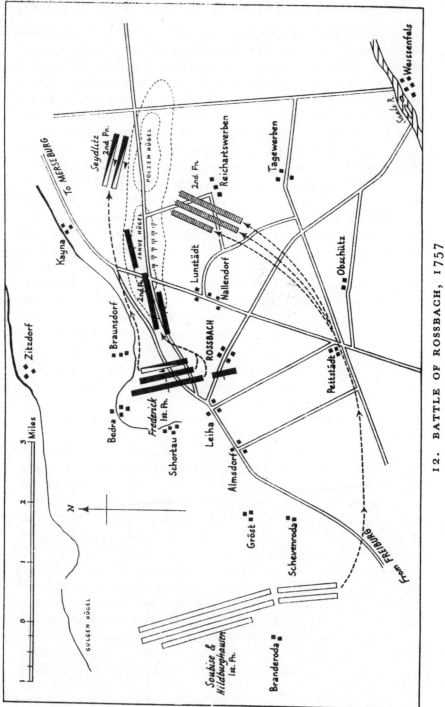

12. BATTLE OF ROSSBACH, 1757

that "it was like a change of scene in the Opéra". By 3 p.m. the camp was struck, the tents were loaded and the troops had fallen in. As they did so, General Seydlitz, then aged 33, at the head of 38 squadrons of cavalry, left at the trot. He moved up the Rossbach stream, and except for a few vedettes on his right flank his advance was covered from view. He made for the Janus and Pölzen Hills, and was followed by the infantry and a battery of 18 heavy guns; the latter Frederick ordered to take up position on the Janus Hill, between the left of the infantry and the right of Seydlitz's horse. Seven squadrons were left at Rossbach to watch St. Germain.

Instead of the rapidity of these movements opening Soubise's eyes to what was taking place, they conveyed to him the idea that the Prussians were in full retreat. He, therefore, ordered his advanced guard to hasten on and make for the Janus Hill, and so hurried were his orders that no instructions were issued where and when to deploy, nor were the soldiers relieved of their packs and camp kettles. So "the infantry moved off in three long columns, at the head of which were the French regiments of Piedmont and Mailly. On the flanks and front of the right column marched two regiments of Austrian cuirassiers and the Imperial cavalry; ten French squadrons were in reserve, and twelve others protected the left flank. No ground reconnaissances were made, there was no advanced guard; the army marched forward– blind".[1]

The tactical picture now changes: Soubise and Hildburg-hausen had thought to turn Frederick's oblique order of attack against himself. Their argument was: as we are numerically superior and he has lost the initiative, all we need do is to march round his left flank and attack him, when victory is ours. Yet, what had really happened? Though they did not grasp it, by 3.30 p.m. they were offering a flank—the heads of their advancing columns—to Frederick to attack; for by then he was in position to do so. To make their position worse, about this time, still thinking that the Prussians were in full retreat, Soubise brought forward his reserve cavalry, under de Broglie, and thereby increased the size of the Prussian target.

Meanwhile, Seydlitz, with his 4,000 horsemen, well behind the Pölzen Hill, watched the slowly moving heads of the allied columns approach. As they neared, without waiting for orders,

[1] *La Guerre de Sept Ans*, Richard Waddington, vol. I, p. 622.

he led his men forward at the trot. A few minutes later he cantered into sight, and as signal for the attack he flung his tobacco-pipe into the air. "Then," says M. de Castries, a French cavalry officer, "barely had we formed up, when the whole of the Prussian cavalry advanced compact like a wall and at an incredible speed. With its right it attacked the Austrian cavalry, which was in column and was unable to place in battle more than three or four squadrons. With its left it charged us."[1] In a blaze of rapid steel four times the Prussian horsemen cut their way through the undeployed mass, and drove their enemy in rout toward Freiburg. At length, Seydlitz steadied his men and re-formed them in the dip of Tagewerben.

When this action was fought, the battery on the Janus Hill opened on the allied infantry, still in columns of route, and, under cover of its fire, Prince Henry of Prussia advanced seven infantry battalions[2] at the double to support the cavalry by an attack on the leading enemy regiments. His attack proved decisive, for in the words of a Württemberg dragoon: "The artillery tore down whole ranks of us; the Prussian musketry did terrible execution."[3] Thrown back in confusion on their supporting battalions, the allied infantry found it impossible to deploy; when Seydlitz seized the opportunity, advanced from the Tagewerben hollow and burst "terribly compact and furious" upon their rear and drove them in rout across the field. Of the part played by the Prussian artillery, Decker writes: "we may say, with all assurance, that the success of the day belonged to the Artillery. If, as at Kolin, it had remained inactive, the enemy's infantry could have formed and advanced; its defeat would not have been so complete, and the success of the cavalry would have been less brilliant."[4]

At 4.30 p.m. the action was decided. Frederick's right was then at Lundstädt, and his left, at Reichartswerben, was "advancing with cannon in the van on the turmoil into which the combined army had been reduced".[5] The retreat became a rout, and "the country for forty miles round", writes St. Germain, "was covered with our soldiers: they plundered, murdered, violated women,

---

[1] Quoted from Waddington, vol. 1, p. 623.
[2] These were the sole Prussian battalions used during the entire battle. See: *Oeuvres de Frédéric le Grand*, vol. 1, p. 154.
[3] *Frederick the Great*, Colonel C. B. Brakenbury (1884), p. 171.
[4] *Ibid.*, p. 173, quoting Decker's *Seven Years' War* (French Edition, 1839), p. 115.
[5] *La Guerre de Sept Ans*, Richard Waddington, vol. 1, p. 626.

robbed and committed all possible abominations".[1] The truth is that throughout the campaign the French showed a grievous lack of discipline; and though there was no pursuit, not only because night was approaching, but because Frederick had to hasten to Silesia, this lack of discipline submerged the French and Imperialists and reduced them to panic-stricken rabble.

The Prussian losses were 165 killed and 376 wounded, but those of the allies were 3,000 killed and wounded, 5,000 prisoners, including eight generals and 300 officers, 67 cannon, seven pairs of colours, 15 standards, and much baggage.

Politically, few battles have led to greater consequences. For well over 100 years, ever since Cardinal Richelieu embroiled France in the Thirty Years War, eastwardly expansion into Germany had been the French aim. Time and again had the Palatinate been invaded, pillaged and burnt, and, like a phoenix from out of its ashes, had emerged the spirit of German nationalism, which found its focal point in the person of Frederick on the field of Rossbach.

Though Europe could not foresee the future that Rossbach held in store, all European nations were suddenly brought to realize that the French army was rotten to the core; that its invincibility was a myth and its grandeur–tinsel. "No battle, during the whole course of the war," writes General Tempelhoff, "caused such a particular impression as that of Rossbach. Friends and foes laughed at the Generals of the combined armies," and they laughed still more heartily, when shortly after his defeat Soubise was made a Marshal of France by Louis XV.[2]

When the news of Frederick's victory was received in England, bonfires were set ablaze throughout the land, and Parliament, which in 1757 had reluctantly voted Frederick £164,000, in 1758 granted him £1,200,000, which in terms of money is evidence of what the English thought. Nevertheless, the immediate consequences of the battle were restricted, for with the rout of Soubise and Hildburghausen, Frederick's task was but half accomplished, and the situation in Silesia was critical in the extreme.

After a week's pause to refit his army, on November 13, with 13,000 men, Frederick marched from Leipzig and arrived at Parchwitz, 170 miles distant, on November 28. Meanwhile, on

---

[1] Quoted from *Frederick the Great: His Court and Times*, Thomas Campbell, vol. III, p. 122.

[2] *The History of the Seven Years' War in Germany*, Generals Lloyd and Tempelhoff, vol. I, p. 271.

November 14, Schweidnitz had capitulated to the Austrians, and, on November 22, Bevern had been defeated at Breslau and had abandoned the town. At Parchwitz, Frederick put General Ziethen in command of Bevern's beaten army and ordered a concentration on Parchwitz for December 3. On the same day Frederick advanced on Neumarkt, and captured it by a light cavalry *coup de main*. At Neumarkt, he obtained positive information that Prince Charles and Marshal Daun had left their camp at Lohe and had advanced to Lissa, where their right rested on the village of Nippern and their left on that of Sagschütz. Frederick's rapid advance had surprised them, for they had considered that after Rossbach he would go into winter quarters.

On December 4, their heavy guns left at Breslau, Charles and Daun hurriedly crossed the Schweidnitz stream and took up a position on the west of that river. Their army consisted of 84 battalions, 144 squadrons, and 210 guns; in all between 60,000 to 80,000 men drawn up in two lines. Its right, under Lucchessi, was covered by the bogs of Nippern; its centre was at Leuthen; and its left, under Nadasti, behind Sagschütz, thrown back *en potence* and protected by abattis. The right wing cavalry was at Guckerwitz and the left at Leuthen. Defensively the position was strong, though over-extended, for from flank to flank it measured five and a half miles. To this formidable array Frederick could only oppose 36,000 men; 24,000 infantry in 48 battalions and 12,000 cavalry in 128 squadrons. He had with him 167 guns, of which 61 were heavy and 10 super-heavy pieces. The field of battle was open plain land, over which Frederick had manœuvred during peace time, therefore he knew it well.

On December 5, at 5 a.m. the Prussian army advanced from Neumarkt, with Frederick in the van. About halfway between that town and Leuthen he halted the army, assembled his generals by a birch tree and gave out his orders. "I should think that I had done nothing", he said, "if I were to leave the Austrians in possession of Silesia. Let me then apprise you that I shall attack, against all the rules of the art, the army of Prince Charles, nearly thrice as strong as our own, wherever I find it. . . . I must venture upon this step, or all is lost: we must beat the enemy, or all perish before his batteries. So I think—so will I act. . . . Now go . . . and repeat to the regiments what I have said to you."[1]

---

[1] *Frederick the Great his Court and Times*, edited by Thomas Campbell, vol. III, pp. 134–136.

Frederick's plan was to advance straight up the Breslau road, to feint at the Austrian right, and then to take advantage of his enemy's extended position, march across his front, attack his left flank and drive him off his communications. In his own words, he resolved "to place his whole army on the left flank of the Imperialists, to strike the hardest with his right and to refuse his left, with such precautions that there should be no fear of mistakes like those which had been made in the battle of Prague, and which had caused the loss of that of Kolin."[1]

After his troops had rested, Frederick ordered the advance to continue direct on to the village of Borne. The advanced guard consisted of 10 battalions and 60 squadrons—Frederick in the van—and the main body followed in four columns with regimental bands playing. As the men began to sing the hymn—

> Grant that I do whate'er I ought to do,
> What for my station is by Thee decreed;
> And cheerfully and promptly do it too,
> And when I do it, grant that it succeed!

an officer asked the King whether he should stop them. Frederick replied: "Not on any account, with such men God will certainly give me the victory to-day."[2]

At Borne, contact was made with the enemy. Dawn was breaking and a haze covered the ground. Through it a long line of cavalry was seen stretched across the high road, its left disappearing in the mist. At first it was thought to be the Austrian right wing; but to make certain, it was charged in front and flank, when it was discovered to be General Nostitz and five regiments. They were at once scattered and 800 were taken prisoners[3] including Nostitz, who was mortally wounded. Next a halt was made, and shortly after the mist cleared and the whole Austrian army was seen stretched from Nippern to Sagschütz, so distinctly "that one could have counted it man by man".[4]

The loss of the village of Borne was an important factor in the Austrian defeat, not only because Frederick could examine the whole of his enemy's dispositions from it, but also because a rise in the ground hid from view the Prussians who advanced

[1] *Oeuvres Posthumes de Frédéric II* (1788), vol. III, p. 238.
[2] *Frederick the Great his Court and Times*, edited by Thomas Campbell, vol. III, p. 138. See also Thomas Carlyle, *History of Frederick the Great*.
[3] *Oeuvres Posthumes de Frédéric II*, vol. III, pp. 235–236.
[4] *Ibid.*, p. 236.

toward Borne in four columns. As they approached, Frederick sent forward his advanced guard cavalry in pursuit of Nostitz, that is, toward the Austrian right wing, commanded by Count Lucchessi, who watched their advance, imagined that he was about to be attacked in force, and called for aid so urgently that Marshal Daun sent to his support the reserve cavalry and part of the cavalry of the left wing. While this took place, the four Prussian columns were formed into two, and when they reached Borne they were wheeled to the right under cover of the rise, and advanced southward. Tempelhoff writes: "It was impossible to witness a more beautiful sight; all the heads of the columns were parallel to each other, and in exact distances to form line, and the divisions marched with such precision, that they seemed to be at a review, ready to wheel into line in a moment."[1] The order of march was as follows: Right wing in advance, Ziethen with 43 squadrons and six battalions under Prince Maurice of Dessau, preceded by an advanced guard of three battalions under General Wedel. The left wing, following under General Retzow, consisted of the rest of the infantry, flanked by 40 squadrons under General Driesen. Each body of cavalry was supported by 10 squadrons of hussars, and the rearguard, under Prince Eugene of Würtemberg, consisted of 25 squadrons.

As Frederick's army vanished from sight, Prince Charles and Marshal Daun, who were standing on the mill of Frobelwitz, imagined that it was in full retreat. "The Prussians are off," said the latter, "don't disturb them!" Then a little after noon their head was seen advancing between Lobetinz and Sagschütz, from where it threatened the Austrian weakened left wing.

Suddenly confronted by an overwhelmingly superior force, Nadasti sent galloper after galloper to Charles for reinforcements. But it was too late; at about 1 p.m., Wedel, supported by a battery of six guns and followed by Prince Maurice, advanced and stormed the defences of Sagschütz; and at the same time Nadasti charged Ziethen's leading squadrons and drove them southward upon the six supporting battalions, and while their fire held back the Austrian horse, Ziethen disentangled his men from the difficult ground, turned about, charged Nadasti and drove him and his men into the Rathener Wood.

By 1.30 Nadasti's wing was routed, and the entire field between

[1] *The History of the Seven Years' War in Germany*, Generals Lloyd and Tempelhoff, vol. I, p. 341.

Sagschütz and Leuthen covered with fugitives pursued by the Prussian hussars, behind whom the infantry advanced in double line. On the right was Wedel, in the centre Maurice, and on the left Retzow, the whole supported by the heavy artillery, which took the flying Austrians in enfilade.

While this advance was made, Charles, taken by surprise,

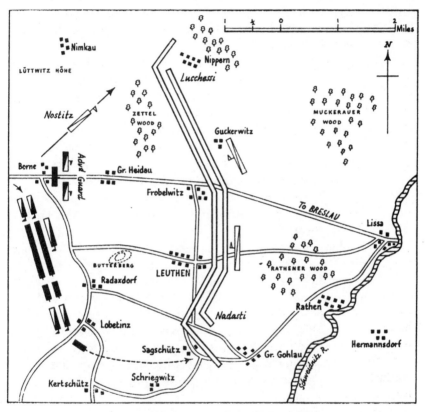

13. BATTLE OF LEUTHEN, 1757

hastily recalled the cavalry which had reinforced Lucchessi, and while awaiting its arrival, sent forward his infantry piecemeal. Nevertheless, though Leuthen was weakly garrisoned, a determined stand was made there, in part thus described by the Prince de Ligne, then a captain in an Austrian regiment of foot:

"We ran what we could run. Our Lieutenant-Colonel fell killed almost at the first; beyond this we lost our Major, and indeed all the Officers but three. . . . We had crossed two successive ditches, which lay in an orchard to the left of the first houses in Leuthen; and were beginning to form in front of the village. But there was no standing of it. Besides a general cannonade such as can hardly be imagined, there was a rain of case-shot upon this Battalion, of which I, as there was no Colonel left, had to take command. . . . Two officers of the Grenadiers brought me what they still had. Some Hungarians, too, were luckily got together. But at last, as, with all helps and the remnants of my own brave Battalion, I had come down to at most 200, I drew back to the Height where the Windmill is."[1]

The overcrowding in Leuthen was as bad as it had been in Blenheim; so jammed together were the troops that in places they stood 30 to 100 ranks deep. Nevertheless, as Tempelhoff writes, "A murderous conflict ensued; the enemy made the resistance of despair; one battalion followed upon another against it without success, till the King was obliged to bring his left wing, which, according to his orders, had kept out of musket-shot, into action. At length the guards, led by their senior Captain, now General Möllendorf, pushed forward with irresistible valour, and after a further resistance of half an hour, forced the enemy to abandon his post."[2]

The problem now was how to debouch from the village, for the Austrians had advanced a battery on to the ridge north of it, under the fire of which their infantry deployed at right angles to their original front. To do so, Frederick ordered the remainder of his left wing to advance; but, as it was driven back by the fire of these guns, he established a battery, including his super-heavy cannon, on the Butterberg and swept the Austrians back. In his *Memoirs*, Horace St. Paul says that it was this formidable artillery, more so than the Prussian infantry, which won the battle.[3]

It was four o'clock when the Austrians were swept back, and as twilight fell Lucchessi, who had assembled the Austrian right wing cavalry at Frobelwitz, saw Retzow's infantry held up and moved forward to charge them in flank. Unfortunately for Lucchessi, behind the village of Radaxdorf Driesen's 40 squadrons were hidden from his sight. Suddenly, under cover of the Butter-

---

[1] Quoted from Carlyle's *Frederick the Great*, Book XVIII, chap. x.
[2] *The History of the Seven Years' War in Germany*, Generals Lloyd and Tempelhoff, vol. I, p. 343.
[3] *A Journal of the First Two Campaigns of the Seven Years' War*, Horace St. Paul (1914), p. 394.

berg battery, they rode into the open, and while 30 squadrons charged Lucchessi in front, the Bayreuth Dragoons struck him in flank and the Puttkammer Hussars galloped round his rear. The result was decisive, Lucchessi was killed and his troopers scattered. Next, Driesen wheeled to his right and charged the Austrian infantry in rear, while Wedel attacked them in flank from near Leuthen. As night closed in the Austrians broke and their retreat rapidly became a *sauve qui peut*.

Frederick followed up the rout and pushed on to Lissa. There he found the small town crowded with fugitives, and as he rode into the courtyard of the château he was met by several Austrian officers with candles in their hands. He dismounted and turned to them and said: "Good evening, Gentlemen, I dare say you did not expect me here. Can one get a night's lodging along with you?"[1]

On December 6 he ordered a day of rest, and the following day advanced on Breslau, sending Ziethen and half the cavalry with nine battalions and the light troops in pursuit of Charles. They followed him until December 9, and captured more than 2,000 prisoners. Breslau surrendered on December 19 with 17,000 men and 81 guns.

As with nearly all battles, the losses at Leuthen are variously given, but probably the Prussians lost 6,000 men killed and wounded, and the Austrians 10,000 as well as 21,000 prisoners, 116 guns, 51 colours, and some 4,000 wagons. According to the *Oeuvres de Frédéric* their total losses during the campaign were 41,442 men, and according to Tempelhoff, 56,446. In either case the loss was annihilating, and not only was the whole of Silesia, except for the fortress of Schweidnitz, rewon, but Prussia emerged as the most formidable military power in Europe. Of the battle Tempelhoff writes:—

"Ancient history scarcely furnishes a single instance, and modern times none, that can be compared, either in the execution or consequences, with the battle of Leuthen. It forms an epoch in military science, and exhibits not only the theory, but also the practice of a system of which the King was the sole inventor."[2]

Napoleon writes:—

"The battle of Leuthen is a masterpiece of movements, manœuvres, and resolution. Alone it is sufficient to immortalize

---

[1] *Frederick the Great his Court and Times,* edited by Thomas Campbell, vol. III, p. 149.
[2] *The History of the Seven Years' War in Germany,* Generals Lloyd and Tempelhoff, vol. I, p. 346.

Frederick, and place him in the rank of the greatest generals. All his manœuvres at this battle are in conformity with the principles of war. He made no flank march in sight of his enemy, for his columns were not in sight. The Austrians expected him, after the combat at Borne, to take position on the heights in front of them, and while they thus waited for him, covered by rising grounds and fogs, and masked by his advanced guard, he continued his march and attacked the extreme left."[1]

It is of interest to compare the two battles which have been discussed in this chapter, for they represent the oblique order of attack at its worst and at its best. At Rossbach there was no generalship; the combined commanders had no plan, and instead of holding the line of the Saale and continuing on the defensive, which must have ended in Frederick's ruin, they abandoned it and did exactly what he wanted—offered him battle. They were novices at manœuvre, and mere copyists of a system they did not understand. They advanced in full sight of their enemy, across his flank and without an advanced guard; there was no co-operation between the three arms, and St. Germain never tried to discover what his enemy was doing. At Leuthen, Frederick moved, concentrated, surprised and hit. Co-operation was perfect, and so were the dispositions of the three arms. Nevertheless, above all, what gave Frederick the victory was that his men had confidence in him as a general.

Though after this superb victory the war continued for five years, in spite of the disasters Frederick suffered during them he emerged from the seven-year conflict the greatest general of his age, to take his place among the few Great Captains of all ages. In 1758, on August 25, he overthrew the Russians at Zorndorf, but on October 14, was surprised and defeated by the Austrians at Hochkirchen; nevertheless, he drove them out of Saxony and Silesia. The following year, on August 12, he suffered an overwhelming defeat at the hands of the Russians at Kunersdorf, and though Berlin was occupied by them, he held back the French. In 1760, undefeatable as he always was in spirit, on August 15, he beat the Austrians at Liegnitz, and, again, on November 3, at Torgau.[2] In 1761 misfortune returned, and in

---

[1] *Correspondance de Napoléon 1er*, vol. XXXII, p. 184.
[2] In estimating Frederick's generalship in these battles, it should always be remembered that numerically he was vastly inferior to his opponent. At Zorndorf, 36,000 to 52,000; at Hochkirchen, 37,000 to 90,000; at Kunersdorf, 26,000 to 70,000; at Liegnitz, 30,000 to 90,000; and at Torgau, 44,000 to 65,000.

1762 England abandoned him and sought a separate peace with France, a defection which 13 years later left England unable to find a single ally in Europe when her American Colonies rebelled. This in itself, though a momentous result of the war, cannot be credited to Frederick.

But what can be is that, not only did the battles of Rossbach and Leuthen in all probability save Prussia from extinction, but that the memories of them have ever since they were fought dominated German history and through history the German mind. Out of them arose that sense of national unity and superiority which enabled the German peoples to survive the Napoleonic Wars, and out of that, step by step, emerged a united Germany which replaced France as the most formidable continental power, terminated the Anglo-French rivalry of 600 years, and thereby opened a new epoch in world history.

The expansion of the British empire in India

The years between the Treaty of Westphalia, in 1648, and the Treaty of Utrecht, in 1713, were, for England and France, both in India and North America, years of gradual colonial expansion. Up to the date of the Restoration, in 1660, the more important acquisitions of the English East India Company were the lease of Madras in 1639 and the establishment of a factory at Hugli in 1651. But it was not until 1662, when the Portuguese settlement of Bombay became part of the dowry brought by Catharine of Braganza to Charles II, that the Company began to prosper. Six years later, Bombay was transferred to the Company for an annual rental of £10. Meanwhile, in 1664, at the instance of Colbert, the French *Compagnie Des Indes Orientales* had been founded, which, in 1674-1676, obtained trading rights at Pondicherry and Chandernagore, and, in 1690, the English Company obtained similar rights at Calcutta (Kalikata).

Throughout these years, the Mogul emperor was master of India and the power with whom the companies negotiated. But on the death of Aurungzeb, in 1707, the Mogul empire rapidly began to disintegrate, and a ring of semi-independent principalities sprang up around its decaying centre, much to the profit of the European companies, which increasingly were able to extend their trade by bargaining with the separate potentates. As an instance of their increasing wealth, the population of Calcutta, which in 1706 numbered 10,000, by 1735 rose to 100,000, and the Company's annual trade turnover topped £1,000,000.

In 1740, on the outbreak of the War of the Austrian Succession, Madras and Pondicherry were the chief trading posts of the English and French on the Coromandel coast, and in addition the English held Fort St. David, a little to the south of Pondicherry. Each was fortified, and as all were on the coast they could be supplied and reinforced from oversea, which put the English and French at an advantage over the potentates, who had no warships. Also it meant that whichever of the two main trading powers – English or French – held command of the Indian seas, it could starve out its competitor. Sea power was, therefore, the key to the colonial problem.

When England became involved in the War of the Austrian Succession, technically the two companies were placed in a state of war. As this did not suit the French, in 1742 the Marquis of Dupleix, who the year before had been appointed Governor-General of French India, and who wished to maintain neutrality, opened negotiations with the English authorities in India. But they refused to consider his proposals because they had no control over the English navy. The result was the outbreak of the First Carnatic War in 1744, which was opened when Commodore Barnet and his squadron threatened Pondicherry; the French at the time had no fleet in Indian waters. Dupleix feared that Pondicherry would be blockaded and appealed to Anwar-ud-din, Nawab of the Carnatic, for help, and also sent a dispatch to the Count of Labourdonnais, Governor of Mauritius, to come to his aid. This the latter did. He set out in March, 1746, with a fleet of eight ships of the line, carrying 1,200 reinforcements, which on arrival in June forced the English squadron to withdraw to Hugli. After this, on September 2, Dupleix laid siege to Madras while Labourdonnais blockaded it. In their turn the English appealed to the Nawab of the Carnatic, who ordered Dupleix to raise the siege, and when he refused to do so, the Nawab sent an army against him. This army arrived to find that Madras had surrendered on September 10, and laid siege to the French within the city. In no way daunted, the tiny French garrison sallied out and scattered the Nawab's unwieldy horde.

Next, Labourdonnais opened negotiations with the English to ransom Madras for £420,000. Dupleix objected to this and there was a violent quarrel, during which a hurricane scattered Labourdonnais's fleet and forced its return to Mauritius. Dupleix renounced the ransom treaty and invested Fort St. David, but as the command of the sea had again passed to his adversary, after an 18-month siege he was forced to raise it. In 1747, a powerful fleet of 13 ships of the line, under Rear-Admiral Boscawen, was sent from England to avenge the capture of Madras. On its arrival siege was laid to Pondicherry in August, 1748; but in October, on the approach of the monsoon, the siege was discontinued, and before it could be renewed the Treaty of Aix-la-Chapelle had brought the war to an end. By its terms, Madras was returned to England in exchange for Cape Breton.

Although nothing was accomplished by the First Carnatic War, much had been learnt, above all that whoever commanded the sea could in time control the land. Therefore, in the struggle for trade supremacy in India, because the English were better placed than the French to gain command of the Indian seas, the latter stood at a permanent disadvantage. Incidentally, this disadvantage encompassed all French colonial adventures; for France, a continental power, could not simultaneously be supreme in Europe and hold fast to a great colonial empire in face of England. England, protected as she was by the sea, could enter and withdraw from a continental war at will; but France could not, and once involved in one, her main effort had to be directed toward winning it or else to risk invasion; therefore the security of her colonies took second place. That she tried to do both–to be supreme in Europe and to extend her colonial empire–at one and the same time, was her undoing; for not only did this impossible task help England to become mistress of the seas, but it also contributed to secure the predominance of Prussia in Germany.

Though Dupleix well enough understood the importance of sea power, he was in no way dismayed by its loss. A man of vision, the complete discomfiture of Anwar-ud-din's horde before Madras had fired his imagination, for it had revealed to him that no native army, however numerous, could hope to match a handful of disciplined European soldiers. Therefore, in his small army he had an effective weapon which would prove decisive in any quarrel between the Indian princes, for any one of them would be eager to offer whatever price Dupleix might ask for its help. With a powerful potentate as his ally, Dupleix felt that ultimately he would be more than a match for the English on land, and in spite of their sea power.

No sooner had he decided upon his plan than fortune enabled him to put it to the test. In 1743, on the death of Dost Ali, Nawab of the Carnatic, Nizam-ul-mulk Asaf Jah, Subahdar of the Deccan, had appointed Anwar-ud-din in his place. At the time, Dost Ali's son-in-law, Chanda Sahib, who claimed succession, was a prisoner, but on his release in 1748 he began to conspire to gain his father-in-law's throne. In the same year, Asaf Jah died and was succeeded by his son Nasir Jang, who was opposed by his son Muzaffar Jung, who laid claim to the throne as the Moghul emperor's appointee. Here was Dupleix's chance, and he seized it.

With the view to oust Anwar-ud-din and Nasir Jang, Dupleix concluded a secret treaty with both claimants, and on August 3, 1749, the three allies defeated and killed Anwar-ud-din at the battle of Ambur, and Chanda Sahib replaced him. Thus started the Second Carnatic War.

The English realized the danger they were in, and appealed to Nasir Jang to reconquer the Carnatic, with the result that after some initial successes, Nasir Jang was assassinated in December, 1750. Dupleix then proclaimed Muzaffar Jung Subahdar of the Deccan, who in gratitude appointed Dupleix governor of all the Mogul lands from the Krishna River to Cape Comorin, in return for which Dupleix placed a small army under the Marquis de Bussy at Muzaffar Jung's disposal.

When the English saw that Dupleix was the real ruler of the Carnatic and de Bussy paramount at the court of the new Nizam, they were compelled to realize that they were faced with a life-and-death struggle. Fortunately for them, in 1750, Thomas Saunders, a man of outstanding energy, was appointed Governor of Madras. He saw that the rocky citadel of Trichinopoly dominated the great plain of the Carnatic; it was held by Mohammad Ali, a connexion of the late Anwar-ud-din, and it was decided to make it the rallying point of opposition against the French.

In the spring of 1751 Dupleix sent an army under Jacques François Law to take it. Robert Clive, who had recently joined the English Army in Madras, on the suggestion of Mohammad Ali, proposed an expedition against Arcot as the best means to relieve the pressure on Trichinopoly; and to this Saunders gave his consent. With 200 English soldiers and 300 sepoys Clive occupied Arcot. At once Chanda Sahib sent a relieving force from the siege lines at Trichinopoly to regain his capital. For 53 days Clive heroically held out, until, exhausted, the besiegers withdrew. This setback immensely raised English prestige and profoundly lowered that of the French, and coupled with Clive's victories at Arni and Coveripak in the autumn and winter, the French cause rapidly declined. In June, 1752, Law was forced to surrender to Lawrence and Clive before Trichinopoly, and his ally, Chanda Sahib, was put to death. For two years fighting continued in the Deccan, but in spite of de Bussy's brilliant successes there, because of French failure in the Carnatic, the French were unable to extend their control over the Nizam's territories. Thus, slowly French dominion crumbled, until the

Court of France, tired of Dupleix's failures, decided on his recall.

In the summer of 1753, Godeheu, a director of the French East India Company, was sent out to supersede Dupleix. He landed in India in August, 1754, and when in October Dupleix sailed for France, he concluded a three-month truce, which in January, 1755, was followed by the publication of a provisional treaty, to become valid only if ratified by the companies at home. Because of the outbreak of the Seven Years War, ratification never took place.

CHAPTER 7

The Battle of Plassey, 1757

While the English and French contended for supremacy in the Carnatic, a similar struggle brewed in Bengal, which, like the Deccan, was ruled by a nominal subahdar of the Mogul, the Nawab Alivardi Khan, who had succeeded to the throne in 1740. Toward the end of his reign friction had arisen with the English over the fortifications of Calcutta, which had been added to without his permission. Thus matters stood when he died on April 9, 1756, and was succeeded by his son-in-law, Siraj-ud-daulah, a pleasure-loving and erratic young man, aged about 20, who, though he possessed vigour and ability, lacked decision and was easily led astray by the profligates of his court.

During the reign of his father-in-law, Siraj-ud-daulah had raised the question of the Calcutta fortifications with Mr. W. Watts, chief of the English factory of Cassimbazar, and immediately after his succession he received an evasive reply to a letter he had addressed to Mr. Roger Drake, Governor of Calcutta, in which he had ordered him to demolish the additional fortifications. The new Nawab knew that Calcutta was garrisoned by no more than 264 soldiers and 250 armed civilians, of whom only 174 were Europeans, and on June 4 he set out from his capital, Murshidabad, and seized Cassimbazar. From there he marched on to Calcutta, and on June 16 appeared before the Maratha wall, which protected its landward side.

At once most of the European population was evacuated; but when the ships were fired on, Governor Drake lost his head and shamefully abandoned the remainder who, when his flight was discovered, appointed Mr. Holwell, a member of the Council, in command. On June 20 Holwell was forced to capitulate, and though Siraj-ud-daulah promised in no way to molest him and his people, it would seem that, unknown to the Nawab, at the instigation of Omichand, a rich merchant, the remnants of the garrison, 146 in all, were, during the night of June 20-21, incarcerated in the Black Hole of Fort William. Of these unfortunates 123 are said to have been suffocated or trampled to death.[1]

Once Calcutta was his, Siraj-ud-daulah returned to Murshidabad, from where he marched against Shaukat Jang, a claimant of his throne, and defeated and killed him. He failed to appreciate that their command of the sea gave the English the advantage over him, never suspected that they would attempt to retake Calcutta, and left in it a weak garrison under Manikchand. Meanwhile Drake and the English from Calcutta had taken refuge in Fulta, from where, by intrigue, they won over to their cause Manikchand, Omichand, and Jagat Seth, a rich banker, and other leading men of the Nawab's court.

On July 15, when the news of the Nawab's advance on Cassimbazar was first received in Madras, Major Kilpatrick and 230 soldiers were sent north to reinforce Calcutta. But when, on August 5, the news of the disaster percolated through, the Madras Council was thrown into consternation, for war between England and France was in the air and the approach of a powerful French fleet was expected. But the Council did not lose its head, and fortunately a well equipped army and navy, the former under Robert Clive, and the latter commanded by Admiral Charles Watson, which had been made ready for an expedition against the French, were available. On the suggestion of one of the Councillors, Robert Orme—the historian—it was decided to send both to Bengal, a decision which was to prove one of the most momentous in British history. On October 16 the expedition set out. It consisted of six warships and transports carrying 900 regular soldiers and 1,500 sepoys.

After a chequered voyage, during which two vessels were

---

[1] The fullest account of this incident is given by J. S. Holwell himself in his "A Genuine Narrative of the Deplorable Deaths of the English Gentlemen and Others, who were suffocated in the Black Hole in Fort William, at Calcutta, in the Kingdom of Bengal; in the Night succeeding the 20th Day of June, 1756": See *India Tracts*, by Mr. Holwell (1764), pp. 253–276. The Black Hole was a prisoners' cell "a cube of about eighteen feet" (Holwell, p. 258), and these cells were so designated down to 1868, when they were abolished. As regards Omichand, Mr. Holwell gives his reasons for suspecting him on p. 268. Sir George Forrest in his *The Life of Lord Clive* (1918), vol. I, p. 331, adopts this view and supplies further proof of its correctness. An Indian view is given by R. C. Majumdar, H. C. Raychandhuri and Kalikinkar Datta in *An Advanced History of India* (1946), p. 658, which reads: "The truth of this story has been doubted on good grounds. That some prisoners were put into the Black Hole and a few of them, wounded in the course of the fight, died there, may be accepted as true. But the tragic details, designed to suit a magnified number of prisoners, must almost certainly be ascribed to the fertile imagination of Holwell, on whose authority the story primarily rests. In any case, it is agreed on all hands that Siraj-ud-daulah was not in any way personally responsible for the incident."

driven out of their course—one to Ceylon—on November 16 the expedition approached the mouth of the Hugli, from where Watson courageously decided to sail up the river, then almost unknown; a feat which Mountstuart Elphinstone says was "one of the most gallant parts of the whole enterprise."[1] The expedition arrived at Fulta after a hazardous voyage on December 15. There a landing was made and a junction effected with Kilpatrick's force, through sickness reduced to 120 men.

Meanwhile Drake at Fulta had received instructions from England appointing him and three of his former council to conduct affairs in Bengal, and as they were ignorant that an expedition was on its way and had opened negotiations with Siraj-ud-daulah, on the arrival of Clive and Watson, Drake and his colleagues did their utmost to persuade them to desist from warlike operations against the Nawab. Watson paid no attention to their plea and on December 17 addressed a letter to Siraj-ud-daulah, in which he demanded the restoration of the ancient rights and immunities of the Company as well as compensation for the losses suffered. What the Nawab's reply was is unknown, but the outcome was that, on December 27, the fleet proceeded upstream, and on January 1, 1757, arrived at Calcutta. On the following day Manikchand fled to Murshidabad, and Clive recovered Calcutta without any serious fighting.

The situation which faced Clive was extremely anxious. At Chandernagore, a few miles north of Calcutta, there were 600 French, of whom 300 were soldiers, and the nearest of de Bussy's stations was only 200 miles distant from Bengal. Should the French throw in their lot with the Nawab, the superiority against the English might prove overwhelming. Again, should the struggle be protracted, as the Carnatic was now defenceless, Madras might easily be lost. The Nawab was in doubt, he hated all Europeans, yet believed that the total inhabitants of Europe numbered no more than 10,000. But the great banking house of Jagat Seth (the Rothschilds of Bengal) favoured peace, because these moneylenders wanted to re-establish their Calcutta trade; so also did Omichand. At first the Nawab toyed with the idea, then he changed his mind and decided to advance again on Calcutta.

The story now reads like an Arabian Night's romance, and its hero was born on September 29, 1725, at Market Drayton,

[1] *The Rise of the British Power in the East*, Hon. Mountstuart Elphinstone (1887), p. 281.

in Shropshire. In his eighteenth year Robert Clive entered the service of the East India Company as a writer, a profession he liked so little that on two occasions he attempted suicide. Next, aged 21, he obtained an ensign's commission in the Company's army, and, as already related, rose to fame as a soldier. Superseded by Major Lawrence, 28 years his senior, he served loyally under that officer, and on his return to England, in 1753, so highly did Clive hold him in respect that he refused to accept a sword set with diamonds, presented to him by the Company, unless a similar one were bestowed upon Lawrence. In 1755, he returned to India as a regular lieutenant-colonel.

As a man Clive was decisive in whatever he undertook, but never obstinate. He always saw clearly his goal; and, as circumstances changed, he could rapidly change his means without losing sight of it. In temperament he was retired, daring and modest. Though autocratic when roused, he was never impatient when under military command. Major Lawrence writes of him: "He was a man of undaunted resolution, of a cool temper, and a presence of mind which never left him in the greatest danger. Born a soldier; for without a military education of any sort, or much conversing with any of the profession, from his judgment and good sense he led an army like an experienced officer and a brave soldier, with a prudence that certainly warranted success."[1] He realized, as Macaulay says, "that he had to deal with men destitute of what in Europe is called honour", and as a statesman Clive was Machiavellian. Like Gloucester he might on more than one occasion have said:

> I can add colours to the chameleon,
> Change shapes with Proteus, for advantages,
> And set the murd'rous Machiavel to school.[2]

As a soldier his will was of iron. No odds ever overcame his determination to conquer, and no difficulties appeared to him to be insurmountable. Should he make a mistake, which was seldom, he never failed with astonishing rapidity to turn it to his advantage, mainly because he read the Oriental like an open book. As Colonel Malleson says: "His conceptions were always brilliant, his plans were always masterly, his execution was always effective."[3] Nevertheless, in no one of his many battles

[1] *Ibid.*, pp. 159–160.   [2] Shakespeare's *King Henry VI*, Pt. 3, III, ii.
[3] *Lord Clive*, Colonel G. B. Malleson (1882), p. 479.

did his courage shine so brightly as when, in 1766, having abolished the system of pay and allowances known as "double batta", he was faced by a mutiny of the Company's officers supported by the civil service. "In this fearful predicament," writes Mr. P. E. Roberts, "he never faltered, and his supreme mastery over men was never better exemplified. . . . In a few days, by amazing promptness of action and pure inflexibility of will, he had shamed the mutineers into submission. It is in a crisis of this nature that Clive appears almost a Titanic figure. He matched all the resources of his wonderful personality against a rebellious Council, an army in open mutiny, a foreign position of extreme peril, and won the day."[1]

In January, 1767, he left India for good. In 1772 he was attacked in Parliament, as he said, like a "sheep-stealer", by the "corrupt Bengal gang" who had followed him to England. He defended himself in the House of Commons with scorn and courage, and, in 1774, broken by abuse and suffering from insomnia, in his fiftieth year he took his own life on November 22.

While the Nawab again prepared to move south from Murshidabad, the Committee decided to occupy Hugli, and to effect this, on January 6 Major Kilpatrick with four ships carrying 150 regulars and 200 sepoys was sent upstream. They arrived at Hugli on January 10, and with little difficulty the town was occupied by an able officer named Eyre Coote.[2] It was during this expedition that definite news "arrived from Aleppo, that war had been declared (in August) between Great Britain and France".[3]

Meanwhile Clive remained at Calcutta, strengthened the fortifications of Fort William, and raised a new battalion of sepoys, the 1st Regiment of Bengal Native Infantry, known as the *Lal Paltan* or "Red Regiment", which originated the Bengal Native Army.[4] Next, on January 30, the Nawab's army approached and crossed the river 10 miles north of Hugli. With it came Omichand, who was anxious to recover his shattered fortunes, and as he owned many of the best houses in Calcutta he "was solicitious to regain his former influence amongst the

---

[1] *The Cambridge Modern History*, vol. VI, p. 565.
[2] Later famous as General Sir Eyre Coote (1726–1783). Victor of Wandiwash in 1760, and Porto Novo, Pollilur and Sholingarh in 1781.
[3] *A History of the Military Transactions of the British Nation in Indostan from the Year MDCCXLV*, Robert Orme (1778), vol. II, p. 127.
[4] *An Historical Account of the Rise and Progress of the Bengal Native Army*, Captain Williams (1817), pp. 4, 165–166.

English, by promoting the pacification."[1] Clive, whose position was precarious, also favoured peace, and already during the Nawab's advance he had entered into correspondence with him on that subject; but as the latter continued his march, and, on February 3, occupied the ground along the Maratha ditch, Clive decided to strike. He assembled a force of 650 regulars, 800 sepoys, 600 seamen, and six guns manned by 100 gunners, and at two o'clock on the morning of February 7, he marched out against his enemy's 18,000 cavalry, 12,000 infantry, 40 guns, and 50 elephants, determined to gain a decisive victory. Probably he would have done so, and in spite of his numerical inferiority, had not a mist arisen which was so dense that objects two to three yards distant were obscured. Then a most extraordinary action took place; the guides lost their way; Clive's army wandered through the centre of the enemy's camp, firing to right and left in almost pitch darkness, and eventually regained its own lines at seven o'clock that evening.[2]

The losses on both sides were considerable, the Nawab's were 1,300 killed and wounded as well as 500 horses and four elephants, and Clive's, 57 killed and 117 wounded. But worse than the casualties they suffered, Clive's men were dispirited, though this was in part set-off by the Nawab's panic; for, according to Orme, his whole army passed the succeeding night on the watch, "firing cannon and musketry until daylight, in order to encourage themselves, and to deter the English from attacking them again."[3]

Siraj-ud-daulah was so paralysed by this surprise attack that, on February 9, he concluded with Clive the Treaty of Alinagar, according to which the past privileges of the Company were recognized and compensation paid for damage done.

The reason why Clive decided on a cessation of hostilities was that he feared the French might throw in their lot with the Nawab, which would have frustrated his policy of keeping them separated in order to deal with each in turn. Further, he realized that until French power in Bengal was destroyed, it would not be safe for him and his army to return to Madras. Thus it came about that, scarcely were the signatures on the treaty dry, than he sought the Nawab's permission to advance on Chandernagore.

---

[1] Robert Orme, vol. II, p. 128.
[2] For a full account of this strange battle see Orme, vol. II, pp. 131–134.
[3] Ibid., vol. II, p. 135.

Though the Nawab replied that he could never allow one section of his subjects to be molested by another, he decided to temporize, and pretending that de Bussy was about to invade Bengal, he asked Clive to come to his help. Further, he requested that Mr. Watts, whom he considered to be a mild man, be sent to his court as the Company's representative. This done, he returned to Murshidabad.

Though Clive knew that the de Bussy scare was a blind, he agreed to Watts's appointment, and with him he sent Omichand, who had assisted in negotiating the peace treaty. The two then set out, and when, on February 18, they were at Hugli, Omichand discovered that the Nawab had sent 100,000 rupees to the Governor of Chandernagore and that one of his agents, Nuncomar (Nanda-Kumar), an astute Bengali brahmin, had been hurried there to help the French in every way. At once Omichand bought this man off for 12,000 rupees, after which he and Watts proceeded to the capital to find that, on February 22, the Nawab had written to Clive peremptorily to forbid an attack on Chandernagore, and had stated that, should the English advance against it, he would march to the support of the French. Coincidently with this prohibition came a request from the Governor of Chandernagore for a treaty of neutrality between the French and the English in Bengal, which, on February 25, resulted in a meeting of the two parties at Calcutta, where articles were drafted. But Admiral Watson refused to sign them unless they were sanctioned by the Supreme Government at Pondicherry, and because on the same day reinforcements arrived by sea, Clive, deemed himself now strong enough to take Chandernagore, dismissed the French deputies and, provided the Nawab's consent were first obtained, decided on an immediate attack.

When these things were in progress, the Nawab received intelligence (possibly concocted by Watts or Omichand) that the Afghans, under the dreaded Ahmad Shah Durrani, were marching from Delhi to invade Bengal. Terrified, he hastily wrote to Clive supplicating his assistance and offered to pay him 100,000 rupees a month for the hire of his troops. This was an opportunity which Clive did not miss, and again he pressed for permission to march on Chandernagore; but as no reply was received, and he learnt that the Nawab was negotiating with de Bussy, he decided to advance, and, on March 8, broke camp and marched north. Next, on March 13, Admiral Watson received a letter from the Nawab which decided the fate of the French settlement. In it was written: "If an enemy comes to you and implores your mercy with a clear heart, his life should be spared; but if you mistrust his sincerity, act according to the time and occasion."[1] According to Ives, "It was this paragraph that encouraged the admiral and colonel to proceed in their attack of Chandernagore."[2]

Immediately after this letter was received, Clive wrote to M. Renault, Governor of Chandernagore, to demand the surrender of the settlement, which was protected by Fort d'Orléans, situated about 30 yards from the Hugli. As no notice was taken of the summons, Clive decided to attack. Batteries were planted, and, on March 18, the fleet anchored off the Prussian Octagon. Again a summons of surrender was sent and refused, and "at length", writed Ives, "the *glorious* morning of the 23rd of March arrived, and upon the ships getting under sail, the Colonel's battery, which had been finished behind a dead wall, began firing away on the S.E. bastion. . . . The fire now became general on both sides, and was kept up with extraordinary spirit." Three hours later, at 9 a.m., "the parapets of the north and south bastions" were "almost beaten down", the French "hung out the white flag",[3] and the settlement capitulated.

"The siege and defence of Chandernagore," writes Sir George Forrest, "derives its importance from the immense and far-reaching effect it had on the extension of British dominion in India. It dealt a blow which shook the faith of the native princes and chiefs of Western India in the French Power. The capture of Fort D'Orleans secured the safety of Calcutta, our base on the sea, and made us masters of the gate of the great waterway which led to the rich provinces of Bengal, Behar, and Orissa, and from thence further northwards to the great central plain which stretches to the foot of the Himalayas. The rout at Plassey was a corollary of the conquest of the fortified station of Chandernagore."[4]

Once Chandernagore was in British hands, Clive, who deeply distrusted the shifty Siraj-ud-daulah, decided, contrary to his orders, to remain in Bengal instead of returning to Madras.

---

[1] *Ibid.*, vol. II, p. 140.
[2] *A Voyage from England to India, etc.* (1773), p. 125.
[3] *Ibid.*, pp. 128–130.
[4] *The Life of Lord Clive*, Sir George Forrest, vol. I, p. 394.

Further, because his entire policy revolved round the total expulsion of the French, as long as de Bussy was in a position to support the Nawab, it could not be attained. On March 29 he wrote to Siraj-ud-daulah to insist that he should surrender to him all the French settlements, and particularly that in Cassimbazar, near Murshidabad. This the Nawab had no intention of doing, for he hoped, once the monsoon was at an end, that Clive would be compelled to return to Madras. He decided, therefore, to obstruct and temporize. He took the French into his service, wrote that he had ordered them out of his country, and to protect himself against surprise he moved Mir Jafar, his commander-in-chief, and 15,000 troops to Plassey, some 30 miles south of Murshidabad.

Outwardly the Nawab's position was a strong one, because Madras wanted Clive, and Clive was too weak to plunge into action. Inwardly, within his court and his camp, his brutality, treachery and avarice had provoked treason.[1] After his occupation of Calcutta he had made Jagat Seth his enemy by striking him in the face, and since then had continually insulted him by threats to have him circumcised.[2] To revenge himself, Jagat Seth, through his friend and brother extortioner, Omichand, got into touch with one of the Nawab's generals, and through him with Mir Jafar, whom he found willing to support Clive in over-throwing Suraj-ud-daulah.

By April 26 the conspiracy had so far developed that Watts, who was in close touch with Omichand, wrote to Clive: "If you approve of this scheme . . . he (Meer Jaffeer) requests you will write your proposals of what money, what land you want, and what treaties you will engage in."[3] Five days later Clive went to Calcutta and placed the proposal before the Committee, which agreed to support Mir Jafar, and the next day he communicated his plan of action to Watts.

In order to lull Siraj-ud-daulah into a false sense of security, Clive sent him a "soothing letter" to inform him that he was moving his troops to Calcutta, and to deceive him he had them embarked. Next, he suggested that Mir Jafar—still at Plassey—should be withdrawn, and finally he wrote to Watts: "Tell Mur Jaffeir to fear nothing, that I will join him with 5,000 Men who

[1] See *The Seir Mutaqherin, or View of Modern Times*, Ghulam Husain Khan (1789), vol. 1, pt. 2, p. 763.

[2] *Ibid.*, p. 759.

[3] Quoted from *The Life of Lord Clive*, Sir George Forrest, vol. 1, p. 412.

never turn'd their Backs and that if he fails seizing him [the Nawab] we shall be strong enough to drive him out of the Country, assure him I will march night and Day to his assistance and stand by him as long as I have a man left. . . ."[1]

In spite of Clive's letter, Siraj-ud-daulah remained unsoothed and highly suspicious; he prevaricated and kept Mir Jafar at Plassey. Then the unexpected happened in its full Oriental way. Watts showed the proposals to Omichand, who refused to agree to them unless he received as his share of the booty five per cent. of the Nawab's treasure, which quite erroneously was supposed to total £45,000,000, as well as a quarter of his jewels. As further inquiries reduced this sum to £4,500,000, Watts inserted in the proposed articles, £300,000 in all as Omichand's share, and was compelled to do so because that wily Hindu suddenly "double-crossed" him, and said that, if he did not receive the five per cent., he would divulge the conspiracy to the Nawab. Also, as Sir George Forrest writes: "If Clive allowed himself to be blackmailed by Omichand, and complied with his terms, the Seths and Meer Jaffier, he had every reason to think, would, according to Watts's letter, refuse to agree to the treaty and the enterprise meant massacre and the destruction of the British settlements in Bengal."[2]

But Clive was a match for the crafty Bengali, and to deal with Oriental cunning he fitted his means to that end. He received Watts's letter concerning Omichand on May 16. The day following he went to Calcutta, and at a meeting of the Committee decided that Omichand should receive nothing. As this did not solve the problem, on May 18 Clive placed before the Committee two draft Articles of Agreement–a real and a fictitious one. In the former, which was to be delivered to Mir Jafar, all mention of a reward to Omichand was omitted; "but, in the fictitious treaty, which was to be shown to Omichand," was to be inserted, "an article stipulating for him a present of two millions of rupees."[3] The two drafts, the real one on white paper and the fictitious one on red, were accepted and signed by all the members except Admiral Watson, who refused to place his signature to the letter, but made no objection to his name being forged by a Mr. Lushington. The two drafts were then sent to Watts.

---

[1] *Ibid.*, p. 414. For summary of proposals see p. 415.　　　　[2] *Ibid.*, p. 418.
[3] Robert Orme, vol. II, p. 154. "The forged document in favour of Omichand is no doubt a stain on his (Clive's) character, but considering the circumstances in which he was placed, and the moral standards òf the age in which he lived, these things should be looked at in proper perspective" (*An Advanced History of India*, p. 665).

Meanwhile Omichand, to make certain of all the gain he could, visited the Nawab secretly, and on his return told Watts that he had informed him that de Bussy and Clive had agreed between themselves to join forces and divide Bengal between France and England, and by this lie he had extracted from him a reward of £80,000. Though, so far as the reward went, this was true, for that night he was found counting out half of it, Watts suspected that, instead of lying about de Bussy, he had divulged to the Nawab as much of the plot as might be confided without endangering his own skin. That he had done so is all but certain, for, on May 30, the Nawab received Mir Jafar with marked distrust, and a few days later removed him from his command. The disgruntled commander-in-chief retired to his residence and fortified it.

By now Omichand's treachery had become so dangerous that it was imperative to get him out of Murshidabad, and at length Watts persuaded him to leave by palanquin with Mr. Scrafton, a Company agent, for Calcutta. On May 30 they set out, but were delayed at Cassimbazar, where the avaricious old man halted awhile in order to extract more money. At Plassey he disappeared when Scrafton was asleep, and by a friend was told "that no stipulation had been made for him in the agreements with Meer Jaffier."[1] He hurried on to Calcutta, where he arrived on June 8, and was received by Clive in so friendly a manner that he regained his confidence. Nevertheless, he bribed the Persian scribe of the Council to inform him if any deceit had been practised. Seemingly he learnt nothing to his disadvantage.

As soon as he and Scrafton left Murshidabad, Mir Jafar sent a messenger to Watts, to whom Watts handed the two treaties with a message to explain the deceit practised on Omichand. Both were signed by Mir Jafar on June 4. This done, it was still necessary that Mir Jafar should take an oath to observe what he had agreed, and as his house was closely watched by the Nawab's spies, Watts was conveyed there in a covered palanquin "such as carry women of distinction" and was deposited in the seraglio. There Mir Jafar informed him that Clive should immediately take the field, and that on his approach "he [Mir Jafar] would regulate his conduct according to the station which he should chance to occupy; if in the van, he would, on the approach of the English, beat his great drum, display his standard, march off with

[1] Robert Orme, vol. II, p. 159.

all the troops under his command, and join them on the right; if on either of the wings, or in the rear, he would display a white flag, charge the main body of the Nabob's army as soon as the English began to attack. . . .[1]

His task accomplished, Watts sent the treaties by a trusted messenger, Omar Beg, to Calcutta, where they were received on June 11.[2] The day following, with three Englishmen, he escaped from Murshidabad, and, after an exciting and perilous journey, on June 13 reached Clive's camp at Kalna, 15 miles north of Hugli. At once Clive decided to strike, so he sent Siraj-ud-daulah a letter which was tantamount to a declaration of war.

The Nawab was in no mood to receive such a communication, for the flight of Mr. Watts had astonished and frightened him so much that he was convinced that Mir Jafar was a traitor, and it was when he was about to lay siege to his residence that Clive's ultimatum arrived. He then abandoned the enterprise and determined to separate his enemies by treating with Mir Jafar. A reconciliation followed and was sealed by mutual oaths on the Koran. This done, on June 15 he sent back to Clive a fiery reply and ordered the whole of his own army to concentrate at Plassey. But his troubles were not ended, for his troops mutinied, and refused to march until they were paid their arrears. Money was distributed, and the army set out. It arrived at the village of Daudpur, a few miles north of Plassey, on June 21.

Meanwhile, on June 13, Clive left 100 seamen to hold Chander-nagore and set out on his hazardous march. "The Europeans with the field-pieces, stores and ammunition, proceeded in 200 boats, which were towed by the Indian rowers against the stream;"[3] for the tide flowed no further than Hugli. His army comprised 613 European infantry,[4] 48 Bengal topasses,[5] 43 Bombay topasses, 171 gunners (including 57 sailors), 2,100 sepoys, eight six-pounders and two small howitzers. In all, he had approximately 3,000 soldiers.

On the afternoon of June 14 the army arrived at Kalna, and,

---

[1] Robert Orme, vol. II, pp. 160–161.

[2] When the treaties were received, we learn that as usual Omichand was on the watch and again visited the Persian scribe; but as this man had only been entrusted with the fictitious treaty, Omichand was satisfied, and "resolved to proceed with the army to Muxadavad [Murshidabad]" (Orme, vol. II, p. 163).

[3] *Ibid.*, vol. II, pp. 163–164.

[4] Made up of a detachment of the 39th Foot (Dorsetshire Regt.) and detachments of Bengal, Madras and Bombay battalions.

[5] A "topass" is a half-caste Christian, usually Portuguese.

on June 17, at Pattlee, which lies on the western bank of the Cassimbazar (Bhagirathi) River. From there, on June 18, Clive sent Major Eyre Coote with 200 regulars and 500 sepoys to seize the fortress of Katwa, not only because much grain was stored in it, but because if a retreat should become necessary, it would provide the army with a strong base to fall back upon. The following day the whole army assembled at Katwa, where, while it pitched camp, the monsoon burst upon it with tremendous violence.

This, then, was the situation that faced Clive. The ground would soon become impassable; a rapid river lay between him and his enemy, and in a few days it would become unfordable. Either he had to cross it immediately or not at all, and if he crossed it he must inevitably be cut off from his base should he be forced to retreat. Further, and most important: what was the intention of Mir Jafar, who now commanded 10,000 men? On June 17 Clive had received an ambiguous note from him; to which he had replied the day following: "If I meet the Nabob's army, what part will you act, and how am I to act? . . . Of all things take care of yourself that you be not undone by treachery before my arrival."[1] On June 19, he wrote again: "So long as I have been on my march you have not given me the least information what measures it is necessary for me to take, nor do I know what is going forward at Muxadavad. . . . I shall wait here till I have proper encouragement to proceed. I think it absolutely necessary that you should join my army as soon as possible. . . . Come over to me at Plassey or any other place you judge proper. . . . Even a thousand horse will be sufficient. . . . I prefer conquering by open force."[2] No reply was received, and as Clive had no cavalry, on June 20 he wrote to the Rajah of Burdwan asking him to send him 200 or 300 "good horse". At length two letters were received from Mir Jafar which increased Clive's distrust in him, and before night fell a report "that the whole affair had been discovered and that the Nabob and Mir Jafar were one."[3] Such was Clive's situation on the night of June 20-21.

Because in these circumstances the risks of an advance were terrible, Clive decided to consult his officers. A council of war was assembled and he put the following question: "Whether in our present situation without assistance and on our own bottom it

[1] Quoted from *The Life of Lord Clive*, Sir George Forrest, vol. i, p. 441.
[2] *Ibid.*, p. 441.   [3] *Ibid.*, p. 443. (See also Orme, vol. ii, pp. 169–170.)

would be prudent to attack the Nabob, or whether we should wait 'till joined by some Country Power?"[1] Clive voted for delay and so did Kilpatrick and eight other officers, but Major Eyre Coote and six others voted for immediate attack.[2] Clive's idea was not to abandon the campaign, but instead to remain at Katwa until assured of Mir Jafar's assistance. He saw the problem from its political point of view; Eyre Coote saw it solely from the military angle. He saw that defeat meant the loss of Bengal; Coote saw only the rising river. Nevertheless, he was perplexed, for the decision of the council in no wise alleviated his anxieties, and, "as soon as it broke up, he retired alone into the adjoining grove, where he remained near an hour in deep meditation, which convinced him of the absurdity of stopping where he was; and acting now entirely from himself, he gave orders, on his return to his headquarters, that the army should cross the river the next morning."[3]

The night passed, but no answer was received from Mir Jafar until the following day, when in a letter he replied: "The Nabob's intention is to have his intrenchment at Moncurra, therefore the sooner you march to fall on him the better. . . . When you come near I shall then be able to join you. . . . When I am arrived near the army I will send you privately all the intelligence. Let me have previous notice of the time you intend to fight." This news was sufficiently definite for Clive, therefore he ordered his army to cross the river at 5 p.m.[4] and advance on Plassey, where, after a fatiguing march through the pouring rain, it arrived about midnight. There "The army immediately took possession of the adjoining grove, when, to their great surprise, the continual sound of drums, clarions, and cymbals, which always accompany the night watches of an Indian camp, convinced them that they were within a mile of the Nabob's army."[5] It consisted of 35,000 infantry, 15,000 cavalry, 53 guns (mostly 32-pounders and 24-pounders) and some elephants.[6]

[1] *Ibid.*, p. 443.
[2] For full particulars, see Sir George Forrest, vol. I, pp. 443–444, and Orme, vol. II, pp. 169–170.
[3] Orme, vol. II, p. 171.
[4] Part of the army may have crossed earlier. Ives (p. 150) says: "At 6 o'clock in the morning the army crossed the river, and marched about two miles further, to a large tope (or grove) where they halted till the evening." Luke Scrafton (*Reflections on the Government of Indostan*, 1763, p. 85) says: "On the twenty-second of June the Colonel received a letter from Meer Jaffeir which determined him to hazard a battle, and he passed the river at five in the evening."
[5] Robert Orme, vol. II, p. 172.
[6] Orme (p. 173) says: 50,000 foot, 18,000 horse, and 50 cannon.

At dawn on June 23, Clive mounted to the roof of the Nawab's hunting lodge on the eastern bank of the Bhagirathi, in order to examine the stage of the approaching battle. A wide green plain stretched at his feet. On his right front rose a mango grove surrounded by a mud wall, and on his left the river swung westward in the form of a great "S", from the lower bend of which stretched across the plain the line of the Nawab's entrenchments. Their right rested on the river and was protected by a redoubt and a hillock, south of which were two water tanks.

As the sun rose, the enemy began to march out of his works through gaps left in their parapets, "and what with the number of elephants all covered with scarlet cloth and embroidery; their horse with their drawn swords glittering in the sun; their heavy cannon drawn by vast trains of oxen; and their standards flying, they made a most pompous and formidable appearance."[1] They advanced in dense columns of cavalry and infantry with heavy guns in the intervals, each drawn by 40 or 50 white oxen "bred in the country of Purnea, and behind every gun walked an elephant, trained to assist at difficult tugs, by shoving with his forehead against the hinder part of the carriage." On the right was Rai Durlabh, in the centre Yar Lu'f Khan, and on the left Mir Jafar. The whole advanced in a huge crescent formation that stretched from the hillock on the right to within half a mile of the mango grove on the left. Some 50 "vagabond" French, under M. St. Frais, with four guns had taken up position near the southernmost of the two water tanks—north of the mango grove, with two heavy guns on their right and Mir Madan and Mohanlal with 5,000 horse and 7,000 foot in support of them.

With assurance Clive surveyed the horde; "but judging, that if his troops remained in the grove, the enemy would impute the caution to fear, and grow bolder, he drew them up in a line with the hunting-house, and facing to the nearest tank",[2] which was occupied by the French. The whole line[3] extended about 1,000 yards. "The *Europeans* he told off in four divisions; the 1st he put under the command of Major *Kilpatrick*, the 2nd under Major *Grant*, the 3rd under Major *Coote* and the 4th under Captain *Gaupp*. The *Sepoys* were formed on the right and left."[4]

---

[1] *Reflections on the Government of Indostan*, Luke Scrafton, p. 91. See also Orme, vol. II, p. 175.
[2] Robert Orme, vol. II, p. 174.
[3] Orme (vol. II, p. 174) gives Clive's total strength at 3,250 all ranks.
[4] *A Voyage from England to India, etc.*, Edward Ives, p. 151.

As Fortescue writes: "Its strength lay in the group of white faces in the centre, and the strength of that group lay in the will of one man. It was the first time that British troops faced such odds; but it was not to be the last."[1] On the left of his line Clive threw forward a small group of sepoys with two six-pounders and two howitzers. This done, at 7 a.m., he wrote a hasty note to Mir Jafar to say: "Whatever could be done by me I have done, I can do no more. If you will come to Daudipore I will march from Placis to meet you, but if you won't comply even with this, pardon me, I shall make it up with the Nabob."[2]

At 8 a.m., the first round was fired by the French, a signal for the whole of the Nawab's artillery to open, and though most of the shot flew high, men began to fall, and Clive, unable to silence the heavy guns with his six-pounders, ordered his men to withdraw behind the mud wall of the grove. No sooner had they done so than Mir Madan, the only really loyal general in the Nawab's army, was mortally wounded,[3] and his place was taken by Mohanlal.

Once under the cover of the wall, with the eight guns firing from behind it, Clive's little army was well protected, and his two howitzers kept the French under a sustained fire. Then a fortunate event occurred: at noon a peal of thunder rolled over the plain, and down came a drenching storm of rain, which silenced the enemy's guns, for unlike Clive's gunners the Indians had no tarpaulins to keep their powder dry. Disheartened by this, the Nawab's men began to retire to their entrenchments, except for a strong body of horse on the left, which was seen to move in a manner that created doubt whether its aim was to gain possession of the village of Plassey.

About 3 p.m., Clive, drenched to the skin, retired to the hunting-lodge to change. His idea was to remain on the defensive until nightfall, and then to attack under cover of darkness. But, before retiring, he left orders with Kilpatrick that should the enemy make a forward move during his absence he was at once to be informed. What then was his surprise when a little later he learnt that Kilpatrick had ordered out a detachment with two field guns to renew the attack on the French.

---

[1] *A History of the British Army*, the Hon. J. W. Fortescue, vol. II, p. 420.
[2] Quoted from *The Life of Lord Clive*, Sir George Forrest, vol. I, p. 453.
[3] Scrafton (p. 93) says: "One great cause of our success was, that in the very beginning of the action, we had the good fortune to kill Meer Modun, one of the Soubah's best and most faithful officers."

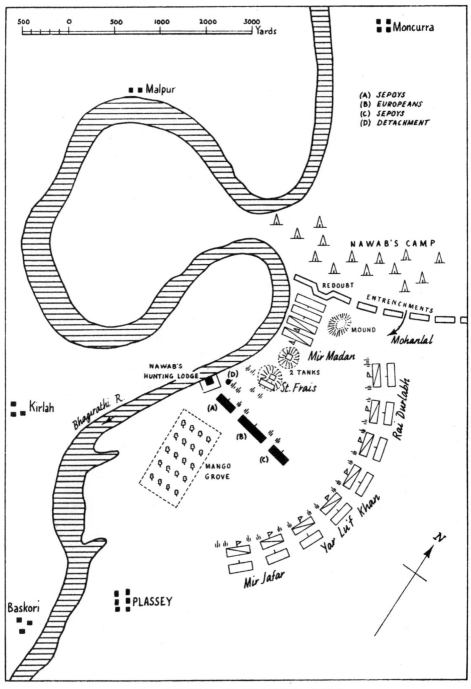

14. BATTLE OF PLASSEY, 1759

He hurried after this small force, caught up with it as it reached the first tank, and there upbraided Kilpatrick for having moved without orders. Then he realized that a second retirement before Orientals might be disastrous and determined to take advantage of the mistake. He sent Kilpatrick back for reinforcements, headed the detachment–two companies and two field pieces–and drove St. Frais back from the further tank to the redoubt. Next, he ordered up Eyre Coote and his division and left Major Grant to watch the Indian horse that still hovered near Plassey. Clive feinted at Mohanlal's left and succeeded in drawing him out of his entrenchments, when he opened the hottest possible fire upon him and killed many men, horses, and artillery oxen, as well as four "principal officers", until confusion set in and the elephants grew unruly. As this action was in progress, Clive noticed that the enemy horse on the Nawab's extreme left appeared to be on the move away from the field of battle–that is, away from the rest of the Nawab's army. This convinced him that it was commanded by Mir Jafar and he decided to strike his decisive blow. He ordered Eyre Coote to storm the mound and he detailed another party to take the redoubt, which was carried at little or no loss, because the French had received orders to retire. Thus, at 5 p.m., the whole English army swarmed into the enemy's camp, and there Clive learnt that the Nawab had fled.

Why had he taken so fatal a course? The answer is, that when Mir Madan was wounded his followers carried him to Siraj-ud-daulah's tent, and the sight of the dying man so unhinged the Nawab that he sent for Mir Jafar, who came to him strongly guarded. The meeting was followed by an abject scene. The Nawab took off his turban, placed it at the feet of his general, and pleaded for his support.[1] But Mir Jafar answered him haughtily, rode back to his troops, and forthwith sent a message to Clive; which, because of the English fire, was not received until the battle was nearly at an end. Next, Siraj-ud-daulah sought the counsel of Rai Durlabh, another of the conspirators, who advised him to withdraw his army within the entrenchments. It was this withdrawal, more especially on the extreme right of the army, which Kilpatrick had seized upon to follow up, and which in its turn had led, first to Clive's anger and secondly to the general

---

[1] See *The Mutaqherin, or View of Modern Times*, Ghulam Husain Khan, vol. 1, pp. 767–768.

advance. When the Nawab heard of it he mounted a fleet riding camel, and, followed by 2,000 horsemen, made straight for Murshidabad. Thus, like Darius, he deserted his army.

As Clive's men swept into the entrenched camp, the note written by Mir Jafar arrived. Clive hastily scribbled a reply to instruct him to meet him at Daudpore the next morning, after which with all speed he pressed on to that village, from where he pushed forward Eyre Coote to observe the enemy should he rally. Wisely, before the battle opened, Clive had promised his men a donation, therefore they had not scattered to plunder the camp.

Thus ended the battle of Plassey, in which, according to Clive, his enemy lost some 500 in killed and wounded. What did it cost him? Four Europeans and fourteen sepoys killed, nine Europeans and 36 sepoys wounded, and two European sentinels missing: in all, 65 soldiers.

The following morning Mir Jafar presented himself at Daudpore and was cordially received by Clive, who saluted him Subahdar of Bengal, Behar and Orissa. Next, he ordered a rapid march on Murshidabad to save it from pillage. When he arrived there that evening he learnt that Siraj-ud-daulah had sent away his women, had disguised himself in a mean dress, and had gone, secretly at ten o'clock at night out of a window, carrying a casket of his most precious jewels, and attended only by his favourite concubine and eunuch.[1] A few days later the unfortunate Nawab was discovered by a fakir whose nose and ears he had cut off. This man betrayed him to Mir Jafar's brother, and he was put to death by Mir Jafar's son, Miran, on July 2, and his remains were "exposed on an elephant round the city".[2]

Meanwhile, at Murshidabad, the final act of this empire-making drama was played. Watts visited the Seths, when Rai Durlabh informed him that the whole of Siraj-ud-daulah's treasure fell short of the 22,000,000 Secca rupees (£2,750,000)[3] which, according to the treaty, were to be paid. At length, after a variety of discussions, on July 6, the Committee received in silver coin 7,271,666 rupees, which were packed in 700 chests, and laden on 100 boats and sent to Calcutta. "Never before", writes Orme, "did the English nation at one time obtain such a prize in solid money; for it amounted (in the unit) to 800,000

---

[1] Robert Orme, vol. II, p. 179.
[2] *A Voyage from England to India, etc.*, Edward Ives, p. 154.
[3] Robert Orme, vol. II, p. 180.

pounds sterling."[1] By August 30 a total of 10,765,737 rupees had been paid, and the immediate result was that "commerce revived throughout the settlement, and affluence began to spread in every house".[2]

When the division of the spoil was made, Omichand, who thought himself in high esteem, awaited his reward. Clive turned to Scrafton and exclaimed: " 'It is now time to undeceive Omichand,' on which Scrafton said to him in the Indostan language, 'Omichand, the red paper is a trick: you are to have nothing.' These words overpowered him like a blast of sulphur; he sank back fainting, and would have fallen to the ground, had not one of his attendants caught him in his arms; they carried him to his palanquin, in which they conveyed him to his house, where he remained some hours in stupid melancholy, and began to shew some symptoms of insanity."[3]

Two points alone remain to be mentioned before we consider the influences of this battle. On August 16, Admiral Watson, Clive's gallant comrade-in-arms, died of a "malignant fever", probably typhoid, and the agent selected by Clive to reside at Mir Jafar's court was Warren Hastings, then aged 25.

What did this small battle, little more than a skirmish, accomplish? A world change in its way unparalleled since on October 31, 331 B.C., Alexander the Great overthrew Darius on the field of Arbela. Colonel Malleson, a sober writer says: "There never was a battle in which the consequences were so vast, so immediate and so permanent."[4] And in his *Lord Clive* he writes: "The work of Clive was, all things considered, as great as that of Alexander."[5] This is true; for Clive realized that the path of dominion lay open. "It is scarcely hyperbole to say," he wrote, "that tomorrow the whole Moghul empire is in our power."[6]

Yet this victory, on the shifting banks of the Bhagirathi, produced deeper changes still. From the opening of the eighteenth century, the western world had been big with ideas, and the most world-changing was that of the use of steam as power. Savery, Papin and Newcomen all struggled with the embryo of this monster, which one day was to breathe power over the entire world. All that was lacking was gold to fertilize it, and it was Clive who undammed the yellow stream.

---

[1] Robert Orme, p. 188.   [2] *Ibid.*, p. 189.   [3] *Ibid.*, p. 182.
[4] *The Decisive Battles of India* (1883), p. 68.   [5] *Ibid.* p. 495.
[6] Quoted from *The Cambridge Modern History*, vol. VI, p. 564.

"As to Clive," writes Macaulay, "there was no limit to his acquisitions but his own moderation. The treasury of Bengal was thrown open to him. There was piled up, after the usage of Indian princes, immense masses of coin, among which might not seldom be detected the florins, and byzants with which, before any European ship had turned the Cape of Good Hope, the Venetians purchased the stuffs and spices of the East. Clive walked between heaps of gold and silver, crowned with rubies and diamonds, and was at liberty to help himself."[1]

India, the great reservoir and sink of precious metals, was thus opened, and from 1757 enormous fortunes were made in the East, to be brought home to England to finance the rising industrial age, to supply it with its life blood, and through it to create a new and Titanic world. As Alexander had unleashed the hoarded gold of Persia, and the Roman proconsuls had seized upon the spoil of Greece and Pontus, and the Conquistadores the silver of Peru, so now did the English nabobs, merchant princes and adventurers, followers and imitators of the Seths and the Omichands, unthaw the frozen treasure of Hindustan and pour it into England. "It is not too much to say," writes Brooks Adams, "that the destiny of Europe hinged upon the conquest of Bengal."[2]

The effect was immediate and miraculous. Before 1757 the machinery for spinning cotton[3] in England was almost as primitive as in India, and the iron industry was in a decline. Suddenly all changed. In 1760 the flying shuttle appeared; in 1764 Hargreaves' spinning-jenny; in 1768 Cartwright's power-loom. "But though these machines served as outlets for the accelerating movement of the time, they did not cause that acceleration. In themselves inventions are passive, many of the most important having lain dormant for centuries, waiting for a sufficient store of force to have accumulated to set them working. That store must always take the shape of money, not hoarded, but, in motion."[4]

Further, after 1760 "a complex system of credit sprang up, based on a metallic treasure".[5] In 1750 Burke[6] informs us that there were not "twelve Bankers shops" in the provinces, while in 1796 they were to be found "in almost every market town". In

[1] *Essay on Clive* (edit. 1903), p. 53.
[2] *The Law of Civilization and Decay*, Brooks Adams (edit. 1921), p. 305.
[3] *History of the Cotton Manufacture*, Sir Edward Baines (1835), p. 115.
[4] *The Law of Civilization and Decay*, Brooks Adams, p. 314.
[5] *Ibid.*, p. 317.
[6] *Two Letters on the Proposals for Peace with the Regicide Directory of France*, Edmund Burke (1796), Letter 1, p. 80.

1756 the national debt stood at £74,575,000, and in 1815 at £861,000,000, and though between 1710 and 1760 only 335,000 acres of common land were enclosed, between 1760 and 1843 7,000,000 acres were. So the story lengthens out, profit heaped upon profit. "Possibly since the world began," writes Brooks Adams, "no investment has ever yielded the profit reaped from the Indian plunder, because for nearly fifty years Great Britain stood without a competitor."[1]

Thus it came about that out of the field of Plassey and the victors' 18 dead there sprouted forth the power of the nineteenth century. Mammon now strode into supremacy to become the unchallenged god of the western world. Once in the lands of the rising sun western man had sought the Holy Sepulchre. That sun had long set, and now in those spiritually arid regions he found the almighty sovereign. What the Cross had failed to achieve, in a few blood-red years the trinity of piston, sword, and coin accomplished: the subjection of the East and for a span of nearly 200 years the economic serfdom of the Oriental world.

[1] *The Law of Civilization and Decay*, p. 317.

The struggle between England and France in North America

When the French planted their first permanent colony in Canada in 1608, rivalry with the English began, and though, after years of border forays, it was to be decided by battle, fundamentally it was determined by the methods of colonization adopted by the French and English. That of France was largely missionary in effort, it aimed at the conversion and civilization of the Red Indians; England's was a commercial enterprise—the occupation of the Indian hunting-grounds and their conversion into prosperous settlements. The former sought collaboration with the Indians, the latter was antagonistic to them, and the issue was that, while the French colonists became traders and hunters scattered over a vast area, the English became farmers and townsmen, stayed concentrated in ever-expanding groups, and rapidly outstepped the French in population. The growth of the English colonies was further accelerated because the Puritan exodus from England to America was unrivalled by a Huguenot migration to the French colonies. Forbidden to seek refuge from persecution in Canada, Acadie (Nova Scotia) and Louisiana—founded by La Salle in 1682—because Louis XIV would not tolerate the formation of heretical French settlements in America, the Huguenots flocked to the Carolinas. By 1713, when the Treaty of Utrecht was signed, the Canadians numbered no more than 20,000, and were opposed by 158,000 settlers in New England and 218,000 in the other British American colonies. Thirty-five years later, the French in Canada numbered 80,000 and the white inhabitants of the English colonies a million.

Shortly after the Treaty of Utrecht was signed, as an offset to the loss of Acadie and Newfoundland, the French, at the cost of 30,000,000 livres, built the great fortress of Louisbourg on Cape Breton Island, and from then onward the situation between the two groups of colonists became increasingly strained. In 1745, France and England were at war, and the New England colonists, under the direction of William Shirley, Governor of Massachusetts, helped by Admiral Warren and four warships, after a five-week siege captured Louisbourg. Nevertheless, in 1748, according to the terms of the Treaty of Aix-la-Chapelle, it was returned to France.

Scarcely was the ink of this treaty dry than de la Gallisonière, Governor of Canada, revived La Salle's scheme and initiated a policy of aggression by sending an expedition into the region of the Ohio to claim it in the name of Louis XV. His aim was to confine the English colonists to the area between the Atlantic and the Alleghanies by planting French settlements in the Ohio valley and linking up Canada with Louisiana by a chain of forts. To frustrate this attempt to box in the English colonists, in 1753 Robert Dinwiddie, Governor of Virginia, sent a young man, George Washington (1732–1799), with a party of soldiers to build a fort at the junction of the Alleghany and Monongahela rivers. Again in the following year Washington was sent out with some 400 soldiers and Indians, and outnumbered, after a series of skirmishes, he was forced to surrender to the French at the Great Meadows.

Aroused by these events, the British Parliament decided to take vigorous action, and in the spring of 1755 two regiments were sent to Alexandria in Virginia, from where, under General Braddock, accompanied by Washington, they were to advance on Fort Duquesne, which had been built by the French on the site selected by Washington two years earlier. The expedition consisted of 1,400 Regulars and 600 Provincials, and it set out in June. It met with disaster, for Braddock, though a gallant soldier, was ambushed in the tangle of the forests on the Monongahela River and routed at a loss of 863 killed and wounded and himself died of his wounds. In May, 1756, war was formally declared between England and France, and the Marquis of Montcalm was sent out to Quebec to take over command of the French forces in Canada, which was under the governorship of the Marquis of Vaudreuil.

A month before Montcalm sailed, Lord Loudon, accompanied by General James Abercrombie, had been sent out to New York as commander-in-chief. He lacked vigour, and Sir Horace Walpole's remark, "I do not augur very well of the ensuing summer; a detachment is going to America under a commander whom a child might outwit or terrify with a pop-gun," proved only too true. He wasted the summer in preparing to take Ticonderoga (Carillon), after which he decided to attack Louisbourg, but when he found the French fleet superior to the English, he abandoned the project. Meanwhile Montcalm had assembled 8,000 French Canadians and Indians at Ticonderoga, and had laid siege to Fort William Henry (later named Fort George) and forced its surrender.

The following year, William Pitt, who had joined the Newcastle administration in June, and was virtual head of the government, saw that the quarrel between England and France was not to be decided in Europe and determined once and for all to crush the French in America. He set traditional methods aside, sought out the ablest soldiers and sailors he could find, and replaced Loudon by Abercrombie and recalled General Amherst from Germany to help him. His plan for 1758 was to wrest from France the three pivots of her power – Louisbourg, Ticonderoga, and Fort Duquesne.

The first was the front door of the St. Lawrence. Its fortifications had been repaired and strengthened since 1748, and its garrison now numbered 3,000 regular soldiers under the Chevalier de Drucour, who was supported by a fleet of 12 warships. To capture this formidable stronghold, Pitt raised a fleet of 22 ships of the line, 15 frigates, and 120 transports, under Admiral Boscawen, to carry and escort 14 battalions with artillery and engineers, under the command of Amherst, to Halifax.

Accompanied by Brigadier-General Whitmore, Brigadier-General Lawrence and Brigadier-General James Wolfe, Amherst set sail from Portsmouth on February 19 and arrived at Halifax on May 28. He found all in readiness, put to sea again, and on June 2 cast anchor in Gabarus Bay. The troops landed at the spot selected by the New England colonists in 1745. On June 12 Drucour destroyed the Grand Battery, and the next day Wolfe advanced round the harbour and seized Lighthouse Point. From then on the siege was pressed, and on July 26 Drucour surrendered at discretion. The passage to the St. Lawrence open, Amherst pressed Boscawen to proceed to Quebec; but as the latter did not consider it a feasible enterprise, it was abandoned, and shortly after Wolfe left for England on sick leave.

For the capture of Fort Duquesne, the gateway to the west, Pitt selected Brigadier-General John Forbes and allotted him a force of 1,500 regular troops – mostly Highlanders – and 4,800 Provincials. His leading subordinate was the noted Colonel Henry Bouquet, and he was also accompanied by Washington.

Forbes set out early in July and advanced cautiously, his van led by Bouquet, for he was so ill throughout most of the campaign that he had to be carried on a litter. When he reached Raystown (near Bedford) Forbes halted the main body and sent Bouquet forward to beyond Loyalhannan. From there, Bouquet detached Major Grant and 800 Highlanders to reconnoitre Fort Duquesne. This Grant set out to do, and, on September 14, he arrived at a hill within half a mile of the fort, since called Grant's Hill, now part of Pittsburgh. There, like Braddock, he was ambushed and lost 300 men. In spite of this disaster, Forbes pushed on, and on November 25, when he found the fort burnt and evacuated, he occupied it and renamed it Fort Pitt, later to be changed to Pittsburgh.

Pitt's third objective—Ticonderoga—was the side door to the St. Lawrence, through which he hoped to launch an expedition against Montreal and Quebec. This operation he left to Abercrombie, but doubtful of his abilities, he gave him as second-in-command Lord Augustus Howe, an exceptionally able officer who had been trained in Indian tactics by the famous American Ranger, Robert Rogers. The expedition, the largest as yet assembled in America, consisted of 6,350 Regulars and 9,000 Provincials.

Toward the end of June Abercrombie broke camp at Albany, and marched to the ruins of Fort William Henry. There, on July 5, he embarked his army in 1,035 boats on Lake George. The following day Howe landed in order to reconnoitre, and most unfortunately was killed, for on his fall the expedition lost its real leader and Abercrombie the little resolution he had.

On July 8, the army, now ashore, came up against a formidable entrenchment protected by abbatis, which had been built by Montcalm as an outwork of Ticonderoga. Abercrombie did not wait for his artillery to come up, but ordered a frontal attack. Seven assaults were made in which 2,000 soldiers fell, and when the retreat was sounded, panic sent the troops in wild disorder to the landing-place.

This disastrous campaign was partly mitigated by a brilliant exploit carried out by Colonel Bradstreet. On his own initiative, he advanced up the Mohawk river at the head of 3,000 men, gained Lake Ontario, crossed it, and burnt Fort Frontenac (Kingston).

Thus ended Pitt's three campaigns of 1758. The tide had turned, Louisbourg and Fort Duquesne were in British hands, and Frontenac was in ashes: the road to Canada had been opened.

CHAPTER 8

The Battle of the Plains of Abraham, 1759

When the winter of 1758 set in, Pitt decided that the following year's operations in Canada should be made on a wider front, this time from the mouth of the St. Lawrence to Lake Erie. Early in December he communicated his plan to the governors of the northern and southern colonies. It was, while Amherst drove the French from Ticonderoga, and by way of Lake Champlain moved on Montreal, Wolfe–his youthful Brigadier–supported by a powerful fleet, should take Quebec. Simultaneously a third army, under General Prideaux, was to advance up the Mohawk River, clear Lake Ontario, occupy Niagara, and so unbar the trade route to Lake Erie and the west.

The selection of Wolfe was remarkable, because, thus far, he had not held an independent command; he was only 32, and though subordinate to Amherst his operation was far and away the most difficult and important of the three.

Born at Westerham, in Kent, on January 2, 1727, James Wolfe came of military stock, his father had fought in the wars under Marlborough. Gazetted an ensign in 1741, he distinguished himself at the battles of Dettingen (1743) and Lauffeld (1747), and during the Forty-five was present at Falkirk and Culloden. Unlike so many of his fellow officers, of whom he was bitingly critical, he was an ardent and highly educated soldier, and though possessed of an indomitable spirit, which never bent before danger or adversity, physically he was frail, and throughout life was a martyr to rheumatism and the stone. He loved men of daring; held in high contempt the Provincial Militia, and considered that Red Indians were only fit to be exterminated. This was unfortunate, because these two opinions undoubtedly misled his countrymen in 1775.

Much of his worth as a soldier may be gleaned from his *General Orders*, issued between May 16 and September 12, 1759–that is, during the Quebec expedition. From them we see clearly the care and trouble he took to form his small army into as perfect an instrument of war as time and circumstances would permit.

The object of the campaign is first laid down: it is "to compleat ye conquest of Canada and to finish the war in America." For this operation, and much of it would have to take place in thickly wooded country infested with Indians, we are told that "care and precaution" are "next to valour", and "the best quality in a fighting man are vigalance and caution". Care of arms is strictly enjoined, plundering is as strictly forbidden; "any officer or non-commission officer who shall suffer himself to be surprised ... must not expect to be forgiven." Discipline and behaviour are insisted upon; swearing is prohibited; scalping, "except when the enemy are Indians, or Canads dressed like Indians", is forbidden; and camps are to be kept clear of "all offall and filth of every kind", which is to be "buried deep under ground". "No churches, houses, or buildings of any kind are to be burned or destroy'd without orders", and "the peasants who yet remain in their habitations, their women and children are to be treated with humanity; if any violence is offer'd to a woman, the offender shall be punish'd with death."[1]

Wolfe objected to flogging and his maintenance of discipline was unorthodox, as this example, dated August 22, shows: Two men, Darby and Everson, who had taken alarm during the night and shown "evident tokens of fear," were punished as follows: they were made to "stand one hour at ye necessary house [latrine] each with a woman's cap upon his head ... as a small punishment for the dishonour they have brought upon the corps and their brother soldiers." Such a humiliation must have been far more effective than the usual five score of lashes.

Wolfe's tactics were also unconventional and show that he had studied Braddock's disaster and probably also the elastic square system devised by Bouquet, for in his *General Orders* we read:—

"The regiment will march by files from the left, and is to be form'd two deep; if the front is attacked, the company that leads is immediately to form to ye front two deep and advance upon the enemy; the next is to do the same. Inclining to ye right of the first, the next to ye left if the ground will permit of it, and so on to ye right and left, until an extensive front is form'd, by which the enemy may be surrounded. And as an attack may be sudden, and time lost in sending orders, these movements are to be made

---

[1] "General Orders in Wolfe's Army during the Expedition up the River St. Lawrence, 1759," *Historical Documents, Literary and Historical Society of Quebec*, 4th Series (1875), pp. 14–30.

in such a case by the several officers without waiting for any. If the column is attack'd on ye left, the whole are to face to ye left and attack ye enemy, on ye right ye same; if in ye rear, the rear is to act as the front was order'd, the whole going to the right about; if on the right and left, the two ranks are to face outwards, if in ye front and rear, ye first and last companies front both ways" (pp. 35-36).

Once the general plan was decided upon, Pitt set to work. The first problem was of sea and not of land power, and to solve it, in consultation with Admiral Anson he selected Admiral Saunders, Admiral Holmes, and Admiral Durell. The first two were exceptionally able sailors, whose object was to co-operate with Wolfe's army, and the third was to move ahead of the expedition and block the St. Lawrence, in order to prevent French reinforcements and supplies entering Quebec. Saunders had accompanied Anson on his voyage round the world, in company with Jervis, Palliser, and Cook, all of whom were to make their mark in history. Of Saunders, Walpole writes: "That admiral was a pattern of most sturdy bravery, united with the most unaffected modesty. No man said less, or deserved more. Simplicity in his manners, generosity, and good nature, adorned his genuine love of his country."[1] The fleet allotted to him consisted of 22 sail of the line, five frigates, 18 sloops, and many transports and other craft; and to Durell were entrusted eight of the line and six frigates. The entire armament comprised 170 sail manned by some 18,000 seamen.

This great fleet was the engine from which Wolfe's army was to be projected against Canada. The latter consisted of the following formations and units:—

First Brigade: 15th Regt. Amherst's–594; 43rd Regt. Kennedy's –715; 58th Regt. Anstruther's–616; and 78th Regt. Simon Fraser's–1,269.

Second Brigade: 28th Regt. Bragg's–591; 47th Regt. Lascelles's– 679; and 2/60th Regt.[2] Monckton's–581.

Third Brigade: 35th Regt. Otway's–899; 48th Regt. Webb's– 852; and 3/60th Regt. Lawrence's–607.

---

[1] *Memoirs of the Reign of King George II*, Horace Walpole (1847), vol. III, p. 231.

[2] The 60th Regiment (Royal Americans) "were provided with Tomahawks," see "Journal of the Siege of Quebec", John Montrésor, *Collections of the New York Historical Society for the Year 1881*, p. 208. Montrésor was an engineer by training; when a lieutenant of the 48th Regiment he was wounded in the battle of the Monongahela River (Braddock's defeat) and took part in the siege of Louisbourg.

There were also three companies of the Louisbourg Grenadiers and the following companies of Rangers: Murray's–326; Gorham's–95; Stark's–95; Brewer's–85; Hazzans's–89; Rogers's–112; also Royal Artillery, Wilkinson's–330.

The army totalled 384 officers, 411 non-commissioned officers, and 7,740 rank and file.[1]

As regards his immediate subordinates, Pitt gave Wolfe *carte-blanche* to appoint whomsoever he liked, and he selected as his three brigadiers, Monckton, Townshend, and Murray. Except for the second all his senior officers were under 30 years old: "it was", as Corbett writes, "a boy's campaign."[2]

While Wolfe made ready, Montcalm, who little dreamt where the main blow would fall, prepared to resist Amherst on the lines of Lake Champlain and Fort Niagara. His task was immeasurably more difficult than his opponent's. Not only was Canada vastly inferior in man-power to the American colonies, the former inhabited by 82,000 people and the latter by 1,300,000; but the royal government at Versailles depended on a corrupt and ill-paid bureaucracy to manage its colonial affairs. For instance, Vaudreuil, the Governor-General of Canada, received a yearly salary of £272 1s. 8d., "out of which he was to clothe, maintain and pay a guard for himself, consisting of two serjeants and twenty-five soldiers, furnishing them with firing in winter, and with other necessary articles."[3] This parsimony led to universal peculation and corruption, and the head brigand was François Bigot, Intendant of Canada, who pillaged the government, settlers, and Indians. Of these rogues, Montcalm says: "Everybody appears to be in a hurry to make his fortune before the colony is lost; which event many perhaps desire as an impenetrable veil over their conduct."[4] "This enormous dishonesty," writes Warburton, "brought down its own punishment; agriculture and trade were paralysed, loyalty shaken, while diminished resources; and a discontented people, hastened the inevitable catastrophe of British triumph."[5] And to make matters worse, Montcalm was not on speaking terms with Vaudreuil.

But for an unforeseeable event Montcalm would have been

[1] Compiled mainly from the Embarkation Return given in *The History of Canada*, William Kingsford (1888), vol. IV, p. 235.

[2] *England in the Seven Years' War*, Julian S. Corbett (1907), vol. I, p. 409.

[3] *Travels in Canada*, Heriot, p. 98.

[4] See *The American Colonies in the Eighteenth Century*, Herbert L. Osgood (1904), vol. IV, pp. 436–441.

[5] *The Conquest of Canada*, G. D. Warburton (1849), vol. II, p. 126.

caught napping; it was that Durell failed in his mission. Because of the ice he feared to enter the St. Lawrence and hung about Louisbourg. In consequence Admiral de Léry's fleet of 18 sail reached Quebec. In one of these ships Louis Antoine de Bougain-ville,[1] brought a copy of an intercepted letter from Amherst which disclosed in detail the British plan. When he knew this, Montcalm hastened to Quebec, and in the exceedingly short time at his disposal set to work to carry out those masterly arrangements[2] which nearly brought Wolfe's operations to ruin.

Forthwith Montcalm assembled his forces–five regular bat-talions, the Militia[3] and 1,000 Redskins–at Quebec; a total of between 10,000 and 14,000 armed men. The city was considered impregnable to assault because it stood on a rocky headland between the St. Lawrence and the St. Charles rivers and on the left bank of the former. Also, its landward supply was secure as long as an enemy fleet did not pass westward of it, and this Montcalm did not believe any hostile ship would dare to do. He decided therefore on a Fabian policy–to play for time– because by October at latest, the autumn gales and fogs would compel the English fleet to withdraw and with it would go the invading army. Therefore he sent his ships upstream to be out of harm's way, and decided to push his left out to the gorge of Montmorenci, seven miles below Quebec, to establish his right on the St. Charles with his headquarters at Beauport, while the Chevalier de Ramesay held Quebec with 1,000 to 2,000 men.

Quebec was protected by 106 guns; in its harbour were a few gunboats and fire ships; a pontoon bridge spanned the St. Charles River, and along the Beauport front, as far as the Falls of Montmorenci, a line of earthworks and redoubts had been thrown up. From this it will be seen that Montcalm's plan was wholly defensive, based on the assumption that his enemy would not dare to force the river immediately south of Quebec, and on the possibility that his own small, ill-organized and ill-disciplined army would hold seven to eight miles of entrenchments.[4]

[1] The celebrated circumnavigator, appointed aide-de-camp to Montcalm in 1756.
[2] See "Journal de Foligné" and "Journal de Johannes", *The Siege of Quebec and the Battle of the Plains of Abraham*, A. Doughty (1901), Vol. IV, pp. 164 and 220. Also *La Guerre de Sept Ans*, Richard Waddington (1899), vol. III, pp. 260 *et seq.*
[3] All males from 10 to 60 years of age were enrolled by companies in the Provincial Militia, which was little more than an armed rabble.
[4] The Chevalier Johnstone in his "A Dialogue in Hades", p. 8, considers Mont-calm's front over-extended. Johnstone was a Scottish Jacobite who had fled to France after the battle of Culloden. He was on Montcalm's staff (see *Literary and Historical Society of Quebec*, 2nd Series).

On February 14, 70 sail escorted by six ships of the line and nine frigates, under Holmes, stood out from Spithead and were followed by Saunders, with whom was Wolfe. But it was not until the end of April that Cape Breton was sighted, and Durell found still at anchor. Unable, because of the ice, to enter Louisbourg, the fleet put into Halifax, from where, on May 5, Durell set out, and, as related, failed in his mission and cast anchor off the Ile aux Coudres on June 6. On May 17 the transports under escort arrived at Louisbourg, where Wolfe decided on his plan of attack. It was to land at Beauport, where Sir William Phipps had landed in 1690, and from there to push across the St. Charles River, and so gain the rear of the fortress with his right on the St. Lawrence and his communications with the fleet maintained by a line of entrenched posts extending from his left, on the St. Charles, to Beauport.[1]

When the French were feverishly at work, on June 4 Wolfe set sail. The fleet was divided into three squadrons—Red, White, and Blue[2]—and it entered the Gulf of St. Lawrence on June 9.

It was a daring move. According to Corbett, never before had a battle fleet been taken up the river, a move which was considered impracticable by the French. Fog was a real danger; nevertheless, as an unnamed officer of Wolfe's army wrote: "The French Account of the Navigation of the River of St. Lawrence we found to be a mere Bugbear."[3] The ships tacked upstream, and on June 23 anchor was cast "nigh the Ile aux Coudres", not far from the Isle of Orleans.

By June 26, the whole fleet had come up, and on the following day a landing on the Isle of Orleans was effected. On the night of June 28, the French launched some fire-ships[4] downstream which, though they provided the invaders with a magnificent spectacle, did them no harm.

Meanwhile Wolfe proceeded to the western extremity of the island, and his first glance at Quebec and the Beauport entrenchments convinced him that his hypothetical plan was impracticable. Saunders realized the importance of securing the south side of

---

[1] See *Life of Major-General J. Wolfe*, R. Wright (1864), p. 498.
[2] *Montrésor's Journal*, p. 196.
[3] *Military Affairs in North America 1748–1765*, Stanley Pargellis (1936), p. 433.
[4] The seven fire ships used in this attack were equipped at a cost of one million francs. In a report contained in Pargellis (pp. 411–418) dated July 9, 1758, we read: "The Baron Diesko and his Aid de Camp talked of an invention, the French had discovered for infallibly destroying ships going up the river; at Quebec we found this invention to be, what they call fire Rafts. . . ."

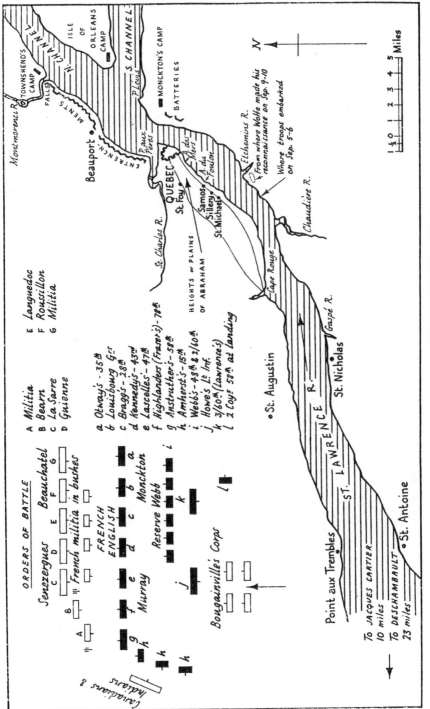

15. OPERATIONS AGAINST QUEBEC, 1759

the Narrows immediately south of Quebec (three-quarters of a mile to one mile broad), and suggested the occupation of Point Lévis, to which place on June 30 Wolfe ordered Monckton and his brigade. They occupied it easily, for little opposition[1] was met with, and Monckton's men at once began to throw up entrench-ments and erect batteries. On July 2[2] Wolfe visited Monckton and carefully examined Quebec and its surroundings from Point aux Pères.

This reconnaissance led Wolfe to formulate his second plan, which was to compel Montcalm to attack him, and to induce him to do so he decided to occupy the high ground east of the Falls of Montmorenci, from where he would threaten his enemy's left. Simultaneously he and Saunders discovered that it was possible to pass ships upstream to the west of the fortress; but the latter believed this was not a practical move until Monckton's batteries were ready to silence the French fire. Therefore, on July 9, Wolfe left a small detachment to protect his base on the Isle of Orleans and had Murray's and Townshend's brigades ferried over to the left bank, where they took up a position immediately east of the Montmorenci gorge.[3]

Now began a tussle of wits between the two commanders-in-chief which was to last for three months. Montcalm penetrated his adversary's intention, and on July 12–the day Monckton opened his bombardment–he ordered Dumas (of Monongahela fame) to take a force of some 2,000 militia and regulars over the St. Lawrence, well above Monckton's position, and from there by moving eastward to attack him in flank. This threat at once brought Wolfe back to Point Lévis; but unfortunately for Monckton, when Dumas's men approached his works, Monckton's men panicked and retired so hastily that no decision was possible. At once Wolfe returned to Montmorenci, and on July 14, with "the Quarter Master General and an Engineer escorted by a party of Light Infantry, Commanded by Col. Howe [later Sir William]", he reconnoitred "up the River Montmorency in order to find a passage over, either by fording or otherwise."[4] On July 16,

---

[1] Montrésor (p. 207) says: "On their landing the Irregulars took 2 Scalps, killed 3 other men and took 3 Prisoners which were brought over to Major-Genl. Wolfe and were examined."

[2] See Malcolm Fraser's Journal, p. 4. *Literary and Historical Society of Quebec*, 2nd Series. Montrésor (p. 207) says that Wolfe attempted to visit Point Lévis on June 30, but had to turn back because of French fire.

[3] See *The General History of the Late War*, John Entick (1763), vol. IV, p. 102.

[4] Montrésor, p. 212.

"between 11 and 12 o'clock part of the Town of Quebec was set on fire by a shell from our Batteries on Point Pères which continued in flames till 1 o'clock at night".[1] Next, Saunders ordered "Capt. *Rous* of the *Sutherland*, to proceed, with the first fair wind and night tide, above *Quebec*, and to take the *Diana* and *Squirrel*, with two armed sloops, and two catts [a kind of lugger] armed and loaded with provisions."[2] This Rous did on the night of July 18 and Wolfe accompanied the expedition, which was highly successful. Not only did it prove that the Narrows could be negotiated, but it compelled Montcalm to send 600 men to Cape Rouge, eight miles upstream from Quebec, and thereby to accentuate his over-extension.

The following day, with Holmes, Wolfe renewed his reconnaissance, and, according to Entick,[3] considered landing a force at St. Michael on the northern bank of the river, about four miles above the city. Orders were, then, sent to Townshend to dispatch nine companies of grenadiers and all his guns and howitzers to Point Lévis.[4] But, when part had arrived, suddenly the whole movement was counter-ordered, possibly because, on second thought, Wolfe realized that, should he land between the fortress and Cape Rouge, he would be unable to reinforce his first flight of troops before it was attacked by a superior force. He set the project aside, and on July 21 ordered Colonel Carleton and a detachment to land at Point aux Trembles, some 27 miles west of Quebec, in order, as he reported in his dispatch to Pitt, "to divide the enemy's force, and to draw their attention as high up the river as possible." This was done; "two scalps, 100 head of cattle and a Jesuit priest being taken."[5]

Wolfe, who had thus substituted a feint for a full-dress landing and so had drawn Montcalm's attention toward his right, returned to his Montmorenci project. On July 23 he assembled a council of war on Saunders's flagship; but, as no minutes have survived, we can only conjecture that it concerned itself with the Montmorenci operation. If so, when it was in preparation, the French, on July 28, launched a second fire-ship attack, which

---

[1] *Ibid.*, p. 213.

[2] Admiral Saunders' dispatch, September 5, 1759. See *The Gentleman's Magazine* (October, 1759), vol. XXIX, p. 470.

[3] Vol. IV, p. 103.

[4] "Townshend Papers", Doughty, vol. V, pp. 194, 250, 273.

[5] "A Journal of the Expedition up the River St. Lawrence", p. 8 (*Literary and Historical Society of Quebec*, 4th Series). Probably by the Hon. George Alsopp, private secretary to General Carleton.

proved as abortive as the first. Three days later, the attack, which became known as the Battle of Montmorenci, was launched. It was a muddled affair, over-impulsively begun,[1] and might well have ended in a major disaster,[2] as Braddock's had done four years before, had not a deluge of rain put a stop to it. Wolfe's losses were heavy, about 30 officers and 400 men killed and wounded, many of whom fell into the hands of the Indians and were massacred and scalped.

The French were elated by the repulse of their enemy. "Every-body," says Commissary Berniers, "thought that the campaign was as good as ended."[3] Instead, it had only begun. At once Wolfe changed his tactics; he had discovered that, in spite of his contempt for Provincials, as the Chevalier Johnstone says, in operations in wooded country "a Canadian is worth three disciplined soldiers, as a soldier in a plain is worth three Canadians."[4]

Because Wolfe's only hope lay in the composition of Mont-calm's army, and because that general refused to come out of his lines, Wolfe now decided to lay waste the country,[5] with the threefold aim of forcing the French to attack him, of compelling the militia to desert in order to protect their homes, and by restricting supplies reduce Quebec through starvation. In modern terminology, he opened a campaign of "frightfulness", which up to a point was legitimate, because he knew that his enemy's main problem was supply.

Meanwhile the bombardment of the city continued, and with terrible effect, for the lower town was completely destroyed and the cathedral laid in ashes. On August 23, writes Montrésor, "was killed and scalped the Priest who commanded a party of men at Joichim (St. Joachim) and 20 of his party."[6] On August 24 "Our

---

[1] See "Journal of Major Moncrief", Doughty, vol. v, p. 42. An anonymous parti-cipant writes: "We were all in our Flat Bottom Boats at Noon, rowing backwards and forwards, in sight of the Enemy, and exposed to their shells for six hours, waiting I believe till the Batterys were silenced, (which the ships could not Effect) and till the Water was low enough to Cross at the Falls. . . . The General Ordered the Grenadiers March to Beat, which Animated our men so much we could not restrain them". . . . (Pargellis, p. 434). Montrésor (p. 227) writes: "Our Commander in Chief was not a little exasperated at his Grenadiers, he says he accuses them of everything but want of spirit as they did not wait for his Orders."
[2] See "Memoirs of the Quarter Mas'r Sergeant", Doughty, vol. v, p. 94.
[3] Quoted from *Montcalm and Wolfe*, Francis Parkman (1901), vol. II, p. 270.
[4] *A Dialogue in Hades*, p. 14.   [5] See Doughty, vol. II, p. 123.
[6] This atrocity was the work of Captain Alexander Montgomery of the 43rd Foot, see *An Historical Journal of the Campaign in North America for the Years 1759–60*, Captain J. Knox – of the 43rd Foot – (1769), vol. II, p. 32.

parties continued burning the village of St. Ange Gardien." On August 25, "The Parties on the North side ordered to burn and destroy all the settlements to the Encampment . . .", and on September 1, "L'Ange Gardien set on fire and all the settlements to this Camp."[1] The effects of this devastation and bombardment were tactically profitable; when Quebec was taken, only supplies for two days were found there. "The reason of this was that the enemy never had above a fortnight's provisions in the garrison at a time, lest they might be burnt."[2]

No sooner had Wolfe's attack at Montmorenci failed than an event of high importance came to his help; it was Amherst's advance up Lake George and Lake Champlain.

When, on July 26, Amherst forced the French to evacuate Ticonderoga, Montcalm had been obliged to send the Chevalier de Lévis–his ablest officer–to Montreal. When Wolfe learnt this, and in the knowledge that Montcalm had withdrawn the French ships to the foot of the Richelieu Rapids, some seven miles above Point aux Ecureils, he resolved to destroy them in order to open communication with Amherst. To do so, on August 5 he ordered Holmes to take 20 flat-bottomed boats upstream, while Murray led 1,200 men westward along the southern bank of the river. Alarmed by this, Montcalm sent Bougainville and 1,500 men from Beauport to Ecureils. Next, on August 8, Murray made an abortive landing at Point aux Trembles, and eight days later he suddenly appeared at Deschambault, at the foot of the Richelieu Rapids, where he burnt a number of magazines. Since this blow against the French communications and ships could not be ignored, at length Montcalm was goaded into action. He left Quebec and hastened to join Bougainville, but arrived to learn that Murray had withdrawn.

Meanwhile Wolfe busily considered a new plan of attack,[3] and, though its nature is not known, it involved the return of Murray and his raiding force, which was back in its camp at St. Antoine on August 30, from where it set out to return to Point Lévis, burning and ravaging as it went.

On August 20, five days after he had mentioned his new plan to Townshend, Wolfe fell ill, and whatever the plan may have been, it was abandoned. For a week he lay completely incapaci-

---

[1] Montrésor, p. 231.
[2] "Journal of Major Moncrief", Doughty, vol. v, p. 56.
[3] "Townshend's Diary", August 15, Doughty, vol. IV, p. 258.

tated in his farmhouse at Montmorenci, but by August 29 had sufficiently recovered to request his three brigadiers to put their heads together and consider what best should be done. He placed before them three courses of action: (1) To march up the Montmorenci River, cross it and take Beauport in rear; (2) to attack the Montmorenci position in rear and front simultaneously; or (3) to attack it in flank and in front.[1]

The brigadiers set these suggestions aside and placed before him the following proposal:—

"We, therefore, are of opinion that the most probable method of striking an effectual Blow is by bringing the Troops to the South shore and directing our operations above the Town. When we have established ourselves on the North shore, of which there is very little doubt, the M. de Montcalm must fight us upon our terms, we are between Him and his provisions and betwixt him and the French army opposing General Amherst. If He gives us Battle and we defeat Him Quebec will be ours, and which is more all Canada must submit to His Majesty's arms. . . ."[2]

This plan, which was approved by Saunders and Holmes, meant the end of Wolfe's cherished dream; nevertheless he at once accepted it, for though it was audacious it was in no way foolhardy because the command of the river was his, and though, should the landing be successful, he would place himself between two hostile armies, as they would have to meet him in the open he had little to fear because of the superior discipline of his men. Further, something had to be done and quickly, for the season was advancing and his admirals were already fretting to clear the St. Lawrence before the autumn storms broke. Therefore, on August 31, he issued orders for the withdrawal of his troops at Montmorenci, and their concentration by September 3 at Point Lévis and to the west of it. On September 2, he sent his final dispatch to Pitt.[3]

Because of the precipitous cliffs, which from Quebec westward skirt the north shore of the St. Lawrence, Wolfe's problem centred in where he should land his men, and until this was settled little could be done.

On September 4 the news was out; for on that day Knox writes

---

[1] Wolfe's instructions are given in Doughty, vol. VI, pp. 90–91.
[2] *Ibid.*, vol. VI, p. 92. For the Brigadier's plan to effect concentration of troops, see p. 93.
[3] Given in full in *The Gentleman's Magazine*, October, 1759, pp. 466–470. See also Knox, vol. II, pp. 41–49.

in his *Journal* that "an expedition is on foot ... the General will command in person." Next, on September 5: "Fair wind and weather to-day: the boats passed the town last night undiscovered." On September 6: "We had an uncommon storm of rain last night; to-day showery weather and wind variable"; and lastly: "The General joined the Army and the upper fleet this night".[1] This was Admiral Holmes's squadron; Saunders's remained meanwhile below Quebec.

On September 7, 1,500 troops embarked in the ships and 30 flat-bottomed boats; and in fine and warm weather the fleet drifted up to Cape Rouge, where Bougainville had his head-quarters. In the afternoon fire was opened on the French camp, and, as a feint, the men took to their boats and rowed upstream as if looking for a landing-place. From then until September 9, Holmes took advantage of the tides and drifted down and up the river between Cape Rouge and Quebec, compelling Bougainville to follow him and exhaust his troops as well as wear-out their boots in forced marches. Meanwhile, Wolfe went up to Point aux Trembles and fixed upon a place a little below it "for making a descent".[2] And, on September 9, when his brigadiers were sent there to examine it, he rowed downstream and "found out another place more to his mind."[3] The weather now broke and became so bad that the troops were disembarked at St. Nicholas on the right bank of the St. Lawrence.

On September 10, Moncrief informs us that "the general carried Admiral Holmes, Brigadier Generals Monckton and Townshend with some other officers [Colonel Carleton and Captain Delaune], to reconnoitre the place he had fixed upon."[4] Further, Knox tells us that Wolfe called for an escort of one officer and 30 men of the 43rd Regiment, and for "six grenadiers' coats", apparently so that he might disguise himself and his five officers.[5] Moncrief continues:—

"The place is called Foulon [Anse (cove) du Foulon, now Wolfe's Cove]; they reconnoitred it from a rising on the south side of the river, below the mouth of the Etchemins River, from whence there was a fair view, not only of the place itself, but

---

[1] Knox, vol. II, pp. 51–54.
[2] "Journal of Major Moncrief", Doughty, vol. v, p. 48.
[3] *Ibid.*, vol. v, p. 48.   [4] *Ibid.*, vol. v, p. 48.
[5] Knox, vol. II, p. 61. The French officer in command at Sillery penetrated the disguise, for when they opened their coats their gold braid, etc., could be seen (Doughty, vol. IV, p. 121).

likewise of a considerable part of the ground between it and the town, which is a mile and a half below; as the place is laid down upon the plan, it requires little or no description, but it must be observed that the bank which runs along the shore is very steep and woody, and was thought so impracticable by the French themselves, that they had only a single picket to defend it. This picket, which we supposed might be about 100 men, was encamped upon the bank near the top of a narrow path, which runs up from the shore; this path was broken by the enemy themselves, and barricaded with an abattis, but about 200 yards to the right [east] there appeared to be a slope in the bank, which was thought might answer the purpose. These circumstances and the distance of the place from succour seemed to promise a fair chance of success."[1]

Admiral Holmes version is as follows:—

"This alteration of the plan of operations . . . had been proposed to him (Wolfe) a month before, when the first ships passed the town. . . . He now laid hold of it when it was highly improbable he should succeed. . . . The care of landing the troops and sustaining them by the ships fell to my share . . . the most hazardous and difficult task I was ever engaged in. For the distance of the landing-place, the impetuosity of the tide, the darkness of the night, and the great chance of exactly hitting the very spot intended without discovery or alarm, made the whole extremely difficult."[2]

This is true; nevertheless on September 11 orders were issued to the troops to be assembled on the beach at five o'clock the next morning: "*The army to hold themselves to land and attack the enemy.*" The 30 flat-bottomed boats were allotted as follows: 1st flotilla— The Light Infantry under Howe; 2nd–28th Regt.; 3rd–43rd Regt.; 4th–47th Regt.; 5th–58th Regt.; and 6th–a detachment of Highlanders and American Grenadiers. Embarkation was to be at about 9 p.m., "or when it is pretty near high tide."[3] All men not embarked were to march under Colonel Burton at nightfall

---

[1] "Journal of Major Moncrief," Doughty, vol. v, pp. 48–49. Winsor (*Narrative and Critical History of America*, 1889, vol. v, p. 546) says that it was Robert Sobo (taken prisoner after the fall of Fort Necessity) who directed Wolfe's attention to this cove. Corbett (vol. 1, 462) writes: "It was a stroke of genius, an example of a penetrating *coup d'oeil* as subtle as the plan of the brigadier's was obvious." He says that as Wolfe had pinned his faith on Montcalm's left flank, the brigadiers had pinned theirs on his right flank. This is true, but he is incorrect when he supposes that this meant a landing at Point aux Trembles, or Cape Rouge, for no specific locality is mentioned in their report. To suggest that Wolfe did not follow their plan is incorrect.

[2] Doughty, vol. IV, p. 296.   [3] Knox, vol. II, pp. 62–64.

up the south bank of the river, and wait to be ferried over, and Admiral Saunders and his fleet were to make a determined feint on Beauport.

On September 12, off Cape Rouge, Wolfe issued his final orders. "A vigorous blow struck at this juncture," he writes, "may determine the fate of Canada. . . . The first body that gets on shore is to march directly to ye enemy, and drive yem from any little post they may occupy. . . . The officers and men will remember what their country expects from them, and what a determined body of soldiers inured to war are capable of doing against five weak bats, mingled with disorderly peasantry. The soldiers must be attentive and obedient to ye officers, and resolute in ye execution of their duty."[1]

The same day a fortunate event occurred; two French deserters came in from Bougainville's camp with the information that Montcalm did not expect an attack near the city, and that a convoy of provisions was that night to pass down the river to Quebec.[2]

Meanwhile, what took place in the enemy's camp? As it happened, on September 5 Wolfe's boats did not pass Quebec undiscovered, as Knox had imagined, for we find that Montcalm informed Bougainville of the movement, and warned him to look to the safety of his line of communications. Further, in order to help him to do so, he informed him that he was going to move the Regiment of Guienne to Sillery, which unfortunately for him he never did. That same day Vaudreuil also wrote to him to say that the safety of the colony was in his hands. He enclosed a distribution of posts, according to which 150 men were to be posted between Anse des Mers (close to Quebec) and Anse du Foulon; 30 with a battery at Samos; 50 at St. Michael; 50 at Sillery; and 200 at Cape Rouge. He also mentions 2,100 for posts further west, including the Regiment of Guienne–500 men. On September 6 he wrote again to state that M. de Vergor with 100 men were to replace M. St. Martin and the 150 between Anse des Mers and Anse du Foulon, and the following day Montcalm wrote to Bougainville to impress upon him the importance of marching parallel to Wolfe's boats wherever they went.[3]

It would appear that Vergor was a bad choice. He did not

---

[1] "General Orders in Wolfe's Army", pp. 53–54.

[2] According to Mante's *History of the Late Wars in America* (1772), p. 262, though these deserters informed Captain Smith of the *Hunter* of the provision convoy, he never passed this information on to headquarters, and very nearly fired on Wolfe's boats when they came down stream.

[3] See "Correspondance de Bougainville", pp. 93–109, Doughty, vol. IV.

believe that the Anse du Foulon was a possible landing place and allowed some of his men, probably 40 in all,[1] to go to the village of Lorette to help in the harvesting. After he had posted his sentries he went to bed, little dreaming of what the morrow had in store for him.

The story of the provision boats is also of interest. On September 9, Cadet, a French army contractor, wrote to Bougainville that, on September 10, he was sending four calkers to Cape Rouge to calk the provision barges, which were to proceed as soon as possible to Quebec. On September 12, he wrote again: "I beg you to be so good as to pass the boats down-stream to-night . . . because I urgently need them."[2] Seemingly the calking took longer than was expected, for though the French sentries had been warned that the barges would pass downstream that night, they never did; yet the warning was not countermanded. This was most fortunate for Wolfe.

As night closed in, Admiral Saunders slowly moved out from his anchorage, brought his ships into line with the shore, and ordered their boats to be manned and lowered; then fire was opened on Beauport. This feint attack was eminently successful, for Montcalm at once concentrated to meet it, and, while he did so, Holmes's squadron, followed by the flat-bottomed boats carrying the advanced guard, drifted up the river, to be followed by Bougainville on the left bank. Toward two o'clock on the morning of September 12 the tide began to ebb, when two lanterns were raised on the maintop shroud of the *Sutherland*. It was the signal to drift downstream, and Bougainville, who thought it to be a repetition of the feint which had annoyed him during the past few days, ceased to follow.

In the leading boat were the Light Infantry under Colonel Howe, the forlorn hope of which consisted of 24 picked men commanded by Captain Delaune. When she and the boats immediately in her rear neared the cove, the current bore them inshore close to the cliff which gloomed out of the darkness on their left. Suddenly the silence was broken by a cry of *Qui vive?* To which Captain Donald McDonald,[3] of Fraser's Regiment, called

---

[1] According to the "Journal of Foligné", at this time Vergor's whole force was only 60 men (Doughty, vol. IV, p. 203).

[2] "Correspondance de Bougainville", pp. 115–126, Doughty, vol. IV.

[3] According to "The Townshend Papers" (Doughty, vol. V, p. 214), it was Captain Fraser who cried out, "*La France et vive le Roy*", on which the French sentinels ran along the shore in the dark crying: "*Laisser les passer ils sont nos gens avec les provisions.*"

back in French: "*France!*" "*A quel regiment?*" came the reply, and he answered: "*De la Reine*"–one of Bougainville's units. This satisfied the sentry, so the boats drifted on, and when off the heights of Samos a man was seen running toward the shore. He halted, and called out: "Who are you?" McDonald answered: "Provision boats. Don't make a noise; the English will hear us,"[1] for the sloop-of-war *Hunter* was anchored in the stream not far off. Again the sentry let the boats pass, and a few minutes later they rounded the headland west of the Anse du Foulon.

The current was now so strong that it carried the leading boats a quarter of a mile beyond the selected landing-place. This was fortunate, for though east of it the cliffs are more precipitous, the point the Light Infantry landed at was well away from the barricaded path upon which a French post was established. As the first boat grounded, Wolfe "leaped out upon the beach; and when he saw the difficulty, or rather the seeming impossibility of getting up the Steep Ascent which hung over his head, he cried out: 'I don't think we can with any possible means get up here, but however we must use our best endeavour.' "[2] Nevertheless, Delaune and his 24 men scrambled up and unnoticed gained the summit.

They saw in the twilight a group of tents, crept toward it and then rushed it. Vergor, suddenly roused from sleep, seized his pistols and fired them into the night. Then three shots and a cheer rang out. When Wolfe heard them, he at once ordered his men to land and clear the barricaded path. This was done, and two brass six-pounders[3] were dragged up it. At once a party was sent to capture the enemy's battery at Samos. The main landing now took place and the boats were rowed backwards and forward to the ships and to the right bank of the St. Lawrence to fetch over 1,200 troops who had not been embarked.[4] It was now broad daylight.

While Wolfe's little army drifted down the river, Montcalm was at Beauport. At midnight, he was informed that boats were seen near the shore and left his house, taking with him the Chevalier Johnstone. Then Johnstone makes him say: "Not a soul having come to me from the right of our camp since midnight when I sent there Marcel [his A.D.C.], I set out with Johnstone between six and seven in the morning. Heavens, what was my surprise, when,

[1] *Montcalm and Wolfe*, Francis Parkman (1901), vol. II, p. 298.
[2] "Memoirs of a Quarter Mas'r Sergeant", Doughty, vol. v, p. 102.
[3] Pargellis, p. 438.
[4] See "Letters of Admiral Holmes", September 18, 1759, Doughty, vol. v, p. 297.

opposite to M. de Vaudreuil's lodgings, the first news of what had passed during the night was the sight of your army upon the heights of Abraham. . . ."[1] True, the surprise was as complete as any in history, because Saunders's feint had entirely misled him.

Montcalm ordered the troops at Beauport and east of it to march to Quebec, but at once ran into difficulties because the French command was divided between him and Vaudreuil, Governor and Commander-in-Chief, and the Chevalier de Ramesay, Garrison Commander of Quebec. Vaudreuil would not release the troops east of Beauport, for he still considered the landing reported at the Anse du Foulon a feint. When Montcalm asked for 25 field piece, Ramesay, in his turn, sent him only three. Orders and counter-orders clashed, and in the resultant confusion Montcalm summoned a council of war.

A profusion of suggestions were made. Some said that the enemy was entrenching, others that he would seize the bridge over the St. Charles River and cut Vaudreuil from Quebec, and still others urged an immediate attack. At length the last suggestion was agreed to, and though Montcalm has often been blamed for accepting it, in truth he had no choice. If he made a mistake, it was in not delaying the battle for a few hours, in order to gain time for Vaudreuil and Bougainville to come up. The news of the landing only reached the latter at 9 a.m.

The reasons which forced him to assume the offensive were that he had only two days' supplies in Quebec, and that Wolfe now threatened his line of communications with the interior; that every hour strengthened Wolfe's position, and, were his enemy to entrench, by the following day he could bring into action on the heights so formidable an array of heavy cannon that in a few hours he would be able to batter down the rotten walls of Quebec. Montcalm had, therefore, to fight, starve, or surrender, and, like the brave soldier he was, he chose to fight. Therefore the *Générale* was sounded; perhaps after all he might win a second Montmorenci on the Plains of Abraham.

These plains or heights, named after Abraham Martin, a French pilot who had once owned the ground, consisted of a track of grassland, slightly broken in places and dotted here and there with clumps of bushes, bounded on the south by the cliffs of the St. Lawrence and on the north by the St. Foy Road, beyond which flowed the St. Charles River. On the plateau, about a mile

[1] *A Dialogue in Hades*, p. 39.

in breadth, Montcalm marshalled his troops in the following order: on the St. Foy Road he drew up a battalion of militia, 350 strong, and then in succession the regiments of Bèarn, (200), and of La Sarre, (340). On either side of the Sillery Road he posted the regiments of Guienne (200) and Languedoc (320), and next to them on their left the Roussillon Regiment (230) and a battalion of militia (300). To his front, among the bushes, he threw forward parties of militiamen and Indians, also a strong force of these men on his right front. His total strength was a little under 4,000, though some say 5,000.

According to Knox, it was about six o'clock in showery weather when the French "first made their appearance on the heights."[1] At once Wolfe began to form his order of battle, and drew up his line two-deep.[2] The right he formed close to the cliff, and there posted the 35th (519 men), and then in succession on its left the Louisbourg Grenadiers (241), the 28th (421), 43rd (327), 47th (360), 78th (662) and 58th (335). Through his centre ran the Sillery Road, on which he advanced his two six-pounders. On the extreme left, beyond the 58th, he drew back the 15th Foot (406) *en potence*. In reserve he held the 2/60th (322) and the 48th (683). He left two companies of the 58th at the Cove, and linked them with his reserve by means of the 3/60th (540), and finally drew up Howe's Light Infantry (400) well in rear in order to face Bougainville should he advance. His total fighting strength, given by Doughty,[3] was 4,829, of which 3,111 men were actually engaged in the battle.

Though in numbers slightly superior to his adversary, Wolfe's men were beyond comparison better soldiers. More important still, he was supported by probably the finest body of English officers which has ever taken the field.

By about nine o'clock Montcalm's line of battle—formed some 600 yards from his enemy—began to advance, covered by skirmishers. As they darted forward among the bushes, Wolfe ordered his men to lie down and threw out his skirmishers. On the English right, the French sharpshooters could make little impression, but on the left they became so active that Townshend brought up the 2/60th on the left of the 48th, as well as the Light Infantry to support the 15th Foot.

[1] Knox, vol. II, p. 69.
[2] "Memoirs of the Quarter Mas'r Sergeant", Doughty, vol. V, p. 107.
[3] Doughty, vol. III, pp. 122-123.

At 10 o'clock the French moved forward to the assault and the English line arose. The French, 200 paces distant, opened fire; but as the Canadian militiamen would throw themselves on the ground in order to reload, their line became disordered. It was during this action that Wolfe received his first wound. He was hit in the wrist by a ball, but wrapped his handkerchief round it and took no further notice of his injury. The French redressed their line and again moved forward cheering, while the English stood silent like a wall.

This was undoubtedly because of Wolfe's method of training; for when in command of the 20th Foot at Canterbury, in 1755, he had laid down the following instructions: "The Battalion is not to halloo, or cry out, upon any account whatever . . . till they are ordered to charge with their bayonets." And as regards firing: "There is no necessity for firing very fast; a cool, well-levelled fire, with pieces carefully loaded, is much more destructive and formidable than the quickest fire in confusion. . . ."[1] Also: "When the [enemy's] column is within about twenty yards, they [the men] must fire with a good aim."[2]

These instructions were put into practice, and before the battle opened we are told that it was Wolfe's "express Orders not to fire till they [the French] came within twenty yeards of us."[3] Also, "When the General formed the line of battle, he ordered the regiments to load with an additional ball."[4]

The French pressed on "briskly in three columns, with loud shouts and recovered arms, two of them inclining to the left of our army, and the third towards our right, firing obliquely at the two extremities of our line, from the distance of one hundred and thirty–until they came within forty yards; which our troops withstood with the greatest intrepidity and firmness, still reserving their fire, and paying the strictest obedience to their officers. . . ."[5]

It would appear that, when the two lines were 100 yards apart, Wolfe's men marched forward and "reserved their fire till within 40 yards,"[6] when a volley rang out which to the French "sounded like a cannon shot." "With one deafening crash," writes Fortescue, "the most perfect volley ever fired on battlefield burst forth as if from a single monstrous weapon, from end to end of the British

---

[1] "Journal of Major Moncrief", Doughty, vol. v, p. 53.
[2] Entick, vol. iv, pp. 92–97.
[3] "The Sergeant-Major's Journal", Doughty, vol. v, p. 10.
[4] Knox, vol. ii, p. 71.   [5] *Ibid.*, vol. ii, p. 70.
[6] "Townshend's Journal", Doughty, vol. iv, p. 269.

line,"[1] and a dense cloud of smoke drifted over the field. Under its cover the English reloaded, stepped forward and fired again, and continued to do so for six to eight minutes, writes Fraser. Then, as the field began to clear, "we observed the main body of the Enemy retreating in great confusion towards the Town, and the rest towards the River St. Charles."[2] The battle had lasted "hardly a quarter of an hour:"[3] the pursuit followed. "*The Louisbourg Grenadiers, Bragg's* and *Lascelles's*, pressed on with their bayonets; Brigadier *Murray* advancing briskly, with the troops under his command, completed the rout on this side; when the *Highlanders*, supported by *Anstruther's*, took to their broadswords, and drove part into the town, and part to the works at the bridge on the river St. Charles."[4]

Both generals-in-chief were mortally wounded; Wolfe died comparatively early in the engagement. When at the head of the 28th Foot, a bullet struck him in the groin. For a moment he faltered, then pressed on and was hit again, this time in the breast; whereat he gasped: "Support me, support me, lest my gallant fellows should see me fall."

Knox's account of the event is generally accepted as the most authentic; he writes: "The General was then carried to the rear, and 'being asked if he would have a Surgeon?' he replied, 'it is needless; it is all over with me.' One of them cried out, 'they run, see how they run!' 'Who runs?' demanded our hero, with great earnestness, like a person roused from sleep. The officer answered, 'The enemy, Sir; Egad they give way every-where.' Thereupon the General rejoined, 'Go one of you, my lads, to Colonel Burton; tell him to march Webb's regiment with all speed down to Charles's river, to cut off the retreat of the fugitives from the bridge.' Then, turning on his side, he added, 'Now God be praised, I will die in peace'; and thus expired."[5]

Montcalm was equally unfortunate. During the rout, as he neared the city walls, a shot passed through his body. Held up in the saddle by two soldiers, he entered by the St. Louis Gate, when one of the excited crowd recognized him and cried out: "*O mon Dieu! mon Dieu! le Marquis est tué!*" To which he replied: "*Ce n'est rien, ce n'est rien; ne vous affligez pas pour moi, mes bonnes*

---

[1] *A History of the British Army*, J. W. Fortescue, vol. ii, p. 381.
[2] *Fraser's Journal*, p. 21.
[3] "Letters of Admiral Holmes", Doughty, vol. iv, p. 298.
[4] "Townshend's Journal", Doughty, vol. iv, p. 270.
[5] Knox, vol. ii, p. 79.

amies." He died that evening, and at 8 o'clock the following morning was buried in a shell hole in the churchyard of the Ursulines.

And what of M. de Bougainville and his 2,000 men? We left him tired and worn out, halted near Cape Rouge, when early in the morning the tide turned and Holmes with his ships and boats began to drift downstream. At 6.45 a.m. Vaudreuil had sent him a message to notify him of the landing. He received it at 9 o'clock, and at once marched eastward. He came up on the St. Foy Road between noon and 1 p.m. in rear of the left of Wolfe's line. Townshend turned about the 48th, which, supported by the 3/60th, the Light Infantry, and two guns, drove him back.

As Townshend–now in command, for Monckton (next senior to Wolfe) had been wounded–began to invest Quebec, Vaudreuil called a council of war, which decided on a retreat, and at 9 p.m. the French streamed away "in disorderly and disgraceful flight" to Jacques Cartier, 30 miles up the St. Lawrence.

Thus ended the crowning battle in the long struggle between England and France for supremacy in north America. In killed the English losses numbered 10 officers and 48 men; in wounded 37 officers and 535 men; a total of 630. The French losses are unknown.

The abandonment of the city by Vaudreuil, coupled with the lack of supplies, led to its capitulation by Ramesay on September 17. On the following day, Townshend entered it and at once set to work to strengthen its defences and to stock it against the winter. About a month later Admiral Saunders and Admiral Holmes, without whose loyal and complete co-operation the campaign would have been impossible, sailed for England. On November 20 Admiral Sir Edward Hawke decisively defeated Admiral Conflans at Quiberon Bay, broke the naval strength of France and won for England the full command of the Atlantic.

Meanwhile Murray was left in command at Quebec, where he and his men passed a terrible winter among its ruins; the garrison was reduced through sickness to barely 3,000 strong. In April, 1760, when he learnt that Lévis intended to attack, Murray occupied the mouth of the Cape Rouge River. On April 26, when Lévis at the head of 9,000 Regulars and Provincials advanced, he fell back, and, on April 28, with 3,000 men and 23 field pieces and howitzers, attacked Lévis at St. Foy, but was compelled to retire after he had lost a third of his force. Quebec was then besieged, but on May 16, it was relieved by the reappearance of the English fleet.

Spring arrived and Amherst, now in supreme command, invaded Canada from east, west, and south. Murray was ordered to ascend the St. Lawrence, Haviland to move north from Lake Champlain, while Amherst himself advanced down the St. Lawrence from Lake Ontario. Though the campaign opened ill it ended successfully, and Montreal capitulated on September 8. Thus was the work of Wolfe completed by the final conquest of Canada. Of Amherst, Fortescue writes: "He was the greatest military administrator produced by England since the death of Marlborough, and remained the greatest until the rise of Wellington."[1]

When, in January, 1763, John Carteret, Earl of Granville, President of the Council, lay dying, he requested Robert Wood, the Under-Secretary, to read to him the preliminaries of the Treaty of Paris which concluded the Seven Years War. And when he heard what they contained he murmured: "This has been the most glorious war and the most triumphant peace that England ever knew."

The treaty was ratified on February 10, 1763. France ceded to England the whole of Canada and in India was left with but five towns—Mahé, Pondicherry, Chandernagore, Karikal, and Yanaon. The treaty secured not only the maritime supremacy of England but also the prestige of Prussia: a greater empire was born and a greater kingdom was founded; the former to control the oceans, the latter to perplex the lands. France not only lost her colonial empire and her navy, but was left in that financial ruin out of which emerged the French Revolution. "Thus then has France disappeared from North America," exclaims Chateaubriand, "like those Indian tribes with which she sympathized."[2] And "All, and more than all, that France had lost," writes Parkman, "England had won. Now, for the first time, she was beyond dispute the greatest of maritime and Colonial Powers."[3]

Nevertheless, the most important immediate result of Wolfe's victory was the removal of the fear of France from the minds of the colonists of New England, of Virginia, of Pennsylvania, and the other colonies. It was a result realized by many at the time,

[1] *A History of the British Army*, the Hon. J. W. Fortescue, vol. ii, p. 405.
[2] *Travels in America*, Chateaubriand (1828), vol. ii, p. 207.
[3] *Montcalm and Wolfe* (1884), vol. ii, p. 426.

including the Duke of Bedford, who, on May 9, 1761, had written as follows to Newcastle: "Indeed, my lord, I don't know whether the neighbourhood of the French to our North American colonies was not the greatest security for their dependence on the mother country, which I feel will be slighted by them when their apprehension of the French is removed."[1]

[1] Indeed prophetic words. Quoted from Corbett, vol. II, p. 173. Edward Channing, (*History of the United States*, 1920, vol. II, p. 603) quotes two remarkable forecasts, the one by Choiseul in 1761, and the other by M. de Vergennes, early in 1763. The first expressed his wonder that "our great Pitt should be so attached to the cession of Canada; for the inferiority of its population, he observed, would never suffer it to be dangerous in the hands of France; and being in the hands of France, to us it would always be of service, to keep our Colonies in that dependence which they would not fail to shake off the moment Canada should be ceded." The second said: "Delivered from a neighbour whom they always feared, your other colonies will soon discover, that they stand no longer in need of your protection. You will call on them to contribute towards supporting the burthen which they have helped to bring on you, they will answer you by shaking off all dependence." Another interesting prediction, highly satirical, is to be found in *The Gentleman's Magazine*, 1759, p. 620. It reads: "Canada ought to be restored in order that England may have another war; that the French and Indians may keep on scalping the colonists, and thereby stint their growth; for otherwise the children will be as tall as their mother. . . ."

The revolt of the American Colonies

By doubling British colonial responsibilities, the exclusion of the French from north America brought to the fore the problem of imperial control. Thus far, the empire had been a commercial undertaking run on mercantile lines, in which the colonies contributed to the wealth of Great Britain. But now, unseen by king and parliament, the vast acquisitions gained during the Seven Years War introduced a transition from commercial to territorial imperialism, and although, according to the former, the colonies were little more than oversea investments of the homeland, according to the latter, they were potential homelands of their own. The result was that, while king and parliament continued to think in terms of trade, the American colonists began to think in those of liberty, and where the one talked of duties, the other talked of rights. What the motherland looked for was not the servitude of her colonial children, but their obedience, and what the children aspired to was not complete independence, but what to-day is called "Dominion status". Thus, in 1774, when this new idea had become rooted, we find James Wilson of Pennsylvania stating: "All the different members of the British Empire are distinct States, independent of each other, but connected together under the same sovereign in right of the same Crown."

Unfortunately, this new conception of empire, which meant, as one writer has said, that "the colonies could not forever remain half in, half out of the Empire, professing allegiance while refusing obedience", was as incomprehensible to the home government, as government without a king had been during the days of the Great Rebellion. Yet what was appreciated was that, although the war had disposed of the French menace, the Indian menace remained, and that it was a very real one, the Pontiac Conspiracy, which immediately followed the ratification of the Treaty of Paris, made tragically clear. Except for Detroit and Pittsburgh, every western fort was captured by the Red Indians, hundreds of families were brutally massacred, and the frontier from Niagara to Virginia was ravaged. But the most conspicuous fact in this upheaval was that it was the British red-coats and not the colonists who quelled the rising. The latter, who possessed no central government, were unable to combine in their own defence; therefore their protection devolved on the British Government, and its provision carried with it the question of revenue to pay for it.

This was the problem which confronted the Grenville ministry when it succeeded to Lord Bute's on April 8, 1763, and economy after the long war was essential, were any ministry to remain in power.

The National Debt stood at £130,000,000, nearly twice what it had been in 1756, and the military establishments in America, which in 1748 had cost £70,000 a year, were costing £350,000. Therefore Grenville felt that to increase the revenue from the American colonies, in order in part to meet the cost of maintaining some 10,000 officers and men in north America, was both necessary and just. To effect this, he decided to tighten up the Customs Service and to introduce stamp duties which would bring in £60,000 a year. On March 25, 1765, the Stamp and Revenue Act was given royal assent, and was followed by the Quartering Act, according to which the colonists were required to provide barracks for the troops. In retaliation, the colonists formed "Non-Importation Associations" and refused to accept all goods "which are, or shall hereafter be taxed by act of parliament for the purpose of raising revenue in America". The boycott proved so successful that trade with the mother country fell by £600,000, and the merchants in London were so hard hit that the pressure they brought on the Government caused its fall and led to the accession of the Rockingham ministry, which, in March, 1766, repealed the Stamp Act. At the same time Parliament passed a Declaratory Act, asserting the power of king and parliament to "make laws and statutes of sufficient force and validity to bind the colonies in all cases whatsoever". But in America the colonists so busily celebrated the repeal of the Stamp Act that this draconic decree went nearly unnoticed.

In July, 1766, the Rockingham ministry was succeeded by the Duke of Grafton's, in which William Pitt–the real master in the ministry–took the Privy Seal and a seat in the House of Lords as Earl of Chatham. Soon after, he was stricken down by a prolonged attack of manic-depressive insanity aggravated by gout, and because Grafton was an indolent man, power passed into the hands of Charles Townshend, the Chancellor of the Exchequer.

When he opened his budget address for 1767, Townshend proposed to reduce the land tax and meet the resulting deficit of some £400,000 partly by reducing the military establishments in the colonies, and partly by increasing the revenue derived from the colonies by laying new duties on imported goods, such as paper, glass, and tea, which were expected to yield the trumpery sum of £40,000 a year. In order to collect them, the Customs Service was strengthened, and a Board of Commissioners of Customs established at Boston. But, and most important, instead of the revenue thus raised being used to support the garrisons, Townshend proposed to use it to create a colonial civil list. This meant that the royal governors and judges would be independent of the colonial assemblies.

There was so violent an opposition in Boston to this that, in July, 1768, the Customs Commissioners requested General Gage to send troops there to help the revenue officers to enforce the law. When he refused to do so, two regiments were sent out by the home government, and an attempt to enforce the Quartering Act led to further disturbances and a return to the boycott of English goods. At length, on March 5, 1770, came the inevitable clash: in a riot between the troops and the populace four citizens were shot dead and seven wounded. This affray was at once named the "Boston Massacre".

Meanwhile, in January, the Duke of Grafton had resigned and had been succeeded by Lord North (2nd Earl of Guilford), who, although little more than a stalking-horse for the king, wisely initiated a policy of conciliation. He removed all the American import duties except that on tea, which he retained as a sop to the East India Company, and as an assertion of parliamentary right to tax the colonies, he said: "To repeal the tea duty would stamp us with timidity."

In spite of this folly and the "Boston Massacre", things were quieter until 1772, when a further attempt to enforce the Acts of Trade–the root of all troubles in America–resulted in a new outbreak of lawlessness in which, on June 9, the revenue schooner *Gaspee* was burnt.

The next incident was more serious. On December 16, 1773, a band of men, disguised as Mohawk Indians, boarded some East India Company ships and threw their cargoes of tea overboard;

an incident which has gone down to history as the "Boston tea-party". Its importance was that it committed the American patriots to a policy of violence and inflamed public opinion in England.

Lord North was roused, and on March 7, 1774, he asked Parliament to provide means to put down disorder and secure the "dependence of the colonies upon the Crown and Parliament of Great Britain". A week later he moved that leave be given to bring in a Bill for removing the Customs House from Boston until £15,000 was paid to the East India Company for the tea which had been destroyed. This Bill, known as the Boston Port Act, came into operation on June 1, and as it meant the virtual blockade of the city, the inhabitants of Boston appealed to the other colonies for aid.

Simultaneously General Gage was appointed, by the King, Governor of Massachusetts, in spite of the fact that Gage had warned him and North that coercion would mean war. He was not listened to, and when he took over his governorship was at once obstructed; the citizens of Boston refused to build barracks or supply his men with food. In order to secure his position, he started to fortify the narrow neck of land which connected the city, as it then was, to the countryside.

The psychosis created by these events went far to consolidate the rebellion and led to a decisive step; Samuel Adams, in the autumn of 1773, launched a campaign in favour of the creation of a Continental Congress. The outcome was the assembly of the first Continental Congress at Philadelphia on September 5, 1774, at which an Agreement of Association was passed. According to this the colonies bound themselves to boycott English goods and to cease trading with England. This agreement should have warned Parliament that the rebellion was no local affair; but Lord North failed to realize it, and on November 18, he told the King that as "the New England Governments are in a state of rebellion, blows must decide whether they are to be subject to this country or independent".

As winter approached, Gage sent out agents to discover where military stores were being collected, and on April 18, 1775, he ordered a detachment under Colonel Smith to seize and destroy those reported to be at Concord. When Lexington was reached there was a skirmish with the local militia in which 18 men were killed. The troops entered Concord and destroyed the stores, while the entire population turned out under arms. Reinforced by Lord Percy and 1,400 men, the British were engaged in a running fight until they reached Boston, during which 259 were killed and wounded.

The immediate result of this first action of the War of the American Independence was that the whole countryside rushed to arms and blockaded Gage in Boston, and a wave of enthusiasm swept from its outworks to Savannah.

The Second Continental Congress, which assembled at Philadelphia on May 10, was a true revolutionary body. It took over the soldiers blockading Boston and formed them into the "Army of the United Colonies." Further, it appointed Washington commander-in-chief.

Simultaneously an extraordinary man stepped into the arena, Captain Benedict Arnold, one of the greatest leaders in this war, and also, because of his eventual treason, one of the most despised. He saw that the works which were being built around Boston lacked cannon, and on May 10, with 83 men he took possession of Ticonderoga by ruse and seized 120 light and heavy pieces. Next, he occupied Crown Point, overpowered the garrison at St. John, and when he learnt there that General Carleton at Montreal had only two British battalions, he forthwith determined to reduce the whole of Canada.

When this expedition was under way, Boston was reinforced, and with the troops sent from England came General Sir William Howe, General John Burgoyne, and General Henry Clinton. To secure his position and the harbour, Gage decided to occupy the Charlestown peninsula immediately to the north of Boston, upon which rose two hills—Bunker and Breed's. But on June 16 he was forestalled by the rebels and ordered Howe to storm their entrenchment on Bunker Hill (actually Breed's) on the following day. The attack was badly conceived though gallantly executed. Two assaults were beaten back by the rebels, the third succeeded because they ran out of ammunition.

The cost of the victory was devastating, for out of the 2,500 attackers, 1,054 officers and men were killed and wounded; nor were the defenders' losses light—441 in killed, wounded and prisoners.

The influences of this bloody engagement were prodigious. It convinced the rebels that a regular military organization was unnecessary, and so added enormously to Washington's difficulties, and its memory made an indelible impression on General Howe, who henceforth failed to press his victories.

Meanwhile Arnold, with the full support of Washington, matured his audacious scheme. In September, with 1,050 men he plunged into the wilderness of Maine, while Montgomery with 1,200 crossed Lake Champlain, forced the surrender of St. John, pushed on to Montreal, and occupied it on November 12; General Carleton escaped by boat to Quebec. Arnold also pressed on, but unfortunately for him a letter he sent by an Indian to General Schuyler was taken direct to Carleton who, when he learnt of the danger which threatened Quebec, at once collected every armed man he could.

Arnold reached the St. Lawrence, crossed it at Wolfe's Cove, and when Montgomery joined him, on December 21 together they advanced on Quebec in a driving snowstorm.

The attack that followed was a complete failure: Montgomery was killed, Arnold severely wounded in the leg, and 500 men were lost, of whom 426 were captured. Thus ended an operation which, though wild-cat in character, might well have proved successful if the letter to Schuyler had remained unwritten. "Had it succeeded," writes General Francis Vinton Greene, "it would probably have united Canada to the Thirteen Colonies, and changed the whole course and outcome of the war."

The fall of Ticonderoga led to the replacement of General Gage by Sir William Howe, and the battle of Bunker Hill spurred the English government to ransack Europe for mercenaries. A plan of campaign had to be decided upon, and Gage was of opinion that, were the line of the Hudson occupied, the rebellion would collapse. In England, the leading military authority, General Harvey, the Adjutant-General, differed. His opinion was that land operations would prove futile, and that instead the American coast should be blockaded until the rebels gave in.

Unfortunately for England, Lord George Germaine had, in November, been appointed Secretary of State for War. He had disgraced himself at the Battle of Minden in 1759, and was held in high contempt by the army. This, together with the contempt he had for the rebels, placed Howe in a difficult situation, which the latter in no way improved upon by his inaction. The outcome was that, when, on March 2, Washington suddenly occupied Dorchester Heights to the south of Boston, Howe's position became untenable. Compelled to abandon the city, on March 17

Howe carried his army—9,000 strong—to Halifax, where he arrived on April 2.

In May, the third Congress met again in Philadelphia to discuss the "Declaration of Independence", drafted by Thomas Jefferson. It was adopted on July 2 and proclaimed two days later.

The immediate effect of this most famous of all American documents was that as it made loyalty to King George treason, it split the colonists into two factions—the patriots who were determined to solve the problem by force, and the loyalists (Tories) who hoped to solve it by compromise. The latter were to be found in every colony, and though they were weakest in Virginia, Maryland, and Massachusetts, in New York, New Jersey, and Georgia, they probably comprised a majority of the population, and in Pennsylvania and the Carolinas were strongly represented. That they constituted a powerful opposition to cession is borne out by the fact that more than 70,000 of them left the colonies during the Revolution, and it is admitted that this figure is but a fraction of their total strength.

The second effect of the Declaration, following the battle of Bunker Hill and Arnold's invasion of Canada, gave the rebellion the status of war, and therefore brought the home government face to face with the problem of conquest.

The theatre of war was a long ribbon of land that stretched for over 1,200 miles between the St. Lawrence and Florida, with an average breadth of about 150 miles. It lacked roads and, still largely undeveloped, it was strategically a good defensive country, and therefore difficult to subdue. For convenience, it may be split into three sectors, the northern, central, and southern. The first included New Hampshire, Massachusetts, Rhode Island, Connecticut, and New York; the second New Jersey, Pennsylvania, Delaware, Maryland, and Virginia; and the third the two Carolinas and Georgia. Simultaneously to subdue all three was beyond the resources of Great Britain to contemplate, therefore strategy demanded that the British should concentrate on one at a time. As the northern sector was not only politically the most important, but strategiclly the easiest to invade because Canada could be used as a base of operations, could the rebellion be extinguished in New England and New York, and the British Army was powerful enough to effect this, the probabilities were that, even should the central and southern sectors continue to hold out, they would in time be subdued piecemeal. The northern sector was, therefore, what Clausewitz would have called "the strategical centre of gravity of the war."

In June, 1776, Howe, at the head of 32,000 men, set out from Halifax by sea, and on July 3 disembarked his army on Staten Island. On August 22 he crossed over to Long Island, defeated Washington, and forced him to withdraw to Manhattan Island. Nevertheless, it was not until September 15 that Howe crossed over to the latter island; when Washington's men took panic and fell back.

Dilatory as usual, Howe remained in New York until October 12, when he again advanced against Washington, and when he crossed to the Jersey shore, Washington withdrew behind the Delaware River pursued by Lord Cornwallis, who arrived at Trenton on December 8. There the army was ordered into winter quarters, covered by a line of posts, of which Trenton, occupied by Colonel Rall and some 1,300 Hessians, was the most important.

Washington's position was now critical, for of his 10,106 rank and file 5,399 were sick. Nevertheless, on Christmas Day he set out, and early on the following morning surprised Rall and captured 909 of his men. Next, on January 1, 1777, he moved against Princeton, fell upon Colonel Marwood, and routed his detachment.

These two small victories, as if by magic, changed the entire campaign. Germaine exclaimed when he heard of the first, "All our hopes were blasted by the unhappy affair at Trenton." Above all they added immensely to Washington's prestige. In 14 days he had "snatched victory out of the jaws of death", and both in America and Europe had, once and for all, established his reputation as a general and a leader of men.

CHAPTER 9

The Capitulation of Saratoga, 1777

When Howe was engaged on his New York and New Jersey campaigns, Sir Guy Carleton, commanding the British forces in Canada, with whom was Burgoyne, set out to invade New York State by way of Lake Champlain. He moved forward in October, 1776, and appeared before Ticonderoga, but he considered the season too advanced and decided to take his army back to Canada. Bitterly disappointed by this decision, Burgoyne sailed for England in November with his mind made up on how the war might be brought to a speedy end.

Howe knew of Burgoyne's idea, and when, on November 30, the former wrote to Germaine to set forth his plan for 1777, it was accepted. In brief, it was as follows:

The Army from Canada was to move by way of Lake Champlain to Albany, where it was to arrive by September. Then, "in order, if possible, to finish the war in one year", Howe proposed the following operations with his own army: (1) 10,000 men under Clinton to move on Boston and reduce it; (2) 10,000 men to move from New York up the North River (Hudson) to Albany; (3) "A defensive Army of eight thousand men to cover Jersey, and to keep the Southern Army [Washington's] in check, by giving a jealousy to *Philadelphia*, which", he writes, "I would propose to attack in the autumn" provided the other operations succeeded. For these movements he asked for an additional 15,000 men.[1] This plan was received by Germaine on December 30.

Three weeks later—on December 20—Howe changed his plan as follows:

" ... the opinions of people being much changed in *Pennsylvania*, and their minds in general, from the late progress of the Army, disposed to peace, in which sentiment they would be confirmed by our getting possession of *Philadelphia*, I am for this consideration fully persuaded the principal Army should act offensively on that side. ...

"By this change, the offensive plan towards *Boston* must be deferred until the proposed reinforcements arrive from *Europe*,

[1] *The Narrative of Lieut.-General Sir William Howe* (1780), pp. 9–10.

that there may be a corps to act defensively upon the lower part of Hudson's river, to cover *Jersey* on that side, as well as to facilitate, in some degree, the approach of the Army of *Canada*.

"We must not look for the Northern [Canadian] Army to reach *Albany* before the middle of *September*. Of course the subsequent operations of that corps will depend upon the state of things at the time."[1]

This letter was received by Germaine on February 23, 1777.

Meanwhile Burgoyne had landed in England on December 13. He frequently discussed the situation with Germaine and the King, and, on February 16, submitted a project entitled, "*Thoughts for Conducting the War from the Side of Canada*". In brief his scheme was as follows:—

(1) To assemble at least 8,000 men at Crown Point, as well as artillery, "a corps of watermen, two thousand Canadians including hatchet-men and other workmen and one thousand or more savages." This column was to move on Ticonderoga.

(2) Simultaneously, Howe was to send an army up the Hudson, "the only object of the Canada army" was "to effect a junction with that force." And again, a little further on: "These ideas are formed upon the supposition that it be the sole purpose of the Canada army to effect a junction with General Howe, or after co-operating so far as to get possession of Albany and open the communication to New York, to remain upon the Hudson's River, and thereby enable that general to act with his whole force to the southwards."

(3) Simultaneously, a force was to move from Oswego down the Mohawk River in order to join hands with the above two forces at Albany.

If the forces to be employed should be considered insufficient "for proceeding upon the above ideas with a fair prospect of success, the alternative remains of embarking the army at Quebec, in order to effect a junction with General Howe by sea."[2]

Although the distance to be travelled by the Canada Army was about 200 miles through most difficult country, Burgoyne's plan was a sound one. His aim was to operate against the heart of the rebellion, to cut off the New England states by occupying the Ticonderoga–Hudson line and holding it with blockhouses,

---

[1] *The Narrative of Lieut.-General Sir William Howe* (1780), p. 12.
[2] *A State of the Expedition from Canada as laid before the House of Commons*, Lieut.-General Burgoyne (1780), Appendix, pp. iii–vii.

then to conquer New England, and lastly, should the southern states still remain in arms, to fall upon them. Strategically, its greatest recommendation was that, except for a break of a dozen miles between Lake George and the Hudson, water transport could be used all the way from Quebec to New York.

This plan was accepted both by the King and Germaine, who nevertheless also held to Howe's plan of December 20. On March 26 Germaine wrote to Sir Guy Carleton as follows: While he (Carleton) held Quebec with 3,770 men, on his return Burgoyne and 7,173 men were "to proceed with all possible expedition" to join General Howe at Albany. There Burgoyne would come under Howe's command. Simultaneously Lieutenant-Colonel St. Leger and 675 men were "to make a diversion on the Mohawk River," and also proceed to Albany. Then he writes: "I shall write to Sir William Howe from hence by the first packet; but you will nevertheless endeavour to give him the earliest intelligence of this measure, and also direct Lieutenant-General Burgoyne, and Lieutenant-Colonel St. Leger to neglect no opportunity of doing the same, that they may receive instructions from Sir William Howe . . . they must never lose view of their intended junction with Sir William Howe as their principal object."[1]

This dispatch posted, a copy of it was handed to Burgoyne, who considered that all was arranged and set out for Plymouth on his return to Canada. Yet this was not so, for though, as it would seem, Germaine had instructed his clerk to draft a somewhat similar letter to Sir William Howe, in which positive orders were to be given him to move up the Hudson, it was not ready when he called at his office to sign it. Instead of waiting until it had been penned, he left it unsigned, and it was pigeon-holed or mislaid.[2]

To make matters worse, on April 2, when Burgoyne was at sea, Howe again changed his plan, because only 2,900 of the 15,000 reinforcements he had asked for were available. He informed Germaine that he had relinquished the idea of all the expeditions "except that to the Southward, and a diversion

---

[1] *A State of the Expedition, etc.*, Appendix, pp. vii–ix.

[2] See *Life of William, Earl of Shelburne* (1876), vol. I, p. 358 *et seq*. Howe writes (see his *Narrative*, p. 15): "On the 5th of June I received a copy of the Secretary of State's letter to Sir Guy Carleton, dated the 26th of March, 1777, wherein he communicates to him the plan of the northern expedition, and adds, 'that he will write to Sir William Howe by the first packet'. I must observe that this copy of a letter to Sir Guy Carleton, though transmitted to me, was not accompanied with any instructions whatsoever; and that the letter intended to have been written to me by the first packet, and which was probably to have contained some instructions, was never sent."

occasionally upon Hudson's River," and, that instead of a move overland on Philadelphia, the southward Army would proceed there by sea. To this letter Germaine replied on May 18 and agreed with the new proposal, but, as apparently he had discovered that his unsigned letter had never been sent to Howe, he added that he trusted "whatever he [Sir William Howe] may meditate, it will be executed in time to co-operate with the army ordered to proceed from Canada."[1] Where Howe was when this letter was received, and what Burgoyne was doing will be related later.

On May 6 Burgoyne arrived at Quebec and immediately wrote to Howe "that under the present precision of my orders, I should really have no view but that of joining him [Howe] nor think myself justified by any temptation to delay the most expeditious means I could find to effect that purpose."[2] On May 12, he proceeded to Montreal, where Carleton, who had been abominably insulted by Germaine, welcomed him. "Had that officer been acting for himself, or for his brother," writes Burgoyne, "he could not have shown more indefatigable zeal than he did, to comply with and expedite my requisitions and desires."[3] Next, Burgoyne wrote another letter to Howe in which he again mentioned the juncture of the two armies at Albany.

In spite of Carleton's unselfish assistance, Burgoyne was at once faced with all but insuperable difficulties. Nothing could be kept secret. On May 19 he wrote to General Harvey in London: "I had the surprise and mortification to find a paper handed about at Montreal, publishing the whole design of the campaign, almost as accurately as if it had been copied from the Secretary of State's letter,"[4] and he attributed the leakage to people in England. Worse still, the Canadians hung back; a paralysing lack of transport was discovered, and there were not enough horses to haul the guns.[5] Five hundred two-wheeled carts had to

---

[1] *A State of the Expedition, etc.*, p. 139.   [2] *Ibid.*, p. 6.
[3] *Ibid.*, p. 6. See also "History of Europe", *Annual Register*, 1777, chapter viii.
[4] *Ibid.*, Appendix, pp. xxi–xxii. Anburey writes from Montreal, May 20, 1777: "We have more dangerous enemies at home, than any we have to encounter abroad, for all the transactions that are to take place are publicly known long before they are officially given out in orders, and I make no doubt you will be much surprised as the General [Burgoyne] was, when I tell you that the whole operations of the ensuing campaign were canvassed for several days before he arrived. . . ." (*Travels through the Interior Parts of America*, Captain Thomas Anburey, 1791, vol. i, p. 181).
[5] Anburey (p. 188) writes: "Another great disadvantage which we experience in the prosecution of this war, and which the Americans avoid is, that we have to transport all our provisions with us, whereas they have magazines stored with great abundance, every thirty or forty miles. . . . Added to this, the Americans are by much our superiors at wood fighting. . . ."

be made at once and out of green wood. Thus began Burgoyne's crucial problem—supply; for it should be remembered that eighteenth-century armies seldom lived on the country. Foraging in any case would prove nearly impossible in so sparsely inhabited a land as that along his line of march.

Unfortunately for Burgoyne, he, like other British officers, held his enemy in contempt. It is true that, throughout the country, particularly in the New England states, men of military age were loth to enlist, except in the militia, and, unless danger immediately threatened them, they would seldom leave their home localities or remain for any length of time under arms.[1] Nevertheless they could mobilize rapidly, and in so broken a country as New England, the protection afforded them by the woods, mountains and ravines went far to compensate for their lack of discipline. Madame de Riedesel calls the New Englanders "natural soldiers," and Lord Balcarres, who commanded Burgoyne's light infantry, says: "they fought at all times with courage and obstinacy,"[2] which is all the more remarkable because they were shockingly equipped. This disadvantage was more than offset by the fact that they knew the terrain and instinctively adapted their tactics to the nature of the country.[3] Many were unsurpassed as marksmen, and when armed with rifles they completely outclassed their enemy; for although this weapon was slow to load, its accuracy was beyond comparison with the smooth-bore musket. On one occasion Colonel George Hanger informs us that he saw an American rifleman fire at him and Colonel Tarleton, and kill an orderly's horse, which was standing close by them; the rifleman was at least 400 yards away.[4] Burgoyne also tells us: "The enemy had with their army great numbers of marksmen, armed with rifle-barrel pieces: these, during an engagement, hovered upon the flanks in small detachments, and were very expert in securing

[1] General Schuyler writes: "Nothing can surpass the impatience of the troops from the New England colonies to get to their firesides. Near three hundred of them arrived a few days ago, unable to do any duty; but as soon as I administered that grand specific, they instantly acquired health; and, rather than be detained a few days to cross Lake George, they undertook a march from here of two hundred miles with the greatest alacrity." (Quoted from *The American Revolution*, Sir George Otto Trevelyan (1907), Part III, p. 101.)

[2] *A State of the Expedition, etc.*, p. 36.

[3] Captain Anburey writes: "This war is very different to the last in Germany; in this the life of an individual is sought with as much avidity as the obtaining a victory over an army of thousands" (vol. I, p. 293); and "In this action [Hubbardtown] I found all manual exercises is but an ornament" (p. 295).

[4] *The Book of the Rifle*, the Hon. T. F. Freemantle (1901), p. 30. The smooth-bore musket was accurate up to about 50 yards.

themselves, and in shifting their ground. In this action [September 19, 1777] many placed themselves in high trees in the rear of their own line, and there was seldom a minute's interval of smoke in any part of our line without officers being taken off by single shot."[1]

As the rebels possessed little artillery, and as Balcarres informs us, they "were always indefatigable in securing themselves by entrenchments, and in general they added an abbatis,"[2] the importance of cannon on the British side was considerable. Bunker Hill had been an eye-opener, and its significance was fully appreciated by Burgoyne, who never attempted to apply European tactics to forest and bush fighting. In one place we read: "The Major-General desires the utmost Alertness and Dispatch in all the different Movements of the Army, and particularly upon coming to fresh Ground, and in a Campaign such as this, that officers act, from their own lights, and not tediously wait for first Intelligence, and new Orders. . . ."[3]

His men trained in common sense tactics, early in June, Burgoyne, then in his fifty-sixth year began to assemble his army on the Richelieu River, to the north of Lake Champlain. It consisted of the 9th, 20th, 21st, 24th, 47th, 53rd, and 62nd Regiments, and the Grenadiers and Light Infantry Companies of the 29th, 31st, and 34th Regiments, all British, and which numbered 3,724 men; five regiments of Germans (most Brunswickers) – 3,016 strong; gunners – 357; recruits – 154; Canadians – 148; and Indians – 500; a total of 7,899, and with officers added, about 8,200.[4] The ordnance for the field army consisted of 38 pieces of field artillery, two 24-pounders and four howitzers.[5]

It is interesting to note what the British soldier of that day carried with him in campaign. Anburey tells us: " . . . a knapsack, a blanket, a haversack that contains his provisions, a canteen for water, a hatchet and a proportion of the equipage belonging to his tent," which with "accoutrements, arms and sixty round of

---

[1] *A State of the Expedition, etc.*, p. 122.   [2] *Ibid.*, p. 30.
[3] *Hadden's Journal and Orderly Book*, James M. Hadden (1884), p. 308.
[4] These figures are extracted from Burgoyne's *A State of the Expedition, etc.* Appendix, pp. xxvii–xxviii, dated July 1. More information may be obtained from Hadden's *Orderly Book*, pp. 44–46, and from Fonblanque's *Political and Military Episodes* (1876), Appendix D. Lieutenant Digby in his *Journal* (edit. James Phinny Baxter, 1887), p. 201, gives a total of 6,904.
[5] " . . . the brass train that was sent out upon this expedition, was perhaps the finest, and probably the most excellently supplied as to officers and private men, that has ever been allotted to second the operations of any army" (*The Annual Register* 1777, p. 143).

ammunition" weighed about 60 lb.[1] A heavy load; yet, if Stedman is to be believed, the English soldiers were certainly more fortunate than their Brunswick comrades; for, according to him, "Their very hats and swords weighed very nearly as much as the whole equipment of one of our soldiers. The worst British regiment in the service would with ease have marched two miles for their one."[2]

The Indians were a perpetual source of trouble and annoyance. Against Carleton's advice, Germaine had insisted upon employing them.[3] They were treacherous and brutal, friend or foe was scalped indiscriminately. On their arrival Burgoyne addressed them,[4] and did his utmost to curb their cruelty, but to no great purpose. His estimate of their fighting was that "not a man of them was to be brought within the sound of a rifle shot."[5]

Under Burgoyne came Major-General Phillips and Major-General Riedesel[6] and Brigadier-General Fraser, all able officers. The first was an expert gunner, the second the leader of the German contingent, and the third was in command of the brigaded Grenadier and Light Infantry Companies, the latter were led by Lord Balcarres and the former by Major Acland.

From all accounts the troops were in every way worthy of their officers. Sergeant Lamb, a member of the expedition, writes: "The soldiers were in a high state of discipline, and had been kept in their winter quarters with the greatest care, in order to prepare them for this expedition."[7] And Anburey writes: "As to our army, I can only say if good discipline, joined to health and spirit among the men at being led by General Burgoyne, who is universally esteemed and respected, can ensure success, it may be expected."[8]

---

[1] Anburey, vol. I, p. 335.

[2] *The History of the Origin, Progress, and Termination of the American War*, C. Stedman (1794), vol. I, p. 331.

[3] Anburey writes: " . . . our employing Indians in the war is reprobated in England . . ." (vol. I, p. 248).

[4] *A State of the Expedition, etc.*, Appendix, pp. xii–xiii.

[5] *Ibid.*, p. 122.

[6] Count von Bernstorff, German Ambassador to the United States in 1917, was descended from one of his daughters.

[7] *An Original and Authentic Journal of Occurrences during the late American War from its Commencement to the Year 1783*, R. Lamb (1809), p. 135.

[8] Anburey, vol. I, pp. 180–181. Throughout the campaign discipline continued good. From *Burgoyne's Orderly Book* (1860) we learn that there was some friction between the English and German soldiers (p. 45); several complaints concerned unauthorized baggage (pp. 56, 64, 105), and that on three occasions 1,000 lashes were awarded as punishment (pp. 74 and 118).

In short, this was no ordinary army, as the following notes, extracted from Hadden's *Orderly Book*, will show:

"The Men are to clean and oil their Feet and Shoes, and take every means to re-fresh, and be prepared for long marches" (p. 185).

"The clothing of such men as have not been properly fitted, are to be immediately completed" (p. 193).

Artillery training to be carried out, "an Examination will be held before the Campaign on the Lakes, which the Second Lieutenants are to prepare themselves for" (pp. 219–222).

"As the Rain laying upon the surface of the Ground in Camp is extremely prejudicial to the Health of the men, drains are to be made ... to carry it off ... The Carpenters, etc ... are to be employed in collecting any material to lay at the bottoms of the Tents, that may tend to keep the ground dry" (p. 240).

"New and convenient Necessaries are to be made in the Rear of every Cantonment and Encampment every week, and the old ones filled up; at least six inches depth of Earth should also be thrown into the Necessaries in use every Morning" (p. 256).

"All orders to be most Carefully read to the men every day, and the particulars explained to them by an officer" (p. 309).

From these various quotations it will be seen that Burgoyne's army was exceptional for its day.

On June 20, from his camp at Bouquet Ferry, Burgoyne issued a pedantically worded proclamation to the civil inhabitants,[1] and, on June 30, a General Order to his troops in which he informed them that "the Services required of this particular Expedition are critical and conspicuous. During our progress occasions may occur, in which nor difficulty, nor labour, nor life are to be regarded. THIS ARMY MUST NOT RETREAT."[2]

At dawn the next day the "General" was beaten and the doomed adventure set out for Ticonderoga.

The advance up Lake Champlain was as spectacular as Alexander's down the Indus. First in their canoes came the Indians in full war-paint; next the advanced guard of little warships, followed by the 1st, 2nd and German brigades, with the camp followers, sutlers and women in rear. It must have been a splendid spectacle; the British infantry in scarlet, the artillery-men and the Germans in blue, the Jägers in green, the British

---

[1] See *Hadden's Orderly Book*, pp. 59–62.
[2] *Burgoyne's Orderly Book*, p. 17.

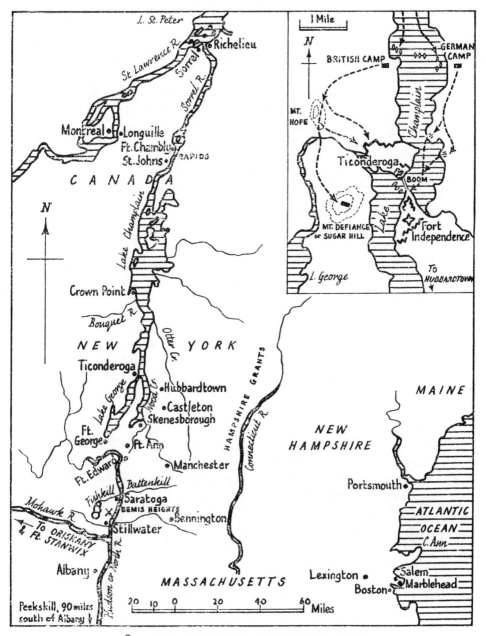

16. THE SARATOGA CAMPAIGN, 1777

grenadiers in their bearskins, and the light infantry with small caps of black leather.

Ticonderoga had been named the Gibraltar of America, but it was nothing of the kind, for though its works were extensive enough to hold 10,000 men, they were indifferently sited. In March, Congress had sent General Gates to repair them; now they were held by Colonel St. Clair, who had under his command 2,546 Continentals and 900 militia.

St. Clair came under the orders of Major-General Philip Schuyler, whose remaining troops were scattered in small detachments at Skenesborough (now Whitehall), Fort Ann, Fort Edward, and at Albany. Unfortunately for the American cause, Schuyler was a gentleman by taste and feeling, and too well bred either for Congress[1] or the New Englanders, whose officers were peculiarly democratic. After Burgoyne's capitulation, Madame de Riedesel relates: "Some [of the American officers] had been shoemakers, who on our halts made boots for our officers, and sometimes even mended our soldiers' shoes."[2] On August 4 this year, Schuyler wrote to Washington: "Too many of our officers would be a disgrace to the most contemptible troops that ever collected, and have so little sense of honour that cashiering them seems no punishment. They have stood by, and suffered the most scandalous depredations to be committed upon the poor, distressed, ruined, and flying inhabitants."[3] Such outspokenness did not make him popular.

When Burgoyne's army landed some four miles north of Ticonderoga, St. Clair was taken by surprise. He had not expected so formidable an expedition and was short of supplies and therefore in no position to withstand a siege. On July 3, his enemy occupied Mount Hope, immediately north of the fortress.

The position held by St. Clair was a weak one; it consisted of three fortified localities separated by water and dominated by Mount Defiance (Sugar Hill), which, because of the difficulty of its ascent, had not been entrenched. At once Burgoyne recognized it to be the key to the position, and, on July 4, he sent out Lieutenant Twiss to reconnoitre it. As this officer's report was

---

[1] "Congress ousted Schuyler, insulted Greene and Knox, reprimanded Stark, snubbed Benedict Arnold, court-martialled Sullivan, St. Clair, Wayne, and Matthews, and promoted a cabal against Washington himself" (*The First American Civil War*, Henry Belcher (1911), vol. II, p. 322).

[2] *Letters and Journals relating to the War of the American Revolution*, Baroness von Riedesel (1827), p. 194.

[3] *Washington Letters*, Sparks (1837), pp. 392-395.

favourable, General Phillips remarked: "Where a goat can go a man can go, and where a man can go he can drag a gun."[1] By daybreak on July 6, the hill was occupied and guns posted on it. Convinced that his position was now untenable, St. Clair forthwith ordered his boats and such cannon as they could carry to fall back on Skenesborough (called after Philip Skene). Simultaneously he withdrew with the garrison by way of Hubbardtown to Castleton.

Directly Burgoyne discovered St. Clair's withdrawal, he set out in pursuit. His boats were rowed down Wood Creek, while Fraser and his brigade, followed by Riedesel's, moved by the Hubbardtown Road. They came up with the Americans early on the morning of July 7 and a fierce engagement resulted. Fraser was heavily outnumbered until Riedesel arrived, when St. Clair fell back on Skenesborough. Attacked there by Burgoyne, he fell back on Fort Ann, and was ordered by General Schuyler to withdraw to Saratoga and to evacuate Fort Edward on the way.

It was now that Burgoyne committed an error which, even more than Howe's delinquency, ruined his campaign. Instead of returning to Ticonderoga and sailing down Lake George to Fort George, whence a wagon road led to Fort Edward, he decided to press straight on. "Had he", writes Stedman, "returned to Ticonderoga, and crossed Lake St. George, he would have reached Fort Edward at least ten or twelve days sooner. He should have detached General Fraser from Skenesborough to Fort George; by which means a quantity of provisions and stores, destined by the Americans for Ticonderoga, would have been secured, as well as a supply of carts, waggons and draft bullocks. This conduct would have enabled him to have penetrated to Albany before the enemy were sufficiently powerful to oppose him."[2]

It would seem that Burgoyne was so elated by his initial success that he decided to plunge on into nearly trackless wilderness;[3] to keep up the pursuit; to occupy Albany without a serious battle; and there to entrench his army and await the arrival of Sir

---

[1] Quoted from *The Turning-Point of the Revolution*, Hoffman Nickerson (1928), p. 144.
[2] Stedman, vol. I, p. 354. See also *History of America*, Justin Winsor (1889), vol. VI, p. 313. Digby in his *Journal* (p. 227) is of the same opinion.
[3] See *The Annual Register*, 1777, p. 152. The difficulties of the country are fully described in *The Gentleman's Magazine* for October, 1777, in an article entitled "Some of the Circumstances which inevitably retard the Progress of the Northern Army through the uninhabited countries of America."

William Howe.[1] This plan fell through, for he was unable to occupy Fort Edward until July 30, during which time his enemy recovered.

For this long halt Burgoyne was blamed, not only by Germaine, but by most historians since. Yet, accepting his line of advance, an impartial examination of the conditions with which he was faced convince one that Fortescue is right when he states that, though Burgoyne assembled his army at Skenesborough on July 10, it was no small feat that he should have reached Fort Edward on July 30.[2] What were these conditions? Sergeant Lamb's answer is:

"The British were now obliged to suspend all operations for some time, and wait at Skeensborough for the arrival of provisions and tents; but they employed this interval clearing a passage for the troops, to proceed against the enemy. This was attended with incredible toil. The Americans, now under the direction of General Schuyler, were constantly employed in cutting down large trees on both sides of every road, which was in the line of march. The face of the country was likewise so broken with creeks and marshes, that there was no less than forty bridges to construct, one of which was over a morass two miles in extent."[3]

Coupled with these difficulties were Burgoyne's deficiencies in transport. On July 10 he wrote: "The army very much fatigued (many parts of it having wanted their provisions for two days, almost the whole of their tents and baggage) . . ."[4] The 500 Canada carts seem to have broken up rapidly: according to Captain Money, when asked by the Parliamentary Committee, "How many carts and ox-teams could be mustered at any one time?" his answer was, "I think only 180 carts . . . the number of ox-carts I really forget, but I believe between 20 and 30."[5] Although a garrison of 910 men was left at Ticonderoga, in order to protect the line of communications, it was imperative for Burgoyne to collect supplies before plunging into the forest. He says: "In the first place, it was necessary to bring forward to

---

[1] When he learnt of the fall of Ticonderoga, "Washington believed that Burgoyne would not proceed further southward until he knew Howe's drums had sounded the advance up the river" (*George Washington, A Biography*, Douglas Southall Freeman, 1951, vol. IV, p. 443).

[2] *A History of the British Army*, the Hon. J. W. Fortescue, vol. III, p. 226.

[3] *Lamb's Journal*, p. 144.

[4] *A State of the Expedition*, etc., Appendix, p. xix.

[5] *Ibid.*, p. 41. Money was Burgoyne's Quarter-Master-General. For a brief note on him see footnote 208 on p. 290 of *Lieutenant Digby's Journal*.

Fort Edward four score or a hundred boats, as mere carriage-vessels for the provisions, each boat made a hard day's work for six or more horses. . . . At the next carrying place . . . it was necessary to place a considerable relay of horses to draw over, first, a portion of carriage-boats, and afterwards the provisions . . ." as well as a "great number of other boats . . . to form bridges, to carry baggage and ammunition, and the number of carriages framed to transport the boats themselves at the ensuing carrying places. . . ."[1] Horses and oxen were unobtainable from the countryside and it rained incessantly.

On July 24, supplies had been collected and the main body marched to Fort Ann and encamped there; Fraser and the advanced guard moved on to within two miles of Fort Edward. On July 29, the army set out again and arrived at the Hudson the next day. Lieutenant W. Digby writes: "We moved on further to a rising ground, about a mile south of Fort Edward, and encamped on a beautiful situation, from whence you saw the most romantic prospect of the Hudson's River interspersed with many small islands."[2]

Meanwhile much happened to the south of the little islands, which it was not possible for either Digby or Burgoyne to see. The latter, however, knew that in armies that consisted principally of militia, a setback is nearly always magnified into an overwhelming disaster, and this is what happened on the fall of Ticonderoga. Consternation overwhelmed Congress and roared through the land. But Burgoyne did not know that Washington, scores of miles to the south, was concerned not so much by its loss as by conflicting reports on Howe's movements.

Schuyler, meanwhile, had fallen back to Stillwater, although not without further disaster. Two of his Massachusetts' regiments deserted, and worse still, John Adams impeded him in every way, while General Gates was hard at work convincing Congress that he alone could bring victory to the American arms. In this welter of panic and intrigue one man alone kept his nerve, and that man was Washington, who again rose above disaster.

Three days before Ticonderoga fell, he had gauged the British

---

[1] *Ibid.*, p. 14. Burgoyne has been much blamed for taking with him so powerful a train of artillery. His answer was: "I could not have proceeded any given ten miles (without it), but at heavy expense to my troops. When it was found that I was provided with that forcible arm, the enemy invariably quitted their entrenchments ♠ ." (*ibid.*, p. 96). His park artillery brigade and stores proceeded *via* Lake George.

[2] *Lieutenant Digby's Journal*, p. 240.

plan. On July 2, writing to Governor Trumbull of Burgoyne's advance, he said: "If it is not merely a diversion, but a serious attack, of which it bears strongly the appearance, it is certain proof, that the next step of General Howe's army will be towards Peekskill, and very suddenly, if possible to get possession of the passes in the Highlands, before this army can have time to form a junction with the troops already there."[1] On July 18, directly after he had learnt of the evacuation of the fortress, he sent Arnold to Schuyler, recommending his bravery, and at the same time wrote to the brigadier generals of militia in the western parts of Massachusetts and Connecticut to point out the danger should Howe join Burgoyne, and to urge them to come to the aid of Schuyler and Arnold.[2]

Nine-tenths of Washington's difficulties are traceable to his enemy holding command of the sea. This may be gathered from his letter of July 25 to Congress, in which he wrote: "The amazing advantage the Enemy derive from their ships and the command of the Water, keeps us in a state of constant perplexity and the most anxious conjecture. . . ."[3] On the day he wrote this, he decided to go north, but when he received an intercepted letter of Howe's, addressed to Burgoyne, which he recognized to be a blind, he wrote: "I am persuaded more than ever, that Philadelphia is" Howe's "place of destination".[4] On July 30 he informed General Gates that Howe was probably going to the Delaware, and added: "General Howe's in a manner abandoning General Burgoyne is so unaccountable a matter that, till I am fully assured it is so, I cannot help casting my Eyes occasionally behind me". The next day he informed Trumbull that Congress had notified him that "the enemy's fleet consisting of two hundred and twenty-eight sail were at the Capes of Delaware yesterday in the forenoon."[5] Nevertheless, he was still in doubt, for on August 1, he wrote to General Putnam: "The importance of preventing Mr. Howe's getting possession of the Highlands by a *coup de main* is infinite to America. . . . The possibility of his going eastward is exceedingly small, and the ill effects that might attend such a step inconsiderable in comparison with those, that

---

[1] *The Writings of George Washington*, Worthington Chauncey Ford (1889–93), vol. v, p. 459.
[2] *Ibid.*, vol. v, pp. 490 and 492. On July 24 General Lincoln was also sent north (p. 511).
[3] *Ibid.*, vol. v, p. 515.   [4] *Ibid.*, vol. v, pp. 513–514.
[5] *Ibid.*, vol. v, pp. 518, 521.

would inevitably attend a successful stroke upon the Highlands."
The same day he ordered Governor George Clinton to "call in
every man of the militia that you possibly can to strengthen the
Highland posts."[1] At length, on August 11, he again wrote to
Putnam that Howe's fleet had been seen on August 7 "sixteen
Leagues to the southward of the Capes of Delaware"; but that
General Sir Henry Clinton would now probably move from New
York to the support of Burgoyne.[2] Finally, on August 22 he learnt
that his enemy's fleet had entered Chesapeake Bay, and on
August 25 that Howe had begun to land his army about "Six
miles below Head of Elk."[3]

From this correspondence it will be seen, not only how clearly
Washington fathomed his enemy's plan, but how dangerous
he considered it to be, which is as flattering to Burgoyne as it
is unflattering to Howe, whose lack of strategical perception
ruined it. Further, Washington's advice to Schuyler was pre-
eminently sound. On July 22 he wrote: "From your accounts he
[Burgoyne] appears to be pursuing that line of conduct, which of
all others is most favourable to us; I mean acting in Detachments.
This conduct will certainly give room to Enterprise on our part,
and expose his parties to great hazard. Could we be so happy, as
to cut one of them off, supposing it should not exceed four, five,
or six hundred men, it would inspirit the people and do away
much of their present anxiety. In such an Event . . . they would
fly to arms and afford every aid in their power."[4] Again, two days
later: "As they can never think of advancing, without securing
their rear by leaving garrisons in the fortresses behind, the force
with which they can come against you will be greatly reduced by
the detachments necessary for the purpose. . ."[5] This, as we shall
see, is what happened, and to help to bring it about, on August 16
Washington sent Colonel Daniel Morgan[6] and his 500 riflemen
north to the aid of Schuyler.

Meanwhile, what of Burgoyne? The question of supply had
become his dominant problem, and, as usual, it was closely

[1] *The Writings of George Washington*, Worthington Chauncey Ford (1889–93), vol.
VI, p. 2.
[2] *Ibid.*, vol. VI, p. 28.   [3] *Ibid.*, vol. VI, pp. 49, 52.
[4] *Ibid.*, vol. VI, pp. 504–505.   [5] *Ibid.*, vol. VI, p. 508.
[6] Certainly the finest light infantry of the day. Though frequently called "Morgan's
Virginians" they were largely composed of men from the western frontier of Pennsylvania of Scotch-Irish stock. They marched exceedingly light, refused all wheeled
transport, and on one occasion covered 600 miles within three weeks. They were
armed with the long barrel flintlock rifle.

related to the problem of transport. When he arrived at the Hudson, he determined to collect all the animals he could, if possible sufficient to mount his German dragoons as well as to make good his casualties in draught horses. Persuaded by Major Skene, a brave but unreliable Loyalist who had gained his confidence, he reluctantly determined to raid the country on the Connecticut River for cattle and horses. He was gravely misinformed by Skene, who led him to suppose that on a small show of force the Loyalists would flock to his standard. The outcome was that, on August 9, Burgoyne selected Lieutenant-Colonel Baum to lead an expedition to the Connecticut, in spite of the fact that Baum could speak only German. To make matters worse, Burgoyne gave him the most detailed instructions,[1] and, on August 11, as Baum set out from Fort Miller, he galloped up to him and changed his destination from Manchester to Bennington, because, as he informed him, a large depôt of horses and cattle was established there. Bennington lies at the foot of the Green Mountains, and some 30 miles to the south-east of Fort Edward.

Baum's force was not only too small for so risky an enterprise, but also internally weak because of its make-up. It consisted of 170 unmounted Brunswick dragoons, about 100 German infantry, a detachment of gunners with two 3-pounders, and 50 of Fraser's marksmen: in all 374 regular soldiers accompanied by some 300 Loyalists, Canadians, and Indians.

Baum failed to appreciate that speed was essential and advanced slowly, misled by Skene's optimism. That night and the following, Baum "allowed people to go and come from his camp, readily believing the professions of sympathy with the royal cause, and imparting to them most full and completely all information as to his strength and designs".[2] Be this as it may, for he spoke no English, one thing is certain—that his Indians behaved in a most disgraceful way. Not only did they plunder everything and everybody, but they completely nullified the purpose of his raid by slaughtering herds of fine cattle, bringing nothing back with them except the cowbells.

Slowly the advance continued until August 14, when Baum heard that the Americans were in strength at Bennington and

---

[1] See *Hadden's Orderly Book*, pp. 111–117; also *Diary of the American Revolution*, Frank Moore (1860), vol. 1, pp. 488–489, in which these orders are **heavily** criticized by the *Pennsylvania Evening Post* of August 28, 1777.

[2] *The Centennial History of the Battle of Bennington*, F. W. Coborn (1877), p. 88.

sent back to Burgoyne for reinforcements. Colonel Breyman and 550 German dragoons, accompanied by two 6-pounders, were sent out to him on August 15; but, because of the rain and their ponderous equipment, they failed to cover much ground that day. Meanwhile Baum, who had advanced to the Walloomsac Creek, entrenched his men on its northern bank and awaited the arrival of Breyman.

Shortly before Baum set out, John Stark—one of those many intractable Americans who could command, but who could not

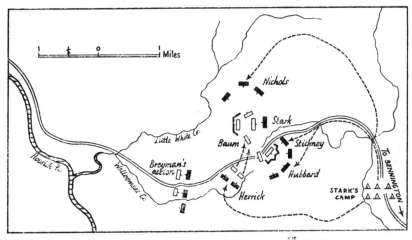

17. BATTLE OF BENNINGTON, 1777

be commanded, and who had fought against Gage at Bunker Hill and with Rogers and Abercrombie during the Seven Years War—gathered in the men of New Hampshire. On August 8, he marched into Bennington at the head of some 1,500 followers.[1] Near there, on the morning of August 16, he came into contact with Baum, who at first mistook his men for a party of Loyalists on their way to tender their services to the king,[2] and instead of opening fire on them, allowed them to wander round his position.

With his enemy thus peacefully picketed, Stark divided his command into three small columns. The central one under himself, supported by Colonel Stickney and Colonel Hubbard, was to move down the Walloomsac and launch a frontal attack

[1] Freeman (*George Washington*, vol. IV, p. 461) says 2,000.
[2] See *The Annual Register*, 1777, p. 159.

on Baum, while the other two–the right under Colonel Nichols and the left under Colonel Herrick–were to move out to the flanks and then close in on the enemy's rear. The result of this distribution was that Baum was surrounded before he realized it, and his Indians fled, clanging their cow-bells.

With a shout of "We will gain the victory, or Molly Stark shall be a widow to-night,"[1] Stark launched his attack with the greatest impetuosity. It was now between three and four o'clock, and an eye witness writes:

"The action was extremely hot for between one and two hours; the flanking parties had carried their points with great ease, when the front pressed on their breastwork with an ardor and a patience beyond expectation. The blaze of the guns of the contending parties reached each other, the fire was so extremely hot, and our men easily surmounting their breastworks, amidst peals of thunder and flashes of lightening from their guns, without regarding the roar of their field-pieces that the enemy at once deserted their covers and ran: and in about five minutes their whole camp was in the utmost confusion and disorder, all their battalions were broken in pieces, and fled most precipitately; at which instant our whole army pressed after with redoubled ardor, pursued them for a mile, made considerable slaughter amongst them, and took many prisoners."[2]

Had Breyman been present, events would undoubtedly have been different, for he was an able soldier; but although he was within six miles of Bennington early on August 16, he did not approach the scene of action until after Baum's force had been destroyed. When he did, he found Stark's men plundering their enemy's camp; upon which he extended his men and swept them out of it. Most fortunately for Stark, as his men were breaking back, Colonel Seth Warner, at the head of a battalion of Green Mountain Boys–who had been roughly handled at Hubbard-town–suddenly appeared in the field. The courage of Stark's militiamen revived, and Breyman was forced to retire under cover of darkness.

The British losses in these two encounters were extremely heavy; 596 men killed and missing, and Baum was mortally wounded. Stark lost 30 killed and 40 wounded, and for his gallant

---

[1] *Life of Stark,* Edward Everett, p. 86.
[2] *Moore's Diary,* p. 480. Extracted from *The Pennsylvania Evening Post,* September 4, 1777.

action was presented by the Board of War of New Hampshire with "a compleat suit of clothes . . . together with a piece of Linen!"

Stark deserved better than this, for his small yet dramatic victory over the dreaded Germans was electric. Every newspaper throughout the States simultaneously glorified him and ridiculed his enemy. Thus, for example, the *Pennsylvania Evening Post* of August 28 exclaimed: "They say poor General Burgoyne is gone STARK MAD."[1]

Nor was Burgoyne under any illusion about the meaning of Baum's defeat. Not only did it teach him how formidable the Americans could be, but he realized that, should he press on, his communications would have to be abandoned, and that he could not burn his boats until he had accumulated at least a month's supplies. With his wretched transport, this would take a long time, and while he was thus employed his adversary would daily become numerically and morally more formidable. On August 20 he wrote a despondent letter to Germaine to state he had heard from Howe that he intended to go to Pennsylvania. "Had I latitude in my orders", he said, "I should think it my duty to wait in this position . . . I little foresaw that I was to be left to pursue my way through such a tract of country, and hosts of foes, without any co-operation from New York. . . ."[2]

The difficulty of his situation was enormously aggravated by the frenzied campaign of propaganda which swept through America. From the opening of the war an intense feeling had existed because the British employed Indians, in spite of the fact that the Americans did the same.[3] Most unfortunately for Burgoyne, on July 27, a Miss Jane MacCrea, the daughter of a clergyman, was brutally murdered and scalped by one of his Indians—the Wyandot Panther[4]—and though Burgoyne was in no way to blame,[5] very naturally a howl of indignation was let loose. *Saunders' News Letter* of August 14, 1777, proclaimed that

---

[1] *Ibid.*, vol. I, p. 491. See also *The Annual Register*, 1777, p. 163.

[2] *A State of the Expedition*, etc., Appendix, pp. xxiv–xxvi.

[3] *Burgoyne's Orderly Book*, p. 123. Under date September 30, 1777, we read "that seven men of those who deserted have been scalped by the Enemy's Indians".

[4] For a full account of this murder see *The Annual Register*, 1777, p. 117, and Lieut. Digby's *Journal*, pp. 235–237.

[5] Washington Irving exculpates him in his *Life of George Washington* (1855–1859), vol. III, p. 191, so also does Miss MacCrea's brother (*Life and Correspondence of Burgoyne*, E. B. Fonblanque, 1898, p. 259). The Indians were quite impossible to restrain. General Heath quotes the following incident: "A British officer sending his waiter to a spring for some cool water, in a few minutes an Indian came in with the scalp of the waiter smoking in his hand" (*Memoirs of Major-General Heath* (1904), p. 135).

Burgoyne's Indians "conjointly with the English Light Infantry" had "scalped 700 men, women and children", in an area which, incidentally, possessed "not more than ten human dwellings".[1]

Here is a more poetic example, signed "John Burgoyne."

> I will let loose the dogs of hell,
> Ten thousand Indians, who shall yell
> And foam and tear, and grin and roar,
> And drench their moccasins in gore:
> To these I'll give full scope and play
> From Ticonderog to Florida . . .[2]

While this propaganda stimulated recruiting, Congress, on August 1, ordered Washington to remove General Schuyler and to replace him by General Gates. Gates, whom Burgoyne calls "an old midwife", arrived at Stillwater on August 19, at the moment when another reverse was to overwhelm the British.

It will be remembered that the second part of the plan of invasion was an advance down the Mohawk Valley, and that it was to be carried out by Colonel St. Leger who, after he had reduced Fort Stanwix (near the present city of Rome), was to advance to the Hudson and link up with the main army. Stanwix, which had been built at the portage between Wood Creek and the Mohawk River, was held by Colonel Gansevoort and Lieutenant-Colonel Willett, who had renamed it Fort Schuyler.

St. Leger set out on July 25 from Oswego and came up before the fort on August 3. His force comprised 850 Regulars, Tories and Canadians, accompanied by 1,000 Indians under Sir John Johnson—son of the noted Sir William Johnson—and the celebrated Mohawk chief Joseph Brant (Thayendanega).[3] Meanwhile General Herkimer roused the militia of Tryon county to rally to the rescue, and, on August 6, he tumbled headlong into an ambush laid by Brant at Oriskany. There the Americans would in all probability have suffered the fate of Braddock's army, had not the contest suddenly been interrupted by a drenching rain storm. Meanwhile Willett set out from the fort to fall upon the Indian camp, now denuded of men. Brant's Indians heard the firing in rear of them and at once fled the field. Then St. Leger

---

[1] See Fonblanque, p. 224, and Lamb's *Journal*, p. 158.
[2] Quoted from the Introduction to *Burgoyne's Orderly Book*, p. xxii.
[3] See *Life of Joseph Brant, Thayendanega*, William L. Stone (1838). Also Stone's *The Expedition of Lieut.-Col. Barry St. Leger* (Albany, 1877).

surrounded the fort, but because of his inadequate artillery, could make little impression on it.[1]

Schuyler heard that Gansevoort was hard pressed, and sent out Benedict Arnold and 1,200 men – mostly Continentals – to his relief. Arnold advanced rapidly to German Flats, some 15 miles east of Fort Stanwix, captured a Mohawk Dutchman, a semi-imbecile named Hon Yost,[2] sentenced him to death and then promised to reprieve him if he would proceed to St. Leger's camp and inform his Indians that the Americans were advancing in overwhelming numbers. Yost carried out his orders with such effect that the Indians took panic and abandoned St. Leger who, in consequence, was compelled on August 22 to raise the siege and retire to Oswego.

On the same day, as we have seen, Sir William Howe cast anchor in Chesapeake Bay. He had, on August 15, notified General Clinton, in command at New York, that should he "see occasion to act offensively", he was to do so. On August 25 he received Germaine's letter of May 18, and again wrote to Clinton to say: "if you can make any diversion in favour of General Burgoyne approaching Albany . . . I need not point out the utility of such a measure."[3]

After the disaster at Bennington, Burgoyne was compelled to remain encamped on the Hudson in order to accumulate supplies, because he saw that, once a forward movement was made, he would be forced to abandon his line of communications. He still believed that Howe would support him, and by September 11 he had accumulated "5 weeks' Provisions for the Army", all "forwarded from *Quebec* upwards of four hundred Miles by Land or water".[4] Finally, on September 13, he set out on his last lap, and left only two posts behind him, one at Ticonderoga and the other on Diamond Island in Lake George. His army consisted of 2,635 British rank and file, 1,711 Germans and 300 reinforcements, in all 4,646 combatants, not counting gunners, Tories and Indians.[5] It crossed the Hudson by a bridge of boats, after which the bridge was broken and the boats used to augment the supply and transport vessels.

---

[1] See Stedman, vol. i, p. 335.

[2] Among the Indians lunatics were always treated with great respect.

[3] *The Narrative of Lieut.-General Sir William Howe*, p. 22.

[4] *Hadden's Orderly Book*, p. 143.

[5] *A State of the Expedition*, etc., p. 78. According to Hadden, Burgoyne's total strength including everybody was 6,000, or in effectives, including officers, "nearly 5,000". (See his *Orderly Book*, p. 153).

Meanwhile Gates had been reinforced by Arnold and 1,200 men, as well as by Morgan and his 500 riflemen. On September 12 his whole army occupied Bemis Heights at Stillwater, which Kosciusko, the Polish engineer, at once proceeded to fortify. No sooner was it in position than Gates sent out James Wilkinson and some scouts, who soon discovered Burgoyne's approach. A series of outpost actions followed, much to the advantage of the Americans.

Burgoyne, who had to all intents and purposes burned his boats, was left with no alternative other than to fight his way southward. So he moved slowly down the track which skirted the western bank of the Hudson toward his enemy's position at Stillwater.

He reconnoitred it, and when he found that to the immediate west lay a height which dominated it and which was neither fortified nor occupied, he decided, under cover of a demonstration against Gates's right and centre, to occupy this height, and to drive his opponent into the river. Although this meant a division of his small army, his plan, though a daring one, was tactically sound. Gates's plan was decidedly inactive. It consisted in the concentration of the whole of his force, now some 12,000 strong, behind his fortifications and there to await attack.

On September 15 Burgoyne issued his orders, and the army moved forward to Dovegat (or Dovecote), halfway between Saratoga and Stillwater; two days later it reached Sword House, and on the morning of September 19 the whole force was organized into three groups—a right wing, a centre, and a left wing—under General Fraser, General Hamilton, and General Phillips respectively, with Riedesel in support of the last named commander.[1]

As the three columns advanced, the glitter of their weapons and the scarlet of their uniforms were to be seen between the trees by the American scouts. Yet Gates sat tight behind his entrenchments, and, according to Lossing, "gave no orders and evinced no disposition to fight."[2] His officers were impatient, and Arnold "urged, begged and entreated" to be allowed to advance. At length he obtained permission to send forward Morgan's riflemen and Dearborn's infantry. A little later, according to Gates's Adjutant-General, Wilkinson, "Gates and Arnold were

---

[1] *Burgoyne's Orderly Book*, p. 114.
[2] *Life of Philip Schuyler*, B. J. Lossing (1884), vol. II, p. 344.

together in front of the camp. Major Lewis came in from the scene of action, and announced that its progress was undecisive. Arnold immediately exclaimed: 'By G—d! I will soon put an end to it'—and clapping spurs to his horse galloped off at full speed."[1] Gates in consternation sent Wilkinson after him to order him back. Of Arnold, Samuel Downing, who fought with him at Bemis Heights, says: "He was dark-skinned, with black hair, and middling height: there wasn't any waste of timber in him, he was our fighting general, and a bloody fellow he was. He didn't care for nothing; he'd ride right in. It was 'Come on boys'—it wasn't 'Go, boys'. He was as brave a man as ever lived."[2]

Arnold reached the front not far from Freeman's Farm, to find Morgan's riflemen hard pressed by Fraser's light infantry. He flung himself on Fraser and drove in his skirmishers, then lost control, regained it, swung his men to the right and flung himself on Hamilton's column. Sergeant Lamb, an eye-witness, describes what followed:

"Here the conflict was dreadful; for four hours a constant blaze of fire was kept up. . . . Men, and particularly officers, dropped every moment on each side. Several of the Americans placed themselves in high trees, and as often as they could distinguish a British officer's uniform, took him off by deliberately aiming at his person . . . Major General Phillips, upon hearing the firing, made his way through a difficult part of the wood to the scene of action, and brought up with him Major Williams and four pieces of artillery; this reinforcement animated our troops in the centre, which at that moment were critically pressed by a great superiority of fire, and to which the major general led up the 20th Regiment at the most personal hazard. Major General Riedesel then brought forward part of the left wing, and arrived in time to charge the enemy, with regularity and bravery."[3]

Victory was now to the general who could bring up the last reserves. Burgoyne had none; Gates had approximately 9,000. Of his astonishing reticence in grasping victory, Fortescue writes: "Had Gates sent to Arnold the reinforcements for which he asked, Arnold must certainly have broken the British centre,"[4] and Lossing says: "Had he [Arnold] been seconded by his commander, and strengthened by reinforcement . . . he would

---

[1] *Wilkinson's Memoirs*, vol. I, p. 245, quoted by J. N. Arnold in *Life of Benedict Arnold* (1880), p. 173.
[2] Quoted from Arnold's *Arnold*, p. 29.
[3] Lamb's *Journal*, pp. 159–160.   [4] Fortescue, vol. III, p. 233.

doubtless have secured a complete victory." Then he adds: "But for Arnold, on that eventful day, Burgoyne would doubtless have marched into Albany at the autumnal equinox a victor".[1] Darkness put an end to the conflict, when "large packs of wolves made night hideous by their howls. Indians prowled through the surrounding forest, scalping the dead and dying who had fallen among the brushwood, and were with difficulty restrained from invading that open space, covered with English bodies, where the prey which they coveted was to be found in the greatest abundance."[2]

In this stubborn and well contested battle, in which the British troops were not a little surprised at the boldness of their adversaries,[3] the British losses were heavy; some 600 killed and wounded –that is, about 33 per cent. of those engaged. The American losses were light; 65 killed, 218 wounded, and 33 missing, under 10 per cent. of the total engaged.

In spite of these paralysing losses, Burgoyne's first intention was to renew the attack on September 20; but when he found this out of the question, he postponed it until the following day. Meanwhile Gates, now intensely jealous of Arnold, after a stormy interview with him deprived him of his command. Then, instead of attacking on September 20, which he should have done, he contented himself with merely sniping at his enemy and pushing out posts on to the left bank of the Hudson. Meanwhile Stark again appeared and took Fort Edward. On September 21, two unexpected factors caused Burgoyne again to postpone his advance. The first was a letter from General Clinton, and the second news that on September 18 General Lincoln had surprised and occupied Sugar Hill at Ticonderoga and had captured most of Burgoyne's supply fleet on Lake Champlain. This meant that Burgoyne's communications were definitely cut.

Clinton's letter, dated September 12, was in cypher.[4] It informed Burgoyne that it was Clinton's intention to attack Fort Montgomery (near Peekskill on the narrows of the lower Hudson) in about 10 days' time. Burgoyne at once answered, described the situation, and asked Clinton to hasten his advance. This

---

[1] Lossing's *Schuyler*, vol. II, p. 348.
[2] Trevelyan, Part III, pp. 181–182.
[3] See *The Annual Register*, 1777, p. 165.
[4] *A State of the Expedition*, Appendix, p. xlix. Trevelyan (p. 184) states that this letter was as follows: "You know my poverty, but if with 2,000 men, which is all I can spare from this important post [New York] I can do anything to facilitate your operations, I will make an attack upon Fort Montgomery, if you will let me know your wishes."

reply was secreted in a silver bullet, but unfortunately the
messenger was caught and shot.[1]

When Howe sailed for the Delaware, Clinton was too weak to
act upon his vague hints to proceed north. His circumstances did
not improve until September 24, when 3,000 reinforcements
arrived from England and brought his total force up to some
7,000 men. He at once set out with 3,000, and on October 5,
when near Peekskill, received a message from Burgoyne to inform
him that his provisions would last until October 29. "He asked
for orders as to whether he should attack or retreat. He desired
Clinton's positive answer whether the latter could reach Albany.
... If no answer were received by October 12, he would retreat."[2]
On October 6 Clinton took forts Clinton and Montgomery, cut
his way through the boom, and sent Burgoyne the following
message: "*Nous y voici* and nothing now between us and Gates ...
I heartily wish you success."[3]

His advance decided Burgoyne to attack. On October 3 rations
had been reduced, and as forage grew scarce a move became
imperative. Added to this, the sniping of the enemy's riflemen had
become intolerable. On October 4 Burgoyne summoned a council
of war, and the following day it met again, when both Riedesel
and Fraser proposed an immediate withdrawal, while Phillips
offered no opinion. Burgoyne stood out for an advance, because,
as he said, should pressure be taken off Gates, that general would
be in a position to lead 14,000 men to Washington's support,
which might easily result in Howe's defeat. He proposed to leave
800 men in camp and with 4,000 again try to turn his enemy's
left flank. As his officers objected to his plan, he substituted for it
a reconnaissance in force by 1,500 men, in order to discover the
best place to attack. Should none be found, then a retreat would
take place on October 11. This plan was radically unsound,
because the enemy was not only strongly entrenched, but now
numbered nearly 20,000. It was the blind throw of a gambler.

Thus it came about that, between 10 and 11 o'clock on the
morning of October 7, Burgoyne moved out of his entrenched
camp accompanied by Fraser, Phillips, Riedesel, and Balcarres.
He halted in a field of corn and deployed his small force: Balcarres
with the Light Infantry on the right, the 24th Regiment and some

---

[1] Lamb's *Journal*, p. 162.
[2] *The Turning-Point of the Revolution*, Hoffman Nickerson, pp. 344–345.
[3] *Ibid.*, p. 352.

weak German battalions in the centre, and on the left, Acland's Grenadiers.

When his approach was reported to Gates, Gates ordered Morgan with 1,500 men to turn the enemy's right, while Poor and 1,000 attacked the left and Learned and 2,000 the centre. A hot engagement took place in which Morgan drove in the British Light Infantry under Balcarres, and Poor took heavy toll of Acland's Grenadiers. Burgoyne then ordered a withdrawal.

Meanwhile Arnold, now without a command and totally ignored by Gates, fretted behind the works on Bemis Heights. As the roar of battle grew louder and louder, he could restrain himself no longer. He turned to his aide-de-camp and exclaimed: "No man shall keep me in my tent to-day. If I am without command, I will fight in the ranks; but the soldiers, God bless them, will follow my lead. Come on," he shouted, "victory or death!"[1] He leapt into the saddle and galloped toward the battle.

He caught up with Learned's brigade, rushed it forward, and led it against the Germans, who withstood his frenzied attack. Next he galloped to the American left and led on Morgan's riflemen against Balcarres, whose men, when Fraser was mortally wounded by a sharpshooter, fell back to their works near Freeman's Farm; whereon Arnold attempted to storm them.

Next, he galloped towards the British right, exposed to the cross fire of the contending armies, and again met Learned's brigade and led it forward. He drove back his enemy's centre and rode direct for a redoubt on its right, which was held by Colonel Breyman, and stormed and carried it. During this action his horse was killed and he was severely wounded in the leg.

With his fall and the closing in of night the battle ended. The most astonishing thing about it is that, although the British were outnumbered by three to one, it had lasted for over five hours. Of it, Anburey writes: "In order that you may form some idea with what obstinacy the enemy assaulted the lines, from the commencement . . . till they were repulsed, there was a continual sheet of fire along the lines, and in this attack we were fully convinced of what essential service our artillery was".[2] It was undoubtedly the British gunners who saved Burgoyne from annihilation, and it was undoubtedly Arnold and his frantic leadership which saved Gates in the two battles of Freeman's

---

[1] Quoted from Arnold's *Arnold*, p. 198.   [2] Anburey, vol. I, p. 319.

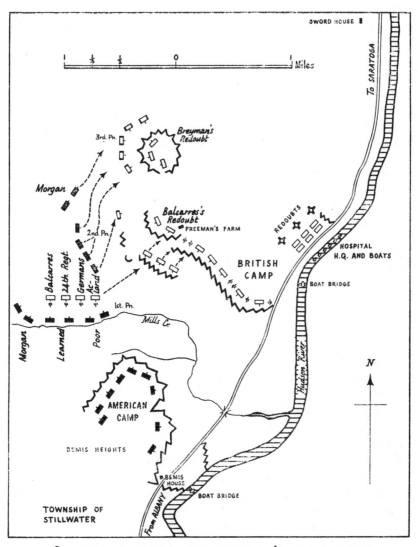

18. SECOND BATTLE OF FREEMAN'S FARM, 1777

Farm. During the second, Gates did nothing, or rather he sat arguing on the merits of the American Revolution with a wounded British officer–Sir Francis Clarke. "Losing his temper in the discussion, Gates called his adjutant–Wilkinson–out of the room and asked him, 'Did you ever hear so impudent a son of a b—h?' And this seems to have been all that the commanding general contributed to the crowning victory of Saratoga."[1] "It is a curious fact", writes one American historian, "that an officer who really had no command in the army, was the leader in one of the most spirited and important battles of the Revolution."[2]

The losses in the battle are not known exactly. According to Winsor, the Americans lost 50 killed and 150 wounded and the British 176 killed, 250 wounded, and 200 prisoners. Among the prisoners was Acland, badly wounded, and among the dead were the gallant Fraser, who died of his wound, and Colonel Breyman, who was shot dead while defending his redoubt.

Burgoyne knew that the game was up, and that nothing short of a miracle could save him.

When dawn broke on October 8, and he found that during the night his enemy had entrenched himself on the high ground east of the Hudson, he was left no option but to withdraw. Soon after sunset the beaten army set out and slowly moved northward over the sodden ground, impeded by its supply barges, which moved snake-like through the darkness upstream. Yet, the morale of the men was as high as ever. Sergeant Lamb says: "The men were willing and ready to face any danger, when led on by officers whom they loved and respected and who shared with them in every toil and hardship."[3]

To make matters worse, it rained in torrents.[4] So exhausting became the retreat that, at 5 a.m. on October 9, Burgoyne called a halt and rested his men for 11 hours; this also gave "time to the

---

[1] *The American Revolution*, John Fiske (1891), vol. I, p. 333. Sparks writes: "Gates was not on the field, nor did he leave his encampment during either of the battles of Bemis' Heights" (*Life of Arnold*, p. 119).
[2] *Life and Treason of Benedict Arnold*, Jared Sparks (1835), p. 118.
[3] Lamb's *Journal*, p. 166. Anburey (p. 413) also praises Burgoyne.
[4] Anburey does not altogether agree. He writes: "The incessant rain during our retreat was rather a favourable circumstance, for though it impeded the army in their march, and increased its difficulties, it served at the same time to retard, and in a great measure prevented, the pursuit of the enemy.... The heavy rain offered another consolation ... which was, in the case the enemy had attacked us, the fate of the day would have rested solely upon the bayonet" (p. 401). See also Lieut. Digby's *Journal*, p. 302.

batteaux loaded with provisions . . . to come a-breast".[1] At 10 p.m. the army reached Schuyler's Farm, and next morning crossed the Fishkill.

Though Gates now had under his command 1,698 officers and 18,624 men, of whom 14,914 were present for duty,[2] he did not attempt to follow up, and as Elijah Fisher remarks, he "gave the Enemy three Days to git off with themselves".[3] True, he was short of supplies and Arnold's victory had disorganized his half-disciplined men. At length he set out, and, on the afternoon of October 10, caught up with the British rearguard. At once Burgoyne prepared to attack him and drew up his men on the rising ground overlooking Fishkill Creek. But on October 12, when he found himself three-quarters surrounded, Burgoyne summoned a council of war, which decided to abandon all transport and guns, to load six days' rations on each soldier, and to retreat that night. It was too late. While the council debated, the trap closed and retreat became impossible.

On the decision of another council of war, on October 13 a flag of truce was sent to Gates. The answer received was: "Unconditional surrender." Burgoyne immediately rejected this and demanded that his troops should march out of their camp with the honours of war.[4] To this Gates agreed, probably because Clinton was now moving toward his rear, and he wanted to be free to meet him. Further, it was agreed: "A free Passage to be granted to the Army under Lieut.-General Burgoyne to Great Britain, on Condition of not serving again in North America during the present Contest. . . ."[5] This was the vital clause of the Convention of Saratoga, signed on October 16.

The Convention concluded, Burgoyne asked for an interview with Gates. Gates received him courteously and behaved with the highest chivalry, as also did General Schuyler.[6] With marked

---

[1] *A State of the Expedition*, etc., p. 126.
[2] *Ibid.*, Appendix CIV. Probably exaggerated.   [3] Fisher's *Journal*, p. 6.
[4] For details see *Burgoyne's Orderly Book*, pp. 132–151.
[5] *Ibid.*, p. 145. Washington's views on this question were that, though a free passage should be adhered to, because it had been laid down that Burgoyne's army should be embarked at Boston, on no account should another port be substituted for it. His reason was that, as Boston would be closed by ice, the embarkation would be delayed until the following spring, and the British Government thereby prevented from immediately relieving garrisons at home by the returning troops for service in America (Freeman's *George Washington*, vol. IV, pp. 554–555).
[6] See *Life of Joseph Brant*, pp. 276 and xlviii–xlix. Madame de Riedesel says: "The reception, however, which we met from General Schuyler, his wife and daughter, was not like the reception of enemies, but of the most intimate friends." Also Digby's *Journal*, pp. 242 and 321.

delicacy Gates confined his troops to their camps[1] when, on October 17, Burgoyne's 3,500 men marched to their appointed place to pile their arms.[2]

However, the terms of the Convention were not honourably kept, for they were repudiated by Congress. So disgraceful was this act that it will be left to an American writer to comment on it. The conduct of Congress, writes John Fiske, "can be justified upon no grounds save such as would equally justify firing upon flags of truce".[3] The troops were never restored to their native lands.[4]

When one reviews this decisive campaign, one of the most fateful in British history, it is apparent that, though as a general Burgoyne does not stand in the front rank, few British oversea expeditions have been commanded by an abler man. When summing up his adventure, Fortescue says "that no more honourable attempt of British officers and men to achieve the impossible is on record". And, "but for Arnold", he "might have made his way to Albany".[5]

Throughout those perilous months–June to October, 1777– Burgoyne's loyalty to his men was unbroken, and was only equalled by their loyalty to him. After the Convention had been signed, Lamb still could write: "He possessed the confidence and affection of his army in an extraordinary degree, that no loss or misfortune could shake the one, or distress or affliction the other . . . not a voice was heard through the army, to upbraid, to censure or blame their general. . . ."[6] Very different was the attitude of the politicians in England, who heaped abuse on him. Germaine, who more than any other man was responsible for the disaster, remained in office.[7] Burgoyne's reputation was

---

[1] Stedman (vol. I, p. 352) writes: "General Gates's conduct in this melancholy event was peculiarly generous and humane. It is said that when the British troops piled their arms he would not suffer his own men to be witness to the sad spectacle."

[2] Digby (*Journal*, p. 317) denotes October 17 as "A day famous in the annals of America". He gives Gates's strength on that day as 22,348, and Burgoyne's as 5,581 (pp. 354–355).

[3] *The American Revolution*, Fiske (1891), vol. I, p. 342.

[4] A point of interest is that Congress " . . . would not recede from their order that all Loyalists taken in arms, after voluntary enlistment with the British, be confined closely in jail and then be turned over to the States for punishment in accordance with a resolve of Dec. 30, 1777" (Freeman's *George Washington*, vol. IV, p. 623).

[5] Fortescue, vol. III, pp. 241–242.   [6] Lamb's *Journal*, p. 183.

[7] Walpole records in his *Journal of the Reign of George III from 1771 to 1783* (1859), vol. II, p. 160, that "Lord George Germaine owned that General Howe had defeated all his views by going to Maryland instead of waiting to join Burgoyne"; nevertheless he did all in his power to deny Burgoyne justice (See *A State of the Expedition, etc.*, pp. 116–118).

eventually cleared; yet when he died, on August 4, 1792, and was buried in the cloister of Westminster Abbey, only one coach followed his body, and from that day to this no stone marks the spot where his remains are interred.

Consequences more important than his victimization arose out of his defeat; for the surrender at Saratoga was the unbottling of the djinn. With the loss of Ticonderoga and the Highlands, all the British had to show for a strenuous year's campaigning was the occupation of Philadelphia, a city empty of military or political significance, and Gates was free to reinforce Washington. More important, France reinforced America and soon dragged Spain and Holland into the war.

On November 1, a fast sailing ship cleared Boston, and in 30 days cast anchor off Nantes. On December 4, Franklin had the news of Burgoyne's surrender, and the next day it rocked Paris to its political foundations. On December 6 Louis XVI approved of an alliance with the United States, and by December 17 it was known that France would support the insurrection. A treaty with the United States was signed on February 6, 1778, and on March 11, Great Britain and France were at war. Thus, at Saratoga, the sword of Damocles fell, not only on Great Britain, but, because of the fervour of the American Revolution, upon most part of the western world.

The progress of the rebellion, 1778-1781

At the end of Howe's 1777 campaign, Washington withdrew his army to Valley Forge, where it spent a terrible winter. There he was joined by Baron von Steuben, who in the Seven Years War had served on the personal staff of Frederick the Great. As he was an exceptionally able administrator, Washington appointed him his Inspector-General, and as such he at once set to work to organize, discipline, and train all branches of the army.

Meanwhile events moved rapidly in England. First, in answer to the American-French alliance, the British Ministry offered the rebellious colonies everything they had asked for, short of independence. Next, a peace commission, headed by the Earl of Carlisle, was sent to Philadelphia, and when nothing but ridicule came of it, early in June, 1778, Sir William Howe was replaced by Sir Henry Clinton, who forthwith evacuated Philadelphia. At once Washington broke camp at Valley Forge and marched toward his enemy. On June 27 contact between the two armies was made at Monmouth Court House, and on the following day an indecisive engagement was fought in such intense heat that many men died of sunstroke. When the last British assault failed, Clinton retired to Sandy Hook and from there carried his army by sea to New York.

While these events took place, Admiral Count d'Estaing, with 12 sail of the line and five frigates, carrying 4,000 French soldiers, sailed from Toulon and on July 8 arrived off the Delaware. Four days later he was faced by Admiral Lord Howe who, though his fleet was inferior to his enemy's, at once manœuvred for battle. But a storm scattered the two fleets, and Howe was forced to withdraw to New York to refit and d'Estaing to put into Newport. There the latter remained until November 4, when he sailed for Martinique. Meanwhile Washington cantoned his army in a semicircle of 40 miles radius around New York.

Again Germaine enters the picture. Baffled in the north by Burgoyne's capitulation, he decided, without abandoning the Hudson, to turn his attention to the south. First, he proposed to conquer Florida and Georgia; next the Carolinas; and lastly Virginia, after which he assumed that the isolation of the northern states would cause them to collapse through exhaustion. His belief was that in North Carolina many of the inhabitants would flock to the King's standard, and should, at the same time, diversions be made in Virginia and Maryland, "it might not be too much to expect," he wrote, "that all America to the south of the Susquehanna would return to its allegiance". This proposal which, as we shall see, was destined to lead to the greatest catastrophe of the war, was sent to Clinton on March 8.

Clinton at once fell in with Germaine's idea, and in June received instructions from him to send 5,000 men to St. Lucia, and 3,000 to Georgia and Florida. On November 27 he sent south a further 3,500, under Lieutenant-Colonel Archibald Campbell, who arrived safely at Tybee Island, at the mouth of the Savannah River, on December 23.

The new campaign opened with a startling success, Savannah was captured on December 29, and within six weeks the conquest of Georgia was completed. Meanwhile General Lincoln had arrived at Charleston on December 19. Not disposed to surrender South Carolina, in February, 1779, he assumed the offensive, and on March 3, was defeated by General Prevost at Briar Creek. This victory destroyed all possibility of an American recovery of Georgia.

Prevost next advanced on Charleston and appeared before it on May 5, and though Lincoln marched to its relief, the intense heat put a stop to operations until September. On September 4 d'Estaing returned from the West Indies with 6,000 French soldiers, and on September 13 he demanded the surrender of Savannah. As this was refused, he laid siege to the town, and on October 9, in an attempt to assault it, was repulsed at a loss of 837 officers and men killed and wounded—six times the British casualties. Eleven days later he raised the siege and sailed for France.

In the meantime Clinton, who found it impossible to draw Washington into an engagement south of the Highlands, heard of d'Estaing's failure and decided to leave General Knyphausen in command of New York and to proceed to the south accompanied by Lord Cornwallis as his second-in-command. On December 26 he set out with 8,500 men carried in 90 transports, escorted by Admiral Arbuthnot's fleet of five ships of the line

21

and nine frigates. He met with such bad weather that one ship, carrying Hessians, was driven across the Atlantic to be beached on the coast of Cornwall. The rest of his fleet arrived at Tybee Island on January 30, 1780.

Clinton landed on John's Island, about 30 miles south of Charleston, on February 11, but did not lay siege to Charleston—then held by Lincoln—until March 29. On May 12 it capitulated, and seven general officers, 290 other officers and 5,159 rank and file surrendered. This was the greatest disaster suffered by the Americans throughout the war.

Clinton believed South Carolina to be fully conquered, and he left Cornwallis in command with 8,500 men, and returned to New York early in June. Simultaneously, Congress, when it learnt of the disaster, without consulting Washington, appointed Gates to take command of the Southern Army, which he did on July 15, and forthwith set out on a 120 mile march to seize the British post at Camden, then held by Lord Rawdon, who at once called Cornwallis to his assistance.

Cornwallis hurried up from Charleston with some 3,000 men, 800 of whom were prostrated by the intense heat, and arrived at Camden on August 13, to face Gates at the head of about 3,000. On August 16 he vigorously attacked and routed him and captured all his artillery, baggage, and supplies, and nearly all his muskets and ammunition. Two days after this victory, Colonel Tarleton, who commanded the British Legion, surprised Sumter in his camp at Fishing Creek, and at a loss of six killed and nine wounded, killed and wounded 150 of his men, took 300 prisoners, and dispersed the remainder of his force.

In spite of these American disasters, the tide of defeat was about to turn, and its ebb was heralded by two events; the appearance of one of the greatest of small war leaders, and a perfect little victory won by the backwoodsmen of the Alleghanies.

To succeed Gates as commander of the Southern Army, Washington selected Nathaniel Greene, and with him came Baron von Steuben as his second-in-command. Greene arrived at Charlotte (Charlottetown) on December 4, to find that his army was only 2,307 strong, of whom 1,482 men were present for duty and only 800 sufficiently well equipped to fight.

Meanwhile, between Gates's defeat and Greene's appointment, Cornwallis had set out for Charlotte and Clinton had sent General Leslie and 3,000 men to the Chesapeake to act under his orders.

Some 30 miles west of Charlotte the second event happened. Major Ferguson, a gallant and skilful officer, with 1,100 men – mostly Tory militia – were surrounded at King's Mountain by an equal force of backwoodsmen, and annihilated; Ferguson was shot dead.

The news of this small though decisive victory set ablaze the back settlements, and at once brought out the militias of North Carolina and Virginia. Cornwallis, who found himself surrounded by a hostile people, retired to Winnsborough, 90 miles to the south of Charlotte, and because this retrograde movement rendered cooperation with Leslie impossible, Leslie and his men were brought round by sea to join him.

While this took place, Greene assumed the offensive; but as battle was out of the question, wisely he restricted himself to a guerrilla war. Thus ended the year 1780.

No sooner had the New Year opened than, in order to support Cornwallis, Clinton sent Benedict Arnold, now in the British service (his treason had occurred in September, 1780) and 1,600 men to the Chesapeake, and in reply Washington sent Lafayette and a slightly smaller force to oppose him.

When Greene split up his small army into guerrilla bands, Cornwallis, instead of concentrating his forces – now in all over 11,000 strong – followed suit, and on January 2, 1781, sent out Tarleton and his Legion – 1,000 strong – to round-up Morgan, then operating in the vicinity of King's Mountain, the scene of Ferguson's defeat. On January 17 the two met at Cowpens, where Morgan, by means of an able tactical distribution and at a loss of 12 killed and 60 wounded, nearly annihilated his enemy; Tarleton lost 100 killed, 229 wounded, and 600 unwounded prisoners. Morgan next fell back to the Catawaba River, which Cornwallis crossed on February 1, and then, deciding to abandon North Carolina, he moved north-east to Hillsborough to rest his exhausted troops.

Meanwhile, Greene and Steuben, who had built up a respectable little army from 4,500 to 5,500 strong, set out to follow Cornwallis's track. On March 2 the two armies came into contact on the Haw River, where a series of manœuvres took place which, on March 15, led to the Battle of Guildford. Though the Americans were numerically superior – Greene had 4,441 men present for duty, whereas Cornwallis could bring but a little over half that number into action – soon after the battle opened,

Greene's militiamen were seized by panic and bolted from the field. Greene then found himself faced by a numerically equal but more highly disciplined force, did not wish to risk defeat, and fell back behind the Haw River.

Though Greene lost this battle he won the campaign, because Cornwallis's losses were so great that he decided to abandon the interior and march to the coast at Wilmington—some 200 miles south-east of Guildford—while Rawdon, then at Camden, was left to confront Greene, who shortly after his defeat set out for South Carolina to regain that State. These two decisions bring us to the threshold of the Yorktown campaign.

CHAPTER 10

The Battle of the Chesapeake and the Siege of Yorktown, 1781

O nce the French-American alliance was cemented, the war ceased to be wholly a land operation and became largely a problem of sea power, a change which was further accentuated when, on April 12, 1779, Spain allied herself with France and two months later declared war on England. From then onward, except in North America itself, England was forced on to the defensive, and compelled to surrender the initiative to Spain and France, who, in December, 1780, were joined by Holland.[1]

The reason was that, although, in 1776, the English navy was adequate to fulfil its immediate task of securing the Atlantic sailing lines, it was inadequate to meet possible eventualities, the most probable of which was that, once England was fully embroiled with her American colonies, France would seize the opportunity to recover what she had lost in the Seven Years War.

This unusual position for England was because of the deterioration of her fleet since 1771, under the corrupt and inefficient administration of Lord Sandwich, First Lord of the Admiralty, and notwithstanding that on paper it was, in 1778, still more numerous than the French, the latter was the more efficient. It comprised 63 ships of the line of 64 guns and upward, as well as 67,000 sailors. Therefore, the issue was that, with the entrance of France into the war, England's strategical situation was changed completely; for her government found themselves faced, not only with a threat to her sea lines, but also with invasion, which became still more threatening when France was joined by Spain and Holland. This was so rude an awakening that, in November,

---

[1] The dangers arising out of this anti-British alliance were, in 1780, augmented when Catherine II of Russia formed a league of Baltic kingdoms, known as "The Armed Neutrality", against Great Britain. Although its aim was to enforce the rights of ships of neutral powers to carry goods belonging to the subjects of a belligerent, its main danger to England lay in its threat to her naval stores, more particularly masts, now no longer procurable in America. To cut off their supply from the Baltic countries would have wrecked British naval power, and France, realizing this, was unquestionably behind Catherine's policy.

1779, Parliament voted a sum of £21,196,000 for the Services and raised the establishment of the seamen and marines to 85,000.[1]

Of all men watching this change, Washington most clearly saw that his cause would in the end be lost unless command of the sea could be gained, if only for a brief period. As early as July 15, 1780, he had sent by Lafayette to the Comte de Rochambeau a "Memorandum for concerting a plan of operations with the French army", which in part reads: "In any operation, and under all circumstances, a decisive naval superiority is to be considered as a fundamental principle, and the basis upon which every hope of success must ultimately depend."[2] Again, six months later, when he sent Lieutenant John Laurens to France, he addressed a long letter to Rochambeau in which he outlined the situation at the moment. He wrote:

"That, next to a loan of money, a constant naval superiority on these coasts is the object most interesting. This would instantly reduce the enemy to a difficult defensive, and, by removing all prospect of extending their acquisitions, would take away the motives for prosecuting the war. Indeed it is not to be conceived how they could subsist a large force in this country, if we had the command of the seas, to interrupt the regular transmission of supplies from Europe. . . . With respect to us, it seems to be one of *two* deciding points; and it appears, too, to be the interest of our allies, abstracted from the immediate benefits to this country, to transfer the naval war to America."[3]

For Washington, 1781 opened disastrously: first the Pennsylvania Line mutinied;[4] next the Jersey Line followed suit;[5] and in the south General Greene reported that his army was "literally naked".[6] Nevertheless, there was a saving clause, the British command lacked unity; for though Sir Henry Clinton was commander-in-chief in America, he was tied to the apron strings of Germaine–3,000 miles away. Also, because of distance and the length of time it took to communicate with Lord Cornwallis in the south, the link with him was slight. Added to this, though all combinations depended on naval power, Arbuthnot, who

---

[1] *The British Navy in Adversity: A Study of the War of American Independence*, Rear-Admiral W. M. James (1933), p. 187.

[2] *The Writings of George Washington*, Ford (1889–1893), vol. VIII, p. 345.

[3] *Ibid.*, vol. IX, pp. 106–107. For other similar remarks see letters to Jefferson, June 8; to Rochambeau, June 13, and to Lafayette, November 15, in vol. IX, pp. 274, 280, and 405.

[4] *Ibid.*, vol. IX, p. 91.   [5] *Ibid.*, vol. IX, p. 117.   [6] *Ibid.*, vol. IX, p. 93.

commanded the British fleet in American waters, was not under his orders nor those of Germaine. On April 30 Clinton wrote to Germaine bitterly complaining of this, and added: "For I must be free to own to Your Lordship, that I cannot place any Confidence in Vice Admiral Arbuthnot, who from Age, Temper, and Inconsistency of Conduct, is really so little to be depended on. . . ."[1]

Meanwhile Germaine, who assumed that the Carolinas had been conquered and that Greene's army was no more than a rabble, had written to Clinton on March 7 to say: "I doubt not You will avail Yourself of his [Washington's] Weakness, and Your own great Superiority, to send a considerable Force to the Head of the Chesapeak as soon as the Season will permit Operations to be carried on in that Quarter. . . ."[2] His aim, now that the Carolinas were assumed to have collapsed, was to push the war in Virginia, which was also Cornwallis's idea, for on April 18 he wrote to Germaine in the same strain, and said: "I take the liberty of giving it as my opinion, that a serious attempt upon Virginia would be the most solid plan, Because successfull operations might not only be attended with important consequences there; but would tend to the security of South Carolina, and ultimately to the submission of North Carolina."[3]

Clinton adopted a diametrically opposite point of view, and wrote to Cornwallis on April 13, "except as a visitor I shall not probably move to Chesapeak, unless Washington goes thither in great force".[4] Ten days later, he wrote to Germaine: "But I must beg leave, my Lord, in this place to observe that I cannot agree to the opinion given me by Lord Cornwallis in his last Letter, that the Chesapeake should become the Seat of War, even (if necessary) at the Expence of abandoning New York: as I must ever regard this post to be of the utmost Consequence, whilst it is thought necessary to hold Canada, with which, and the Northern Indians, it is so materially connected."[5] This letter crossed with one written to him by Germaine on May 5, in which Germaine, after mentioning "the vast Importance of the Possession of Virginia", wrote:—

---

[1] *The Campaign in Virginia 1781, Clinton-Cornwallis Controversy*, Benjamin Franklin Stevens (1888), vol. I, p. 448. On the same day he wrote to General Phillips that should the report that Arbuthnot was to be recalled prove untrue, "I shall probably retire and leave him to Lord Cornwallis's management" (vol. I, p. 452).
[2] *Ibid.*, vol. I, p. 334.　　　　　　　[3] *Ibid.*, vol. I, pp. 417–418.
[4] *Ibid.*, vol. I, p. 406.　　　　　　　[5] *Ibid.*, vol. I, p. 459.

"Your Ideas therefore of the Importance of recovering that Province [Virginia] appearing to be so different from mine, I thought it proper to ask the Advice of His Majesty's other Servants upon the Subject, and their Opinion concurring entirely with mine, it has been submitted to the King, and I am commanded by His Majesty to acquaint you, that the Recovery of the Southern Provinces, and the Prosecution of the War by pushing Our Conquests from South to North, is to be considered as the Chief and principal Object for the Employment of all the Forces under your Command, which can be spared from the defence of the Places in His Majesty's Possession, until it is accomplished . . . the Reduction of the Southern Provinces, must give the Death Wound to the Rebellion notwithstanding any Assistance the french may be able to give it, and if that were the Case, a general Peace would soon follow, and this Country be delivered from the most burthensome and expensive War it was ever engaged in."[1]

While Cornwallis marched toward Wilmington, Clinton had various conversations with Major-General William Phillips—whom we first met under Burgoyne—which were destined to have an important influence on the campaign. These referred "to a station for the protection of the King's ships". Clinton suggested to Cornwallis that there was "no place so proper as York Town", which he considered might be held by "one thousand men", and he also mentioned Old Point Comfort at the mouth of the James River.[2] Finally he decided to send Phillips south to reinforce Arnold. Accordingly Phillips and 2,600 men set out on March 10 and arrived on the Chesapeake 16 days later.[3] Meanwhile Washington, who, as early as February 6, had considered the possibility that Clinton might establish a post in Virginia, had decided to send Lafayette and 1,200 men "towards the Head of Elk River" to operate against Arnold, whose capture, he thought, "would be an event particularly agreeable" and of "immense importance".[4]

Next, when he heard of Cornwallis's arrival at Wilmington, Clinton, on April 26, wrote to Phillips to point out that this

---

[1] *The Campaign in Virginia 1781, Clinton-Cornwallis Controversy*, Benjamin Franklin Stevens (1888), vol. I, pp. 465–469.
[2] *Ibid.*, vol. I, pp. 431–432.
[3] *The History of the Origin, Progress and Termination of the American War*, C. Stedman (1794), vol. II, p. 383.
[4] *Ford*, vol. IX, pp. 136, 141–143.

unexpected move had considerably changed the complexion of affairs, and that "all operations to the northward must probably give place" to Cornwallis's. Further, that before he had learnt of Cornwallis's move, he had hoped "that his Lordship would have been in a condition to have spared a considerable part of his army from Carolina for the operations in Chesapeak". Also he informed Phillips that he proposed to send him yet another detachment, in order to render him strong enough to cooperate with Cornwallis in Carolina. Then, suddenly, he switched to quite a different operation, "which if successful would be most solidly decisive in its consequences". It was to transfer the war to Virginia, Maryland, and Pennsylvania, and to subdue those states. He wrote: "but the inhabitants of Pennsylvania on both sides of the Susquehannah, York, Lancaster, Chester, and the Peninsula between Chesapeak and Delaware, are represented to me to be friendly. There or thereabouts I think this experiment should now be tried."[1]

In the meantime Cornwallis, then in camp near Wilmington, put forward a similar suggestion, for on April 10 he wrote to Clinton: "I am very anxious to receive your Excellency's commands, being as yet totally in the dark, as to the intended operations of the Summer. I cannot help expressing my wishes, that the Chesapeak may become the Seat of War, even (if necessary) at the expence of abandoning New York: until Virginia is in a manner subdued, our hold of the Carolines must be difficult, if not precarious."[2] This idea, as we have seen, he communicated on April 18 to Germaine, with whom he corresponded directly. Next, on April 23, in a letter to Clinton, he hinted at "a junction with General Phillips", and on the following day informed him that he intended to join him, and at the same time forwarded a copy of a letter he had written to Phillips in which he said: "Send every possible intelligence to me by the Cypher I inclose, and make every Movement in your power to facilitate our Meeting which must be somewhere near Petersburg, with safety to your Army".[3]

Because it would have taken weeks to get a reply from Clinton, and as he had made up his mind, Cornwallis set out on a march of 223 miles to join Phillips and Arnold. He arrived at Petersburg on May 20 to learn that Phillips had died of fever on May 13.

---

[1] *Clinton-Cornwallis*, vol. I, pp. 437–439.
[2] *Ibid.*, vol. I, pp. 398–399.   [3] *Ibid.*, vol. I, pp. 425, 426 and 429.

There, on May 24, he received a copy of the "Conversations" Clinton had had with Phillips, also his letter to him of April 26, as well as his instructions to him of March 10, in which Phillips was bidden to occupy Yorktown or Old Point Comfort, should he be in a position to do so without risk.[1] In the meantime, Clinton, who knew nothing of Cornwallis's march north, had written to Germaine on May 20: "But should Lord Cornwallis persist in his intention of joining Major-General Phillips . . . I shall be under some apprehension for every part of South Carolina, except Charlestown, and even for Georgia. . . ."[2] He wrote again on May 22, to express his belief that such a move would be "replete with the worst Consequences to our Southern Possessions, in their present State".[3] Next, when he had received Cornwallis's letter of April 24, on May 29 Clinton replied: "I cannot therefore conceal from your Lordship the apprehensions I felt . . . that you should probably attempt to effect a junction with Major-General Phillips . . . I shall dread what may be the consequence of your Lordship's move, unless a reinforcement arrives very soon in South Carolina . . . ", and added, "I have in the most pressing terms requested the Admiral's [Arbuthnot] attention to the Chesapeak, having repeatedly told him, that should the enemy possess it even for forty-eight hours your Lordship's operations there may be exposed to most imminent danger."[4]

When this correspondence is considered, it should be borne in mind that, between posting and receipt, not only days but often weeks intervened; therefore, more often than not, this see-saw of letters confused the operations they were intended to assist. The truth is, that in this war there was no operative commander-in-chief. Cornwallis was to all intents and purposes his own supreme head, therefore he had to decide for himself: yet, as we shall see, he failed to realize this.

When he entered Petersburg, Cornwallis found himself at the head of 7,000 men, with Lafayette and 1,200 watching him from Richmond. The latter had been instructed by General Greene to take over the command of all troops in Virginia;[5] but, as they were few in number, all he could do, as Lafayette himself

---

[1] *An Answer to that Part of the Narrative of Lieutenant-General Sir Henry Clinton, K.B.*, etc. Earl Cornwallis (1783), pp. 63, 175, 176.
[2] *Clinton-Cornwallis*, vol. I, p. 475.   [3] *Ibid.*, vol. I, p. 480.
[4] *Ibid.*, vol. I, pp. 493, 494, 947.
[5] *Life of General Greene*, F. V. Greene (1893), vol. III, p. 556.

says, was "to skirmish" and "not to engage too far".[1] Therefore, on May 27, he evacuated Richmond and headed for Fredericksburg, so that he might draw Cornwallis north and simultaneously augment his own strength. Cornwallis, who realized that he was not strong enough to conquer Virginia, had the day before written to Clinton to say that, after he had dislodged his enemy and destroyed all stores in the neighbourhood of Richmond, he intended to move to Williamsburg, and, as he wrote, "keep myself unengaged from operations, which might interfere with your plan for the Campaign untill I have the Satisfaction of hearing from you. . . . At present I am inclined to think well of York: The objections to Portsmouth are, that it cannot be made strong, without an Army to defend it, that it is remarkably unhealthy, and can give no protection to a Ship of the Line."[2] Then he crossed the James River and camped near White Oak Swamp, from where he slowly followed Lafayette and arrived in the neighbourhood of Hanover Junction on June 1. On June 4 he sent out his mounted units under Simcoe and Tarleton to destroy stores at Charlotteville,[3] where they nearly caught Jefferson. A fortnight later, when he heard that Wayne and 1,000 men had reinforced Lafayette, he retired from Elk Head, by way of Richmond, to Williamsburg, followed by his enemy, who by then had been reinforced by Steuben.

Cornwallis arrived at Williamsburg on June 26 to find awaiting him a letter from Clinton dated June 11, which informed him that, as Washington was about to lay siege to New York, he should send forthwith to that city some 3,000 men.[4] Because so large a detachment would leave him insufficiently strong to hold Yorktown and Gloucester, Cornwallis decided to retire to Portsmouth, from where he could comfortably proceed south. Therefore, on June 30, he informed Clinton that, as Lord Rawdon was sick, he was "willing to repair to Charlestown".[5] This meant the abandonment of the Virginia campaign.

Cornwallis did not wait for Clinton's reply, which would have taken many days to arrive, but set out from Williamsburg to Jamestown on his way to Portsmouth. On July 6, Lafayette,

[1] *The Yorktown Campaign and the Surrender of Cornwallis 1781*, Henry P. Johnston (1881), p. 37.
[2] *Clinton-Cornwallis*, vol. I, p. 488.
[3] See Stedman, vol. II, pp. 387–389.
[4] *Clinton-Cornwallis*, vol. II, pp. 20–21. (See also Clinton's letters dated June 15 and 19, pp. 24–25 and 26–28).
[5] *Ibid.*, vol. II, p. 37.

then following him, was so severely handled by the British rear guard at Green Springs that Tarleton was of opinion that, had Cornwallis turned with his whole army on his adversary, in all probability he would have annihilated him.[1] However, except for a long distance raid carried out by Tarleton on Bedford,[2] nothing but letter writing occupied the following month.

On July 8 Clinton wrote to Cornwallis to say that the 3,000 men he had asked for need no longer be sent, and that Old Point Comfort should be occupied in order to secure Hampton Road.[3] Also, on the same day, Cornwallis wrote to Clinton to suggest the abandonment of the campaign.[4] Clinton wrote to him again on July 11, pointing out the absolute necessity of holding a station on the Chesapeake for ships of the line, and ended by saying: "I beg leave to request that you will without loss of time examine Old Point Comfort and fortify it."[5] The next day Admiral Graves—who had replaced Arbuthnot—made a similar request.[6] Then, when he received Germaine's letter of May 2—which ordered him to hold fast to Virginia—as well as Cornwallis's letter of June 30, Clinton wrote on July 15 to the latter that he was mortified to hear he had crossed the James and retired to Portsmouth. "To which I will moreover add," he said, "it ever has been, is, and ever will be, my firm and unalterable opinion, that it is of the first consequence to his Majesty's affairs in this continent, that we take possession of the Chesapeak, and that we do not afterwards relinquish it."[7] In the meantime, Cornwallis sent Lieutenant Sutherland, an engineer, to examine Old Point Comfort. Because he reported it unsuitable, Cornwallis wrote to Admiral Graves that "I shall immediately seize and fortify the posts of York and Gloucester."[8] This decision he communicated to Clinton the next morning.[9]

In 1781 Yorktown on the southern and Gloucester on the northern bank of the river York were villages, the former consisted of "about 60 houses", and the latter of 20.[10] Cornwallis

---

[1] For this interesting action, see *A History of the Campaign of 1780 and 1781 in the Southern Provinces of North America.* Lieutenant-Colonel Tarleton (1787), pp. 354–357. Also: *Original and Authentic Journal*, etc., R. Lamb, p. 373; Stedman, vol. II, p. 394, and Johnston's *Yorktown Campaign*, pp. 61–68.

[2] See Tarleton, pp. 358–359.   [3] *Clinton-Cornwallis*, vol. II, pp. 51–53.

[4] *Ibid.*, pp. 57, 58.   [5] *Ibid.*, pp. 63, 64.   [6] *Ibid.*, p. 68.

[7] *Ibid.*, pp. 74–75.   [8] *Ibid.*, p. 100.   [9] *Ibid.*, p. 108.

[10] "Journal of the Siege of York in Virginia, by a Chaplain of the American Army", *Collection of the Massachusetts Historical Society* (1804), vol. IX, pp. 103–104.

began to move in their direction a few days after he had written the above-mentioned letter to Clinton.

Fortescue comments on this correspondence:

"The truth was that Clinton, Cornwallis and Germaine were all of them in favour of a campaign in the Middle Colonies. Clinton . . . wished to await the arrival of reinforcements and of a covering fleet, and meanwhile secure a naval base. Cornwallis was for evacuating New York, transferring the principal base of the British to the Chesapeake, and opening the campaign there at once. Germaine desired to combine both designs after some incomprehensible fashion of his own. . . ."[1]

The result was a repetition of the muddle of 1777, when Germaine favoured two variant plans and precipitated the disaster of Saratoga.

Washington's idea was still to drive the English out of New York. His main forces were posted at White Plains and were supported by four strong regiments of foot, a battalion of artillery, and the Duc de Lauzun's Legion, under the command of Lieutenant-General the Comte de Rochambeau, who had sailed from France on May 2, 1780, and had disembarked his army at Newport, Rhode Island, on the following July 11.

Though this French reinforcement was most welcome, it did not solve Washington's main difficulty—naval support. It was, therefore, an immense relief for him when early in May, 1781, Admiral the Count de Barras with a small French squadron sailed into Newport, for though he was at once bottled-up there, he brought with him the welcome tidings that Admiral the Count de Grasse was on his way from France with a powerful fleet.

The war at sea was being fought mainly around the Lesser Antilles; the strategic aim of the French was more to deprive Great Britain of her valuable sugar trade than to help the Americans.

In November, 1779, Admiral Sir George Rodney was appointed to the command of the Leeward Island Station, and in January, 1781, when he was joined at St. Lucia by Rear-Admiral Sir Samuel Hood with eight ships of the line, his fleet was brought up to a strength of 21 sail. On February 3 Rodney forced the surrender of the island of St. Eustatius, and while he collected the enormous booty captured there, which was valued at

[1] *A History of the British Army*, the Hon. J. W. Fortescue, vol. III, pp. 396–397.

£3,000,000, on March 17 he ordered Hood with 17 ships to blockade four French ships in Fort Royal Bay, Martinique. Hood was there when early on April 28 a frigate off the southernmost point of the island signalled "enemy in sight", and by noon Hood had information that he was in the presence of a French fleet of 20 ships of the line – including one of 110 guns and three of 80 – and a convoy of 150 sail. It was de Grasse, who had cleared from Brest on March 22.

On April 29 a long range action opened between the two fleets, and in the meantime the four French ships in Fort Royal Bay slipped out and joined de Grasse to give him a superiority of seven ships. Nevertheless, de Grasse did not intend to come to close quarters, and the result was that, on April 30, Hood stood out northward, and, on May 11, joined forces with Rodney between St. Kitts and Antigua, and de Grasse anchored at Fort Royal on May 6. For Rodney and Hood it was a regrettable event, caused by laxity on the part of the Admiralty, for had Brest been effectively watched, the sailing of de Grasse's fleet could have been reported to Rodney well before its arrival, in which case he could have linked up with Hood and probably have defeated de Grasse.

On May 9, de Grasse made an abortive attack on St. Lucia, and, on May 23, forced the capitulation of Tobago. After some desultory manœuvres, on June 18, he was back at Fort Royal.

On July 5, when a frigate reported to Rodney that de Grasse, with 27 of the line and nearly 200 homeward-bound merchantmen, had been seen coming out of Fort Royal Bay, he at once sent sloops to New York and Jamaica to inform the authorities there of de Grasse's movement. Simultaneously, because of ill health, he decided to proceed home and sent orders to Hood to hold himself in readiness to proceed to New York with most of the fleet. It would appear that Rodney was convinced that de Grasse would convoy the homeward-bound trade from Cape François in San Domingo with a strong squadron, and detach no more than 12 or 14 sail for operations in north American waters, and that, therefore, if he allotted 14 of the line to Hood, when once Hood had linked up with Graves at New York, together they would be capable of defeating de Grasse. This he did, and on August 1 set out with the rest of the fleet to convoy 150 merchantmen to England. It was a most unfortunate decision.

On July 16 de Grasse had put in at Cape François. There he

received an urgent request from Washington and Rochambeau to proceed with his fleet to Sandy Hook or the Chesapeake. He postponed the sailing of the convoy, and, while he embarked 3,000 troops and some guns, sent the *Concorde* with letters to Rochambeau, Washington, and de Barras, to inform them of his intention to help them. After which, by way of the Old Bahama Channel, an unfrequented route, he stood out for the north.

On August 3, when off Antigua, Hood received despatches from Clinton and Graves, dated June 28, to inform him that, from intercepted letters, they had learned that de Grasse was expected on the American coast "in the hurricane season, if not before, with all the sea and land forces he can assemble";[1] that they had no doubt a combined attack would be made on New York, and, therefore, they urged that the fleet should come north. When he had read this, on August 10, Hood set out for the American coast.

When Washington received the news from de Barras that de Grasse was on his way from France, he set out from his headquarters at New Windsor (Newburg), and on May 22 met Rochambeau at Wethersfield, near Hartford, Connecticut. Together they drew up a dispatch for de Grasse, which would find him on his arrival at Cape François. They suggested in this that he either sail for Sandy Hook, in order to support an attack on New York, or else to the Chesapeake. Washington favoured the former course, and Rochambeau, somewhat doubtfully, the latter destination.[2] On the following day a dispatch was sent to the Chevalier de la Luzerne to pass this information on to de Grasse. But doubt seems to have been in the air, for, on June 1, de la Luzerne wrote to Rochambeau as follows:

"The situation of the Marquis de Lafayette and that of General Greene is most embarrassing, since Lord Cornwallis has joined the English division of the Chesapeake. If Virginia is not helped in time, the English will have reached the goal which they have assigned to themselves ... they will soon have really conquered the Southern States."[3]

That same day Washington wrote to Greene:

"I have lately had an interview with Count de Rochambeau at Weathersfield. Our affairs were very attentively considered in every point of view, and it was finally determined to make

[1] *The British Navy in Adversity*, p. 265.   [2] Ford, vol. IX, pp. 251–254.
[3] *With Americans of Past and Present Days*, J. J. Jusserand (1916), pp. 62–63.

an attempt at New York with its present garrison, in preference to a southern operation, as we had not the decided command of the water."[1]

In the meantime, on May 27, Washington had written to the President of Congress to inform him of the impending New York operation;[2] but the express that carried it was captured by the English. Clinton learnt "of the enterprise in agitation . . . made a requisition of part of the troops under Lord Cornwallis's command in Virginia, and directed that they should be sent to New York".[3] Such was the origin of his letter of June 11.

Next, on June 13, Washington received a letter from Rochambeau, dated June 9, to inform him that news of de Grasse had been received, and that he was expected in American waters about midsummer. Also Washington learnt from Lafayette that there could be no doubt that Cornwallis had abandoned North Carolina. These developments persuaded the allied commanders to reconsider the question of how best to utilize the approaching fleet and their respective land forces in order to relieve the south.

On receipt of Rochambeau's letter about de Grasse's expected arrival, Washington replied as follows:

"Your Excellency will be pleased to recollect that New York was looked upon by us as the only practicable object under present circumstances: but should we be able to secure a *naval superiority* we may perhaps find others more practicable and equally advisable. If the frigate should not have sailed, I wish you to explain this matter to the Count of Grasse. . . . In the letter which was written to the minister from Weathersfield, in which he was requested to urge the *Count* to come this way with his *whole fleet*, Sandy Hook was mentioned as the most desirable point. . . . Should the *British fleet* not be there, he could follow them to the Chesapeak. . . ."[4]

The outcome of this somewhat ambiguous reply was that, on July 20, Rochambeau asked Washington for a "definitive plan of Campaign",[5] upon which Washington considered three proposals. The first was, should Clinton reinforce Cornwallis, to attack New York; the second, should Cornwallis reinforce

---

[1] Ford, vol. IX, pp. 265–266.   [2] *Ibid.*, vol. IX, pp. 259–262.
[3] Stedman, vol. II, pp. 392–393.
[4] Ford, vol. IX, pp. 282–284. In *Mémoires militaires, historiques et politiques de Rochambeau* (1809), vol. II, p. 277, Rochambeau states that after the Wethersfield meeting he privately informed de Grasse "that an enterprise in the Chesapeak Bay against Lord Cornwallis would be the most practicable".
[5] *The Diaries of George Washington*, John C. Fitzpatrick (1925), vol. II, p. 240.

Clinton, to attack Virginia; and the third, if conditions were favourable, to besiege Charleston.

He adhered to the first until August 1, at which date all should have been ready to set on foot an operation against New York. But the States failed to support him. " . . . not more than half the number [of men] asked of them," he wrote, "have joined the Army and of 6,200 . . . continuously called for to be with the army by the 15th of last Month, only 176 had arrived from Connecticut. . . . Therefore, I turned my views more seriously (than I had done before) to an operation to the Southward and, in consequence, sent to make inquiry, indirectly, of the principal Merchants to Eastward what number, and what time Transports could be provided to convey a force to the Southward, if it should be found necessary to change our plans."[1]

On August 11, he heard that Clinton had been reinforced by a draft of 2,880 Germans, and three days later he received a dispatch from Count de Barras "announcing the departure of the Count de Grasse from Cape François with between 25 and 29 Sail of the line and 3,200 land Troops on the 3rd Instant for Chesapeak bay. . . . Matters having now come to a crisis . . . I was obliged . . . to give up all idea of attacking New York; and instead thereof to remove the French Troops and a detachment from the American Army to the Head of Elk to be transported to Virginia for the purpose of co-operating with the force from the West Indies. . . ."[2] The following day he wrote to Lafayette "to prevent if possible the Retreat of Cornwallis towards Carolina",[3] and on the morrow heard from him that Cornwallis had landed at "York and Gloucester Town" on August 6.[4] On August 17, a letter, jointly signed by Washington and Rochambeau, was sent to de Grasse to notify him that a Franco-American Army would march to the Chesapeake, and to ask him on his arrival to send up to Elk River all the transports he could spare in order to carry the French and American troops down the bay.[5]

Speed was now paramount, and rapid measures were taken to prepare for what was destined to be the most famous march made during the war.

General Heath and some 3,000 men were left at West Point to amuse Clinton and his 16,000, and on Monday, August 20,

[1] *The Diaries of George Washington*, John C. Fitzpatrick (1925)., pp. 248–249. (See also Ford, vol. IX, pp. 332–333).
[2] *Ibid.*, pp. 253–264.   [3] *Ibid.*, p. 254 (see also Ford, vol. IX, pp. 334–336).
[4] *Ibid.*, p. 255.   [5] Ford, vol. IX, pp. 336–340.

the allied armies–2,000 American and 4,000 French soldiers–
began to cross the Hudson at King's Ferry, some 12 miles south
of West Point.[1] From there the advance was made in such a way
that Clinton was induced to believe that these forces were making
for Staten Island to threaten New York from the south.[2]

The next day Washington issued a "Circular Letter to the
States" to inform them of his plan, and stated that it would
give them "the fairest opportunity to reduce the whole British
force in the south, and to ruin their boasted expectations in that
quarter".[3] The allies then set out on their 400-mile march; the
Americans took the river road, and the French the way by
Northcastle, Pine's Bridge, and Crompond.

On August 29, when the Americans bivouacked at Brunswick
and the French at Bullion's Tavern, it was no longer possible
to hide their destination and the march became an open movement.[4] The following day, Washington and Rochambeau rode
ahead of their men to Philadelphia, and entered it amid the
universal acclamations of its citizens. From Philadelphia, as he
had heard nothing further of de Grasse, Washington wrote to
Lafayette on September 2:—

"But, my dear Marquis, I am distressed beyond expression
to know what has become of the Count de Grasse, and for fear that
the English fleet, by occupying the Chesapeak (towards which my
last accounts say they were steering) may frustrate all our flattering
prospects in that quarter.... Adieu, my dear Marquis, if you
get anything new from any quarter, send it I pray you, *on the
spur of speed* for I am almost all impatience and anxiety...."[5]

On September 5, when he had halted his troops at Elk Head,
Washington at length heard of "the safe arrival of the Count de
Grasse in the Bay of Chesapeak with 28 Sail of the line, and four
frigates, with 3,000 land Troops...."[6] The troops left Philadelphia for Head of Elk, and by September 18 they were being
carried down the Chesapeake to the landings nearest to Williams-

---

[1] The French did not all cross until August 26.

[2] Lieutenant-Colonel Jonathan Trumbull writes in his diary, August 21: "... By
these manœuvres and the correspondent march of the Troops, our own army no
less than the Enemy are completely deceived. No movement perhaps was ever
attended with more conjectures, or such as were more curious than this. Some were
indeed laughable enow'; but not one, I believe, penetrated the real design." (*Massachusetts Historical Society Proceedings*, vol. xiv, p. 332.)

[3] Ford, vol. ix, p. 352.   [4] See Fitzpatrick, p. 257.

[5] Ford, vol. ix, pp. 358–359.

[6] Fitzpatrick, p. 258. "No person is more interested than I am in the arrival of
M. de Grasse in these seas." (See also *Mémoires de Rochambeau*, vol. i, p. 276.)

burg where, on September 26, all the forces of Washington, Rochambeau, and Lafayette, were concentrated.

On August 27, three days before the arrival of de Grasse, Admiral Hood, on his way north, stood into Chesapeake Bay, but heard nothing of de Grasse and made for New York.[1] There he joined Admiral Graves, who had at his disposal five ships of the line. He, also, had heard nothing of de Grasse, but informed Hood

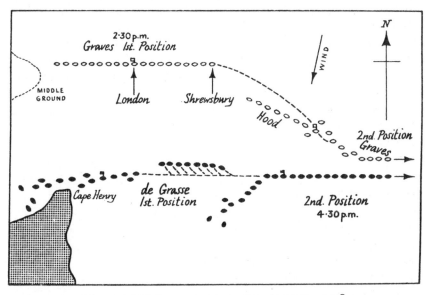

19. BATTLE OF THE CHESAPEAKE, 1781

that de Barras, with eight sail of the line and a convoy of 18 transports, had sailed from Rhode Island on the previous day. With no apprehension that the sea communications were threatened by a superior force, on September 31 the two fleets put to sea under Graves–the senior admiral–and stood out for the Chesapeake in order to intercept Barras. But unfortunately for Graves, de Grasse had sailed into Chesapeake Bay the day before.

De Grasse at once disembarked his 3,000 soldiers, who were under the command of the Marquis de St. Simon, and next ordered his transports to proceed up the Chesapeake to the Head of Elk. Then he cast anchor in Lynnhaven Bay, immediately to the west of Cape Henry, which lies about 10 miles south of

[1] See *Letters and Papers of Charles, Lord Barham* (1907, Navy Record Society), vol. I, pp. 121–124.

Cape Charles, and is separated from it by a shoal called the Middle Ground. There he was when, at 8 a.m. on September 5, one of his look-out frigates signalled a fleet approaching. At first it was thought to be Barras, but soon 19 sail of the line[1] were reported, from which de Grasse realized that it must be Admiral Graves.

At noon, with the ebb-tide, the French ships slipped their cables and got under way; but as many had to make several tacks in order to clear Cape Henry, their line was late in forming or, as Stedman writes, they were compelled to "form the line prom-iscuously as they could get up."[2] It was then that Admiral Hood, who was leading the British van, says that Graves should have attacked. He writes: "Soon after they [the French] began to come out in a line of battle ahead, but by no means regular and connected, which afforded the British fleet a most glorious open-ing for making a close attack to manifest advantage, but it was not embraced."[3] According to Corbett, this is correct comment, for he says that "Graves, instead of signalling 'General Chase' or one of its modified forms, so as to attack the French before they could form, continued to stand in shore, so as to extend his line parallel with theirs".[4] However, Graves himself informs us: "My aim was to get close, to form parallel, extend with them, and attack all together; to this end I kept on until the van drew so near a shoal called the Middle Ground as to be in danger."[5] He therefore signalled for the whole fleet to wear together, by which it was put about on the same tack with the enemy, when Hood's division became the rear. This took place at 1 p.m. An hour later, the French van was three miles to the south of the *London*–Graves's flagship–and abreast the British centre, and, in order to allow it to come abreast of his own van, at 2.30 p.m. Graves made the signal for the van ship (the *Shrewsbury*) to lead more to starboard toward the enemy.

When, on July 2, Arbuthnot left for England, Graves continued to use his signals and instructions with additional ones of his own,

---

[1] A list of the British ships is given in *The Royal Navy*, Wm. Laird Clowes (1898–1899), vol. III, p. 497.

[2] Stedman, vol. II, p. 400. See also *Gordon's History* (1788), vol. IV, p. 182.

[3] *Letters written by Sir Samuel Hood, 1781–1783* (1895, Navy Record Society), p. 28. See also *The Private Papers of John, Earl of Sandwich, 1771–1782* (1938, Navy Record Society), vol. IV, p. 186.

[4] *Signals and Instructions, 1776–1794*, Julian S. Corbett (1908, Navy Record Society), p. 54.

[5] *The Private Papers of John, Earl of Sandwich, 1771–1782*, (1938, Navy Record Society), vol. IV, pp. 181–182.

and it seems probable that Hood and his officers had not had sufficient time to assimilate them. Two now were simultaneously flown, namely "close action" and "line ahead at half a cable", with the result that, while the British van bore down on the French, the British centre and rear, instead of closing, followed the van and therefore accentuated the distance between themselves and their enemy's centre and rear. This happened at 3.45 p.m., when both vans became engaged, but the rest of the two fleets to all intents and purposes remained out of action. At 4.27 p.m. the signal of "line ahead" was hauled down; yet it was not until 5.20 p.m. that Hood at length bore down on the French, who by bearing up avoided close engagement. At sunset, the battle ended; the British had lost 90 killed and 246 wounded to the French 221.

That night Graves used his best endeavours to keep up the line, in order to renew the action in the morning; but September 6 was calm all day, and on September 7 and 8 the enemy bore to windward and refused to engage. On September 9 Hood wrote: " ... the French carried a press of sail, which proved to me beyond a doubt that De Grasse had other views than fighting".[1] The next day Graves learnt that Barras and his fleet had arrived with eight line-of-battle ships and had brought with him the siege artillery and stores indispensable for the siege of Yorktown. This augmentation of his enemy's strength persuaded him to call a council of war on September 13. It was decided the fleet should return to New York, where it arrived on September 19.

This indecisive and fateful engagement led to the doom of Cornwallis, and consequently must take its place among the decisive battles of the world.

Whatever the cause of Graves's failure, it cannot be denied that the outcome of the engagement was largely because of Rodney's initial miscalculation of de Grasse's probable movements from Cape François and because of Hood's pigheadedness during the battle.[2] In the eyes of Graves, "the fiasco was entirely due to the fact that his captains, and particularly Hood and his squadron", writes Corbett, "were too hide-bound in the stereotyped tradition of the old Fighting Instructions to interpret his signals intelligently, or to act with a reasonable initiative." Further, Corbett comments:

[1] *Letters written by Sir Samuel Hood, 1781–1783*, pp. 29–30.
[2] Both Rodney and Hood disliked Graves.

"Why Hood of all people did not show more initiative, it is difficult to understand, but he chose to keep the line as it was formed, obliquely to the enemy. It may be he hoped still to see a concentration of De Grasse's centre and van, or that he was so much out of heart and temper at the chance that had been missed that he would do nothing but obey the order for the line literally. . . .

" . . . Had Hood but acted with one-half of the spirit that Nelson showed at St. Vincent, would De Grasse have been able to get back to the Chesapeake? And if he had not, what then?"[1]

Four days before Admiral Graves sailed from Sandy Hook, Clinton wrote to Cornwallis: "I cannot well ascertain Mr. Washington's real intentions by this move of his army."[2] Three days later, he wrote again: " . . . unless Mr. Washington should send a considerable part of his army to the southward, I shall not judge it necessary until then to detach thither".[3] Not until September 2 did he discover what had happened, when he wrote to Cornwallis:

"By intelligence which I have this day received, it would seem that Mr. Washington is moving an army to the southward, with an appearance of haste, and gives out that he expects the co-operation of a considerable French armament. Your Lordship, however, may be assured, that if this should be the case, I shall either endeavour to reinforce the army under your command by all the means within the compass of my power, or make every possible diversion in your favour."[4]

This same day Cornwallis also discovered his predicament, for he sent a cypher message to Clinton that: "Comte de Grasse's fleet is within the Capes of the Chesapeak."[5]

True to his word, Clinton carried out a diversion. He sent Arnold to New London, where, on September 6, he stormed two forts. That day Clinton sent a dispatch to Cornwallis saying: " . . . I think the best way to relieve you, is to join you as soon as possible, with all the Force that can be spared from hence, which is about 4,000 Men. They are already embarked, and will proceed the Instant I receive Information from the Admiral that we may venture. . . ."[6] It was a vain hope, for already the Battle of the Chesapeake had put a stop to this proposal. Not until six weeks later did the expedition sail.

[1] *Signals and Instructions*, pp. 54–56.   [2] *Clinton-Cornwallis*, vol. II, p. 142.
[3] *Ibid.*, vol. II, p. 145.   [4] *Ibid.*, vol. II, p. 149.
[5] *Ibid.*, vol. II, p. 148.   [6] *Ibid.*, vol. II, pp. 152–153.

When this proposal was made, Cornwallis lay at Yorktown with 7,000 men, watched by Lafayette with 5,000. Obviously Cornwallis could have attacked him and in all probability have beaten him before the arrival of Washington and Rochambeau. For not having done so, he has been severely censured by both Tarleton and Stedman, and also for not having withdrawn into North Carolina.[1] Even as late as September 16 and 17, when he hinted at a withdrawal and informed Clinton that his position was desperate, he could have slipped away.[2] That he did not do so is difficult to explain, because he must have appreciated the seriousness of the naval situation. On September 29 he received a dispatch from Clinton, dated September 24, saying that he hoped to set out on October 5 with a fleet of 23 sail.[3] Next, on September 25, Clinton informed him that "repairs of the fleet" would detain him, and on September 30 he wrote that he hoped to "pass the bar by the 12th of October".[4]

During these delays all was activity in the enemy's camp. On September 17 Washington had already visited de Grasse,[5] and on September 25 he successfully induced him to remain in Chesapeake Bay until Yorktown had surrendered, and not to proceed north as, on September 23 he had intimated he intended to do.[6] On September 27, he assembled his army at Williamsburg: it consisted of 16,645 men[7] organized into three divisions, under Lincoln, Lafayette, and Steuben. The following day the army advanced to within two miles of its goal, and on September 29, as the anonymous American Chaplain informs us, "Our troops lay on their arms the last night, and expected an attack from the enemy; but they did not disturb us."[8] Thus the famous siege opened.

The positions of Yorktown and Gloucester were not favourable to defence without command of the sea, and it cannot be doubted that Cornwallis would have abandoned them if he had realized, as he should have done, that naval supremacy had passed to the French. Their defences, natural and artificial, are described by Tarleton as follows:

Yorktown. "The right rests on the swamp which covered the

---

[1] See Tarleton, pp. 368–370 and Stedman, vol. II, pp. 407–408.
[2] *Clinton-Cornwallis*, vol. II, pp. 157–158.
[3] *Ibid.*, vol. II, p. 160.   [4] *Ibid.*, vol. II, pp. 163 and 172.
[5] Fitzpatrick, p. 260.   [6] Ford, vol. IX, pp. 367–368.
[7] Continentals–5,645; Militia–3,200, and French–7,800. A full description of the opposing armies is to be found in Johnston's *The Yorktown Campaign*, pp. 109-119.
[8] *Massachusetts Historical Society*, vol. IX (1st Series), p. 104.

right of the town: A large redoubt was constructed beyond it, close to the river road from Williamsburg, and completed with fraizing and abbatis. The Charon, Guadaloupe, and other armed vessels, were moored opposite to the swamp; and the town batteries commanded all the roads and causeways which approached it. On the right, at the head of the morass, two redoubts were placed, one on each side of the Williamsburgh road. The center was protected by a thin wood, whose front was cut down, with the branches facing outwards. A field work, mounted with cannon, was erected on the left of the center, to command the Hampton road. A deep ravine, and a creek, which increased till it reached York river, covered the left. Trees were felled, fleches were thrown up, and batteries were constructed, at the points which were deemed most vulnerable. The distance between the heads of the swamp and creek, which embraced the flanks of the town, did not exceed half a mile. The face of the country, in front of this line, was cut near the center by a morass, and, excepting this break, the ground was plain and open for near two thousand yards."

.   .   .   .   .

Gloucester. "This village is situated on a point of land on the north side of York river, and consisted at that time of about a dozen houses. A marshy creek extends along part of the right flank: The ground is clear and level for a mile in front: At that distance stands a wood: The space which it occupies is narrowed by the river on the left, and a creek on the right: Beyond the gorge the country is open and cultivated."[1]

Beyond the immediate defences of Yorktown lay an outer ring of works, which Cornwallis, on receipt of Clinton's letter of September 24, notifying him that he would sail south on October 5, most foolishly abandoned[2] during the night of September 29. The next day they were occupied by his enemy.[3] Washington suspected that Cornwallis was trying to escape, and urged de Grasse to pass up the York River and so prevent him from seeking shelter between the Pamunky and Mattapony rivers.[4] This request was refused.

To make such an escape more difficult, the Duc de Lauzun and his legion—300 cavalry and 300 infantry—as well as 700

[1] Tarleton, pp. 371–372 and 361–362.   [2] See Tarleton, p. 374.
[3] Ford, vol. IX, p. 272.   [4] *Ibid.*, vol. IX, p. 375.

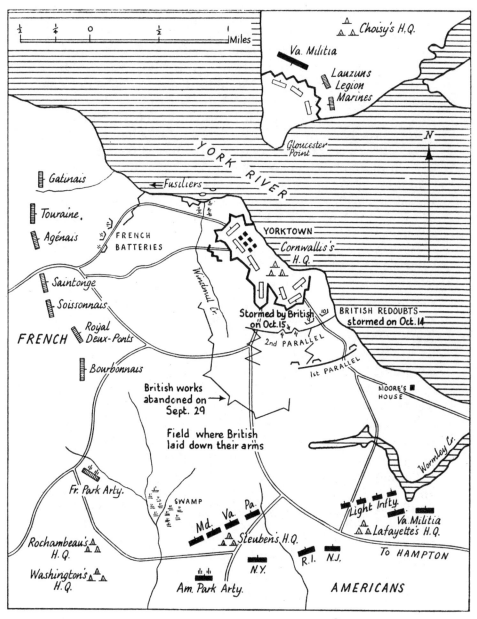

20. SIEGE OF YORKTOWN, 1781

Marines were sent to Gloucester to reinforce M. de Choisy, who was blockading it. There, on October 3, a spirited cavalry encounter took place between de Lauzun and Colonel Tarleton, in which the latter was unhorsed and nearly captured. On the Yorktown side little happened until the night of October 6, when, under the direction of General von Steuben, the first parallel was opened at about 600 yards distance from the British left. Three days later, when the batteries and redoubts had been finished, "a general discharge of 24- and 18-pounders and of 10-inch mortars commenced by the Americans on the right, and continued all night without intermission. The next morning, the French opened their batteries on the left, and a tremendous roar of cannon and mortars was continued for 6 or 8 hours without ceasing."[1]

Of October 10, Washington wrote:

"The fire now became so excessively heavy, that the enemy withdrew their cannon from their embrasures, placed them behind the merlins [that part of the parapet which lies between two embrasures], and scarcely fired a shot during the whole day. In the evening the Charon frigate of forty-four guns was set on fire by a hot ball from the French battery on the left, and entirely consumed. Her guns and stores had been taken out. By the report of a deserter, our shells, which were thrown with the utmost degree of precision, did much mischief in the course of the day."[2]

Next night the second parallel was opened 300 yards in advance of the first (it was 750 yards long, $3\frac{1}{2}$ ft. deep and 7 ft. wide), and 52 pieces opened fire. It was at this moment that Cornwallis received Clinton's letter of September 25, to inform him that his start was delayed. It was then suggested to Cornwallis that he should carry the Yorktown garrison over to Gloucester and attempt to cut his way out, as Washington feared he might do. According to Tarleton this was a feasible operation.

"The army had, exclusive of the navy", he wrote, "many boats and much small craft, which, properly manned, could transport twelve hundred infantry at a trip, and with the assistance of the navy, above two thousand. No difficulties occur, therefore, to impede a great part of the troops withdrawing in the night, embarking, crossing the river, and destroying the boats

---

[1] *The History of the Rise, Progress and Establishment of the Independence of the United States of America*, William Gordon (1788), vol. IV, p. 191.
[2] *Ford*, vol. IX, p. 381.

after the passage. Gloucester was not besieged: Brigadier de Choisy only blockaded that post with the Duke de Lauzun's legion (three hundred and fifty men) seven hundred marines and twelve hundred militia. . . ."[1]

It was Cornwallis's last chance of escape, yet for some unknown reason he did not take it, and that day (October 11) he wrote to Clinton: "We have lost about seventy men, and many of our works are considerably damaged: with such works on disadvantageous ground against so powerful an attack we cannot hope to make a very long resistance."[2]

On October 12 and 13 the bombardment continued, and as a direct approach was held up by Redoubts No. 9 and No. 10–on the extreme British left–the allied command decided to carry them by assault. This was done on the night of October 14, No. 9 was stormed by the French and No. 10 by the Americans. Their loss sealed the doom of Cornwallis; yet, ironically, it was on this day that Clinton wrote to him to suggest various courses of action, and ended by saying: "I expect we shall certainly sail in a day or two."[3]

The next day, Cornwallis, who fully realized that his position was untenable, but who did not wish to surrender without some show of fight, ordered a detachment of 400 men to storm two American batteries, which they gallantly did, but at no great profit. Finally, on October 16–a week too late–he decided to abandon Yorktown and carry such troops as he could over to Gloucester. Embarkation began at 11 p.m., but when part of the army had been carried over, a sudden storm scattered the boats and put a stop to the evacuation. "Thus," writes Tarleton, "expired the last hope of the British army."[4]

On October 17–the anniversary of Burgoyne's surrender at Saratoga–at 10 o'clock in the morning, under cover of a white flag, a drummer in red mounted the parapet on the left of the Yorktown works and beat a "parley". As Johnston writes, he was indeed a momentous figure. "He seemed publicly to confess the end of British domination in America, and proclaim the success of the 'rebel' Revolution."[5] The cannon then ceased to fire, and a little while later the following note from Cornwallis was handed to Washington:

[1] Tarleton, p. 380. [2] *Clinton-Cornwallis*, vol. II, p. 177.
[3] *Ibid.*, vol. II, p. 186. [4] Tarleton, p. 388.
[5] Johnston's *Yorktown Campaign*, p. 151. This incident is mentioned by Washington in his *Diary*, see Fitzpatrick, p. 268.

"I propose a cessation of hostilities for twenty-four hours, and that two officers may be appointed by each side, to meet at Mr. Moore's house, to settle terms for the surrender of the posts of York and Gloucester."[1]

Later came a longer letter to request that, so long as they undertook not to fight again against the allies, the British should be sent to Britain and the Germans to Germany.[2] Remembering the trouble which had arisen out of the Capitulation of Saratoga, Washington would not agree to this, and demanded that all officers and men were to be surrendered as prisoners of war.[3] These terms[4] were accepted, and the unnamed chaplain wrote in his diary–"Hallelujah!"[5]

The number surrendered was 7,157 soldiers, 840 seamen, and 80 camp followers–in all 8,077.[6] During the siege the British lost 156 killed and 326 wounded, and the allies–75 killed and 199 wounded, and as two-thirds of these casualties were French, for the Americans it was an exceedingly cheap victory.

When, on October 19, Cornwallis's men marched out to pile arms, they did so to the appropriate tune of "The World Turned Upside Down". Henry Lee (Light-Horse Harry), who was present, says of the march past: "Universal silence was observed amidst the vast concourse, and the utmost decency prevailed, exhibiting in demeanour an awful sense of the vicissitudes of human life, mingled with commiseration for the unhappy."[7]

On October 20, Cornwallis sent to Clinton his final dispatch,[8] and Washington asked de Grasse to move to the relief of Charleston. This de Grasse refused to do, because he had to return to the West Indies.[9] Four days later, Colonel Tilghman–Washington's aide–galloped into Philadelphia to announce the news of the victory. In the meantime Clinton, who at length had set out on October 19, arrived off Cape Charles and Cape Henry–five days too late. There was nothing he could do but return to New York.

Thus ended the crowning campaign of the war, which after prolonged negotiations was brought to its conclusion by the

---

[1] *Clinton-Cornwallis*, vol. II, p. 189.   [2] *Ibid.*, vol. II, p. 192.
[3] *Ibid.*, vol. II, p. 193.
[4] For articles of capitulations, see *ibid.*, vol. II, pp. 199–203.
[5] *Massachusetts Historical Society*, vol. IX (1st Series), p. 107.
[6] *The Revolutionary War*, Francis Vinton Greene, pp. 275–276. Fortescue (vol. III, p. 401) says 6,630, including 2,000 sick and 2,500 Germans; Tarleton says–7,427.
[7] *Memoirs of the War in the Southern Department of the United States*, Henry Lee (1812), vol. II, p. 343.
[8] *Clinton-Cornwallis*, vol. II, p. 205.   [9] Ford, vol. IX, pp. 389, 391.

Treaty of Versailles, signed on November 3, 1783. By its terms the independence of the United States of America was established and the 13 colonies granted unlimited power to expand westward. A new nation, in potentials rivalling all the nations of Europe combined, was added to the western world, and a great empire, possessed of a new imperialism, was born, which in a little over a century was to take its place among the world's great powers, and half a century later still, in wealth and might exceed them all.

More immediately important, the War of American Independence brought to a close the Age of the Reformation. What Luther and Calvin had created, and what the Thirty Years War and the Puritan Rebellion in England had developed was brought to its final expression in the Declaration of Independence, drafted by Thomas Jefferson, the disciple of John Locke. In this epoch-shattering document may be read:

"We hold these truths to be self-evident, that all men are created equal, that they are endowed by their Creator with certain inalienable rights, that among these are life, liberty, and the pursuit of happiness. That to secure these rights governments are instituted among men, deriving their just powers from the consent of the governed. That whenever any form of government becomes destructive to these ends, it is the right of the people to alter or abolish it, and to institute new government, laying its foundations on such principles and organizing its powers in such form, as to them shall seem most likely to effect their safety and happiness."

This was a challenge not only to the government of the King of England, but to absolutism throughout the western world. Thus it came about that when, on December 6, 1777, Louis XVI wrote "approved" on Vergenne's proposals for an American alliance, he signed his death warrant, and when Spain entered the war, she abrogated her colonial empire.

It was not in France but in America that the French Revolution sprang to life. It was from America that the French soldiers brought home with them the seed of liberty, equality and fraternity. Summing up his impressions of the war, the youthful Saint-Simon exclaimed:

"I felt that the American Revolution marked the beginning of a new political era; that this revolution would necessarily set moving an important progress in general civilization, and that it would, before long, occasion great changes in the social order then existing in Europe."[1]

And Mathieu Dumas wrote:

"We listened with avidity to 'Doctor Cooper', who, while applauding our enthusiasm for liberty said to us: 'Take care, take care, young men, that the triumph of the cause on this virgin soil does not influence overmuch your hopes; you will carry away with you the germ of these generous sentiments, but if you attempt to fecund them on your native soil, after so many centuries of corruption, you will have to surmount many more obstacles; it cost us much blood to conquer liberty; but you will shed torrents before you establish it in your old Europe'."[2]

[1] *Œuvres de Saint-Simon* (1865–1878), vol. I, p. 12.
[2] *Souvenirs du Lieutenant-Général Comte Mathieu Dumas* (1839), vol. I, p. 108. In his *Memoirs* the Chevalier de Pontgibaud, aide-de-camp to Lafayette, writes: "When we think of the false notions of government and philanthropy which these youths acquired in America, and propagated in France with so much enthusiasm, and such deplorable success – for this mania of imitation powerfully aided the French Revolution, though it was not the sole cause of it, – we are bound to confess that it would have been better, both for themselves and us, if these young philosophers in red-heeled shoes had stayed at home. . . ." (Quoted by Trevelyan in his *George the Third and Charles Fox*, 1912, vol. II, pp. 401–402.)

The coming of the French Revolution

Although it was the American Revolution that set the French Revolution vibrating, no two countries could have been less alike than the United States and France in 1789. The one was a vast, undeveloped land that offered boundless opportunities to a free and democratically-minded people; the other an ancient, monarchial state shackled by traditions and privileges. In America, taxation–the cause of the rebellion of 1775–was decided by representation, in France it was determined by the king and paid by the Third Estate–that is, by everybody except the nobility and clergy. The grievances caused by this lack of equity were stimulated instead of mitigated by the rising prosperity of France, because every increase in wealth was at once cancelled out by increased debt and additional taxation. It was not the poverty-stricken proletariat, but the well-to-do middle classes–the wealth producers–who were hardest hit, and it was their demands for social justice and a place in the direction of national affairs which resulted in the revolution.

To pay for the part played by France in the War of the American Independence, Louis XVI (1774-1792) had summoned to his counsels the Genevese banker Jacques Necker, and he, to avoid increased taxation, had adopted the expedient of financing the war on loans, until interest on them could no longer be paid without increased taxation. It was debt which precipitated the flood predicted by Louis's grandfather, Louis XV, when he is reputed to have exclaimed: *"Après moi le déluge."*

In 1781 Necker was dismissed, and soon after was replaced by Charles Alexandre de Calonne who, to stay the crisis, persuaded Louis to assemble the *Notables* (deputies of the nobility and clergy). They met in 1787, but when they found that Calonne's financial reforms struck at their privileges, they refused to sanction them. Next, on August 8, 1788, Louis, with much trepidation, was persuaded by the *Parlement* of Paris[1] to summon the States General for the following year. They had not met since 1614.

---

[1] The *Parlements* (Municipal Councils) had been abolished by Louis XV, and were recalled by Louis XVI on his accession.

What the people wanted was a constitutional monarchy, under which their representatives would meet periodically and grant supplies, and it was with these ideas in mind that the States General assembled in Versailles and held their first session on May 5, 1789.

The representatives of the Third Estate refused to sit as a separate order, and invited the deputies of the nobility and clergy to deliberate with them, and because few were willing to do so, on June 10, the representatives declared themselves a National Assembly. Ten days later, in the famous Tennis Court, they took an oath that they would not separate until they had decided upon a new constitution. To appease them, Louis ordered all deputies of the privileged orders to join the Commons, but simultaneously, to forestall trouble, he instructed the Duc de Broglie to form a camp of Swiss and German troops at Versailles, and he dismissed Necker, whom he had called back some time before.

This thinly disguised threat put the Paris mob, the tool of the capitalists, who held that Necker was the only man who could effect a recovery, in a frenzy. The outcome was that, on July 14, the rabble stormed the Bastille and massacred its garrison. When the news was brought to Louis he exclaimed: "This is a great revolt." The Duc de Liancourt replied: "No, Sire, it is a great revolution."

The immediate effects of this outbreak were the recall of Necker and the formation of the National Guard under the Marquis de Lafayette.

In order to reassure the people, on August 26 the National Assembly issued a declaration known as "The Rights of Man", which closely resembled the American "Declaration of Independence". As Louis hesitated to ratify it, on October 5, Lafayette, with a detachment of the National Guard, followed by a howling mob, brought the royal family from Versailles to the capital. Thereon the King's youngest brother, the Comte d'Artois, fled the country with the first wave of *émigrés*, who at once began to plot the overthrow of the Revolution. Their intrigues with foreign powers were one of the main causes of eventual war.

As the country was bankrupt, on the suggestion of the Bishop of Autun (Talleyrand)–lover of Necker's daughter Madame de Staël–the Assembly set out to reform the Church in order to appropriate its vast estates. It declared that the bishops and clergy should henceforth be elected by the representatives of the people. Next, Mirabeau urged that money in the form of *assignats* be issued against the confiscated Church lands. But Necker out-jockeyed him and obtained vast tracts of ecclesiastical property as security for his promises to pay in gold and silver; but as neither existed his notes were refused and a run on the exchanges followed. Necker then fled the country, and under Mirabeau's influence the land-money was issued.

This anti-religious legislation cut Louis to the quick. "I had rather be King of Metz," he exclaimed, "than rule over France on such terms." The result was that, shortly after it had come into force, he began to contemplate flight, not to loyal Normandy or Brittany, as Mirabeau had suggested, but to the *émigrés* at Metz. In this he was ardently supported by the Queen–Marie Antoinette –daughter of Maria Theresa and sister of the Austrian Emperor Leopold II (1790–1792).

On the night of June 20–21, Louis and his family gave their guardians the slip and set out on the road to Montmédy, but they were recognized and arrested at Varennes, and sent back to Paris. When the news reached Leopold, he declared that the King's arrest "compromised directly the honour of all sovereigns and the security of every government". On August 27, in con-junction with Frederick William II of Prussia (1786–1797), he issued the "Declaration of Pilnitz", in which the two monarchs stated that they were ready to join other European rulers should they support Louis. Leopold's aims were far from disinterested, for shortly before the declaration was issued he had concerted a plan with Frederick William to partition France: Austria was to take Alsace and Lorraine and Prussia the duchies of Jülich and Berg and be given a share in the contemplated partition of Poland.

On September 14, the National Assembly, which had decided on a new constitution, dissolved itself and was replaced by the Legislative Assembly provided for by the Constitution. It held its first session on October 1, 1791.

Its leadership passed into the hands of a group of young middle-class enthusiasts, known as the Girondins, because many came from the Gironde. They were violently opposed to the *émigrés*, Leopold and Marie Antoinette. Fearful of, and insulted by, the assembly of small *émigré* armies on the eastern frontiers of France, they argued that war with Austria would unite the nation and compel Louis to show his hand.

In December, this enthusiasm for war led to the organization of the troops along the eastern frontier of France into three armies: the Army of the North under Rochambeau, the Army of the Centre under Lafayette, both of whom had served in America, and the Army of the Rhine, under Marshal Nicolaus Luckner, an old German hussar. These were the first armies of the Revolution.

Increasingly, the Paris press stimulated the warlike passion of the people, and at the Jacobins[1] and in the Assembly Brissot excited enmity toward the court and belief in the necessity of war. War was required not only to consolidate the people and keep them subservient to the will of the Assembly, but also because, as Hérault de Sechelles said, "in time of war measures can be taken that would appear too stern in time of peace" – a forecast of the approaching Terror.

When the Bastille was stormed there was no idea in Europe of a crusade against France. The problem which then held the attention of the courts was Poland and not the Revolution. With the death of Leopold on March 1, 1792, a change rapidly set in; for his son Francis–Francis II and last of the Holy Roman Emperors (1792–1835)–took up the challenge of the Girondins and was eager to vindicate the honour of his aunt. At the same time, Frederick William looked upon France as easy prey and saw in the Revolution an excuse to extend his realm, while Catherine II of Russia (1762–1796) sought to entangle both Vienna and Berlin in the affairs of France, so that she might gain elbow-room in Poland, which was on the verge of its second partition. Finally, the monarchial party in France saw in an Austrian irruption and the scattering of the French levies the sole means of saving Louis. Such was the situation when on April 20, 1792, under a Girondin Ministry, Louis XVI, its captive, proposed to his captors a declaration of war against Austria, in order that they might be overthrown and himself released.

France was quite unprepared for war: her treasury was empty, her army chaotic and her people hysterical. On July 11 a general call to arms was made and a rabble of volunteers enrolled. A fortnight later, Prussia declared war on her, and the Duke of Brunswick, who had been appointed to the command of the

---

[1] When the Assembly moved to Paris, certain representatives of the Third Estate rented a large room in the monastery of the Jacobins, hence the name of the most famous of the revolutionary clubs.

Prussian army, issued an ill-advised manifesto, concocted by the *émigrés*, which threw Paris into a frenzy. On August 10, the Tuileries was stormed, and a decree issued that abolished the Constitution of 1791 deprived Louis of all his powers and established universal suffrage. The Legislative Assembly was succeeded by the Convention.

In the midst of this chaos, the gravest peril came from the army, 82,000 strong, excluding frontier garrisons. On the left, the Army of the North, now under Lafayette, covered the frontier from Dunkirk to Malmédy, and was split into two groups, one (24,000) in camps on the Flemish border, and the other (19,000), known as the Army of the Ardennes, near Sedan. On its right stretched the Army of the Centre—also called the Army of Metz—(17,000) from Montmédy to the Vosges, under Marshal Luckner. And on his right lay the Army of the Rhine (22,000) from the Vosges to Basle, under General Biron (formerly the Duc de Lauzun). In the rear, around Soissons, there was also a rabble of unorganized and insubordinate volunteers, known as the Reserve Army.

When, on August 11, Lafayette, then at Sedan, learnt of the decree of the day before, he at once ordered General Arthur Dillon, at Pont-sur-Sambre, and General Dumouriez, at the Camp of Maulde, to march on Paris. Though the former—a Royalist—agreed, the latter—a friend of the Girondins—refused to do so. The Assembly learnt of the mutiny and sent commissaries to Sedan, who were seized by Lafayette and imprisoned. Others were then sent, and on August 18 they placed Dumouriez in command of the Army of the North. The next day, when he found that his army had lost confidence in him, Lafayette and many of his officers crossed the Luxemburg border and surrendered to the Austrians. At the same time, Luckner at Metz—a friend of Lafayette—refused to accept the decree and was replaced by General François Christophe Kellermann and sent to Châlons to command second line troops. Nearly all Luckner's principal officers were dismissed, and in the Army of the Rhine, Biron alone among its generals full-heartedly accepted the decree. Such was the state of the army when Dumouriez succeeded Lafayette.

CHAPTER II

The Cannonade of Valmy, 1792

The Cannonade of Valmy was more than a military event; it drew a sharp line between the form war had taken since 1648 and the form it was to assume after 1792. In the earlier period, as previously related, war became more and more limited both politically and militarily. With a few notable exceptions, campaigns were methodical, leisurely, and punctuated by an accepted etiquette. Writing in 1677, the Earl of Orrery observes that "we make war more like Foxes than Lyons, and you have twenty sieges for one Battel".[1] Some 20 years later we find Daniel Defoe writing: "Now it is frequent to have armies of fifty thousand men of a side stand at bay within view of one another, and spend a whole campaign in dodging, or, as it is genteely called, observing one another, and then march off into winter quarters."[2] A hundred years later it is much the same. Lazare Carnot notes that, "What was taught in the military schools was no longer the art of defending strong places, but that of surrendering them honourably, after certain conventional formalities."[3]

At the siege of Pizzighetone, in 1733, we are offered a perfect example of idyllic war. A truce had been arranged and, we read:

"A bridge thrown over the breach afforded a communication between the besiegers and the besieged: tables were spread in every quarter, and the officers entertained one another by turns: within and without, under tents and arbours, there was nothing but balls, entertainments and concerts. All the people of the environs flocked there on foot, on horse back, and in carriages: provisions arrived from every quarter, abundance was seen in a moment, and there was no want of stage doctors and tumblers. It was a charming fair, a delightful rendezvous."[4]

A hundred years after Carnot's observation, and when the new form of war approached its zenith, Marshal Foch castigated these

---

[1] *A Treatise of the Art of War, etc.* (1677), p. 15.
[2] "An Enquiry upon Projects" in *The Earlier Life aud Chief Earlier Works of Daniel Defoe*, Henry Morley (1889), p. 135.
[3] *De la defense des places fortes* (1812), p. xiii.
[4] *Memoirs of Goldoni*, trans. John Black (1814), vol. 1, p. 207.

"antiquated methods . . . in which there is no decisive solution, nothing but a limited end . . .", and poured scorn on Maurice de Saxe (1696–1750) for having said: "I am not in favour of giving battle, especially at the outset of a war. I am even convinced that a clever general can wage war his whole life without being compelled to do so."[1]

Nevertheless, the reasons for these "antiquated methods" were ignored by Foch. They were not only abhorrence of the unlimited barbarities of the Thirty Years War and the realization that wars between gentlemen are preferable to wars between cads, but also the growing cost of regular, standing armies coupled with the deficiencies of their commissariat and the slowness of supply by requisitioning. These restrictions led to the avoidance of battles, which at the close musket range of this period were extremely costly in life, and also to the frequency of sieges, in order to establish supply depôts at intervals along the lines of march. Basically, the pace-maker was cost–that is, money–and this was realized by Guibert as early as 1770. He considered that wars of punctilious courtesies, of bloodless manœuvres and honourable surrenders were only superficially cheap because they led to no grand political solutions. In their place he suggested a very different kind of conflict.

"But let us suppose," he writes, "that a vigorous people were to arise in Europe: a people of genius, of resources and of political understanding: a people who united with these stirling virtues and with a national militia a fixed plan of aggrandizement, and never lost sight of it: a people who knows how to make war cheaply and sustain itself on its victories. Such a people would not be compelled to limit its fighting by financial calculations. One would see this people subjugate its neighbours, and overthrow our feeble Constitutions, like the north wind bends the frail reeds."[2]

Valmy was the herald of the type of war Guibert had in mind, and one year after its cannonade had thundered and two years after Guibert was dead, in order to assure the "permanent requisition of all Frenchmen for the defence of the country", on

---

[1] *The Principles of War*, trans. Hilaire Belloc (1918), pp. 27–28. Well may it be asked: if wars are to be, are not limited ends preferable to unlimited ones? Is not the behaviour at Pizzighetone wiser and more rational than the behaviour at the Battle of the Somme in 1916, or at the bombing of Hiroshima in 1945?

[2] In "Discours Préliminaire" of his *Essai Général de Tactique*, 1770. (See *Oeuvres Militaires de Guibert*, 1803, vol. I, pp. 15–16.) A point to note here is the introduction of the idea of amorality into war; force becomes the dominant factor.

August 23, 1793, the National Convention passed a law whereby unlimited warfare became the order of the day.

"The young men shall fight", we read; "the married men shall forge weapons and transport supplies; the women will make tents and clothes and will serve in the hospitals; the children will make up old linen into lint; the old men will have themselves carried in to the public squares and rouse the courage of the fighting men, to preach hatred against kings and the unity of the Republic.

"The public buildings shall be turned into barracks, the public squares into munition factories. . . . All fire-arms of suitable calibre shall be turned over to the troops: the interior shall be policed with shot guns and cold steel. All saddle horses shall be seized for the cavalry; all draft horses not employed in cultivation will draw the artillery and supply wagons."[1]

Such was the birth-cry of total war.

It was these two forms of war—the limited and unlimited—which were brought into clinch during the French Revolution, and both are well exemplified by the leaders in the initial clash—Charles William Ferdinand Duke of Brunswick on the one hand, and Charles François Dumouriez on the other.

Brunswick was born in 1735 and Dumouriez in 1739; they were therefore approximately of the same age, which was their sole common link. The one was a *grand seigneur* and a nephew of Frederick the Great; the other an astute political and military adventurer, son of a French commissary. In 1792, Brunswick was held to be the greatest soldier in Europe; Dumouriez believed himself to be such. He had an unbounded confidence in himself, saw in the Revolution a career exactly suited to his talents, and instinctively felt that to make the most of its fanatical spirit, audacity was the highest prudence; of principles he had none, other than opportunism. On one occasion he proposed a plan to save the monarchy. It was simple and audacious. In order to defeat the Jacobins, he said, all that was necessary was to become one. "Think as they do, adopt their spirit and language, and then turn upon them."[2] In the field he was completely fearless, made light of difficulties, showed an indefatigable activity and possessed that most precious gift—ability to electrify his men. He was

[1] Quoted from *Mémoires sur Lazare Carnot*, Lazare Hippolyte Carnot (1907), vol. I, p. 379.
[2] *Valmy*, Arthur Chuquet (n.d.), p. 12.

a brilliant and talented military gambler, imaginative, quick-witted, foreseeing and as optimistic as Candide.

Brunswick was a learned, highly cultivated pedant, cautious, painstaking, and apt to examine every problem in such minute detail that the problem itself vanished from sight. His reputation was founded largely on his 1787 campaign in Holland. It was so completely bloodless that in the eyes of his contemporaries it appeared to be an example of perfect generalship. And so it actually was, for within the narrow limits of methodical warfare, Brunswick, like an expert chess player, could foresee every move, as long as his opponent observed every rule. He invariably magnified his own difficulties and seldom considered those of his adversary, and usually was as loth to express an opinion of his own, as under pressure he was yielding to the opinions of others. Unfortunately for him, Frederick William–an impulsive and shallow-minded man–tried to play the part of Frederick the Great, and Brunswick, who considered that the first duty of a Prussian field-marshal was to obey his prince, against his better judgment complied with his wishes. Further, Brunswick intensely disliked the Austrians; looked upon France as Prussia's true ally, and held the *émigrés* in abhorrence. So highly was he thought of by both the Girondins and Jacobins that, early in 1792, the Revolutionary Government offered him the supreme command of the French army,[1] which, had he accepted it, would have made Dumouriez his collaborator instead of his opponent.

The armies commanded by these two men were also very different. The Prussian and Austrian were the obedient tools of their respective monarchs. The French, though still largely composed of the soldiers of the old Royal Army, was a national army animated by a national spirit. Under leaders who knew how to exploit its spirit, it could display wonderful *élan*, and under those who could not, it was subject to panics and mutinies. Though lamentably deficient of officers, more especially in the infantry and cavalry, for thousands had become *émigrés*, thanks to its magnificent corps of long service non-commissioned officers, officers could readily be promoted. At the time of Valmy, we find, either in command or in the ranks, many of the famous names of the Empire, names such as Jourdan, Lecourbe, Oudinot, Victor, Macdonald, Davout, Gouvion-Saint Cyr, Mortier, Soult,

---

[1] See *Charles William Ferdinand, Duke of Brunswick*, Lord Edmond Fitzmaurice (1901), pp. 45-49.

Leclerc, Lannes, Masséna, Berthier, Bessières, Suchet, Laharpe, Friant, Lefebvre and Kellermann (the elder).

The French artillery was the best in Europe, for though the father of modern gunnery was an Englishman, Benjamin Robins, who in his *New Principles of Gunnery* (1742) advocated the breech-loading rifled gun and placed gunnery on a scientific footing, the greatest progress in artillery was made in France under the direction of Gribeauval. In 1776, when appointed Inspector-General of Artillery, he reorganized the French artillery from top to bottom. He restricted field artillery to 4-pounder regimental guns, and for the reserve (divisional artillery) to 8- and 12-pounder guns and 6-in. howitzers. For garrison and siege work he adopted 16- and 12-pounder guns, 8-in. howitzers and 10-in. mortars. He introduced limber-boxes and had gun-carriages constructed on a uniform model, their parts, as far as possible, were interchangeable.

These improvements[1] influenced artillery as radically as the introduction of the bayonet had influenced infantry a century earlier, and led to the increasing dominance of the cannon over the musket. Two effects are to be noted. The first was that the increasing use of artillery involved an increase in the number of horses and wagons, and therefore to the lengthening of columns on the line of march, and to the necessity of protecting them by light troops—*chasseurs à pied* and *à cheval*. The second was the rise in the cost of armies and the ever-increasing demands put upon industry for standardized arms and equipment.

Though in the Prussian army the infantry and cavalry were excellent, the artillery was indifferent and the commissariat antiquated. Many of the generals were old, and not a few of the younger officers favoured the Revolution. But the weakest link was its command, for between Frederick William and Brunswick there was no unity of thought. The latter detested the *émigrés*; the former was subservient to them. They exaggerated the monarchial sentiments of the French people and boasted of their good understanding with the French officers. " 'I', said Bouillé, 'can answer for the taking of fortresses, for I have the keys of all of them in my

---

[1] Two notable inventions of this period—both English—were Mercier's "operative gun shell", a 5.5-in. mortar shell fired from a 24-pounder gun, first used at the siege of Gibraltar (1779–1783), and Henry Shrapnel's "spherical case" ("shrapnel shell"), invented in 1784, but not adopted by the British army until 1803. The one was destined to render obsolete the wooden battleship, and the other to revolutionize artillery tactics.

pocket'."[1] These claims led Frederick William to believe that all he had do was to march straight on Paris, and there be received with plaudits by its loyal citizens.

Brunswick thought not, for he not only distrusted the *émigrés* but was opposed to the war. His idea was to limit the first campaign to the capture of the fortresses of Longwy, Montmédy, and Sedan; next, to establish depôts at them, outmanœuvre any French army which might come to their relief, and lastly go into winter quarters and prepare for next year's campaign. To wage an autumn campaign in France, with uncaptured fortresses in his rear and in a country which might prove hostile, terrified him. Further, he knew that his commissariat prohibited a rapid advance, and in this he was right, for as Massenbach, one of his staff officers, later said: "The question of supply hung like a dead weight on our legs."[2]

The plan finally decided upon was to invade Lorraine with three armies: (1) Brunswick with 42,000 Prussians, 5,500 Hessians, and 4,500 *émigrés* was to move from Coblenz into Lorraine between Kellermann's army at Metz and Dumouriez's at Sedan; (2) 15,000 Austrians, under Clerfayt, based on Belgium, were to advance southward on the Prussian right flank; and (3), an equal number, under Prince Hohenlohe-Kirchberg, based on the Palatinate, was to move on the Prussian left flank. When the three armies joined in Lorraine, the Meuse was to be crossed and the road to Paris gained.

The Prussians took 20 days to march from Coblenz to the French frontier and it was not until August 23 that they arrived before the border fortress of Longwy, and, after a short bombardment, forced its capitulation.

Dumouriez was then urging Servan, the French Minister of War, to invade the Netherlands. His plan was that while Dillon at Sedan and Kellermann at Metz held back the Prussians, from Valenciennes he would deal with the Austrians under Clerfayt. This was an *idée fixe* with Dumouriez, and he likened himself to Agathocles and Scipio. "It is thus", he wrote in a letter to the Assembly, "that the Roman people carried their war into Africa, when Hannibal was at the gates of Rome."[3]

---

[1] Quoted from *History of the French Revolution*, Heinrich von Sybel (1867), vol. II, p. 112. The Marquis de Bouillé was the French general Louis XVI hoped to join in his flight to Varennes.

[2] Quoted by Fitzmaurice in his *Duke of Brunswick*, p. 67.

[3] Quoted in *Valmy*, p. 25.

Strategically, he may have been right, for he had measured Brunswick's worth pretty accurately. But politically he was wrong, because, had he marched north, the citizens of Paris would have imagined the eastern roads to the capital unbarred, and would at once have cried "treason!" Fully aware of this, on August 22, Servan urged Dumouriez to cooperate with Kellermann, then falling back before Hohenlohe. And when, on August 24, Paris was thrown into consternation by the news that Longwy was invested, he ordered Dumouriez to proceed to Sedan.

Dumouriez arrived at Sedan on August 28 to find, as he writes, "an army without generals or senior officers, and divided into factions. More than half the soldiers regretted a chief [Lafayette] they had loved, and looked upon his successor as his personal enemy and the author of his ruin."[1]

Next day, when he paraded his men, instead of the customary cheers, he was met by silence and scowls. At length a grenadier cried out: *"C'est ce b . . . là qui a fait déclarer la guerre!"* "Do you think", replied Dumouriez, "that liberty can be won without fighting?" When another soldier shouted *"A bas le général!"* Dumouriez drew his sword and challenged him to fight, and when the culprit slunk back, suddenly Dumouriez realized that his unconventional behaviour had won over his men to him.[2]

Next, when he learnt that Verdun was threatened, he sent Lieutenant-Colonel Galbaud and two battalions to reinforce its garrison. They failed to reach the fortress and retired on St. Ménehould. That night he wrote as follows to Servan: "The army is in the most deplorable state. If we retire, I fear it will disband itself, and if we advance, as it appears to wish to do, we shall certainly be beaten . . . it has neither clothing, nor shoes, nor hats . . . and is short of many muskets."[3]

Still obsessed by his Netherlands plan, on August 30 he summoned a council of war which, in spite of what he writes in his *Mémoires*,[4] approved of it. But in Paris, Servan, who thought that Dumouriez had dropped it, on September 1 wrote to urge him to fall back on the Argonne and at the same time informed him that Kellermann was under orders to march to his support. On the following day, while in Paris the tocsin rang in the

[1] *La Vie et les Mémoires du Général Dumouriez* (1822), vol. II, p. 385.
[2] *Ibid.*, vol. II, p. 383, and *Valmy*, pp. 36–37.
[3] Quoted from *L'Europe et la Révolution Française*, Albert Sorel (1891), vol. III, p. 29.
[4] See vol. II, pp. 387–391.

September Massacres, and Danton thundered, "*il nous faut de l'audace, et encore de l'audace, et toujours de l'audace, et la France est sauvée*", Servan wrote to Dumouriez again: "In the name of the fatherland . . . lead your army to between the Meuse and the Marne. Move to St. Ménehould or its vicinity, or even on Châlons. . . ."[1]

In the meantime, on August 31 – that is, before either of these letters had been written – Dumouriez, at Bazeilles, heard gunfire from the direction of Verdun[2] and at the same time learnt that Clerfayt with 15,000 to 18,000 men was about to cross the Meuse at Stenay, and at length saw that his invasion plan was impossible, for his right flank was threatened and Sedan was therefore no longer tenable. "Never", he wrote to Servan, "has the danger to France been so great in any war. . . . To avoid greater evils I shall perhaps be compelled to leave Montmédy and Verdun to their garrisons; abandon the whole length of the Meuse and by the shortest road retire . . . to the river Aire and defend the gap of Autry."[3]

This meant falling back on the Forest of the Argonne, which skirts the right bank of the upper Aisne. It consists of low hills, thickly wooded, and cut up by streams and marshes. In 1792, it was a more difficult country for troops to operate in than it is to-day, for the roads were then unkept and in rainy weather the soft clay soil over which they ran was rapidly churned into mud. For an army followed by an artillery and a supply train, the forest could be crossed only by five roads that ran through the following five defiles: (1) Les Islettes, the Verdun-Clermont-St. Ménehould-Châlons-Paris road; (2) La Chalade, the Verdun-Rheims Road; (3) Grandpré, the Varennes-Vouziers Road; (4) Croix-aux-Bois, the Stenay-Vouziers Road; and (5) Chesne-Populeux, the Sedan-Rethel Road.

For Dumouriez who, at Sedan, was farther away from the two main defiles of Grandpré and Les Islettes than were Clerfayt at Stenay and Brunswick at Verdun, haste was imperative. He

---

[1] Quoted in *Valmy*, p. 36.

[2] Writing on August 31, Goethe mentions the use of rockets in the bombardment of Verdun. He writes: "These tailed fire-meteors, we had only to observe quite quietly gliding through the air, and shortly afterwards a part of the town was seen in flames." (*Campaign in France in the Year 1792*, trans. Robert Farie (1859), p. 31.)

[3] Sorel, vol. III, p. 30. It would appear that the idea of retiring to the Argonne was first suggested by General Money at the council of war on August 30. Money was an English soldier who had fought in the Seven Years War and had served under General Burgoyne in America. (See *The History of the Campaign of 1792, etc.*, J. Money, 1794, pp. 38–41.) He has already been mentioned in the Saratoga campaign, chap. xxix.

realized that he had not sufficient troops to hold all five defiles in strength and ordered Duval with 6,000 men[1] at the camp of

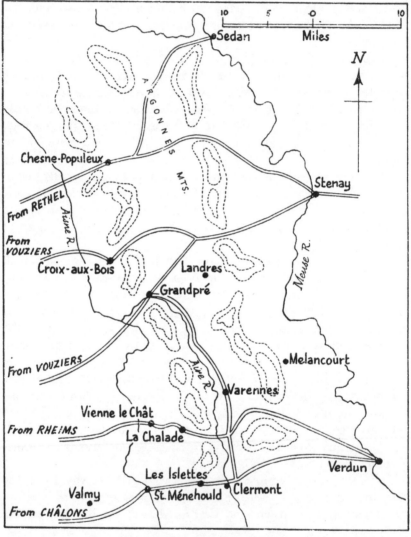

21. THE ARGONNE, 1792

Pont-sur-Sambre and Beurnonville with 10,000 at the camp of Maulde, to march with all speed to Rethel, the former to arrive there on September 7 and the latter on September 13.

[1] Dumouriez's *Mémoires*, vol. II, p. 394. Chuquet (*Valmy*, p. 98) says 3,050.

Dumouriez left Chesne-Populeux and Croix-aux-Bois for the time being unguarded, and on September 1 he sent Dillon forward with the advanced guard (6,000) to take over Les Islettes and La Chalade, and with the main body (13,000) he followed the shortest road, marched across Clerfayt's front, and arrived at Grandpré on September 4. Dillon arrived at Les Islettes on the following day.

From Grandpré, on September 5, Dumouriez sent the following heroic dispatch to Servan: "Verdun is taken, I await the Prussians. The Camps of Grandpré and les Islettes are Thermopylaes, but I shall be more fortunate than Leonidas."[1]

But what of Brunswick? On September 2 Verdun capitulated, but instead of pushing on he remained in camp there until September 11. True, the weather was appalling, and heavy rain had fallen ever since the allies had crossed the frontier. On August 28, Goethe jotted down in his journal "frightful weather"; on September 6, "everything was sunk into bottomless mud", and on September 12, "it rained incessantly".[2] Also hundreds of men were dying of dysentery in the Prussian camp.[3] Though, as Goethe points out on September 4: "Mention was often made of the Islettes, the important pass between Verdun and St. Ménehould. Nobody could understand why it was not taken possession of, and why it had not been occupied before."[4] The reason was that Brunswick and Frederick William were unable to agree upon what next to do.

With Verdun taken, Brunswick's plan was to occupy Sedan, to go into winter quarters around Montmédy, Mézières and Givet, and to establish a solid base for the next year's campaign. But the King would not listen to this, and not only was he supported by the émigrés, but also by several of Brunswick's officers. What the King and his supporters saw, was that at bottom the war was a political rather than a strategical operation, and that they were confronted by a revolutionary and not a normal army. Therefore the idea of establishing magazines at Verdun and Longwy and of going into winter quarters, was quite unsuitable. Instead, they urged, what was needed was to burst into Champagne like a torrent and submerge the French in one

[1] Dumouriez's *Mémoires*, vol. III, p. 2.
[2] *Campaign in France*, pp. 17, 49 and 53.
[3] An eyewitness states that the whole front of the camp was covered with excrement (*Valmy*, p. 7⁵).
[4] *Campaign in France*, p. 47.

great battle, the winning of which was assured by the superior discipline of the Prussians. Only thus could a decisive political victory be won in time to save Louis XVI and Marie Antoinette.

Though so unconventional a procedure shocked Brunswick, because of the state of his army, of the roads, and of his commissariat, he knew that a rapid advance could not be made. Nevertheless, obediently he abandoned his own plan for the King's; yet he did not order an immediate advance, but wasted his time in detailed preparations. At length, on September 7, he and the King rode forward to Clermont and reconnoitred Les Islettes. Brunswick saw many enemy troops among the woods, and when he learnt from a peasant that the French were entrenched, he feared that a frontal attack would prove too costly and suggested a turning movement. Ultimately it was agreed to force one of the five defiles, and to do so the following distribution was decided on. Les Islettes to be masked by Hohenlohe's Austrians and the Hessians, while the Prussian army marched on Grandpré. The cavalry and corps of *émigrés* were to move on Chesne-Populeux, and Clerfayt, supported by Kalkreuth, was to secure the defile of Croix-aux-Bois.

At length, on September 10, Brunswick issued his orders to advance, and on the following morning, in pouring rain, the Prussians marched out of their sodden camp and took the road to Melancourt. There they halted for the night, and on September 12 marched on to Landres; on the way they were much perturbed to find the countryside deserted, for this made subsistence still more difficult. To fight the French army was one thing, but to fight it in a deserted country was another, and this depressed the allies, as also did the indescribable condition of the camp at Landres, which became known as the *Drecklager* ("filth camp"). On the left, Hohenlohe's Austrians and the Hessians masked the eastern side of Les Islettes, and on the right, Clerfayt's army from Stenay faced the defile of Croix-aux-Bois.

Croix-aux-Bois was held by two battalions, a squadron and four guns under Colonel Colomb, a veteran of the American war. On September 11 he informed Dumouriez that his position was impregnable, and in consequence the latter, who considered that the main enemy effort would be made against Grandpré, ordered him to leave 100 men under a captain to hold the defile, and bring the remainder to Grandpré.[1]

---

[1] Dumouriez's *Mémoires*, vol. III, pp. 19–20.

Unfortunately for Dumouriez, Clerfayt learnt of the withdrawal from a peasant and on September 12 sent out a detachment of chasseurs and hussars which rushed the defile and captured it, and because its loss threatened the southern flank of Chesne-Populeux, its commander, Colonel Dubouquet, withdrew its garrison. At 5 p.m., the arrival of fugitives at Grandpré was the first intimation Dumouriez received of the disaster, and as he realized how serious was the loss of Croix-aux-Bois, he ordered General Chazot with eight battalions, five squadrons and four guns to march from Grandpré by way of Vouziers and retake the defile on September 13. The road was in so bad a condition that Chazot only reached Vouziers at nightfall. He set out again the next morning and retook the defile, but shortly after was driven out of it by an Austrian counter-attack, and returned to Vouziers. The astonishing thing about this action was that he was not pursued. As Jomini points out,[1] had Clerfayt pushed on, and had Brunswick simultaneously attacked Grandpré, Dumouriez's army would in all probability have been destroyed.

The situation of the French was at its worst; Dumouriez was at his best. He reckoned on the slowness of the Prussians, as well as on the execrable weather to add to their delay,[2] and at once decided, while holding fast to Les Islettes and La Chalade, to pull out of Grandpré, fall back on St. Ménehould, and place his army in a position facing the rear of his enemy once he had advanced through the abandoned defiles. It was a stroke of genius, and in order to trap his sluggish opponent, aides and messengers were sent galloping in all directions. First a detachment was sent out to mask Croix-aux-Bois, then Chazot was ordered to move from Vouziers at midnight and rejoin the main body on the plain of Montcheutin. Beurnonville and his 10,000 men at Rethel were ordered up to St. Ménehould, and an aide was sent to Kellermann, then near Bar-le-Duc, to hasten his march northward. Instructions were sent to Dillon at Les Islettes to resist the Austrians to the death, and urgent requests were made to General Sparre at Châlons to send forward reinforcements, and to General d'Harville to collect all remaining troops at Rheims, Epernay, and Soissons.[3]

Brunswick, astonished to find the Argonne still held, decided to

[1] *Histoire Critique et Militaire des Guerres de la Révolution*, Jomini (1820), vol. II, pp. 119–120. See also Dumouriez's *Mémoires*, vol. III, p. 25.
[2] Dumouriez's *Mémoires*, vol. III, p. 27.
[3] *Ibid.*, vol. III, pp. 24–25.

enter into negotiations with Dumouriez, and to effect this he sent out Colonel Massenbach to arrange an interview. From the French outposts Massenbach was taken to General Duval's headquarters, but Dumouriez refused to see him. While with Duval, Massenbach had noticed great activity in his camp, and on his return he informed Brunswick that, in his opinion, the French were preparing to retire. Brunswick was overjoyed, for it meant that his manœuvre had succeeded, and according to his code of war, a successful manœuvre was equivalent to a victory. Immediately after, Massenbach met the King, and when the latter learnt that the French were on the point of retiring, he flew into a violent rage, for he wanted a victory and not a manœuvre. He galloped away, cursing, toward Grandpré.

Massenbach was right, Dumouriez did intend to withdraw, but not to the river Marne as Massenbach suspected, but to St. Ménehould, and this Dumouriez set out to do at 3 a.m. on September 15. At 8 a.m. Autry on the Aisne was reached, from where the main body marched on to Dommartin-sous-Hans on the Bionne.

In accordance with his instructions, Chazot should have set out from Vouziers at midnight September 14, in order to reach the plain of Montcheutin ahead of the main body and under cover of its rear guard. But his men were so exhausted by their exertions of the morning and afternoon, that he did not set out until dawn September 15, and when some hours later his corps debouched into the plain of Montcheutin it was attacked by a body of 1,500 Prussian hussars. Though at first his men beat off their enemy, suddenly some of them were seized by panic and scattered in all directions, shouting: "*Sauve qui peut! Nous sommes trahis! Nous sommes coupés.*" Next Chazot's whole corps – 10,000 strong – disbanded itself, and, as Dumouriez informs us, more than 2,000 of them fled as far as Rethel, Rheims, Châlons, and Vitry, where they proclaimed that the army had been annihilated and that Dumouriez and all his generals had gone over to the enemy.[1] In their headlong flight they met reinforcements on their way up from Châlons, which at once turned tail and fled back to that town.

When the panic occurred, Dumouriez was tracing out his camp at Dommartin-sous-Hans, when again, as in the Croix-aux-Bois mishap, the first news of the disaster was brought to

[1] *Ibid.*, vol. III, pp. 31–32.

him by fugitives yelling: "All is lost! The Army is in rout! The enemy is at our heels!"[1] He galloped forward and met General Miranda,[2] who was rallying the infantry. A few hours later, on returning to Dommartin and when about to sit down to dinner, for no accountable reason a second panic suddenly exploded, this time in his own camp, and which, after causing inextricable confusion, was only stayed by his energetic action.[3] Much of the following day—September 16—was spent in disentangling the disorder.

To the west of St. Ménehould and to the north of the Châlons Road rises a plateau which extends from the latter to the village of Neuville-au-Pont on the Aisne. On this plateau Dumouriez encamped his troops, their right about Maffrecourt, their centre west of Chaude Fontaine, and their left on the Châlons Road, in part protected by a marsh called L'Etang-le-Roi. Westward of the camp, at Braux-St. Cohière, he posted an advanced guard under General Stengel, with outposts on the Tourbe stream, which runs north of, and parallel to, the Bionne. In front of his camp he drew up his batteries to sweep the low ground, and along the right bank of the Aisne he threw out a line of strong posts to link his right with Dillon's left at La Chalade. Lastly, he selected St. Ménehould as his headquarters, because it lay half way between his camp and Dillon's.[4]

That he was able to do this was entirely due to the slowness of his enemy, for had the Prussians attacked him between September 16 and 18—that is, immediately after the panic and before he was reinforced—his army would most certainly have been routed. Even as things were, his situation was critical, for Beurnonville, who had arrived at Rethel on September 13, on September 16 approached the village of Auve and heard of the panic. Afraid of finding himself in the midst of the enemy, at once he withdrew to Châlons. There he received an urgent call from Dumouriez, and he set out again on September 18 to arrive at St. Ménehould the following day.

A somewhat similar incident delayed the arrival of Kellermann. On September 12 his army had reached Bar-le-Duc, but when, on the following day, he received Dumouriez's dispatch informing him of the loss of Croix-aux-Bois, he did not wish to get

---

[1] *Valmy*, p. 139.
[2] Spanish-American adventurer in the French service. (See footnote Dumouriez's *Mémoires*, vol. III, pp. 10–11.)
[3] *Ibid.*, vol. III, p. 30.   [4] *Ibid.*, vol. III, pp. 35–36.

involved in a defeat and instead of hurrying on to support Dumouriez, he switched his march westward to Vitry-le-François. Not until September 15, when he received a peremptory order from Marshal Luckner[1] to proceed by forced marches to St. Méne-hould, did he again set out. On September 18 he reached Dampierre-sur-Auve, and the following day crossed the river Auve and went into camp on the Châlons Road at Dommartin-la-Planchette. He brought with him 17 battalions and 30 squadrons; in all, 16,000 men.

Brunswick had missed two opportunities to destroy his enemy: the first at Croix-aux-Bois, and the second on September 15 when he sent forward only 1,500 hussars instead of the whole of his advanced guard. Now he missed a third, for though he occupied Grandpré on September 16, instead of advancing his main body, still in the camp at Landres, he kept it there until September 18. The reason for this was that he could not move it until his supply train had brought bread from Verdun. "The indifferent arrangement that had been made for subsistence," says Nassau-Siegen, "compelled us to halt and lose time at Grandpré as at Verdun."[2]

At length, on September 18, the bread had come up and Brunswick began to contemplate a plan of action. Again it was by means of an envelopment to turn the enemy out of his position and force him to withdraw. Late that day he and Massenbach rode forward to reconnoitre, and afterward, Brunswick decided to march the Prussians by way of Grandpré against the western side of the La Chalade and Les Islettes position, while the Austrians pressed its eastern side. This, he considered, would force Dumouriez to abandon his camp. "Our left wing," he said to Massenbach, "will advance, we must hunt the enemy out of the Argonne. We will take les Islettes and without much bloodshed. As you know we must economize our men, for we are not over numerous."[3]

The following morning the Prussian army set out, but at noon, as the King was about to eat, a messenger arrived with the news that the French were evacuating St. Ménehould. Assuming that Dumouriez was about to retire, Frederick William in a rage turned to Massenbach, and though Brunswick was present, he did not even consult him, but ordered the army to move directly toward

---

[1] Kellermann was an independent commander, and not under Dumouriez.
[2] Quoted from *Valmy*, pp. 169–170.
[3] *Ibid.*, p. 173. See also Sybel, vol. II, p. 134.

the Châlons Road, and by cutting the French line of retreat bring the enemy to battle. Though this completely upset Brunswick's grand manœuvre, he raised no objection. Soon after, another message was received to cancel the previous one; nevertheless, the King adhered to his order, and therefore must bear full responsibility for the ultimate fiasco.

"Thus," writes Chuquet, " . . . the Prussians with heads down, moved straight forward toward the French, without carrying out a single reconnaissance, without sending forward a single officer to examine the ground and without a plan of battle."[1]

That night the Prussians bivouacked along the road leading from Suippes to Valmy, with their main body about Somme-Tourbe on the Tourbe, south of which ran the Bionne stream.

South of the Bionne lay the battlefield of Valmy, bordered on its eastern flank by the river Aisne and on its southern by the river Auve. North of the latter ran the St. Ménehould-Châlons highway, passing through Dumouriez's left flank at L'Etang-le-Roi and also through Dommartin-la-Planchette, where Kellermann was now encamped. About a mile and a half west of Dommartin was the posting-house of Orbeval, from where westward the highway rose to a tavern named La Lune, at which a branch road from Somme-Bionne joined it. East of the branch road rose a ridge, the northern part of which was called Mont Yron (or Hyron) and the southern the *butte* or *tertre* (mound or hillock) of Valmy. On the mound stood a windmill—where the monument now stands—and a little to the north of it lay the village of Valmy. From La Lune, Orbeval, Dommartin, and the mound of Valmy could clearly be seen, and east of them in the distance the high ground of the Argonne.

No sooner had Kellermann encamped at Dommartin-la-Planchette than he rode over to St. Ménehould and told Dumouriez that he considered his position insecure because the swampy Auve ran immediately in the rear of it, and that therefore on the following morning he intended to recross the Auve and occupy the villages of Dampièrre and Voilement. Dumouriez suggested that it would be better to occupy La Lune and the high ground about Valmy; but Kellermann disagreed and the withdrawal was decided upon. In order to cover his camp during the night, Kellermann instructed his advanced guard, under General Deprez-Crassier, to move forward toward the Bionne,

[1] *Valmy*, p. 180.

and on his way to contact Dumouriez's advanced guard, under
Stengel, whose outposts had retired before Prussian cavalry
from the Tourbe to Mt. Yron and Valmy.

Between six and seven o'clock on the morning of September 20,
when Kellermann was about to recross the Auve, the Prussian

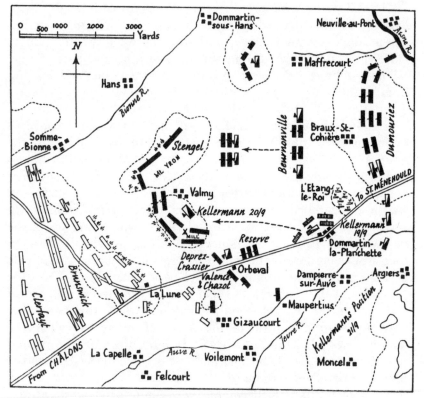

22. BATTLE OF VALMY, 1792

advanced guard, under Prince Hohenlohe, set out from Somme-
Bionne to cut the Châlons Road. A cold drizzling rain[1] fell
and a dense fog obscured the countryside. The van had not
marched far before gunfire was heard from the direction of
Mt. Yron–it was the cannon of Deprez-Crassier. No notice was
taken of it, and the advanced guard slowly continued to move
southward. Next, a hail of shot fell short of its left flank. It came
from a French battery at La Lune, for early that morning, in

[1] *Campaign in France*, p. 72.

order to support Deprez-Crassier, Kellermann had sent forward
to the tavern his reserve corps under General Valence.

He had done this because at 7 a.m. news had been received of
the Prussian advance, and as he realized that he would not have
sufficient time to cross the Auve before the Prussians fell upon him,
he counter-ordered the withdrawal and substituted for it Dumouriez's suggestion of the evening before. He hastily fell in his men,
and under cover of the fog and Deprez-Crassier's and Valence's
guns, ordered his second line and 18 guns, under Muratel, to
advance and occupy the mound of Valmy and take over its
defence from Stengel. Next, not being able, because of the fog,
to judge the extent of the high ground, which was restricted, he
ordered his first line, with another 18 guns, to follow the second,
and then, for some reason unknown, instead of keeping his
cavalry on the low ground about Orbeval, he ordered it to follow
the first line. The result was that in the fog his infantry, cavalry,
and artillery were jammed together in a confused mass around
the windmill. Fortunately for Kellermann the fog obscured the
confusion from the Prussians, and equally fortunate, at that
time Valence's guns at La Lune put to flight three Prussian
squadrons, which in the fog had ridden into them. After this
repulse Hohenlohe halted his advanced guard until some batteries
could be brought forward to fire on La Lune, which gained for
Kellermann time to straighten his army.

When Hohenlohe's guns opened fire, Deprez-Crassier and
Valence fell back to a position close to Orbeval, in order to protect
the left flank of the Valmy position and fill in the gap between it
and the strong detachments posted by Kellermann in the Château
of Maupertius and the village of Gizaucourt on the Auve.

Thus it came about that the French line of battle, which
stretched from Mt. Yron to Maupertius, assumed a semicircular
form. On the right stood Stengel's advanced guard on Mt. Yron;
in the centre the mass of Kellermann's army on the mound, and on
the left, from below the windmill to Orbeval, the troops of
Deprez-Crassier and Valence, with the detachments at Maupertius and Gizaucourt on their left and south of the Châlons Road.

Thus it also came about that, instead of Kellermann's army
prolonging Dumouriez's left and covering his communications
with Vitry-le-François, it was isolated in front of its left centre,
which meant that, were it attacked, it would receive the full
shock of the enemy's assault. In order to mitigate this, Dumouriez

ordered Stengel to move forward to the western edge of Mt. Yron, and to support him he brought up in rear of him 16 battalions under Beurnonville. To strengthen Kellermann's left, he sent forward nine battalions and several squadrons to reinforce Valence and drew up 12 battalions and six squadrons on the Châlons Road east of Orbeval as a reserve.

Though the French had been caught unprepared and were forced on the defensive, Dumouriez had no intention of abandoning the offensive altogether. He decided on two audacious manœuvres. Firstly, he instructed General le Veneur, with 12 battalions and eight squadrons, to cross the Aisne above Neuville-au-Pont, advance on Berzieux and Virginy, and fall upon the rear of the Prussians and Austrians. Secondly, he ordered Duval, at Vienne-le-Château, also to cross the Aisne and attack the Prussian baggage train, then drawn up in wagon-laager (*Wagenburg*)[1] at Maison-de-Champagne.

When Valence fell back and the fog in places began to lift, Massenbach, accompanied by Brunswick's natural son the Count of Forstenburg, rode forward from the advanced guard to La Lune. At once they recognized its tactical importance, for from it the highroad to Orbeval could be swept by gunfire and the mound of Valmy taken in flank, and galloped back and informed Brunswick, who ordered forward a battery to La Lune. About the same time, Dumouriez, who also had recognized its importance, ordered General Chazot to occupy it; but when he approached it he found it too strongly held to attack and withdrew.

While La Lune was occupied by Hohenlohe, the Prussian main body came up in two columns, which slowly formed face toward Mt. Yron and Valmy, their right rested on La Lune and their left on the Bionne. At noon, while the deployment was completed, the fog thinned, and to their surprise, Frederick William, Brunswick, and Goethe, at La Lune, saw before them, not as they had expected an enemy in precipitate retreat, but an army drawn up in ordered line of battle. Nor were they encouraged, when Kellermann, at the windmill, saw them, raised his hat, decorated with a tricolor plume, on his sword, and cried out, "*Vive la nation!*" To which a roar of "*Vive la nation! Vive la France! Vive notre général!*" swept down the French ranks.[2]

When this incident occurred, the Prussian artillery—58 guns—

---

[1] See *Valmy*, p. 177.   [2] *Valmy*, p. 207.

commanded by General Tempelhoff, had been drawn up in battery position from La Lune northward, and faced Kellermann's 40 pieces, under General d'Aboville, on the Valmy ridge. The range was about 1,300 yards.

Suddenly a strong wind began to blow, the fog dissipated, and the sun shone out brightly. "Now", writes Goethe, "commenced the cannonade of which so much has been spoken, but the violence of which at the time it is impossible to describe."[1] Money says it "was heavier than I ever heard".[2] It reached its height at 1 p.m., and, according to Goethe, the whole battlefield trembled.[3] Yet, in spite of the intensity of the fire – Dumouriez says that each side expended more than 20,000 shot[4] – casualties were slight. Not only was 1,300 yards a long range for cannon of that day, but the clayey soil was so sodden that most of the shot buried itself in it instead of ricochetting.

Though the cannonade had not produced the effect Brunswick's staff had expected, it was agreed that there was only one thing now to do, that was, to assault the Valmy position.

While this question was discussed, Brunswick carefully examined his enemy through a telescope. He had marched 30 odd miles to avoid attacking Les Islettes, and now, ironically, he was faced with an attack on Valmy. This, certainly, did not fit in with his strategy; nevertheless he ordered the attack to be made.

At once the Prussian infantry, under cover of the smoke of their batteries, began to form up into two lines of attack. But no sooner had they begun to advance than the whole of Kellermann's artillery was turned upon them and some of the battalions wavered and lost their dressing. Brunswick, who though he had ordered the attack was at heart opposed to it, found sufficient excuse in this to halt it before it had covered more than 200 paces. At the time this order was given, Dumouriez rode up to Kellermann at the windmill, and the enemy's sudden halt made him certain that Brunswick would not attempt an assault.

At about 2 p.m. a Prussian shell blew up three ammunition wagons behind Kellermann's line, the noise of the explosion resounded over the battlefield. A thick cloud of smoke enveloped the French gunners, who ceased firing, as also did the Prussian gunners, whose target was obscured. Two French regiments broke back, at once to be rallied by Kellermann, but the artillery

[1] *Campaign in France*, pp. 72–73.   [2] *The History of the Campaign of 1792*, p. 88.
[3] *Campaign in France*, p. 77.   [4] Dumouriez's *Mémoires*, vol. III, p. 44.

wagoners, who were undisciplined civilians, in flight streamed toward the rear: it was a critical moment.

Massenbach, then at La Lune, saw the commotion around the windmill, thought that the battle was as good as won, and rode to the King and Brunswick to urge them to reinforce the right of the halted attack and carry the mound of Valmy by storm.

No sooner had he spoken than the cannonade began again, and it was seen that the French had recovered their ranks. Impressed by the steadiness of the French infantry, and noticing that in the plain between Orbeval and the Auve the French troopers stood to their horses, Brunswick turned to those around him and said: "Gentlemen, you see by what kind of troops we are faced. Those Frenchmen are only waiting for us to advance before mounting their horses and charging us."[1] Then he paused, as if turning over in his mind whether to resume the attack or await the arrival of Clerfayt, whom he had ordered with all speed to join him. He glanced again at the French, then summoned a council of war, at which the King and a few senior officers were present. For the first time in the campaign he assumed the full authority of a commander-in-chief, and as the guns thundered, he pronounced his decision: "*Hier schlagen wir nicht*" ("We do not fight here"). Hohenlohe, Manstein (the King's A.D.C.) and General Grawert agreed with him, and when Brunswick declared that the assault would fail, and even should it succeed, no good could come of it, the King gave way.[2]

In the meantime, on the left, Kalkreuth bombarded Mt. Yron, on which, as Chuquet points out, the resistance put up by Stengel, which prevented Kellermann's right being turned, was not the least of the factors which contributed to French success.[3]

The assault was called off and at 4 p.m. the Prussians moved across the highway to cut off their enemy from Châlons and Paris. The cannonade ceased, and as evening closed in a drenching storm of rain swept over the battlefield. A few hours later, Kellermann, under cover of night, withdrew his army to Dampièrre and Voilement, in order to cover the Vitry-le-François Road.

Thus ended the Battle of Valmy, in which 34,000 Prussians

---

[1] *Valmy*, p. 215.
[2] In *Dumouriez and the Defence of England against Invasion* (1909), p. 129, J. Holland Rose and A. M. Broadly suggest that Duval's raid on the Prussian baggage train may have contributed to Brunswick's decision to call off the battle.
[3] *Valmy*, p. 217.

faced 52,000 Frenchmen, of whom 36,000 of the latter were engaged. The casualties were insignificant; the French lost about 300 officers and men and the Prussians 184. Many of the wounded died on the battlefield.

There can be little doubt that, though Brunswick's generalship, emasculated as it was by the interferences of Frederick William, was beneath contempt, his decision not to fight was a wise one. His army was reduced by dysentery; winter was approaching and the roads would increasingly become worse. His line of communications was insecure, and his commissariat was so inefficient that a rapid march on Paris was out of the question. Even were it reached, by then his army would have become so weak and worn that it would have risked annihilation. The aim of the campaign had become unattainable and the campaign itself had been reduced to an absurdity, a condition Brunswick had foreseen from the start. But the overruling reason which led to his decision was that, in spite of its panics and its mutinies, he felt—though he would never have acknowledged it—that the French generals and their men were superior to him and his slow-moving unthinking troops.

"The enemy", wrote Lombard, the King's private secretary, "had disappointed our hopes. Dumouriez and Kellermann had proved themselves generals not to be despised. They had chosen excellent positions; they had under their orders all that remained of the old French troops of the line; the volunteers helped by their numbers, and were in a position to render real service when attached to the veteran troops; their light cavalry was excellent and quite fresh. Their army lacked nothing, and we—we lacked everything. They were well fortified in their positions, both front and rear, and their artillery was at least equal to ours. This is what prevented a decisive blow being struck."[1]

The writer of this illuminating *aperçu* played an important part in bringing the campaign to its end. On September 30 he was captured by General le Veneur in his daring raid on the rear of the Prussian army, and at the particular request of Frederick William, Dumouriez released him, and took the opportunity to send by means of him a memorandum[2] to the King setting forth his reasons why the war should be terminated. Also, as he heard that the King was without coffee and sugar, as a gift he sent him 12 lb.[3]

[1] Quoted from *Ibid.*, pp. 242–243.
[2] See Dumouriez's *Mémoires*, vol. III, Appendix A,   [3] *Ibid.*, vol. III, p. 66.

Brunswick with eagerness seized upon the idea, and was supported by the King who had just received perturbing news from Poland. A week of negotiations followed, and on September 27 Dumouriez sent a second memorandum in which the separation of Prussia from Austria was his sole theme. The King indignantly refused to consider it, and though this brought the truce to an end, on September 29 Dumouriez urged upon Lebrun, Minister of Foreign Affairs in Paris, the need of moderation, because, as he wrote, "a general peace, which we might obtain on glorious conditions, would be better for us than the dangers of a long war. . . ."[1] But the Revolutionary Government would not listen to this, and defiantly declared that: "The Republic does not discuss terms until its territory is evacuated."

On the night of September 30–October 1, Brunswick struck camp at La Lune and skilfully withdrew his army to the right bank of the Meuse. Dumouriez, who on September 27 had been appointed Commander-in-Chief of the French armies, then returned to his plan of invading the Netherlands. He took over command of the Army of the North at Valenciennes, marched into Belgium, and on November 6, to the consternation of Europe, defeated Albert Duke of Saxe-Teschen and Clerfayt at Jemappes.

Valmy was the Marathon of the French Revolutionary and Napoleonic Wars. Faced by the most formidable armies in Europe, led by the most noted general of the day, the French under Dumouriez and Kellermann had repulsed the one and discredited the other. "After Valmy", writes Chuquet, "every Frenchman who held sword or musket in hand, looked upon himself as the champion of a cause which was destined to triumph."[2] Valmy was the deathbed of the Old Régime and, spiritually, the cradle of the New Republic which, in the fond dreams of Camille Desmoulins and others, was to carry liberty, equality, and fraternity into the enslaved countries, in order that kings might perish and paradise be realized on earth.

Though this alluring dream was soon to give way to a nightmare, some at the time sensed that the thunder of the cannonade heralded a portent. Massenbach wrote: "You will see how those little cocks will raise themselves on their spurs. They have undergone their baptism of fire. . . . We have lost more than a battle. The 20th September has changed the course of history. It is the

---

[1] Quoted from Sybel, vol. II, p. 173.   [2] *Valmy*, p. 232.

most important day of the century."[1] And on the evening of that day, when Goethe's dejected companions gathered around him and asked what he thought, he replied: "From this place and from this day forth commences a new era in the world's history, and you can all say that you were present at its birth,"[2]

[1] Quoted by Sorel, vol. III, p. 50. [2] *Campaign in France*, p. 81.

The maritime struggle between France and England

After the battle of Valmy, two ideas directed the foreign policy of the Revolution: that of the visionaries and that of the realists. The former were Alexandrian in outlook and offered to the world a new dispensation based on the brotherhood of man. The latter were Caesarians who sought in the conquest of neighbouring countries, not only a means to consolidate France, but also to mend her shattered finances. Both ideas urged the Revolution outward, the one to share with other peoples the freedom France had won, and the other to plunder them and lay them under tribute.

Whether Dumouriez was aware of it or not, both these causes of expansion lay at the bottom of his *idée fixe*, for the Austrian Netherlands was both a rich country and one eager to cast off Austrian rule. Further, could the mouth of the Scheldt be brought under French control, in time Antwerp might rival, if not oust London as the centre of world trade. That, at least in part, this was realized is supported by the fact that, immediately after Dumouriez's victory at Jemappes, the National Convention declared that the Scheldt was open to commerce, and also that military aid would be accorded to all peoples striving after liberty. This threat to the Low Countries, which had brought England into war during the previous hundred years, coupled with the thinly veiled declaration of war on all monarchies was, on January 21, 1793, sealed by the execution of Louis XVI. It made the meaning of the Revolution unmistakable, and so shocked the government of England that two days later, the Marquis de Chauvelin, the French envoy in London, was given eight days' notice to leave the kingdom. His peremptory dismissal so infuriated the Convention that the day after his departure it declared war on Great Britain and Holland, and a month later hurled an ultimatum at Spain. Thus was opened a war which, except for one short spell, was to last for 22 years.

Though the proportions of this conflict were vast—it eventually was to embrace most of Europe–for France its central problem was how to force England to terms, either directly by gaining command of the English Channel, or indirectly by strangling England's continental and colonial trade. But it was not until the First Coalition against France collapsed in 1795, and until in the following year the National Convention gave way to the Directory, that events began to reveal it.

The five Directors resolved that a continuation of the war would consolidate their power and they pressed on with it. Under their pilotage the year 1796 witnessed a series of French triumphs which, in 1797, culminated in Bonaparte's conquest of northern Italy and the acceptance by Austria of the Treaty of Campo Formio, which ceded Lombardy and the Austrian Netherlands to France. In the meantime, in June, 1796, the Directors had turned their attention to an oversea attack on Great Britain and Ireland, which in December resulted in an abortive invasion of the latter, and in February, 1797, in Colonel Tate's farcical landing in Wales.

One of the most critical moments in British history followed. On April 15, the Channel Fleet at Spithead mutinied, and on May 2, Admiral Duncan's North Sea Fleet at the Nore followed suit. At this time the Dutch fleet, under French control, expected to find the main British fleet drawn toward Ireland and was preparing to sail with 42 transports to invade England, and Duncan, then lying off Yarmouth, was ordered to blockade the Dutch or bring them to battle. Because of the mutiny, he was able to induce only two of his ships to put to sea. Nevertheless, with them he proceeded to blockade the Texel, and thus matters stood until June 21, on which date the Directory urged the Dutch to carry 20,000 men to Ireland, while another fleet carried 6,000 more from Brest.

Nothing happened until October 9, when Duncan, who learned that the Dutch had sailed with the intention of disembarking a force in the Clyde in order to draw British troops from Ireland, on October 11 brought 16 Dutch ships to action off Camperdown and captured nine of them. Immediately after this defeat, the Directory appointed General Bonaparte to command the army designated to invade England.

Bonaparte reached Dunkirk on February 11, 1798, and at once inspected the coastal establishments, issued orders for the building of a flotilla of flat-bottomed boats, and on February 23 reported to the Directors: "Make what effort we will, we shall not for many years gain naval supremacy. To make a descent on England, without being master of the sea, is the boldest and most difficult task imaginable." Always ready with an alternative, he suggested that, until naval preparations were adequate, the correct course to take was to strike at England's eastern trade by seizing Malta, occupying Egypt, and invading India. This proposal was accepted.

Fired by the exploits of Alexander the Great, on May 19 Bonaparte set out from Toulon with 13 sail of the line, 300 transports, and upward of 35,000 troops and 15,000 sailors and civilians. In chief naval command was Admiral Brueys, accompanied by Admirals Ganteaume, Villeneuve, and Decrès. Malta was occupied on June 12; the army landed at Alexandria on July 2, and on July 21 the Battle of the Pyramids was won. Then, as Bonaparte organized his conquests, suddenly he learnt that on August 1–2 Nelson had destroyed his fleet in Aboukir Bay and won the Battle of the Nile.

The news of this decisive victory brought into being the Second Coalition, a combination of England, Naples, Austria, Russia, and Turkey, and while Bonaparte warred in Syria its members took the offensive. The Franco-Italian republics were overrun by Suvarov, Holland was assailed by a joint British-Russian army, and Switzerland was invaded by a joint Russian-Austrian one. So critical was the French situation that the Directory recalled Bonaparte. He handed over his army to Kléber, and on the night of August 22–23 he set sail from Alexandria, eluded the English ships, and on October 9 landed in France at Fréjus. Meanwhile, Suvarov had been driven out of Switzerland and the British and Russians out of Holland.

When Bonaparte arrived in Paris, he was at once placed in command of its garrison, and as he sensed that the Army and the people were behind him, with the aid of his brother Lucien, then President of the Council of Five Hundred, and one of the Directors, the Abbé Sieyès, he carried out the *coup d'état* of the 18th Brumaire (November 9). The Directory was abolished and a new constitution voted which made him the first of three consuls appointed to rule France for 10 years. On December 15, the new constitution was promulgated and shortly after confirmed by a plebiscite of 3,011,007 votes to 1,562. Thus ended the democratic revolution, henceforward the drill-sergeant was to govern France.

Bonaparte had made himself all but dictator and was ready to face the forces of the Second Coalition. Craftily, in order to justify his intentions in the eyes of the people, he appealed to George III and the Emperor Francis to end the war. Nothing came of this and on May 6, 1800, he left Paris for Geneva; crossed the Alps at the Great St. Bernard, and on June 14 fell upon the rear of the Austrians under Melas in Piedmont and routed them at Marengo. Routed again on December 2 by Moreau at Hohenlinden, the war of the Second Coalition collapsed and the Austrians accepted the Peace of Lunéville on February 9, 1801.

Freed from Austria, Bonaparte at once returned to his project of striking at England. Already, on December 12, 1800, he had persuaded Russia, Prussia, Denmark, and Sweden to form, on the lines adopted by Catherine II in 1780, a League of Armed Neutrality against England, but soon after it was brought to ruin by the assassination of Paul I of Russia, and by Nelson's decisive victory on April 2, 1801, over the Danish fleet at Copenhagen.

It was when the above maritime alliance was being formed that Bonaparte began to grapple in earnest with the problem of subduing England. In February he addressed a letter to Talleyrand in which he outlined a vast programme of naval expeditions to be undertaken by the fleets of France, Spain, and Holland, supported by Russia and Denmark. The central idea was to decoy the main British fleet to Egypt; for the French navy was too weak to dispute with England the mastery of the seas. A return was made therefore to the idea of slipping a force across the English Channel, once the English fleet had been inveigled away. To effect this, Admiral Decrès was made Minister of Marine, and, as planned, the army of invasion was to number 114,554 officers and men carried in more than 2,000 small craft.

But the collapse of the Armed Neutrality, coupled with the formation of the Addington Ministry in England, in October led to the preliminaries of peace which culminated in the signing of the Treaty of Amiens on March 27, 1802. Peace was proclaimed between France, Spain, and the Batavian Republic (Holland) on the one part, and by Great Britain and Ireland on the other. Its main terms were that England was to retain Ceylon and Trinidad and restore all other colonies taken from France and her allies, and that Malta was to be evacuated by the English, and France was to withdraw her troops from Taranto and the States of the Church.

The Peace of Amiens left France arbiter of Europe, and the gratitude of the people toward Bonaparte was shown when, on May 10, the Council of State put to the nation the following question: "Is Napoleon Bonaparte to be made Consul for Life?" It was answered by a plebiscite of 3,568,885 "ayes" to 8,374 "nays". Bonaparte became "Napoleon" to France and to history.

The peace was no more than a truce which neither side strictly observed. Causes of friction at once arose and the main ones were the protectionist policy of Napoleon, which crippled English trade; the refusal of England to evacuate Malta; and the refusal of Napoleon to withdraw his garrison from Holland. After a year of contentious wrangling, on May 2, 1803, Lord Whitworth, British Ambassador in Paris, sent for his passports; on May 17 he crossed the Strait of Dover, and the next day England declared war on France.

The French navy, which had never recovered from the shock of the Revolution, then consisted of 23 ships of the line, 25 frigates and 107 corvettes, etc., ready for service; also 167 small craft belonging to the invasion flotilla of 1800. Forty-five sail of the line were under construction, and in addition, France had at her call the Batavian fleet of 15 sail of the line, of which only five were fit for service.

Facing these two fleets was the English, commanded by men who had scored victory after victory. In January, 1803, it comprised 34 sail of the line in commission, supported by 86 50-gun ships and frigates, and behind it in reserve were 77 sail of the line and 49 50-gun ships and frigates. On the declaration of war, Earl St. Vincent, First Lord of the Admiralty, at once ordered the blockade of the main French naval ports. Nelson was chosen for the Mediterranean command, Lord Keith to watch the North Sea and Strait of Dover, and Cornwallis to blockade Brest.

With so great a disparity between the French and English naval forces, and with most of the French fleet bottled-up, Napoleon was left with the flotilla project as his sole hope. He rightly realized that the strategical centre of gravity of every continental war in which England was engaged lay in the English Channel, and it was not long before he appreciated that a flotilla of *prames*, *chaloups* and *cannonières*, which had already gained for him the soubriquet of "*Don Quixote de la Manche*", was not in itself sufficient to master it. But that this project, as some suppose, was from first to last only a bluff to cover the raising of armies against Austria and Russia, has little support.[1] That eventually the Army of England was used against Austria in no way sustains the hoax theory, for Napoleon never worked to a fixed plan, but always had one or more alternatives up his strategical sleeve.

That the threat of invasion roused England is proved by the immense effort made to raise regular and volunteer troops. The official returns of December 9, 1803, show that by then, 463,000 men had been enrolled, and those of January 1, 1805, that this figure had been increased to 590,000, a tremendous effort for a country of some ten million inhabitants.

In the autumn of 1803 the Russian Government had made overtures to Great Britain and Austria with reference to French designs on Turkey, and after William Pitt was returned to office in May, 1804, this proposal was actively considered. Pitt realized that it was impossible for Great Britain single-handed to wage a successful offensive against Napoleon and he saw in the overtures a means to establish yet another coalition against France, but as Russia wanted to dismember Turkey in Europe, in order to annex Moldavia and Constantinople, and split up the rest into separate states under Russian protection, as well as obtain Malta, the outcome was a prolonged diplomatic wrangle which ended on April 11, 1805, in a treaty between Great Britain and Russia. According to this it was agreed to form a European league for the restoration of peace and the balance of power. A little before this treaty was signed, Pitt decided to send a force under Sir James Craig to garrison Malta, and thereby set free some 8,000 seasoned troops to occupy Sicily, who, with the assistance of Nelson, were to prevent it falling into French hands.

No fighting occurred in 1803, nor during the opening months of 1804. Both England and France prepared for a contest to the death, and to add to French prestige, exactly a year after the declaration of war, the *Senatus Consultum* of the 28th Floréal, year XII (May 18, 1804,) awarded to Napoleon the title of Emperor of the French. In Notre Dame, on December 2, he gently waved aside Pope Pius VII, and with his own hands crowned himself to the chant of *Vivat in aerternum semper Augustus.*

[1] In January, 1805, according to Miot de Mélito (*Memoirs*, vol. II, p. 244), Napoleon told his Council that his preparations for the invasion of England were only a pretext to cover the assembly of a great army with which to invade Austria. What would seem more likely is, that this information was vouched his Council in order to mislead his enemies.

CHAPTER 12

The Battle of Trafalgar, 1805

The renewal of the war found England in the weakest position she had held since 1781. Not only was she now faced with the combined fleets of France and Holland, but the alliance of Spain was guaranteed to France by treaty. This meant that Napoleon had at his call all the ports from the Texel to Genoa for shipbuilding and refuge. Further, it was clearly apparent that he had every intention to invade England, for the ports of France rang with the blows of the shipwright's hammer.[1] Nor was his assertion that he intended gradually to create a French navy of 130 sail of the line, supported by 60 Spanish, 20 Dutch, and 15 Genoese ships, altogether an empty one; for, in spite of his numerous campaigns from 1805 onward, by 1815 the French fleet had grown to 103 sail of the line and 55 frigates.[2]

The English naval problem was, therefore, not merely one of meeting the allied fleet in the Channel, but also of preventing allied ships—then existing and as they were built—from leaving their ports and putting to sea. This meant blockade carried out in such a way that the escape of any one impounded squadron would not lead to a chain-reaction—that is, to the releasing of the other squadrons—a problem which became still more difficult to solve when, on December 12, 1804, Spain declared war on England.

The allied ships of the line were then distributed as follows: Toulon—11; Cartagena—5; Cadiz—10; Ferrol—9; Rochefort—5; Brest—21; and at the Texel—6. The first two were blockaded by Nelson with 12 sail of the line; the third by Sir John Orde with five; the forth, fifth, and sixth by Cornwallis and his subordinates with 37 off Ushant and in the Bay of Biscay, and the seventh by Lord Keith with nine off the Downs and in the North Sea. Besides these ships there were five of the line in British ports and 12 in the East and West Indies. In European waters therefore, British numerical superiority over that of the allies was slight.

This lack of strength was more than made good by the British

---

[1] By August, 1805, 2,343 landing craft had been built (*Napoleon and the Invasion of England*, H. F. B. Wheeler and A. M. Broadley, 1908, vol. II, p. 233).

[2] *Mémoires pour servir à l'historie de Napoléon 1er*. Claude François Méneval (1894), vol. I, p. 366. By 1814 the British Navy numbered 240 of the line, 317 frigates and 611 smaller craft (*The Cambridge Modern History*, vol. IX, p. 243).

Admiralty's adherence to England's traditional naval policy of holding in force the western mouth of the Channel. As long as a powerful fleet rode off Ushant, no flotilla invasion was possible in face of Keith at the Downs. Therefore it was laid down by the Admiralty as an inflexible principle that, should a blockaded squadron escape and should the blockading fleet be unable to bring it to battle, the latter was at once to rally off Ushant and thereby increase the strength of the fleet stationed there.[1] Ushant, therefore, was the centre of gravity of British naval defence, and, in consequence, Cornwallis's fleet excelled all others in importance. Were he defeated, Keith would be uncovered, and should Keith be defeated, except for the weather, there was next to nothing to prevent the Boulogne flotilla from fulfilling its purpose. Napoleon understood this full well, and though he had little grasp of naval tactics and paid scant respect to wind and tide, as a naval strategist he had nothing to learn because the principles of strategy are universal.

Though the campaign which culminated in the battle of Trafalgar sprang from Napoleon's instructions of March 2, 1805,[2] given to Vice-Admiral Ganteaume at Brest and Vice-Admiral Villeneuve at Toulon, in order to clarify events it is as well to return to December 12, 1804, the day Spain declared war on England.

On that day Napoleon ordered Villeneuve to break out of Toulon, sail for the West Indies and at Martinique link up with Admiral Missiessy, who was to break out of Rochefort and join him. Next, after a stay of 60 days, in which he was to do all possible damage to British possessions, Villeneuve was to sail for Ferrol, free Captain Gourdon's (or Gordon) squadron of five of the line and two frigates blockaded there, and then proceed to Rochefort.[3]

On January 11, Missiessy escaped from Rochefort with five of the line and four frigates and sailed for Martinique. A week later, when Nelson had taken his squadron to Maddalena Islands, in the Strait of Bonifacio, Villeneuve, with 11 sail of the line and nine frigates, stood out from Toulon. When he learnt of his escape, "regardless of probabilities,"[4] Nelson concluded that Villeneuve

---

[1] See *La Campagne Maritime de 1805, Trafalgar*, Edouard Desbrière (1907), pp. 3 and 79.

[2] *Correspondance de Napoléon 1er*, Nos. 8379 and 8381, vol. x, pp. 182, 185.

[3] *Ibid.*, Nos. 8206 and 8231, vol. x, pp. 63 and 78.

[4] See *Nelson the Sailor*, Captain Russell Grenfell (1949), p. 172.

was bound for Malta or Egypt, and forthwith sailed eastward to arrive at Alexandria on February 7. When he found nothing there, he set sail for Malta, where he learnt that Villeneuve had been forced back to Toulon by a storm. Still convinced that Villeneuve's goal was Egypt, on March 26, in order to intercept Villeneuve the next time he set out, Nelson anchored his squadron off the south of Sardinia. Four days later he received the news that Villeneuve had put to sea again, for unknown to Nelson Villeneuve was carrying out Napoleon's instructions of March 2.

The aim of these instructions was to assemble a fleet of over 40 sail of the line at Martinique, the main contingents to be Ganteaume's Brest squadron of 21 sail of the line and six frigates and Villeneuve's Toulon squadron of 11 and six respectively. On the way out, the former was to release Gourdon's squadron of four of the line and two frigates at Ferrol, and the latter the Cadiz squadron, under the Spanish Admiral Gravina, of about seven of the line. At Martinique, Missiessy, with five of the line and four frigates, was to join them, and once this union was effected Ganteaume was to take over the supreme command of the combined fleets, sail for Ushant, attack the English fleet there, and make for Boulogne. Villeneuve was instructed that should he reach Martinique ahead of Ganteaume, he was to wait 40 days for him, and if by then he had not arrived, he was to sail to Cadiz, where orders would await him.

Here it is convenient, before the tussle that was to lead to Trafalgar began, briefly to measure the characters of the two men who were to play the major parts in it–Villeneuve and Nelson.

Villeneuve, who was five years younger than Nelson–the one born in 1763 and the other in 1758–was of the French *noblesse*, and one of the few well-born French naval officers to survive the Revolution, hence his rapid promotion. He was an educated and studious sailor, who might have done good work at the French Admiralty, but was unfitted for command. Though he in no way lacked personal courage, by temperament he was a defeatist. He did not believe in Napoleon's project of invading England; he had no confidence either in his subordinates or his allies, and worst of all he had none in himself. At the battle of the Nile he had commanded the *Guillaume Tell*, one of the two French ships of the line which had escaped, and from then on *le souvenir d'Aboukir* paralysed him; ever after he was haunted by the spectre of Nelson.

Nelson stood at the opposite pole. He was a bold and imaginative tactician, independent in outlook, ambitious, sensitive of his reputation, at times vainglorious and frequently violent in his dislikes. His moral courage was extraordinary, as his action when he left the line and single-handedly attacked the Spanish van at the battle of St. Vincent shows. Captain Grenfell says of it that it was "a piece of individual initiative . . . unsurpassed in naval history . . . an act of supreme valour,"[1] His pugnacity at the Nile, Copenhagen, and Trafalgar has seldom been equalled; nevertheless he was an indifferent strategist because he failed to realize that strategy is a science, and though not an exact one, one at least based on facts and not on intuitions. In 1804–1805, the uppermost strategical fact was Napoleon's naval threat to England; yet in Nelson's dispatches and letters of these years the word "invasion" occurs but once, and then incidentally and after Napoleon had abandoned his project.[2] The reason was that his gaze was always fixed on the Mediterranean, and because of this, unwittingly Villeneuve succeeded in outwitting him. What Nelson failed to grasp was that in 1804–1805 the strategical centre of gravity lay in the English Channel and not off Sardinia or at the mouth of the Nile. Nevertheless, in spite of this defect, he was the greatest fighting admiral England has ever had.

On March 10 Nelson, with his squadron, was in the Gulf of Palmas, at the south-western corner of Sardinia, and when he learnt that Villeneuve was embarking his troops, he set sail for Toulon. He found there every appearance that Villeneuve was about to put to sea and jumped to the conclusion that his most probable destination was Egypt, and in consequence returned to Palmas, from where he could cover Naples and Sicily, block the main seaway to Egypt, and be well placed to strike westward, should Villeneuve's aim be to make for the Atlantic. There he was when, on March 30, in accordance with Napoleon's instructions, Villeneuve stood out from Toulon for Cadiz to pick up Gravina's squadron before sailing for the West Indies.

The first news Nelson received of his departure was on April 4, when from one of his frigates he learnt that, on March 31, she had sighted Villeneuve's squadron some 60 miles south by west of Toulon–that is, some 300 miles west of Palmas. This news Nelson sent by dispatch to the Admiralty, saying "I shall push

---

[1] See *Nelson the Sailor*, p. 66.
[2] *The Dispatches and Letters of Vice-Admiral Lord Viscount Nelson*, Sir Nicholas Harris Nicholas (1856), vol. VII, p. 87.

for Egypt."[1] Next, with Egypt still in mind, believing that Ville-neuve would make for the island of Galita–off Bizerta–and attempt to reach Alexandria by hugging the African coast, he took up position with his squadron between Sardinia and Galita. But no sooner had he done so than, afraid that Villeneuve would round the north of Sardinia, he shifted his position to the island of Ustica, 50 miles north of Palermo, and arrived there on April 7.

On the same day Villeneuve was off Cartagena, and Sir John Orde, who was blockading Gravina in Cadiz, was warned by Sir Richard Strachan, who had been sent by Nelson to escort a homeward-bound convoy past Algeciras, that on April 8 he had seen Villeneuve coming out of the Strait. As Orde had but four of the line with him, this news placed him in a most perplexing situation. Should he stay where he was and await Nelson, or should he close in on Ushant? This question was decided when Strachan informed him that Nelson was occupied with Egypt. Orde left his frigates to keep touch with Villeneuve, and after sending a dispatch to the Admiralty, stood out for the north.

His dispatch is illuminating, for it shows that he–the man Nelson traduced in violent terms[2]–had a far clearer appreciation of the strategical situation than Nelson. This dispatch reads: "I am persuaded the enemy will not remain long in Cadiz, and I think the chances are great in favour of their destination being westward where by a sudden concentration of several detach-ments, Bonaparte may hope to gain a temporary superiority in the Channel, and availing himself of it to strike his enemy a mortal blow."[3] This was exactly what Napoleon intended, and when he penetrated his enemy's scheme, Orde set out to reinforce the centre of gravity–Ushant.

On April 9 Villeneuve anchored outside Cadiz and signalled Gravina to come out. But his fear that Nelson was on his tracks was so great that, at 1 p.m. he waited no longer for Gravina, but weighed anchor and left the Spaniards to straggle after him.

Soon after this, as Villeneuve did not appear in the Tyrrhenian Sea, Nelson shifted his position from Ustica to Toro, a small island

---

[1] *The Dispatches and Letters of Vice-Admiral Lord Viscount Nelson*, Sir Nicholas Harris Nicholas (1856), vol. VI, p. 397.

[2] Due to an old quarrel which started in 1798, and was accentuated when, in 1804, Orde was appointed to blockade Cadiz, a profitable command because of prize money, and one which Nelson coveted.

[3] Quoted by Corbett in his *Trafalgar*, p. 64.

near the Gulf of Palmas, and on April 18, when he learnt that Villeneuve's squadron had been sighted off Gibraltar on April 8, he informed the Admiralty that because of his "vigilance" the enemy had found "it impossible to undertake any Expedition in the Mediterranean,"[1] and the next day he sent another dispatch in which he stated that, as he was satisfied that Villeneuve was not bound for the West Indies, but more likely for Ireland and Brest, he was proceeding off the Scilly Islands.[2] Though late in the day, this was strictly in accordance with the Admiralty principle already defined.

Delayed by foul weather, Nelson did not reach Gibraltar until May 6. There he fell in with Rear-Admiral Donald Campbell, then in the Portuguese service, who informed him that Villeneuve was on his way to the West Indies. Nelson, always impulsive and pugnacious, made up his mind, and on May 10, with his 10 sail of the line and three frigates, set out to cross the Atlantic.

Commenting on this, Captain Russell Grenfell remarks:

"It is a debatable point whether Nelson's decision to make for the West Indies was a sound one. With the 'Army of England' making its noisy preparations at Boulogne, there was an inescapable possibility that Villeneuve's movements were connected with the transport of that army across the Channel. Wherever Villeneuve had gone, he was a month ahead of Nelson, and if, as it was both reasonable and prudent to assume, the Franco-Spanish fleet was engaged in a feint designed to draw British squadrons away from the Channel, it could well be thought likely that a decoy fleet which had disappeared westward or southwestward that length of time before might now be on its way back towards its final and decisive destination. There was therefore a considerable risk that by starting off for the West Indies so long after Villeneuve had vanished, Nelson was but playing into the enemy's hand. It can be plausibly argued that, on a broad survey of the whole strategical field, Nelson should have steered for Brest, to be on the safe side of a very uncertain and precarious situation."[3]

There was another reason, as Captain Grenfell points out, why Nelson should have joined Cornwallis. It was that by May 10 his dispatch of April 19, which notified his intention to sail for the Scilly Islands, would have been received by the Admiralty, who, should they have learned of Villeneuve's true movements, might

[1] *Nelson's Dispatches and Letters*, vol. VI, p. 407.
[2] *Ibid.*, vol. VI, p. 411.   [3] *Nelson the Sailor*, p. 180.

well have made their own arrangements to follow him up. In these circumstances, were Nelson to sail for the West Indies, two squadrons instead of one would be in pursuit. This is what very nearly happened, for when the Admiralty learnt from Orde (on April 30) as well as from agents that Villeneuve was bound for the West Indies, Lord Barham, First Lord of the Admiralty, ordered 11 of the line under Vice-Admiral Collingwood to proceed there, and only by accident,[1] when he was on his way, did he learn that Nelson was already in pursuit. Had this accident not occurred, 21 battleships would have gone on a wild-goose chase.

On June 4, after a rapid voyage, Nelson put in at Barbados, where he was joined by Rear-Admiral Cochrane and two sail of the line. There he was wrongly informed that the French fleet had been seen to windward of St. Lucia, and the result was that he missed his enemy. Villeneuve had reached Martinique on May 14 to find that Missiessy had returned to Rochefort and that Ganteaume had not arrived. The latter was still blockaded at Brest, and Napoleon, brooking no further delay, had, on April 29, sent off Rear-Admiral Magnon and two of the line with orders to Villeneuve instructing him to remain in the West Indies for 35 days after their receipt, and if by then Ganteaume had not joined him, he was to sail for Ferrol, pick up the 15 ships blockaded there, next release the 21 at Brest, and lastly, "*avec cette armée navale*", enter the English Channel and appear before Boulogne.[2]

Magnon arrived on June 4, and on June 7 the news was received that Nelson was in the West Indies. It so unnerved Villeneuve that, regardless of his new orders, on June 10[3] with all haste he stood out for Europe. Two days later Nelson reached Antigua, and rightly guessed that Villeneuve was returning to Europe— either to Cadiz or Toulon, more probably the latter, because, as he wrote at the time, "They may fancy they will get to Egypt without any interruption"[4]—and he decided to return to Gibraltar.

---

[1] At Gibraltar, Nelson had detached Sir Richard Bickerton in the *Royal Sovereign* to assist in covering General Craig's passage to Malta. Next, an Admiralty Order instructed Bickerton to reinforce Calder at Ferrol. On May 17 Bickerton sailed north, and 10 days later, as he neared Finisterre, he met Collingwood coming down, and informed him that Nelson with 10 of the line was already in pursuit.

[2] *Correspondance*, No. 8583, vol. x, p. 321.

[3] *The Campaign of Trafalgar*. Julian S. Corbett (1910), p. 167. Desbrière (*Trafalgar*, p. 42) says June 11 and Captain Grenfell (*Nelson the Sailor*, p. 183) says June 8.

[4] *Dispatches and Letters*, vol. VI, p. 454. Napoleon seems to have been aware of Nelson's obsession. On April 20 (No. 8603) he wrote to Decrès, "Nelson will probably make a second voyage to Egypt," and again on April 23 (No. 8617), "Publish in the Dutch papers that a French squadron has disembarked 10,000 men in Egypt, and that the French admiral has skilfully manœuvred to deceive Nelson."

Before he set out, Nelson sent back to England the brig *Curieux* commanded by Captain Bettesworth, to notify the Admiralty of his return, and during her voyage home, on June 19, the French fleet was sighted on a course well to the north of the Mediterranean. This could only mean that Villeneuve was making for the Bay of Biscay and not, as Nelson supposed, for the Strait of Gibraltar. On July 7 the *Curieux* arrived at Plymouth, and on July 19 Nelson cast anchor at Gibraltar.

On July 18, when off Cape Spartel, Nelson had communicated with Collingwood, then blockading Cadiz, and had received from him a reply which should have enlightened him on the strategical situation. What Collingwood said was, that he believed Napoleon's aim to be Ireland, and that Villeneuve's fleet would "now liberate the Ferrol Squadron . . . make the round of the Bay, and, taking the Rochefort people with them, appear off Ushant, perhaps with thirty-four sail, there to be joined by twenty more. . . . The French Government", he added, "never aim at little things while great objects are in view. . . . Their flight to the West Indies was to take off the naval force, which proved the great impediment to their undertaking. This summer is big with events."[1]

On July 20 Nelson went ashore (at Gibraltar) "for the first time since 16th June, 1803,"[2] and in a letter of the same date to Lord Barham he says that, unless Russian frigates replaced Collingwood's, now withdrawn "from the upper part of the Mediterranean . . . the French will, whenever they please, convey an Army to Sardinia, Sicily, the Morea, or Egypt . . . for which service I have repeatedly applied for many, many more Frigates and Sloops of War".[3] The mention of these places shows that even Collingwood's illuminating letter of July 18 had not altered Nelson's ideas. On August 3 he was ordered to sail to Ushant to join Cornwallis.[4]

In the meantime important political events had taken place which were profoundly to influence Napoleon's project. On May 12, 1804, Pitt had returned to office, and his controlling idea was to build up another coalition. In part his project was based on Dumouriez's "General Reflections of the Defence of England" of

---

[1] *Dispatches and Letters*, vol. VI, p. 472, and *Public and Private Correspondence of Vice-Admiral Lord Collingwood*, G. L. Newnham Collingwood (1829), pp. 107–108. In the former the letter is dated July 18 and in the latter July 21. The two versions differ in places.
[2] *Dispatches and Letters*, vol. VI, p. 475. [3] *Ibid.*, vol. VI, p. 476.
[4] Corbett's *Trafalgar*, p. 230.

1804.[1] The members were to be England, Russia, Austria, Sweden, and Naples, and after a year's negotiations, on April 11, 1805, a treaty between England and Russia was signed, to be followed, on August 9, by another between Russia and Austria. Prussia was also approached, but refused to become a partner. These treaties provided that Russia would put into the field 180,000 men, Austria 315,000 and Sweden 12,000, and that England would pay an annual subsidy of £1,250,000 for each 100,000 soldiers, up to a total of 400,000, employed by her allies against France and Spain.

When the *Curieux* arrived at Plymouth, Captain Bettesworth posted to London, and reported to Lord Barham on July 9. The latter at once appreciated the importance of Bettesworth's information and forthwith sent a dispatch to Cornwallis instructing him to order Rear-Admiral Stirling to raise the Rochefort blockade and reinforce Sir Robert Calder off Ferrol. Also Cornwallis was to instruct Calder, once he had been reinforced, "to proceed without loss of time off Cape Finisterre, from whence he is to cruise for the enemy to the distance of 30 or 40 leagues to the westwards for the space of six or seven days".[2] Thus, in the middle of July, 1805, Napoleon's strategical aim was more than half attained. Except for Brest and Cadiz, all the French and Spanish ports were free from blockade.

Villeneuve had passed the Azores on July 2, and on July 22 approached Cape Finisterre in a dense fog. Had it continued, he might have sailed past Calder's 15 sail unobserved, and have effected a junction with Ganteaume at Brest. But at noon the fog lifted, one of Calder's look-out frigates reported the French fleet in sight, and at 5 p.m. an indecisive engagement was fought, in which two of Villeneuve's ships struck their colours. Though on July 23 the two fleets kept in sight, they did not re-engage, and the following day when Calder bore northward to join Cornwallis, Villeneuve crowded on sail and made for Vigo Bay, where he arrived on July 28. From there he sailed for Ferrol, which he reached on August 1.

The moral effect of this action was decisive, for the little faith Villeneuve had in his fleet now oozed out of the soles of his shoes. On August 6 he wrote: "In the fog our captains, without ex-

---

[1] See *Dumouriez and the Defence of England against Napoleon*, J. Holland Rose and A. M. Broadley (1909), pp. 240–261, particularly pp. 260–261.

[2] Quoted from Corbett's *Trafalgar*, p. 184.

perience of an action or of fleet tactics, had no better idea than to follow their second ahead, and here we are the laughing-stock of Europe."[1] The action palsied him.

At Ferrol Villeneuve received Napoleon's dispatch of July 16, in which he was ordered to raise the blockade of Ferrol, and "manœuvre in such a way as to render us masters of the Strait of Dover, either by uniting with the Rochefort and Brest squadrons or by uniting with the Brest squadron alone, or the Rochefort squadron alone, and then with this fleet double Ireland and Scotland in order to join up with the Dutch squadron at the Texel". Further, if, because of battle or some other cause Villeneuve was unable to accomplish this task, on no account was he to enter the port of Ferrol, but instead proceed to Cadiz.[2]

With a man of Villeneuve's disposition, this last injunction was a fatal error on the part of Napoleon; for to get to Cadiz—as far away as possible from Brest—was the master thought in Villeneuve's mind. Forbidden to enter Ferrol, he left three damaged ships there, then put in at Coruña, where he was strengthened by 14 sail of the line.

When Admiral Stirling withdrew from Rochefort in order to reinforce Calder, on July 17 Rear-Admiral Allemand, who had replaced Missiessy, slipped out of Rochefort under orders to unite with Villeneuve on August 13. But because Decrès omitted to notify Villeneuve of this,[3] an extraordinary sequence of misadventures followed, which culminated in fiasco on August 13.

That day Villeneuve put to sea, and when he sighted some frigates he assumed them to be English and altered course southward to avoid them. They belonged to Allemand's squadron, which was searching for him. Had Villeneuve united with Allemand, he would have brought his fleet up to 34 sail, and had he then borne north instead of south, fortune might have favoured him, for on August 16 Cornwallis had split his fleet of 35 sail into two, and had sent one of these (18 sail) under Calder to Ferrol. Therefore, had Villeneuve, in accordance with his orders, sailed northward, and had he by good fortune eluded Calder, he might have raised the Brest blockade.

"What a chance Villeneuve has missed!" wrote Napoleon. "By coming down upon Brest from the open he might have played

[1] *Projets et Tentatives de Débarquement aux Îles Britanniques*. E. Desbrière (1900–1902), vol. v, p. 776.
[2] *Correspondance*, No. 8985, vol. xi, p. 18.
[3] Desbrière's *Projets et Tentatives*, vol. v, pp. 727–728.

prisoners' base with Calder's squadron and fallen upon Cornwallis; or with his thirty of the line have beaten the English twenty, and obtained a decisive superiority."[1] Though, theoretically, this may be correct,[2] actually it is extremely doubtful, for Cornwallis had retained with him 10 three-deckers, and, according to the computation of that day, one three-decker was equivalent to two two-deckers in fighting value.

Villeneuve continued southward, and on August 20 entered Cadiz, and there was blockaded by Collingwood's three sail of the line. On August 22 Collingwood was reinforced by Sir Richard Bickerton's four of the line, and on August 30 by Calder and his 18.

On August 3 Napoleon arrived at Boulogne. Time pressed, for already there were indications that a coalition was forming in his rear: Austria was massing troops in Venetia and the Tyrol, and a levy *en masse* of the Neapolitan militia was reported by St. Cyr. On August 13, having by then heard of Villeneuve's action with Calder, on which he congratulated him, Napoleon instructed him to unite with Allemand, sweep everything before him, intermingle his French and Spanish ships, and come to the Channel.[3] Also he wrote to Decrès to complain of Villeneuve's slowness,[4] and on August 22 to Ganteaume to state that Villeneuve was on his way to join him, and that on his arrival not a day was to be lost in setting sail up the Channel, in order that six centuries of England's insults might be avenged.[5] This same day he wrote again to Villeneuve, addressing his letter to Brest: "I trust you are now at Brest. Sail, do not lose a moment, and with my squadrons reunited enter the Channel. England is ours. We are ready and embarked. Appear for forty-eight hours, and all will be ended."[6]

Next day, still ignorant that Villeneuve was at Cadiz, he wrote to Talleyrand: "The more I reflect on the situation of Europe, the more I see how urgent it is to take a decisive step." If Villeneuve with his 34 ships "follows my instructions and unites with the Brest squadron and enters the Channel, there is still time: I am master of England. Otherwise I shall raise my camp at Boulogne

[1] *Correspondance*, No. 9160, vol. XI, p. 161.

[2] Whereas Mahan (*The Influence of Sea Power upon the French Revolution and Empire*, vol. II, p. 576) stigmatizes it a blunder, Corbett (*The Campaign of Trafalgar*, pp. 246-254) considers it a masterstroke.

[3] *Correspondance*, No. 9073, vol. XI, 87.   [4] *Ibid.*, No. 9071, vol. XI, p. 85.

[5] *Ibid.*, Nos. 9113 and 9114, vol. XI, p. 115.   [6] *Ibid.*, No. 9115, vol. XI, p. 115.

and march on Vienna."[1] At last, on August 26 he made up his mind and instructed Berthier to prepare to move the army at Boulogne against Austria,[2] and on August 31 to Duroc he wrote: "The army is in full movement . . . I shall be ready on 27th September. I have given the Army of Italy to Masséna. Austria is very insolent, she is redoubling her preparations. My squadron has entered Cadiz. Keep this secret, it is for you alone. Collect all the maps you can of the Danube, the Main and Bohemia, and let me have the organization of the Austrian and Russian armies."[3] On September 2 he left Boulogne. Thus the Army of England became the Grand Army, and instead of crossing the Channel it set out to cross the Rhine.

It was related earlier that Nelson on August 3 was sailing northward to Ushant, off which, on August 15, when he had saluted Cornwallis's flag, he received a signal to proceed with the *Victory* to Portsmouth, where he cast anchor on August 18. In England he spent his time between London and Merton, and on September 2, news was brought by Captain Blackwood of the frigate *Euryalus* that Villeneuve had entered Cadiz and Nelson's brief holiday was cut short. On September 5 he sent his heavy baggage to Portsmouth, and on September 14 arrived there himself. The next day the *Victory*, accompanied by the *Euryalus*, set sail, and when he joined Collingwood on September 28, Nelson took over command of his fleet.

The following day was his forty-seventh birthday, and in a letter to some unknown friend he wrote: "The reception I met with on joining the Fleet caused the sweetest sensation of my life. The officers who came on board to welcome my return, forgot my rank as Commander-in-Chief in the enthusiasm with which they greeted me."[4] Nelson assembled his Captains and explained to them the plan of battle he had worked out when at Merton,[5] contained in what is usually called his "Secret Memorandum".

Before we turn to it, it is as well to glance at an earlier plan, which he had thought out on his way to the West Indies, because of the two it more clearly reveals the factor which, as a fighting admiral, differentiates Nelson from the admirals of his day.

The essence of the earlier memorandum is that in a "close and decisive battle"–always Nelson's aim–subordinates must not

[1] *Correspondance*, No. 9117, vol. XI, p. 117.
[2] *Ibid.*, No. 9137, vol. XI, p. 141.
[3] *Ibid.*, No. 9155, vol. XI, p. 157.
[4] *Dispatches and Letters*, vol. VII, pp. 66–67.
[5] *Ibid.*, vol. VII, p. 241.

wait for signals, but act on their own initiative, and to enable them to do so without risk of upsetting the battle, they must be fully acquainted with the commander-in-chief's "mode" of attack.[1] Nelson did not fight in order to carry out a plan, instead he planned in order to carry out a fight, and between the two there is a vast difference.

The novelty in this memorandum does not lie in the "modes" of attack, of which two are mentioned, for of necessity they vary according to circumstances, but in the liberty of action delegated to subordinates to carry them out. Nelson, as a subordinate, had displayed the highest initiative at the battle of St. Vincent, and he expected his captains to model themselves upon him. Unlike Napoleon, who seldom tolerated initiative on the part of his marshals, Nelson wanted his captains to be Nelsonically-minded. Coupled with his pugnacity, it was not only his own initiative but also the initiative of his subordinates, though the latter ran counter to the rigid naval discipline of the day, which made Nelson England's supreme fighting admiral.

The Secret Memorandum, first discussed with Admiral Sir Richard Keats, when Nelson was at Merton,[2] is based on the supposition that Nelson's fleet numbered 40 sail of the line and Villeneuve's 46, and that it is almost impossible to bring 40 ships into line of battle without much loss of time. Therefore, in order to save time, the fleet was to be organized into two lines of 16 sail each, and an "Advanced Squadron", or reserve line, of eight ships. Again, to save time, the order of sailing was to be the order of battle, and to make the most of opportunities, the two lines were to act independently. One was to be under Nelson and the other under Collingwood, who was to "have the entire direction of his line".

The "mode" of attack was that, while Collingwood attacked the 12 rear ships of the enemy's line, Nelson was to attack the enemy's centre in order to prevent it attacking Collingwood, and at the same time interpose his ships between the enemy's centre and van before the latter could wear about and come to the assistance of the enemy's rear. Meanwhile the Advanced Squadron was to cut in, two or three or four ships ahead of the enemy's centre, "so as to ensure getting at their Commander-in-Chief, on whom every effort must be made to capture", presumably because he was the directing organ and moral centre of

---

[1] *Dispatches and Lettters*, vol. VI, pp. 443–445.   [2] *Ibid.*, vol. VII, p. 241.

his fleet. "Something must be left to chance," writes Nelson, "nothing is sure in a Sea Fight beyond all others. Shot will carry away the masts and yards of friends as well as foes; but I look with confidence to a victory before the van of the enemy could succour their Rear, and then the British Fleet would most of them be ready to receive their twenty Sail of the Line, or to pursue them, should they endeavour to make off."[1]

Nelson's idea is reminiscent of Epaminondas's at Leuctra. In that battle the Theban right wing by threatening the Spartan left wing and centre held them to their ground while the Theban left wing destroyed the Spartan right wing. At Trafalgar, Nelson held back the centre and van of the Franco-Spanish fleet, not by threatening but by attacking, while Collingwood destroyed the enemy's left wing—his rear. Because the tactical idea was, in fact, an ancient one, it in no way detracts from the credit due to Frederick at Leuthen or to Nelson at Trafalgar. In war fundamental ideas are always reborn—they transmigrate from generation to generation.

Of the conference he had with his captains, Nelson wrote to Lady Hamilton: " . . . when I came to explain to them the '*Nelson Touch*', it was like an electric shock. Some shed tears, all approved—'It was new—it was singular—it was simple!'; and, from Admirals downwards, it was repeated—'It must succeed, if ever they will allow us to get at them! You are, my Lord surrounded by friends whom you inspire with confidence'."[2] On October 9 or 10 the Secret Memorandum was circulated in writing.

At Cadiz, Villeneuve found himself in worse straits than ever. His treasure-chest was empty; sea-stores, provisions, even handspikes were difficult to obtain, and besides being 2,000 men short of establishments, he had 1,731 sick. Equally bad, there was constant quarrelling between his French and Spanish officers and men. On September 2 he poured out his grievances to Decrès. Nevertheless, on September 24 he was able to report that he had shipped six months' supplies and was ready to sail.

Napoleon, all idea of invading England abandoned, had devised for Villeneuve—"*un misérable*", as he called him[3]—a new and fatal scheme. From St. Cloud, on September 14, he sent him the following instructions:

[1] For the Memorandum as originally written and subsequently amended see *Admiralty Committee Report* (Cd. 7120 of 1913), pp. 64–65.
[2] *Dispatches and Letters*, vol. VII, p. 60.
[3] *Correspondance*, No. 9174, vol. XI, pp. 176–177.

"Having resolved to make a powerful diversion by directing into the Mediterranean our naval forces concentrated at the port of Cadiz ... we would have you know that our intention is that ... you will seize the first opportunity of sailing with the Combined Fleet and proceeding into that sea.

"You will first make for Cartagena to join the Spanish squadron which is in that port.

"You will then proceed to Naples and disembark on some point of the coast the troops you carry on board to join the army under the orders of General St. Cyr. ...

"The fleet under your command will remain off the Neapolitan shores as long as you may judge necessary, in order to do the utmost harm to the enemy as well as intercept a convoy which they intend to send to Malta.

"After this expedition, the fleet will sail to Toulon to revictual and repair.

"Our intention is that wherever you meet the enemy in inferior force you will attack them without hesitation and obtain a decision against them.

"It will not escape you that the success of these operations depends essentially on the promptness of your leaving Cadiz."[1]

Two days later the Emperor sent instructions to Decrès to replace Villeneuve by Admiral Rosily;[2] but out of consideration for Villeneuve's feelings, Decrès did not communicate this to him. Rosily arrived in Madrid on October 10.

On October 1 Villeneuve began his final preparations, intending to put to sea on October 7, but the wind changed and for 10 days he was kept in port. On October 8 he held a council of war at which he explained to his captains how he proposed to fight the coming battle. He intended, he said, to divide his fleet of 33 sail of the line into two divisions, a *corps de bataille* of 21 ships, under his personal command, and a *corps de reserve* of 12 ships under Admiral Gravina, which would be stationed to windward of the former.[3] With extraordinary accuracy, he next outlined his enemy's probable tactics. "The British Fleet", he said, "will not be formed in a line of battle parallel with the

---

[1] *Correspondance*, No. 9210, vol. xi, p. 195.   [2] *Ibid.*, No. 9220, vol. xi, p. 204.
[3] On October 16 the final order of battle was decided upon. The *corps de bataille* was to consist of three squadrons, each of seven ships: 2nd Squadron (Van) under Vice-Admiral Alava, flagship the *Santa Ana*; 1st Squadron (Centre) under Villeneuve, flagship the *Bucentaure*, and 3rd Squadron (Rear) under Rear-Admiral Dumanoir, flagship the *Duguay Trouin*. *Corps de reserve*, Admiral Gravina, flagship the *Principe de Asturias*.

Combined Fleet ... Nelson ... will seek to break our line, envelop our rear, and overpower with groups of his ships as many of ours as he can isolate and cut off."[1] Of how best to meet this attack he said nothing, apparently because he knew that his captains were only capable of forming line ahead. All he added was, that if the Combined Fleet was to windward, it would bear down on the enemy and engage ship to ship; and if to leeward, it would form a close line ahead and await attack, each captain looking out for himself.

The French and Spanish ships were to be mingled, as Napoleon had ordered him to do. They comprised one four-decker, the *Santissima Trinadad* of 131 guns, then the largest ship afloat; three three-deckers (two of 112 guns and one of 100); six 80-gun ships; twenty-two 74's, one 64 and seven frigates and corvettes. Eighteen of the ships of the line were French and 15 Spanish. They mounted 2,626 broadside guns, exclusive of carronades, and carried 21,580 officers and men. The regiments embarked were drawn from the Cadiz garrison, and among them were the Regimento de Africa (formerly Tercio de Sicilia) and the Regimento de Soria (formerly Tercio de Soria) both of which had fought in the Spanish Armada.

The British fleet should also have numbered 33 sail of the line, but shortly after Nelson took over its command, Rear-Admiral Thomas Louis and his squadron of six of the line had been ordered away with a convoy bound for Malta; hence Nelson found himself with 27 of the line. Of these ships, seven were three-deckers—three of 100 guns and four of 98—and 20 were two-deckers—one of 80 guns, sixteen of 74 and three of 64. Also he had four frigates, a schooner, and a cutter. The fleet was manned by 16,820 officers and men, and, exclusive of carronades, it mounted 2,148 broadside guns.

Because of the absence of Louis's squadron, Nelson dropped his original idea of forming his fleet into three lines, and substituted two, a van or weather column of 12 of the line, under his personal command in the *Victory*, and a rear or lee column of 15 under Collingwood in the *Royal Sovereign*. This was his first deviation from the Secret Memorandum, and as others followed, which since have given rise to much pedantic explanation, it is as well to set down what we believe Nelson had in mind when Trafalgar was fought.

His aim was to gain a decisive victory, to capture or sink

[1] Quoted from *The Enemy at Trafalgar*, Edward Fraser (1906), p. 54.

26

20 of the enemy ships; for, as he said when he was dying: "I bargained for twenty."[1] He realized, as the Secret Memorandum infers, that the old engagements of line ahead in parallel order were generally indecisive because they were so slow and prohibited the concentration of strength against weakness. He looked upon them, we may assume, as contests between two one-armed boxers, and, so far as he was concerned, he intended to fight with two arms. His fleet was to have a left punch and a right punch. The weather column was to protect the right, and the lee column was to knock out the enemy's rear. He selected the rear in preference to the van, because, in order to support the rear, the enemy's van would have to wear about, which would take a long time, whereas had he selected the van, in order to support it, all the enemy's rear would need to have done was to continue on its course.

To give both his punches the maximum of momentum, he did not adhere either to a formal line ahead or abreast. Instead, he substituted for them two groups of ships in order of sailing— that is, coveys and not lines of ships. Of this there can be no doubt, for when he explained his tactics to Admiral Keats at Merton, he said: "It will bring forward a pell-mell Battle, and that is what I want."[2] In support of this, in a letter written two months after Trafalgar, Collingwood says: "Lord Nelson determined to substitute for an exact order an impetuous attack in two distinct divisions. . . . It was executed well, and succeeded admirably; probably its novelty was favourable to us, for the Enemy looked for a time when we should form something like a line."[3] This is what Nelson had foreseen, for at Merton he suddenly turned to Keats and said: "But I'll tell you what *I* think of it. I think it will surprise and confound the Enemy. They won't know what I am about."[4] Surprise was to add to concentration as much as superior gunnery.

The differences between the Secret Memorandum and what occurred are those between idea in mind and idea in action. The tactical aim remained the same, but the means of attaining it varied according to the moment. No pedantry can explain this.

---

[1] *Dispatches and Letters*, vol. VII, p. 251.
[2] *Ibid.*, vol. VII, p. 241.   [3] *Ibid.*, vol. VII, p. 242.
[4] *Ibid.*, vol. VII, p. 241. Lieutenant B. Clement of the *Tonnant* said: "We went down in no order but every Man to take his Bird." (Quoted from Newbolt's *The Year of Trafalgar*, p. 101.)

On October 15 Villeneuve received news from Bayonne that
Admiral Rosily was on his way to Cadiz, and as he knew that
Rosily had not been at sea for over 12 years, he concluded that
he was on an administrative mission. Next, news came from
Madrid that Rosily was to supersede him, and feeling that his
honour was impugned, Villeneuve decided to slip out of Cadiz
before his arrival. On October 17 this intention was fortified when
he learnt–very belatedly–that Admiral Louis's squadron had
been detached from Nelson's fleet. The wind was favourable, and
after a conference with Gravina he ordered the captain of his
flagship to signal "Prepare to sail." No sooner had he done so
than the wind dropped and soon died away altogether.

The next day Nelson wrote in his diary: "Fine weather, wind
Easterly; the Combined Fleet cannot have finer weather to put
to sea."[1] Nevertheless, Villeneuve hesitated, and it was not
until 6 a.m. on October 19 that he signalled his fleet to "Make
sail and proceed."

Two and a half hours later, when lying some 50 miles to the
west-south-west of Cadiz, Nelson received the signal from one
of his inshore frigates that the enemy was coming out of port. At
once he signalled "General chase",[2] as his aim was to cut off the
Combined Fleet from the Mediterranean. Next came the signal,
"Enemy's fleet at sea." This was incorrect, for on October 19
only Admiral Magnon's division got out of Cadiz, and it was not
until noon October 20 that Villeneuve had the whole of his fleet
under way.

By daylight on October 20, when close to the Strait of Gibraltar,
Nelson had seen nothing of his enemy and wore his fleet and made
to the north-west. At 7 a.m. Villeneuve's fleet was sighted, and
at noon was reported to be sailing westward. An hour later the
Victory hove to, and Collingwood came on board to receive final
instructions. Later Nelson learnt that Villeneuve had changed
direction to the south-east, and before sunset he ordered his
frigates to keep sight of the enemy during the night.[3]

At daybreak on Monday, October 21, when the British fleet
was still in no precise order or formation, the enemy in close line
of battle, bearing east by south, was seen 10 to 12 miles away. As
it was still too dark for flags to be distinguished, it was not until
6.10 a.m. that Nelson made the general signal "Form the order

---

[1] *Dispatches and Letters*, vol. VII, p. 126.
[2] *Ibid.*, vol. VII, p. 133.   [3] *Ibid.*, vol. VII, p. 136.

of sailing in two columns," which brought Collingwood's column to the starboard of the van. Immediately after, the signal "Bear up and sail large of E.N.E. course" was run up, and at 6.22 a.m. was followed by "Prepare for battle."[1]

Villeneuve was headed for the Strait of Gibraltar, and when he realized that because of the lightness of the wind it would not be possible to avoid battle, at 8 a.m. he signalled his whole fleet to go about, so that he should have Cadiz harbour under the lee as a refuge for crippled ships. It was an unfortunate last minute change of plan, for not only did it look like a retreat, and therefore was discouraging for his crews, but the wearing about took over two hours and resulted in the formation of a confused line of battle. It was crowded in some places and had gaps in others, its centre sagged to leeward, and the whole line formed an irregular crescent about three miles long. The wearing placed Gravina's squadron behind, instead of to windward of, the line, and Dumanoir's squadron became the van. Once the change of direction was completed, the Combined Fleet moved slowly ahead on a northerly course at the rate of a knot or a little more.

When the Combined Fleet went about, the British in two columns, or rather, groups of ships—the Weather Line under Nelson and the Lee Line under Collingwood—slowly bore down on it under full sail. The wind, from the north-west, was very slight; there was a heavy westwardly ground swell, and the rate of advance, at first estimated at three knots, soon fell to one and a half. As Nelson did not shorten sail, there was no possibility of the two columns forming regular line. Further, like two school-boys, he and Collingwood set out to race each other; the former steered, not for the van of the enemy centre, as originally decided, but for the centre of his van, while Collingwood steered for the van of his rear.

The reasons for Nelson's change of direction would appear to have been that when he saw the enemy wear about, he jumped to the conclusion that Villeneuve was trying to escape to Cadiz. This is borne out by the fact that, shortly before 11.40 a.m.—the time the message was received—he telegraphed Collingwood: "I intend to pass [push] or go through [the end of] the enemy's line to prevent them [from] getting into Cadiz."[2] In other words, to head off their van. Next, at 11.48 a.m., he sent out his famous

---

[1] For signals see *Admiralty Committee* (Cd. 7120) Appx. V.
[2] *Ibid.*, see Signals, p. 102.

general signal: "England expects that every man will do his duty."[1]

When this signal was sent, Collingwood closed in on the enemy's rear, for already at 11.30 a.m. Villeneuve had run up the signal "Open fire!", to be followed at 12.15 p.m. by another: "*Tout capitaine qui n'est pas dans le feu n'est pas à son poste.*"[2] At 11.45 a.m. the first shot was fired by the *Fougueux*, next astern of the *Santa Ana*, and was aimed at the *Royal Sovereign*, then rather more than a quarter of a mile away. Thereon in unison the ships of the two fleets hoisted their colours, "the drums and fifes playing and the soldiers presenting arms" in the French and Spanish ships.[3]

The battle then opened, and may be divided into three distinct actions: Collingwood's attack, Nelson's attack, and Dumanoir's abortive counter-attack. We will follow these in turn.

When the *Fougueux* opened fire on the *Royal Sovereign*, Collingwood's division sailed on the larboard line of bearing,[4] at approximately two cables (about one quarter mile) interval between ships. It was, therefore, in a diagonal, though irregular, line abreast formation which, because of the curvature of the enemy's line, brought it almost parallel with it.

For five to 10 minutes after the *Fougueux* opened the battle, the *Royal Sovereign* held on her course while the *Santa Ana* discharged a broadside at her. Then she closed in and broke through the enemy's line, astern of the *Santa Ana* and ahead of the *Fougueux*, or, as Collingwood says in his dispatch, "about the twelvth [ship] from the rear."[5] When she passed under the stern of the *Santa Ana*, she raked her with a double-shotted broadside, which did her tremendous damage. Next, she fired her starboard broadside at the *Fougueux*, and then sheered up on the starboard quarter of the *Santa Ana* and engaged her at the gun-muzzle.

Collingwood soon found himself surrounded by enemy ships, and within 40 minutes of opening fire the *Royal Sovereign* was

---

[1] *Admiralty Committee* (Cd. 7120) Appx. V, p. 102.

[2] *The Enemy at Trafalgar*, Edward Fraser, p. 114.

[3] *Ibid.*, p. 114. The plan of the battle on page 396 is based on Desbrière's. No two plans, whether contemporary or subsequent, agree, and not a few are fantastic.

[4] "He [Collingwood] changed the formation of his division from an irregular line ahead to an irregular line of bearing. In his *Journal* he writes: 'made the signal for the Lee Division to form the larboard line of bearing and make more sail'. " (*Admiralty Committee*, Cd. 7120, p. xii.)

[5] Collingwood's *Correspondence*, p. 120. Actually it was the fifteenth, because three allied ships were to leeward of the enemy's line and were unseen by Collingwood or mistaken as frigates. (*Admiralty Committee*, Cd. 7120, p. xiii.)

reduced to an unmanageable hulk, and a little after was taken
in tow by the *Euryalus*. At 2.20 p.m. the *Santa Ana*, then com-

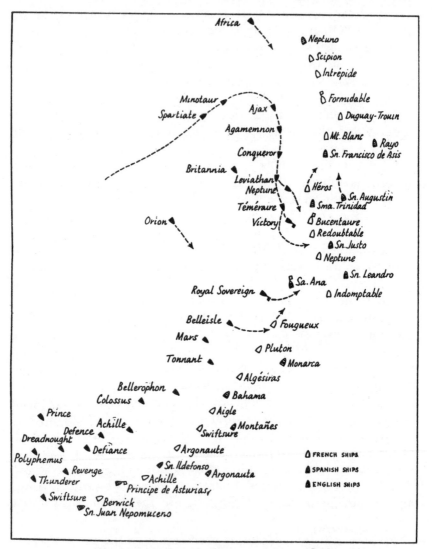

23. BATTLE OF TRAFALGAR, 1805

pletely dismasted and with 104 of her crew killed and 236
wounded, struck her colours, and Captain Blackwood boarded
her and brought back with him to the *Euryalus*, Admiral de
Alava, mortally wounded.

Eight minutes after the *Royal Sovereign* engaged, the *Belleisle* came into action and cut through the enemy's line, astern of the *Fougueux*. Like the *Royal Sovereign* she was at once engaged by several of the enemy's ships, and for a time was unable to fire a gun because of the wreckage of her masts. Nevertheless she kept her ensign flying by nailing it to the stump of her mizen-mast. Later she was relieved by the *Polyphemus*, *Defiance*, and *Swiftsure*.

A quarter of an hour after the *Belleisle*, the *Mars* came into action, and after her, in rapid succession, the *Tonnant*, *Bellerophon*, *Colossus*, and *Achille*. Ship after ship came up, and as they broke through the enemy's line in all parts, each closed with the first enemy ship encountered and engaged her yard-arm to yard-arm. Next, each ship sailed on to leave the pounding of the enemy to ships astern. This resulted in a continuous concentration of fire on the enemy's ships.

Of Collingwood's rear ships, the *Dreadnought* did not engage until an hour after the *Royal Sovereign*, and a quarter of an hour later was followed by the *Defiance*. The *Defence* did not come up until an hour later still, and the last ship of Collingwood's division to enter the battle was the *Prince*, which did not engage until 3 p.m.

When the action of the Lee Column ended, Collingwood's victory was complete. Of the 15 French and Spanish ships he fought, 10 were captured, one–the *Achille*–blew up, and only the *Principe de Asturias*, carrying Admiral Gravina, mortally wounded, the *Algésiras*, *Montañés*, and *Aigle* escaped.

Twenty-five minutes after Collingwood's division engaged, Nelson's went into action. Unlike the former, it retained its irregular line ahead formation, and according to the "Private Log" of Thomas Atkinson, Master of the *Victory*, it was "still standing for the enemy's van."[1] Also in accordance with Atkinson, "At 11.50 [actually 12.10 p.m.] the Enemy began to fire upon us, and at 4 minutes past 12 [12.24 p.m.] open'd our Larboard guns at Enemy's van."[2]

From north to south, the five leading ships of Dumanoir's van were probably the *Neptuno*, *Scipion*, *Intrépide*, *Formidable*, and *Duguay-Trouin*, and, according to Dumanoir, Nelson's leading three three-deckers moved on the centre of his van, and

---

[1] Though no time is given for this entry, according to *Admiralty Committee*, Cd. 7120, pp. xiii and 63, it refers to the period immediately preceding Collingwood's attack.
[2] *Ibid.*, p. 63.

at 12.15 p.m. became engaged with it, and after a cannonade of 40 minutes wore to starboard.[1]

As far as Nelson's three leading ships were concerned, the cannonade was far shorter than Dumanoir states, for immediately after the *Formidable* opened fire, the *Victory* and *Téméraire* wore to starboard, which is mentioned by Lieutenant Conor of the *Héros*, who adds: "Whereas the other ships of the same column kept on the port tack threatening our van."[2] Nelson searched for Villeneuve's flagship, for his overmastering desire was to lay his own ship alongside her. "Although," says James, "every glass on board the *Victory* was out in requisition to discover the flag of the French Commander-in-Chief, all the answers to Nelson's repeated questions on the subject ended in disappointment."[3] The *Victory*, therefore, made for the *Santissima Trinadad* to seek Villeneuve[4] in the largest ship of the enemy's fleet, and, according to the Master of the *Spartiate*, at 12.57 p.m., when the *Victory* bore down on her, to her stern was seen the French Admiral's flag "at the Fore" of a French two-decker (the *Bucentaure*).[5] Raked by the enemy's guns, the *Victory* shortly after passed under the stern of the *Bucentaure* and fired her forecastle carronade–a 68-pdr.–loaded with a round shot and a keg of 500 musket balls, as well as a double-shotted broadside, into her cabin windows, and did her tremendous damage. Next, as the *Neptune* (Br.) and *Conqueror* closed on the *Bucentaure*, the *Victory* put her helm hard to starboard and ran alongside the *Redoubtable*, commanded by Captain Lucas.

At once their rigging became entangled and the two ships were locked together. Both crews then prepared to board, but the Frenchmen were prevented from doing so by the *Victory's* starboard carronade and a broadside from the *Téméraire*, which cut them down in scores. About an hour later, the two ships still interlocked, Nelson was hit by a musket shot aimed from the mizen-top of the *Redoubtable* while he was walking with Captain Hardy on the quarter-deck. The ball struck the epaulette on his left shoulder, penetrated his chest and lodged in his spine. He fell on his face, and when raised from the deck gasped: "They

---

[1] Desbrière's *Trafalgar*, p. 150. Captain Berrenger of the *Scipion* in his "Journal" states that the *Formidable* opened fire at 12.35 p.m.; he also mentions that the head of Nelson's column moved on the centre of the van (*ibid.*, pp. 155–156).

[2] *Ibid.*, p. 168.

[3] *Naval History of Great Britain, 1793–1820* (1886), vol. III, p. 32.

[4] Actually, Nelson believed that Decrès was in command.

[5] *Admiralty Committee* (Cd. 7120), "Log of *Spartiate*", p. 53.

have done for me at last, Hardy . . . my backbone is shot through."[1] He was carried down to the cockpit of his ship, and at 4.30 p.m., in the knowledge that the battle had been won, died.

When the *Victory* engaged the *Redoubtable*, the *Téméraire* steered clear of the former and opened fire on the *Santissima Trinadad*, and next on the *Neptuno* (Fr.) and *Redoubtable*. Shortly after, the *Fougueux*, which after engaging the *Belleisle* crossed the space between the allied rear and centre, bore up to assist the *Redoubtable*, and was grappled by the *Téméraire*. The latter poured into her a full broadside at point-blank range, and immediately caught her fore-rigging and lashed it to her spare anchor. No sooner were the two ships interlocked, than the *Redoubtable's* "main yard and all the wreck fell on the *Téméraire's* poop, which entirely encumbered the after part of the ship". Then, "with a prize lashed on each side and the greater part of her batteries out of action", the *Téméraire* raked the *Santissima Trinadad* for half an hour with her foremost guns.[2]

Ten minutes after the *Victory* broke the enemy's line the *Neptune* (Br.), fired her first broadside into the *Bucentaure*, passed on to the *Santissima Trinadad*, and an hour and a half later, with 254 of her crew killed and 173 wounded, the great four-decker struck her colours. The scene in her, as described by Midshipman Badcock of the *Neptune* (Br.) gives some idea of what early nineteenth century naval fighting was like. "I was on board our prize the Trinidada," he writes, "getting the prisoners out of her. She had between three and four hundred killed and wounded, her beams were covered with Blood, Brains and pieces of Flesh, and the after part of her Decks with wounded, some without legs and some without an Arm."[3]

The *Britannia* next came up, followed by the *Leviathan* and *Conqueror*. The last two came alongside the *Bucentaure*, and at 2.5 p.m. Villeneuve hauled down his flag. The scene on board her is described by Captain Atcherley of the *Conqueror's* marines. "The dead, thrown back as they fell," he writes, "lay along the middle of the decks in heaps, and the shot passing through these, had frightfully mangled the bodies. . . . More than four hundred had been killed and wounded, of whom an extraordinary proportion had lost their heads."[4]

[1] *Dispatches and Letters*, vol. VII, p. 244.
[2] Quoted by Newbolt in *The Year of Trafalgar*, p. 140.
[3] Quoted by Fraser in *The Enemy at Trafalgar*, p. 272.   [4] *Ibid.*, p. 142.

The *Ajax* came into action 40 minutes after the *Victory*, and the *Agamemnon* later still. The *Africa*, a sixty-four and the smallest battleship on either side, had an unusual adventure. During the night of October 20–21 she lost sight of the fleet, and at daybreak was several miles north of it. Directly she discovered its position, she headed for the *Victory*, and a few minutes after the *Royal Sovereign* opened the battle she came within range of the enemy's van. According to her log,[1] at 11.40 she engaged the headmost ship and then ran down the whole of the van and fired at each ship she passed, after which she bore down to assist the *Neptune* (Br.), engaged the *Santissima Trinadad*, and later fought the *Intrépide*.

The *Orion* also played a singular part, for when he saw the enemy ships of the central division more than outmatched by Nelson's, Codrington, her Captain, sailed south to help the *Royal Sovereign*. Next she passed the *Mars*, *Colossus*, and *Tonnant* and then turned north toward the *Victory*. The last two ships of Nelson's division, the *Minotaur* and *Spartiate*, had not engaged when Villeneuve struck.

We come now to Dumanoir's counter-attack, if so it can be called.

At 12.30 p.m., when Nelson bore down on the allied centre, Villeneuve made a general signal to instruct all his ships not then engaged to get into action. To this Dumanoir made no response and Villeneuve took no notice of it. Half an hour later, Dumanoir still bore north and, in consequence, opened up a gap between the van and the centre. Instead of acting on his own initiative, he asked for orders. Nevertheless, Villeneuve sent no reply until 1.50 p.m., when he ordered him to come to the help of the hardly pressed centre.

The wind was very light and Dumanoir had considerable difficulty in going about, and instead of keeping his squadron intact, so that he might hit with full force, he split it into halves.[2] So slow was his manœuvre that it was not until between 3.15 p.m. and 3.30 p.m. that Captain Hardy in the *Victory* noticed that the nearer five of Dumanoir's 10 ships were drawing southward. At once he signalled Nelson's division to make ready to receive them.

---

[1] *Admiralty Committee* (Cd. 7120), p. 6.
[2] Or what seems more probable is that the first five ships which got about sailed on in advance of the other five, or that half the ships disobeyed orders.

The five ships Hardy saw were the *Héros, Intrépide, San Augustin, San Francisco de Asis,* and the *Rayo,* and soon after he had signalled they bore down on the *Conqueror, Ajax, Agamemnon,* and *Leviathan.* A little later the *San Augustin* struck; the *Héros* broke away and made for Cadiz, and the *San Francisco de Asis* and *Rayo* escaped, the one to be wrecked and the other to surrender to the *Leviathan* on October 23. The *Intrépide,* commanded by Captain Infernet, was gallantly attacked by the *Africa,* and then engaged by the *Ajax, Agamemnon,* and *Orion,* and after a tremendous fight surrendered to Captain Codrington.

In the meantime Dumanoir's remaining five ships got about: the *Formidable* and two others had to be towed round by boats. They hauled to wind and came down the line, the *Formidable* in the lead, followed by the *Scipion, Mont Blanc, Duguay-Trouin,* and *Neptuno.* They opened fire on the *Conqueror,* and then passed on and poured their broadsides into the *Victory, Téméraire,* and *Royal Sovereign.* Soon, the *Minotaur* and *Spartiate*—not yet engaged—closed in on them, and cut out the *Neptuno,* which later struck her colours. In the meantime Dumanoir's remaining four ships disappeared to the south, and on November 4 were rounded up and captured by Sir Richard Strachan's squadron.

When, at 4.30 p.m., the battle neared its end, of Villeneuve's 33 ships, nine were on their way to Cadiz; four were flying for the Strait; and of the remaining 20, 17 were totally disabled, 13 in possession of prize crews, and one in flames. As night closed in, the storm which had threatened since the morning broke and blew for four days, and during it many of the damaged ships foundered, including all the British prizes except four. Yet, throughout the battle and storm not a single British ship was lost.

The casualties in life and limb are variously given. According to the *London Gazette* of November 27 and December 3, 1805, the British lost 449 killed and 1,214 wounded. The French and Spanish losses, given by Fraser,[1] are as follows: French, 3,373 killed and drowned and 1,155 wounded; Spanish, 1,022 killed, 1,383 wounded and between 3,000 and 4,000 prisoners. As the French loss in prisoners must, at least, have equalled the Spanish, the total allied losses probably amounted to some 14,000 officers and men. Though a high figure, it was nevertheless small when compared with the losses suffered at the battle of Lepanto.

[1] *The Enemy at Trafalgar,* p. 374.

On both sides the battle was remarkable for its gallantry, the French and Spaniards, though from the first at a heavy discount, fought as stubbornly as the British. Also, when compared with present-day battles and their aftermath, it was remarkable for the chivalry displayed during it and the courtesies meted out after it. For instance, when a prisoner of war, Captain Lucas of the *Redoubtable* was lionized by London society; Captain Infernet of the *Intrépide* paid his compliments to Mrs. Codrington, wife of his captor; and Admiral Villeneuve and Captain Magendie were given permission to attend Nelson's funeral. In spite of the Revolution, war was still the occupation of gentlemen, as the following incident illustrates.

After the battle, Captain Codrington of the *Orion*, in a letter written home gives the following description of life at Gibraltar: "Whilst the Governor of Algeziras (old Gibraltar) is dining with the Governor of the Rock (new Gibraltar), or whilst the Governor of the Rock, with one-half of the officers and many of the private soldiers, is at a horserace in Spain, the Algeziras gunboats are making an attack on a convoy coming in with supplies for the garrison. I was actually, when last here, standing with one of General Fox's aides-de-camp in the Spanish lines observing the Spanish fire at the 'Beagle' sloop of war which happened to come within range of their shot, with the same apparent indifference as would have attended me on seeing them attack a nation hostile to England."[1]

Collingwood's dispatch on the battle was sent home on October 27 in the schooner *Pickle*, commanded by Lieutenant Lapenotière. On November 4, Lapenotière arrived at Falmouth, from where within half an hour he posted to London. He changed horses 19 times on the way and drew up at the gates of the Admiralty at one o'clock on the morning of November 6.[2] A few minutes later he was met by the First Secretary, and the first words he said to him were: "Sir, we have gained a great victory, but we have lost Lord Nelson!"

Nelson's pre-eminence as an admiral largely rests on his break away from the theory of the parallel order of battle, and though he was by no means the first to do so, more clearly than his

---

[1] Quoted by Fraser in *The Enemy at Trafalgar*, pp. 381–382.
[2] Napoleon received the news of Villeneuve's defeat when at Znaym on his march to Austerlitz (*Correspondance*, No. 9507, vol. XI, p. 424). A few months later he paid Nelson the remarkable tribute by directing that "*La France compte que chacun fera son devoir*," should be painted prominently on board every man-of-war.

predecessors he saw that it was based on a purely defensive idea. According to this, a line of battleships could bring so great a superiority of fire to bear against an enemy approaching in line ahead formation, that it was suicidal for him to attempt to do so. But Nelson saw the flaw in this theory, he saw that because of the restricted range and inaccuracy of the guns of his day, the danger of being blasted out of action by a wall of converging fire was limited to the last few hundred yards of the approach. Further, he saw that once contact was gained, superiority of gunnery, far more than numerical superiority or linear formation, was the decisive factor. It was in this respect that the British crews completely outclassed their antagonists, for not only was their fire more accurate, but twice as rapid, and, therefore, more than twice as destructive, as a comparison between the casualties proves. In part, at least, this was because the French and Spaniards had been unable to practise during the blockade, whereas the English could.

When Collingwood commanded the *Dreadnought*, we read that the sailors were so constantly practised "in the exercise of the great guns . . . that few ships companies could equal them in rapidity and precision of firing." And that Collingwood was accustomed to tell them that, "if they could fire three well-directed broadsides in five minutes, no vessel could resist them; and from constant practice, they were enabled to do so in three minutes and a half."[1] What this meant was that, once closely engaged, a ship which could fire twice as rapidly as her opponent was in fire power equivalent to two ships. Therefore, the tactical problem, as Nelson saw it, was to close with the enemy *coûte qu'il coûte*. It was what, to-day, in journalese would be described as "*blitzkrieg* at sea".

In every respect, Trafalgar was a memorable battle and its influence upon history was profound. It shattered for ever Napoleon's dream of an invasion of England. It brought to an end the 100 years struggle between her and France for the lordship of the seas. It gave England the Empire of the Oceans, which was to endure for over a century and make possible the *Pax Britannica*. More immediately important, it showed the world of 1805 that Napoleon was not invincible, and it compelled him to fall back on his Continental System, to seek to establish a universal empire which economically would strangle England,

[1] Collingwood's *Correspondence*, pp. 124–125.

and which instead ended by his own political strangulation. Without Trafalgar there could have been no Peninsular War, and without the Peninsular War it is hard to believe that there would ever have been a Waterloo. Therefore Mr. H. W. Wilson does not exaggerate the importance of this greatest of naval victories when he writes: "Trafalgar was the really decisive battle of the Napoleonic War."[1]

[1] *Cambridge Modern History*, vol. ix, p. 243.

The continental struggle between France and England

Phase I

Though Napoleon's direct attack on England had to be abandoned, the indirect approach remained open, and as the solution of the former hinged on the command of the Channel, that of the latter depended on the command of the coastal ports of Europe. Could he gain control of them, England's foreign trade, the source of her financial power, would be strangled, and without a heavy purse it would be impossible for the English Government to subsidize their continental allies, without whom they could not hope to defeat Napoleon. Therefore, as Mr. Paul H. Emden states in his *Money-Power of Europe in the Nineteenth and Twentieth Centuries*, "The strongest of all the powers allied against Napoleon was the power of British finance."

This was apparent to Charles James Fox and Count Andréossy, the French Ambassador in London. The former, when he urged the evacuation of Malta, had said: "Must we then, to gratify the ambition of our merchants, spill torrents of British blood? . . . I had rather blood should flow for romantic expeditions like that of Alexander, than for the gross cupidity of a few merchants greedy after gold." And the latter, a few weeks before the outbreak of war in 1803, had written to the First Consul to say: "In a country where the main interest is business, and where the merchant class is so prosperous, the Government had to appeal to the merchants for extraordinary funds, and they have the right to insist that their interests should be considered in the policy which is adopted." Because the French embargo on English goods was the cause of an ever-growing trade depression in England, the one thing the merchant-bankers wanted was freer trade.

But Napoleon would not consider this, because he held that free trade would make France become the debtor of England. His economic ideas were those of Rousseau, according to whom, "the perfect state was one that sufficed for all its needs and could do without foreign trade." It was in pursuance of this autarchic idea that, in the autumn of 1793, the Convention had excluded all British goods not carried in French bottoms, and three years later, in order to stimulate French industry, had prohibited the import of all enemy manufactured products.

Not only did Napoleon refuse to modify this policy, but he began to elaborate it into his Continental System – his trade war with England. Two months before the rupture of the Peace of Amiens, in a conversation with Lord Whitworth he had said: "Do you suppose that I want to risk my power and renown in a desperate struggle? If I have a war with Austria, I shall contrive to find my way to Vienna. If I have a war with you, I shall take from you every ally on the Continent; I shall cut you off from all access to it, from the Baltic to the Gulf of Taranto. You will blockade us, but I will blockade you in my turn."

This was not an idle boast, for when the war was renewed in May, one of Napoleon's first acts was to seize Hanover, in order to control the mouth of the Elbe, and to send St. Cyr with a body of troops to occupy Taranto and other ports in the kingdom of Naples, in order to gain a footing in the central Mediterranean. Nevertheless, as we have seen, it was not until August, 1805, when the threat of the Third Coalition matured, that he was compelled to abandon his attempt to invade England.

The forces then assembled against him, though immense, were scattered: 84,000 men in Italy under the Archduke Charles; 34,000 in Tyrol; 58,000 on the Danube under the Archduke Ferdinand and General Mack; and 55,000 Russians under Kutusov, who were expected on the Inn by the middle of October, three weeks before it was reckoned that Napoleon could reach the Danube. Kutusov was to be followed by two armies, one under Bennigsen and the other under Buxhöwden, and in addition 50,000 Russians, Swedes, Danes, Hanoverians and English were to recover Hanover and invade Holland, and 50,000 Russians, English, and Neapolitans were to drive the French out of southern Italy.

Though the allies had observed great secrecy, Napoleon was well aware of their intentions, and in order to prevent Prussia from joining the Coalition, he offered Hanover to Frederick William, and on August 24 sent General Duroc to Berlin with powers to sign a treaty. At the same time he informed Frederick William that he had warned Austria that if her troops were not withdrawn into their peacetime cantonments, he would enter Bavaria at the head of more than 100,000 men.

On September 3 this ultimatum was rejected, and when, on September 8, the Austrian troops crossed the Inn, the Elector of Bavaria withdrew his army to Würzburg and Bamberg to await the French. On September 26 the Grand Army began to cross the Rhine, from where at top speed it set out to fall upon the Austrians, under Ferdinand and Mack, before Kutusov could come to their support.

On October 6 Napoleon reached the Danube, and, on October 17, he repeated his Marengo manœuvre and forced the capitulation of Mack and 15,000 men at Ulm, and at the same time rounded up 13,000 more under General Werneck.

While Frederick William considered whether to accept the offer of Hanover, Bernadotte's corps violated Prussian neutrality by passing through Ansbach. The Tsar was then pressing the king to join the Coalition, and Bernadotte's affront so annoyed the latter that, on November 3, he received Alexander at Potsdam, and in return for Russian support pledged himself to declare war on France if Napoleon did not withdraw from Austrian territory within four weeks of the arrival of his envoy, Count Haugwitz, who, as he was against Prussia's entry into the war, delayed his departure until November 14.

The day before this, Napoleon had entered Vienna, from where, because Francis refused to make peace, he decided to press on. On November 19 Kutusov and Buxhöwden united their armies at Olmütz, and the next day, at the head of 40,000 men—rapidly reinforced to 65,000—Napoleon entered Brunn. His position there was critical, for not only was the bulk of his army still scattered, but at Olmütz, 40 miles to his north-east, he was faced by 82,500 Russians and Austrians, under Alexander and Francis, and by the middle of December their forces would be doubled by the arrival of the armies of Bennigsen and the Archduke Charles. Further, by then 180,000 Prussians might also be in the field.

Fortunately for Napoleon, supplies at Olmütz were short, and in spite of Kutusov's protests, Alexander decided not to wait for Bennigsen, but to attack Napoleon before he could gather in the rest of his army. The result was the battle of Austerlitz, fought on December 2. Lured by Napoleon into a false position, the allied army was cut in two and its left wing annihilated. The allies lost 12,000 men killed and wounded, 15,000 captured, and 180 guns. The French casualties were 6,800. Austerlitz was Napoleon's masterpiece, and of all his battles

27

the one of which he was most proud. Nothing comparable with it had been seen since the days of Frederick.

Morally the allied disaster was so overwhelming that Francis immediately asked for an armistice, which was agreed to on condition that the Russians would withdraw from Austria and the Prussians would be prohibited from entering it. At first, Napoleon was willing to leave Austria intact, if Russia would agree to exclude British goods from the Continent; but as Alexander would not consider this, negotiations were opened and a treaty of peace signed at Pressburg on December 26. For Austria its terms were shattering: Venetia, Istria and Dalmatia were ceded to Napoleon as King of Italy; the Emperor renounced his feudal rights over Bavaria, Würtemberg and Baden; Bavaria and Würtemberg became kingdoms; Augsburg, Nuremberg, Brixen, Trent, Tyrol and Vorarlberg were ceded to Bavaria; Austria received nothing, except Salzburg and Berchtesgaden, and had to pay an indemnity of 40,000,000 francs.

Throughout, Talleyrand was opposed to these severe measures, for he held that Austria should be maintained as a great power because she was "a needful bulwark against the barbarians, the Russians". But Napoleon would not listen to this, for Austria – virtually a landlocked country – was of little importance in his Continental System, and as his aim was to exclude British shipping from the Baltic, his eyes were fixed on Prussia and Russia.

His problem became this. How was he to separate Prussia and Russia and isolate England? Though he had no exact knowledge of the Potsdam compact, his suspicions had been aroused, and in order to gain time, when Haugwitz arrived he had had him kept waiting until after Austerlitz was fought. Then, at Vienna, on December 15, Haugwitz, instead of presenting Frederick William's ultimatum, was compelled to agree to a treaty whereby France and Prussia would enter upon an offensive and defensive alliance, the latter to cede Cleves, Neuchâtel and Ansbach in return for Hanover. Two months later this treaty was superseded by the Treaty of Paris, according to which the alliance was to be wholly defensive, and Prussia was forthwith to annex Hanover and close the mouths of the Ems, Weser and Elbe to England. This treaty was ratified at Berlin on February 24, 1806, and immediately after this England seized 300 Prussian ships and blockaded the Prussian North Sea ports.

Napoleon considered these were satisfactory terms with Prussia, and next set out to establish his dynasty and consolidate his gains. In March he made his brother Joseph, King of the Two Sicilies and his brother Louis, King of Holland. Further, he created a new aristocracy, Berthier, Talleyrand and Bernadotte became princes of Neuchâtel, Benevento, and Ponte Corvo, and other honours were showered on his leading generals. At the same time he dissolved the Empire and founded a league of states to be known as the Confederation of the Rhine. Its more important members were Bavaria, Würtemberg, Baden, Berg and Nassau. Later it was enlarged to include all the territory west of the Elbe and Bohemia (less Baireuth and Hanover) as well as Mecklenburg, east of the Elbe.

The treaty constituting this confederation was ratified at Saint Cloud on July 19 and Napoleon was declared its Protector. On August 1, the Emperor Francis II absolved all electors and princes from allegiance to him, and declared himself Francis I, Emperor of Austria. Thus, after a thousand years, the Holy Roman Empire came to an end.

While Napoleon formed this confederation he also intrigued with Russia and England. From the one he wanted Alexander's recognition of Joseph as King of The two Sicilies, in order to strengthen his position in the Mediterranean and obtain Sicily, then in English hands. To the other he offered to restore Hanover, Prussia to receive compensation in its stead.

The news of these proposals leaked out, and on August 9 Frederick William, under pressure by the Prussian war party—headed by Queen Louise and Prince Louis Ferdinand—ordered a partial mobilization of his army. Next, an incident occurred which detonated war.

In July a Nuremberg bookseller named Palm had circulated an anonymous pamphlet entitled *Germany in her Deep Humiliation.* Napoleon took offence and ordered his arrest, and on August 25 Palm was court-martialled, condemned, and shot. This high-handed act so profoundly stirred Prussia that, on September 6, the king reopened the North Sea ports to British ships. On September 21 the king left Berlin for his army headquarters at Naumburg, and five days later sent an ultimatum to Paris demanding the withdrawal by October 8 of the French armies still cantoned in southern Germany to beyond the Rhine.

CHAPTER 13

The Battles of Jena and Auerstädt, 1806

Among the world's great autocrats and conquerors, Napoleon has but two compeers–Alexander the Great and Augustus. The warrior spirit of the one he shared to the full, as he did the administrative abilities of the other, and though he failed to establish a universal empire, he so completely uprooted the last vestiges of the medieval conception of commonwealth that ever since his day the nations have groped after his dream of unification.

He was fortunate in the year of his birth,[1] for in 1769 a thousand years of European civilization was about to dissolve. The Industrial Revolution was in its cradle; that year James Watt in England patented his steam engine and in France Cugnot drove the first steam-propelled wagon; the American Revolution was simmering, and out of it was to boil the greater revolution in France. A new age was in precipitation, and it awaited a man of genius to seize hold of it and mould it to his will.

Possibly, in 1779, Guibert sensed this when he wrote: "A man will arise, perhaps hitherto lost in the obscurity of the crowd; a man who has not made his name either by speech or writing. A man who has meditated silently; a man, in fact, who has perhaps ignored his own talent and has been only conscious of his power while actually exercising it, one who has studied very little. This man will seize hold of opinions, or circumstances, of chance, and will say to the great theoretician what the practical architect said to the orator: 'All that my rival tells you, I will carry out'."[2]

Such a man was Napoleon, the supreme egoist and architect, the entirely isolated and self-centred man who relied on himself alone and centralized everything. Méneval says of him: "He took not only the initiative in thought, but also attended personally to the detail of every piece of business . . . his genius, superhuman in its activity, carried him away: he felt he possessed the *means* and the *time* to manage everything . . . in reality it was he who did everything."[3]

---

[1] At Ajaccio on August 15, 1769.
[2] *Oeuvres de Guibert* (1803), vol. IV, p. 74.
[3] *Mémoires pour servir a l'histoire de Napoléon Ier* (1894), vol. III, p. 50.

Caulaincourt, the most illuminating of his memorialists, says much the same, but even more penetratingly: "He spared neither pain, care nor trouble to arrive at his end," he writes, "and this applied as much to little things as to great. He was, one may say, totally given over to his object. He always applied all his means, all his faculties, all his attention to the action or discussion of the moment. Into everything he put passion. Hence the enormous advantage he had over his adversaries, for few people are entirely absorbed by one thought or one action at one moment."[1]

This was his secret both as a statesman and a general, and to appreciate the importance of the campaign that culminated in the dual battle of Jena-Auerstädt–the first of a series which was to end with Waterloo–it is necessary to make sure of his political aims.

The first was to make France orderly, prosperous, and above all glorious, and the second–its derivative induced by the opposition of England–to establish a universal empire in the form of a league of kingdoms under the aegis of France. The foundations of the first were laid when he became First Consul and during the Peace of Amiens, when, in order to consolidate his gains, undertake great public works, initiate great legal and social reforms, and stimulate science, art and industry–in short, close the abyss created by the Revolution–he earnestly wished for peace. Yet, as we have seen, the clash between his protectionist policy and England's need for free trading made peace impossible.

The struggle which then began was not between right and wrong, but between two survival values that arose out of the early Industrial Revolution. To remain prosperous and powerful, England had to export her manufactured goods, and to become prosperous and powerful France had to protect her infant industries. As Metternich said: "Everyone knew that England could not give way on this question [the maritime problem], which to her was a matter of life and death."[2] And it was because Napoleon realized this that he relied on his Continental System to strangle England's trade and thereby undermine her credit, without which she could not continue to raise enemies against him.[3]

"The power of the English", he said, ". . . rests only upon the

---

[1] *Memoirs of General de Caulaincourt Duke of Vicenza*, trans. Hamish Miles (1935), vol. I, p. 93.

[2] *Ibid.*, vol. II, p. 10.   [3] *Ibid.*, vol. I, p. 521.

monopoly they exercise over other nations, and can be maintained only by that. Why should they alone reap the benefits which millions of others could reap as well?"[1] And again: "The good of that Europe which seems to envelop her with goodwill counts for nothing with the merchants of London. They would sacrifice every state in Europe, even the whole world, to further one of their speculations. If their debt were not so large they might be more reasonable. It is the necessity of paying this, of maintaining their credit, that drives them on. . . ."[2]

In his struggle with England, he saw "the basic solution of all the questions" that were "agitating the world and even individuals".[3] Therefore, as he told Caulaincourt, England was his sole enemy: "He was working against the English alone," and "since their trade had ramifications everywhere he had to pursue them everywhere".[4] It was out of this pursuit that the idea of a universal empire arose. From a weapon with which to destroy England, the Continental System became an instrument whereby a new world conception could be realized: a veritable Alexandrian vision–Europe united in Concord.

With France as the power-house of his Imperial Continental System, his "grand objects" were: To re-establish the kingdom of Poland as a barrier against "the barbarians of the north". To liberate Spain from superstition and give her a constitution. To form independent republics in England and Ireland. To declare Hungary independent and to liberate Greece. To subdivide Austria, break up Prussia, gain control of Egypt, cut a canal through the isthmus of Suez, partition Turkey, drive the Turks out of Europe and bridle the "Muscovite barbarians"–the one great threat to Europe.[5] In brief, and as Professor Fisher says: to "accomplish a world analogous to that of Leo I and Charles Martel, of Charlemagne and Otto I, who saved the fabric of Greek and Latin civilization from destruction at barbarian hands."[6]

When at St. Helena, he informed the world through Las Casas that his aim had been to unite the great European nations, hitherto "divided and parcelled out by revolution and policy", into one great confederation bound together by "a unity of codes,

---

[1] *Memoirs of General de Caulaincourt Duke of Vicenza*, trans. Hamish Miles (1935), vol. I, p. 438.
[2] *Ibid.*, vol. I, p. 424.   [3] *Ibid.*, vol. I, p. 529.   [4] *Ibid.*, vol. I, p. 429.
[5] "I considered", said Napoleon, "that the barbarians of the North were already too strong, and probably in the course of time would overwhelm all Europe, as I now think they will." (Quoted in *The Cambridge Modern History*, vol. IX, p. 765.)
[6] *Ibid.*, vol. IX, p. 765.

principles, opinions, feelings and interests". At its head, under the aegis of his empire, he had dreamed of establishing a central assembly, modelled on "the American Congress or the Amphictyons of Greece", to watch over the common weal of "the great European family". Though this dream had been dissipated by his ruin, "sooner or later", he said, it would be realized "by the very force of events. The impulse has been given, and I do not think that since my fall and the destruction of my system, any grand equilibrium can possibly be established in Europe, except by the concentration and confederation of the principal nations. The sovereign who, in the first great conflict, shall sincerely embrace the cause of the people, will find himself at the head of all Europe, and may attempt whatever he pleases."[1]

Whatever we may think of this grandiose scheme, it was anathema to England, because she could not hope to survive as the dominant maritime power were Europe federated. Therefore, the clash between her and France was to the death: a struggle in which the generalship of Napoleon was pitted against coalition after coalition. In this his first and greatest asset was, that unity of command was assured him because he was at one and the same time autocrat and commander-in-chief of France. His second was that his insistence upon glory and not terror as the driving force of war fitted the spirit of the Revolution and endowed newborn French nationalism with an heroic faith in its destiny. His third was his genius, and of him, as a general, one of the best portraits has been left to us by General Foy.

"With his passions, and in spite of his errors," he writes, "Napoleon is . . . the greatest warrior of modern times. He carried into battle a stoical courage, a profoundly calculated tenacity, a mind fertile in sudden inspirations, which by unhoped-for resources disconcerted the plans of the enemy. . . . Napoleon possessed in an eminent degree the faculties requisite for the profession of arms; temperate and robust, watching and sleeping at pleasure, appearing unawares where he was least suspected, he did not disregard the details to which important results are sometimes attached. . . . He carried with him into battle a cool and impassible courage; never was a mind so deeply meditative, more fertile in rapid and sudden illuminations."[2]

---

[1] *Journal of the Private Life and Conversations of the Emperor Napoleon at Saint Helena*, Count de Las Casas (1824), vol. IV, Pt. vii, pp. 134–139.
[2] *History of the War in the Peninsula under Napoleon* (1827), vol. I, pp. 110–112.

As a general in the field, his activity was phenomenal. During an advance, he generally remained in rear, but when near the enemy he went forward. He saw everything for himself, for as he said: "A general who has to see things through other people's eyes will never be able to command an army as it should be commanded."[1] Time to him was everything, day for seeing and night for working. "The Emperor", writes Caulaincourt, "always arose at eleven o'clock at night, or at the latest, midnight, when the first dispatches from the army corps came to hand," and after working on them for two or three hours, he issued his orders for the next day.[2] He adopted this method so that the troops should receive orders based on the latest information by reveille. "The loss of time," he once said, "was irreparable in war; reasons alleged for it were always bad, for operations only fail through delays."[3]

As a soldier, Napoleon was doubly fortunate in the year of his birth, for between the end of the Seven Years War and the close of the century, French military organization and, consequently, tactics, were profoundly modified. Though the flintlock was little improved,[4] as we have seen, gunnery was greatly advanced by Gribeauval, and Napoleon was pre-eminently a gunner, who as a youth had studied Benjamin Robins's *New Principles of Gunnery*.[5] In the battles of this period, because of the short effective range of the musket, field artillery could gallop within 350 yards of an enemy and batter his battalions to pieces. Yet, strange to say, the full meaning of this was not completely grasped until late in the Napoleonic Wars.

In 1759, thanks to the experiments of Maurice de Saxe, Marshal de Broglie had introduced the divisional system, which, in 1804, became the basis of Napoleon's army corps—completely self-contained bodies of troops. But the greatest innovation of all was the introduction of conscription, which was finally established by General Jourdan and the Council of Five Hundred in 1798. Though there was nothing new in the idea of compulsory enlistment, under the Directory it was placed on a national footing,

---

[1] *Napoleon in Exile*, B. E. O'Meara (1822), vol. II, p. 377.
[2] Caulaincourt's *Memoirs*, vol. I, p. 599.
[3] *Correspondance*, No. 9997, vol. XII, p. 203.
[4] "With the French flint-musket one misfire might be expected in every nine shots, and one hang-fire in every eighteen. The flint had to be changed every thirty shots." ("Mémoire sur le fusil de guerre", *Oeuvres du Marquis de Chambray*, 1840, vol. v, p. 292.)
[5] See *The Growth of Napoleon*, Norwood Young (1910), p. 166.

every able-bodied male citizen from his twentieth to his twenty-fifth year was by law compelled to serve his country. Not only did conscription render Napoleon's policy of conquest possible, but it radically changed infantry tactics by increasing the average intelligence of the ranks.

Although the training of the French conscripts was negligible, their tactics were individual and elastic, based on man and musket more than on mechanical volley firing. The skirmishers were, Sir Robert Wilson said, "as sharp-sighted as ferrets and as active as squirrels".[1] And the Duke of York's aide-de-damp wrote: "No mobbed fox was ever more put to it to make his escape than we were, being at times nearly surrounded."[2] Of the conscripts, a Prussian officer said: "In the woods, when the soldiers break rank and have no drill movements to carry out, but only to fire under the cover of the trees, they are not only equal but superior to us. Our men, accustomed to fight shoulder to shoulder in the open field, found it difficult to adopt that seeming disorder which was yet necessary if they were not to be targets for the enemy."[3] Equally important, the French soldier lived on the enemy's country, and therefore the French trains needed but a fraction of the animals to be found in the Prussian supply columns. This added enormously to French mobility.

Such was the army Napoleon inherited–active, mobile, intelligent and fanatical, but in discipline weak. "He was ready to grant," says Caulaincourt of the Emperor, "that his system of warfare could not admit of severe discipline, as the troops were forced to subsist without any proper rationing."[4] Nevertheless, it was a dangerous principle to work on; after Eylau there were 60,000 maurauders,[5] and before Wagram thousands of men were drunk.[6] Yet in moral force the spirit of the army remained firm. It was an army inspired rather than trained, and quite unlike the Austrian, Prussian, Russian, and British. Of the last, Gourgaud informs us: "His Majesty finds English discipline rather too rigorous; it doesn't leave sufficient to one's honour."[7]

As a strategist, Napoleon has never been excelled, and in this

---

[1] *Life of Sir Robert Wilson*, H. Randolph (1862), vol. I, p. 86.
[2] *Journals and Correspondence of Sir Henry Calvert* (1853), p. 220.
[3] Quoted from *Les Guerres de la Révolution*, A. Chuquet, vol. II, p. 96.
[4] *Memoirs*, vol. I, pp. 592–593.
[5] *Souvenirs militaires de 1804 à 1814*, Duc de Fézensac (1863), p. 163. ·
[6] *Etude sur l'armée révolutionaire*, Pierre Cantal, p. 118.
[7] *The St. Helena Journal of General Baron Gourgaud*, edit. Norman Edwards (1932), p. 51.

the age in which he lived also favoured him, for roads were being improved by men such as Thésaguet in France and McAdam in England. Increasing prosperity demanded better roads, and, when built, the regions they traversed grew more prosperous and in consequence enabled armies more easily to live on the land they marched through, and therefore to dispense with the old magazine and depôt system that dated from the days of Marlborough and Turenne.

Napoleon, himself a master road-builder, fully appreciated this change and largely founded his strategy upon it. In the Ulm campaign his men said: "The Emperor has discovered a new way of waging war, he makes use of our legs instead of our bayonets."[1] Or, as he himself expressed it: "In the art of war, as in mechanics, time is the grand element between weight and force."[2]

If rapidity be looked upon as the soul of strategy, planning may be likened to its body. Napoleon always had a plan–a strategical, but not necessarily a tactical one–worked out on what he intended to do, and which bore little or no reference to the enemy's probable intentions. In 1807 he said to Soult: "One should never try to guess what the enemy can do. My intention is always the same,"[3] which meant that his initiative was to be given free play. His plan was invariably offensive. "It is an axiom in strategy," he wrote as early as 1793 in *Le Souper de Beaucaire*, "that he who remains behind his entrenchments is beaten; experience and theory are at one on this point." Also in St. Helena he said: "In short, I think like Frederick, one must always be the first to attack."[4]

His tactics were as offensive as his strategy. In all his many campaigns there is only one example of a wholly defensive battle, that of Leipzig on October 18, 1813. One reason for this was his aggressive temperament, another, as he said: "The change from a defensive to an offensive attitude is one of the most delicate of operations."

As a tactician he possessed a wonderful eye. "The fate of a battle," he said, "is a question of a single moment, a single thought . . . the decisive moment arrives, the moral spark is

---

[1] *Correspondance*, No. 9392, vol. xi, p. 336. In the Jena Campaign a day's march in the Prussian army seldom exceeded 12½ to 15 miles. In the French, some of the marches were phenomenal. On one occasion Lannes's corps covered 65 miles in 50 hours, and on another Bernadotte's corps marched 75 miles in 69 hours. Much of Napoleon's success was due to rapid marching.

[2] *Ibid.*, No. 14707, vol. xviii, p. 218.   [3] *Ibid.*, No. 11939, vol. xiv, p. 380.

[4] *Journal de Sainte Hélène*, Genl. G. Gourgaud (1899), vol. ii, p. 336.

kindled, and the smallest reserve force settles the matter."[1] And again: "There is a moment in engagements when the least manœuvre is decisive and gives victory; it is the one drop of water which makes the vessel run over."[2] As a tactician, Caulaincourt writes of him: "Even when chasing the enemy helter-skelter before him, or in the heat of one of his greatest victories, no matter how weary the Emperor was he always had an eye for ground that could be held in the event of a reverse. In this respect he had an astonishing memory for localities. The topography of a country seemed to be modelled in relief in his head. Never did a man combine such a memory with a more creative genius. He seemed to extract men, horses and guns from the very bowels of the earth."[3]

As his wars lengthened, his infantry deteriorated, and though he said that "it is not sufficient that the soldier should shoot, he must shoot well,"[4] he was not much interested in musketry. For instance, in 1800, on the day before crossing the St. Bernard, we find Berthier ordering that all conscripts should fire a few rounds in order "that they may know which eye to aim with and how to load their muskets."[5] Not until 1811 do we hear of Napoleon approving target practice for recruits, and then only if inferior powder were fired.[6] The truth is that throughout he relied more upon gun than musket. "In siege warfare, as in the open field," he said, "it is the gun which plays the chief part; it has effected a complete revolution . . . it is with artillery that war is made."[7] The following figures support this statement: At the battle of Malplaquet the French fired 11,000 cannon shot; at Wagram—71,000; and at Leipzig—175,000; and whereas, under Henry IV, the French cannon numbered 400, under Louis XIV—7,192; under Louis XV—8,683; under Louis XVI—10,007; in 1815 under Napoleon they numbered 27,976.[8]

Strange as it may seem, though Napoleon was a gunner by training, he only slowly evolved his artillery tactics. As late as the battles of Eylau (1807), Friedland (1807) and Aspern (1809) his infantry dashed themselves to pieces against the enemy guns.

[1] *Journal*, Las Casas, vol. I, Pt. ii, p. 6.
[2] *Correspondance*, "Précis des guerres de J. César," vol. XXXII, p. 104.
[3] *Memoirs*, vol. I, p. 600.   [4] *Correspondance*, No. 11390, vol. XIV, p. 35.
[5] *Le Maréchal Berthier*, V. B. Derrécagaix (1904), vol. I, p. 399.
[6] *Correspondance*, No. 18219, vol. XXII, p. 540.
[7] *Ibid.*, "Diplomatie-Guerre", vol. XXX, p. 447.
[8] *Des Changemens survenus dans l'art de la guerre 1700–1815*, Marquis de Chambray (1830), p. 23.

After Aspern he massed his artillery against the point of attack, and at Wagram (1809) and Borodino (1812) he blew great holes in his enemy's lines and columns. "In every case where the services of the artillery, because of the want of this weapon, failed, Napoleon was obliged to have recourse to a series of successive efforts, which cost him infinite forces and time."[1] At Waterloo, the want of howitzers, or their misuse, resulted in his inability to dislodge Wellington from his covered position, and went far to lose him the battle. In his place, Frederick would probably have routed Wellington in a couple of hours.[2] Nevertheless, Napoleon was a very great gunner.

Had Frederick William joined the 1805 coalition against France, he would have been well placed to challenge this re- markable soldier. But to do so in 1806 was the height of folly, for then Austria lay crushed; the Russians had withdrawn beyond the Vistula; England, exasperated by Prussia's occupation of Hanover, had, with Sweden, declared war on her; and Naples, as a power, no longer existed. Further, where in 1805 Napoleon had had to march from Boulogne to the Danube, now his vic- torious army lay cantoned between Frankfort and the Inn, within a fortnight's advance of the Prussian frontier. Under these circum- stances to challenge Napoleon was suicidal.

Why then did Frederick William do so? Because everything in Prussia looked back to the epic days of Frederick. Living on the fat of the Frederician tradition and inhibited by the memory of Rossbach, he, his generals and his people, were blind to the fact that, since 1792, the character of war had changed. It was no longer a duel of honour between ambitious kings, but instead a clash between impassioned nations, in which fanaticism, individual initiative and mobility were to count for more than unthinking obedience, collective action and meticulous manœuvrings.

Tactically the Prussian Army was a museum specimen, organized and ordered to fight ranged battles on level ground–phalanx against phalanx–in which a volley fired by a carefully dressed line of men at 40 to 50 paces from the enemy was the decisive factor. This close-range fighting could be terribly destructive.

[1] *The Influence of Firearms upon Tactics*, Anonymous (English edit., 1876), p. 83.
[2] Regarding the use of howitzers, it is interesting to note that, on August 10, 1813, Frederick William III issued the following instructions: "Should the enemy be on the reverse side of heights or otherwise protected, it will be advantageous to unite the howitzers, as a large number of shells thrown upon one spot produces a fearful effect, which for the most part it would be impossible to withstand." (*Ibid.*, p. 83).

At Crefeld, in 1758, the first Prussian volley is said to have stretched out 75 per cent. of the enemy, and the first volley of the British Guards at Fontenoy (1745) brought down 690 Frenchmen. Though in this type of fighting the French, who lacked the Prussian drill, were inferior to the Prussians, as *tirailleurs* they were vastly superior, and under cover of swarms of skirmishers, their mobile battalion columns were more than a match for the Prussian line. Besides, the Prussians only raised their light infantry on the outbreak of war; they were undisciplined and generally worthless. Added to this, since Frederick's day, his magnificent corps of cavalry had been split up, as had most of his reserve artillery. But victualling by magazines remained, and with it the enormous Prussian supply trains which prohibited rapid movement.

In addition to these defects, the Prussian high command was a hydra. It was divided between the Duke of Brunswick, aged 71, Prince Hohenlohe, and General von Rüchel, with General von Scharnhorst as principal staff officer to the first, and Colonel Massenbach to the second. To allay friction between these five, Frederick William took over nominal command, and as he had no knowledge of war, he selected Field-Marshal von Möllendorf, aged 82, as his confidential adviser, and took with him into the field the *Ober Kriegs Collegium*, or Military Cabinet, which comprised the inspectors-general and heads of departments. As each of the commanders and advisers could submit to the king a plan of his own, the result was perpetual Babel.

According to a confidential report, received by Napoleon on September 28, Brunswick, who feared to compromise his reputation, was opposed to war, and was timid, slow and irresolute. Möllendorf was also afraid to risk his good name; Hohenlohe and Rüchel were eager for war; Kalkreuth was sick and incapable; and Prince Louis Ferdinand—"The Prussian Alcibiades"—a nephew of Frederick the Great, though a man of spirit, was a debauchee who nightly was carried to bed drunk.[1] The only general of note not mentioned in this report was Blücher, aged 64, who possessed great energy and resolution and was a bold cavalry leader.

When mobilization was ordered on August 9, the Prussian Army numbered rather more than 200,000 men, and after deducting reserves and garrisons, the residue was divided into three field armies: the first under Brunswick (70,000), the second under

[1] *La Manœuvre d'Iéna*, General H. Bonal (1904), p. 127.

Hohenlohe (50,000), and the third under Rüchel and Blücher (30,000). In order to augment these forces, Saxony and Hesse-Cassel were approached with a view to alliances, and the former reluctantly agreed to support Prussia. On September 13, Hohenlohe proceeded to Dresden and incorporated into his army two Saxon divisions, each 10,000 strong. Thus his army became numerically as important as Brunswick's, and he himself still more truculent.

Not until September 25, when Brunswick's army lay between Leipzig and Naumburg, Hohenlohe's at Dresden, and Rüchel's at Mühlhausen, with Blücher at Göttingen, was the first of a number of councils of war assembled to consider a plan of operations. Brunswick assumed that Napoleon–of all men–would stand on the defensive, and proposed to move by Erfurt on Würzburg, in order to seize the communications of the French Army and surprise its cantonments, which he believed to be between Würzburg and Amberg. Hohenlohe violently objected to this and instead proposed a move across the Frankenwald on Bamberg. Already, in preparation for this, he had pushed Tauenzien's Saxon division out to Hof as an advanced guard. Lengthy discussions followed, one council of war gave birth to another, until at length Frederick William intervened and decided to adopt both plans. As this pleased no one, another plan was suggested, and when it met with the fate of the previous ones, on October 5, it was agreed to send out Captain Müffling to discover where the French communications lay. When he returned to report that they were uncovered, Brunswick ordered a cavalry reconnaissance on Hildburghausen and Neustädt, supported by the Duke of Weimar's division, which was to occupy Meiningen. At the same time he called in Rüchel and decided to remain stationary on the northern slopes of the Thuringian Forest, with his own army about Erfurt, Rüchel's at Eisenach, and Hohenlohe's at Blankenhain. Because this put an end to an offensive towards Würzburg, Hohenlohe was elated, and at once ordered his two Saxon divisions to Mittel-Pöllnitz (near Auma) and Prince Louis Ferdinand to move from Jena to Saalfeld to cover a general move on the Saale, which, incidentally, had not been decided upon.

It is difficult to fathom what all this meant, and we can only agree with Scharnhorst who, on October 7–the day before Frederick William's ultimatum of September 26 was due to expire –in despair wrote: "What we ought to do I know right well, what we *shall* do only the gods know."[1] What Frederick William should have done was to retire behind the Elbe–the Rhine of Prussia– and to have disputed its passage until joined by the Russians. This is what Dumouriez (now a refugee in England) had urged again and again; he pointed out that the surest way to fight Napoleon was by opposing to him distance, climate, and the difficulties of supply. It was also what Napoleon expected, and he was much surprised when he learnt that the Prussians were concentrating west of the Elbe.[2] Though their forward movement delivered them into his hands, he nevertheless prepared for a long campaign, for he suspected the formation of yet another hostile coalition, in which Austria might join and re-enter the field and England strike at his rear. His first problem was, therefore, to secure his base–France–and his second to defeat the Prussians before the Russians could support them.

When, in August, Frederick William set out to mobilize, the Grand Army, under command of Berthier at Munich, was distributed as follows: Ist Corps (20,000) under Bernadotte, at Ansbach and Nuremberg; IIIrd Corps (27,000) under Davout, near Nördlingen; IVth Corps (32,000) under Soult, on the Inn; Vth Corps (22,000) under Lefebvre (later Lannes), on the Lower Main; VIth Corps (20,000) under Ney, on the Iller and Upper Danube; and VIIth Corps (17,000) under Augereau, around Frankfort. The Imperial Guard and *Corps d'Élite* (16,400) under Oudinot (later Lefebvre), were in Paris, and the Cavalry Corps (28,000) was commanded by Murat. But Napoleon did not issue his first instructions until September 5.

That day he wrote to Berthier and ordered him to have all roads from Bamberg toward Berlin reconnoitred and to be prepared to assemble the IVth, VIth and VIIth Corps at Bamberg within eight days of receiving march orders.[3] Four days later he wrote to him again to inform him that in the event of war, his line of operations would be Strasburg-Mannheim-Mayence-Würzberg,[4] and on the following day that "The Movements of the Prussians continue to be most extraordinary. They want to be taught a lesson. My horses leave to-morrow and the Guard in a few days. . . If the news continues to indicate that the Prussians have lost their heads, I shall go straight to Würzburg or to Bam-

[1] *Der Krieg von 1806–1807*, Lettow-Vorbeck (1892), p. 163.
[2] *Correspondance*, No. 10881, vol. XIII, p. 263.
[3] *Correspondance*, No. 10744, vol. XII, p. 150
[4] *Ibid.*, No. 10756, vol. XIII, p. 160.

berg."[1] This shows, as General Bonal points out,[2] that Napoleon had not as yet decided on his ultimate direction. Should the Prussians move into the valley of the lower Main, he would make Würzburg his centre of assembly, but should they continue to hesitate, it would be Bamberg, whence by way of Dresden or Leipzig he could march on Berlin and force his enemy to fall back and accept battle. On September 13 he wrote again to Berthier to say that, should the Prussians enter Saxony, Würzburg would be the centre of assembly.[3] He changed his mind on September 15 and finally decided that it was to be Bamberg.[4] On September 18 he learnt that the Prussians had entered Saxony on September 13, accepted it as a declaration of war, and at eleven o'clock that night issued orders for the Imperial Guard to move by post chaises from Paris to Mayence.[5] Also he wrote a long letter to his step-son, Prince Eugène, in command of the Army of Italy, to caution him to watch Austria.[6]

Napoleon seemingly had received reassuring news about Austria, and on September 18 and 19, he dictated 102 letters, dispatches and orders to his Minister of War–General Clarke. The most important was "The General Dispositions for the Assembly of the Grand Army"–the basic document of the Jena campaign. According to this, the Grand Army was to occupy the following positions:

> IIIrd Corps (Davout) Bamberg on October 3.
> VIIth Corps (Augereau) Frankfort on October 2.
> Vth Corps (Lefebvre) Köningshofen on October 3.
> IVth Corps (Soult) Amberg on October 4.
> Ist Corps (Bernadotte) Nuremberg on October 2.
> VIth Corps (Ney) Ansbach on October 2.
> Park and Baggage Column at Würzburg on October 3.
> Field Headquarters at Bamberg October 3.

This order was of great length and detail;[7] it was dispatched on September 20 and received in Munich on September 24.

On September 19, Napoleon also dictated a letter to his brother

---

[1] *Correspondance*, No. 10757, vol. XIII, p. 162.   [2] *La Manœuvre d'Iéna*, p. 41.
[3] *Correspondance*, No. 10773, vol. XIII, p. 177.   [4] *Ibid.*, 10787, vol. XIII, p. 188.
[5] *Ibid.*, No. 10801, vol. XIII, p. 210. For details of this remarkable move see Bonal, p. 63, and Thiers's *History of the Consulate, etc.*, vol. vii, p. 20.
[6] *Ibid.*, No. 10809, vol. XIII, p. 204. Consisting of Masséna's corps in N. Italy (70,000) and Marmont's in Dalmatia (12,000).
[7] See Bonal, chap. v, and *Correspondance*, 10818, vol. XIII, p. 217. To have dictated it was a prodigious effort.

Louis, King of Holland, in which he said: "As my intention is that you will not attack, I wish you to open the campaign by threatening the enemy",[1] in order to draw him northwards. Next day he wrote to him again, advising him in his gazette to exaggerate the number of his troops at Wesel. "I wish these troops", he wrote, "to be on the road at the beginning of October, because your operation is a feint to attract the attention of the enemy while I manœuvre to turn him."[2]

On the same day he formed a new corps at Frankfort, the VIIIth, under Mortier, to cooperate with Louis in holding the Rhine.

With his base now fully secured, on the night of September 24–25, accompanied by the Empress and Talleyrand, Napoleon set out from Paris for Mayence, and arrived there on September 28. The following day he heard from Berthier that on September 27 the Prussians were still about Eisenach, Meiningen and Hildburghausen, and that, therefore, there was ample time for the army to cross into Saxony without serious interference. This was exactly what he wanted to know, and on September 29 he instructed Berthier to order Bernadotte to occupy the Saxon defiles and Lefebvre to watch the Fulda Road; for should the enemy attempt to cut his communications, it would be by way of Fulda on Würzburg or Mayence.

Next, he sent a long dispatch to the King of Holland in which he revealed his plan of campaign. It is divided into four "Notes", and in the first one he wrote:

"My intention is to concentrate all my forces on my extreme right, leaving the area between the Rhine and Bamberg entirely unheld, so that I may unite approximately 200,000 men on the same battlefield. Should the enemy push forces between Mayence and Bamberg, it will not worry me, because my line of communications is based on Forcheim, a small fortress, and thence on Würzburg. . . . The nature of the events which may take place is incalculable, because the enemy, who supposes that my left is on the Rhine and my right on Bohemia, and believes that my line of operations is parallel to my battle front, may see great advantage in turning my left, and in that case, I can throw him into the Rhine. . . . By 10th or 12th October, the VIIth Corps will arrive at Mayence, about 18,000–20,000 strong. Its instructions will be,

---

[1] *Correspondance*, No. 10815, vol. XIII, p. 213.
[2] *Ibid.*, No. 10845, vol. XIII, p. 239.

not to let itself be cut off from the Rhine; to make incursions as far as Frankfort, and in case of necessity to retire behind the Rhine and contact the right of your troops."

The second "Note" begins: "The observations in my first note are all of a precautionary nature. My first marches menace the heart of the Prussian monarchy, and the deployment of my forces will be so imposing and rapid, that it is probable that the whole army of Westphalia will retire to Magdeburg, and all will combine by forced marches for the defence of the capital [Berlin]. Then, but only then, it will be necessary for you to throw out an advanced guard and take possession of the Mark, Münster, Osnabrück and East Frisia. . . . For the first part of the war you are only a corps of observation, that is to say until the enemy has been thrown into the Elbe. I only count on your corps as a means of diversion to amuse the enemy up to the 12th October, which is the date on which my plans will be unmasked. . . . Finally, in case of a serious event, such as the loss of a great battle, while I make good my retreat to the Danube, you can defend Wesel and Mayence with your army and the VIIIth Corps, which latter is under no circumstances to withdraw from Mayence and will at the same time hinder the enemy crossing the Rhine and pillaging my estates."

The third and fourth "Notes" develop the two previous ones, and the latter contains this remarkable passage: "The least check to you will cause me anxiety; my measures may thereby be disconcerted, and such an event might leave the whole of the north of my Empire without a head. On the other hand, whatever may happen to me, as long as I know that you are behind the Rhine, I can act with greater freedom; even should some great misfortune overtake me, I shall beat my enemies if I have only 50,000 men left, because free to manœuvre, independent of all lines of operations and tranquil as to the most important points of my Empire, I shall always have resources and means."[1]

The whole of this long letter was based on one of Napoleon's most important maxims: "The whole art of war consists in a well reasoned and extremely circumspect defensive, followed by rapid and audacious attack."[2]

On October 1 Napoleon left Mayence and late the following day arrived at Würzburg. There he took over effective command

---

[1] *Correspondance*, No. 10920, vol. XIII, pp. 292–296.
[2] *Ibid.*, No. 10558, vol. XIII, p. 10.

from Berthier, and on October 3 issued orders for the Ist and IIIrd Corps to advance to Kronach; the IVth and VIth to Forcheim; the VIIth to Würzburg; and the Vth to Schweinfurt. On October 5 Marshal Lannes took over command of the Vth Corps from Lefebvre, and on that day the Emperor sent Soult the following letter, one of the most instructive of the whole campaign, for in it he outlined his grand tactics:

"I have caused Würzburg, Forcheim and Kronach to be armed and provisioned, and I propose to debouch into Saxony with my whole army in three columns. You are at the head of the right column with the corps of Marshal Ney half a day's march behind you, and 10,000 Bavarians another day's march behind him, which makes in all over 50,000 men. Marshal Bernadotte leads the centre column, behind him follows Davout's corps, and the greater part of the Reserve Cavalry, which makes about 70,000 men. He marches by Kronach, Lobenstein and Schleiz. The Vth Corps is at the head of the left column, followed by the VIIth, and the two march by Coburg, Gräfenthal and Saalfeld. This makes another 40,000 men. The day you arrive at Hof, the whole will have reached positions on the same alignment. I shall march with the centre.

"With this immense superiority of force united in so narrow a space, you will feel that I am determined to leave nothing to chance, and can attack the enemy wherever he chooses to stand with nearly double his force. . . .

"If the enemy opposes you with forces not exceeding 30,000 men, you should concert with Marshal Ney and attack him. . . . On reaching Hof, your first care should be to open communications between Lobenstein, Ebersdorf and Schleiz, on that day [October 10] I shall be at Ebersdorf. . . .

"From the news which has come in up to to-day it appears that if the enemy makes any movement, it will be against my left, as the bulk of his forces seems to be about Erfurt.

"I cannot recommend you too earnestly to correspond with me frequently, and keep me fully informed of all you learn from the direction of Dresden.

"You may imagine that it will be a fine thing to move around this place [Dresden] in a battalion square (*bataillon carré*) of 200,000 men. Still, all that demands a little art and certain events."[1]

---

[1] *Correspondance*, No. 10941, vol. XIII, pp. 309–310.

What exactly did Napoleon mean by *"bataillon carré"*? A defensive time and space distribution which, irrespective of the position of the enemy or the direction of his approach, would permit Napoleon to fix him with part of his army offensively, while another part was free to manœuvre against one of his flanks or rear, and a third part remained in reserve.

Thus, in the present case, should the Prussians move against the French left or communications, then the Vth Corps, supported by the VIIth, operating as a general advanced guard, would fix and hold them until the Ist and IIIrd Corps, acting as a *masse de manœuvre*, struck them in flank, while the IVth and VIth Corps remained in reserve. On the contrary, should the Prussians move against the French front, then the Ist Corps, supported by the IIIrd, would become the general advanced guard, and either the Vth and VIIth or IVth and VIth the *masse de manœuvre*.

On the evening of October 7, the Grand Army was disposed as follows: on the right Soult's IVth Corps at Baireuth, with Ney's VIth Corps a march in rear; in the centre Bernadotte's Ist Corps and the bulk of the Reserve Cavalry under Murat were about Kronach, with Davout's IIIrd Corps and the Guard following up; and on the left Lannes's Vth Corps was approaching Coburg, followed by Augereau's VIIth Corps.

On October 8 the Saxon frontier was crossed and Murat's light cavalry made for Lobenstein and Saalburg and drove the Prussian vedettes before them. The following day Bernadotte's leading troops came up with Tauenzien's Saxon division at Schleiz and drove it back in disorder on Mittel-Pöllnitz, where Hohenlohe's main body lay. To support Tauenzien, at first Hohenlohe ordered a general advance across the Saale; next he cancelled it, but too late to enable Prince Louis Ferdinand to withdraw from Saalfeld, where on October 10 he encountered the head of Lannes's corps and was routed and killed. When the news of his defeat and death was received at Jena, the troops there were swept by panic and consternation spread to Weimar.

That evening, when at Schleiz, Napoleon received news from Soult that on the previous evening the enemy had evacuated Plauen and was falling back on Gera. At once he added as a postscript to a letter he had just dictated for him: "The information which you give me . . . allows no further doubt that Gera is the point of union of the enemy's army. I doubt, however, whether he can unite before I can."[1] This postscript was followed by a second letter to Soult saying: "In Gera matters will be cleared up. I believe that I am still able to be at Dresden before them [the Prussians]; but as soon as I feel my left secure, everything will take a rapid turn."[2]

Meanwhile, in view of his enemy's advance, Hohenlohe had fallen back to Kahla, and Frederick William and Brunswick, alarmed for their communications with the Elbe, on receipt of the news of Saalfield decided to collect the whole army at Weimar. Thus, we see that, although Napoleon was unacquainted with his enemy's positions in detail, his general view of the situation was correct—namely, that his manœuvre would compel the Prussian Army to fall back on its communications—therefore an advance on Gera was in the right direction.

From Kahla, Hohenlohe proceeded to Jena, and, on October 12, while his army fell back from the latter, another panic seized it; it was caused by the approach of Lannes's advanced guard from the south. In the meantime rumours were prevalent at Erfurt that the French had occupied Naumburg, and when at 11 p.m. these rumours were confirmed, the King summoned a council of war. It assembled early on October 13 and decided on a retreat to the Elbe by way of Auerstädt, Freiburg, and Merseburg, and on the way to pick up the Duke of Würtemberg's reserves (15,000) at Halle. In order to secure the withdrawal, Hohenlohe was instructed to proceed to Capellendorf, a village on the Weimar-Jena Road half-way between the two towns, and there, supported by Rüchel, who was ordered up to Weimar, he was to act as a flank guard to the main army until it had cleared Auerstädt, when he and Rüchel were to form its rearguard. At about 10 o'clock the main army set out for Auerstädt. Once at Capellendorf, Hohenlohe disposed his forward troops as follows: Tauenzien's division (8,000), three battalions in Closewitz, Lützeroda and Isserstedt Wood; nine battalions behind Closewitz on the Dornberg and in the woods on its western slope; 10 squadrons behind these and two batteries in Lützeroda; Holzendorf's detachment of 5,000 in the villages north-east of Closewitz; and outposts, under Senft, as far out as Dornburg and Camburg.

At about 10 a.m., when he heard, through the fog, firing to the south, Hohenlohe ordered up his Reserve Infantry to close with

---

[1] *Correspondance*, No. 10977, vol. XIII, p. 334.
[2] *Ibid.*, No. 10980, vol. XIII, p. 335.

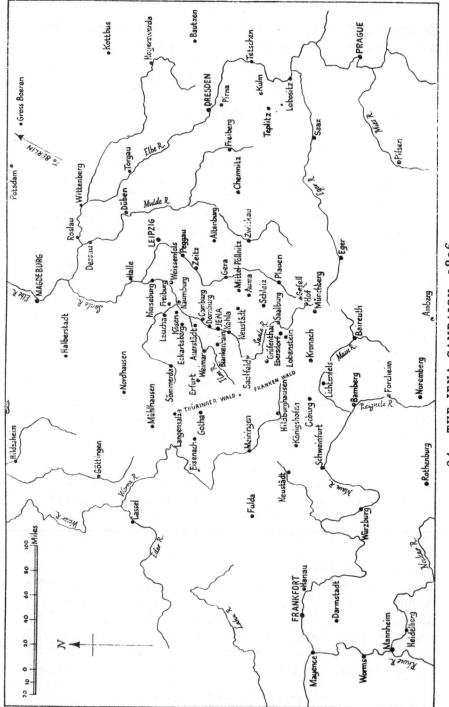

24. THE JENA CAMPAIGN, 1806

the enemy. While this order was carried out, Massenbach rode up with instructions from the King that no serious engagement with the French was to take place, Hohenlohe's task was wholly defensive. For Napoleon this was most fortunate, for had Hohenlohe advanced and occupied in strength the Landgrafenberg, the high plateau overlooking Jena, the battle on October 14 would have taken a very different turn.

In the meantime, between 1 a.m. and 2 a.m. on October 12, Napoleon heard from Murat that the Prussians were not concentrating at Gera, and that from prisoners it had been learnt that the King was still at Erfurt with 200,000 men. From this Napoleon drew two conclusions: the first was that the Prussians intended to accept battle in the vicinity of Erfurt, and the second that they were concentrating there before a withdrawal on Halle, where he knew their reserves to be, and thence on Magdeburg. To meet these two conjectural movements, he decided to detach the Ist and IIIrd Corps and most of the cavalry to carry out a turning movement by way of the right bank of the Saale, and with the remainder of his army force the Saale between Kahla and Jena and advance on Weimar-Erfurt. Then, should the Prussians decide to stand, the main body would fix them and the two detached corps come in on their left flank. Or, should they retire, the main body would pursue them and the detached corps head them off from the Elbe until they were brought to battle. The result was a sequence of orders which led to the following movements: Murat to Naumburg to scout toward Leipzig; the Ist Corps from Gera to Zeitz; the IIIrd Corps from Mittel-Pöllnitz to Naumburg; the IVth Corps from Weyda (south or Gera) to Gera; the VIth Corps from Schleiz to Mittel-Pöllnitz; the Vth Corps from Neustädt to Jena; and the VIIth Corps from Saalfeld to Kahla. All these points were reached on October 12, and Lannes drove an enemy post out of Jena and Davout's advanced guard entered Naumburg.

Napoleon arrived at Gera on October 12 and at 8 p.m. turned in for a few hours' rest and rose again at midnight. No reports of consequence were received until between 7 and 9 a.m. on October 13, when three arrived in rapid succession. The first was from Augereau at Kahla, who reported that the enemy had left Jena for Erfurt, where the King and the main army were. The second, from Davout at Naumburg, reported that from deserters and ·prisoners it had been learnt that the main Prussian army was at

Erfurt and the King at Weimar. The third, from Murat at Zeitz, forwarded an agent's report that troops had been seen all along his route from Fulda to Weimar and that the King and Queen were at Erfurt.[1] Presumably, because Napoleon could not bring himself to believe that the Prussians would commit so gross a folly as to accept battle at Erfurt–that is, facing Berlin with their backs to the Thuringer Wald–he decided that the high probability was that they were about to carry out the second of the above conjectural movements. Nevertheless, in his reply to Murat, in spite of its decisive opening, he still showed doubt. "At length the veil is torn," he said, "the enemy begins his retreat on Magdeburg. Move as quickly as possible with Bernadotte's Corps on Dornburg"; and next, "I believe that the enemy will either strive to attack Marshal Lannes at Jena, or that he will retire. If he attacks Marshal Lannes, your being at Dornburg will permit of you supporting him."[2]

Immediately after he had dictated this dispatch, Napoleon set out for Jena, and at 3 p.m., when near it, he received a message from Lannes to report from 12,000 to 15,000 enemy on the plateau above the town. At once he sent orders to Lefebvre to march the Guard to Jena; Soult and Ney to push on to Jena as rapidly as possible; and Davout to manœuvre against the enemy's left flank from Naumburg. He then continued his journey to Jena, and a little after 4 p.m. met Lannes on the Landgrafenberg, since renamed the Napoleonsberg.

Once there, judging from what he could see, he came to the erroneous conclusion that the Prussians intended to accept battle on the plateau. Therefore he decided to bring the whole of Lannes's corps and the Guard on to the Landgrafenberg, in order to fix the enemy, and next deploy two corps against his flanks while Davout's and Bernadotte's corps fell upon his rear.

Though the Landgrafenberg could be turned by way of the Mühlthal, through which ran the Jena-Weimar Road, it could only directly be approached by a track running out of Jena, which, though negotiable for infantry, was too narrow to permit the passage of artillery and wagons. Engineers were at once set to work to widen its narrower stretches, a task which Napoleon himself superintended with lantern in hand. When he had seen the first guns through, he returned to the Landgrafenberg and ordered his tent to be pitched in the centre of a square formed by

---

[1] Bonal, pp. 412–413.   [2] *Correspondance*, No. 11000, vol. XIII, p. 348.

his Guard, a spot since marked by the Napoleon Stone. From there he could see Hohenlohe's bivouac fires twinkling over the greater part of the plateau, and the glow of Brunswick's in the distance, topped by the old castle of Eckartsberg. This made him doubly certain that, far from retiring, the whole Prussian army intended to offer battle.

Next, by the light of a bivouac fire, he dictated his orders for the following morning; their aim was to gain sufficient space on the plateau to deploy, and not to fight a pitched battle until October 15. Augereau was instructed to advance from Kahla and by way of the Mühlthal turn Tauenzien's right flank; Soult to advance from Gera to Löbstedt and by debouching on Closewitz fall upon Tauenzien's left flank; while Ney and Murat were ordered to hasten forward and support Lannes.[1]

Convinced that the whole Prussian army marched against him, at 10 p.m. Napoleon instructed Berthier to order Davout at Naumberg to push out toward Apolda early on October 14, and take the enemy in flank or rear. Included in this order was the following paragraph: "If the Duke of Ponte-Corvo [Bernadotte] is with you, you can march together. The Emperor hopes, however, that he will be in the position which he has assigned to him at Dornburg." Davout received this order at 3 a.m.[2]

Hohenlohe was also under a misapprehension. He little suspected that he was faced by the bulk of the French Army and believed that, under cover of a flank guard on the Landgrafenberg and at Naumberg, the enemy's main body was hurrying on to Leipzig and Dresden, and that, therefore, he was in no immediate peril.

The morning of October 14 was cold, and when, before day-break, Napoleon set out to visit Lannes's corps, a thick fog covered the plateau. Escorted by torch-bearers, the Emperor rode from unit to unit talking to the officers and men whom he encouraged by telling them that the Prussians were in the same predicament the Austrians had been in at Ulm just a year before. Everywhere his words drew forth shouts of "*Vive l'Empereur!*" and though the fog was thick, the enemy advanced posts were so close that they could see the glow of the torches and when they heard the acclamations the Saxons took alarm.

At six o'clock the order to attack was given. Under cover of the

---

[1] *Ibid.*, No. 11004, vol. XIII, p. 350. No village names are mentioned in this order, presumably because the light of the bivouac fire was insufficient to read the map by.
[2] Bonal, p. 421.

fog, Suchet's division on the right advanced on Closewitz, and on the left Gazan's on Cospeda. By half-past eight both villages, as well as Lützeroda, were in their hands, and half an hour later, on Suchet's right, Soult's leading division debouched from Löbstedt and pushed on to the Zwätener Wood, there to be faced by Holzendorf. At the same time, on Gazan's left Augereau's leading division advanced by way of the Mühlthal toward the Flohberg to deploy on the left of Gazan's division. Thus, at about nine o'clock, when the fog began to thin, Napoleon had realized the first part of his plan: he had gained sufficient room in which to deploy his army. He therefore resolved to halt the attack to give his troops time to reach their positions and form line. The VIth Corps had reached Jena, but impatient to share in the battle, Ney did not wait for orders, but with some 3,000 *élite* troops pushed on toward the fighting.

Met by fugitives of Tauenzien's division, Hohenlohe at length realized that he was faced by more than a flank guard operation. He left three Saxon brigades on the vital Weimar Road to hold it at all costs, moved forward most of his Prussian infantry, under General Grawert, to retake the positions lost by Tauenzien, and to support him he brought up in his rear General Dyherr's Saxon brigade. Tauenzien's shattered division he ordered to rally in rear of the battle and replenish its ammunition, and, when he had sent Rüchel an urgent appeal to advance to his aid, he rode forward with his cavalry and horse artillery to cover Grawert's deployment.

At ten o'clock, when the fog dispersed, Hohenlohe's cavalry, 45 squadrons in all, approached the village of Vierzehnheiligen, split into two wings, and, while they prepared to charge the swarms of skirmishers Suchet and Gazan had thrown forward, were suddenly brought to a halt by a violent attack. It came from neither of the French divisional commanders, but from Ney who, under cover of the fog and unknown to Napoleon, had advanced his 3,000 men between Lannes's left and Augereau's right. Soon he became so heavily engaged with the Prussian cavalry that he was completely cut off and compelled to throw his infantry into squares in order to prevent them being ridden down.

Napoleon, then on the Landgrafenberg, was astonished to hear heavy firing around Vierzehnheiligen, and was still more astonished when he learnt that the battle had been reopened by Ney, whom he supposed to be in rear. At once he sent forward Bertrand with two regiments of cavalry, all he had in hand, for

Murat had not yet come up, and at the same time he sent an order to Lannes to advance. Lannes did so, carried Vierzehn-heiligen, and came face to face with Grawert's line, then deployed on the northern side of the village. Met by crashing volleys, Lannes's men recoiled and fell back to its houses and orchards, and under their cover opened a devastating fire on the Prussians. Hohenlohe's Staff urged him to order Grawert to carry the village by assault, but he refused to do so, and instead decided to await the arrival of Rüchel, to whom he sent Colonel Massenbach to hasten his advance. "Now followed one of the most extra-ordinary and pitiful incidents in military history", writes Colonel Maude. "This line of magnificent Infantry, some 20,000 strong, stood out in the open for two whole hours whilst exposed to the merciless case and skirmishing fire of the French, who behind the garden walls offered no mark at all for their return fire. In places the fronts of the companies were only marked by individual files still loading and firing, whilst all their comrades lay dead and dying around them."[1]

While Grawert's men were uselessly sacrificed, Lannes's and Ney's infantry penetrated the Isserstedter Wood and cut off the Saxon brigades on the Weimar Road from the Prussian centre. To fill this gap, Hohenlohe ordered up Dyherr's brigade as well as some Saxon reserves he still had in hand, and by one o'clock, except for Tauenzien's shattered division, every soldier he had stood in line awaiting the arrival of Rüchel.

Augereau's left was engaged with the Saxons on the Weimar Road at a place called the Schnecke ("Snail")—a series of hairpin bends—and away on the right Soult's leading division, under St. Hilaire, after detaching a few troops to watch Holzendorf, wheeled inward against the extreme Prussian left, while Murat's cavalry began to come up in rear of the Guard, and the main bodies of Ney's and Soult's corps massed on their flanks. Thus, at about 12.30 p.m., exclusive of the 54,000 troops engaged, Napoleon had some 42,000 men in hand as a general reserve.

The Emperor watched the progress of his two wings, and when he judged that the crisis of the battle had arrived he ordered a general advance. His troops, who sensed that victory was in their hands, rapidly moved forward and pressed the enemy down the sloping ground into the valley of the Sulbach. At last Hohenlohe yielded to the inevitable and ordered a withdrawal on Gross and

[1] *The Jena Campaign 1806*, Col. F. N. Maude (1909), p. 156.

Klein Romstedt, but by now his men were so exhausted and disorganized that with the exception of one Saxon battalion square, in which Hohenlohe himself sought refuge, all other units retreated in disorder. At every step prisoners were made by the French, and entire batteries were taken.

Only one thing now could prevent the complete destruction of

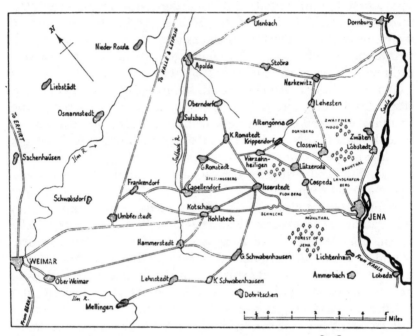

25. THE BATTLEFIELD OF JENA, 1806

Hohenlohe's army, and that was for Rüchel to take up a defensive position on the Sulzbach between Capellendorf and Hammerstedt, behind which its remnants could retire and re-form until night came and a withdrawal could be made. But this was not to be; Massenbach, when he met Rüchel in the neighbourhood of Frankendorf, directed him with all haste to march on Capellendorf and attack the enemy on Hohenlohe's right.

On receipt of Hohenlohe's call for aid, Rüchel had moved out of Weimar, and though when met by Massenbach he was no more than six miles from Capellendorf, his advance was so slow that his leading troops did not reach that village until about 2 p.m. He went through it and deployed the bulk of his men between Gross Romstedt and Kötschau, at the foot of the Sperlingsberg, a ridge a little more than a mile north-west of Isserstedt. No sooner had he done so and begun to advance than some French light batteries appeared on the Sperlingsberg and opened fire with case on his men. Nevertheless, they moved steadily forward, when suddenly swarms of infantry, supported by batteries of guns, poured over the rolling ground and opened a withering fire. Within 15 minutes many of Rüchel's battalions were reduced to half their strength, and a quarter of an hour later, attacked by the French cavalry, the whole mass broke and drifted back in rout toward Weimar. In this engagement Rüchel was mortally wounded.

So rapid was Rüchel's retreat that Hohenlohe's attempt to rally his broken troops and lead them to his support proved fruitless. Instead, he fell back over the river Ilm to Sachenhaüsen and Liebstädt. Meanwhile the Saxons on the Weimar Road put up a most gallant fight, refused to abandon the position entrusted to them, and were either cut down or captured.

By 4 p.m. the battle was over and the French pursuit began. Murat's cavalry were at once pushed on to Weimar, where thousands of routed Prussians were captured. That night Lannes advanced to Umpferstedt, Augereau and Ney to Weimar, and Soult to Schwabsdorf. The Emperor and the Guard set out to return to Jena, the former fully convinced that he had beaten the main Prussian army.

On his way back, Napoleon first attended to the removal of the wounded, and when after nightfall he reached his head-quarters he found Captain Trobriant, an officer of Marshal Davout's staff, awaiting him. From him he learnt that single-handed the IIIrd Corps had defeated 70,000 Prussians, under the King and the Duke of Brunswick, near Auerstädt. He was so astonished by this news that he turned to Trobriant and said: "Your marshal must see double"; but soon convinced that it was true, his praises for Davout and his corps were unbounded. This is what had happened.

While Napoleon fought at Jena a battle which, because of his numerical superiority, he could not lose,[1] in the vicinity of

[1] Even had the King's army marched from Apolda on Jena, though during the early afternoon of October 14 fighting might have been stabilized in front of Vierzehn-heiligen, by 4 p.m. not only had Napoleon brought up 96,000 men, but also, as Foucart points out, the Ist and IIIrd corps (46,000) would have reached the vicinity of Apolda and fallen on the Prussian left flank. (*Campaign de Prusse, 1806*, P. Foucart, 1890, vol. i, p. 671.)

Auerstädt, 13 miles to the north, Davout had been engaged in another which, by all the rules of war, he could not win. On October 13, as related earlier, the Royal Army set out on the Weimar-Naumburg Road. It consisted of five divisions, and comprised 52 battalions, 80 squadrons, and 16 batteries, 40,000 infantry, 10,000 cavalry, and 230 guns, including regimental

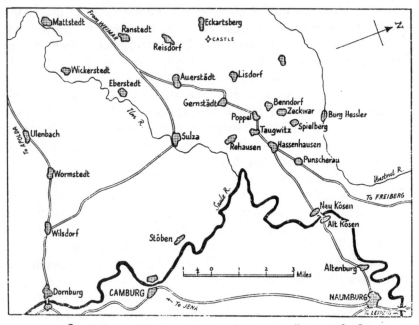

26. THE BATTLEFIELD OF AUERSTÄDT, 1806

pieces. Its leading division was commanded by General Schmettau who, when he reached Apolda, heard cannon fire to the south and called a halt. But as it was considered to be of no consequence, he was ordered to move on. That night the army bivouacked at Auerstädt, by road eight to nine miles west of the bridge of Kösen.

For October 14 the orders were that one division, preceded by a squadron of cavalry, was to advance on Kösen and mask the defile, while the rest of the army, on reaching Hassenhausen, was to branch off northward by the Freiberg Road, cross the Unstrut River and encamp for the night at Freiberg and Laucha. As it was known that the French were at Naumburg, why, early on October 13, Brunswick did not push out a strong force of cavalry, supported by an infantry division, to seize and hold the Kösen defile until the rearguard had cleared Hassenhausen is incomprehensible. What he did do was the worst thing possible. On the evening of October 13 he alarmed his enemy by sending forward a few cavalry patrols which, after exchanging pistol shots with Davout's advanced posts near Taugwitz, retired and reported the defile held.

When this skirmish took place, Davout was at Naumburg, and when he heard of it he at once rode forward and from prisoners learnt that the main body of the Prussian army, headed by the King, approached. At once he sent forward a battalion to reinforce the Kösen bridge.

At Naumburg Davout had 24,500 infantry, 1,500 cavalry, and 44 guns, and his orders were to march on Apolda by the shortest route, which was by Kösen. From there the road zigzagged up the left bank of the Saale to a plateau in the centre of which lay the considerable village of Hassenhausen, about five miles from Auerstädt.

Bernadotte had his headquarters at Naumburg, while his corps was bivouacked along the Naumburg-Dornburg Road. He also had been ordered to march on Apolda, but by way of Dornburg, for at the time the order was written Napoleon was under the impression that he was about to be faced by the whole Prussian army. The news Davout had picked up that half the enemy's army was now at Auerstädt obviously modified the order, and when, at 3 a.m. on October 14, Berthier's order of 10 p.m. the previous day was received by Davout, he repeatedly urged Bernadotte to march with him by way of Kösen. Probably because of jealousy, the latter refused, and insisted on carrying out to the letter the earlier of the two orders. He set out for Dornburg and arrived there at 11 a.m. But though Apolda was only eight to nine miles by road from Dornburg, he did not arrive there until 4 p.m., when the battle of Jena was over.[1]

In spite of Bernadotte's refusal to cooperate, Davout–probably the ablest of Napoleon's generals–did not hesitate to march against the Prussians, 70,000 though he believed them to be. At 6 a.m. he set out with his three divisions, commanded by

[1] In *Correspondance* No. 11060, dated October 23 (vol. XIII, p. 393), Napoleon leaves us in no doubt what he thought of Bernadotte's decision, and when at St. Helena he stated that he had had an order signed for Bernadotte's trial, but had withdrawn it on personal grounds – probably out of regard for his wife. (*Mémoires pour servir à l'histoire de France sous Napoléon, etc.*, 1823, vol. VIII, p. 215.)

Generals Gudin, Friant, and Morand, for Kösen, and at about eight o'clock debouched on the plain surrounding Hassenhausen. There, in a dense fog, Blücher at the head of 600 cavalry stumbled upon him, and in rear of Blücher came Schmettau's division, accompanied by the King, the Duke of Brunswick, and Field Marshal Möllendorf. Thanks to the fog, Davout found time to deploy Gudin's division, which was in the lead. It consisted of the 12th, 21st, 25th, with the 85th in Hassenhausen. Gudin drew up the 21st and 25th in line on the right (north) of the village, and held the 12th in rear of them in reserve.

While Gudin deployed, the King, Brunswick and Möllendorf deliberated on what should be done. Brunswick, ever cautious, was for halting until Wartensleben's division–the next to Schmettau's–came up; but Möllendorf thought an immediate attack should be made, the King agreed, and Schmettau deployed his division. As he did so, the fog lifted, and Gudin's division was discovered. Forthwith it was decided to let loose 2,500 cavalry, under Blücher, against Gudin's right flank; but the latter saw what was intended and at once formed the flanking battalions of the 21st and 25th into squares, with the 12th in a single regimental square behind them. Four times Blücher charged, and each time was repulsed, and when, at 9 a.m., Friant's division came up, Davout saw that the enemy's efforts were directed against his right flank–in order to keep open the Freiberg Road–and drew Gudin's division around Hassenhausen and brought Friant up on his right between Hassenhausen and Spielberg.

Wartensleben's division now came up, followed by the Prince of Orange's: both had been delayed by baggage wagons blocking the road. The former moved toward the south side of Hassenhausen, which was being attacked by Schmettau, and as Morand had not yet arrived, Gudin brought forward the 12th Regiment–his reserve–to reinforce the village. Schmettau was mortally wounded during the attack, and the Duke of Brunswick, who saw how staunch was the French resistance, led forward a regiment of grenadiers to storm the village, but as he did so was shot through both eyes. He was carried off the field and died at Ottensen, near Hamburg, on November 10. The Prussians were virtually without a commander, for the King neither named a successor to Brunswick nor took the lead himself.

Soon after this, the two brigades of Orange's division came up.

The one under Lützow was sent to support Wartensleben's left, and the other, under Prince Henry, to Schmettau's left, where Friant gained ground toward Zeckwar. Morand's division arrived and deployed on the left (south) of Hassenhausen. In spite of the heavy artillery fire it had to face, it gradually pushed back Wartensleben and Lützow. As their withdrawal uncovered the right flank of Schmettau's division, to prevent it from being enveloped, it was ordered to retire.

To halt Morand, the King assembled the whole of his cavalry, under Prince William, in rear of Wartensleben. Thereon Morand formed his battalions into squares; he entered one and Davout another. When the charge came, like all charges against infantry squares, it was beaten back, as also was each successive charge, until exhausted, disorganized and disheartened, the Prussian horse withdrew to Sulza and Auerstädt. Morand then advanced on Rehausen.

When Morand was engaged on Davout's left, Friant, on his right, gained Spielberg; took Poppel, lost and retook it, and next advanced on Lisdorf. Thus by noon, while Gudin still held Hassenhausen, Morand in the south and Friant in the north were enfilading with their artillery and threatening the retreat of Schmettau, Orange, and Wartensleben. As their divisions fell back, Gudin advanced and stormed Taugwitz, and then pressed on toward Gernstädt, where Kalkreuth had assembled the bulk of his two reserve divisions. These, with the whole of the cavalry, Blücher and Kalkreuth now urged the King to throw into the battle; but Frederick William, who believed Hohenlohe's and Rüchel's armies to be still intact, decided to fall back on them, and once he had joined up with them to reopen the battle the following day.

The retreat began at 12.30 p.m. and was pressed no farther than Eçkartsberg by the French, for Davout's troops were exhausted and his cavalry insufficient to drive away the Prussian. In moderately good order, under cover of Kalkreuth's divisions, it was carried out until Mattstedt was reached, from where camp-fires could be seen around Apolda. They were believed to be Hohenlohe's, but soon after panic-stricken fugitives were met with, and from them it was learnt that Hohenlohe's army had been defeated and that the camp fires were those of the French. As this meant that the Weimar Road was blocked, the King ordered his army to turn off northward on the Sömmerda Road.

At Buttelstedt the now demoralized men encountered streams of fugitives withdrawing from Jena, and their confusion became worse. In the belief that the French were at their heels, unit after unit broke and scattered across country. Thus in a single day the three armies Prussia had put into the field were dispersed; the French captured 25,000 prisoners, 200 guns, and 60 standards.

Except for the IIIrd Corps, the casualties in killed and wounded for the joint battles are unknown. That corps lost 258 officers, and 6,794 men, or approximately a quarter of its strength, which shows how severe the fighting was. Gudin's division alone lost 41 per cent., one of the heaviest losses ever recorded for victorious troops in battle.

On October 15, in his Fifth Bulletin Napoleon said: "The battle of Jena wiped out the affront of Rossbach. . . . On our right Marshal Davout's corps did prodigies. Not only did he contain, but he pushed back, while beating, for more than three leagues, the bulk of the enemy's troops, which were to debouch by way of Kösen. This marshal displayed distinguished bravery and firmness of character, the first qualities of the warrior."[1]

On the morning of October 15, there began one of the most famous pursuits in history: Murat, Soult, Ney and Bernadotte set out to follow up the fragments of the beaten armies and annihilate resistance, while Napoleon with Davout, Augereau, Lannes and the Guard took the road to Berlin. Further, Louis and Mortier were ordered to advance into Hesse.

On October 27, Napoleon entered Berlin in triumph, and though conditions of peace were discussed and decided, the King received a dispatch from St. Petersburg to inform him that if he stood by his alliance with Russia, the Tsar would come to his assistance with 140,000 men, and refused to ratify them. In the meantime fortress after fortress surrendered—Erfurt, Prenzlau, Spandau, Stettin, Küstrin, Magdeburg and Hameln, and on November 7 Blücher capitulated at Lübeck. Thus, in 24 days, the entire military might of Prussia and Saxony was destroyed: 25,000 men had been killed and wounded, 100,000 had been made prisoners, and the remainder had disbanded themselves and dispersed. The immense booty included 4,000 cannon, 20,000 horses and 100,000 muskets taken in Berlin alone.

Strategically and tactically, few victories have been so decisive as those of Jena and Auerstädt; nevertheless, politically, Napoleon

[1] *Correspondance*, No. 11009, vol. XIII, p. 357. See also Nos. 11007 and 11014.

failed to attain his aim. The defeat of Prussia did not bring with it the withdrawal of England from the war, and it was because of this that the influence of these two battles on history was to be so profound. They did not bring peace, and in the warring years which followed them Europe became so exhausted that, when finally Napoleon was overthrown, the field was clear for England to become the workshop and the banker of the world, the very thing Napoleon had sought to prevent.

Compared with this, the overthrow of an absolute monarchy, the enforcement of a war contribution of 160,000,000 francs,[1] and the compulsory affiliation of Saxony and Weimar with the Confederation of the Rhine were secondary events. That Napoleon understood this is clear enough, for immediately after his victory he turned to his still unsolved problem, how to deplete the stores of bullion in London that he might undermine and finally destroy British credit.

Firstly, he seized all British merchandise found in Prussia and Saxony;[2] next he ordered Mortier to take possession of Hamburg and other Hanse towns; and lastly, on November 21, he issued his Berlin Decree,[3] the grand instrument with which he intended to destroy British trade. It comprised 11 articles, of which the first eight—the more important—read:

"Article 1: The British Islands are declared in a state of blockade.

"Article 2: All travel and all correspondence with the British Islands are interdicted. . . .

"Article 3: Every individual subject of England . . . who shall be found in the countries occupied by our troops or by those of our allies, shall be made prisoner of war.

"Article 4: Every storehouse, all merchandise, all property of whatever nature it may be, belonging to a subject of England, shall be declared subject to seizure.

"Article 5: Commerce in English merchandise is forbidden, and all merchandise belonging to England, or coming from her factories and from her colonies, is declared subject to seizure.

"Article 6: Half of the product of the confiscations of the

---

[1] *Correspondance*, No. 11010, vol. XIII, p. 359.

[2] In Leipzig, so great a quantity of English cloth was seized that "the Emperor made a present of a complete new uniform to every French officer, and of a cloak and a coat to each soldier." (*Great Captains: Napoleon*, Theodore Ayrault Dodge, 1904, vol. II, p. 418.)

[3] For the Decree see *Correspondance* No. 11283, vol. XIII, pp. 555–557.

merchandise and properties declared subject to seizure by the preceding articles shall be employed to indemnify the tradesmen for the losses they have sustained by the capture of vessels of commerce which have been taken by the English cruisers.

"Article 7: No vessel coming directly from England or from English colonies, or which has been there since the publication of the present decree, shall be received in any port.

"Article 8: Every vessel which by means of a false declaration shall make a breach of the above dispositions shall be seized, and the vessel and the cargo shall be confiscated as if they were English property."

This decree became the cornerstone of Napoleonic policy. Whatever nation accepted it was the friend of France; whatever nation did not was her enemy.

England's counter-attack was immediate. On January 7, 1807, an Order in Council was promulgated that forbade neutrals to trade between any two ports in possession of France or her allies under pain of confiscation of ship and cargo. In answer, on January 27 Napoleon decreed the seizure in the Hanse towns of English goods and colonial produce. Thus the real battle was waged.

But Russia was still in the field, and as Alexander, the Continental champion of the British credit system, refused to come to terms, Napoleon determined to smash him.

Bennigsen lay at Warsaw with 60,000 Russians, and Buxhöwden with 40,000 more would be ready in a month. On November 25 Napoleon had left Berlin for Posen; Murat entered Warsaw on November 28, followed by the Emperor on December 18. By then the two Russian armies had been united under the command of Kamenskoi, and on February 8, 1807, in a blinding snow-storm Napoleon attacked him at Prüssisch-Eylau. A most bloody battle resulted, but with no definite French gain, for the Russians withdrew in good order. For the first time Napoleon had failed in a pitched battle, and on April 26 Russia and Prussia signed the Convention of Bartenstein, by which the Tsar and Frederick William bound themselves to drive the French out of Germany, and were supported by Great Britain, who undertook to pay Prussia a subsidy of £1,000,000, and to send 20,000 troops to Stralsund to reinforce 16,000 Swedes under Gustavus IV.

Next, Napoleon laid siege to Danzig, and immediately after its capitulation Bennigsen foolishly assumed the offensive. On

June 14 he was routed by the French at the battle of Friedland. It was a decisive victory, and the Tsar not only asked for peace, but proposed an alliance with his conqueror.

On June 25 the two emperors met on a raft moored in the middle of the river Niemen, and for three hours discussed terms of peace, while in the rain on the river bank Frederick William awaited their decisions. What, above all, Napoleon desired, was a return to the League of Armed Neutrality of Paul I, which meant the closing of the Baltic to English ships. This was agreed, and on July 7 peace between France and Russia was signed. Two days later peace between France and Prussia was signed at Tilsit, according to the terms of which the latter was deprived of her territory west of the Elbe, of her Polish provinces annexed in 1793, and of the southern part of west Prussia acquired in 1772, and Kottbus was assigned to Saxony. Danzig was made a free city, and Prussia, reduced to half her former size, undertook to take common actions with France and Russia against England. Napoleon's triumph seemed complete.

The continental struggle between France and England

Phase II

Though Napoleon had reached the zenith of his power, his task was far from completed, for England still refused to make peace, and until she did there could be no peace for Europe. Therefore, immediately he returned to Paris he extended the radius of his Continental System. On July 19, 1807, he warned Portugal that it would be to her advantage to close her ports to British shipping by September 1, and on July 31 he sent a somewhat similar warning to Denmark, to be followed on August 16 by a demand that the Danish fleet was to cooperate with the French. But England had set her eyes upon this fleet, and already, on July 26, Admiral Gambier and a powerful expeditionary force had been sent to the Sound to demand its surrender. As the Danes refused to comply, on September 2, and without a declaration of war, Copenhagen was bombarded, and when it capitulated on September 7, 18 sail of the line and 52 other vessels of war were seized. After this high-handed act Denmark joined France and declared war on England.

With the spectacle of Copenhagen before them, the Portuguese refused to close their ports, and to compel them to do so Napoleon made a convention with Spain for a joint invasion of Portugal, and sent General Junot and 28,000 troops through Spain to march on Lisbon. Thus originated the War of the Spanish Peninsula, which in its accumulative effects was to prove as decisive a factor in the eventual overthrow of Napoleon as his disastrous Russian campaign. The Portuguese fleet escaped him, for the Regent, under British persuasion, reluctantly sought refuge in the flagship of Sir Sidney Smith's squadron in the Tagus, and with the Portuguese fleet set sail for Brazil. Annoyed by this rebuff, Napoleon determined to secure the Spanish ports, and particularly Cadiz.

In March, 1808, Charles IV of Spain abdicated in favour of his son Ferdinand VII (1808–1833). Napoleon refused to recognize the latter, enforced his abdication, and in his stead set Joseph Bonaparte, then King of Naples, on the Spanish throne. The appointment was as unwise as it was unfortunate, for Spain was already in insurrection, and Joseph was not the man to suppress revolt, though, besides Junot's army in Portugal, he had some 90,000 French troops in Spain. Napoleon believed the insurrection to be no more than an affair of banditti and instructed his brother to send out flying columns to disperse them. This Joseph did, and ordered the largest, 22,000 strong, under General Dupont, to quell the revolt in Seville and Cadiz. At Baylen, on July 19, 1808, Dupont ran into difficulties, and four days later he disgracefully capitulated to General Castaños.

Baylen was the greatest disaster French arms had suffered since, in 1801, Belliard and Menou capitulated in Egypt, and compared with the latter it was more portentous, for it initiated a revolt, not of the kings, but of the common people against Napoleon's despotism, and without popular support, whatever else might happen, his cause was doomed. The immediate result of Baylen was the evacuation of Madrid on August 1, to be followed two days later by the landing of a British expeditionary force under Sir Arthur Wellesley in Portugal and the defeat of Junot at Vimiero on August 21. In the meantime, Napoleon had ordered three veteran corps under Victor, Mortier, and Ney to march for Spain. Nothing came of a letter jointly signed by himself and the Tsar and addressed to George III, begging him to consider a general peace, and on October 30 the Emperor left Paris, placed himself at the head of 200,000 men, and invaded Spain. He was before Madrid on December 2–the anniversary of Austerlitz.

In the meantime, on October 6, the command of the British forces in Portugal had devolved on Sir John Moore, and he, to draw away Napoleon from the ports of southern Spain, set out to cut the French communications at Burgos. When, on December 23, he reached Sahagun and learnt that Napoleon had left Madrid and was advancing against him, he set out to retire on Vigo and Coruña. The Emperor pursued him as far as Astorga, and there he handed over the army to Soult and hastened back to Paris. The reason for this sudden departure was that he had learnt that Talleyrand, Fouché, and Murat were intriguing with Count Metternich, the Austrian ambassador in Paris, and secretly encouraging Austria to oppose him, and that Josephine was implicated. In this he saw what he called the "invisible hand", his implacable foes, the London and Amsterdam bankers and merchants. Certain that another great conflagration was in preparation, he set about to raise 800,000 men, and in March, when Austria declared war, he had available 300,000 in Spain, 100,000 in France, 200,000 drawn from the Rhenish territories, and 60,000 in Italy. The Austrian field army numbered 265,000.

On April 10, 1809, the Austrians, under the Archduke Charles, crossed the Bavarian frontier, and on April 22 were beaten at Eckmühl and lost nearly 40,000 men. On May 13 Napoleon entered Vienna, and nine days later the sanguinary battle of Aspern-Essling was fought, in which Marshal Lannes was killed. It was a near defeat for Napoleon, and it sent a thrill of hope throughout Europe. On July 5–6 came the stubbornly fought battle of Wagram, in which Charles was defeated. It led to the signing of the peace treaty of Schönbrunn on October 15, by the terms of which Austria ceded large districts to Bavaria, France, Russia, and Saxony; was limited to an army of 150,000 men; and compelled to pay an indemnity of 75,000,000 francs. In January, 1810, a treaty was signed between France and Sweden; and during that month Napoleon divorced Josephine. On March 11 he married Marie Louise, daughter of Francis I, in order to obtain an heir as well as to strengthen his position *vis-à-vis* Russia. In order to tighten the blockade, on July 9, by Imperial edict, Holland was annexed to France, and a month later the Swedish Diet recognized Bernadotte, Prince of Ponte Corvo, heir to the Swedish throne, and in October Sweden declared war on England.

Thus far the war between the French and English "systems" had gone well for Napoleon, and particularly so the annexation of Holland, which led to a severe slump in British trade and to a financial crisis aggravated by the failure of the English harvests in 1809 and 1810. By allowing, subject to heavy duty, the import of corn into England, coupled with the cost of maintaining Wellington's army in Spain, the stores of bullion in London were rapidly depleted, and so pronounced became the drain that France alone had stores of bullion in the bank. As something had to be done to break Napoleon's grip on the City of London, Sir Francis Baring, regarded as the first merchant in Europe, and his friends saw that, unless Alexander could be persuaded to break away from the Continental System, England would be bankrupted into submission.

Napoleon did not want war, he wanted peace, but peace on his own terms, which were the destruction of the English System. Above all, he did not want war with Russia, for the Tsar was not only his ally, but the king-pin in his Continental System.

In 1810, Alexander had begun to weaken and accept English goods. Next, he allowed 600 English merchantmen, which had been chased from the Baltic ports, to land their cargoes in Russia. In retaliation and to tighten the blockade, Napoleon annexed the Duchy of Oldenburg, an action which deeply offended the Tsar, because the Grand Duke was his brother-in-law. The situation then deteriorated so rapidly that Napoleon remarked: "War will occur in spite of me, in spite of the Emperor Alexander, in spite of the interests of France and the interests of Russia. I have so often seen this that it is my experience of the past which unveils the future to me. . . . It is all a scene of the opera and the English control the machinery." When at St. Helena he said to Las Casas: "Russia was the last resource of England. The peace of the whole world rested with Russia. Alas! English gold proved more powerful than my plans."

At length the crisis came. On January 12, 1812, in secret treaty with England, Alexander sent Napoleon an ultimatum to demand that all French troops be withdrawn west of the Oder, a demand which Napoleon could not accept.

Napoleon was well prepared to meet the challenge, for he had raised an immense army of 680,000 men, approximately 500,000 infantry, 100,000 cavalry, and nearly 1,400 field and siege guns. Early in May he assembled 450,000 men on the Vistula. Opposed to him were two Russian armies, the one under Barclay de Tolly and the other under Bagration. The former numbered 127,000 men and was extended on an immense frontage—Schavli—Vilna—Prushany. The latter, entirely separated from the former, was at Lutzk, south of the upper Pripet, and numbered 66,000.

Napoleon's idea, rather than plan, was to advance on Vilna, break through the right wing of Barclay's army; next, fall upon the communications of his centre and left wing, and lastly separate him from Bagration. In the small hours of June 24, 1812, the Grand Army began to cross the Niemen at Kovno, Pilona, and Grodno, and Barclay fell back. On June 28 the French entered Vilna and remained there until July 16. This delay, caused by the breakdown of the supply columns, was fatal, because it enabled the two Russian armies to unite at Smolensk on August 1. Again, at Vitebsk, Napoleon decided to halt for a fortnight, this time in order to rally stragglers and establish magazines. Next, on August 16, 17, and 18 he attacked his enemy, but his failure to cut the Moscow Road enabled the Russians again to withdraw.

It is generally held that at Smolensk Napoleon should have gone into winter-quarters and have reopened the campaign in the following spring. This was not practicable because he could not supply his army there, and also because Bernadotte had joined Russia and was well placed with English assistance to fall upon his rear. Only one of two courses were open to him; either to abandon the campaign or continue it. The former course meant victory for England; the latter was to gamble that the occupation of Moscow would force the Tsar to terms. Here for the first time Napoleon allowed politics to intrude on strategy—the occupation of a geographical point instead of the destruction of his enemy's army became his aim.

Napoleon knew that his enemy was demoralized by constant retreat and that the fiery Kutusov had replaced Barclay, which meant a fight, and he accepted the throw of the dice. On September 7 he fought the bloody and indecisive battle of Borodino (Moskowa), in which he lost 28,000 men killed and wounded and the Russians 45,000. Kutusov fell back through Moscow and abandoned the city, which Napoleon entered and occupied on September 14.

The rest of the story may be written in one word—ruin. Between September 15 and 19 three-quarters of Moscow was burnt, probably accidentally. A formidable guerrilla war had already been launched against the French communications, and as the Tsar would not come to terms, to remain in Moscow was impossible. On October 19 the city was abandoned, and at the head of 108,000 men and 569 guns Napoleon began his return to Smolensk. The next day the first frost set in, and on November 4 it began to snow. On November 28 and 29 was fought the battle of the Beresina, in which 25,000 Frenchmen were killed and wounded. "There," writes the Marquis de Chambray in his *Histoire de l'expédition de Russie*, "ended the career of the Grand Army, which had made Europe tremble; it ceased to exist in a military sense, its only safety now lay in headlong flight." On December 5, at Smorgoni, Napoleon handed over the supreme command to Murat, and accompanied by Caulaincourt and a few others he set out for Paris. On the road, always the invincible optimist, he said to Caulaincourt: "The Russians should be viewed by everyone as a scourge. The war against Russia is a war which is wholly in the interests – if those interests are rightly judged – of the older Europe and of civilization. . . . The reverses that France has just suffered will put an end to all jealousies and quiet all the anxieties that may have sprung from her power or influence. Europe should think of only one enemy. And that enemy is the colossus of Russia."

On the night of December 18, at full gallop the Emperor's carriage bore him through the Arc de Triomphe, and as the clock struck the last quarter before midnight he alighted safe and sound at the central entrance of the Tuileries.

CHAPTER 14

The Battle of Leipzig, 1813

With Napoleon's retreat from Moscow the whole character of the war changed. Except in Spain, hitherto he had been opposed by monarchies, henceforth he was to be opposed by peoples possessed with the spirit of self-reliance which in his youth the French Revolution had awakened in France, and which in 1792 had swept the Duke of Brunswick out of Champagne. Now, in 1813, that same spirit was to hurl back the man who, by raising France to as privileged a position among the nations as the *ancien régime* had held *vis à vis* the French people, had sown revolt throughout his conquered lands. The flames of Moscow spiritually set fire to the entire Continent, hence the struggle on the plains of Leipzig has rightly been called "The Battle of the Nations" a battle out of which a new Europe was to emerge.

This profound change was little realized by Napoleon, and in consequence the situation which faced him on his return to Paris, though complex, appeared to him by no means desperate. Though his prestige had suffered, his military power was only temporarily crippled. Behind him stood France, war-worn yet loyal. Italy, Illyria, the Netherlands, and all Germany, except Prussia, were still his, and both Prussia and Austria were in alliance with him. England and Russia alone were his enemies; the one held his forces in Spain, the other was bankrupt and divided between Kutusov's peace party, which urged that the war should end on the Prussian frontier, and the Tsar's war party, the aim of which was the annihilation of Napoleon. Yet Alexander knew that single-handed he could not carry Russia with him.

For Napoleon, the two doubtful quantities were Prussia and Austria. But the former was militarily so weak that were she to desert him—which appeared probable—he felt confident that he could crush her and Russia combined. The latter posed a more serious problem, for were Austria to join Russia and Prussia he would be faced either by a war on two fronts, or by an overwhelming combination on one. Therefore, on his return to Paris, in order to make certain of Austrian neutrality, he at once opened negotiations with his father-in-law.

England also was then in negotiation with Austria; this Napoleon learnt through Count Otto, his minister in Vienna.[1] But Austria played a double game: she did not want the barbaric Russian hordes to enter and pillage her territories, but she did want to be quit of French tutelage. She was as yet unready for war, therefore her policy was to play for time.

In the meantime, on the Niemen, an event occurred which proved decisive. On December 30, General Yorck von Wartenberg, in command of 30,000 Prussians–half Marshal Macdonald's rearguard–concluded with the Russians the convention of Tauroggen, according to the terms of which his corps was declared neutral.

The results of this unexpected desertion were twofold. Firstly, Murat, still in command of the remnants of the Grand Army, was compelled to fall back, and on January 16, three days after the main Russian army crossed the Niemen, he handed over his command[2] to Prince Eugène, Viceroy of Italy, an incapable palace general. Secondly, Yorck's defection was the signal for a great popular rising in Prussia which, on February 26, induced Frederick William to conclude with Russia an offensive and defensive alliance at Kalisch. By its terms, Russia undertook to provide 150,000 men and Prussia to contribute 80,000. On March 13 the treaty was published and Prussia declared war on France. Thus the aim of the Russian war party was secured.

In Prussia the declaration of war was followed by wild enthusiasm. A *levée en masse* was proclaimed. Every man not in the regular army or *Landwehr* was to support the army by acting against the enemy's communications and rear. The people were to fight to the death and with every means in their power. The enemy was to be harassed, his supplies cut off and his stragglers massacred. No uniforms were to be worn, and on the enemy's approach, after all food stocks had been destroyed, and mills, bridges and boats burnt, the villages were to be abandoned and refuge sought in the woods and the hills. "Such", writes Fain, "are the new means that the . . . enemies of Napoleon propose to employ against him."[3] It was to be a repetition of 1792.

In the meantime, on January 18, the Russians crossed the

---

[1] *Manuscrit de Mil Huit Cent Treize,* Baron Fain (1824), vol. I, p. 39. Fain was Secretary of Napoleon's Cabinet.

[2] About 100,000 men. Out of the 600,000 who had entered Russia, some 200,000 were French, therefore the loss to France was not as great as is often assumed.

[3] Fain, vol. I, p. 108.

Vistula, and on February 7 entered Warsaw. Eugène left garrisons in Danzig, Graudenz, Thorn, Modlin, and other fortresses—54,000 men in all, of whom 33,000 were French—and early in March, fearful of the popular risings and the approaching Russians, he abandoned the line of the Oder and fell back on the Elbe. There he was ordered by Napoleon to evacuate Dresden and concentrate his forces at Magdeburg. On March 12, distance obliged Eugène to abandon Hamburg, which was entered by Tettenborn and his Cossacks amid the rejoicings of its citizens.

Napoleon was busily engaged upon one of his most remarkable feats, the creation of a new army in four months. "France was one vast workshop", writes Caulaincourt, ". . . the entire French nation overlooked his reverse and men vied with one another in showing their zeal and devotion. It was as glorious an example of the French character as it was a personal triumph for the Emperor, who with amazing energy directed all the resources of which his genius was capable into the organization and guidance of this great national endeavour. Things seemed to come into existence by enchantment."[1]

Napoleon's aim was to raise 656,000 men. In the previous November he had ordered a new conscription for 1813, which was reckoned to bring in 137,000 recruits. Earlier still, when on the road to Moscow, in order to add to home security, he had ordered "cohorts" of the National Guard, 80,000 men, to be raised; these he now placed on a foreign service footing. Further, he called out the whole of the 1814 contingent (200,000) as well as the contingents of 1808, 1809 and 1810, which had escaped previous drafting (100,000); drew many veterans and four regiments of the Guard from the 270,000 men he had in Spain;[2] raised 40,000 veteran gunners from the Navy;[3] 3,000 cavalry officers and n.c.o.'s from the Gendarmerie; and ordered Italy to supply a corps (30,000) under General Bertrand. Largely because of desertion these figures were never fully realized.

On the whole, the new infantry would appear to have been good, though Caulaincourt says they were "but an organized mob".[4] But with all deference to Caulaincourt, one cannot but agree with D'Odeleben that, when it came to fighting, "it would be almost impossible to find elsewhere soldiers who braved death

---

[1] *Memoirs of Général Caulaincourt* (1938), vol. II, pp. 611–12. See also *Relation Circonstanciée de La Campagne de 1813 en Saxe*, Baron D'Odeleben (French edit., 1817), vol. I, p. 62.
[2] Fain, vol. I, p. 33.   [3] *Ibid.*, vol. I, p. 35.   [4] *Memoirs*, vol. II, p. 620.

with so much intrepidity and courage, and who, in the midst of all difficulties and dangers, could have shown themselves more devoted to their chief and their service".[1] As before, the artillery was excellent, but the cavalry was insufficient and inefficient, and by April numbered no more than 15,000, of which half was fit for service. The reasons were that practically the whole of the old cavalry had perished in Russia; sufficient suitable chargers were not to be found in France; the younger cavalry officers lacked training, and the new saddles and harness as well as poor horse-mastership put many horses out of service. Napoleon's lack of efficient cavalry hampered him throughout the campaign.

By a decree, issued from the Trianon on March 12,[2] the provisional composition of the new army was laid down as follows: Ist Corps, Marshal Davout (Prince of Eckmühl); IInd Corps, Marshal Victor (Duke of Belluno); IIIrd Corps, Marshal Ney (Prince of Moskova); IVth Corps, General Bertrand; Vth Corps, General Lauriston; VIth Corps, Marshal Marmont (Duke of Ragusa); VIIth Corps, General Reynier; VIIIth Corps, Prince Poniatowski; IXth Corps, Marshal Augereau (Duke of Castiglione); Xth Corps, General Rapp (in Danzig); XIth Corps, Marshal Macdonald (Duke of Taranto); and XIIth Corps, Marshal Oudinot (Duke of Reggio). Besides these there were various German contingents.

By the middle of April, when Napoleon was ready to take the field, he had at his disposal 226,000 officers and men and 457 guns organized in two armies: the Army of the Main, under himself, consisting of the IIIrd, IVth, VIth and XIIth corps, the Guard and the Guard Cavalry; and the Army of the Elbe, under Eugène, comprising the Vth and XIth corps, portions of the Ist, IInd and VIIth corps and the 1st Cavalry Corps.[3]

To raise and equip in so short a time nearly a quarter of a million men and assemble behind them an equivalent number in reserve was a unique effort, and had Napoleon's future depended solely upon physical force, it is highly probable that before the next four months had elapsed he would more than have cancelled out the debt he incurred in Russia. Why he failed to do so is to be attributed, not to lack of physical means, but to the system of command which hitherto had led him from victory to victory.

---

[1] Vol. I, pp. 210–211. Baron D'Odeleben was a Saxon officer attached to Napoleon's headquarters as an interpreter. He is an exceedingly impartial eyewitness.
[2] *Correspondance*, No. 19,698, vol. xxv, p. 63, with slight modification.
[3] See Lanrezac's *La Manœuvre de Lützen*, p. 116. Lanrezac's total strength is 202,000.

Conditions had changed since Wagram. Armies had grown in size, and theatres of operations had become so extended that it was no longer practicable for a single commander, even when operating on interior lines, to direct all troop movements. This was true, not only strategically, but also tactically; for at the battle of Leipzig numbers were too great and the situation too complex for Napoleon's personal system of command.

Equally important, hitherto he had always acted on the offensive and used his army like a thunderbolt. But in 1813 he was compelled to act on the defensive, and, be it noted, in a theatre of war in which the inhabitants were violently hostile. Their hostility not only forced him to employ more troops on his lines of communication and entrench depôts and bridgeheads, but it made the gathering of information most difficult, a difficulty increased by his lack of light cavalry. On this question D'Odeleben says, that ". . . all the efforts of Napoleon's generals were useless, either because of the hostility of the inhabitants . . ., who had been ill-treated [by the French], or because of the raids of the Cossacks, who were everywhere to be found. The little that was learnt was almost exclusively based on the reports of prisoners, which in number were few and undetailed. In short, we only knew what was happening in the districts the enemy had withdrawn from. Though, in offensive warfare, suchlike information may suffice, it is worthless when a defensive war is in question."[1]

Another important factor was that his previous successes had rendered him more and more dictatorial. He considered himself to be invincible and the only general in the world fit to command a great army. This led him to despise his enemy, and, like Charles XII, to believe that no obstacle was insurmountable. Listen to Fézensac: "His orders had to be executed whatever the means at command. This habit of undertaking everything with insufficient means, this determination not to recognize any impossibilities, this boundless assurance of success, which in the beginning were the causes of our triumphs, in the end became fatal to us."[2]

Several historians, when considering the last years of Napoleon's generalship, have jumped to the conclusion that his lack of success is to be explained either by ill-health or physical degeneracy caused by indulgence and increasing bodily weight. There is

---

[1] D'Odeleben, vol. I, p. 167.
[2] *Souvenirs Militaires de 1804 à 1814* (1863), pp. 118–119.

little to support this contention and much to refute it.[1] During his 1812 campaign in Russia many instances of his ceaseless activity are noted by Caulaincourt, such as: "The Emperor showed incredible activity during his stay at Wilna. Twenty-four hours did not give him a long enough day. . . ." "He spent the day in the saddle, reconnoitred the terrain in every direction, even at a considerable distance, and returned to his tent very late, having actually seen and checked everything for himself. . . ." "He worked all day and part of the night. France was administered, Germany and Poland felt the impulse of his mind, just as if he had been at the Tuileries."[2] In 1813, the same activity is remarked upon by D'Odeleben.[3]

The truth is, that it was his activity, not his lethargy, which was as much the cause of his fall as of his rise, for it led him to believe that in his person he could combine the duties of commander-in-chief and chief of staff, and the result was that, when the army had grown so large that skilled staff officers were needed, they were not to be found. Again, listen to Caulaincourt. In 1812 he informs us that "The staff foresaw nothing, but on the other hand, as the Emperor wanted to do everything himself, and to give every order, no one, not even the general staff, dared to assume the responsibility of giving the most trifling order."[4] Though, in 1812, Napoleon had written to Berthier: "The General Staff is organized in such a manner that it cannot be relied upon for anything",[5] in 1813 we find D'Odeleben writing: "It appears that in this campaign the officers of Berthier's headquarter staff were not so skilful or so experienced as those who had formerly surrounded him. . . . As a whole, the army in this campaign was a too complicated and imperfect machine to allow of coordination being established. Promotions, reforms, the replenishment of supplies; in a word, the multiplicity of movements which later on took place, gave birth to difficulties which all the authority of Napoleon could not always surmount."[6]

Napoleon's marshals had not been brought up to command, but solely to obey, they were followers and not leaders, vassal

---

[1] Before setting out on the Leipzig campaign, Napoleon, as reported by D'Odeleben, said: "I shall carry out this campaign as General Bonaparte and not as Emperor", and in greater part he did.

[2] *Memoirs*, vol. I, pp. 135, 141 and 245. In 1809, though an indifferent horseman, Napoleon rode from Valladolid to Burgos, a distance of 77 miles, in five hours.

[3] See, notably, vol. I, p. 224.

[4] *Memoirs*, vol. I, p. 155.   [5] *Correspondance*, No. 18,884, vol. XXIV, p. 7.

[6] D'Odeleben, vol. II, pp. 363-364.

princes many of whom had been raised in rank for dynastic, political and personal reasons. Many were of humble origin. Thus Masséna was the son of a publican, as was Murat; Ney, of a cooper; Lefebvre, of a miller; Lannes, of a groom; and Augereau of a mason, and *folie de grandeur* went to their heads. The Emperor heaped wealth and rank on these men, gave them incomes up to a million francs, and made them dukes and princes. After his fall and just before he left France for Elba, he told Caulaincourt that: "He found fault with himself for having made so much use of the marshals in these latter days, since they had become too rich, too much the *grands seigneurs*, and had grown war-weary. Things, according to him, would have been in a much better state if he had placed good generals of division, with their batons yet to win, in command."[1]

Opposed to the new French army were the armies of Russia and Prussia. The former numbered about 110,000 men, of whom 30,000 were cavalry and Cossacks. The latter were undisciplined horsemen, the terror not only of the French rear services but also of the German peasantry; among them were many Baskirs and Tartars still armed with bow and arrow.[2]

The Prussian army was the offspring of the degradation following the battle of Jena, which transformed Prussia from a feudal into a semi-liberal State. On October 9, 1807, serfdom was abolished by the Edict of Emancipation; the semi-feudal organization of the army was scrapped and civil patriotism inculcated as the moral basis of military service. Though by the Convention of Paris of September 8, 1808, Napoleon had, on a 10 years' enlistment, limited the strength of the Prussian army to 42,000 officers and men, by means of the *Krümpersystem*, introduced by Scharnhorst, recruits were rapidly and secretly passed through the line into the reserve. Throughout, Scharnhorst's aim was to create a true national army, but actually this did not take place until 1814.

At the time of Yorck's defection, there were no more than 38,000 soldiers left in Prussia; but before this, in order to make good the wastage incurred in Russia, Napoleon had instructed Frederick William to raise an additional 30,000. Next, by a decree issued on February 9, 1813, the *Landwehr*—a conscript militia—was created, and volunteer *Jäger* units were raised as well as a number of "free companies", largely recruited from

[1] *Memoirs*, vol. II, pp. 363–364.   [2] Fain, vol. II, p. 361.

foreigners. By the middle of April, when Napoleon was ready to take the field, the Prussian army numbered 80,000 men.

On March 11, the Emperor explained his first plan of operations to Eugène,[1] and though it was never implemented, it is of considerable interest, for throughout the campaign it was never entirely forgotten. It was to cross the Elbe at Havelberg, carry 300,000 men to Stettin, and next relieve Danzig. This would gain an additional 30,000 men. But there was far more in it than that, for a campaign in the north would carry war into the heart of Prussia, would place Berlin at Napoleon's mercy, and would completely upset Prussian recruiting. Further, by threatening from the north the Russian communications through Poland, it would draw both the Prussian and Russian armies northward – that is, away from Austria and thus isolate her. Further still, were Napoleon to out-march his enemies, which was probable, by coming down on their rear he might create an opportunity to fight another Jena, this time with his front facing France. As Count Yorck von Wartenberg says, it was a plan which "need not fear comparison with his best, either in point of boldness or of brilliancy".[2]

It was never carried out because by May, when the movement was contemplated, Napoleon had barely two-thirds of the 300,000 men he required, and none to pin down his enemy within the Dresden area while he moved on Havelberg and Stettin. Also by then it had become apparent to him that the growing unrest in the States of the Rhenish Confederation prohibited a move so far away from them. Already the rising spirit of nationalism throughout Germany began to limit his strategy.

Napoleon's second plan was to advance directly on Leipzig and thence on Dresden, and thereby compel his enemies either to accept battle or fall back behind the Elbe.[3] Because his weakness in cavalry prevented him from screening his movements and adequately protecting his base and lines of communication, as an alternative he was compelled to rely on defended river lines. Should the allies, of whose whereabouts he was by no means certain, decide to advance against him, Eugène was to strike at their right flank; but should they advance against Eugène, he himself would fall upon their left. As we shall see, Plan 2 was not

---

[1] *Correspondance*, No. 19697, vol. xxv, pp. 61–63.
[2] *Napoleon as a General* (1902), vol. II, p. 242.
[3] See *Correspondance*, No. 19902, vol. xxv, pp. 225–226.

so much an alternative as a preliminary step toward accomplishing Plan 1; the need to seize Berlin and operate in the north remained Napoleon's controlling idea. But to realize it demanded first a decisive victory in the south which would re-establish his prestige throughout Germany.

On April 15 Napoleon left St. Cloud for Mayence, where he arrived in two days. On April 25 he pushed on to Erfurt, the point of assembly for all but Bertrand's corps, and according to D'Odeleben "he appeared very uneasy,"[1] apparently because his lack of cavalry prevented him from discovering what the enemy was doing.[2] He moved on to Eckartsberg, and on April 28 we read that the grooms with the led horses were long delayed by "the swarms of the enemy's light horse which infested the road"[3]– an ominous opening of the campaign.

On the evening of April 30 the Army of the Elbe (62,000) was in position around Merseburg, and the bulk of the Army of the Main was in the neighbourhood of Naumburg and west of it. In the meantime the allied forces–64,000 infantry, 24,000 cavalry, and 552 guns–under the command of the Russian Field-Marshal Prince Wittgenstein (Kutusov had died on April 28) were assembled in the area Zwenkau–Altenburg, south of the Naum-burg–Leipzig Road. Napoleon could immediately oppose to them 145,000 men and 372 guns, but only 7,500 of these were cavalry. He badly needed a quick and decisive victory, not only to blood his young troops, but to reinstate his prestige.

On May 1, the Army of the Elbe was ordered to advance from Merseburg to Schladebach, and the corps of the Army of the Main to move as follows: the IIIrd (Ney) with the cavalry of the Guard from Weissenfels toward Lützen, with the VIth (Marmont) in support; the Guard to move to Weissenfels; and the IVth (Bertrand) and XIIth (Oudinot) to march on Naumburg. This day Marshal Bessières was killed by a cannon shot, and on its close Napoleon entered Lützen.

On May 2 Ney was ordered to stand fast at Lützen and hold in strength the villages of Klein and Gross Görschen, Rahna and Kaja, south of Lützen, in order to cover the advance of the Army of the Elbe on Leipzig and the rear elements of the Army of the Main as they closed on Lützen. In case of an attack from the

[1] D'Odeleben, vol. 1, p. 34.
[2] See *Correspondance*, No. 19873, vol. xxv, pp. 204–205.
[3] D'Odeleben, vol. 1, p. 35.

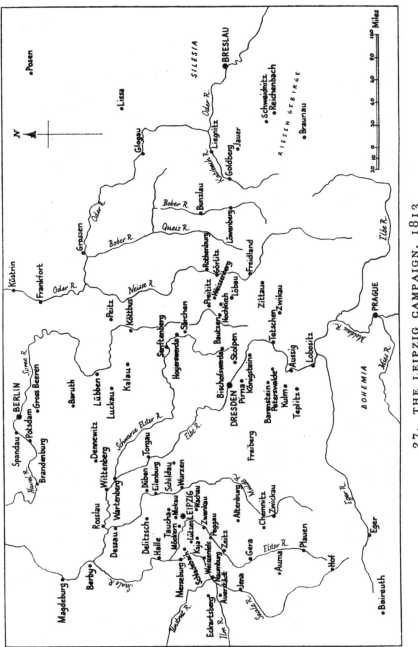

27. THE LEIPZIG CAMPAIGN, 1813

direction of Zwenkau, Ney's flank guard was to become an advanced guard, which, when it fixed the enemy, would gain time for the remainder of the army to manœuvre around it.

Meanwhile the Russian cavalry had reported to Allied Head-quarters that the French were spread out in column of march from Weissenfels to Leipzig, with a weak flank guard at Kaja. This was correct, because Ney had neglected to reconnoitre in the direction of Peggau and Zwenkau, which at 4 a.m. he had been ordered to do,[1] and instead of concentrating the bulk of his corps in the Kaja area, had left three of his five divisions at Lützen. Further, his outposts were so inert that they failed to discover the enemy, who was only two miles distant from them. When he received the cavalry report, Wittgenstein decided to destroy the French flank guard, cut his enemy in half, and drive all east of Lützen into the swamps of the Elster.

Napoleon did not expect to be attacked on May 2,[2] and at about 9 a.m. he left Lützen and rode forward to join Lauriston, who had been ordered to drive Kleist out of Lindenau and occupy Leipzig. When at 11 a.m., accompanied by Eugène and Ney, he was approaching Leipzig, suddenly a violent cannonade was heard in the direction of Kaja.[3] At once Ney galloped back to his corps, and the Emperor, after he had ordered all troops on the Leipzig Road to turn about and march on Kaja, and Marmont and Bertrand, still west of Lützen, to do the same, returned to Lützen.

In the meantime desperate fighting took place in Rahna and Gross and Klein Görschen, and when, at 2.30 p.m., Napoleon galloped up he found the IIIrd Corps in a critical situation, but as always his presence had a magical effect on his men. From all sides there rang out the cry of "*Vive l'Empereur!*" "Hardly a wounded man passed before Bonaparte", writes D'Odeleben, "without saluting him with the accustomed '*vivat*'. Even those who had lost a limb, who in a few hours would be the prey of death, rendered him this homage."[4] The Emperor encouraged Ney's men and led them forward. "This is probably the day of all his career," writes Marmont, "on which Napoleon incurred the greatest personal danger on the battlefield. . . . He exposed him-self constantly, leading back to the charge the defeated troops of

[1] *Correspondance*, No. 19942, vol. xxv, p. 254.
[2] D'Odeleben, vol. 1, p. 49, and *Mémoires du Maréchal Marmont Duc de Raguse* (1865), vol. v, p. 15.
[3] Fain, vol. 1, p. 348. [4] Vol. 1, p. 51.

the IIIrd Corps."[1] In the desperate fighting that followed General Scharnhorst was mortally wounded.

At about 5.30 p.m., while Macdonald was closed in on the right of the allied Army and Bertrand[2] and Marmont on its left, Napoleon ordered Drouot to form a battery of 80 guns a little to the south-west of Kaja.[3] Next he drew up the Young Guard in four columns, supported by the Old Guard and Guard Cavalry, and at 6.30 p.m. the order rang out, *"La garde au feu!"* Thereupon Rahna, Gross and Klein Görschen were carried by storm, and with the fall of night the battle ended. The allies learnt that Kleist had been driven out of Leipzig, and afraid that their line of retreat would be cut, they decided to fall back, which they did in perfect order, carrying away their wounded and covered by their cavalry.

The victory won by the French was in no way decisive. With two more hours of daylight it would certainly have been so, for nothing short of a miracle could have prevented the allies from being driven into the Elster and annihilated. There was no pursuit, for the French cavalry was incapable of facing the Russian. The victory was a costly one; the French lost 18,000 in killed, wounded and prisoners, of whom 12,000 were accountable to Ney's corps, and the allies lost 11,500.

At 3 a.m. on May 3 Napoleon ordered Ney to rest his corps at Lützen for 24 hours, and then march by way of Wittenberg on Berlin, while the Army of the Elbe pursued the allies, who were now in full retreat on Dresden. Bülow was left with some 30,000 Prussians to protect Berlin, and after much quarrelling and argument the Russians and Prussians withdrew by way of Dresden on Bautzen, where they were reinforced by 13,000 Russians under Barclay.

On May 8 Napoleon entered Dresden, where he decided to establish his main advanced depôt. His line of communications ran from Mayence to Weimar and thence bifurcated by way of Jena and Altenburg to Dresden, and by Naumburg to Leipzig. Next, as reinforcements steadily arrived, he began to reorganize his army in such a way that it could simultaneously operate against Berlin and Bautzen. He sent the incapable Eugène to Italy, first

---

[1] *Mémoires*, vol. v, p. 26.

[2] At 1 p.m. Bertrand's leading division was less than four miles from Kaja, but instead of marching on the cannon he halted until 3 p.m. to await further orders. This is typical of the lack of initiative on the part of Napoleon's generals.

[3] At Lützen the French fired 39,000 cannon shot (Fain, vol. i, p. 367).

amalgamated the Armies of the Elbe and Main, and then split the total into two separate armies, the one under Ney and the other under himself. The first comprised the IIIrd (Ney), Vth (Lauriston), VIIth (Reynier) and IInd (Victor) corps, a light cavalry division and the 2nd Cavalry Corps (79,500 infantry and 4,800 cavalry); and the second the IVth (Bertrand), VIth (Marmont), XIth (Macdonald) and XIIth (Oudinot) corps, the Guard, Guard Cavalry and 1st Cavalry Corps (107,000 infantry and 12,000 cavalry).

When thus engaged, he learnt that the Austrians had been negotiating with the Russians and Prussians, but because of the allied defeat at Lützen were now marking time.[1] He saw in this an opening leading toward his dominant aim, the establishment of a general peace, and on May 17 he instructed Caulaincourt to proceed to the enemy's outposts and request to be presented to the Tsar, to whom he was to propose an armistice as a preliminary to the assembly of a peace conference at Prague.[2] Simultaneously and in order to force the pace, convinced that the allies would accept battle at Bautzen, he ordered the XIth, VIth and IVth corps, supported by the XIIth, to advance on that town, and at the same time instructed Ney, while advancing with the IIIrd and Vth by way of Hoyerswerda on Bautzen, to move the VIIth and IIIrd on Berlin. Shortly after this he cancelled the last movement and directed Ney to march his whole army on Bautzen. Unfortunately, Ney had already halted Reynier and sent Victor off, and, in spite of the counter-order, this meant that the IInd Corps and probably also the VIIth would be kept out of the forthcoming battle. Berlin, at best, was but a secondary objective, for were the allies decisively beaten at Bautzen, the fall of Berlin must inevitably have followed. It is strange that Napoleon failed to see this when he issued his first order to Ney. Had he done so, instead of being a second Lützen, the battle of Bautzen might have gained for him the peace he so ardently desired.

On May 19, after he had reconnoitred the allied position at Bautzen, which lay on the eastern bank of the Spree and was held by 64,000 Russians and 32,000 Prussians under the nominal command of Wittgenstein, Napoleon decided to fix his enemies by a frontal attack on May 20, and the following day, bring Ney's army down from the north to fall upon their rear, sever their communications,

---

[1] Fain, vol. I, pp. 388–390.
[2] See *Correspondance*, Nos. 20017 and 20031, vol. xxv, pp. 299 and 390.

and drive them against the Bohemian mountains. Were this done, Austria, still unready, would not dare to move, and without Austrian assistance the shattered Russians and Prussians would be forced to accept a dictated peace.

On May 20 the battle went entirely in Napoleon's favour, for the Tsar, who invariably ignored his commanding generals, believed that his enemy's intention was to turn the allied left and drive it northward away from Austria and played straight into Napoleon's hands by insisting on reinforcing the left to the detriment of the centre and right. In the meantime Ney's army advanced by forced marches, and on the evening of May 20 reached the following places: IIIrd Corps, Sdier; Vth, Särchen; VIIth, Hoyerswerda; and IInd, Senftenberg. The first two were close to the Spree, the third was 35 miles distant from it and the last more than 50.

At 4 a.m. on May 21 Ney received an order to march on Weissenberg and halt at Preititz at 11 a.m., where he was to be prepared to fall upon the allied rear when, at that hour, Napoleon launched his final and general assault. The IIIrd and Vth Corps left their bivouacs between 4 and 5 a.m., crossed the Spree at Klix, and reached Preititz at 10 a.m. There Ney halted them and awaited the general assault. But it did not develop until 3 p.m., and when it did, instead of pressing on toward Weissenberg, Ney got involved with the enemy's right wing. Had Ney had the whole of his army up, this would not have mattered, for then he could have directed the IInd and VIIth corps on Weissenberg.

The allies realized the danger they were in and at 4 p.m. broke off the battle and, covered by their powerful cavalry, fell back in good order on Görlitz. Nevertheless, their condition was critical, for they had lost faith in each other, violent dissensions had broken out between them, and had Napoleon been in a position to carry out a powerful cavalry pursuit, it would seem nearly certain that they would rapidly have disintegrated.

The failure by the French to gain a decisive victory must be shared between Napoleon and Ney. The fatal initial order of the one deprived the other of Victor's corps, and led to the arrival of Reynier's only as the battle ended. And the obtuseness of Ney, who never in his whole career grasped the meaning of Napoleonic strategy, led to the muddle at Preititz. Well may it be asked, since Ney was to deliver the decisive blow, should not Napoleon on the morning of May 21 have ridden over to Klix—eight to nine miles from Bautzen–and personally have superintended Ney's attack?

The French and allied losses are variously given, probably they amounted to about 20,000 on each side. At such a price the French gain was meagre. Like Lützen, Bautzen was another Pyrrhic victory, and Napoleon recognized it as such, for as he watched his enemies retire, he remarked: *"Comment! après une telle boucherie aucun resultat! point de prisonniers! Ces gens–là ne me laisseront pas un clou!"*[1] A few minutes later, Marshal Duroc, who had been with him when he uttered these words, was mortally wounded by a cannon ball. The shock of his death so profoundly affected the Emperor that he ordered the cease-fire to be sounded.

On May 22, when the pursuit was taken up, Oudinot was left behind to gather in his corps and then march on Berlin. On May 27 he reached Hoyerswerda, and on the same day the main army crossed the Katzbach and the allies fell back on Silesia in order to keep touch with Austria. Two days later Davout and Vandamme reoccupied Hamburg, and on June 1, with the allies withdrawn to Schweidnitz, Napoleon entered Breslau.

Although on May 19 the Tsar had refused to grant Caulaincourt an interview,[2] on June 1 an armistice was agreed to by all three belligerents, which at Pläswitz, on June 6, was extended to July 20 and later to August 16, in order to enable peace terms to be discussed at Prague.

Although Lord Burghersh, who was the British representative accredited to allied headquarters, considered that the armistice was greatly in Napoleon's favour,[3] Jomini[4] believed that it was the greatest blunder in Napoleon's career, and since then, with the notable exception of Colonel F. N. Maude, nearly every historian of the campaign has thought the same.

Should the strategical situation alone be considered, undoubtedly they are right, for had the allies at Schweidnitz accepted battle, which unknown to Napoleon they had resolved to do, all he need to have done was to hold them in front, turn their right flank and drive them pell-mell into the Riesen Gebirge. What, then, were Napoleon's reasons for this astonishing cessation of hostilities? They are given in a letter dated June 2 and addressed to General Clarke in Paris. "I decided for it [the armistice]", he

---

[1] Fain, vol. i, pp. 421–422. [2] *Ibid.*, vol. i, p. 402.
[3] *Memoir of the Operations of the Allied Armies, 1813–1814* (1822), p. 2.
[4] Jomini had been Ney's chief of Staff at Lützen, but shortly after had deserted to the allies.

said, "on two grounds. First, because of my want of cavalry, which prevented me dealing great blows, and secondly, because of the assumption of a hostile attitude on the part of Austria."[1] When quoting this passage, Yorck von Wartenberg adds: "We doubt whether these two reasons fully explain this surprising act."[2] They do not, and of the many students of this campaign, Colonel Maude is one of the very few who has troubled to examine them. What he points out is this: Because at the time 90,000 of Napoleon's men were on the sick list,[3] and because his losses to date had exceeded those of his opponents by 25,000 men, he had not sufficient forces left to fight another battle, and a defeat would at once have brought Austria into the war. Further, a powerful and efficient force of cavalry was indispensable for Napoleon's method of waging war. "His artillery", writes Maude, "might tear out gaps in the enemy's line with case fire, but in the face of the enemy's superior cavalry, his infantry could only avail themselves of the lanes of death thus formed by marching in dense columns, ready to form square at a moment's notice. This, he knew, meant delay, which the enemy utilized to break off the fighting." Without cavalry, there could be no decision. Equally important, " . . . he had left Dresden with only ammunition enough for 'un jour de bataille,' and his march had been so rapid that his trains could not overtake the troops."[4] Further still, his lines of communication were infested with Cossacks and partisans. On May 25, Halle had been raided, and though on June 1 Napoleon did not yet know of it, on May 30 an artillery convoy, escorted by 1,600 troops, had been intercepted and captured near Halberstadt. Therefore, the truth would appear to be that, in spite of the deplorable strategical position of the allies, Napoleon's momentum was exhausted, and like Pyrrhus he had to abandon his campaign.

On June 10 Napoleon returned to Dresden, and as he held the crossings of the Elbe between Hamburg and Dresden, he decided to make that river his supply base.[5] "What is important," he wrote later to St. Cyr, "is not to be cut off from Dresden and the Elbe. I care little whether I am cut off from France."[6]

· [1] Correspondance, No. 20070, vol. I, p. 346.
[2] Napoleon as a General, vol. II, p. 268.
[3] The Cambridge Modern History, vol. IX, p. 521, says 30,000.
[4] The Leipzig Campaign 1813, Col. F. N. Maude (1908), pp. 142–143.
[5] See Correspondance, No. 20142, vol. XXV, pp. 393–397.
[6] Ibid., No. 20398, vol. XXVI, p. 78.

In the meantime his enemies were not idle. On June 15, England by treaty granted Russia and Prussia a subsidy of £2,000,000 and offered Austria £500,000 should she join them. On July 7, Bernadotte, Crown Prince of Sweden, was won over to the allied cause, and on July 19, at Reichenbach, Austria also. There, by treaty, it was agreed that under no circumstance was any one of the allied powers to incur the risk of a single-handed battle with Napoleon in person. Whichever army met him was at once to retire until all forces in the field could be united against him. Shortly after, Austria offered France peace on the following terms: that the Grand Duchy of Warsaw and the Confederation of the Rhine be abolished; that the Illyrian provinces be restored to Austria; and Prussia replaced in the position she held in 1805. As these terms were unacceptable to Napoleon, on August 10 the armistice was renounced by Russia and Prussia, and two days later Austria declared war on France.[1]

On August 15–the last day of the armistice–D'Odeleben informs us that Napoleon was "extremely grave and pensive".[2] He certainly had every reason to be, for the forces gathering were enormous. By then he had assembled 442,000 men, of whom over 40,000 were cavalry. They were marshalled in 559 battalions, and 395 squadrons, and were supported by 1,284 guns. In addition Napoleon had 26,000 men garrisoning the fortresses of the Elbe; 55,000 holding those in Poland and Prussia, and 43,000 men in second line. Opposed to him were the field forces of Russia, 184,000; of Prussia, 162,000; of Austria, 127,000; and of Sweden, 39,000; as well as an Anglo-German contingent 9,000 strong, which included a British rocket battery commanded by Captain Bogue. The four field forces comprised 556 battalions, 572 squadrons, 68 regiments of Cossacks and 1,380 guns. Behind them were available reserves and besieging forces numbering 143,000 men, and 112,000 more garrisoning the fortresses in Prussia and Bohemia. The allied field forces were divided into three armies: the Army of Bohemia, under Prince Schwarzenberg; the Army of Silesia, commanded by Prince Blücher and the Army of the North under Bernadotte.

These strengths were unknown to Napoleon who, at Dresden on August 12, believed that the main enemy army, 200,000 strong under the Tsar and King of Prussia, was in Silesia, and that, because Austria would have to watch the French forces on the

---

[1] See *Correspondance*, No. 20300, vol. XXVI, p. 34.   [2] Vol. I, p. 231.

Inn and Izonzo, she was unlikely to mass more than 100,000 in
Bohemia. In order to meet this problematical distribution, he
decided on two operations, a defensive in the south based on
Dresden and an offensive in the north based on Hamburg. The
first was to comprise the Ist Corps (Vandamme) to arrive at
Dresden on August 17, the IInd Corps (Victor) at Rothenburg;
the IIIrd Corps (Ney) at Liegnitz; the Vth Corps (Lauriston) at
Goldberg; the VIth Corps (Marmont) at Bunzlau; the XIth
Corps (Macdonald) at Löwenberg; the XIVth Corps (Gouvion-
St. Cyr) at Pirna; the Guard at Dresden, and the 1st, 2nd, 4th
and 5th Cavalry Corps. The first task of this force was to flank
the lines of march of the Army of Silesia leading northward to
Berlin and southward towards Bohemia.

The offensive operation, under Oudinot, was to be directed
against Berlin and supported by Davout operating from Hamburg.
The former was given the IVth Corps (Bertrand) at Peitz; the
VIIth Corps (Reynier) at Kalau; the XIIth Corps (Oudinot) at
Baruth and the 3rd Cavalry Corps; and the latter the XIIIth
Corps (Davout) near Hamburg, with Girard's division.[1]

Marshal St. Cyr was opposed to an offensive on Berlin, as also
was Marshal Marmont. The former pointed out to Napoleon that
he had greatly underestimated the strength and fighting value of
Bernadotte's army,[2] and the latter, prophetically, said to him:
"I fear greatly lest on the day on which your Majesty has gained
a victory, and believe you have won a decisive battle, you may
learn that you have lost two."[3] In his *Memoirs*[4] Marmont tells us
that it was passion which prompted Napoleon to act quickly
against Prussia; yet a better reason would appear to be that, as
in his project of March 11, a move on Berlin might draw the
Prussians and Russians northward, and therefore away from
Austria.

On August 15 Napoleon and the Guard left Dresden for
Bautzen, where, on August 17, news was received that a considerable force of Russians had been detached from Blücher's
army and was *en route* for Bohemia. Forthwith Napoleon decided
to move against Blücher, and, once he had beaten him, to turn
against the armies of Bohemia and the North and destroy them
in detail.[5] To help in this, he ordered up Vandamme to Bautzen,

---

[1] See *Correspondance*, Nos. 20357, 20360 and 20365, vol. xxvi, pp. 32, 34 and 37.
[2] *Mémoires pour servir à l'Histoire, etc.* (1831), vol. iv, p. 59.
[3] *Mémoires du Maréchal Marmont* (1851), vol. v, pp. 140, 207.
[4] *Ibid.*, vol. v, p. 139.   [5] *Correspondance*, No. 20398, vol. xxvi, pp. 77-78.

intending either to move him to Zittau, or, should the enemy meanwhile threaten Dresden, to send him there to support St. Cyr. To the latter he allotted the following task: "to gain time, dispute the ground and hold Dresden, and keep up secure and active communications with Vandamme and General Headquarters."[1]

At Görlitz, on August 18, when he received confirmation that 40,000 Russians were on their way from Silesia to Bohemia, Napoleon decided to go to Zittau and attack them in flank when on the line of march. However, on August 20, he learnt that Blücher was advancing on the IIIrd, Vth and VIth corps, and set this project aside, turned against him, and crossed the Bober on August 21. But immediately Blücher learnt of his presence, in accordance with the Reichenbach plan, he at once fell back. Apparently Napoleon failed to realize that this was a planned strategical manœuvre.

On August 22 Napoleon was at Löwenberg, and from there he sent a letter to Maret in Paris in which the following illuminating words occur: "The worst feature, generally speaking, of our situation is the little confidence my generals have in themselves. Whenever I am not present, they exaggerate the enemy's strength."[2] Possibly this referred to a message he had received from Dresden in which St. Cyr informed him that the Army of Bohemia was approaching and that Dresden was in danger. Be this as it may, Napoleon at once handed over the chief command in Silesia to Macdonald, and ordered him to push back Blücher to Jauer and then occupy a defensive position on the Bober, in order to flank Blücher should he attempt to march either on Berlin or Dresden. Next, he committed an error which was to cost him the campaign. Suddenly he saw, as if in a vision, the possibility of a tremendous manœuvre, and overlooking St. Cyr's precarious position, instead of sending Vandamme to his support, he ordered him to carry his corps to Stolpen.[3]

What was this grand manœuvre? It was to concentrate the Guard, the 1st Cavalry Corps and the Ist, IInd and VIth corps at Stolpen on August 25, and on the following night advance 100,000 men over the Elbe at Königstein, occupy Pirna, fall upon the rear of the Army of Bohemia, annihilate it, and then march on Prague and force Austria out of the war.[4]

[1] *Correspondance*, No. 20398, vol. xxvi, pp. 77–78.
[2] *Ibid.*, No. 20437, vol. xxvi, pp. 112–113.
[3] *Ibid.*, No. 20446, vol. xxvi, p. 119. See also Fain, vol. ii, p. 234.
[4] *Ibid.*, No. 20449, vol. xxvi, pp. 121–122.

At 1 a.m. on August 25 Napoleon set out for Stolpen, from where he sent General Gourgaud to Dresden to ascertain St. Cyr's situation. In the afternoon he received a rumour that, on August 23, Oudinot had been defeated by Bernadotte and Bülow at Gross Beeren, a few miles south of Berlin, and was retiring on Wittenberg. At 11 p.m. Gourgaud returned and reported that the situation at Dresden was critical. As he did not dare to risk the loss of Dresden[1] – his main supply depôt – he forthwith decided to march direct on the Saxon capital, and at 1 a.m. on August 26 he issued orders to that effect: the Guard and 1st Cavalry Corps were to start at 4 a.m., while Vandamme continued in the direction of Pirna,[2] and on their arrival at Stolpen, Marmont and Victor were immediately to follow the Guard. Then, as D'Odeleben writes, "the army advanced like a torrent".[3] At 9 a.m. Napoleon rode into Dresden to the frantic cries of "*Vive l'Empereur!*" At 10 a.m. the Guard began to arrive – they had marched 120 miles in the past four days – and during the night came Victor and Marmont.

When we review these rapid changes, there can be little doubt that had Napoleon reinforced St. Cyr with Vandamme's corps, as was his original intention, the high probability is that the two together would have been able to hold fast to Dresden until August 28, and that, in consequence, there would have been no need to whittle down the Pirna manœuvre, which under Napoleon's personal direction must have led to the destruction of the Army of Bohemia. But, as we shall see, though by marching direct on Dresden he made certain of saving his main depôt, by sending Vandamme single-handed to Pirna he lost the campaign. Had he but reinforced Vandamme with either Victor's or Marmont's corps, he might well have won a second Jena, and again have been master of Europe. This possibility shows that the armistice was not such a blunder on his part as so many historians have supposed.

When Napoleon turned against Blücher, Schwarzenberg set out to strike at Leipzig, in order to sever the French communications, which erroneously he believed to be vital to Napoleon. But, on August 20, when he heard that the Emperor was at Zittau, and afraid that he was about to march on Prague, he

---

[1] See Fain, vol. II, pp. 258–259.
[2] *Correspondance*, No. 20472, vol. XXVI, p. 139, and Fain, vol. II, p. 258.
[3] Vol. I, p. 250.

wheeled his army toward Dresden and arrived before that city on August 25.

The next day he decided to attack it at 4 p.m.—the signal for which was to be three cannon shot. On the morning of August 26 the three monarchs (Francis, Frederick William, and Alexander) rode out to watch his preparations, and at 9 o'clock to their consternation through the mist came a great cheer of "*Vive l'Empereur!*"—Napoleon had arrived! At once a council of war was assembled which, after a prolonged argument, decided on a retreat, when someone fired the signal guns, and without further orders the attack launched itself.

Though Napoleon had 70,000 men to face his enemy's 150,000, he easily repulsed them,[1] and shortly after the fighting ended at 9 p.m. Marmont and Victor began to arrive. Meanwhile Vandamme had crossed the Elbe at Königstein and had driven an allied detachment, commanded by Prince Eugene of Würtemberg, back in Peterswalde.

For August 27, Napoleon's plan was to hold the enemy's centre, attack both his wings and drive him into the mountains while Vandamme marched on Teplitz and blocked his line of retreat.

At 6 a.m. the battle reopened in torrents of rain.[2] The allied left wing was practically annihilated, over 13,000 prisoners were taken, and at 4 p.m. the allies began to withdraw. Drenched to the skin,[3] Napoleon returned to Dresden in the belief that the battle would be continued on the next day.[4] That night he wrote the following three lines to Cambacérès in Paris: "I am so tired and busy that I cannot write to you at length. The Duke of Bassano [Maret] will do so. Things here are going very well."[5] This clearly explains what historians have called "his lethargy".

Early on August 28 the French took up the pursuit and Napoleon rode forward. Abandoned arms and other signs of a precipitated withdrawal convinced him that the enemy was badly beaten, and feeling unwell he got into his coach and returned to Dresden; the pursuit was left in the hands of his corps commanders.[6] This also explains his inaction on August 28,

---

[1] Commenting on this action, Yorck von Wartenberg writes: "I know of no example in war which furnishes clearer evidence, that the numbers and *moral* of troops, important factors as these are, may be over-matched by the weight of one person of genius." (*Napoleon as a General*, vol. II, p. 246.)

[2] Fain, vol. II, pp. 277.   [3] D'Odeleben, vol. I, p. 261.

[4] *Correspondance*, No. 20480, vol. XXVI, p. 144.

[5] *Ibid.*, No. 20482, vol. XXVI, p. 147.   [6] Fain, vol. II, p. 297.

which has been so severely criticized. At 4 p.m. he ordered Vandamme, then at Hellendorf, to press on to Tetschen, Aussig, and Teplitz and strike at the enemy's rear. At 8.30 p.m. he received the news that Macdonald had been routed by Blücher on the Katzbach and had lost 15,000 men captured and over 100 guns. In addition, the rumour of Oudinot's defeat was confirmed, he had lost 3,000 men.

On August 29, when Napoleon was still at Dresden, Vandamme advanced to Kulm, and there at 8 a.m. on August 30, when he tried to push back a Russian corps, through a fortuitous accident he was attacked in rear and his corps dispersed at a loss of some 13,000 prisoners, including Vandamme. The news of this defeat was received by Napoleon at 2 a.m. on August 31. "Thoughtfully," writes Fain, "he again gazed at the map, and idly picking up a pair of dividers, audibly repeated these lines which came back to mind:

> J'ai servi, commandé, vaincu quarante années;
> Du monde entre mes mains j'ai vu les destinées;
> Et j'ai toujours connu qu'en chaque événement
> Le destin des états dépendent d'un moment.[1]

"The battle of Kulm", wrote Colonel Butturlin, the Tsar's aide-de-camp, "changed into a cry of joy the despair which was spreading through the valleys of Bohemia."[2] This was indeed true, for following as this battle did on the heels of Grossbeeren and Katzbach, not only did it thrill all Germany, but it also confirmed the allegiance of Austria to the Triple Alliance.

Strange as it may seem, this succession of defeats did not induce Napoleon to set aside his project to occupy Berlin, which had played so important a part in distracting his strategy. Eager to arrest the Army of the North from marching on the Elbe, he replaced Oudinot by Ney, and on September 2 ordered the latter to march on Baruth by September 6, on which day he would be at Luckau to support him, and next from Baruth to advance on Berlin and occupy it on September 9 or 10.[3] But the following day Napoleon was compelled to abandon his part in the joint project, for he received an urgent appeal from Macdonald, who was hard pressed on the Bober.

On September 3, he set out from Dresden to Bautzen, and

[1] Fain, vol. II, p. 320.   [2] *Ibid.*, vol. II, p. 321.
[3] *Correspondance*, No. 20502, vol. XXVI, p. 162.

headed Macdonald's shattered army in an advance to Hochkirch. Blücher judged from the impetuosity of the French attack that Napoleon was again in command, and at once retired. This, writes D'Odeleben, put Napoleon in a very bad temper.[1]

On September 6, an alarmist report from St. Cyr brought him back to Dresden, and there on September 8 he learnt that Ney on September 6 had met with a catastrophic defeat at Dennewitz, and had lost 22,000 men, of whom 13,000 were captured. Nevertheless, says St. Cyr, he discussed it "with all the coolness he could have brought to a discussion of events in China. . . ."[2]

Dennewitz, following the other allied victories, led to Tyrol declaring for Austria, and to Bavaria's decision to desert. In the meantime Cossacks were active in Hanover, Hartz, and Westphalia: Tettenborn seized Bremen; Dornburg surprised a French division near Hamburg; and Czernichev penetrated into Brunswick. Wherever the Cossacks went, insurrections followed.[3] The whole of Germany was rising against Napoleon.

By September 5, when Napoleon pressed back Blücher, the Army of Bohemia had sufficiently recovered for Schwarzenberg again to advance on Dresden. But no sooner had he set out than he learnt that the Emperor had returned, and forthwith fell back to Teplitz. On September 10 Napoleon advanced against him, but he found his position too strong to attack, and he left St. Cyr to mask it and went back to Dresden.

Four days later Schwarzenberg advanced again, whereon Napoleon went to Pirna and reconnoitred the allied positions on September 17 and 18. When thus engaged, he received from Ney a premature report that Bernadotte had crossed 80,000 men over the Elbe at Rosslau. He returned to Dresden on September 21, and on the following day with the Guard he joined Macdonald and drove Blücher back to a strong position he had prepared near Bautzen. Next, as he faced him there, he received a second premature report from Ney that Bernadotte had bridged the Elbe at Wartenberg. Thereon he decided to abandon all territory east of the Elbe, except the bridgeheads, and ordered Macdonald to retire to the left bank. This step was forced upon him by the state of his army. Since August 16 he had lost 150,000 men and 300 guns; 50,000 were sick and many of the remainder half-starved. On September 23 he wrote a long, detailed letter on the

[1] D'Odeleben, vol. I, p. 270.   [2] *Mémoires*, vol. IV, p. 148.
[3] Fain, vol. II, pp. 353–356.

question of supplies to Count Daru, Director of Administration, and in it said: "The army is not nourished. It would be an illusion to regard matters otherwise."[1] Nevertheless, by the end of September he was still able to put 256,000 men and 784 guns into the field; but many of his men were raw, untrained conscripts.

Bernadotte, who had reached the Elbe, bridged it at Rosslau and below Wittenberg, and on September 24 appeared in full force before Wartenberg. Blücher then decided on a momentous move, to march north and join him, and at the same time Schwarzenberg made up his mind to cease operations against Dresden and to advance on Leipzig. On October 3, Blücher, at the head of some 60,000 men, beat Bertrand with 15,000 at Wartenberg, and the following day crossed the Elbe. Bernadotte, with 76,000 men, crossed it that day at Rosslau and Berby and marched up the Mulde. This compelled Ney to fall back on Delitzsch.

Napoleon could mass his 250,000 men against either Blücher and Bernadotte's 140,000 in the north or against Schwarzenberg's 180,000 in the south, and, placed as he was on interior lines, he had every hope of destroying each in turn. He was in no way the hunted animal he has been depicted to be: strategically, he was still master of the situation. On October 2 he handed over to Murat, the IInd (Victor, 16,000); Vth (Lauriston, 14,000) and VIIIth (Poniatowski, 7,000) Corps, as well as the 5th Cavalry Corps, and instructed him, while St. Cyr (XIVth, 28,000) and Lobau (Ist, 12,500) held Dresden, to oppose the advance of the Army of Bohemia on Leipzig. Meanwhile he would march with the main army against Blücher and Bernadotte and destroy them before Schwarzenberg could reach Leipzig.

We now come to the strangest incident of the whole campaign. On the afternoon of October 6, in a long interview with St. Cyr, Napoleon impressed upon him the importance of defending Dresden. Next, at midnight, he sent for him and told him that he had decided to abandon the city and take him and Lobau north. St. Cyr asserts that he said: "I am certainly going to have a battle; if I win it, I shall regret not having all my troops under my hand; if, on the contrary, I suffer a reverse, in leaving you here you will be of no service to me in the battle, and you are hopelessly lost. Moreover, what is Dresden worth to-day?"[2] In consequence, at

---

[1] *Correspondance*, No. 20619, vol. XXVI, pp. 236–238.
[2] *Mémoires*, vol. IV, p. 185.

1 a.m. on October 7 orders were sent to St. Cyr to withdraw from Dresden on October 8 and 9.[1] However, 12 hours later Napoleon again changed his mind, and, in violation of the Napoleonic principle of concentration, he ordered St. Cyr to remain at Dresden.[2] Why? We hazard to suggest that it may have been he feared that were Dresden abandoned, Saxony would declare for the allies.

On October 8, Napoleon concentrated 150,000 men at Wurzen, east of Leipzig; Bertrand at Schildau formed his right wing, and Marmont, with Latour-Maubourg, at Taucha, his left. He rightly believed that Blücher was at Düben and Bernadotte at Dessau, though he underestimated their forces, and on October 9 he set out to attack the former; but when his advanced troops entered Düben, they found that Blücher had again slipped away. Actually, on October 10, and unknown to Napoleon, Blücher linked up with Bernadotte near Halle.

Furious at having the same old trick played on him again, what could he do? He could not indefinitely continue to march northward, because he knew that Schwarzenberg was approaching Leipzig and that Murat could not for long block his way. Should he move rapidly against Schwarzenberg, Schwarzenberg would almost certainly withdraw. Obviously the correct thing to do was to let him advance, and once he was involved with Murat descend upon him like a thunderbolt. In the writer's opinion, Napoleon's alleged lethargy at Düben has been completely misunderstood by all historians. Napoleon pitched his headquarters at Eilenburg, a little to the south of Düben, and remained there until October 14. D'Odeleben says that he saw the Emperor in his room sitting idly on a sofa covering a sheet of paper with large letters,[3] and Fain says that he remained almost constantly shut up in his room consulting his generals.[4] These things may be true, but the fact remains that between October 10 and October 13 he dictated 62 letters, which cover 42 pages of the *Correspondance*, and in the meantime heard that Bavaria had gone over to his enemies. On October 12 he abandoned the idea of a pursuit of Blücher and Bernadotte and informed Marmont that he had decided to march on Leipzig and concentrate 200,000 men there on October 14;[5] also he wrote to Maret to the same effect.[6] At 3 a.m. on October

[1] *Correspondance*, No. 20711, vol. xxvi, pp. 299–300.
[2] *Ibid.*, No. 20719, vol. xxvi, p. 304.   [3] Vol. ii, p. 9.
[4] Vol. ii, pp. 272–273.   [5] *Correspondance*, No. 20775, vol. xxvi, p. 339.
[6] *Ibid.*, No. 20776. See also 20771 and 20772, vol. xxvi, pp. 336–338.

14 orders were issued for the move,[1] and at 7 p.m. he wrote to Macdonald, "There can be no doubt that tomorrow, 15th, we shall be attacked by the Army of Bohemia and by the Army of Silesia."[2]

At noon, October 14, Napoleon arrived at Leipzig, from where he heard Murat's guns thunder in the south. That day at Liebertwolkwitz the greatest cavalry battle of the campaign was fought, but with no decisive result. On the morning of October 15, accompanied by Murat, the Emperor reconnoitred the whole field, and by nightfall the French were posted as follows:

IVth (Bertrand) at Entritzsch; VIth (Marmont) at Lindenthal; VIIIth (Poniatowski) at Markkleeberg and Dösen; IInd (Victor) at Wachau; Vth (Lauriston) at Liebertwolkwitz; IXth (Augereau) at Zuckelhausen; IIIrd (Souham) at Mokau and Düben; XIth (Macdonald) at Taucha; and VIIth (Relynier) at Düben. The Guards were in general reserve at Reudnitz and Crottendorf; the 5th Cavalry Corps (L'Héritier) on the right of the southern front, the 1st and 4th (Latour-Maubourg and Kellermann) behind its centre, and the 2nd (Sebastiani) on its left.

Strange things happened in the allied camps. Blücher was at Halle and Bernadotte some 15 miles to the north of him. The former wanted to close on Napoleon from the north directly the Army of Bohemia began to do so from the south. The latter, who dreaded Napoleon, wished to avoid him, and instead proposed to protect his line of communications with Berlin. The outcome was that Blücher marched off on his own, and later Bernadotte reluctantly followed, to arrive too late for the vital battle on October 16.

Schwarzenberg, with 160,000 men, had set out on September 26, but marched so slowly that he did not reach Altenburg until October 14, 17 days to cover 70 miles. He also wanted to avoid a direct clash with Napoleon, preferring manœuvre to battle, but on October 13, when he received the following message from Blücher, "The three armies are now so close together that a simultaneous attack, on the point where the enemy has concentrated his forces, might be undertaken", the Tsar intervened, and Wittgenstein with a large force of cavalry was sent out to make a reconnaissance in force. This led to the great cavalry battle with Murat. October 15 was devoted by the allies to

---

[1] *Correspondance*, No. 20799, vol. XXVI, pp. 356–357.
[2] *Ibid.*, No. 20801, vol. XXVI, p. 358.

preparations for battle the following day, and Blücher was ordered to hasten his march and effect a junction with the Army of Bohemia at Markranstädt, nine miles south-west of Leipzig.

In 1813, Leipzig, then a city of some 30,000 inhabitants, was surrounded by antiquated fortifications, beyond which lay many suburbs. On its western side it was skirted by the rivers Pleisse and Elster, which ran through a network of channels spanned by bridges; the main one was at Lindenau, whence roads ran to Merseburg and Weissenfels. On its northern side flowed the Partha, which joined the Pleisse at the village of Paffendorf. To the south lay a succession of low ridges, the highest of which was the Galgenberg, a little to the west of Liebertwolkwitz.

The allied plan of attack, as devised by Schwarzenberg and amended by the Tsar, was that while Blücher and 54,000 men advanced on the north-western side of Leipzig, three separate forces were to advance upon the city from the west and south. Gyulai with 19,000 was to attack Lindenau and cut the French communications; Meerveldt with 28,000 was to advance from Zwenkau northward between the Pleisse and the Elster; and Wittgenstein with 96,000, with his left on the Pleisse, was to attack the position Murat had taken up on October 14, the centre of which lay at Wachau. This wide distribution led to four separate engagements, those of Möckern and Lindenau in the north, and of Dölitz and Wachau in the south.

As regards the first, Napoleon, in spite of his message to Macdonald, did not believe that Blücher would engage in battle on October 16. Throughout the campaign he never credited him with the energy and pugnacity he possessed, and this occurred again in 1815. At 10 p.m. on October 15 he wrote to Marmont, then at Lindenthal, that Bernadotte was reported to be at Merseburg, and that many camp fires were to be seen at Markranstädt, "which makes me believe", he added, "that the enemy will not advance by the Halle Road, but by that of Weissenfels, in order to unite with the Army of Bohemia at Zwenkau or Peggu."[1] He assumed that this was so and at 7 a.m. on October 16 he instructed Marmont to move his corps to a position halfway between Leipzig and Liebertwolkwitz, from where he could either move on Lindenau, should it be attacked – "which seems to me to be absurd" – or move south when called upon to do so.[2] The reason

---

[1] *Correspondance*, No. 20812, vol. XXVI, p. 362.
[2] *Ibid.*, No. 20814, vol. XXVI, pp. 364–365.

for the second move was that Napoleon had decided to turn the right flank of the allies on the Wachau front with Macdonald's corps; therefore, in order to make certain of this flank attack, he wanted Marmont to support Macdonald.

Unfortunately for Napoleon, his assumption was wrong, and though on the night of October 15-16, from the church tower at Lindenthal Marmont had clearly seen the glow of Blücher's camp fires in the distance, on receipt of the above order he reluctantly set out to comply with it. Barely had he begun to move than Blücher's advanced guard drove the French posts out of Radefeld, Stahmeln and Wahren. Marmont realized that it was now impossible to carry out the order and turned about and took up a defensive position between Möckern and the Elster. He then appealed to Ney, who was in supreme command of the northern front. Next, at about 10 a.m. Ney directed Bertrand with the IVth Corps to take Marmont's place and proceed to the half-way *rendez-vous*. This Bertrand set out to do, but when on the way he received an urgent call for help from Arrighi at Lindenau, as he was being violently attacked by superior forces under Gyulai. Bertrand knew how vital the Lindenau bridge was to the whole army and immediately complied. He advanced on Gyulai and drove him back. Later, when Souham's IIIrd Corps came up from Düben, Ney sent one of his divisions to support Marmont, and the remaining two to carry out Bertrand's original task. They set out, but when near Macdonald, Marmont's situation became so critical that one aide after another was sent at a gallop to call them back. As Fain says, the result was that during the whole of the day they wandered between the two battlefields without firing a shot on either. "In the eyes of the Emperor," he adds, "this was the calamity of the day."[1]

At Möckern, Marmont was fiercely attacked by Yorck's corps; again and again the village changed hands, but at length at 5 p.m., after he had lost a third of his men, Yorck established himself in it and Marmont fell back to Gohlis and Eutritzsch.

Sometime after daybreak, Napoleon and Murat again rode out to the Galgenberg. The morning was cold and rainy, and a thick mist covered the ground. At nine o'clock, as it began to clear, "three cannon shot fired at regular intervals announced the opening of the allied attack. . . . Next, followed a terrific cannonade on both sides, which continued without break for five hours."[2]

[1] Fain, vol. II, p. 404.   [2] D'Odeleben, vol. II, pp. 19-20.

Under cover of their cannon, the allies moved forward in four columns on a wide frontage, a faulty distribution because they

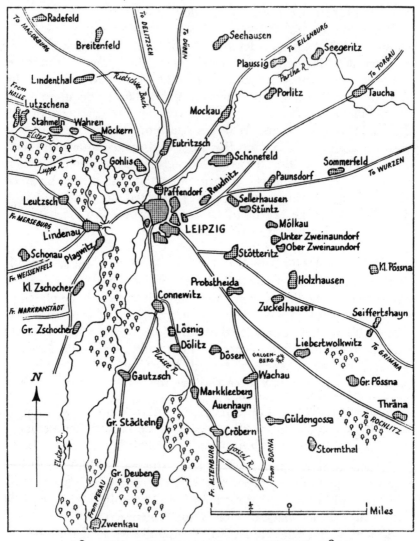

28. THE BATTLEFIELD OF LEIPZIG, 1813

could not see each other, and, therefore, could not coordinate their attacks. Eugene of Wurtemberg advanced on Wachau, where furious hand-to-hand fighting took place until 11 a.m. Finally, his men were driven out of the village. On Eugene's left,

Kleist stormed Markkleeberg, but was pinned down there by the French artillery; and on Eugene's right, Gortchakov advanced on Liebertwolkwitz, to be driven back by blasts of gunfire. This repulse opened a gap between him and Klenau's columns, which at 10 a.m. had begun to advance on Gross Pössna. Lastly, between the Pleisse and Elster, Meerveldt was repulsed and thrown on the defensive.

At 11 a.m. the position of the French was as follows: Poniatowski held Markkleeberg, Connewitz and Dölitz, and Augereau at Dösen supported him. Victor held Wachau, and Lauriston, Liebertwolkwitz, with Mortier and Oudinot, each commanding two divisions of the Young Guard, in reserve. The Old Guard was in rear of the Galgenberg, and Macdonald, at Holzhausen, awaited the arrival of Marmont. Drouot, meanwhile, had been ordered to mass a great battery of 150 guns between Wachau and Liebertwolkwitz in preparation for the decisive attack.

Napoleon's intention was to break through the enemy's centre in the region of Güldengossa with all his cavalry, less Sebastiani's corps, and follow up the confusion with an infantry attack in columns, while Macdonald, directly Souham came up, struck at the allied right flank and drove it on to the shattered centre.

At a little before 2 p.m., Napoleon was no longer able to wait for Souham, and ordered the advance, when, covered by Drouot's battery, some 10,000 to 12,000 cavalry, led by Murat, rode forward, while the infantry massed in their rear and Macdonald advanced on Seiffertshayn.

At first Murat swept all before him and rode down two infantry battalions and captured 26 guns. Had the infantry immediately followed on the heels of his horse, the probability is that the battle would have been won. But at the critical moment a distant rumbling was heard in the north. Berthier thought it was a far away thunder storm, but Napoleon at once recognized it to be gunfire. He turned his horse about and rode for Möckern, hence his absence at the moment he was most needed at Wachau.

By the time Murat had penetrated to well south of Güldengossa, Victor had stormed and taken the sheep farm of Auenhayn; Oudinot was advancing on Cröbern, Mortier on the University Wood, Lauriston on Güldengossa, and Macdonald on Seiffertshayn. But in the meantime the allies had called up their reserves, and Murat, whose horses were now blown, was violently attacked in flank by 13 squadrons of Russian cuirassiers and with Lauriston's Corps was driven pell-mell back to Drouot's battery. On the French side, the confusion became general: Victor was compelled to abandon the sheep farm and Oudinot was forced out of Seiffertshayn, while on the French right, Meerveldt, who had crossed the Pleisse and got into Dölitz, was ejected and himself captured.

When the fighting was over, Napoleon ordered his headquarters tents to be pitched in a dried-up pond at Stötteritz,[1] where as usual he was surrounded by the Old Guard. He then sent for General Meerveldt, with whom he was acquainted, and from him he learnt that the Bavarian General Wrede had joined the Austrians on the Inn, and intended to march against the French communications at Mayence and Frankfort. This convinced him that retreat was inevitable, and, in order to gain time, he decided to send Meerveldt back to allied headquarters with a proposal to open negotiations.[2] Nothing, of course, came of this.

That Napoleon decided to retire, seems to us to be beyond dispute, because at 7 p.m. he ordered Bertrand with the IVth Corps to be prepared to set out and secure the passages of the Saale and Unstrut at Merseburg, Freiberg, Weissenfels and Kösen; Mortier with two divisions of the Young Guard to replace him at Lindenau. But, so it would seem, through personal pique he did not intend to do so until October 18. This was a fatal blunder, for he still could muster 160,000 men, and if, on October 17, he had set out for the Rhine, though it would have meant the abandonment of Germany, there is little doubt that he would have been able to secure the eastern frontier of France and have been in an incomparably better situation than he eventually found himself in in 1814.

On October 17 very little fighting took place, both sides spent the day in preparing for the morrow. At 2 a.m. on October 18, rain still fell and, the French pulled out of their bivouacs and withdrew to the line Connewitz-Dölitz-Probstheida-Zuckelhausen-Holzhausen-Zweinaundorf-Paunsdorf-Schönefeld, and thence along the Partha to Paffendorf and Gohlis. Reynier's corps arrived during the day.

Like the French, the allies remained where they were on

---

[1] D'Odeleben, vol. II, p. 23.
[2] See Fain, vol. II, pp. 409–411, and for Meerveldt's report, Burghersh, Appendix III, pp. 349–353.

October 17 awaiting the arrival of Colloredo, Bernadotte, and Bennigsen, who brought the allied strength up to 295,000 men and 1,466 guns. Schwarzenberg's plan for October 18 was to attack in six columns: the Prince of Hessen-Homburg on Lösnig; Barclay on Probstheida; Bennigsen on Zuckelhausen-Holzhausen; Blücher north-east of Leipzig; Gyulai on Lindenau, and Bernadotte between him and Blücher.

At 11 p.m. on October 17 Napoleon ordered his headquarters to be moved to the tobacco mill at Stötteritz, and three hours later he drove to Probstheida and from there to Reudnitz to see Marshal Ney. At Reudnitz he remained until 5 a.m., and then went on to Lindenau, where, according to Baron Fain, he gave orders for additional bridges to be built.[1] At 8 a.m. he was in Stötteritz, and while at breakfast the enemy's guns began to fire. At once he sent Bertrand his final orders to set out for the Saale.

Up to 2 p.m. the French advanced posts were slowly driven back; the allied forces advanced with caution. Only the allied left column, under Hessen-Homburg, experienced severe fighting at Dölitz and Dösen, which were taken. Next he advanced on Connewitz, but was repulsed by Poniatowski's Poles. Barclay, on Hessen-Homburg's right, advanced on Probstheida, but suffered heavy losses from the French batteries and halted to await Bennigsen who, still far in rear, made his way slowly on Zweinaundorf. But there were as yet no signs of Bernadotte's approach. Meanwhile at Lindenau Bertrand completely defeated Gyulai, and then pushed on to Weissenfels.

At 2 p.m. fierce fighting broke out around Lösnig, but Augereau and Poniatowski held fast to Connewitz, while at Probstheida, Victor's corps, supported by Lauriston's, repeatedly hurled back Barclay's columns. Assault on assault was made, until Schwarzenberg ordered Barclay to go on the defensive. Meanwhile Bennigsen, who was vastly superior to Macdonald, after desperate fighting, occupied Holzhausen and Zuckelhausen. He pushed on and took Zweinaundorf, but at Stötteritz was repulsed. Bernadotte had at last come up on his right, and together, at 3 p.m., they stormed Mölkau. Next, supported by tremendous gun fire and by Captain Bogue's rocket battery, an advance was made on Paunsdorf, which was also stormed. Shortly after, Napoleon retook it with the Young and Old Guard, but he found it untenable, and Ney withdrew his

[1] Fain, vol. II, pp. 415 and 440. See also D'Odeleben, vol. II, p. 40.

right wing to Schönefeld, Sellerhausen and Stüntz. While this withdrawal was under way, two of Reynier's Saxon brigades and a Saxon field battery, which had been posted in front of Sellerhausen, deserted to the enemy,[1] and the French cavalry, who thought that they were advancing to the attack, cheered them as they passed by.

Though Connewitz, Probstheida and Stötteritz held firm, as evening set in, at other points the French had been forced back on to the outskirts of Leipzig. Marmont had been driven out of Schönefeld and had fallen back on Reudnitz, and at 4 p.m. Ney and Souham had been wounded. By then Napoleon recognized that his position was no longer tenable, and, as night closed in, at a camp fire, "with his usual precision",[2] he dictated his orders for the retreat. These orders have since been lost, but the order of march set down in them was that the Old Guard, followed by Oudinot's two divisions of the Young Guard, the 4th Cavalry Corps, and IXth and IInd Corps, and lastly the 2nd Cavalry Corps, should at once begin to retreat by Lindenau, under cover of the rest of the army. Until 8 p.m. Napoleon remained at his bivouac, and then rode to the Rossplatz in Leipzig and put up at the Hotel de Prusse. There he worked with the Duke of Bassano (Maret) far into the night.[3]

Blücher learnt that evening that Bertrand was on his way to the Saale, and at once ordered Yorck with his corps to set out and occupy Merseburg and Halle.

When fighting ended on October 18, no decision had been reached. The French line held firm from Connewitz to Probstheida, Stötteritz, Crottendoft, Reudnitz to the north of Leipzig, and to the west Napoleon's line of retreat was still open. The scene that night is graphically described by Danilewski:

"Night fell; the sky glowed red, Stötteritz, Schönefeld, Dölitz, and one of the suburbs of Leipzig were in flames. Whilst with us (the allies) all were intoxicated with joy, and messengers of victory sped in every direction, indescribable confusion reigned in the enemy's army. Their baggage, their artillery, their broken regiments, the soldiers of which had been for days without food, were stopped for want of bridges over the streams round Leipzig. In the narrow streets resounded the cries of innumerable wounded, as our shot and shell fell upon them. Over the battlefield, so recently

---

[1] See *Correspondance*, No. 20830, vol. xxvi, pp. 274–279.
[2] D'Odeleben, vol. ii, p. 34. [3] *Ibid.*, vol. ii, p. 37.

filled with the thunder of 2,000 guns there reigned the stillness of the grave. The silence ensuing after a battle has something terrible in it which inspires the soul with an unspeakable feeling."[1]

On the evening of October 18, Schwarzenberg issued his orders for the following day. As usual, there was to be a wholly line abreast attack; for, like all his previous attack orders, no attempt was made to concentrate against any one point. Further, except for the step Blücher had already taken, nothing was done to cut the French line of retreat or prepare for a pursuit.

At 2 a.m. on October 19, the French left outposts and camp-fires burning at Connewitz, Probstheida and Stötteritz, and withdrew from those villages, and Macdonald with the VIIth, VIIIth and XIth Corps—30,000 men in all—was ordered to cover the retreat by holding Leipzig. Orders were also sent to St. Cyr to effect his escape if he could.

At 7 a.m. on October 19 the allies renewed their advance, and shortly after, a pause occurred in order to negotiate for the surrender of the city, because the Tsar wished to spare it batter and storm. At the same hour Napoleon heard that Bertrand had successfully established himself at Weissenfels. At nine o'clock he bade farewell to his ally the King of Saxony, and then rode to the Lindenau bridge through a scene of anarchy, thus described by D'Odeleben: "Ammunition wagons, vivandiers, gendarmes, cannon, cows and sheep, women, grenadiers, post chaises, soldiers —unharmed, wounded and dying—pell-mell struggled together in so great a confusion that it was all but impossible to continue on the march, and much less to defend oneself."[2]

In this confusion General Château met, not far from the bridge, "a man of peculiar dress and with only a small retinue; he was whistling the air of 'Malbrook s'en va-t-en guerre', although he was deeply lost in thought. Château thought he was a burgher and was on the point of approaching him to ask a question. . . . It was the Emperor, who, with his usual phlegm, seemed to be perfectly callous to the scenes of destruction which surrounded him."[3]

Napoleon crossed the bridge at 11 a.m., dismounted at the Lindenau mill, and after dictating orders, fell asleep. In the meantime the Tsar's negotiations had come to nothing and

[1] Quoted by Petre in *Napoleon's Last Campaign in Germany 1813* (1912), p. 369, from Danilewski's *Denkwürdigkeiten aus dem Kriege 1813* (1837), pp. 259–260.

[2] Vol. II, p. 39.

[3] *Précis politique et militaire des campagnes de 1812 à 1814*, Jomini (1886), vol. II, p. 207.

fighting broke out in Leipzig, where the French and Poles fought with the ferocity of despair.

A little before one o'clock, while Napoleon was asleep, undisturbed by the thunder of the guns, suddenly he was awakened by a terrific explosion. It was the premature blowing up of the Lindenau bridge by a sapper corporal, whose colonel had ridden forward to ascertain which corps would be the last to cross. To what remained of the French rearguard it was a cruel blow, for the sole supplementary bridge which had been built had already collapsed. Macdonald, Poniatowski, and other officers, as well as many men, plunged into the river. Macdonald succeeded in reaching its western bank, but Poniatowski, who the day before had been promoted Marshal of France on the field of honour, was drowned. Soon after, on the eastern side of the Elster, the fighting ended in a general surrender.

On October 20 the main body of the defeated army crossed the Saale at Weissenfels. On October 23 it entered Erfurt and remained there until October 26 to replenish its supplies. When there, Napoleon found his line of retreat blocked at Hanau by Prince von Wrede and 40,000 Bavarians. He advanced against him, and between October 28 and 31 severely defeated him at a loss of over 9,000 men. The Emperor pushed on through Frankfort and reached Mayence on November 2. There he halted until November 7, when he left for Paris and arrived at St. Cloud on November 9. Two days later, St. Cyr in Dresden capitulated. Thus ended the campaign.

The casualties suffered on October 18 are not known exactly; probably they amounted to about 25,000 on each side. Between October 16 and 19 it has been estimated that the allies lost 54,000 in killed and wounded and the French 38,000, or with prisoners, sick in hospital, and deserters, nearly twice this figure. The trophies captured by the allies were immense, including 28 flags and eagles, 325 guns, 900 ammunition wagons and 40,000 muskets. Of the leading French generals, six were killed in battle and 12 wounded; 36 generals were captured, including Lauriston and Reynier. Further, Fain informs us that on October 18 the French fired 95,000 cannon shots, and between October 16 and 19 more than 200,000. On October 19 only 16,000 rounds remained in the artillery reserve.[1]

"For the first time in his life," as D'Odeleben writes, "the

[1] Vol. II, pp. 428–429.

leader of the French had been beaten under the eyes and in the centre of civilized Europe. . . . In one word, he had lost a decisive battle."[1] This time there could be no excuses, no Polish mud or Russian winter. He had lost a second Trafalgar, this time on land: his initiative was gone.

Though he bore the shock heroically, it was a mortal blow from which he could never recover; for the victory of the allied powers lit a new candle in European history. Nothing was to be exactly what it had been before this victory was won. The joy that swept the continent was as ecstatic as it had been after Lepanto. The sluice gates of invective were opened, and, like a corrosive acid, a deluge of vitriolic propaganda swept the nations, a presage of the degradation of wars to come. "London was illuminated, and every town and village lit its bonfire and burnt Napoleon in effigy as Guy Fawkes, whilst the Press vomited forth a cacophony never as yet heard. . . . 'The First and Last, by the Wrath of Heaven, Emperor of Jacobins, Protector of the Confederation of Rogues, Mediator of the Hellish League, Grand Cross of the Legion of Horror, etc.'." According to General Dupont's statements, "he (Napoleon) commenced his career of murder at the age of sixteen, by poisoning a young woman, at Brienne, who was with child by him, etc."[2]

Yet the influences of the Battle of the Nations—to-day commemorated by a colossal and barbaric monument—were more notable than these ravings: they were the victory of the English System, the rise of modern Prussia and the decay of France. Further, they predicted that the struggles between individual powers were increasingly to become a thing of the past, and that the time was approaching when these politically primitive conflicts would give way to wars of world dimensions.

Napoleon's strategy failed, not only because his means were inadequate, or because his presumption was inordinate, but because his policy was out of tune with the spirit of his age. He had aimed at establishing a universal empire and had followed in the footsteps of the great conquerors of the past. But times had changed. No longer was Europe a conglomeration of tribes and peoples, but instead a mass of crystallizing nations, each seeking its separate path towards the illusive pinnacle of a new presumption—its personal deification.

[1] Vol. II, pp. 36–37.
[2] *Napoleon in Caricature 1795–1821*, A. M. Broadley (1909), vol. II, pp. 246–248.

At Jena, Napoleon destroyed not only a feudal army, but the last vestiges of the feudal idea, and out of the ashes arose a national army, which at Leipzig destroyed him. On the corpse-strewn fields by the Elster, present-day Europe writhed out of its medieval shell.

The campaign of 1814

A
lthough England had played an insignificant part in the 1813 campaign, had it not been for her war in Spain, which since 1808 had placed Napoleon between two hostile fronts, the crowning battle of Leipzig would never have been won, nor would it have been won without the assistance of her subsidies. Towering above her allies, she was both the permanent and dominant factor in Napoleon's overthrow, and had been ever since Trafalgar. Throughout, her aim had been commercial as much as political, and with peace in sight, her statesmen—who never forgot that for England all the greater continental powers are potential enemies—set out to attain that aim by re-establishing the balance of power. It did not demand the partition or debilitation of France, but instead a return to her geographical frontiers—the Rhine, the Alps, and the Pyrenees.

This policy was favoured by Austria, who feared the growing power of Russia and Prussia, and though it was opposed by the Tsar, who was eager to wash out Napoleon's affront to Moscow by dictating peace in Paris, on November 16, 1813, England's policy was tentatively accepted and its terms communicated to Napoleon. But, as his reply was evasive, they were at once withdrawn and a declaration substituted that the allied powers would invade France and overthrow Napoleon, but that they hoped "to find peace before touching her soil". This proclamation did not win over the war-weary French people, instead its sole effect was to reawaken the spirit of 1792. The sacred soil was in danger; France sprang to arms.

The position of France was desperate, for under Macdonald in the north and Marmont in the south, there were only 53,000 soldiers available to hold 300 miles of the Rhine. Five armies faced France: in the north Bernadotte's and Blücher's, respectively 102,000 and 82,000 strong; in the centre Schwarzenberg, with 200,000 men; and in the south an Austro-Italian army of 55,000, and in Gascony, Wellington, with 80,000.

Napoleon had calculated that his enemies would not move forward until the spring of 1814. In this he was in error, and no sooner had the new year opened than one disaster followed another. On January 11, Murat, King of Naples, deserted to the allies, and three days later Frederick VI of Denmark followed suit. Worse still, in the north and east the allies began to advance with unexpected speed: Bülow and Graham (Lord Lynedoch) overran Holland; Schwarzenberg and the main allied army moved forward through Basle and Belfort on Langres, while Blücher with the Army of Silesia advanced into Lorraine and drove Victor out of Nancy. On January 25 Schwarzenberg, with 150,000 men, was between Langres and Bar-sur-Aube, and Blücher, who had crossed the Marne at St. Dizier, was near Brienne, then held by Victor and Macdonald.

On this same day the Emperor left Paris for Châlons-sur-Marne, to open a campaign which in brilliance was to equal any he had so far fought. He had 42,000 men near St. Dizier, Macdonald was approaching with 10,000, and Mortier was at Troyes with 20,000. At once he scattered an enemy division near St. Dizier, and then, on January 29, fell upon Blücher in the hope that he would prevent him linking up with Schwarzenberg. In this he failed; Blücher withdrew to Bar-sur-Aube, and, on February 1, severely repulsed Napoleon at La Rothière and the latter withdrew to Troyes. The allies believed that Napoleon's power was now shattered and they looked upon the war as won, but though they invited each other to dinner at the Palais Royal in a week's time, their rickety combination was at breaking point.

While Napoleon fell back on Troyes, the allies held a council of war at which they decided that, while Blücher with 50,000 men advanced from the north-west on Paris, Schwarzenberg with 150,000 would approach the capital from the south-west by way of Sens. The reason for this unstrategic division of forces was political. Austria was gravely alarmed by Russian ambitions; like England, she did not want an emasculated France. But the Tsar wanted a weak France in order to tilt the balance of power in his favour, because his aim was to gain the whole of Poland, and to indemnify Prussia for the loss of her Polish lands by giving her Saxony.

Lord Castlereagh, the British Foreign Minister, who was then at allied headquarters, vigorously opposed the Russian policy, for he saw that the only sure pledge of a lasting peace was the establishment of a moderately strong France, preferably under the rule of her old dynasty. Metternich supported Castlereagh, but the Tsar, who did not trust Metternich, decided to push on to Paris, but agreed to leave the French free to select their future ruler.

Nothing could better have suited Napoleon than this division of forces, for as he was operating on interior lines, it enabled his small army to deal with his enemies in detail, an operation rendered still more inviting because Blücher, whose forces were now mainly Russian, was advancing in three separated columns. To achieve their overthrow, on February 7 the Emperor ordered Marmont to occupy Sézanne, and on February 9 he set out to support him. The next day Marmont and Ney fell upon Alsusiev's corps at Champaubert, and virtually annihilated it, and on the following day with 20,000 men Napoleon struck at Sacken's corps at Montmirail, defeated it and drove it northward over the Marne at Château-Thierry. Mortier was left to pursue Sacken, and on the night of February 13 Napoleon set out to reinforce Marmont at Vauchamps, then hard pressed by Blücher's third column. He fell upon it and after a stubborn fight drove it back on Bergères. Thus, in four days and with less than 30,000 men, he had scattered Blücher's 50,000 and inflicted upon him 15,000 casualties. The effect of these victories was electric: Paris recovered her nerve and the peasants rose against the invaders, cut off their foragers and ambushed their patrols.

No sooner had Blücher been dealt with, than Napoleon learnt that Schwarzenberg was advancing in two columns, one by Bray-sur-Seine and the other on Fontainebleau. Furious because he had to abandon his pursuit of Blücher, he turned southward and, on February 18, fell upon Eugene of Würtemberg at Montereau, drove him back, and retook the vital bridge over the Seine.

Pride ruined his splendid strategy. Aware that Alexander's ambitions excited alarm, he sought to detach Austria from the Coalition, but because he refused to surrender Belgium and the Rhine frontier, negotiations failed, and on March 1, at Chaumont, the allies bound themselves not to treat with him singly, and to continue the war until France accepted her old frontiers. In these negotiations England's main part was to grant her allies a further subsidy of £5,000,000.

In the meantime Blücher resumed his advance, and when on February 25 Napoleon, at Troyes, learnt of this, he set out against him, but on his approach the former skilfully withdrew northward and, delayed for 36 hours at La Ferté-sous-Jouarre by a broken bridge, Napoleon was unable to catch up with him until March 7, when he attacked him at Craonne, and drove him back on Laon. There, on the night of March 9 and 10, Blücher surprised Marmont and routed him, whereon Napoleon withdrew to Soissons, and on March 17 learnt that to the south of him Schwarzenberg was again advancing on Paris. He marched against him, and on March 20 the desperate and bloody battle of Arcis-sur-Aube was fought between 23,000 Frenchmen and 60,000 Austrians. It ended when the Emperor had to withdraw to Sézanne.

Napoleon did not possess force enough to head Schwarzenberg off from Paris, and he decided to move into Lorraine, rally its fortress garrisons, and then, by falling on Schwarzenberg's rear and communications, force him to turn about. It was a desperate gamble. At St. Dizier he proclaimed a *levée en masse* and ordered the Lorraine garrisons to cut their way out and join him. But on March 23, one of his couriers, who carried to Paris a letter to the Empress, was captured by a Cossack patrol, and when the Tsar learnt from it what Napoleon had in mind, he persuaded Schwarzenberg—already in retreat—to turn about, abandon for the time being his communications, link up with Blücher, and with him advance on Paris. Thus, instead of compelling the Austrians to fall back, all Napoleon's manœuvre accomplished was to unbar the road to Paris.

On March 25, Schwarzenberg set out, while Blücher marched parallel with him from Châlons. On that day Marmont's and Mortier's corps were routed at La Fère-Champenoise, and near there General Pacthod's division of National Guards, 4,500 strong, after an epic fight, the most heroic in this remarkable campaign, was all but annihilated. Nothing remained but the wreck of Marmont's and Mortier's corps to defend Paris, which under the weak leadership of the Emperor's brother Joseph was in a state of panic.

At the foot of Montmartre the two marshals drew up their forces, and there, on March 30, the last battle of the campaign was fought. When Joseph and his brother Jérôme saw from the heights above that it was lost, they directed Marmont and Mortier to treat with the enemy. An armistice was agreed upon, and Paris was granted honourable terms of surrender.

Napoleon was at Vitry, and when he learnt that Paris was in danger, he hastened ahead of his troops to Fontainebleau. There he learnt that Marmont had gone over to the enemy, and as his marshals refused to follow him, on April 11 he abdicated. On April 20 he bade farewell to his Guard, and on the night of April 28, at Fréjus, accompanied by Bertrand and Drouot, he embarked in the British frigate *Undaunted*, which bore him to Elba.

On May 30, a series of treaties, collectively known as the First Treaty of Paris, was signed, which fixed the frontiers of France as they stood on November 1, 1792. According to one of its terms, a congress of all belligerents was to be held in Vienna to determine a general peace settlement. In September the Congress assembled and soon brought the allies to the brink of war; the Tsar demanded the whole of Poland. Castlereagh, supported by Metternich and Talleyrand, led the opposition. England, Austria, and France, distrusted the growing strength of Russia, and considered, should her boundaries be pushed westward into Germany, the balance of power would be completely upset, so on January 3, 1815, they formed a secret compact to raise 450,000 men to wage war on Russia. The Congress was still sitting when, on March 4, news was received that Napoleon had escaped from Elba.

While the Congress was in session, Napoleon had been kept well informed of its quarrels, and when, on February 13, he learnt that Fouché was plotting the overthrow of Louis XVIII, he decided to hazard his fortune by a return to France. On the night of Sunday February 26, at Porto Ferrajo, with 1,050 officers and men of his bodyguard he embarked in the brig *l'Inconstant* and six small craft, eluded the French guard ship and landed in the Bay of St. Juan on March 1.

On March 7, near Grenoble, he found the defile of Laffrey held by the 5th Regiment, and as he approached it a Royalist officer called out: "There he is: fire on him!" Napoleon turned to Colonel Mallet, in command of his bodyguard, and said: "Order the soldiers to put their muskets under their left arms, muzzles down". Then he stepped forward and said: "Soldiers of the 5th, do you know me? Here is your Emperor. Who will may shoot." A shout of "*Vive l'Empereur!*" burst forth. The first round of the Waterloo campaign was won. On March 20, he was back again in Paris; it was the birthday of his son.

CHAPTER 15

The Battle of Waterloo, 1815

The Waterloo campaign has been so thoroughly investigated and criticized that the errors committed in it are apt to appear exceptional and glaring. They were not, they were the usual errors to be found in most campaigns. But what was exceptional is that the two most noted captains of their age met in clinch for the first time in a war of 22 years' duration, and that both were outstanding generals. Thus far, except for the Archduke Charles, Napoleon had faced and fought leaders of only moderate abilities, and, in his turn, so had Wellington. Now the two great protagonists were to meet face to face, and in consequence the errors they and their subordinates committed have been spotlighted by their personal renown and exceptional abilities.

That the greater of the two went down before the lesser has given rise to the myth that Napoleon's genius was on the wane, and that he was either a sick man or had grown lethargic. Such evidence that has been raked up in support of these contentions is as forced as it is distorted; for he was no better or worse than he had been at Marengo, Austerlitz, Jena, and Leipzig; a man so mastered by his genius that at times he lived in a land of illusions.[1] So convinced was he of his own powers and good fortune that, as Caulaincourt once said: "He had a wholly incalculable antipathy for any thoughts or ideas about what he disliked."[2] When, on June 21, after his defeat at Waterloo, he alighted at the Elysée, he said to Caulaincourt: "Well, Caulaincourt, here is a pretty to-do! A battle lost! How will the country bear this reverse? All the material is lost. It is a frightful disaster. The day was won. The army had performed prodigies; the enemy was beaten at every point; only the English centre still held. Just as all was over the army was seized with panic. It is inexplicable. . . ."[3] It was nothing of the sort; it was the logical end of his illusions that personally he could control and do everything, and that a perfect

---

[1] "Once he had an idea implanted in his head, the Emperor was carried away by his own illusion. He cherished it, caressed it, became obsessed with it. . . . " (*The Memoirs of Caulaincourt*, 1935, vol. I, p. 93.)

[2] *Ibid.*, vol. I, p. 602.　　　　　　　　　　[3] *Ibid.*, vol. II, p. 423.

plan, irrespective of the means at hand, could not fail to lead to a perfect solution.

In Wellington he met a soldier very different from himself and a general whose armies had been small and compact, and in which command could be centralized; obedience and not initiative was required of subordinates. Though as autocratic and dictatorial as Napoleon, because Wellington possessed the faculty of combining foresight with common sense, his imagination seldom ran away with his reason. His armies usually were numerically inferior to his opponent's, he was compelled to be prudent. Yet it is a great mistake to assume, as many have done and as Napoleon himself did, that he was no more than a cautious general. Though a master of defensive warfare, he could, when conditions were favourable, be audacious in the extreme, as he was at Assaye and Argaum in 1803, in the Vimiero and Talavera campaigns, and in the storming of Ciudad Rodrigo and Badajoz. His Fabian tactics were common sense: when conditions demanded prudence, he was prudent, and when they did not, he could strike like a thunderbolt.

Few generals of his age understood the ingredients of tactics so thoroughly as he did. He grasped the limitations of the musket of his day, that it was a deadly weapon at point-blank range, but nearly useless at a distance. He realized that the dominant characteristics of the English soldier were steadiness and stolidity, and that the French soldier did not possess them. Therefore he welcomed meeting column by two-deep line, which meant that he could multiply his fire power at least fourfold. In order to protect his men as well as to mystify his enemy, he seldom failed to make the fullest use of cover by ground. Because of this, at Vimiero, Junôt was completely deceived, and at Busaco, Masséna mistook the British centre for its right. At Salamanca it was the same, and also at Waterloo.

In the main his grand tactics were of a defensive-offensive order; that is to say, he encouraged the enemy to attack, and when he was in confusion, under cover of the smoke of his muskets, he attacked him in turn. He seldom massed his guns, not only because he seldom had a sufficiency of them, but because his line tactics demanded artillery dispersion and not concentration. Also, he seldom pursued a beaten foe, because generally his cavalry was weak and indifferent. One other fact must be mentioned, for, combined with his use of ground, it raised him to the position of supreme tactical artist. It was that he saw everything for himself and only when it was impossible to do so did he rely upon secondhand information. As he once said: "The real reason why I succeeded . . . is because I was always on the spot–I saw everything, and did everything myself." Like Napoleon, he combined the duties of chief of staff with those of commander-in-chief, and because of this his command was, in fact, Napoleonic. But had he been called upon to command a large army, split into several independent or semi-independent bodies, it goes without saying that his centralized system would have proved as defective as Napoleon's increasingly did after Austerlitz.

Once back in Paris, Napoleon set to work on his Herculean task of raising his last great army. Men were plentiful, for France was thronged with disbanded veterans and returned prisoners of war; but muskets, equipment, horses, and ammunition were lamentably deficient, and the Royal Army, about 100,000 strong, was decrepit. But his main problem was the selection of his principal officers, for many of his marshals and generals, including Soult, Berthier, Macdonald, St. Cyr, Suchet, Augereau, and Ney, had sworn allegiance to Louis XVIII, and not a few of those who rejoined him had little confidence in the triumph of his cause. Equally bad, there was mutual suspicion between those who had or had not served Louis.[1]

For the effective execution of his grand tactics, he needed at least four men who thoroughly understood his *bataillon carré* system: a chief of staff who could express his ideas clearly in written orders; a cavalry general who could handle masses of horsemen; and two wing commanders who, when he was not present, could carry out his aim. Hitherto he had relied on Berthier as his chief of staff, and though that able head clerk was willing to return to him, on June 1 he met with a fatal accident. In his place, Napoleon selected Soult. It was a thoroughly bad choice, for though an able commander, Soult had never held the office of chief of staff of any army or even of a corps, and the campaign was lost largely through bad staff work.

Napoleon refused to take back Murat as his cavalry leader, and chose Grouchy. But no sooner had the campaign opened than he appointed the latter to the command of his right wing. This

---

[1] See the report of the Chevalier d'Artez of May 6, 1815, on conditions in France (Wellington's *Supplementary Despatches*, 1863, vol. x, pp. 247–256). It is, however, so exaggerated that, instead of helping Wellington, it probably misled him.

again was a bad choice, for though Grouchy was a skilful cavalry general, he had never commanded a corps, let alone an army wing. Equally bad, he gave the command of his left wing to Ney, of whom, in 1808, he had said that he was as ignorant of his projects "as the last-joined drummer boy".[1]

These four appointments were the most fatal of all the errors Napoleon committed during the Hundred Days, and it is no exaggeration to say that they were the chief cause of his defeat. At St. Helena he realized this, for he told Las Casas that, had he had Murat with him, victory would have been his,[2] and he told Gourgaud that Soult did not serve him well,[3] that "it was a great mistake to employ Ney",[4] and that he ought to have given the command of the right wing to Suchet and not to Grouchy.[5]

One man he did not mention, and that was Davout, probably the most skilful officer he ever had. He left him at Paris as Governor because, as he said to him, he could not entrust the capital to anyone else. Yet surely Davout was right when he replied: "But, sire, if you are the victor, Paris will be yours, and if you are beaten, neither I nor any one else can do anything for you."[6]

What the French marshals lacked in ardour was in no way made good by the wild enthusiasm of the regimental officers and men. A spy, writing to Wellington, compared them with the soldiers of 1792, and Houssaye, summing up the disposition of the Army of 1815, writes that it was "impressionable, critical, without discipline, and without confidence in its leaders, haunted by the dread of treason, and on that account, perhaps, liable to sudden fits of panic . . . it was capable of heroic efforts and furious impulses. . . . Napoleon had never before handled an instrument of war, which was at once so formidable, and so fragile.[7]

In spite of all difficulties, by the end of May Napoleon had raised the strength of the active army to 284,000 men, supported by an auxiliary army of 222,000 strong;[8] but in both many men were no more than figures borne on the registers. Of the former,

---

[1] *Lettres Inédites de Napoléon 1er*, Léon Lecestre (1897), vol. I, No. 217, p. 142.
[2] *Mémorial de Sainte Hélène* (1923), vol. II, p. 276.
[3] *Sainte-Hélène, Journal inédit* (1899), vol. I, p. 505.
[4] *Ibid.*, vol. II, p. 276.   [5] *Ibid.*, vol. I, p. 502 and vol. II, p. 424.
[6] *Histoire de la Vie Militaire, etc., du Maréchal Davout*, L. J. Gabriel de Chenier (1866), p. 540.
[7] *1815 Waterloo*, Henry Houssaye (English edit. 1900), p. 48. (See also Wellington's *Supplementary Despatches*, vol. x, pp. 364–366.)
[8] See Houssaye's *1815 Waterloo*, pp. 21 and 310–311.

124,500 were formed into the Army of the North under his personal command; the remainder was split between the Armies of the Rhine, Loire, Alps and Pyrenees, as well as other formations, depôts and fortresses.

The Army of the North was organized into five infantry corps, the Imperial Guard, and reserve cavalry. The first comprised the Ist Corps (d'Erlon) 19,939 men; the IInd (Reille) 24,361; the IIIrd (Vandamme) 19,160; the IVth (Gérard) 15,995; and the VIth (Lobau) 10,465. The second consisted of the Old Guard (*grenadiers*) under Friant; the Middle Guard (*chasseurs*) under Morand; and the Young Guard (*voltigeurs*) under Duhesme, which, with Guyot's and the Lefebvre-Desnouettes's divisions of Guard Cavalry, numbered in all 20,884 officers and men. The Reserve Cavalry, under Grouchy, was divided into four divisions: 1st (Pajol) 3,046 men; 2nd (Exelmans) 3,515; 3rd (Kellermann) 3,679; and 4th (Milhaud) 3,544. In all, the army consisted of 89,415 infantry, 23,595 cavalry, and 11,578 artillery with 344 guns.[1]

In Vienna, the allies, who had formed the Seventh Coalition, were engaged upon raising five armies: an Anglo-Dutch Army (93,000 men under Wellington) and a Prussian Army (117,000 men under Blücher) in Belgium; an Austrian Army (210,000 men under Schwarzenberg) on the Upper Rhine; a Russian Army (150,000 men under Barclay de Tolly) on the Middle Rhine; and an Austro-Italian Army (75,000 men under Frimont) in northern Italy.

In brief, their plan, as devised by Gneisenau, was to crush Napoleon by force of numbers. Wellington, Blücher, and Schwarzenberg were to march straight on Paris, and should one of them be beaten or forced to retire, Barclay was to come to his help while the remaining two continued their advance.[2] Frimont's army was to move on Lyons and not on Paris; Wellington was to command all forces in Belgium; and the French frontier was to be crossed simultaneously by all armies between June 27 and July 1.

Early in April, Wellington set out from Vienna for Brussels, and on May 3 he met Blücher at Tirlemont. Though neither believed that Napoleon would assume the offensive, it would seem they

---

[1] These figures are taken from *Histoire de la Campagne de 1815*, Lt.-Colonel Charras (5me edit.), vol. I, pp. 65–68.
[2] See Wellington's *Supplementary Despatches*, vol. x, pp. 196–197.

29. NAPOLEON'S CONCENTRATION, JUNE 15-19, 1815

agreed that, should he do so, they would concentrate their armies on the line Quatre-Bras-Sombreffe. Whether this was so or not, on the following day Blücher moved his headquarters from Liège to Namur, and ordered his four corps forward; the Ist (32,692 men under Ziethen) to Fleurus; the IInd (32,704 under Pirch) to Namur; the IIIrd (24,456 under Thielemann) to Huy; and the IVth (31,102 under Bülow) to Liège. Blücher's army contained 99,715 infantry, 11,879 cavalry, and 9,360 artillery with 312 guns.[1]

Wellington's army was a heterogeneous body of troops and consisted of 31,253 British; 6,387 men of the King's German Legion; 15,935 Hanoverians; 29,214 Dutch-Belgians; 6,808 Brunswickers; 2,880 Nassauers; and 1,240 engineers, etc. In all he had 69,829 infantry, 14,482 cavalry, 8,166 artillery with 196 guns, and 1,240 engineers, etc. Nominally, his infantry was organized into two corps and a reserve: the Ist Corps (25,233 men) under the Prince of Orange; the IInd (24,033 men) under Lord Hill; and the Reserve (20,563) under Wellington's direct command.[2] By the end of May the Ist Corps occupied Mons, Roeulx, Frasnes, Seneffe, Nivelles, Genappe, Soignies, Enghien, and Braine-le-Comte, and the IInd Corps occupied Leuze, Ath, Grammont, Ghent, Alost, and Oudenarde. The cavalry, under Lord Uxbridge, was encamped along the Dender, and the Reserve was cantoned around Brussels, where Wellington had established his headquarters.

Fully aware of the over-extended distribution of the allies in Belgium, and rightly judging that they would not be ready to advance before July 1, Napoleon decided to seize the initiative, enter Belgium and beat in turn the English and Prussians before they could unite their forces. After this, he reckoned, the Belgians –pro-French at heart–would rise in his favour and the English Ministry would fall and be replaced by one more friendly to France. Should the destruction of the Anglo-Prussian armies not end the war, he would next unite with the Army of the Rhine (23,000 men under Rapp) in Alsace, and fall upon the Austrians and Russians.[3] As in 1814, he planned to make the most of his central position, and what he desired above all things was a startling and glorious victory at the very outset of the war in order to consolidate France and demoralize her enemies.

[1] For strengths see Charras, vol. 1, pp. 81–82.
[2] For strengths see Siborne's *History of the War in France and Belgium in 1815* (1844), vol. 1, pp. 28–29.
[3] *Commentaires de Napoléon 1er* (1867), vol. v, pp. 116–117.

Early in June, the Army of the North was ordered to concentrate in the area Maubeuge-Avesnes-Rocroi-Chimay, and on June 12, at 3.30 a.m., when its corps approached their destinations, Napoleon set out for Avesnes. There he was joined by Marshal Ney, who three months earlier had boasted that he would deliver the Emperor to Louis in an iron cage. At Avesnes he issued a stirring Order of the Day, which opened: "Soldiers, to-day is the anniversary of Marengo and Friedland", and which ended—"the moment has come to conquer or perish!"[1] On June 14 he moved his headquarters to Beaumont, and by nightfall, except for the IVth Corps, the concentration was virtually completed.

While the French massed, oblivious of what was in progress, the English and Prussians lay scattered in their cantonments. Not until the night of June 13–14, when Ziethen's outposts on the Sambre reported to him that many bivouac fires were to be seen around Beaumont, did he suspect what was happening.[2] He forwarded the news to Blücher, who on the evening of June 14—presumably depending on the Tirlemont agreement that Wellington would come to his support—ordered his IInd, IIIrd and IVth Corps to concentrate at Sombreffe. He also instructed Ziethen to cover their concentration by a stubborn resistance, and if pushed back to retire on Fleurus. Strategically, this forward concentration within striking distance of the enemy was a most foolhardy undertaking, for it presented Napoleon with a grand opportunity victoriously to end the campaign within 48 hours of its opening. Though Blücher was working in the dark, on June 15 his eyes were opened, for early that day General de Bourmont, who commanded the leading division of Gérard's corps, deserted to Ziethen and revealed to him Napoleon's orders and strength. But Blücher, who deemed himself invincible, remained blind, and sped from Namur to Sombreffe where he arrived at 4 p.m., determined to accept battle.

At 3 a.m.[3] on June 15 Napoleon mounted his horse, and at noon rode into Charleroi amid scenes of frantic excitement. There, a little after 3 p.m., he was rejoined by Ney, who through lack of horses had been delayed at Avesnes. The Emperor greeted him in a friendly way and forthwith gave him command of the Ist and IInd corps as well as Lefebvre-Desnouettes's cavalry division, and

[1] *Correspondance de Napoléon 1er*, No. 22052, vol. XXVII, p. 281.
[2] Certain rumours had been received earlier, see *Supplementary Despatches*, vol. X, pp. 470–471.
[3] *Correspondance*, No. 22055, vol. XXVIII, p. 286.

ordered him to "Go and pursue the enemy".[1] There can be little doubt that he must have said more than this, and, according to Gourgaud, he instructed him to sweep the enemy off the Charleroi-Brussels Road and occupy Quatre-Bras.[2] The probability of the last injunction is supported by the statement in the Bulletin of June 15 that "The Emperor has given the command of the left to the Prince of Moskova, who this evening established his head-quarters at Quatre-Chemins on the Brussels Road".[3] Though Ney did not do so, this statement indicates that Napoleon intended that he should.

As Ney rode away to take over his command, Grouchy appeared upon the scene, and shortly after was given command of the IIIrd and IVth Corps as well as Pajol's and Exelmans's divisions. Napoleon ordered him to push back the Prussians toward Sombreffe, but Grouchy was so dilatory that, at 5.30 p.m., Napoleon grew uneasy and rode forward to urge him on. A vigorous attack followed, and the bulk of Ziethen's corps was driven back to Fleurus. In the meantime Ney drove a Prussian detachment out of Gosselies, but then he ceased to be the Ney of Jena, yielded to prudence, and halted Reille's corps and sent forward Lefebvre-Desnouettes unsupported. At 6.30 p.m. the latter came under fire of a detachment of Dutch-Belgians of Prince Bernard of Saxe-Weimar's Nassau Brigade at Frasnes, which withdrew to Quatre-Bras. Lefebvre followed it up but found it too strongly posted to attack with cavalry alone and fell back to Frasnes.

That night, in three columns, the French Army bivouacked in a square of ten miles by ten, and, says Napoleon, "was disposed in such a way that it could manœuvre with equal facility against the Prussian Army or against the Anglo-Dutch Army, for it was already placed between them".[4] In the square the three columns were located as follows: *Ney's*–Lefebvre-Desnouettes's cavalry division at Frasnes; Reille's IInd Corps between Gosselies and Frasnes with Girard's division pushed out on the Fleurus Road, and d'Erlon's Ist Corps between Marchienne and Gosselies. *Grouchy's*–Pajol's and Exelmans's cavalry divisions around Lambusart (south of Fleurus); Vandamme's IIIrd Corps and Reserve Cavalry between Charleroi and Fleurus, and Gérard's IVth Corps astride the Sambre at Châtelet. *Reserves*–Guards

---

[1] Colonel Heymès "Relation", *Documents Inédits sur la Campagne de 1815*, duc d'Elchingen (1840), p. 4. Heymès was Ney's first A.D.C.
[2] *Campagne de Dix-Huit Cent Quinze* (1818), pp. 46–47.
[3] *Commentaires*, vol. v, p. 136.   [4] *Ibid.*, vol. v, p. 136.

between Charleroi and Gilly, and Lobau's VIth Corps south of Charleroi.

At 9 p.m. Napoleon returned to his headquarters at Charleroi

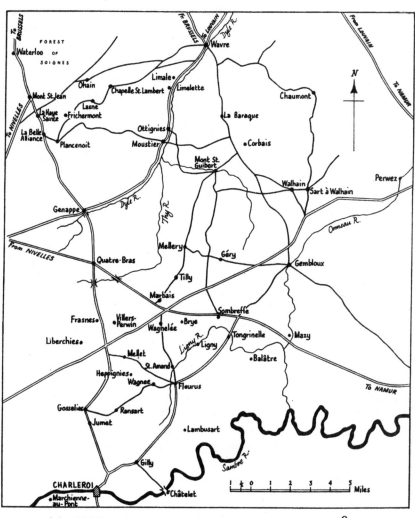

30. AREA OF OPERATIONS, JUNE 15–19, 1815

exhausted—he had been in the saddle since 3 a.m.—and at once lay down to rest.[1] At midnight he was aroused by the arrival of Ney, who stayed with him until 2 a.m. on June 16. Of this interview Colonel Heymès writes: "The Emperor made him stay to

[1] *Correspondance*, No. 22055, vol. XXVIII, p. 286.

supper, gave him his orders" and "unfolded to him his projects and his hopes for the day of the 16th. . . ."[1] Therefore, it goes without saying that Ney must have told the Emperor why he had not occupied Quatre-Bras, and that the latter must have instructed him to occupy it early on June 16. This is common sense, for should Wellington come to the support of Blücher, it was vital to Napoleon's project of dealing with one hostile army at the time that the Nivelles-Namur Road should be blocked. To assume otherwise is to write Napoleon down as a strategic dunce.

In the meantime, what was Wellington doing? Though his actions have been minutely analysed by all competent historians of the campaign, the only certain fact which has emerged is that he was totally unprepared to face the situation. He did not believe that Napoleon would assume the offensive,[2] and, it would seem, had become so involved in the gay life of Brussels that, on June 13, a rumour that Napoleon was at Maubeuge so little disturbed him that "he took Lady Jane Lennox to Enghien for a cricket match and brought her back at night, apparently having gone for no other object but to amuse her".[3] Though further rumours reached him on June 14, it was not until 3 p.m. the following day that a definite report was received to announce that the Prussian outposts near Thuin had been attacked. Possessed by the idea that Napoleon's intention was to advance by way of Mons and fall upon the Anglo-Dutch communications,[4] between 5 and 7 p.m.,[5] Wellington ordered his divisions to concentrate at the points already designated for them and hold themselves in readiness to march at the shortest notice.[6] According to this order, the Prince of Orange was to collect his 2nd and 3rd Divisions (Perponcher and Chassé) at Nivelles.

Next, in the evening, a dispatch came in from Blücher to announce the concentration of his army at Sombreffe.[7] Thereon, at 10 p.m., the Duke issued a second set of orders, according to which the 3rd Division (Alten) was to move from Braine-le-

---

[1] Heymès "Relation," p. 6.

[2] See his letter to Lord Lynedoch on June 13 (*The Dispatches of the Duke of Wellington.* Gurwood, 1838, vol. xii, p. 462).

[3] Quoted from a letter written at Brussels, on June 13, by the Rev. Spencer Madan, tutor to the young Lennoxes (*The Life of Wellington,* Sir Herbert Maxwell (1900), vol. ii, p. 10).

[4] An extraordinary misconception of Napoleonic strategy, because such a move would have driven Wellington and Blücher not apart but together.

[5] *Supplementary Despatches,* vol. x, p. 509.   [6] *Dispatches,* vol. xii, pp. 472–473.

[7] See *Passages from my Life,* etc., Baron von Müffling (1853), p. 229. Müffling was Blücher's liaison officer attached to Wellington's headquarters.

Comte to Nivelles; the 1st (Cooke) from Enghien to Braine-le-Comte; the 2nd (Clinton) and 4th (Colville) from Ath and Oudenarde to Enghien; and the cavalry, under Lord Uxbridge, from Ninhove to Enghien.[1] This meant a concentration away from Blücher and was clearly intended to cover the roads leading from Mons and Ath to Brussels, and not in order to cooperate with him.

Immediately after these orders had been sent, the Duke went to the Duchess of Richmond's ball and remained there until 2 a.m. Toward midnight he received a report from General Dörnberg at Mons to inform him that Napoleon had moved with all his forces on Charleroi and that there was nothing in front of Mons. At length Wellington's fears for his right were laid at rest, and in his official report he informs us that he then directed "the whole army to march upon Les Quatre Bras".[2]

This decision is corroborated by Captain (later General Sir George) Bowles. He says that at supper time Wellington and the Duke of Richmond left the table and went into the study to examine a map. Closing the door, Wellington said: "Napoleon has humbugged me, by G—! he has gained twenty-four hours march on me." When Richmond asked what he intended to do, he replied: " 'I have [? will] ordered the army to concentrate at Quatre-Bras; but we shall not stop him there, and if so, I must fight him *here*' (at the same time passing his thumb-nail over the position of Waterloo)."[3] Immediately after this Wellington left, and at 7.30 a.m. set out for Quatre-Bras.

Should the experiences of Captain Mercer be typical, then the forward concentration of the Anglo-Dutch Army, distracted as it was by orders and counter-orders, was carried out in extreme confusion. Some units received no orders at all, others defective ones; some officers were still in ballroom dress, and many had no idea of what was happening. At Nivelles, writes Mercer, "The

---

[1] *Dispatches*, vol. XII, p. 474.

[2] *Dispatches*, vol. XII, p. 479. See also Müffling's *Passages*, p. 230, and *Supplementary Despatches*, vol. x, p. 510. Some time after 2 a.m. June 16.

[3] See *Letters of the First Earl of Malmesbury* (1870), vol. II, p. 445. Bowles says that the Duke of Richmond repeated this conversation to him two minutes after it had taken place. With reference to it, and when combined with Wellington's social proclivities, it is illuminating to read that, at 3 a.m. on June 18–a few hours before the battle of Waterloo opened–the Duke wrote to Lady Frances Webster–"A very pretty woman"–that she should be prepared "to remove from Bruxelles to Antwerp in case such a measure should be necessary" (*Supplementary Despatches*, vol. x, p. 501), and that at 8.30 a.m. on June 19 he wrote to her again that she could "remain in Bruxelles in perfect security". (*Ibid.*, vol. x, p. 531.) Well may it be asked, was it Napoleon who had done the humbugging?

road was covered with soldiers, many of them wounded but also many apparently untouched. The numbers thus leaving the field appeared extraordinary. Many of the wounded had six, eight, ten and even more, attendants. When questioned about the battle and why they left it, the answer was invariably, 'Monsieur, tout est perdu! les Anglais sont abimés, en déroute, abimés, tous, tous, tous!' "[1] The battle of Quatre-Bras had begun.

When Wellington was on his way to Quatre-Bras, 25 miles to the South of Brussels, Ziethen's corps occupied a salient along the Ligny brook, its right at Wagnelée, its centre at St. Amand and its left at Ligny. There it remained unsupported until noon, when the IInd Corps, under Pirch, and the IIIrd, under Thielemann, began to arrive. The former was posted immediately in rear of Ziethen's Corps and the latter was deployed on its left between Sombreffe and Mazy with a strong covering force along the Ligny brook. Bülow's IVth Corps was far behind, therefore Blücher was only able to concentrate 84,000 men on the field of Ligny.

In the meantime, assuming that the allies would behave according to the rules of war – that is, fall back in order to secure their concentration – Napoleon jumped to the conclusion that Wellington would withdraw on Brussels. He therefore decided to advance on that city and fight Wellington should he stand, or drive him on to Antwerp – that is, away from Blücher, who was based on Liège. But before this could be done, it was necessary to push Ziethen back beyond Gembloux, in order to deny Blücher the use of the Namur-Wavre-Brussels Road. With this in mind, at about 6 a.m. Napoleon dictated two letters, one for Ney and the other for Grouchy, to explain his intentions.[2]

In his letter to Grouchy he wrote that, should the Prussians be at Sombreffe or Gembloux, he would attack them, and once he had occupied Gembloux he would next swing his reserves over to Ney and operate against Wellington. He restated this in his letter to Ney and instructed him to be ready to march on Brussels directly the reserves joined him, and that meanwhile he was to push one division five miles north of Quatre-Bras, hold six at Quatre-Bras, and send one to Marbais to link up with Grouchy's left. Also he told him that Kellermann's division would replace Lefebvre-Desnouettes's. Then, so it would seem, he remembered

---

[1] *Journal of the Waterloo Campaign*, General Cavalie Mercer (1870), vol. i, chapter xi, and p. 250.

[2] See *Correspondance*, Nos. 22058 and 22059, vol. xxviii, pp. 289–292.

how thick-headed was Ney and explained to him the method of his manœuvre. "I have adopted for this campaign," he wrote, "the following general principle, to divide my army into two wings and a reserve. . . . The Guard will form the reserve, and I shall bring it into action on either wing as circumstances may dictate. . . . Also, according to circumstances, I shall draw troops from one wing to strengthen my reserve."

Shortly after these letters were dispatched (about 8 a.m.) Napoleon received a message from Grouchy to inform him that strong columns had been seen to approach Sombreffe from the direction of Namur. This pointed to the probability that the whole, or most, of the Prussian army would assemble at Sombreffe, and therefore to the further probability that the Anglo-Dutch army would come to the support of Blücher. As this disrupted Napoleon's plan, he refused to believe it, modified nothing, and set out from Charleroi and arrived at Fleurus shortly before 11 a.m. There he found Vandamme's corps in line facing St. Amand–the western side of Ziethen's salient–and learnt that Gérard's was still far in rear, due, it would appear, to faulty staff work. At once Napoleon reconnoitred the enemy position, and though he could see only Ziethen's corps, its dispositions convinced him that it was no rear guard, but instead a force covering a general advance, as well as one securing the Sombreffe-Quatre-Bras Road–that is, the only main road by which Wellington could approach.[1] In an instant all was clear; in spite of his fixed idea and the rules of war, it was apparent that the allies were concentrating forward, and, therefore intended to unite. But until Gérard's corps came up, which it began to do at 1 p.m., Napoleon did not feel strong enough to attack. Meanwhile Pirch and Thielemann deployed, and overjoyed when he saw that he had to deal with more than one corps, he decided to settle accounts with Blücher that afternoon.

His plan–a truly brilliant one–was first to contain Blücher's left (Thielemann's corps) with Pajol's and Exelmans's cavalry, and secondly to annihilate his right and centre (Ziethen and Pirch). The latter operation he intended to carry out by engaging the Prussian centre and right frontally, so as to compel Blücher to exhaust his reserves, and meanwhile to call in Ney from Quatre-Bras to fall upon the rear of Blücher's right wing while the Guard smashed through his centre. By these means he expected to destroy

[1] Gourgaud, *Campagne de 1815*, pp. 55–56.

two-thirds of Blücher's army and compel the remaining third to fall back on Liège–that is, away from Wellington.

At 2 p.m. he instructed Soult to inform Ney that Grouchy would attack the enemy between Sombreffe and Brye at 2.30 p.m. Next, we read: "His Majesty's intention is that you also will attack whatever force is in front of you, and after having vigorously pushed it back, you will turn in our direction, so as to bring about the envelopment of that body of the enemy's troops whom I have just mentioned to you. If the latter is overthrown first, then His Majesty will manœuvre in your direction, so as to assist your operation in a similar way."[1]

Then he turned to Gérard, whose corps was deploying against Ligny–the southern face of Ziethen's salient–and said: "It is possible that three hours hence the fate of the war may be decided. If Ney carries out his orders thoroughly, not a gun of the Prussian Army will get away: it is taken in the very act (*prise en flagrant délit*)."[2]

At 2.30 p.m., while Grouchy's cavalry contained Thielemann, Vandamme and Girard[3] vigorously attacked St. Amand while Gérard assaulted Ligny. But the Prussian resistance was so stubborn that, at 3.15 p.m., Napoleon instructed Soult to send the following message to Ney:

"His Majesty desires me to tell you that you are to manœuvre immediately in such a manner as to envelop the enemy's right and fall upon his rear; the army in our front is lost if you act with energy. The fate of France is in your hands.

"Thus do not hesitate even for a moment to carry out the manœuvre . . . and direct your advance on the heights of Brye and St. Amand so as to co-operate in a victory that may well turn out to be decisive. . . ."[4]

Immediately after its dispatch, Napoleon heard from Lobau, at Charleroi, that Ney was confronted by a force 20,000 strong. He feared that the 3.15 p.m. order might not be sufficiently explicit, and assuming that, with Reille's corps alone, Ney should be able to hold the enemy back, Napoleon sent by Count de la Bédoyère his celebrated "pencil note"[5] to him. As circumstances prevented Ney advancing with his whole army on Brye, he in-

---

[1] *Documents Inédits*, duc d'Elchingen, No. XIII, p. 40.
[2] *Commentaires*, vol. v, pp. 140–141.
[3] On the night of June 15–16 Girard's division of Reille's corps, as we have seen, bivouacked on the Fleurus Road. On June 16 it was attached to Vandamme's corps.
[4] *Documents Inédits*, duc d'Elchingen, No. xiv, p. 42.
[5] This note has since been lost.

structed him to order d'Erlon's corps alone to march against the Prussian rear. At the same time he sent an order to Lobau to advance his corps to Fleurus.

This last order introduces Napoleon's crucial blunder on June 16. When, at about 10 a.m., he set out from Charleroi for Fleurus, he should, at the same time, have ordered Lobau forward. Had he done so, and had Lobau started at, say, noon, since Fleurus is eight miles from Charleroi, the head of his corps would have reached Fleurus by 3.30 p.m.; in which case there would have been no need to send the "pencil note" to Ney. Should it be suggested that, at 10 a.m., Napoleon could not tell where he might need to employ Lobau, then he should have ordered him to Mellet, near the junction of the Roman and Charleroi-Brussels roads, where he would have been far better placed than at Charleroi either to assist Ney or himself. Actually, Lobau reached Fleurus at 7.30 p.m., and as Fleurus is more than four miles from Wagnelée, it was then too late for him to move against Blücher's right rear. The eventual wanderings of d'Erlon's corps were a serious but not an unusual incident, somewhat similar mishaps occurred at Jena and Leipzig. But on the morning of June 16 to leave Lobau at Charleroi was an inexcusable blunder.

In the meantime, the battle continued furiously; Girard was killed assaulting St. Amand, and Gérard stormed into Ligny. So hard pressed was the Prussian right that Blücher was compelled repeatedly to draw on his reserves, until at 5 p.m. they were nearly exhausted. By then, out of the 68,000 troops which Napoleon had brought on to the field, he had used no more than 58,000, and with them had fixed Blücher's 84,000. The time, therefore, had come to strike the decisive blow, and calculating that, at 6 p.m. he would hear the roar of d'Erlon's guns in rear of the Prussian right wing, he prepared to launch the Guard against the enemy centre at Ligny; smash through it, cut off Blücher's right from Sombreffe and annihilate Ziethen and Pirch.

While the Guards prepared for their grand assault, suddenly Vandamme rode up to the Emperor with alarming news. Two and a half miles to the rear, he said, an enemy column, 20,000 to 30,000 strong, had been sighted approaching Fleurus. Was it Ney? Was it d'Erlon? Vandamme was positive that it was hostile.[1]

---

[1] Vandamme had sent out an officer to reconnoitre the column, but he merely approached it, and then galloped back exclaiming: "They are enemies." It is strange that d'Erlon did not send forward a galloper announcing his arrival.

Napoleon was perplexed, for he expected d'Erlon to move to Brye by the Roman Road and not on Fleurus, which lay to the south of the Prussian centre. At once he suspended the movements of the Guard, made dispositions to meet the advancing column, and sent Duhesme's division of the Young Guard to support Vandamme, whose men bordered on panic. At the same time he sent an aide-de-damp to ascertain to whom the column belonged. At 6.30 p.m. the aide-de-camp returned,[1] and reported it to be d'Erlon's. Forthwith, so it would seem, another aide-de-camp was sent galloping to d'Erlon with orders to press on to Wagnelée, but when he arrived he found that, except for his leading division (Durutte's), the rest of his corps was in full retreat—in compliance with orders sent by Ney. To send out yet another aide to order d'Erlon to counter-march was useless, for nearly three hours would be required to bring him to Wagnelée, and by then it would be dark.

Too frequently it has gone unrecognized that d'Erlon's expected approach in the least expected of directions nearly cost Napoleon the battle. It so completely unhinged the morale of Vandamme's corps that General Lefol, one of his divisional commanders, in order to arrest the flight of his men, turned his cannon on the fugitives.[2] The Prussians took advantage of the French disorder and vigorously assaulted St. Amand, and had it not been for the arrival of the Young Guard, who counter-attacked with superb *élan*, it is probable that the whole of Vandamme's corps would have taken to flight. The net result of the d'Erlon fiasco was that, once the situation again was stabilized, Napoleon was left with so little time[3] that, even should the final assault of the Guard on Ligny prove successful, it was improbable that it would prove decisive. This is what happened, for not until 7.30 p.m. was Napoleon again ready to launch his final assault.

Though the sun was still high above the horizon, great, rolling storm clouds now shrouded the battlefield in blackness. Then, as the storm broke, and the thunder drowned the roar of the cannonade, in sheets of rain and with cries of "*Vive l'Empereur!*" the Guard advanced at the charge, for the deluge rendered firing impossible; like an avalanche of steel they swept the Prussians out of Ligny.

[1] Gourgaud, *Campagne de 1815*, p. 59.
[2] See Houssaye's *1815 Waterloo*, pp. 99–100, quoting Lefol's *Souvenirs*.
[3] The sun set at 8.20 p.m., and the battle ended in the dark at 9.30 p.m.

When the rain ceased and the last rays of the setting sun gleamed between the scattering clouds, at full gallop Blücher arrived on the field. He counted on Röder's cavalry – 32 squadrons in all – to repel the French, placed himself at their head, and ordered them to charge the squares of the Guard, then slowly advancing toward the mill of Bussy (south of Brye). In the resulting mêlée Blücher's horse was struck by a bullet and rolled over its rider. His aide-de-camp, Nostiz, sprang from his horse and came to Blücher's help. Though surrounded by the 9th Regiment of Cuirassiers, under cover of the increasing gloom and the confusion of innumerable fugitives, he dragged the 73-year-old field-marshal, bruised and half-conscious, to safety. Had he not done so, Waterloo would never have been fought.

Though Blücher's centre was completely shattered and his right wing severed from his left, under cover of night the broken Ist and IInd corps fell back in disorder to between Sombreffe and the Roman Road. Had d'Erlon been in their rear, they would have been destroyed. But what is equally probable is, with two hours more daylight the Guard alone would have accomplished as much. Captain Becke in no way exaggerates what this would have led to when he writes: "The news of such a victory . . . would have shaken Europe to its foundations, and at the same time have raised France to a pitch of enthusiasm that must have carried Napoleon on to ultimate victory."[1] Nevertheless, Ligny was a great victory and it presented Napoleon with the opportunity to attack Wellington on the next day without fear of Prussian interference.

Toward 11 p.m. the Emperor returned to Fleurus, and under cover of its outposts the whole French Army bivouacked on the left bank of the Ligny brook. As usual, the casualties are variously given, but it would appear that those of the Prussians in killed, wounded and prisoners amounted to about 16,000, and of the French to between 11,000 and 12,000. To the Prussian losses must be added between 8,000 and 10,000 men who during the night abandoned their colours and fled toward Liège.[2] This flight had an extraordinary repercussion on June 17, and was worth to Blücher at least an additional army corps.

In the meantime, what had taken place at Quatre-Bras? At

---

[1] *Napoleon at Waterloo* (1914), vol. I, p. 270.

[2] According to Ropes (*The Campaign of Waterloo*, 1910, p. 159), quoting Gneisenau, "These men belonged to provinces which had formerly been part of the French Empire, and their sympathies were with Napoleon."

10 a.m., when Wellington arrived there, he found Saxe-Weimar's and Bylandt's brigades holding the cross-roads and hamlet. Though this concentration of Perponcher's Division contravened Wellington's 5 p.m. order of June 15, it was fortunate for the Duke, for had his order been obeyed it is highly unlikely that he would ever have reached Quatre-Bras. What had happened was this:

When the Prince of Orange left Nivelles to attend the Duchess of Richmond's ball, General Rebecque, his Chief of Staff, heard that Saxe-Weimar's brigade had been attacked and had fallen back on Quatre-Bras and ordered Perponcher with his remaining brigade–Bylandt's–to support him. Next, at 11 p.m., when Wellington's 5 p.m. order was received by Rebecque, he passed it on to Perponcher without comment, and on his own initiative the latter set it aside, and instead of concentrating his division at Nivelles, concentrated it at Quatre-Bras. Little suspected by him at the time, this act of intelligent disobedience saved Blücher; for had he complied with the order Ney would have found Quatre-Bras unheld, and therefore would have been able to carry out the Emperor's 6 a.m. instruction to the letter, and later those contained in Soult's 2 p.m. dispatch.

Wellington found little in front of him and at 10.30 a.m. wrote to Blücher[1] to inform him of his troop movements. These appear to have been based on a memorandum[2] which had been handed to him before leaving Brussels by Colonel De Lancey, his Chief of Staff. It was a thoroughly slipshod document, for several of the units mentioned in it were nowhere near the positions assigned to them, therefore their arrival at Genappe and Quatre-Bras could not be correctly timed. Some time after this letter was sent, all remained quiet, Wellington rode over to Brye and at 1 p.m. met Blücher at the Bussy windmill.

What took place during the interview is uncertain, but, according to Müffling,[3] Wellington agreed to come to Blücher's support provided he himself was not attacked. What he thought of Blücher's dispositions is made clear in the reply to a question posed to him by Sir Henry Hardinge, his military attaché at Blücher's headquarters. When the latter asked him what he thought of Blücher's deployment, the Duke replied: "If they fight here they will be damnably mauled."[3]

[1] See The Campaign of Waterloo, Ropes, p. 106.
[2] Supplementary Despatches, vol. x, p. 496.   [3] Passages, p. 237.
[3] Notes of Conversations with the Duke of Wellington, 1831–1851. Philip Henry, 5th Earl of Stanhope (1886), p. 109.

Some time after 2 p.m. Wellington set out on his return, and when at three o'clock he was back at Quatre-Bras, because of the De Lancey memorandum he found his own dispositions even more damnable than Blücher's. Actually, he was lucky ever to have got back there, which he most certainly would not have done had Ney lived up to his reputation.

When, after his midnight interview with the Emperor, Ney returned to Gosselies, instead of ordering Reille, whom he actually visited, to concentrate his corps as soon as possible after dawn at Frasnes–at the time held by Bachelu's Division and Piré's cavalry–and at the same time sending instructions to d'Erlon to close up on Gosselies, he waited until 11 a.m. before doing so. This quite unnecessary delay of five or six hours was the root cause of all his subsequent predicaments, and it contrasts glaringly with Perponcher's bold initiative.

At 11.45 a.m. Reille set out, and at two o'clock was ordered by Ney to clear the enemy out of the woods south of Quatre-Bras. Reille feared what he called a "Spanish battle"–that is, that the English were hidden away and would only appear at the critical moment–and advanced with extreme caution. He had in all 19,000 men backed by 3,000 cavalry within call and 60 guns, and in rear, d'Erlon with 20,000 more, though still distant, was approaching. Actually, though Reille was unaware of it, the Prince of Orange then had only 7,800 infantry, supported by 50 horsemen and 14 guns. Therefore, had Reille or Ney displayed but usual boldness, nothing could have saved Quatre-Bras. As it was, when Wellington returned there at 3 p.m., he found the situation critical. The hamlet of Quatre-Bras was nearly lost and would have fallen had not Picton's Division come up by the Brussels Road and van Merlen's cavalry brigade from Nivelles. Immediately after, the Duke of Brunswick's Corps arrived and Reille was slightly outnumbered.

Shortly before 4 p.m., Ney received Soult's 2 p.m. letter ordering him to press the enemy back and then move against Blücher's right rear. At last Ney realized the importance of gaining Quatre-Bras and ordered a general forward movement, during which the Duke of Brunswick was mortally wounded, as his father had been at Auerstädt.

Ney, who counted on d'Erlon to support Reille, impatiently awaited his arrival, and long before this he would have been at hand had he set out earlier. Actually, the head of d'Erlon's column

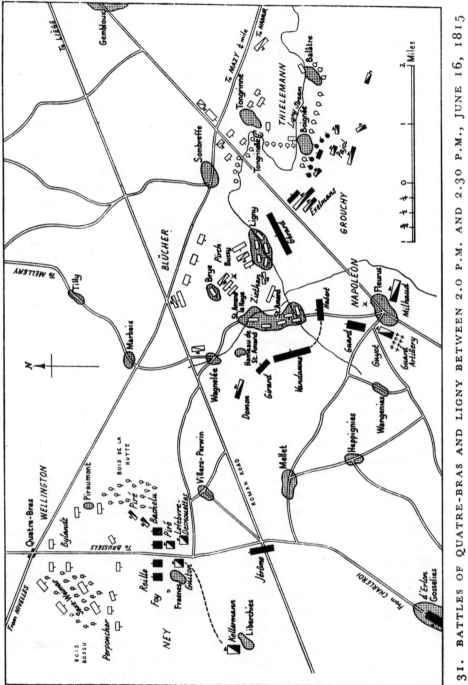

31. BATTLES OF QUATRE-BRAS AND LIGNY BETWEEN 2.0 P.M. AND 2.30 P.M., JUNE 16, 1815

was not far away, for between four and a quarter past four o'clock, half his corps was already north of the Roman Road, and he himself had ridden forward to reconnoitre Quatre-Bras. It was while he was away that General de la Bédoyère galloped up with the "pencil note" for Ney, and instead of warning the commander of the van of its purport, and then taking the note on to Ney, on his own initiative he "ordered the column to move in the direction of Ligny".[1] The "pencil note", it would seem, was an all but illegible scrawl, and de la Bédoyère read it incorrectly and instead of directing the column on Wagnelée, instructed it to march on St. Amand.

On his return, d'Erlon learnt of this change of direction and at once sent his Chief of Staff, General Delacombre, to inform Ney what had happened. Ney, who increasingly was outnumbered, relied on d'Erlon to win his battle, and when he was acquainted with what had transpired he flew into a violent passion which was raised to still higher pitch when a few minutes later the officer carrying Soult's 3.15 p.m. dispatch—"the fate of France is in your hands"—arrived. To make matters worse, at this moment the van of Alten's division debouched from Quatre-Bras and, maddened by the sight and blinded with rage, Ney cast the Emperor's orders aside. He did not for a moment consider that tactically d'Erlon's corps was now beyond profitable recall, and sent Delacambre back with an imperative order to d'Erlon to countermarch his corps. This the latter did and rejoined Ney after nightfall.

For Ney, the irony of this fiasco was that, had not d'Erlon's corps been diverted, in all probability Wellington would have suffered a severe defeat. And for Napoleon that, had the "pencil note" been legible, there would have been no alarm, and Blücher would not have gained a breathing-space in which to prepare to meet Napoleon's final assault, which would have been launched two hours earlier, and therefore would have permitted a pursuit to follow.

Both these lost chances were due to failures to concentrate in time: Gérard's IVth Corps was at least three hours late in arriving at Fleurus, and Reille's IInd Corps over five hours late in concentrating at Frasnes. As it happened, of all the corps commanders engaged in the two battles, d'Erlon was the least to blame,

---

[1] *Le Maréchal Drouet, Comte d'Erlon* (1844), pp. 95–96. Also *Documents Inédits*, duc d'Elchingen, pp. 95–96.

though when Delacombre caught up with him near Villers Perwin, he should have disobeyed Ney's frantic order, because lack of time did not permit it profitably to be carried out.

Deprived of d'Erlon, Ney not only lost his temper, but also his judgment. He called up Kellermann and ordered him with a single brigade of cuirassiers to charge Wellington's infantry squares and trample them under foot. This Kellermann most gallantly set out to do, and after he had scattered Halkett's 69th Regiment and had driven his 33rd into the woods, though repulsed by the 30th and 73rd[1] he nevertheless succeeded in penetrating as far as the cross roads.[2]

When this heroic[3] though fruitless charge was under way, Major Badus, who had been sent by the Emperor with a verbal message to Ney, came up. The message was that, whatever Ney's circumstances might be, the order to d'Erlon must be executed absolutely.[4] Maddened with rage, Ney abruptly turned from him, rushed into the midst of his routed infantry, and succeeded in rallying them.

At nine o'clock the battle ended in a draw, both armies retook the positions they had held in the morning. Even by the close of the day, thanks to his delays on June 15 and the De Lancey memorandum, Wellington had succeeded only in concentrating less than half his infantry, a third of his artillery, and only one-seventh of his cavalry, in all 31,000 men. Nevertheless, Ney had done no better, for out of the 43,000 men entrusted to him he assembled only 22,000. The casualties were about equal, between 4,000 and 5,000 on either side.

Thus far Napoleon's plan had worked well enough. He had beaten Blücher, therefore all that remained was to beat Wellington. How to defeat his army now became the problem, consequently on his return to Fleurus at 11 p.m., as he had heard nothing from Ney throughout the day,[5] he should have sent an

---

[1] See *Waterloo Letters*, Major-General H. T. Siborne (1891), pp. 318–337.

[2] Mercer (*Journal of the Waterloo Campaign*, vol. I, p. 263) writes: "Just in front of the farm of Quatre Bras there was a fearful scene of slaughter—Highlanders and cuirassiers lying thickly strewn about...."

[3] In *Letters of Colonel Sir Augustus Simon Frazer, K.C.B.* (1859), p. 540, Frazer writes: "The enemy's lancers and cuirassiers are the finest fellows I ever saw;—they made several bold charges, and repeatedly advanced in the very teeth of our infantry."

[4] See Houssaye's *1815 Waterloo*, p. 122.

[5] In Soult's 2 p.m. letter Ney was instructed to inform the Emperor of his dispositions and what happened on his front. This he did not do until 10 p.m., when he sent in a report on Quatre-Bras which was so meagre as to be valueless. (See *Napoleon and Waterloo*, Captain A. F. Becke, vol. II, Appx. II, p. 287.)

officer to Frasnes to obtain for him a report on Ney's situation, also he should have instructed Ney to keep him hourly informed of Wellington's movements. That he did not do so may have been because of complete exhaustion,[1] in which case Soult, on his own initiative, should have acted for him, or what is equally possible, he assumed that Blücher would fall back on his base at Liège and that Wellington would retire from Quatre-Bras during the night, as he should have done, but apparently delayed doing because he had so little cavalry and artillery at hand to cover his retreat.

The first of these illusions was strengthened when, at 7 a.m. on June 17, he learnt that at 2.30 a.m. Grouchy had sent out Pajol's cavalry, which at 4 a.m. had reported that the enemy was in full retreat on Liège. Actually what Pajol's squadrons had come up against were the thousands of deserters who had fled the field of Ligny. This news was received when the Emperor was at breakfast, and at the same time General Flahaut, an aide who had carried a dispatch to Ney on the previous day, returned from Frasnes with news of the battle of Quatre-Bras and that Wellington was still in position there. At once Soult wrote to Ney to inform him of Blücher's defeat and retreat. Next, he wrote:

"The Emperor is going to the mill of Brye, where the highway leading from Namur to Quatre-Bras passes. This makes it impossible that the English Army should act in front of you. In the latter event, the Emperor would march directly on it by the Quatre-Bras road, while you would attack it from the front, and this army would be destroyed in an instant. . . .

"His Majesty's wishes are, that you should take up your position at Quatre-Bras; but if this is impossible . . . send information immediately with full details, and the Emperor will act there as I have told you. If, on the contrary, there is only a rearguard, attack it and seize the position.

"To-day it is necessary to end this operation, and complete the military stores, to rally scattered soldiers and summon back all detachments."[2]

---

[1] On June 15 Napoleon rose at 3 a.m., rested at Charleroi between 9 p.m. and midnight, interviewed Ney from midnight to 2 a.m. June 16, and presumably rested between 2 a.m. and 4 a.m. (Houssaye, p. 346, footnote 7). At 10 a.m. he left Charleroi for Fleurus, returned to Fleurus at 11 p.m. and rested until about 6.30 a.m. on June 17. Therefore, between 3 a.m. on June 15 and 6.30 a.m. on June 17, in all 51½ hours, he rested for 12¼. This was not excessive for a man who, as Caulaincourt says, "needed much sleep" (Memoirs, vol. 1, p. 599). Fain (Mémoires, 1908, p. 290) says, "It was his habit to sleep about seven hours out of the twenty-four; but it was always in several naps."

[2] Documents Inédits, duc d'Elchingen, No. XVII, pp. 45–47.

This is an extraordinary document, for it shows that, though Napoleon was uncertain whether the whole of Wellington's army was still at Quatre-Bras, he was in no way certain that it was not. Therefore, knowing that Blücher was retreating, whether Wellington's army were retiring or not, he should forthwith have ordered Ney to attack whatever was in front of him and simultaneously have carried the VIth Corps and the Guard to his support. Instead he ordered Lobau to assist Pajol on the Namur Road, and sent out a cavalry reconnaissance to Quatre-Bras to make certain whether the English were still there. After this he got into his coach, drove to Grouchy's headquarters, visited the wounded and reviewed his troops. While thus engaged, between 10 and 11 a.m., the officer in command of the reconnaissance returned and reported that the English were still at Quatre-Bras,[1] and at the same time Pajol reported that the Prussians were massing at Gembloux. At last Napoleon awoke from his trance, made up his mind, and sent orders to Lobau and Drouot to march the VIth Corps and Guard to Marbais in order to support Ney's attack on Quatre-Bras. Next, he dictated two letters, one for Grouchy, to whom he had already given verbal orders, and the other for Ney. In the first, we read: "Proceed to Gembloux with the cavalry . . . and the IIIrd and IVth corps of infantry . . . You will explore in the directions of Namur and Maestricht [i.e. south-east and north-east of Sombreffe] and you will pursue the enemy. Explore his march, and instruct me respecting his manœuvres, so that I may be able to penetrate what he is intending to do. . . . It is important to penetrate what the enemy is intending to do; whether they are separating themselves from the English, or whether they are intending still to unite, to cover Brussels or Liège, in trying the fate of another battle. . . ."[2]

The letter to Ney, which is timed midday, reads:

"The Emperor has just ordered a corps of infantry and the Imperial Guard to Marbais. His Majesty has directed me to inform you that his intention is that you are to attack the enemy at Quatre-Bras and drive him from his position and that the force which is at Marbais will second your operations. His Majesty is about to proceed to Marbais, and awaits your reports with impatience."[3]

---

[1] Gourgaud, *Campagne de 1815*, p. 74.
[2] See Ropes, *The Campaign of Waterloo*, pp. 209–210 and 358.
[3] *Documents Inédits*, duc d'Elchingen, No. XVI, pp. 44–45.

When Blücher was incapacitated, Gneisenau had ordered the Prussian Army to retire on Tilly and Wavre, not in order to keep contact with Wellington, but because most of the army had been driven north of the Nivelles-Namur Road, and therefore it was safer to fall back on Louvain and from there reopen communication with Liège than to attempt a direct withdrawal on Liège. Later, when Blücher had been carried to Mellery–a mile or two north of Tilly–and had sufficiently recovered, he discussed the next move with Gneisenau, his Chief of Staff, and Grölmann, his Quarter Master General. Gneisenau, who did not trust Wellington and considered him to be a knave, urged that the army should fall back on Liège, but Blücher, still full of fire and supported by Grölmann, disagreed, and it was decided to maintain contact with the English.[1]

When this decisive argument took place, Wellington was at Genappe, and as he had heard nothing from Blücher since 2 p.m., at 2 a.m. on June 17 he sent Colonel Gordon and a troop of cavalry to discover what had happened. Gordon returned at 7.30 a.m. and reported that he had contacted Ziethen and had learnt that the Prussians had been beaten and were retiring on Wavre. Wellington then decided that he must also retire. Next, at 9 a.m., when his army was prepared to do so, an officer arrived from Blücher to confirm what Gordon had said. Further, he informed Wellington that the Field-Marshal was anxious to know his intentions. The Duke replied that he was falling back on Mont St. Jean, and there would offer Napoleon battle if Blücher would support him with one army corps.[2] At 10 a.m., covered by Lord Uxbridge's cavalry, the retreat on Mont St. Jean began.

That Wellington was able to retire unmolested was entirely because of Ney's inactivity. Though the latter had been ordered to attack, he did nothing, and at noon, when his enemy was in full retreat, his men sat about preparing their mid-day meal.[3]

While they were thus peacefully engaged, the Emperor set out from Brye and reached Marbais at about one o'clock. Because he did not hear a cannonade at Quatre-Bras he was much perturbed, and when he pressed on with his cavalry and debouched on the Brussels Road he was astonished to find Ney's army still in bivouac.[4] At once he ordered all troops to fall in, but it was not

---

[1] See Stanhope's *Conversations*, pp. 108–110.   [2] Müffling, *Passages*, p. 241.
[3] *Waterloo Letters*, No. 75, p. 166.   [4] Gourgaud, *Campagne de 1815*, p. 77.

until two o'clock that the head of d'Erlon's Corps came up.
Napoleon realized the magnitude of his lost opportunity and
said to d'Erlon: "France has been ruined; go, my dear General,
and place yourself at the head of the cavalry, and press the
English rearguard vigorously."[1] Next, when he saw Milhaud's
horsemen drawn up alongside the road, the Emperor led them
forward at breakneck speed toward Genappe.

When the French pursuit began, "The sky", writes Mercer,
"had become overcast since the morning, and at this moment . . .
large isolated masses of thundercloud, of the deepest, almost inky
black . . . hung suspended over us, involving our position and
everything on it in deep and gloomy obscurity; whilst the distant
hill lately occupied by the French army still lay bathed in brilliant
sunshine." Next, he says:

"Lord Uxbridge was yet speaking when a single horseman
[Napoleon] immediately followed by several others, mounted the
plateau I had left at a gallop, their dark figures thrown forward
in strong relief from the illuminated distance, making them
appear much nearer to us than they really were. For an instant
they pulled up and regarded us, when several squadrons, coming
up rapidly on the plateau, Lord Uxbridge cried out, 'Fire!–fire!'
. . . The first gun that was fired seemed to burst the clouds over-
head, for its report was instantly followed by an awful clap of
thunder, and lightning that almost blinded us, whilst the rain
came down as if a water-spout had broken over us."[2]

In part, at least, this terrific storm of rain saved Wellington, for
it so drenched the ground that the French were unable to advance
across country, and were, in consequence, tied to the Brussels
Road.[3] Had they been able, as was Napoleon's wont, to advance
in extended order, it is probable that, in spite of the late start,
the Emperor would have caught up with his enemy by five or
six o'clock. Had he done so, and had he attacked Wellington and
fixed him to his position when not fully deployed, it is also possible
that he might have beaten him during the next morning, or what
is more likely, have forced him to retire during the night.

[1] *Le Maréchal Drouet, Comte d'Erlon*, p. 96.
[2] Mercer's *Journal*, vol. I, pp. 268-270. The rain at once extinguished every slow-
match in the brigade.
[3] Captain W. B. Ingliby, R.H.A. writes: "The road and ground became so quickly
deluged with the heavy rain . . . that it became impracticable for the French
Cavalry to press our columns in any force. In fact, out of the road in the track of our
own Cavalry, the ground was poached into a complete puddle." (*Waterloo Letters*,
No. 81, p. 196.)

From Quatre-Bras, the pursuit and retreat resembled a "fox-hunt". "Lord Uxbridge urging us on", writes Mercer, "and crying 'Make haste!–make haste! for God's sake, gallop or you will be taken' . . . away we went, helter-skelter–guns, gun-detachments, and hussars mixed pêle-mêle, going like mad."[1] Genappe with its single narrow bridge was reached, the rain stopped, and toward 6.30 p.m. Napoleon with the van of his cavalry rode on to the heights of La Belle Alliance,[2] which were separated by a shallow valley from a parallel range of heights, behind which, unseen to Napoleon, Wellington's army lay. At once the Emperor ordered up four horse batteries and under cover of their fire Milhaud's cuirassiers charged up the slope to discover that the whole of the Anglo-Dutch Army was in position. Napoleon pointed to the sun and exclaimed: "What would I not give to-day to have had Joshua's power to have slowed down the enemy's march by two hours."[3] Though he himself was by no means free of blame, had Ney attacked his enemy early in the morning those two hours, and more, would have been gained.

Napoleon turned about and rode to his headquarters, which had been established in the farm of Le Caillou, a mile and a half south of La Belle Alliance, and about 9 p.m. he received a report from Milhaud that one of his patrols had sighted a Prussian column retiring from Géry toward Wavre. This did not perturb him, for he could not bring himself to believe that, in face of Grouchy's 33,000 men, Blücher would dare to attempt a flank march across his front in order to join Wellington.

After resting for an hour or two, at 1 a.m. on June 18 Napoleon set out in torrents of rain to ride round his outposts. He returned to his headquarters at dawn to find that at 2 a.m. a dispatch, timed 10 p.m. June 17, had come in from Grouchy. It informed him that the Prussians appeared to be withdrawing in two columns, one on Wavre and the other on Perwez, and it added: "Perhaps it may be inferred that one portion is going to join Wellington, whilst the centre, under Blücher, retires on Liège; another column, accompanied by guns, has already retreated to Namur. This evening General Exelmans is pushing six squadrons of cavalry towards Sart-à-Walhain, and three to Perwez. When their reports are at hand, then if I find the mass of the Prussians is retiring on

[1] Mercer's *Journal*, vol. 1, pp. 270–274.
[2] Gourgaud, *Campagne de 1815*, p. 79. The leading French infantry were still several miles in rear.
[3] *Commentaires*, vol. v, p. 200.

Wavre I shall follow them, so as to prevent them gaining Brussels and to separate them from Wellington."[1]

Coupled with Milhaud's report, this dispatch should at once have been answered.[2] Yet it was not until 10 a.m. that a reply was sent off to inform Grouchy "that at this moment His Majesty is going to attack the English Army, which has taken up its position at Waterloo. His Majesty desires that you will head for Wavre in order to draw near to us, and to place yourself in touch with our operations and to keep up your communications with us, pushing before you those portions of the Prussian Army which have taken this direction, and which have halted at Wavre; this place you ought to reach as soon as possible."[3]

For a man of Grouchy's limited intelligence, it was a badly worded message. All that was necessary was: "Draw near to us and prevent the Prussians marching to Wellington's assistance", and had Soult accepted the responsibility of sending it out at 3 a.m., it would have reached Grouchy at Gembloux by 8 a.m. at latest. Even had Napoleon sent it out between 4 and 5 a.m., Grouchy would have received it when, as will be related, he was at Walhain. In which case, at most, only one Prussian corps could have come to Wellington's assistance.

At the identical hour that Grouchy's message was delivered at Imperial Headquarters, Wellington received an answer to his 10 a.m. message to Blücher. It informed him that, at daybreak June 18, Bülow's corps would march to his aid, immediately followed by Pirch's, and that the Ist and IIIrd Corps would hold themselves in readiness to follow Pirch. This was indeed more than Wellington had expected, and he at once determined to accept battle and await Bülow's arrival.

It is time now to return to Grouchy, who at 1 p.m. had received his orders to pursue Blücher. An hour later he set out, but advanced with such incredible slowness that he only reached Gembloux at nightfall. There he collected the information given in his 10 p.m. dispatch to the Emperor, and an hour later, when he learnt from his cavalry that the Prussians were marching on

---

[1] See Becke's *Napoleon and Waterloo*, vol. II, Appx. II, No. 28, p. 292.

[2] Gourgaud says that at 10 p.m. an officer was sent to inform Grouchy that a great battle, south of the Forest of Soignes, would be fought on the following day, and that, should the Prussians remain at Wavre, Grouchy was to move on St. Lambert and join the right of the French Army. Further, that when Grouchy's dispatch was received at 2 a.m., it was answered at 3 a.m., a duplicate of the 10 p.m. dispatch being sent. (*Campagne de 1815*, pp. 82–83.) Neither of these dispatches is traceable.

[3] See Becke's *Napoleon and Waterloo*, vol. II, Appx. II, No. 29, p. 293.

Wavre,[1] he jumped to the conclusion that they only intended to assemble there and then push on to Brussels. Next, instead of deciding to pursue them in flank, by way of Géry and Moustier on Wavre, he determined to follow up their rearguard by advancing on Sart-à-Walhain.[2] Worse, instead of moving off at dawn on June 18, he ordered Vandamme to march at 6 a.m. and Gérard at 8 a.m. Actually they moved off at eight and nine o'clock.

Grouchy left Gembloux between 8 and 9 a.m., and at 10 a.m. caught up with the head of the IIIrd Corps at Walhain. There he entered the house of the local notary, a M. Hollert, in order to write a note to the Emperor to inform him that it appeared that the Prussians intended to concentrate at Chyse, 10 miles south of Louvain, "to give battle to their pursuers, or finally to join hands with Wellington", and therefore, that he would mass his troops at Wavre in order to interpose them "between the Prussian Army and Wellington".[3]

He sent this message off, then sat down to breakfast, and at 11.30 a.m., when strolling with Gérard in the garden, the roar of cannon was heard in the direction of Mont St. Jean. At once Gérard exclaimed: "I think we ought to march on the cannon." This Grouchy refused to consider, as he believed it to be merely a rearguard affair. A violent altercation followed, in which finally Gérard urged that he and his corps be sent off alone. Grouchy would not hear of this, but said that he must obey the Emperor's orders, which from start to finish he utterly failed to understand.[4]

What was the Prussian position at the time? Bülow's van had reached Chapelle-St. Lambert, but the rear of his corps was so far behind that it did not close up until 3 p.m. Pirch was to start in half an hour, so was Ziethen, who was to advance on Ohain, and Thielemann's corps was in position at Wavre. Therefore, at 11.30 a.m. three-quarters of the Prussian army was still at, or near, Wavre. Consequently, had Grouchy acted on Gérard's suggestion and at noon set out for Moustier and Ottignies on the Dyle, both eight miles away, in spite of the bad roads, he would have reached them between 4 and 5 p.m. and have placed himself on Blücher's left flank and rear. Instead, in a single column he

---

[1] See Houssaye's *1815 Waterloo*, p. 164.
[2] Whether it was Sart-à-Walhain or Walhain is disputed. (See Houssaye's *1815 Waterloo*, pp. 396–398.)
[3] See Becke's *Napoleon and Waterloo*, vol. II, Appx. II, No. 32, p. 295.
[4] For this conversation, see Houssaye's *1815 Waterloo*, pp. 167–170.

continued his march by way of Corbaix on Wavre, and at 2 p.m. reached La Baraque—three and a half miles east of Moustier and Ottignies, where the bridges were still standing and unguarded. From La Baraque, or near by, the Prussians were seen marching toward the field of Waterloo, and, as Ropes points out, had Grouchy even then masked Thielemann at Wavre with his cavalry, he could have moved his two corps on the Dyle bridges, and had he done so "he would have certainly arrested the march of Bülow and Pirch", though not of Ziethen.[1] With such subordinates as Grouchy and Ney, Michael and all his angels would have lost the campaign.

Between 4 and 5 a.m. orders were issued by Soult for all troops to be in position to attack at 9 a.m. precisely,[2] but because of the rain, preparations were so much delayed that this was found to be impracticable. Between 7 and 8 a.m. the rain ceased, and when the Emperor sat down to breakfast, Soult, who since the evening before had been perturbed about Grouchy, suggested to Napoleon that at least part of Grouchy's command should at once be re-called. This advice was rudely brushed aside, and when Jérôme remarked that at supper the night before, the waiter who served him, and who had served Wellington that morning, informed him that one of the Duke's aides had spoken of a junction be-tween the English and Prussians, the sole answer Napoleon vouchsafed was "nonsense!"[3] Nothing would shift the fixed ideas which possessed him, that after Ligny the Prussians were in-capable of intervention, and that Wellington's polyglot army could be smashed by a single blow.

Breakfast at an end, the Emperor called for his horses, and with Drouot set out to examine the ground and the enemy. When thus engaged, Drouot, an experienced artillery officer, advised him to postpone the attack for two or three hours, because, he urged, the ground was as yet too wet for rapid artillery movements.[4] Napoleon, also an expert artillerist, agreed to this, and postponed the attack until 1 p.m. This, Houssaye states, was his most fateful blunder during the campaign, for had he not agreed, "the English army would have been routed before the arrival of the Prussians."[5]

---

[1] The Campaign of Waterloo, p. 261.
[2] See Becke's Napoleon and Waterloo, vol. II, Appx. II, No. 33, pp. 296–297.
[3] Houssaye, 1815 Waterloo, p. 180.
[4] Besides, it should be remembered that round-shot buried themselves in the soft ground instead of richochetting. (See The Diary of a Cavalry Officer, Lieut.-Col. Tomkinson (1895), pp. 297–298.)
[5] 1815 Waterloo, p. 288.

At 10 a.m., when at Rossomme Farm, Napoleon suddenly remembered Grouchy and instructed Soult to reply to his last dispatch, and a few minutes later, as if he half-consciously sensed danger from the east, he ordered Colonel Marbot to take up his position with the 7th Hussars at Frichermont, and send patrols to the bridges of Moustier and Ottignies,[1] apparently to get in touch with Grouchy and send back prompt notice of his approach. After this, when the troops were in their battle positions, Napoleon reviewed his army to frenzied shouts of *"Vive l'Empereur!"*

At 11 a.m. he dictated his very brief attack order,[2] and as his aim was the same as at Ligny–to break his enemy's centre and exploit the penetration–he instructed Ney at 1 p.m. or soon after, on the heels of an intense preliminary artillery bombardment, to advance d'Erlon's corps on the village of Mont St. Jean with Reille's abreast of it on its left flank. A few minutes after, to distract Wellington and cause him to weaken his centre by reinforcing his right, he ordered Reille immediately to send a division against Hougoumont to carry out a powerful demonstration. Meanwhile, a great battery of 80 guns was brought into position in front of, and to the right of, La Belle Alliance, to open fire at noon.[3]

Even for battles of this period, the field of Waterloo was restricted, for its depth from Mont St. Jean to Rossomme was no more than two and a quarter miles, and its extreme width from Braine l'Alleud to the Paris Wood–four miles. Roughly, it was cut into halves by the Charleroi-Brussels Road, and was flanked on the south by a low irregular ridge on both sides of La Belle Alliance, and on the north by another low ridge along which ran the Braine l'Alleud-Wavre Road. The two ridges were separated by a shallow valley, about 45 ft. lower than themselves.

Wellington's main line ran along the second of these ridges, three-quarters of a mile south of the village of Mont St. Jean, and extended for about a mile and a quarter east of the Brussels Road and for nearly a third of a mile west of it. On his left front, from four to eight hundred yards in advance of it, lay the hamlets of Smohain, La Haye and Papelotte; immediately south of his centre stood the farm of La Haye Sainte as well as an extensive

---

[1] *Mémoires (1799–1854)*, le General Baron de Marbot (1891), vol. III, p. 403.
[2] *Correspondance*, No. 22060, vol. XXVIII, p. 392.
[3] Gourgaud, *Campagne de 1815*, p. 92. Kennedy (p. 107) says 74 guns about "600 yards from the Anglo-Allied position."

sandpit, and in advance of his right flank rose the Château of Hougoumont, surrounded by orchards and gardens. Facing Wellington, Napoleon's line ran from a point a mile and three-quarters south of Mont St. Jean on the Mont St. Jean-Nivelles Road across the southern face of Hougoumont to the Château of Frichermont, which faced Papelotte, La Haye and Smohain.

The general distribution of the two armies at 1 p.m. is shown on the diagram, and, according to Siborne,[1] Wellington's army numbered 49,608 infantry, 12,408 cavalry, and 5,645 artillery with 156 guns—67,661 men; and Napoleon's: 48,950 infantry, 15,765 cavalry, and 7,232 artillery with 246 guns—71,947 men. In part compensating Grouchy's detachment, Wellington, still fearful of being turned by way of the Mons-Brussels Road, left at Hal and Tubize 17,000 men and 30 guns under Prince Frederick of the Netherlands. When one considers that, on the morning before, the Duke had asked for the assistance of only one Prussian corps, to leave this strong detachment eight to nine miles away during the whole of June 18 was a blunder of the first magnitude. Without the assistance of Blücher, it might have saved the Anglo-Dutch Army by manœuvring against Napoleon's left flank, and even had it not rained in torrents, with it Wellington would surely have been strong enough to hold his own until Blücher arrived. As it was, these 17,000 men—one-fifth of his whole force—were utterly wasted, and, as Kennedy remarks, it would be "difficult to comprehend how any French force could have got to Tubize and Hal without its advance being previously known".[2]

At half-past eleven o'clock the French batteries opened fire, and Jérôme's division of Reille's Corps advanced against Hougoumont. But instead of restricting his attack to a demonstration, Jérôme at once got involved in an all-out attempt to occupy the *château*. This was the first tactical blunder of several made by the French; for it led to exactly the opposite result Napoleon had intended. Instead of drawing in the English, it drew in the French. Soon a brigade of Foy's division was sent forward to support Jérôme who, instead of destroying the solid buildings with howitzer fire, ordered attack after attack, until "the trees in advance of the *château* were cut to pieces by musketry".[3]

---

[1] *History of the War in France and Belgium in 1815*, vol. I, pp. 460–461.
[2] *Notes on the Battle of Waterloo*, p. 69.
[3] *The Diary of a Cavalry Officer in the Peninsular and Waterloo Campaigns*, Lieut.-Col. W. Tomkinson (1895), p. 318.

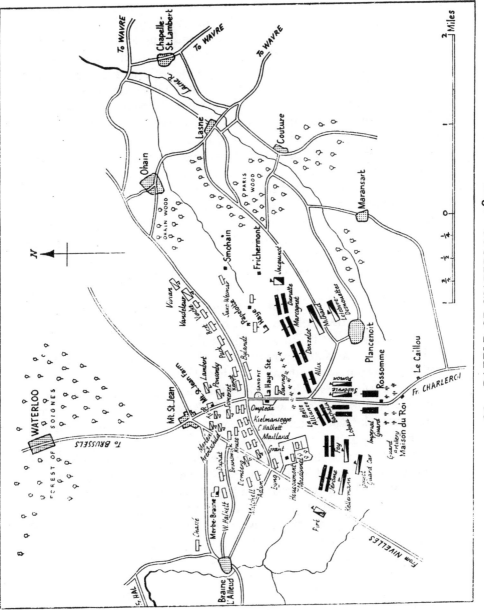

32. BATTLE OF WATERLOO, 1815

While this misplaced operation was in full swing, the Emperor busily prepared d'Erlon's assault on Wellington's centre, and close upon one o'clock, when all was ready, he glanced round the field and noticed in the distance, about four to five miles to the north-east, what looked like a "dark cloud" emerging from the woods of Chapelle-St. Lambert. At once all glasses were turned upon it. Soult said that he could plainly see troops, and at once it was thought that they must be Grouchy's. A moment later the mystery was solved, some of Marbot's Hussars appeared with a captured Prussian dispatch rider, and from his dispatch it was learnt that the "dark cloud" was Bülow's advanced guard.[1] Though this was somewhat of a shock for the Emperor's fixed idea, he was in no way perturbed: to him it was a complication and nothing more. Not for a moment did he doubt that he could ruin Wellington long before Bülow could arrive. Nevertheless the new danger had to be met, and to a letter he had just dictated in reply to one of Grouchy's, he bade Soult add the following postscript:

"A letter which has just been intercepted tells us that General Bülow is to attack our right flank. We believe we can perceive this corps on the heights of Chapelle-Saint Lambert. Therefore do not lose a minute to draw nearer to us and to join us and crush Bülow, whom you will catch in the very act."[2]

According to Gourgaud, the officer sent with this letter could deliver it in less than two hours. This was quite impossible, and the letter did not reach Grouchy until about five o'clock, when he was fully engaged at Wavre with Thielemann. Had the summons been sent early that morning, then Napoleon's complaisance would have been fully justified.

Next, the Emperor ordered the light cavalry divisions of Domont and Subervie to move toward Chapelle-St. Lambert, and under their cover he instructed Lobau to follow them with his corps and hold Bülow in check.[3] With these steps to secure his right flank taken, it was now about half-past one o'clock and he ordered Ney to attack.

In the French army since 1792, in order that the ground might rapidly be crossed without confusion, the approach phase of the attack usually was carried out in column formations. Next, when the enemy was neared, so that the maximum fire power might be

---

[1] *Campagne de 1815*, Gourgaud, p. 89.   [2] See Houssaye's *1815 Waterloo*, p. 192.
[3] *Campagne de 1815*, Gourgaud, p. 90.

developed, the columns deployed into line. To facilitate deployment, columns were usually of battalion strength at half or full
deploying intervals: they were handy, favoured rapid deployment
and, in the event of meeting cavalry, could quickly be formed into
square. The attack was based on the following principles:
(*1*) While the columns advanced, the artillery compelled the
enemy to remain in line–that is, in the least vulnerable formation
to case and round shot fire; (*2*) just before they deployed, the
cavalry, by threatening the enemy, compelled him to form from
line into squares–that is, not only in the securest formations in
which to meet cavalry, but also in a very vulnerable one in which
to meet infantry and artillery fire; (*3*) next, under cover of the
cavalry, the columns deployed in order to bring to bear on the
squares a heavier fire than the squares themselves could deliver,
which was supplemented by case shot fire from the regimental
guns; and (*4*) lastly, when once the squares were thrown into
confusion, the assault with the bayonet was made, and the
cavalry finished off the enemy by annihilating the fugitives.

In the present case, for some reason which has never been
explained, three of d'Erlon's four attacking divisions, instead of
being drawn up in battalion columns, advanced in divisional
columns on a battalion frontage–that is, each battalion extended
in three ranks,[1] one behind the other. As each of the three divisions
which adopted this clumsy formation consisted of eight or nine
battalions, each column had a frontage of some 200 men and
was from 24 to 27 ranks deep. Not only did these heavy columns
make rapid deployment impossible, but their size rendered them
peculiarly vulnerable to the enemy's case and round shot fire.

Unfortunately for Ney and d'Erlon, they were faced by a general
who understood the French tactics, and in part, at least, knew how
to neutralize them. Instead of lining the ridge along which the
Braine l'Alleud-Wavre Road ran, Wellington drew up the bulk
of his forces in rear of it, where they were sheltered from the shot
and shell of the enemy's great battery which, as it was composed
of guns and not howitzers, could not search the rear slope. The
result was that his men suffered little from the preliminary bombardment. All they had to do was to lie down in ranks behind the
ridge, and when the enemy's columns approached its summit,

---

[1] The French maintained the old three ranks system, whereas under Wellington
the English always deployed in two ranks, and thereby increased their fire power by
one-third.

rise, advance a few paces and deliver a crashing volley on their heads before they could deploy. These tactics did not modify the problem of meeting cavalry, which remained that of forming into squares. Throughout the battle, as we shall see, it was the indifferent cooperation between the French cavalry and infantry, even more than the faulty column formation, that wrecked the French assaults.

These brief tactical comments should make clear why d'Erlon's assault failed. It was made in four columns in *échelon*, the left division (Donzelot) led on La Haye Sainte with Traver's brigade of cuirassiers on its left, while the right column (Durutte) advanced on Papelotte, and Allix's and Marcognet's were in between.[1] Papelotte was stormed without great difficulty, but Donzelot failed to take La Haye Sainte, which was most gallantly held by a battalion of the King's German Legion under Major Baring. Meanwhile, in the centre, Allix's and Marcognet's Divisions came under heavy fire as they climbed the ridge. They came up against Bylandt's Dutch-Belgian brigade, the only body of troops Wellington had deployed on the forward slopes of the ridge, and which, in consequence, had already suffered severely from French artillery fire, and drove it back in rout, and at about the same time the three companies of the 95th Rifles, who held the sandpit, found their position untenable and fell back, and the engagement became general. Meanwhile Wellington watched the attack from the post he had taken up at the foot of an old elm tree which stood at the junction of the Braine l'Alleud-Wavre and Charleroi-Brussels roads, while Napoleon at Rossomme was similarly engaged: to the latter and his staff it looked as if d'Erlon's success was certain.

Seldom has a mirage proved more illusory, for the faulty arrangement of d'Erlon's columns, which had already slowed down the approach, now led to disaster. They had become mere masses of men which, when they neared the top of the ridge, were incapable of deploying in any semblance of order, and, as they tried to do so, Picton brought his division (4,000 men) forward. Whereon, when it topped the ridge, Kempt's brigade, at 40 paces distance, poured a crashing volley into the advancing French, while Pack's rushed out from behind the hedge which skirted the Wavre Road and with bayonets fixed charged into the seething masses. A moment later, Picton was shot dead.

[1] Some accounts place Allix on the left and Donzelot next to him. (See Houssaye, pp. 194–195).

The crisis was reached, and Uxbridge seized it. He launched Somerset's and Ponsonby's cavalry brigades into the battle.[1] First, they scattered Traver's brigade of cuirassiers, which had accompanied d'Erlon, and next they charged d'Erlon's disordered infantry and drove them pell-mell down the slope; they captured 3,000 prisoners and two eagles. Borne on by their horses, the English cavalry crossed the valley at full speed, passed through the French outposts and up the opposite slope. In vain Uxbridge sounded the retreat, but nothing could stop them. On they pressed, and were near the great battery when they were charged in flank by Martigue's lancers, and Ponsonby was killed. Next, Farine's brigade of cuirassiers was thrown in, and after they had left over a third of their number on the field, Somerset's and Ponsonby's brigades were driven back in complete disorder. Meanwhile the attack on Hougoumont continued to the steady exhaustion of Reille.

At 3 o'clock the battle died down, and though d'Erlon's attack had failed, Wellington's position was approaching a critical stage: Bylandt's brigade (some 4,000 men) was *hors de combat*, and because of Somerset's and Ponsonby's inconsiderate charge, 2,500 of Wellington's best horsemen had been lost to him. Everything depended on the arrival of Blücher, whose advance was painfully slow.

Napoleon's position was no less anxious, for he had just received Grouchy's 11.30 a.m. dispatch from Walhain, which must have made it clear to him that no help could be expected from that quarter. Though he might have saved his army by retiring,[2] it would have meant not only the loss of the campaign but a political upheaval; therefore he took advantage of Bülow's slowness, and decided to crush Wellington before the Prussians could come into line. At 3.30 p.m., by when d'Erlon had rallied some of his battalions, he ordered Ney to occupy La Haye Sainte, as he contemplated using it as the base from which to launch a grand assault with d'Erlon's and Reille's corps, followed by the bulk of the cavalry and the infantry of the Guard.

The cannonade was intensified, but because of the disorganized state of d'Erlon's corps and the difficulty Reille had in disengaging troops from before Hougoumont, Ney was only able to attack with

---

[1] See Kennedy's *Notes on the Battle of Waterloo*, pp. 110–111.
[2] It is probable that the moral state of his army prohibited a successful retreat. Further, retreats were not Napoleon's strong point. (See Caulaincourt's *Memoirs*, vol. I, p. 601.)

two brigades. Though they were repulsed, he saw between the drifting clouds of smoke numbers of enemy ammunition wagons streaming to the rear–actually they were engaged upon carrying back wounded–and he jumped to the conclusion that his enemy was in retreat. He did not wait for the Emperor's authority to launch the cavalry, but ordered Milhaud and his two divisions forward. As they moved off, Lefebvre-Desnouettes, whose division was in rear of Milhaud, on his own initiative conformed with the movement. Thus some 5,000 horsemen were thrown into the fray *before* La Haye Sainte had been taken, and why Napoleon did not stop this unsound movement was because his attention was then riveted on his right flank. What was happening there?

Though Bülow had reached Chapelle-St. Lambert at one o'clock, it was not until four o'clock that the heads of his columns debouched from the Paris Wood. As they did so, they were checked by Domon's squadrons, which then fell back and un-masked Lobau's infantry. Though outnumbered by three to one, Lobau forthwith attacked the heads of Bülow's two leading divisions, and then fell back on Plancenoit. There, attacked on three sides, he was driven out of the village, and from it the Prussian batteries opened fire on the Brussels Road. Because the loss of Plancenoit threatened the French line of retreat, Napoleon ordered Duhesme to retake it with the Young Guard. This he did, Lobau with the VIth Corps extended to their left to link up with the right of the Ist Corps.

It was while the Emperor was thus occupied that Ney, "carried away by an excess of ardour",[1] between four and a quarter past four o'clock, had placed himself at the head of Milhaud's cuiras-siers and led them forward against Wellington, who had no thought of retiring, for his sole aim was to hold on to his position until the Prussians arrived. Though the allies expected that some time during the day a great cavalry attack would be made on them, to launch it against unbroken infantry came to them as a surprise.[2] At once the allied infantry formed squares and the gunners were ordered to remain in front with their pieces until the last moment, and then with their horses to seek refuge in the squares.

The French cavalry advanced, says Kennedy, "in lines of columns", and filled nearly the whole space between La Haye Sainte and Hougoumont.[3] They came on at a slow canter up the

---

[1] Gourgaud, *Campagne de 1815*, pp. 96–97.
[2] See Kennedy, *Notes on the Battle of Waterloo*, p. 114.   [3] *Ibid.*, p. 116.

slope, and as the supporting French batteries ceased firing the allied batteries opened, their pieces loaded with double-shotted charges.[1] The "Charge" was then sounded, and with cries of "*Vive l'Empereur!*" the 5,000 horsemen surged through the allied batteries. Though all were captured, no preparations had been made to render them ineffective. There were no horses at hand to drag the guns away and no spikes to render them useless. Nothing was done, and it did not even occur to a single officer to have the sponge-staves broken. Had the guns been spiked, which could have been done with headless nails and hammers, the next great cavalry assault would almost certainly have succeeded, for it was more from case and grape shot than from musketry that cavalry suffered in the attack.

Cuirassiers, chasseurs, and lancers charged the squares and surged round them, until the whole plateau was flooded with horsemen. Of this action, Frazer writes: ". . . the French cavalry made some of the boldest charges I ever saw: they sounded the whole extent of our line. . . . Never did cavalry behave so nobly, or was received by infantry so firmly."[2]

Uxbridge, who watched the mêlée, and still had in hand two-thirds of his cavalry fresh, suddenly hurled against the French Dörnberg's, Arenschild's, Brunswick's, van Merlen's and Ghigny's brigades, in all some 5,000 horsemen. As they swept the French back, the allied gunners rushed out from the squares, manned their pieces and poured grape and case shot into the retiring enemy. Undaunted, at the bottom of the slope, Milhaud and Lefebvre-Desnouettes re-formed their squadrons, and again cantered up the slope, only to be volleyed upon by the allied batteries and again driven back.

Though, at Rossomme, those with the Emperor were elated by what they saw, Napoleon was far from being so. Impatiently he turned to Soult and exclaimed: "This is a premature movement, which may well lead to fatal results." Soult replied: "He [Ney] is compromising us as he did at Jena."[3] Nevertheless, in spite of its prematurity, afraid that the repulse of his cavalry might unnerve the army and lead to panic, Napoleon sent General Flahaut to Kellermann to order him to support Ney. Kellermann, who also considered the action premature, expostulated, but while he did so General L'Heritier, who commanded his 1st

---

[1] A round shot with case over it.   [2] Frazer's *Letters*, p. 547.
[3] Gourgaud, *Campagne de 1815*, p. 97.

Division, without awaiting orders set off at a trot; whereon Kellermann followed with Roussel's 2nd Division. Next, Guyot, like Lefebvre-Desnouettes, either without orders or on a wrongly given one, with his division of Guard Cavalry, followed Kellermann. This was a fatal move, for not only did it deprive the Emperor of his last cavalry reserve, but it so completely overcrowded the field with horsemen that to manœuvre became impossible. No wonder, as Kennedy remarks, the allies were amazed to see some 12,000 horsemen[1] massing for an attack on the 1,000 yards frontage between Hougoumont and La Haye Sainte, of which "these horsemen could advance on a front of only 500 yards, as they were obliged to keep at some distance from the enclosures of both Hougoumont and La Haye Sainte".[2]

The advance of Kellermann and Guyot, followed by the now exhausted horsemen of Milhaud, took place at 5.30 p.m., and was unsupported by infantry and badly supported by artillery, for only one battery was brought up in rear of the horsemen to breach the allied squares. Undoubtedly, the heavy, churned-up ground made artillery movement difficult; nevertheless, had but two or three horse artillery batteries been advanced to within case-shot range, nothing could have saved Wellington's army.

Although the second grand assault met with the fate of the first, the stresses and strains it set up in the allied line were severe, and by now Wellington had used up most of his cavalry and most of his infantry reserves. What would he not have given to have in hand the 17,000 men he had left at Hal and Tubize?

But Ney could not take advantage of his enemy's critical situation because the whole of his tactics was at fault–instead of combining his arms, he used them separately. Had he, as he had been ordered, first occupied La Haye Sainte, and next established his batteries in advance of it, he could have riddled his enemy's squares. Further, had he supported his cavalry with infantry, success would have been assured to him. As it was, one French battery, writes Mercer, "established itself on a knoll somewhat higher than the ground we stood on, and only about 400 to 500 yards a little in advance of our left flank. The rapidity and precision of this fire was quite appalling. Every shot took effect, and I certainly expected we should be annihilated . . . the whole livelong day had cost us nothing like this."[3]

---

[1] Actually 9,000 to 10,000.   [2] Kennedy, *Notes on the Battle of Waterloo*, p. 118.
[3] Mercer's *Journal*, vol. 1, pp. 325–326.

Ney had not only forgotten his objective–La Haye Sainte–but also his infantry, and only after Kellermann's fourth charge did he think of using his 6,000 bayonets. At 6 p.m. he advanced Foy's and Bachelu's divisions of Reille's corps, but unsupported by cavalry, they were met, as Foy describes it, by such a "hail of death" that in a few minutes they lost some 1,500 men and were repulsed.

When this attack took place, Napoleon rode along the entire battle front to steady his men, and at the same time he sent an order to Ney to take La Haye Sainte whatever it might cost. This Ney did with part of Donzelot's division; he succeeded very largely because Baring's detachment ran out of ammunition. The sandpit was also lost by the allies.

This time Ney made immediate use of his success; he brought a battery into action near La Haye Sainte and within 300 yards of the allied position, and pushed forward the remnants of Allix's, Donzelot's and Marcognet's divisions and gained a footing on the Wavre Road. But by then his men were too exhausted to advance farther, and in order to support them he sent Colonel Heymès to the Emperor to ask for reinforcements.

"Troops!" cried Napoleon, "Where do you expect me to get them? Do you expect me to make them?"[1] But Ney was right, the decisive moment, which faulty tactics had so long delayed, had been reached. Napoleon, though hard pressed, was not altogether lacking reserves, but apparently he did not realize how desperately critical Wellington's position then was.

In regard to this, Kennedy writes:

"La Haye Sainte was in the hands of the enemy. . . . Ompteda's brigade was nearly annihilated, and Kielmansegge's so thinned, that those two brigades could not hold their position. That part of the field of battle, therefore, which was between Halkett's left and Kempt's right, was unprotected; and being the very centre of the Duke's line of battle, was consequently that point, above all others, which the enemy wished to gain. The danger was imminent; and at no other period of the action was the result so precarious as at this moment. Most fortunately Napoleon did not support the advantage his troops had gained at this point, by bringing forward his reserve. . . .

"Of such gravity did Wellington consider this great gap in the very centre of his line of battle, that he not only ordered the

---

[1] *Documents Inédits*, duc d'Elchingen, p. 18.

Brunswick troops there, but put himself at their head, and it was even then with the greatest difficulty that the ground could be held. . . .

"In no other part of the action was the Duke of Wellington exposed to so much personal risk as on this occasion . . . at no other period of the day were his great qualities as a commander so strongly brought out, for it was the moment of his greatest peril as to the result of the action. . . ."[1]

Napoleon still had in hand eight battalions of the Old Guard and six of the Middle, and had he sent to Ney but half this force, Wellington's centre must inevitably have been overwhelmed; for all it needed was the appearance of a comparatively small force of fresh troops to throw the allies into a panic. But Napoleon's situation was then as critical as Wellington's. The Young Guard had been thrown out of Plancenoit, and overpowered on his right flank, the Emperor was now threatened by an eruption on his rear. Instead of reinforcing Ney, he formed 11 battalions of the Guard into as many squares, and posted them facing Plancenoit from La Belle Alliance to Rossomme; one battalion he kept at Le Caillou, and two he sent under Morand and Pelet to retake Plancenoit.

With drums beating the 1st Battalion of the 2nd Grenadiers and the 1st Battalion of the 2nd Chasseurs advanced on the village, and without deigning to fire a shot, with bayonets fixed, in 20 minutes they swept the Prussians out of it; after which the Young Guard reoccupied Plancenoit.

It was now past seven o'clock, and with Plancenoit again in French hands Napoleon decided to support Ney and strike his final blow before the sun set. He ordered Drouot to bring forward eight battalions[2] of the Guard under Friant, and on their arrival he placed himself at their head, led them forward in advance of La Belle Alliance, and handed them over to Marshal Ney. At the same time he ordered the batteries to intensify their fire, sent instructions to Reille and d'Erlon as well as to the cavalry to support Ney's assault, and, in order to restore his troops' morale,

[1] *Notes on the Battle of Waterloo*, pp. 127–129.
[2] There has been much controversy over the number of battalions actually employed. Ropes (pp. 316–317) favours eight or six, and Houssaye (pp. 223 and 428)–five. Napoleon (*Correspondance*, vol. XXXI, p. 198) says that Friant had four battalions, and Gourgaud (pp. 101–102) says four battalions of the Middle Guard. Ney, who is not likely to have exaggerated the number, in his letter of June 26 to the Duke of Otranto (Fouché) says "four regiments of the Middle Guard"–that is, eight battalions. (See Becke, vol. II, pp. 301–306.)

sent General de la Bédoyère down the front to announce the arrival of Grouchy, whose guns could be heard thundering in the distance. As the Guard formed up under cover of dense clouds of smoke, a cavalry officer deserted to the enemy, and through him Wellington learnt what was in progress.[1]

Actually, the decisive moment had passed, for since Heymès had begged reinforcements of the Emperor, Donzelot's, Allix's and Marcognet's men had been pushed off the plateau, and Wellington, who had regained his former position and who knew that Ziethen's advanced guard had reached Ohain at six o'clock, drew Vandeleur's and Vivian's cavalry brigades from his left to his centre and brought up Chassé's 3rd Dutch Belgian Division from Braine l'Alleud in rear of Maitland's Guards Brigade and Adam's Light Brigade, which, on Wellington's right centre, sheltered behind the banks of the Wavre Road, west of the sand-pit.

Though accounts differ, it would appear that the Guard was marshalled in one column with its battalions formed in close column of grand divisions – that is, on a frontage of two companies, each in the usual three ranks. Because each battalion numbered about 500 men and had four companies, the frontage of the column was 75 to 80 men; the battalions were accompanied by two batteries of horse artillery of six pieces each, which fired as the infantry advanced.

Instead of marching up the Brussels Road, the embankments of which would to some extent have sheltered his men from fire, Ney moved diagonally over the slope between Hougoumont and La Haye Sainte towards his enemy's right centre. The attack was, however, carried out not in one column but in two,[2] and though the reasons for this are obscure, it would seem that either, because the start was hurried,[3] the leading four battalions (grenadiers of the Old Guard) advanced ahead of the four in rear (chasseurs of the Middle Guard), or – as frequently happens – the head of the column stepped out more rapidly than the rear and got ahead of it, with the result that the column broke into two columns, and the rear one inclined to the left rear of the forward one.[4] This is borne

---

[1] Frazer's *Letters*, p. 552.
[2] Possibly three, see *Waterloo Letters*, No. 128, p. 302.
[3] The sun was sinking.
[4] It must be remembered that, in the days of black powder, smoke was frequently so dense that soldiers could not see clearly for more than a few yards. In these circumstances it would be easy for the rear half to diverge from the forward one.

35

out by General Maitland who says: "As the attacking force moved forward it separated, the Chasseurs inclined to their left. The Grenadiers ascended the acclivity towards our position in a more direct course, leaving La Haye Sainte on their right, and moving towards that part of the eminence occupied by the 1st Brigade of Guards."[1]

As is common in nearly all eyewitnesses' descriptions, they vary in accordance with the position of the observer, and when pieced together, as Houssaye has done, detail is apt to obscure the decisive moments. There were two; the destruction of the leading column by Maitland's Guards and of the rear column by Adam's Light Brigade. As regards the first, Captain Powell of the 1st Foot Guards says that before the assault the English Guards sheltered themselves during the cannonade in the ditch and behind the bank along the Wavre Road, and "without the protection of this bank every creature must have perished".[2] Next, he continues:

". . . suddenly the firing ceased, and as the smoke cleared away a superb sight opened on us. A close column of Grenadiers (about seventy in front) . . . were seen ascending the rise *au pas de charge* shouting '*Vive l'Empereur!*' They continued to advance till within fifty or sixty paces of our front, when the Brigade were ordered to stand up. Whether it was from the sudden and unexpected appearance of a Corps so near them, which must have seemed as starting out of the ground, or the tremendous heavy fire we threw into them, *La Garde*, who had never before failed in an attack, *suddenly* stopped."[3]

Maitland's account reads:

"The Brigade suffered by the Enemy's Artillery, but it withheld its fire for the nearer approach of the Column. The latter, after advancing steadily up the slope, halted about twenty paces from the front rank of the Brigade.

"The diminished range of the Enemy's Artillery was now felt most severely in our ranks; the men fell in great numbers before the discharges of grape shot, and the fire of the musketry distributed among the Guns.

"The smoke of the Artillery happily did not envelop the hostile Column, or serve to conceal it from our aim.

---

[1] *Waterloo Letters*, No. 105, p. 244.
[2] In spite of the assault being carried out with eight battalions of Guard, instead of the normal 24, Wellington's position was nevertheless critical. Frazer says of it, "this last struggle was nearly fatal to us". (*Letters*, p. 552.)
[3] *Waterloo Letters*, No. 109, pp. 254–255.

"With what view the Enemy halted in a situation so perilous, and in a position so comparatively helpless, he was not given time to evince.

"The fire of the Brigade opened with terrible effect.

"The Enemy's Column, crippled and broken, retreated with the utmost rapidity, leaving only a heap of dead and dying men to mark the ground which it had occupied."[1]

Had the Grenadiers of the Guard been supported by cavalry it is highly probable that Maitland would have been overwhelmed, for then he would have had to form into squares and his brigade would have been badly mauled by the French horse artillery and musketry.

Meanwhile, in rear and probably obscured by the smoke, the chasseurs of the Middle Guard moved on and came up on the right of Maitland's brigade, some 10 to 15 minutes after the grenadiers were repulsed, to find Adam's Light Brigade deployed on their left front. As they neared the top of the ridge, Colonel Sir John Colborne (later Lord Seaton), ordered his regiment, the 52nd, supported by the 95th, to wheel to the left. This change of front placed it "nearly parallel with the moving Column of the French Imperial Guards". Next, he ordered forward one company in extended order to fire into the column; whereon the column halted, "formed a line facing towards the 52nd", opened fire and caused many casualties in the extended company. At this moment the Duke rode up and ordered Colborne to press forward up a slight rise toward the chasseurs. "At the time," writes Colborne, "the 71st formed on our right flank, and I ordered the bugles to sound the advance, and the whole line charged up the hill; and on our arriving at the edge of the deep road, the opposite side of which the Imperial Guards had occupied, the 52nd fired, at least most of the Companies. . . ."[2]

Next, according to the account given by Lieutenant Gawler of the 52nd:

"The enemy was pressing on with shouts, which rose above the noise of the firing, and his fire was so intense that, with but half the ordinary length of front, *at least* 150 of the 52nd fell in less than four minutes. . . . When the 52nd was nearly parallel to the Enemy's flank, Sir J. Colborne gave the word, 'Charge', 'charge'. It was answered from the Regiment by a loud steady cheer and a hurried dash to the front. In the next ten seconds the Imperial

[1] *Waterloo Letters*, No. 105, pp. 244–245.   [2] *Ibid.*, No. 123, pp. 284–286.

Guard, broken into the wildest confusion, and scarcely firing a shot to cover its retreat, was rushing towards the hollow road in the rear of La Haye Sainte, near to which, according to La Coste's account, Napoleon himself was then standing."[1]

Again, as with the grenadiers, had the chasseurs been supported with cavalry, Adam would have had to throw his brigade into squares, and in consequence this famous counter-attack would never have taken place. It was lack of cavalry, and more particularly Guyot's heavy cavalry of the Guard, that deprived Napoleon of his last chance of victory.

When the final French attack was under way, Ziethen had at last come up on Wellington's left flank to link it to Bülow's corps near Frichermont, and when the two columns of the Guard were repulsed, his troops drove Durutte's and Marcognet's divisions out of La Haye and Papelotte. Lobau then fell back toward Plancenoit, and Wellington, watching his enemy's rapidly increasing confusion, decided to finish the day. He spurred his horse forward to the edge of the plateau, took off his hat and waved it in the air. At once this signal was understood, and a general advance from the left to the right began; 40,000 men gradually poured down the slope with Vivian's hussars and Vandeleur's dragoons in the van.

"I have seen nothing like that moment," writes Frazer, "the sky literally darkened with smoke, the sun just going down, and which till then had not for some hours broken through the gloom of the day, the indescribable shouts of thousands, where it was impossible to distinguish between friend and foe. Every man's arm seemed to be raised against that of every other. Suddenly, after the mingled mass had ebbed and flowed, the enemy began to yield; and cheerings and English huzzas announced that the day must be ours."[2]

Meanwhile, Napoleon, near La Haye Sainte, formed up such troops as he could in order to support the Guard, when suddenly he saw the whole French front give way. At once he formed the shattered and retreating column of the Old Guard into three squares with its right on the Brussels Road, from where it fell back before the advance of Adam's Light Brigade. As Colborne and the 52nd came up, "the Duke of Wellington rode forward", writes Kennedy, "and ordered Colborne to attack them [the squares], remarking that they would not stand. Colborne then

---

[1] *Waterloo Letters*, No. 124, p. 293.   [2] *Letters*, p. 553.

advanced ... routed and dispersed them", [1] and the survivors joined in with the fugitives who poured down the Charleroi Road.

To the south, near de Coster's house, the two battalions of the 1st Grenadiers of the Guard, *élite* of the *élite*, under General Petit, had formed squares, and in that of the 1st Battalion the Emperor sought refuge. Slowly they fell back on each side of the road, and from time to time halted to arrest their pursuers. During one of these halts the Emperor pushed on to Le Caillou, and from there with the 1st Battalion of the 1st Chasseurs he took the road to Charleroi.

At a little after nine o'clock, when the 1st Grenadiers were still close by de Coster's house, Blücher met Wellington at or near La Belle Alliance, and after they had greeted each other it was decided that the Prussians should take over the pursuit.

In spite of the darkness of night, the pursuit was pressed with the utmost vigour, and at Genappe, as at Lindenau in 1813, dammed by the single narrow bridge over the Dyle, the French retreat piled up into a struggling confusion of men, horses, guns and vehicles.

From Genappe, with Soult, Drouot, and Bertrand, Napoleon pushed on to Quatre-Bras, which he reached toward one o'clock on the morning of June 19. He halted for a short spell, and instructed Soult to send a message to Grouchy to fall back on the Sambre. This the latter did most skilfully and carried his army to Givet. Had he during his advance displayed a fraction of the resolution he showed in his retreat, the outcome of the campaign would have been very different.

The Emperor pressed on from Quatre-Bras and reached Charleroi at five o'clock, and Philippeville at nine. There he wrote his last Bulletin, [2] a most revealing document which describes the events of June 16, 17 and 18, and next rode on to Laon where he spent the night. On June 20 he left Laon and the following day was in Paris. Urged by his brother Lucien to collect the few remaining troops in the capital and disperse the Chamber, he refused to do so. He knew that his star had set and the idea of precipitating a civil war was hateful to him: never had he been a leader of the rabble. The next day he abdicated in favour of his son, the King of Rome, and on June 25 retired to Malmaison.

Meanwhile Blücher's army pressed on and ravaged the country

---

[1] *Notes*, p. 145.   [2] *Correspondance*, No. 22061, vol. XXVIII, pp. 293-299.

it passed through. On July 3 it marched into Versailles, Wellington's followed more leisurely in rear, and on July 7 together the allied armies triumphantly entered Paris. Louis XVIII followed on July 8 with their baggage trains.

The casualties of this memorable battle were heavy. "The face of the hill near La Haye Sainte and from thence to Hougoumont", writes Tomkinson on the morning of June 19, "has more the appearance of a breach carried by assault than an extended field of battle",[1] and Kincaid says that "the 2⁷th Regiment (Inniskillings) were lying literally dead in square".[2] The total losses in killed and wounded, so far as can be estimated, for those of the French are only approximately known, were: Wellington's Army, 15,100; Blücher's 7,000; and Napoleon's 25,000, to which must be added some 8,000 captured and 220 guns.[3]

These figures speak for themselves, and Wellington was never under any illusion how close defeat had been, and in spite of Ney's inept tactics. On the night of the battle he said to Lord Fitzroy: "I have never fought such a battle, and I trust I shall never fight such another",[4] and to his brother he wrote: "In all my life I have not experienced such anxiety, for I must confess I have never before been so close to defeat."[5]

Had Napoleon won, and it is as startling as it is ironical that, in spite of his mistakes and those of his Marshals, a few pounds weight of nails and two dozen hammers would have cancelled out one and all, it is almost certain that the Seventh Coalition would have collapsed. Nevertheless it is equally probable that an eighth and possibly a ninth would have followed, and that in the end France would have been overwhelmed.

Though the allied triumph at Leipzig was the strategical climax of the long war, because it left France too exhausted to achieve ultimate victory, Waterloo, its epilogue, was a battle of profound economic and political significance. Where the one led to the triumph of European nationalism over French militarism and hegemony, the other resulted in the triumph of the English System—as Napoleon called it—not only over France, but over Europe and most of the world. For England, Waterloo was the copestone of Trafalgar: the latter assured her command of the sea, the former opened to her the markets of the world. For two

[1] *The Diary of a Cavalry Officer*, p. 317.
[2] *Adventures in the Rifle Brigade* (1909 edit.), p. 170.
[3] Becke's *Napoleon and Waterloo*, vol. II, pp. 134–135.
[4] Frazer's *Letters*, p. 560.   [5] Quoted from Becke, vol. II, p. 136.

generations and more she was to be the world's workshop and banker.

The Second Treaty of Paris, signed on November 20, 1815, redrew the map of Europe. It left France virtually as she had been in 1792, and strong enough to play a part in maintaining the balance of European power, which was essential to England's security. It pushed Prussia westward as a counter-poise to France; but by allotting Finland, and, above all, the greater part of Poland to Russia, like a wedge it thrust Muscovite power between Prussia and Austria—the eastern European bastions which faced "the barbarians of the North". Further, in order to fill the gap created by the dissolution of the Holy Roman Empire, it established a Germanic confederation of 38 sovereign States, and by doing so prepared the future for Sadowa and Sedan.

As her share of the spoils, England gained Malta, the Cape of Good Hope, Mauritius, and Ceylon. But of even greater importance than these, the war left her mistress absolute of the oceans and the seas. "So impressive was the aggrandizement of England beyond the seas," writes Professor H. A. L. Fisher, "that some writers have regarded the augmentation of the British Empire as the most important result of Napoleon's career."[1]

Out of sea power, steam power, money power and the prestige with which Waterloo had crowned England, emerged the *Pax Britannica*, which was destined to survive as long as British sea power and British credit retained their dominance. Actually they did so for a hundred years and controlled extra-European events and localized European wars. During this century, though revolutions were frequent and at times violent, Europe enjoyed the most stable and prosperous peace she had known since the days of the Antonines.

Quoted in Vol. I, Chronicle 8, was the panegyric of the Greek Sophist Aelius Aristides, addressed by him to the Emperor Marcus Aurelius, in which he sang the praises of the *Pax Romana*. Forty-five years after Waterloo, when the *Pax Britannica* had reached its zenith, Mr. Horsman, member for Stroud, in the House of Commons, gave voice to it in the following words:

"We seem to forget that there are great moral as well as material considerations involved in our security . . . the safety of England, in the estimation of every reflecting person in Europe, is the preservation of all that is valuable to the peace and progress of man-

[1] *The Cambridge Modern History*, vol. IX, p. 770.

kind . . . the security of England means the security of the only moderating and tranquillizing Power that exists in Europe. They (foreigners) know that if England should vanish out of existence the whole of the continent of Europe would probably pass under the domination of despotism. If England fell, how long would the nationality of Belgium endure? How long would the independence of Germany remain? How long would Italian unity be anything but a dream? No: the moral influence of England abroad is irresistible in exact proportion to her impregnability at home. Our greatness does not consist merely in our wealth, our commerce, our institutions, our military renown, but in those tributary elements that constitute a gigantic moral force, of which freedom is the animating principle and peace the holy mission. There is not a friend to freedom of thought who does not turn to England as its supporter. . . . Every man who is the friend of his species, looks upon England as the great depository of political truth, her safety as their pride, and the peril of England as their despair. With such considerations, while I value the safety of England as regards the security of our coasts, I value it also for the responsibilities and duties imposed upon us in our relations to humanity at large."[1]

Yet, when these memorable words were spoken, in Europe, in North America and in Asia, rumblings were to be heard of changes to come, which, in a little over half a century, were to put an end to the *Pax Britannica* and blast the entire world with war.

[1] *Parliamentary Debates (Hansard)*, vol. 160, 3rd series, col. 566, for August 2, 1860.

INDEX

Index